Norene's

healthy
kitchen

NORENE GILLETZ

norene's healthy kitchen

EAT *YOUR* WAY TO GOOD HEALTH

whitecap

DEDICATION

This cookbook is dedicated to my family, especially to my parents.

To my mother, Belle Rykiss, my first cooking teacher, who started teaching me how to cook and bake when I was barely tall enough to reach the kitchen table—I'm so lucky to have her love, support, and guidance, both in the kitchen and elsewhere. She cooks or bakes something almost every day and rarely uses a recipe. Mom, you are truly amazing.

To the memory of my father, Max Rykiss, who battled heart disease and lung cancer. Dad loved good food and would have enjoyed the recipes in this book—especially if he could have eaten them with a loaf of bread slathered with butter!

Copyright © 2007 by Norene Gilletz
Whitecap Books

The information in this book is true and complete to the best of our knowledge. All recommendations are made without guarantee on the part of the author or Whitecap Books Ltd. The author and publisher disclaim any liability in connection with the use of this information. For additional information, please contact Whitecap Books Ltd., 351 Lynn Avenue, North Vancouver, British Columbia V7J 2C4. Visit our website at www.whitecap.ca.

Project coordination by Elaine Kaplan
Edited by Nicole de Montbrun
Proofread by Marilyn Bittman
Design & Illustration by Robin Mitchell-Cranfield
Photography by Doug Gilletz

Library and Archives Canada Cataloguing in Publication

Gilletz, Norene
    Norene's healthy kitchen / Norene Gilletz.

Includes index.
ISBN-13: 978-1-55285-802-8
ISBN-10: 1-55285-802-2

    1. Cookery. I. Title.

TX714.G544 2007   641.5'63   C2006-904985-8

The publisher acknowledges the financial support of the Government of Canada through the Book Publishing Industry Development Program (BPIDP) and the Province of British Columbia through the Book Publishing Tax Credit.

Printed in Canada by Friesens.

CONTENTS

ACKNOWLEDGEMENTS

So many wonderful people have contributed their time, knowledge, and experience to make this cookbook a reality. My gratitude and thanks go to the following people for their assistance, advice, and moral support. I couldn't have done this book without you!

Elaine Kaplan, Shirley Millett, Shelley Sefton, and Cindy Beer, what can I say? Thank you to my creative team for all you've done to help me cook up such a fabulous book. I toast you for a job well done. You've "bean" there for me through thick and thin, using your noodles to bring this enormous project to fruition—although at times we were drained and felt like we had reached the boiling point. But the puns we came up with were pan-tastic and helped us laugh away the excess calories from the recipes we tested and tasted. You are such dedicated, hard working, and wonderful women—beyond a "trout!"

Elaine Kaplan—she's small, but mighty! A whiz with words, she spent countless hours at my side, whipping this manuscript into shape. Her sense of humor, positive attitude, organizational skills, and determination are amazing. A special thank you goes to Elaine's husband Marty, who generously shared her with me, day and night.

Shirley Millett—my "e-fish-ent" assistant, runs my office, intercepts my phone calls and helps keep my life organized. She juggles many tasks at a time and can find any file or phone number in record time. Shirley can always anticipate my needs and her devotion is incredible. My coffee cup runneth over!

Shelley Sefton—my recipe tester par excellence cooked up a storm in my test kitchen. She shopped and chopped, cooked and cleaned, and transformed my culinary concepts into the delicious, healthy dishes that grace these pages. Her creativity, bubbly enthusiasm, and love of food were indispensable ingredients in the creation of this book.

Cindy Beer—affectionately known as "eagle eyes." She could catch the smallest errors or inconsistencies and questioned things that might be unclear to readers. Her perseverance, dedication, and helpful suggestions were invaluable.

My friend Cheryl Goldberg, for feeding me countless Friday night dinners and for generously sharing many of her wonderful recipes, even though she hates to measure!

My early morning walking buddies, Kathy Guttman, Frieda Wishinsky, and Anne Perrelli, who encouraged me, shared great recipes and ideas, and kept me on track in more ways than one!

My foodie-friends I've "met through the net," and who shared their favorite recipes and cooking tips over the miles. Special thanks to my "pan-pals" on www.jewish-food-list.com for their inspiration and ideas. Many of their wonderful recipes grace the pages of this book.

Bella Borts, Jocie Bussin, Sharon Fryer, Marilyn Goodman, Bev Gordon, Rhonda Matias, Debbie Morson, Liane Segal, and Faye Zeidman for their feedback, help, and advice.

Elizabeth Braithwaithe and the support team at ESHA Research for answering my many questions so I could provide my readers with an accurate nutrient analysis of my recipes.

To the many dietitians and health care professionals who shared their knowledge and expertise with me and helped guide my journey to the "weigh" I cook today.

Shaun Takata for his "backup" during the many computer crises and crashes I encountered while writing this book.

My dear friend and publisher, Robert McCullough of Whitecap Books, for his vision, patience, and wisdom. Thank you for believing in me.

The Whitecap Bunch for their skills and guidance in shaping this huge manuscript into such a beautiful cookbook.

Stephanie von Hirschberg, for her sage advice, caring, and encouragement. You are an amazing agent and friend.

My family, especially my mother, Belle Rykiss, who taught my sister Rhonda, my brother Bruce, and me that there is nothing better than a home-cooked meal. Mom will never accept the fact that eating out is not just about the food—it's about sharing food with friends and letting someone else do the dishes.

My daughter Jodi and her husband Paul, for their love, help, and encouragement over the miles. I wish we didn't live so far apart so we could cook together more often. My granddaughters Lauren and Camille love to cook with me whenever I visit them, and we always have great fun in the kitchen. Lauren loves to cook and Camille loves to bake—a winning combination!

My son Steven and his wife Cheryl, for their caring and support. They always beg for brisket and homemade cookies when they come to visit. My grandson Max loves my pesto and pasta better than canned spaghetti, but he believes that orange M&M's are a better snack than orange carrots. It's obvious he's inherited my love of sweets.

My son Doug and his wife Ariane, for always being there for me. Doug, who only ate white foods when he was a child, did the fabulous food styling and photography for this cookbook, illustrating his creative culinary talents. Doug, I'm so proud of you! My youngest grandson Sammy loves all kinds of foods and generously shares his Cheerios with my dog Maizie.

My devoted dog Maizie, whose "office" is under my desk and who takes me for long walks. She has a taste for the finer foods in life, including chicken, chickpeas, and Cheerios.

The people who attend my cooking classes and culinary events, my readers, visitors to my website (www.gourmania.com), and the many friends near and far who have contributed to this book in small and large ways. Thank you for all your phone calls, emails, and letters. I always appreciate hearing how much pleasure and enjoyment my recipes have brought to you and your family.

Thank you one and all!

—*Norene Gilletz*

INTRODUCTION

Welcome to *Norene's Healthy Kitchen*! My world revolves around food. I love to cook and bake and believe that eating is one of life's greatest pleasures.

People often ask me how I create my recipes. Sometimes I've tasted a dish at a restaurant or at a party that feeds my creativity, while at other times a photograph in a cookbook or magazine sparks an idea. A trip to the supermarket often inspires me to combine a variety of ingredients in a certain way, or I may wake up in the middle of the night with a concept for a new dish.

People love to share their treasured recipes and ideas with me and these often become a springboard for new recipes. I firmly believe that once someone's name and recipe is in print, that person becomes immortalized and his or her memory will live on, to be enjoyed by future generations through the flavor of memory.

I'm always delighted when people say "Your books are my bibles." The incredible success of *Healthy Helpings* (originally titled *MealLeaniYumm!*) made me realize how hungry people are for quick, easy meals with a healthy focus. This led me to write *Norene's Healthy Kitchen.*

Obesity and diabetes have reached almost epidemic proportions, despite all the health and diet books flooding the market. Most people have difficulty controlling their weight and bounce around from one diet to the next, looking for a quick fix. I speak from experience as I have a family history of diabetes and heart disease. I've struggled with my weight for years and if I didn't cook and eat the way I do today, I'd probably weigh at least a hundred pounds more! I control my blood sugar levels through lifestyle changes by making healthier food choices and by being more active.

Norene's Healthy Kitchen is just what the doctor ordered. It teaches you how to transfer the advice from your doctor or dietitian straight to your plate. You can still enjoy your favorite foods, but now with fewer calories, carbohydrates, and unhealthy fats—and without sacrificing flavor. My motto is "Food that's good for you should taste good!"

The recipes in this book are fast, fabulous, flavorful, and fun. They focus on smart carbs, smart fats, and smart proteins, and feature a wide variety of vegetables, fruits, whole grains, beans, legumes, and nuts. Fish and poultry are more prominent than red meat, and I've also included many vegetarian dishes. There are lots of healthy, delicious desserts. (You'll notice that many of my desserts include chocolate, which comes from the cocoa bean—and everyone knows you should eat beans!)

You'll learn smart strategies to make quick, delicious meals that are good for you and the whole family. Small changes in your diet can add up to significant health benefits. I strongly believe that the simple choices we make each day have the greatest impact on our health and well-being.

My recipes are heart-healthy and weight-loss friendly, offer low glycemic index values (GI), and are suitable for people with diabetes. They're compatible with most of today's popular heart-healthy, smart-carbohydrate diets, including The South Beach Diet, YOU On a Diet, Weight Watchers, The Mediterranean Diet, and The GI Diet.

This book appeals to all palates, from singles to families, from children to seniors, from beginners to well-seasoned cooks.

The recipes in this book work well for the Kosher cook, but you don't have to be Jewish to enjoy my leaner versions of latkes and matzo balls, which will definitely "de-light" your palate.

I've included wonderful recipes for easy entertaining and for Shabbat, as well as for the Jewish holidays. *Norene's Healthy Kitchen* is also Passover-friendly. The Passover chapter, which is almost a cookbook on its own, offers helpful charts for cooking and baking substitutions, as well as a comprehensive list of all the recipes in this book that can be used or modified for Passover.

While writing this book, I could hear your questions: How can I convert my favorite recipes and make them healthier? What can I substitute if my family doesn't like an ingredient? Can I prepare this in advance? Does it freeze well?

I've done my best to answer these questions, and more. Every chapter begins with helpful information and tips. There are Chef's Secrets and Nutrition Notes peppered throughout the book, in bite-sized morsels so you can slowly digest them and apply what you've learned at your own pace.

The recipes have been written to "hold your hand" while you cook. It's the next best thing to having me right beside you in your kitchen! I've shared my culinary secrets with you and hope they will provide you with the tools, knowledge, and confidence to experiment with new ingredients, methods, and recipes.

I prefer to cook from scratch, but there are often times when I'm too busy, too tired, or too lazy to do that, so I use shortcuts. I've streamlined my recipes to save time and clean-up. I love "machine cuisine" and use my food processor, microwave, slow cooker, and grill to save time. I like to develop recipes that can be cooked in advance and refrigerated or frozen until needed, so there are lots of storage and freezing tips.

My recipes are user-friendly. If I can't prepare a recipe quickly or use easy-to-find ingredients, it probably won't be in this book. They also offer lots of variations to allow for different tastes and availability of ingredients. You'll love the helpful charts for substitutions, cooking times and yields, pan sizes, weight, volume and temperature conversions, healthier options . . . and much, much more.

I believe cooking should be fun, so I've combined puns with pots and pans to help you laugh while cooking your way to good health. I hope you use this cookbook often and make it dirty! Put your apron on and start cooking.

From my healthy kitchen to yours . . . enjoy! Eat *your* way to good health!

THINGS YOU WANT TO KNOW

GET SMART

• I've done the detective work for you to help you "get smart!" The following are strategies to help you take control of your food, health, and lifestyle and to help you reach and maintain a healthy weight. You'll learn how to control your cravings rather than have your cravings control you.

• Weight gain is less likely in people who eat an abundance of vegetables and who exercise on a regular basis. So stop vegging out on your sofa and start vegging in your refrigerator. Stop being a couch potato mindlessly munching on potato chips and start walking to pare down the pounds.

SMART SHOPPING

• It all starts out in your shopping cart, so be a smart shopper. Make a grocery list and stick to it. A list will help you avoid impulse decisions and high fat, high-carb, high-sodium temptations. Never shop when you're hungry—it's a recipe for disaster. If it's not in your cart, it won't end up in your kitchen—or in your tummy!

• When shopping, buy perishable foods last. The longer a perishable product sits in your shopping cart, in your car, and on the counter before you refrigerate it, the shorter its shelf life. Always check expiration dates before buying.

• For maximum nutrition, fill your cart with fresh vegetables, fruits, whole grains, beans, and legumes. Frozen or canned vegetables and fruits are nutritious and convenient, but check the label for sodium content and added sugars.

• Dairy-smart choices are skim and 1% milk, nonfat and low-fat yogurts, and part-skim, low-fat, and nonfat cheeses.

• Choose wholegrain cereals (rolled oats, bran), breads, pasta, brown rice, and other grains. Avoid enriched, bleached, or refined white flour.

• Choose lean meats (extra-lean beef or veal), poultry (skinless chicken and turkey), fish (salmon or tilapia), and meat alternatives (tofu), as well as beans and legumes (chickpeas or lentils).

• Choose healthy fats (extra virgin olive oil and canola oil), nuts (walnuts and almonds) and seeds. Avoid hydrogenated oils.

• Read the Nutrition Facts Label carefully. Choose products lower in sodium and saturated fats, and avoid trans-fats. Choose foods that are higher in fiber and which contain important nutrients such as calcium and iron. Don't be fooled: "light" on a label can refer to flavor, color, or texture, not "light" in calories. Fat-free foods often contain added sugars. Any word that ends with "ose" is a sugar—such as sucrose, dextrose, and maltose.

• Avoid foods that contain high-fructose corn syrup (HFCS), which is a sweetener found in processed foods such as fat-free salad dressings, regular soft drinks, and fruit punches. The fructose in HFCS doesn't turn off your hunger signals.

• Check the ingredient list: generally speaking, the less ingredients, the healthier the food. Ingredients are listed on the label in descending order by weight.

• Choose foods that contain less than 4 grams of saturated fat and less than 4 grams of sugar per serving. Look for brands that don't have high-fructose corn syrup or sugar in their first 5 ingredients. Avoid hydrogenated oils, which are added to the product to increase its shelf life—not *your* life!

• Double-check the size of a serving—it should be realistic. The serving size listed on the label is often much smaller than what most people actually eat. If a serving size is $1/4$ cup and you eat a 1 cup portion, that turns out to be 4 servings!

SMART CARBS

• Choose your carbohydrates carefully. The best carbs are nutrient-rich vegetables, fruits, whole grains, beans, and other legumes. Limit your intake of carbs from unhealthy processed, refined starchy foods such as those made with white flour and added sugars. Choose foods that are higher in fiber to help slow down the absorption of carbohydrates. See the Glycemic Index (GI), page 18, for more information. There are 4 calories in each gram of carbohydrate.

• The minimum amount of carbs required for proper brain function is 130 grams a day, mostly in the form of whole, unprocessed foods with a low GI.

• Fruits and vegetables are nutritional powerhouses—they're packed with vitamins, minerals, fiber, and are an excellent source of antioxidants. Strive for 5 to 9 servings of vegetables and fruits each day: that's 3 to 5

vegetables and 2 to 4 fruits. That might seem like a lot, but a serving is actually smaller than you might think. One serving is $1/2$ cup cooked or raw fruit or vegetables or 1 cup raw leafy green vegetables, 1 medium fruit, $1/4$ cup dried fruit, or 6 ounces of vegetable juice. A large salad can easily contain 2 to 3 servings of vegetables.

• Locally grown produce is fresher, so enjoy it in season. If you want fewer pesticides in your body, choose organic fruits and vegetables, which are grown and handled according to strict procedures that prohibit the use of chemical fertilizers and pesticides. Buy unwaxed fruits and vegetables if you plan to eat their peels. Wash all produce thoroughly, even if you don't eat the peel or skin.

• Choose whole grains such as brown rice, wild rice, or bulgar. Your goal for grains should be three servings a day (1 serving is equal to $1/2$ cup cooked).

• Read "How to Switch to a Low GI Diet" (page 25) for more smart tips on carbohydrates.

SMART FIBER

• Fiber is the part of fruits, vegetables, and grains that you can't digest. The higher the fiber content, the more slowly the food is digested, so you feel full longer. Fiber helps slow down the absorption of sugars and fats into your body, reduces surges in insulin, and is a key component of a healthy diet, so make fiber your friend. Fiber has no calories because it isn't digested by the body.

• Fiber comes in two forms: soluble and insoluble. Soluble fiber, found in foods such as oats, peas, beans, barley, apples, and citrus fruits, has been shown to lower blood cholesterol levels. Insoluble fiber, which is "good for your gut," is found in whole wheat breads and cereals and most vegetables.

• How much is enough? You need at least 20 to 35 grams of fiber a day. By increasing your intake of fruits (especially berries), vegetables (especially beans and legumes), whole grains (especially slowly digested grains such as barley), nuts and seeds, you'll boost your fiber intake easily. To avoid bloating and gas, increase your fiber intake gradually, and be sure to drink plenty of water.

• Low-carbohydrate gurus calculate the effective carbohydrate count (ECC) by subtracting the fiber from the total carbohydrate content. For example, 1 cup of raw broccoli contains 3.7 grams of carbohydrate and 2.1 grams come from fiber. Therefore, there are 1.6 grams of "effective carbs" in 1 cup of raw broccoli.

SMART FATS

• Healthy fats are essential to good health. They are a major source of energy and supply the essential fatty acids that the body needs for many chemical activities. You need to get essential fatty acids from the foods you eat—your body can't make them. Fats transport the fat-soluble vitamins (A, D, E, and K) in the body. Fats add flavor to foods, slow down digestion, and keep you feeling full longer. Fats are important for the normal growth and development of children. There are 9 calories in each gram of fat.

• Good fats are liquid at room temperature while bad fats are solid at room temperature. Polyunsaturated fats (especially the Omega-3 fats) and monounsaturated fats are good fats. They are found in plant-based foods, including most vegetable oils. Omega-3 fats are also found in fish. Good fats are found in olive oil, canola oil, salmon, avocado, olives, nuts, and seeds.

• For cooking, choose olive, canola, grapeseed, peanut, walnut, and sesame oil. (Would you believe that if you drizzle your veggies with olive oil, it's healthier than eating them plain?) For baking, use canola oil, walnut oil, or a heart-healthy margarine. Eat less saturated fat by reducing your intake of red meat and full-fat dairy products such as whole milk and cheese.

• Avoid trans-fats whenever possible. Transfat (short for trans-fatty acid) is vegetable oil that has been transformed into a solid fat, such as margarine or shortening, by heating it with hydrogen. This process is called hydrogenation. It extends the shelf life of processed foods (but not your life)! Transfats are worse for you than saturated fat: they raise LDL (bad) cholesterol as much as saturated fat does, but also lower HDL (good) cholesterol. Trans-fats have been linked with heart disease and the risk of Type 2 diabetes. Also avoid foods that contain partially hydrogenated, palm, and coconut oil.

• Olive oil is high in heart-healthy monounsaturated fats and antioxidants. Extra virgin olive oil is less processed than regular olive oil. Extra virgin olive oil is best in uncooked dishes such as salads, salad dressings, sauces, and marinades. Because of its intense flavor, a little goes a long way. Regular olive oil is less expensive than extra virgin olive oil, has a milder flavor, and is a good all-purpose oil to use for cooking as it has a higher smoking point. Store olive oil away from heat and light to prevent rancidity. If stored in the refrigerator, olive oil gets cloudy and thickens slightly, but will become translucent again when it reaches room temperature.

• Canola oil is mainly monounsaturated, but it's also rich in Omega-3 fats, which can help lower LDL (bad) cholesterol levels. Use canola oil when you want a neutral-flavored oil for baking or cooking. Look for expeller-pressed brands, available at health food stores. (Pressure is used to extract the oil, rather than using solvents to chemically extract the oil from the seed.)

• Omega-3 fats are found in canola oil, fish, walnuts, and flaxseeds (grind them first). Omega-3 fats protect the heart, including helping it maintain a strong, steady beat, preventing potentially fatal arrhythmias.

• Shape Matters! Stick margarine, sold wrapped in foil or paper, contains the same number of calories as butter but is loaded with trans-fats. In baking and cooking, choose a soft margarine, sold in plastic tubs, that contains as little saturated fat as possible (2 g or less per serving), no trans-fats, and at least 0.4 g of Omega-3s per serving. Check the label carefully. Some brands are available unsalted. A heart-healthy margarine contains vitamin E and vitamin D. Instead of butter or margarine, switch to a liquid vegetable oil when possible—they are usually interchangeable in recipes. Oils don't contain added salt. If calories are a concern, use fats in moderation. You'll improve your shape as well!

• Nuts to You! Nuts contain healthy fats and should be included in a heart-healthy

diet. Health experts recommend eating up to an ounce of nuts (that's about a handful) 5 or more days a week. Different nuts have different benefits. Read "Nut"-rition Notes following Nutty Baked Chicken (page 204). Also check the Index for more information about nuts.

SMART PROTEINS

• Lean proteins such as chicken, turkey, and fish are healthier options than meat. Red meat is rich in iron, zinc, and B vitamins, but it's also a source of saturated fat, so choose the leanest cuts and enjoy smaller portions. Eat protein from a variety of vegetable sources such as beans, legumes, and nuts, which are low in saturated fat and high in fiber. Eggs, egg whites, soy products, nut butters, and low-fat dairy products provide protein as well. There are 4 calories in each gram of protein.

• Chicken, especially the breast, is a lean protein choice if you skip the skin. Boneless, skinless chicken breasts cook quickly, and leftovers make an easy lunch or dinner. The dark meat is a good source of iron and zinc. Forget about those chicken wings—they're full of fat and calories. Chicken is versatile, so enjoy it grilled, baked, roasted, or stir-fried. Use lean ground chicken or turkey breast instead of ground beef in meatballs, burgers, and casseroles. Turkey cutlets or strips, roast turkey breast, or a whole roast turkey, are also heart-healthy, lean protein choices.

• Eat fish more often. It cooks quickly and is an excellent source of important healthy fats. Omega-3 fatty acids are abundant in salmon, tuna, halibut, cod, tilapia, trout, and herring.

To boost your heart health, enjoy fish 2 or 3 times a week. Canned tuna, salmon, and sardines make quick, easy fish meals.

• Eggs are back on the menu. They're quick and easy to prepare, making them a great choice for time-starved families. They're a good source of protein and contain important nutrients such as polyunsaturated fats, folic acid, and other B vitamins. An egg contains about 200 mg of cholesterol, which is found only in the yolk. Egg whites are cholesterol-free, so use them in an omelet or frittata, or make hard-boiled eggs, then discard the yolks and enjoy the whites. People with diabetes may need to limit their intake of egg yolks to two yolks per week. Health experts believe that up to 7 eggs a week is fine for most people. Check with your health care provider or dietitian for guidance.

• Don't forget about cheese. Leaner choices include nonfat and 1% cottage cheese, reduced-fat or skim varieties such as feta, goat cheese, mozzarella, and Swiss cheeses. Add grated low-fat cheese to casseroles, pancakes, vegetables, salads, sandwiches, and wraps for a protein and calcium boost.

• Cut extra-firm tofu into cubes or strips and add them to a stir-fry. Or cut tofu into thick slices, marinate it, then grill, bake, or broil.

• Protein powders and shakes make a good snack or meal replacement. Use them in smoothies or add them to muffin or pancake batters for a protein boost.

• Your body needs protein to make, maintain, and repair tissue. Protein helps decrease hunger, making you feel satisfied sooner and full longer than if you had eaten carbs or fat. Be smart and eat moderate portions of lean, protein-rich foods at most meals or as a snack. Excess calories from protein are stored in your body as fat, so watch those portions.

SMART MEALS AND SNACKS

• Have three meals a day plus 2 or 3 snacks, so you're never hungry. Eat slowly. It takes about 20 minutes for your brain to know your stomach is full.

• Start your day with a fiber-filled breakfast. Enjoy a bowl of whole grain cereal such as large flake rolled oats. Top with berries, cinnamon, nonfat yogurt and nuts, or flaxseed. Or eat an egg-white omelet filled with spinach, mushrooms, and red peppers. Fiber helps keep you full and prevents hunger later in the day.

• For an easy, healthy lunch, enjoy a green salad with grilled chicken, sliced turkey, salmon or tuna, or combine them in a 100% whole wheat pita or tortilla for a handy meal.

• For dinner, fill your plate with water-rich vegetables (broccoli, cauliflower, green beans, or spinach), with a drizzle of extra virgin olive oil, a lean protein choice (skinless chicken, turkey, or fish), and a serving of whole grains (brown basmati rice, quinoa or kasha).

• It's okay to belong to the Clean Plate Club—just switch to a smaller plate! Use a 7-inch plate for lunch and a 9-inch plate for dinner.

• A smart trick to help curb hunger is to eat 6 walnut halves 20 minutes before a meal. A bowl of vegetable or lentil soup is another smart way to take the edge off your appetite. Or have a salad with tomatoes, extra virgin olive oil, garlic, and lemon juice. The acid in the tomatoes and lemon juice helps slow down gastric emptying.

• If you are feeling hungry between meals, it's possible you didn't eat properly at your last meal. You may be thirsty, so try drinking a glass of water. Often, what you think is hunger is actually frustration or boredom. It may not be what you've been eating—it's what's eating you!

• Be a smart snacker. Have a fiber-filled fruit, such as an apple or pear, with a few nuts.

• Enjoy snacks such as Trail Mix (page 71) or some raw veggies with nonfat yogurt or hummus. Crunch away! Or enjoy a healthy, homemade muffin (pages 356–70) made with less sugar and fat, with a cup of cocoa. Bake a batch of muffins and freeze them as a handy snack to enjoy at home, work, or school. A bowlful of whole-grain cereal makes a terrific after-school snack for kids. Cut a juicy orange into wedges and see your children's smiles turn into big orange grins!

• To help reduce inflammation and obesity, eat foods that have anti-inflammatory and antioxidant properties. Best bets are Omega-3 foods (such as salmon, walnuts, and flaxseed), green tea, turmeric, coffee, and bananas.

• Antioxidants are a group of substances that play different roles in protecting the body from free radicals (a by-product of oxidation) that accelerate aging and lead to disease. Each antioxidant has its own benefits, so eat smart and include a wide variety of foods from plant sources in your diet.

SMART WAYS TO MEASURE SERVING SIZES

3 oz (85 g) cooked meat, poultry, or fish
a deck of cards or the palm of your hand

1/2 cup veggies, fruit, cereal, rice, pasta
a tennis ball or a hockey puck

1 apple or orange
a baseball or a large fist

1 cup salad
a baseball or a large fist

1 tsp butter, margarine, or sugar
the tip of your thumb

1 Tbsp natural peanut butter
half your thumb

1 oz cheese
your thumb

1 oz (1/4 cup) nuts or raisins
a golf ball or a small handful

SMART BEVERAGES

• If you drink only when you're thirsty, you're probably not drinking enough. You need about 64 ounces (8 glasses) of liquid a day for a 2,000 calorie-a-day diet. Most of this can come from water, which is both calorie-free and free (unless you buy bottled water). The rest can come from tea, coffee, soup, or water-rich vegetables and fruits. Don't confuse thirst with hunger.

• Have a glass of water before and/or with each meal, and a glass between meals. Water helps take the edge off your appetite. Add lemon or lime to water to boost the flavor, or have some sparkling water. Hot water with a wedge of lemon is another option.

things you want to know

• Tea is also "tea-riffic!" Make a pitcher of iced tea and keep it in your refrigerator, or brew a pot of hot tea. Tea, especially green tea, contains powerful antioxidants that offer protection against both heart disease and cancer. Experiment and try different varieties of tea—there are so many interesting flavors available. If you're concerned about caffeine, choose decaffeinated versions.

• Coffee, in moderation, doesn't appear to raise health risks and may even have some benefits. It is a major source of antioxidants, acts an antidepressant, and appears to lower the risk of Type 2 diabetes, gallstones, and kidney stones. If caffeine is a problem, choose decaffeinated versions. Add a pinch of ground cinnamon to enhance the flavor of coffee. To protect your bones, add a splash of milk, preferably skim or 1%.

• Skinny Café au Lait: Combine equal portions of brewed coffee with hot skim milk. (If you prefer a skinny latte, process the hot milk in the food processor fitted with the steel blade for 30 seconds, until foamy, then add it to the brewed coffee.) Sweeten to taste and lightly sprinkle with grated dark chocolate and ground cinnamon, if desired.

• The Milky Weigh: An 8-oz glass of whole (3.5%) milk contains 8.0 g fat (5.0 g saturated) and 150 calories. A glass of 2% milk contains 4.8 g fat (3.1 g saturated) and 122 calories. A glass of 1% milk contains 2.4 g fat (1.5 g saturated) and 102 calories. Skim (nonfat) milk contains 0.4 g fat (0.3 g saturated) and 86 calories in an 8-oz glass. Milk contains 300 mg calcium, 12 g carbohydrate and 8 g protein in an 8-oz glass. Calcium-enriched milk contains about 1/3 more calcium than regular milk. Milk contains vitamin A as well as vitamin D, which is necessary for the absorption of calcium. Lactose-free milk and fortified soymilk are excellent alternatives for people who are lactose-intolerant.

• Add a teaspoon or two of unsweetened cocoa powder to a cup of hot milk, along with a little sugar or sweetener. For a delicious calcium boost, enjoy a comforting cup of hot chocolate, and add a cinnamon stick for an antioxidant boost.

• Juices often contain added sugars, so limit your consumption. Choose unsweetened juices and dilute them by adding equal parts of water or club soda. Avoid sugary soft drinks and fruit punches. Did you know that a 12-oz can of soda contains 1/4 cup of sugar? Or that fruit punch often has high-fructose corn syrup as the second or third major ingredient? Diet drinks are really artificially sweetened water. Enjoy vegetable or tomato juice, but choose low-sodium versions.

• Avoid drinking excess alcohol—in addition to the extra empty calories, it lowers your inhibitions, so you may tend to overeat. One 5-oz glass of wine (or any alcohol in moderation) on most days of the week can be beneficial to your health (depending on your health and medical history), lowering the risk of heart attack and stroke. Check with your physician for further guidance.

SMART CALORIES

• Depending on gender, body size, and activity level, most adults need between 2,000 and 3,000 calories a day. Women and less-active people need fewer calories than men or more active people. Current dietary recommendations are flexible, as different individuals have different nutritional needs, medical histories, and lifestyles. For general good health, 45% to 65% of calories should come from carbohydrates, 20% to 35% from fat, and 10% to 35% from protein.

• The number of calories you eat and the number of calories you burn determines weight gain and loss. If you take in fewer calories than you burn, you'll lose weight. If you take in more calories than you burn, you'll gain weight. If you burn as many calories as you eat, then your weight will stay the same. Be smart and make the healthiest possible choices about where you get your calories. Small changes add up to big differences.

• Would you believe that 100 calories a day, either eaten or expended, equals 10 pounds a year? An easy way to lose 10 pounds in a year is to cut out 100 calories a day from your diet (or burn an extra 100 calories a day through exercise). "Weigh" to go!

SMART MOVES

• Exercise is an essential ingredient in successful weight management. It increases your metabolism, improves your mood, reduces stress, helps control food cravings, and improves blood glucose levels.

• Strive for 30 minutes to 1 hour of physical exercise each day. Choose an activity you enjoy so you'll be more likely to continue doing it. Try aerobic exercises such as walking, biking, swimming, dancing, or aerobic classes, or discover the benefits of yoga or Pilates. Weight resistance such as lifting weights is also beneficial. So forget those excuses, get off your "buts," and get moving!

• Walking works. It's easy, inexpensive, and you can do it almost anywhere. Walking has the highest compliance rate of any exercise. Buy a pedometer and clip it on each morning when you get dressed. Start off slowly if you are older or out of shape. Each week, increase the number of daily steps you take. If the weather is bad, walk in an indoor mall. Walk up and down the stairs at the office or at home, or dance with your dog or kids! Stretch for 3 to 5 minutes after you walk.

• Every step counts! The optimum is 10,000 steps a day, with at least 30 minutes of continuous walking. Short on time? Then break it up into chunks of at least 10 continuous minutes. Calculate the average number of steps you walk each day. Each week, add an extra 500 steps per day, until you reach your walking goal. Weigh to goal!

• In addition to walking, there are other ways to add activity to your day—or night. Fifteen minutes of moderate sexual activity is equivalent to 500 steps and vigorous sexual activity is equivalent to 750 steps! Fifteen minutes of washing dishes is equivalent to 900 steps and 15 minutes of grocery shopping is equivalent to 1400 steps. The choice is yours.

• When you lose weight but don't exercise, you lose both muscle and fat. When you gain weight but don't exercise, you gain fat. When you keep losing and gaining weight (yo-yo dieting), you end up gaining more fat because of the muscle loss that takes place every time you diet. Muscle burns more calories than fat, so it's essential to maintain and add muscle to achieve and maintain weight loss. Increased muscle mass means your body burns more calories around the clock, so be smart and build those muscles.

• To help build and maintain muscles, why not try kitchen aerobics? Lift that pot, tote that garbage pail, chop those veggies and you won't fail!

SMART MEASURES

• Focus on "waist" management—which doesn't mean you should eat everything on your plate just because your mother told you that you shouldn't "waste" food. Your waist measurement indicates your level of abdominal fat, which is significant for your health. Belly fat is the most dangerous fat you can carry because of its proximity to your organs.

• Measure the circumference of your waist at your belly button. For women, the ideal measurement is 32^1/$_2$ inches and for men it is 35 inches. Women with a waist circumference of 37 inches or more and men with 40 inches or more increase their risk of heart disease and diabetes.

• Inch your "weigh" to a smaller waistline and a healthier you!

THE GLYCEMIC INDEX (GI)

• The glycemic index (GI) ranks carbohydrate-containing foods on a scale from 0 to 100, according to how quickly they raise your blood sugar levels after eating. It was first developed by Dr. David Jenkins and his colleagues at the University of Toronto in 1981 to help people with diabetes maintain steady blood sugar levels.

• Choosing carbohydrates with low GI values helps reduce the risk of heart disease and diabetes. When people with diabetes consume carbohydrates that have lower GI values, their blood sugar levels are better controlled: these carbs increase the body's sensitivity to insulin and reduce cholesterol levels.

• Low GI diets are also a helpful tool in achieving and maintaining weight loss. Eating mostly carbs with low GI values, which slowly trickle glucose into your blood stream, will help control your hunger by making you feel full longer.

• People who have insulin resistance syndrome or women with PCOS (polycystic ovarian syndrome) may benefit from a low GI diet as it helps reduce weight and has been shown to improve insulin sensitivity in individuals at risk of coronary heart disease.

• The glycemic index is a useful tool for exercise, including endurance sports. Carbs with low GI values prolong physical endurance during exercise while carbs with high GI values help refuel your carbohydrate stores after exercise.

GLYCEMIC INDEX

Low GI = 55 or less (choose most often)
Medium GI = 56 to 69 (choose more often)
High GI = 70 or more (choose less often)

• Carbohydrates with high GI values, such as bagels (72), white bread (70 to 80), a baked russet potato (85), and Rice Krispies (82), are rapidly absorbed, resulting in rapid rises in blood sugar and insulin levels.

• Carbs with medium GI values, such as couscous (65), pita bread (57), basmati rice (58), and raisins (56), have a moderate effect on blood sugar and insulin levels.

• Low GI carbs such as apples (38), oranges (42), strawberries (40), prunes (29), carrots (41), sweet potatoes (44), 100% stone-ground whole wheat bread (53), canned chickpeas (40), barley (25), quinoa (51), and rolled oats (42), are more slowly digested and absorbed, producing gradual rises in blood sugar and insulin levels.

• Don't get hung up on numbers and don't judge a food only by its GI rank. Experts recommend dividing carbohydrates into three categories—those with high, medium, and low GI values—then making the best choices within each category. Even though white and brown basmati rice have a similar GI value, brown rice is a more nutritious choice because it contains more fiber. Vegetables, fruits, legumes, and whole grains offer valuable vitamins, minerals, fiber, and phytochemicals, so enjoy them as part of a healthy lifestyle.

• Switching to carbs with low GI values is just one component of a healthy weight-loss plan. You also need to cut your portion sizes, reduce your daily caloric intake, and increase your physical activity. Effective long-term weight management evolves out of a healthy change in lifestyle, not a brief commitment to eating certain foods because of their GI values!

• For more information about the GI value of specific food groups, refer to *GI Go!* For breads/sandwiches, see page 277, for vegetables, see page 283, for grains, see page 319, and for desserts, see page 410. For baked goods, see Bake Someone Happy, page 22. Additional tips are peppered throughout this book.

• The University of Sydney, Australia, has an excellent searchable database at their website (www.glycemicindex.com) for hundreds of foods showing their glycemic index, glycemic load, and amount of carbohydrates per serving. It's the official website of the glycemic index and GI database, which is updated and maintained by the University's GI Group, headed by Dr. Jennie Brand-Miller, Professor of Human Nutrition. She is considered a leading authority on the glycemic index and is also the co-author of the best-selling *Glucose Revolution* series.

• The *G.I. Diet* series of books by Rick Gallop provides user-friendly food guides based on the colors of the traffic light. Foods in the red-light or "stop" category have high GI values and are often high-calorie foods. Foods in the yellow-light or "caution" category have moderate GI values. Foods in the green-light or "go-ahead" category are the ones that help you lose weight.

• GI values may change or be added to the database as research continues in this field.

FACTORS THAT AFFECT THE GI

• The GI value of food varies depending on when and where it was grown, how ripe it is, how it is stored or processed, the type of starch it contains, its fat or acid content, and whether it's raw or cooked. Even the health of the person consuming it factors into the equation!

• Most foods are eaten in combination with other foods and are affected by other components such as fat, protein, fiber, and acid. These components can change the GI value of the food, making it difficult to determine the GI value of a mixed meal. However, the effect of a low-GI meal will carry over to the next meal, reducing its glycemic impact, so try to include at least one low-GI food per meal.

• Generally, cooked starchy foods have a higher GI value than uncooked starchy foods. Cooking causes the starches to swell, making them easier to digest, so they convert into glucose more quickly. Cooking time also affects the GI value. Pasta cooked *al dente* (still firm to the bite) has a lower GI value than overcooked, mushy pasta.

• The more a food is processed, the higher the GI value will be. Processed instant oatmeal has a higher GI value than traditional rolled oats.

• High-fructose corn syrup (HFCS), which is found in many packaged foods and regular soft drinks, has a high GI value.

• The ripeness of a fruit also affects its GI value. Riper bananas have a higher GI value than less ripe ones.

• Variety can also affect the GI value. Russet (Idaho) potatoes have a higher GI value than new potatoes. As a general rule, the smaller the potato, the lower the GI value.

• Soluble fiber, which is found in apples, rolled oats, oat bran, and legumes, tends to slow digestion, resulting in a lower GI value.

GLYCEMIC INDEX VS GLYCEMIC LOAD

• What is the Glycemic Load? Your blood glucose rises and falls when you eat a meal that contains carbohydrates. How high it rises and how long it remains high depends on

two things: the *quality* of the carbohydrates (its GI value) and the *quantity* of carbohydrate in your meal. The glycemic load (GL) combines both the *quality* and *quantity* of carbohydrate in a typical serving as one number. Here is the formula:

GL = (GI value × the amount of carbohydrate) divided by 100.

For example: a medium orange has a GI value of 42 and contains 15 g carbohydrate.

Therefore:

GL = (42 × 15) divided by 100 = 6.3.
The GL of the orange is about 6.

Another example: a one-cup serving of whole wheat spaghetti also has a GI value of 42 but contains 37 g carbohydrate.

Therefore:

GL = (42 × 37) divided by 100 = 15.5.
The GL of the spaghetti is about 16.

• GI or GL? If you choose carbohydrates with a low GI value, your diet will probably be healthier, containing good-quality, slowly digested carbohydrates. However, if you base your choices on the GL, it's possible you could be eating foods that are low in carbs but that contain unhealthy fats and proteins.

• Eat Smart: Choose foods with a high-nutrient density (nutrients per calorie) and a low GI value, with the best nutrient profile—higher fiber, lower saturated fat, higher protein content, and lower sugar content. Your best choices are foods that contain the most nutrients and the lowest amounts of unhealthy fats. Choose slowly digested carbs (low GI values) over carbs that are quickly digested (high GI values), even if the glycemic load (GL) is the same. Refer to How to Switch to a Low GI Diet (see page 25).

GLYCEMIC LOAD RANGE

Low GL = 10 or less
Medium GL = 11–19
High GL = 20 or more

SMART STRATEGIES TO LOWER THE GI:

• GI Go! Choose at least one healthy low GI food at each meal. The more low GI foods you include in a meal, the lower the overall GI value of that meal.

• High and Low: Mix foods with higher and lower GI values at each meal to achieve a moderate overall GI value. Combine lentils with rice, or fill a 100% whole wheat pita with tabbouleh.

• Start with Soup: A bowlful of vegetable soup will make you feel full longer than if you drink a glass of water and eat the vegetables separately. Vegetables, beans, or legumes with low GI values make a "souper" soup that will fill you up without filling you out.

• Balance your Meals: Eat an abundance of vegetables and lean protein in reasonable amounts, and choose healthy fats (olive oil versus butter).

• Step Up to the Plate: Fill half your plate with vegetables and fruit, one-quarter with whole grains, and one-quarter with lean protein. For protein, choose from lean meats, chicken, turkey, fish, eggs, cheese, legumes, and tofu.

• Fill 'er Up: Pile up half your plate with greens or salad vegetables. Strive to have at least 5 servings of vegetables a day. This recommendation doesn't include starchy vegetables such as potatoes.

• Spuds or Duds? Don't eliminate potatoes from your diet just because they have a high GI value—potatoes contain other nutritional benefits. Choose boiled small new potatoes instead of larger, starchy mashed potatoes, which are digested more quickly. Eat potatoes less often, or combine them with other low GI vegetables, or add a drizzle of extra virgin olive oil.

• The Slow-Down: Acidic foods slow down gastric emptying, slowing down the release of glucose into the bloodstream. Eat a mixed salad with tomatoes and a vinaigrette dressing, sprinkle lemon juice on cooked vegetables, or add yogurt to salad dressing, cereal, or fruit.

• Fiber Up: Choose foods that are higher in fiber. The fiber acts as a physical barrier to slow down the absorption of carbohydrates. Good choices are wholegrain breads, rolled oats, barley, beans, lentils, and chickpeas.

• Bean Me Up! Add beans or legumes to salads, soups, casseroles, even stir-fries. Include kidney beans or chickpeas in a salad or eat an apple for dessert to lower the meal's overall GI value.

• Refined Foods Are Not So Fine! Limit your intake of processed refined starchy foods, which have a higher GI value, usually contain high-fructose corn syrup (HFCS), and tend to be low in fiber and other nutrients.

• Portion Distortion! Watch your portion size of carb-rich foods, such as rice and pasta, to limit the overall glycemic load of your diet.

• Using Your Noodle: Choose whole wheat pasta made from whole wheat durum semolina, or white pasta made with hard/durum wheat. Cook pasta until *al dente* (still firm to the bite). Add a lean protein and lots of vegetables with low GI values to expand one cup of cooked pasta into a filling, low GI meal.

• Snack Smart! Choose fresh or frozen fruit, dried fruit and nut mix, yogurt, and skim or low-fat milk. Limit your intake of flour products with high GI values such as cookies, cakes, pastries, and crackers—save these for the occasional treat or bake your own, using the lower GI recipes in this book.

• Bake Someone Happy! To counteract the high GI values of whole wheat and all-purpose flours, add some soluble fiber when baking muffins, cakes, and cookies. Use rolled oats, apples, applesauce, pears, blueberries, wheat germ, or raw carrots. Protein foods such as yogurt or buttermilk, and other acidic ingredients, also help lower the GI.

QUICK MEAL-PLANNING TIPS FOR PEOPLE WITH DIABETES

• If you are following a diabetic diet or are calculating your carb intake, the following guide will help you choose the best recipes in this book when planning meals.

1 carbohydrate/starch choice equals
15 grams carbohydrate

1 protein choice equals
7 grams protein

1 fat choice equals
5 grams fat

• Carbohydrates include breads/starch, milk and milk products, fruits, and vegetables. Starch is found in breads, cereals, crackers, grains, legumes, pasta, and certain vegetables such as potatoes, sweet potatoes, squash, and corn. Non-starchy vegetables such as lettuce, spinach, broccoli, cucumbers, mushrooms, and celery are also carbohydrates, but contain less carbs (5 grams) per serving.

• Carbohydrate Counting: Count 1 bread/starch, 1 fruit, or 1 milk choice (8 ounces milk, or yogurt) as 15 grams carbohydrate. If you consume non-starchy vegetables in sufficient amounts to contain 15 grams of carbohydrate, count them as 1 carb choice. Your dietitian or health care provider can provide further guidance.

• Choose carbs with low glycemic index (GI) values more often to help control your blood glucose levels. Watch your portion sizes.

• Include foods that are high in fiber. Aim for at least 20 to 35 grams per day.

• Stay hydrated by drinking plenty of water throughout the day. Drink a glass between meals and one glass with each meal.

• Choose lean proteins such as skinless poultry, fish, nonfat or low-fat dairy products, legumes, and tofu. Avoid high-saturated fat sources such as beef and high-fat dairy foods.

• Choose heart-healthy unsaturated fats such as olive oil and canola oil. Eat less saturated fat and avoid trans-fats.

• Choose a variety of foods from all food groups. Base your choices primarily on nutrient-rich foods.

• Limit sweets and processed foods.

• In a healthy meal plan, sugar can occasionally be substituted for other carbohydrates such as fruit or vegetables.

• Limit salt, alcohol, and caffeine.

• Space your meals, eating at regular times throughout the day. Keep your blood sugar stable by eating nutrient-rich, high-fiber meals and snacks that take longer to digest. Refer to Smart Meals and Snacks (page 14).

• Always consult your health care professional for guidance in proper meal planning.

• In addition to the meal planning tips suggested above, be as active as possible, exercise daily, and control your weight.

SWEET CHOICES

• Sweet Stuff: Sugar is added to so many of the foods we eat that it's difficult to avoid it. Eat sugars and sweets in moderation—they supply calories, but little else nutritionally. Health experts recommend that no more than 10% of the calories we eat each day should come from added sugars.

• Figure It Out: To calculate the sugar content of a food, divide the grams of sugar on the label by four to get its equivalent in teaspoons. (For example, a cookie with 20 grams of sugar per serving contains 5 tsp of sugar.)

• How Low Can You Go? In some recipes, sugar can be safely cut by 1/4 to 1/3. Cookies and cakes may not turn out as well or will be less moist when the sugar is reduced. Refrigerate baked goods to retain moisture and freshness.

• Sucralose, sold as Splenda, is heat-stable and can be used successfully in many stove-top and oven recipes that call for sugar including sauces, cookies, cakes, desserts, and other baked goods. Splenda can also be used successfully in marinades and salad dressings. There's also a brown sugar version.

• Aspartame, sold as Equal or Nutrasweet, breaks down when exposed to heat and air, so it's unsuitable for cooking and baking.

• Saccharin is heat-stable but may leave a metallic aftertaste. It's sold in tablet, powder, or liquid form.

• Cyclamate is heat-stable, so it can be used in cooking and baking. It's sold in tablet, powder, or liquid form; there's also a brown sugar version.

• Sweet 'N Low, sold in the U.S., contains saccharin, not cyclamate, but in Canada, it contains cyclamate. Conversely, Sugar Twin, which is the brand-name cyclamate sweetener in Canada, contains saccharin in the U.S.

• What's the Difference? Splenda and other artificial sweeteners don't add texture or bulk to baked goods, so the end result will be smaller in volume and less moist. Baking time often needs to be reduced, so check for doneness a few minutes earlier than the time indicated in the recipe. Baked goods made with Splenda don't brown like those made with sugar.

• Passover Substitute: For Passover, you can substitute 1 packet of Passover sugar substitute (such as Sweet N'Low) for 1 packet (1 g) of Splenda or 2 tsp of sugar.

• Cover Up: Cinnamon and lemon or orange juice help mask the taste of artificial sweeteners.

• Sweet Tooth? If you like things sweeter, add a little additional artificial sweetener. It won't affect the texture or bulk of baked goods and your recipe will still turn out fine.

• When to Use? Artificial sweeteners work best in cooked foods that don't need sugar for color, texture, or moistness.

• Sweet Switch: For people with diabetes or who are insulin resistant, artificial sweeteners can be helpful. Four packets or 8 tsp of granular Splenda are considered a "free food."

• Surprise! Many people with diabetes are reluctant to eat foods or baked goods made with sugar. What they don't realize is that most of the carbs in baked goods come from the flour, not the sugar!

• Sweet News: Sugar can be enjoyed in moderation by people with diabetes. However, sugars should be substituted for other carbohydrates, not added to the meal. Spread your sugar intake throughout the day as part of slowly digested meals and snacks that include lean proteins, healthy fats, and fiber-rich carbohydrates. Balance with extra exercise.

• Craving Sugar? To help stop sugar cravings, try replacing sugary foods or refined carbs with higher protein foods for several days. It may help put the brakes on your sugar breaks!

• Sweet Trick: Try this trick to stop a sugar craving. Place a few granules of sugar on the tip of your finger. Tap the sugar granules into a glass of water and then drink the water. In a few minutes, the sugar craving should disappear.

SPLENDA CONVERSIONS:

• If you buy Splenda in individual packets or sold loose in boxes and labeled as "granular Splenda," here's some useful information:

• 1 packet of Splenda is equal in sweetening power (but not in volume) to 2 tsp of granular Splenda (the kind that measures like sugar) and also has the same amount of carbohydrates.

• Granular Splenda contains maltodextrin and sucralose. One teaspoon contains 0.5 g carbohydrate, 2 calories and 6 mg sucralose.

• Splenda packets contain dextrose, maltodextrin and sucralose. One packet contains 1 g carbohydrate, 4 calories, and 12 mg sucralose.

SPLENDA PACKETS	GRANULAR SPLENDA
24 packets	1 cup
12 packets	$1/2$ cup
8 packets	$1/3$ cup
6 packets	$1/4$ cup
3 packets	2 Tbsp
$1^1/2$ packets	1 Tbsp
1 packet	2 tsp
$1/2$ packet	1 tsp

HOW TO SWITCH TO A LOW GI DIET

Switch "this" for "that" by replacing high GI carbs with low GI carbs. Most foods with low GI values are also low in calories and fat, high in fiber and nutrients, and will keep you feeling full longer. The following chart will help you make healthy smart-carb choices and will be especially helpful for people with diabetes or who are insulin resistant.

SWITCH "THIS"	FOR "THAT"
Instant oatmeal	Large flake rolled oats, oat bran
Rice Krispies, corn flakes, sweetened cereals	All-Bran, Bran Buds, or Special K cereal
White bread, rolls, bagels, croissants	Wholegrain, multi-grain, pumpernickel, or sourdough bread
White hamburger buns	100% whole wheat pita bread
Corn or white flour tortillas	100% whole wheat flour tortillas
Regular crackers, rice cakes	Wholegrain crackers (with no trans-fats)
English muffins	Whole wheat pita bread or grilled portobello mushrooms (used as a base for mini pizzas)
Cheese pizza (thick crust)	Whole wheat vegetable pizza (thin crust)
Lasagna noodles	Eggplant or zucchini slices
Spaghetti	Spaghetti squash
White pasta (well-cooked)	Whole wheat pasta (cooked al dente)
Instant, short-grain, or jasmine rice, risotto	Basmati (brown or white), converted long-grain rice
Potatoes (most varieties)	Small new potatoes
Mashed potatoes	Mashed sweet potatoes or cauliflower
French fries	Sweet potato "fries" (baked)
Potato latkes (fried)	Vegetable latkes (baked)
Baked, mashed, or fried potatoes	Corn on the cob
Potatoes or starchy side dishes	Whole grains (barley, couscous, quinoa) or legumes (baked, black, or kidney beans)
Starchy side dishes	Roasted, grilled, steamed, or stir-fried vegetables, salad with tomatoes, or coleslaw
Creamy salad dressings	Vinaigrette salad dressings (low-calorie)
Bottled salad dressings	Extra virgin olive oil plus lemon juice
Butter or margarine (on vegetables or bread)	Extra virgin olive oil
Regular mayonnaise	Light mayonnaise, mustard, mashed avocado

SWITCH "THIS"   FOR "THAT" (*Continued*)

SWITCH "THIS"	FOR "THAT"
Light peanut butter (contains sugars/fillers)	Natural peanut butter (watch portion size)
Higher-fat cheeses	Low-fat or part-skim cheeses
Bagel, lox, and cream cheese	Pita, lox, and light cream or cottage cheese with tomato and cucumber
Deli meat sandwich (on a roll or bagel)	Chicken or turkey breast, salmon, tuna, or veggie deli (on wholegrain bread or salad)
Cream-based soups, instant noodle soups	Vegetable, lentil, barley, or broth-based soups
Sugar-sweetened beverages	Water, herbal, or iced tea (with lemon)
Fruit juices or punch	Tomato or vegetable juice (low sodium)
Fruit juices	Fresh fruit (apples, berries, grapes, oranges)
Cantaloupe, honeydew, watermelon	Apples, berries, grapefruit, pears, plums
Raisins, dried cranberries	Frozen grapes
Jujubes, licorice	Dried fruit and nut mix
Gummy bears, jelly beans	Prunes or dried apricots
Milk chocolate bar	Bittersweet (dark) chocolate (1 oz)
Pretzels, potato chips	Almonds, walnuts, or pistachios (a handful)
Potato chips	Air-popped popcorn
Potato chips with dip	Carrots or celery sticks with hummus
Tortilla chips with salsa	Pepper strips or grape tomatoes with salsa
Sugar (white or brown)	Honey (pure floral), pure maple syrup, or artificial sweetener
Ice cream	Frozen nonfat or low-fat yogurt
Fruit-bottom or flavored yogurt	Nonfat plain yogurt (add your own fruit)
Store-bought muffins, cakes, or cookies	Homemade muffins, cakes, or cookies (with healthy oils and less sugar)

SHAKING THE SALT HABIT

• How Much is Enough? The current recommended sodium intake is about 2,400 mg a day (about 1 tsp), but less is better (1,500 mg or less), especially for middle-age and older adults, and for people with high blood pressure. Most people eat around 4,000 to 5,000 mg of sodium a day, about 2 tsp of salt. Blood pressure creeps up as we age, so cutting back on salt can prevent or delay the inevitable rise.

• Shake It Up, Baby! A healthy lifestyle including weight maintenance though diet, exercise, and reduced alcohol consumption can help to reduce your risk for high blood pressure, heart disease, and stroke.

• What's the Difference? Table salt contains additives, including iodine. Kosher salt is additive-free and coarse-grained. Many chefs prefer the clean taste and texture of Kosher salt.

• Weighing in on Salt: Did you know that 1 tsp of Kosher salt contains less sodium than 1 tsp of table salt? That's because Kosher salt has a larger grain, so less salt fits in the spoon! If you measure by volume, the sodium content will be lower for Kosher salt than for table salt. If you measure by weight, the sodium content will be the same.

• "Sea"-soning! Sea salt, either fine-grained or large crystals, is produced by the evaporation of sea water. Sea salt contains trace amounts of minerals. The sodium content of fine-grain sea salt is comparable to table salt. The sodium content of coarse sea salt is comparable to Kosher salt. Chefs use sea salt as a finishing salt, adding it to foods just before serving.

• Analyze This! When a specific amount of salt is called for in my recipes, sodium is calculated in the analysis. When a recipe doesn't give a specific measurement, then salt is not calculated in the nutrient analysis.

• Go Slow: The best approach is to gradually reduce the amount of salt you use when preparing foods. Try using half to one-quarter of the amount stated in the recipe. You can always add salt at the table.

• Shake It Up? Each shake of the salt shaker equals about 40 mg of sodium!

• Skipping Salt: Instead of adding salt to foods, add a squeeze of lemon or lime, a splash of vinegar, a drizzle of low-sodium soy sauce, a dash of pepper, or a sprinkling of different herbs. Mrs. Dash makes a variety of salt-free products.

• Soak Solution: To reduce the sodium content of Kosher meat and poultry (which are prepared with Kosher salt), soak in cold water plus a little lemon juice for 1/2 hour before cooking. (Don't try this with ground meat or poultry!) Rinse and drain thoroughly. If water is called for in your recipe, don't add salt to the water.

• Hide and Salt! Salt-free doesn't mean sodium-free. Foods with no salt added can still contain sodium, which can be in many forms—not just as table salt or sodium chloride. It also comes as sodium benzoate (a preservative), sodium nitrate (found in processed meats), and monosodium glutamate (known as MSG). Even baking powder, baking soda, diet colas, sport drinks, and sparkling mineral water contain sodium.

• A-Salt and Buttery? Use unsalted butter or margarine (in small amounts), or switch to extra virgin olive oil and canola oil.

• Un-Canny: Rinse canned legumes and vegetables well to reduce the sodium.

• Salt on the Side: Restaurant food is generally loaded with salt. Ask if they can prepare your dish without added salt. Choose grilled, baked, broiled, or steamed options from the menu instead of seasoned, marinated, or sauce-topped dishes.

• Smart Choices: The easiest way to avoid excess sodium is to choose fresh fruits, vegetables, whole grains, unsalted nuts, meat, poultry, and fish.

HIDDEN SALT ON THE SUPERMARKET SHELF

Processed foods are the main source of hidden sodium. Read labels carefully and look for low-sodium or sodium-free varieties. These foods are often high in sodium:

• Canned or packaged soups and soup mixes
• Tomato juice, vegetable juice
• Canned tomatoes, tomato sauces
• Prepared sauces such as pesto, salsa, barbecue sauce, and pasta sauce
• Soy sauce, tamari sauce
• Bottled salad dressings, mayonnaise
• Commercially prepared dips and spreads
• Condiments such as mustard, ketchup, relish, pickles, and olives
• Seasonings such as spice blends, seasoning salt, garlic salt, and lemon pepper
• Baking soda, baking powder, and monosodium glutamate (MSG)
• Canned vegetables and legumes
• Canned salmon, tuna, sardines, lox, and herring

• Cheese
• Kosher poultry and meats
• Deli and luncheon meats
• Frozen TV entrees and side dishes
• Commercially prepared salads and grains
• Rice and pasta mixes
• Packaged crunchy snacks such as chips, pretzels, popcorn, and crackers
• Nuts and dried fruits
• Packaged cereals
• Breads, rolls, and baked goods
• Soft drinks and sparkling mineral water

FOOD STORAGE TIPS

• Pack Date: This is the date the item was packed by the manufacturer. The cryptic codes, used on many cans and packaged products, are often difficult to decipher. If you have a questionable product in your cupboard, call the manufacturer's toll-free number for guidance.

• Expiration Date: If you haven't used a perishable product by the expiration date on the package, you should probably throw it out, especially if it hasn't been refrigerated the whole time. (If in doubt, throw it out.)

• Best Before Date: This date indicates how long the unopened product will retain its freshness and quality. Once opened, the "best before" date no longer applies.

• Canned foods and jars should be stored in a cool, dark place—preferably at 65°F or lower. Most will last up to a year. Once opened, they keep 2 to 3 days in an airtight container in the refrigerator. For best taste

TIME LIMITS FOR FOOD STORAGE	REFRIGERATOR (40°F)	FREEZER (0°F)
Soups and stews (meat-based)	3 to 4 days	3 to 4 months
Soups and stews (vegetable-based)	3 to 4 days	3 to 4 months
Fresh beef (roasts, steaks)	3 to 4 days	6 to 12 months
Fresh ground meat	1 to 2 days	2 to 3 months
Cooked ground meat	1 to 2 days	2 to 3 months
Cooked meat, meat dishes	3 to 4 days	2 to 3 months
Fresh chicken, turkey (whole, pieces)	1 to 2 days	6 to 9 months
Fresh ground poultry	1 to 2 days	2 to 3 months
Cooked ground poultry	1 to 2 days	2 to 3 months
Cooked chicken, poultry dishes	3 to 4 days	4 to 6 months
Poultry (pieces) with gravy or sauce	2 to 3 days	4 to 6 months
Fresh lean fish (sole)	2 to 3 days	6 months
Fresh fatty fish (salmon)	2 to 3 days	2 to 3 months

and texture, follow the guidelines suggested.

• Most people keep their refrigerator temperature at about 40°F, rather than 34°F, which is the refrigerator temperature at your supermarket. To ensure safe food storage, invest in a refrigerator thermometer. Don't leave the refrigerator door open longer than absolutely necessary—it's not an efficient way to get rid of your "hot flashes!"

FOOD STORAGE GUIDELINES

• Chocolate keeps for 1 year from its production date. (But it doesn't last that long in my kitchen!)

• Cereals keep 6 to 12 months unopened. Once opened, they keep about 4 months. Place in an airtight container or in a large, re-sealable plastic bag.

• Cooking oil keeps for 18 months from its production date, or check the "best before" date on the label. Once opened, it keeps for about 3 months in a cool, dark place.

• Dried herbs and spices keep 12 to 24 months unopened. Once opened, they keep for 12 months in an airtight container in a cool, dark place.

• Eggs keep for 4 weeks in the refrigerator after the date on the package. Store them in their original carton or container, not on the door of the refrigerator. Refer to How to Test if an Egg Is Fresh (see page 479).

• Flours and grains may become rancid with time. Check "best before" date. Once opened, store in an airtight container or large re-sealable plastic bag in a cool, dry place. Storage times vary.

• Jams and jellies keep for 12 months un-opened. Once opened, they keep for 3 to 4 months in the refrigerator.

• Bottled juice keeps for 8 months from production date, if unopened. Once opened, it keeps for 1 week.

• Ketchup keeps for 1 year unopened. Once opened, it keeps for 4 months in the refrigerator.

• Mayonnaise keeps for 3 years unopened. Once opened, it keeps for 2 months in the refrigerator.

• Milk keeps for 7 days after the "best be-fore" date. Once opened, it keeps for 4 to 6 days in the refrigerator.

• Bottled mustard keeps for 2 years un-opened. Once opened, it keeps for 6 months in the refrigerator.

• Dried pasta keeps for 6 to 8 months. Place boxed pasta in re-sealable plastic bags to avoid insect infestation.

• Peanut butter keeps for 2 years unopened. Once opened, it keeps for 3 months in the refrigerator.

• Canned tomatoes and canned or bottled tomato sauce keep for 6 to 12 months unopened. Once opened, they keep 4 or 5 days in the refrigerator.

• Salad dressing keeps for 6 months after the "best before" date. Once opened, it keeps for 6 months in the refrigerator.

• Canned salmon or tuna keeps for 1 year unopened. Once opened, it keeps 3 days in an airtight container (not in the can) in the refrigerator.

KITCHEN EQUIPMENT

• Welcome to my kitchen! I actually have two kitchens. The main one is average in size, functional, and busy. I also have another kitchen, next to my office, where I test recipes for my cookbooks and teach cooking classes.

• I believe in "machine cuisine." Some of my favorite appliances are the food processor, microwave oven, slow cooker, outdoor gas grill, and indoor electric grill. I've provided suggestions and tips (pages 31–36) to help you make better use of these appliances.

• Although my bread machine is wonder-ful for mixing up bread dough in minutes, I prefer to bake my yeast breads in the oven instead of the bread machine because I pre-fer the final results. See page 341 for helpful tips on using a bread machine.

• I use an immersion stick blender to purée soups and sauces to the desired consistency, and I use a high-speed blender when mak-ing smoothies and silky-smooth soups. My heavy-duty electric stand mixer is excellent for whipping egg whites and other baking tasks. I use my mini-processor to mince herbs and chop nuts. My coffee grinder is great when I need to grind flaxseed. My rice cooker cooks grains perfectly.

• It's important to have the right tools for the right task. I have a collection of good qual-ity knives in various sizes, including several chef's knives, paring and utility knives, and an assortment of cutting boards. I also have a few vegetable peelers and garlic presses, and I use an instant-read thermometer to check the internal temperature of meats and poultry.

• I have skillets (nonstick and regular), pots and pans in a variety of sizes, and a large nonstick wok. I have glass and ceramic baking dishes and casseroles, large, rimmed aluminum baking sheets, assorted baking pans, loaf pans, and pie plates. My muffin pans range in size from mini to maxi—I also have muffin top pans. I collect rubber and metal spatulas in all sizes and shapes, lots of measuring equipment, mixing bowls, strainers . . . and the list goes on.

• My advice? It's better to own fewer pieces of good quality, versatile kitchen equipment and use them rather than collect gadgets, cookware, and appliances that you never use. Remember, form follows function. Focus on quality, not quantity.

FOOD PROCESSOR POWER

• A Cut Above the Rest: The steel blade for your food processor is the "do-almost-every-thing" blade. Use it to chop foods with quick on/off pulses. You can also mince, grind, pu-rée, emulsify, mix, blend, knead, and whip by letting the machine run until the desired results are achieved.

• Keep it Dry: When chopping or mincing, make sure the bowl, blade, and food are dry.

• Don't Fill 'er Up: When you want to chop, mince, or purée fruits and vegetables, don't fill the work bowl more than 1/3 to 1/2 full. For larger quantities, process in batches. If you overload the processor bowl, you may end up with mush!

• Order, Please! Process the hard or dry ingredients first, then the soft or wet ingredients. Never process foods that are too hard to cut with a knife. You could damage the blade or the machine.

• Drop and Chop: Small or very hard foods such as garlic should be dropped in through the feed tube while the motor is running. Very hard foods, such as chocolate and almonds, make a loud noise at first, so don't be alarmed.

• Size Counts: For uniform chopping, cut the foods being processed into chunks that are similar in size, about 1 to 1 1/2 inches. Instead of using a ruler, use this quick way to measure: make a circle with your thumb and index finger—the food portion should be equal in diameter to that circle.

• Let Your Eye be Your Guide: Processing times vary according to texture, temperature, and size of food. Quick on/off pulses will help you control the texture and prevent foods from becoming overprocessed. Onions, zucchini, bell peppers, and other foods with a high water content will quickly become puréed if you aren't careful.

• Time It Right: Mincing takes 6 to 8 seconds, mixing cake and muffin batters takes 1 1/2 to 2 minutes, and kneading yeast dough takes less than a minute. You may have to stop the processor once or twice to scrape down the sides of the bowl with a rubber spatula.

• Flour Power: When adding flour to cakes, muffins, and cookies, blend it in using on/off pulses, just until it disappears. Overprocessing results in poor volume or heavy baked goods.

• Purée Power: For smoother purées, process the solids first, then slowly add the liquids through the feed tube while the motor is running.

• Vegetable Power: Leftover cooked vegetables will thicken gravies, sauces, and soups with minimal calories and carbs. Purée until smooth and creamy.

• Thick or Thin: The thicker the mixture, the more you can process in one batch without it leaking from the bowl. If the mixture is thin and the bowl is filled past the top of the hub of the steel blade, the mixture may leak out between the top of the bowl and the cover when the motor is running.

• Grate News: You can "grate" food by chopping it finely on the steel blade when appearance is not important (e.g., cheese for sauces, vegetables for soups).

• Be Prepared: To save time and clean-up, process more food than you need, such as grated chocolate, cheese, nuts, and onions, and refrigerate or freeze extras for future use.

• In a Spin? Always wait for the blades to stop spinning before removing the cover.

• Give It a Whirl! Empty contents of the bowl, then return the bowl and blade to the base of the machine, replace the cover, and turn on the processor. The blade will spin itself clean in moments!

• Avoid Ring Around the Counter: When you uncover the processor bowl, place the cover upside-down on your counter. Saves on clean-up.

• Quick Clean-up: Paper towels are handy to wipe out the processor bowl between steps.

• Keep It Clean: Rinse the bowl, the cover, and the blade(s) immediately after use. A dish brush simplifies clean-up. Never let the blade(s) soak in soapy water—you can accidentally cut yourself by reaching in blindly. Most processor parts are dishwasher-safe, but it's best to check your manual.

BE A MICROWAVE MAVEN

• Contain Yourself: To reduce your exposure to harmful chemicals, don't microwave foods in plastic bags, plastic wrap, or disposable plastic containers from the prepared food department of the supermarket. When subjected to heat, chemicals from the plastic can leach and migrate into foods, especially fatty foods.

• Don't Take the Wrap! Never cover food that is being cooked or heated in the microwave with plastic cling wrap (see Contain Yourself, above). After microwaving, wait until the food has cooled completely before covering it with plastic cling wrap and storing it in the refrigerator.

• Pan-tastic! Glass baking dishes are oven-proof and microwaveable. Use the casserole cover, a microwaveable dinner plate, or parchment paper to cover the dish.

• Be Flexible: To make parchment paper more flexible, place it briefly under running lukewarm water. You can then mold it easily around the dish or casserole as a covering.

• Store It Right: Don't store hot food in disposable plastic containers or re-sealable plastic bags. Instead, use heat-resistant glass or ceramic containers such as those made by Pyrex and Corning Ware.

• Dish-Stressed? Freeze food in a microwaveable baking dish that has been lined with heavy-duty foil. When it's completely frozen, remove the foil-wrapped food from the dish. Now your casserole is free to use for other recipes. To defrost or reheat, unwrap the food and place it back in the original baking dish.

• Time It Right: Always check food shortly before the estimated cooking time is over. Food will continue to cook from residual heat after the cooking time is completed—this is known as "standing time."

• Get Adjusted: Microwave ovens vary, so cooking times may need to be adjusted. Times in this book are based on a 700-watt microwave oven. (1 cup of water boils in 2 to 2¼ minutes on high.)

• Timing Tips: To double the recipe, allow ½ to ⅔ more cooking time. To make half the recipe, allow ⅓ less cooking time.

• Hot Stuff! To test if a food is fully heated, insert the blade of a knife into the center of the food. When you remove the knife, it should feel hot to the touch.

• Frozen Assets: To defrost or reheat frozen foods, transfer them to a heat-resistant glass or ceramic container to thaw or heat. An easy way to remove frozen food from its original container is to place the tightly covered container under running water for a minute or two, then unmold the food from the container.

SLOW COOKERS

• The Low-Down on Slow Cookers: Electric slow cookers, such as Crock-Pots, come in a variety of sizes and shapes. They are easy to clean and are usually dishwasher-safe. A good choice for a medium-sized family is one with a 5- to 7-quart capacity, which is large enough to allow for leftovers. (I use a 6-quart oval slow cooker, which is ideal for my needs.) The keep-warm feature is also useful.

• Love Me Tender: A slow cooker is excellent for tough cuts of meat and fibrous vegetables that are usually cooked on top of the stove or braised in the oven. The slow cooker cooks them at a low heat, ranging from 200–300°F, in a tightly sealed, moist environment. It's also excellent for stews, meatballs, cabbage rolls, chili, spaghetti sauces, and soups.

• Lower the Liquid: When converting a recipe and cooking it in a slow cooker, reduce the amount of liquid to compensate for the fact that there will be little evaporation during cooking.

• Carefree Cooking: An electric slow cooker is wonderful for make-ahead meals. Just combine the ingredients in the removable pot (spray it first with cooking spray) and store in the refrigerator overnight. The next day, put the pot into the heating unit and set the timer.

• Conversion Times: If your recipe calls for 15 to 30 minutes of cooking, cook it for 4 to 8 hours on the low setting, or 1½ to 2 hours on the high setting. If your recipe calls for 30 to 60 minutes, cook it for 6 to 8 hours on the low setting, or 3 to 4 hours on the high setting.

• No Peeking, Please! Each time you lift the lid, it will prolong the cooking time by an additional 20 minutes.

• Late for Dinner? Timing isn't crucial—if you're late for dinner, an extra hour of cooking in the slow cooker usually won't affect the recipe.

• Is It Done Yet? Meat and poultry should be tender when done, and easily pierced by a knife. For soups and stews, do a taste-check to determine if the flavors are fully developed.

• Liquid Assets: If there's excess liquid left in the pot at the end of the cooking time, drain it into a small saucepan to make a sauce. Simmer it over medium heat, uncovered, for a few minutes or until it has reduced and thickened to the desired consistency.

• It's in the Bag! Disposable slow cooker liners save on clean-up and come in a variety of sizes. If you don't have any on hand, you can line your slow cooker with a commercial cooking bag. Fill it with the ingredients and close the bag. Make several slits in the top of the bag to allow the steam to escape.

• Hot Stuff! Some of the newer models of slow cookers are much hotter than older models, even on the low setting. The following trick should help prevent any problems, especially when making cholent (page 152 and page 185 for recipes): put an inch of water in the bottom of the remove-able pot before lining it with a disposable slow cooker liner or cooking bag. The water forms a barrier between the heating unit and the bag containing the food which is being cooked. The bag will bob up and down during cooking, but that's okay.

GRILL IT RIGHT

GAS AND CHARCOAL GRILLS

• Don't Let the Flames Begin! Heterocyclic aromatic amines (HCAs) are formed when meat, poultry, or fish—grilled or broiled at very high temperatures—become charred. HCAs are carcinogenic, so remove all charred or blackened portions before eating.

• Good News: HCAs don't form on grilled vegetables or fruits, so grill them often.

• Don't be a Drip: When meat, poultry, and fish are grilled, the fat drips down onto the hot coals or stones, forming carcinogens that are deposited back onto the food by smoke and flare-ups. Choose lean cuts of meat and poultry and trim them well to reduce drips and flare-ups.

• Rare Findings: The National Cancer Institute has found that people who ate well-cooked meats (medium-well or well-done) had triple the risk of stomach cancer compared to those who ate rare or medium-rare meats. Eating well-done barbecued or fried meats several times a week may be associated with an increased risk of developing certain cancers. Just be sure to cook food to a safe eating temperature (refer to Temperature's Rising, page 35, for guidelines).

• Get Skewed: Add grilled vegetable skewers to your meal. Arrange the veggies on separate skewers from the meat or chicken and grill until tender and golden. This ensures even cooking of meat and veggies. Skewered kabobs grill quickly, which helps to minimize health risks.

• Piercing Is Out, Tongs Are In: Don't pierce meat with a fork when turning or moving it during grilling as the fat and juices will be released and drip down. Use long-handled tongs, which also help prevent burns.

• The Heat's On: Don't grill over direct or high heat. When using a charcoal grill, place food around the hot coals, not directly over them. When using a gas grill, turn on one burner, then cook the food on the other side of the grill. Grill over medium to medium-high heat.

• Hand-y Tips! To check the heat, place your hand 3 to 4 inches above the top of the cooking grate and count the seconds until the heat forces you to pull your hand away.

1 to 2 seconds means high heat.

3 seconds means medium-high heat.

4 to 5 seconds means medium heat.

• Open or Closed? Closing the lid traps heat, adds flavor, and decreases cooking time. Lift the lid only when you have to turn the food. As a general rule, if the cooking time is 25 minutes or less, leave the lid open. Close the lid if the cooking time is longer than 25 minutes.

• Time-Saver: Precook meat or poultry in the oven, using 3/4 of the recommended cooking time as a guideline. You can also precook it in the microwave, allowing 4 minutes per pound on high. Transfer the meat or poultry immediately to a hot grill to finish cooking and to create grill marks.

• Temperature's Rising: Insert an instant meat thermometer into the center of chicken or meat to ensure that it's properly cooked. Cook chicken to an internal temperature of 165°F throughout. Large cuts of meat, such as London broil or steak, should be cooked from 145°F (medium-rare) to 160°F (medium). Cook burgers to an internal temperature of 165°F.

• Keep It Clean: Wash your hands before and after handling food. To avoid cross-contamination, use separate cutting boards, dishes, and utensils. Clean all surfaces with disposable paper towels.

• Parchment Power: Place raw foods on a parchment paper-lined platter. Transfer foods to the hot grill and discard the parchment paper. Line the platter with a new piece of parchment paper before placing the cooked food back on the platter to prevent cross-contamination and save on clean-up.

• Clean It Twice: A metal grill brush is excellent for cleaning the grill. Clean the grill once before cooking and once after cooking. Better safe than sorry!

• Barbecue Bonus: Grill extra portions of chicken or steak, undercooking slightly. When cool, wrap the meat and freeze. Thaw and heat in the microwave for that "just-cooked" taste.

• Sweet News: Grilled fruit makes a delicious and healthy dessert. Try slices or skewers of pineapple, peaches, mangoes, and/or bananas, and boost your intake of fruit. Ready in minutes!

ELECTRIC GRILLS

• Grilling Anytime, Anywhere: Electric grills are wonderful when the weather's not! They're quick and easy to use and have a non-stick surface, so clean-up is easy. Some brands come with removable grilling plates that are dishwasher-safe. Use your grill to cook meat, poultry, fish, sandwiches, vegetables, even fruits. So versatile!

• Spaced Out: Electric grills are affordable and compact—they're great for small kitchens with limited counter or cabinet space, or for use in student dorms and studio apartments.

• Size Counts: Electric grills come in a variety of sizes. If you're cooking for one or two, or do very little cooking, buy a small grill. If you have guests or like leftovers, choose one with a medium-sized grilling surface. If you like to entertain or have a larger family, buy one with a large grilling surface.

• Temperature Rising: Some electric grills come with variable temperature controls, while others have one setting with a fixed temperature that ranges from 350–450°F, depending on the wattage.

• Fat Facts: Nonstick grilling surfaces let you grill low-fat foods without sticking and the excess fat within the food drips away as it grills.

• Timely Tips: Electric grills preheat in 10 minutes, so use that time to prepare your recipe. Two-sided grills cook in half the time of a charcoal or gas grill, so most foods will cook in 5 to 10 minutes—perfect for hurried households!

• Open and Shut Case: Food cooked on a two-sided contact grill will be moist and juicy. When you close the lid, the food is pressed between the hot grilling plates, trapping the moisture and creating attractive grill marks.

• Keep It Hot: Grills that work on a timer cool down quickly when the cooking time is up. If you are cooking several batches of food, leave the timer on so the grill will stay hot.

• Is It Done Yet? Check for doneness. An instant-read meat thermometer is useful. Cook fish to an internal temperature between 140–145°F, steak to anywhere between 145–160°F, and chicken and burgers to 165°F.

• Clean-up Time: After removing cooked food from the grill, turn off the heat and let the grill cool slightly. Place a moist, soapy paper towel between the warm (not hot) grill plates. When you have finished eating, the grill will be a snap to wipe clean. Be sure to rinse off any soapy residue. This is a terrific trick if your grill plates aren't removable!

• Trade-Offs: Electric grills don't have the smoky flavor of charcoal or gas grills, but you also don't get the flare-ups that happen when the fat drips down onto the hot coals or stones, forming carcinogens that are deposited back onto the food.

MARIN-AIDES

• Marinating Solutions: Marinating helps create a barrier against heat that significantly lowers the formation of carcinogenic HCAS (see Gas and Charcoal Grills, page 34). Marinating meats and poultry before cooking also makes them more tender and flavorful.

• Bowl Them Over: If using an acid-based marinade, such as vinegar or citrus juice, place the meat, fish, or vegetables and the marinade in a non-reactive (glass, ceramic, or stainless steel) bowl.

• Cheater's Marinade: Use your favorite salad dressing (regular or low-calorie) as a quick marinade for meat, poultry, fish, or vegetables. Good choices are balsamic or vinaigrette. Dressings that are high in sugar or that contain tomatoes have a tendency to burn. Avoid fat-free salad dressings—they usually contain high-fructose corn syrup (HFCS).

• It's in the Bag! Marinating foods in a heavy-duty re-sealable plastic bag allows for a more thorough coating of poultry, meat, fish, or vegetables—you'll also use less marinade.

• Shake It Up: If using marinade in a bag, shake the bag and turn the meat or massage it so it's evenly coated.

• Time to Marinate: Marinate meats or poultry at room temperature for 30 to 60 minutes, or in the refrigerator for a day or two. Don't marinate fish for more than an hour before cooking or it will start to "cook."

• Brush Up: Use separate brushes to baste raw and cooked meats, poultry, or fish. Silicone basting brushes are easy to clean and are dishwasher-safe. When brushing foods with marinade during cooking, make sure to cook the food 2 to 3 minutes longer after brushing it with marinade.

• First Aid Marinade: Drain the marinade before grilling. To use the leftover marinade for basting or as a sauce, bring it to a boil, then simmer it for 5 minutes before drizzling it over the cooked food. *Never* use leftover marinade, which contains bacteria, without boiling it first.

FOOD SAFETY

• Refrigerate foods and leftovers within two hours after cooking. Bacteria multiply rapidly between 40°F and 140°F. Split leftovers into smaller portions and store them in shallow containers in the refrigerator so they'll cool quickly. Use within 2 to 3 days.

• When reheating leftovers, heat them to 165°F. Soups and sauces should be brought to a full, rolling boil.

• Don't defrost food at room temperature. Use your refrigerator instead, allowing 6 hours for each pound of food. If you defrost food in the microwave, cook it immediately after defrosting.

• Foods stored in an upright or chest freezer will keep for a longer time than if stored in the freezer compartment of your refrigerator.

• Although foods may be safe to eat if frozen beyond the recommended time, the taste or texture may be affected. Refer to Time Limits for Food Storage (page 29) for basic guidelines.

PAN SIZES

PAN SIZES	METRIC	CAPACITY
8-inch square pan	20- × 20- × 5 cm	2 liters (8 cups)
9-inch square pan	23- × 23- × 5 cm	2.5 liters (10 cups)
9- × 5-inch loaf pan	23- × 13- × 6 cm	2 liters (8 cups)
12-cup fluted tube (Bundt) pan	25- × 9 cm	3 liters (12 cups)
10-inch tube pan	25- × 10 cm	4 liters (16 cups)
8-inch round layer pan	20- × 5 cm	1.5 liters (6 cups)
9-inch round layer pan	23- × 5 cm	2 liters (8 cups)
7- × 11-inch glass baking dish	18- × 28- × 5 cm	2 liters (8 cups)
9- × 13-inch glass baking dish	22- × 33- × 5 cm	3.5 liters (15 cups)
9-inch pie plate	23- × 4 cm	1 liter (4 cups)
10- × 15- × 1-inch rimmed baking sheet	25- × 38- × 3 cm	2.5 liters (10 cups)
9-inch springform pan	23 cm	2.5 liters (10 cups)
10-inch springform pan	25 cm	3 liters (12 cups)

LENGTH MEASUREMENTS

One inch equals 2.5 centimetres (cm).
Each 5 cm is 2 inches.

0.3 cm	1/8 inch
0.6 cm	1/4 inch
1.2 cm	1/2 inch
2.5 cm	1 inch
10 cm	4 inches
20 cm	8 inches
30 cm	12 inches

TEMPERATURE CONVERSIONS

To convert from °F to °C:
(°F–32) divided by 1.8 = °C

To convert from °C to °F:
(1.8 × °C) plus 32 = °F

Freezer temperature	–18°C	0°F
Water freezes	0°C	32°F
Refrigerator temperature	4°C	40°F
Room temperature	20°C	68°F
Water temperature to proof yeast	41–46°C	105–115°F
Safe temperature for cooking ground beef	71°C	160°F
Safe minimum temperature for cooking poultry	74–77°C	165–170°F
Safe temperature for poultry (well-done)	79°C	175°F
Water boils	100°C	212°F

OVEN TEMPERATURE EQUIVALENTS

When baking in glass dishes, or in black or dark-colored baking pans, reduce temperature by 25°F (10°C).

120°C	250°F
135°C	275°F
150°C	300°F
160°C	325°F
180°C	350°F
190°C	375°F
200°C	400°F
220°C	425°F
230°C	450°F
245°C	475°F
260°C	500°F

VOLUME & WEIGHT CONVERSIONS

TO OUNCES
Drop the last digit from the number of milliliters (mL) or grams (g) and divide by 3. For example, 156 mL is about 5 oz (15 divided by 3 = 5).

TO MILLILITERS OR GRAMS
Multiply the number of ounces by 30. For example, 1 ounce is about 30 mL or grams.

VOLUME MEASUREMENTS	METRIC	IMPERIAL
1/4 tsp	1 mL	—
1/2 tsp	2 mL	—
1 tsp	5 mL	—
1 Tbsp	15 mL	—
2 Tbsp	30 mL	1 fluid oz
1/4 cup	60 mL	2 fluid oz
1/3 cup	80 mL	3 fluid oz
1/2 cup	125 mL	4 fluid oz
3/4 cup	175 mL	6 fluid oz
1 cup	250 mL	8 fluid oz
4 cups	1 liter	32 fluid oz
	(actual is 35.2 oz)	

WEIGHT MEASUREMENTS IMPERIAL	METRIC
1 oz	30 g (actual is 28.4 g)
2 oz	60 g
3 oz	85 g
3^1/$_2$ oz	100 g
4 oz (^{1}/$_4$ lb)	115 g
6 oz	170 g
8 oz (^{1}/$_2$ lb)	250 g (actual is 227 g)
12 oz (^{3}/$_4$ lb)	375 g (actual is 340 g)
16 oz (1 lb)	500 g (actual is 454 g)
2 generous lb	1 kg (2.2 lb)

COOKING/BAKING SUBSTITUTIONS

(Also see Passover Cooking/Baking Substitutions on page 450)

FOR:	USE:
1 tsp baking powder	^{1}/$_2$ tsp cream of tartar plus ^{1}/$_4$ tsp baking soda
1 cup broth (chicken or vegetable)	^{1}/$_2$ to 1 tsp instant chicken-flavored soup mix plus 1 cup water (use pareve brands for vegetarian or dairy-free dishes)
1 Tbsp butter (in baking)	1 Tbsp canola, grapeseed, or walnut oil OR soft tub margarine such as Becel (contains dairy), Earth Balance Buttery Spread (dairy-free) or Fleischmann's (dairy-free). Light margarine can be used for streusel toppings, but not for regular baking.
1 Tbsp butter or margarine (in cooking)	1 Tbsp olive, canola, or grapeseed oil (or spray cookware with cooking spray)
1 cup butter, margarine or oil (in baking)	^{1}/$_2$ cup canola oil or soft tub margarine plus ^{1}/$_2$ cup fruit purée such as unsweetened applesauce, Banana Purée, or Prune Purée (page 373). You might be able to use a ratio of ^{1}/$_3$ cup oil or margarine to ^{2}/$_3$ cup fruit purée in some recipes.

FOR:	**USE:** (*Continued*)
1 cup buttermilk	1 Tbsp lemon juice or vinegar plus skim milk, soy, or rice milk to make 1 cup OR 1/2 cup nonfat yogurt or light sour cream mixed with 1/2 cup skim milk
1 oz dark, bittersweet or semi-sweet chocolate	1/4 cup chocolate chips
1 oz unsweetened chocolate	3 Tbsp unsweetened cocoa plus 1/2 Tbsp canola or vegetable oil OR 1 1/2 oz dark, bittersweet, or semi-sweet chocolate (reduce sugar in recipes by 2 Tbsp)
1 cup cream cheese (dairy)	1 cup light cream cheese or ricotta cheese, cottage cheese (pressed or smooth-texture), Homemade Cottage Cheese (page 177) or Firm Yogurt Cheese (page 178)
1 cup cream cheese (dairy-free)	1 cup Tofutti imitation cream cheese
1 large egg (in baking or cooking)	2 egg whites OR 1/4 cup pasteurized liquid egg whites OR 1/4 cup low-cholesterol liquid egg substitute For 2 large eggs, use 1 egg plus 2 whites
1 large egg (in baking)	1/4 cup mashed banana, soft tofu, yogurt, or light sour cream. (Baked goods may be more dense and heavier than those with eggs.)
1 large egg (in baking—flaxseed alternative)	Use ground flaxseed (or grind whole flaxseed in a coffee grinder or spice mill). For 1 large egg, combine 1 Tbsp ground flaxseed with 3 Tbsp hot water in a small bowl. Let stand until thick, 2 to 3 minutes. (Store leftover flaxseed in refrigerator or freezer.)
2 Tbsp flour (for thickening)	1 Tbsp cornstarch or potato starch

COOKING/BAKING SUBSTITUTIONS (*Continued*)

FOR:	USE: (*Continued*)
1 cup all-purpose flour	1/2 cup all-purpose flour plus 1/2 cup whole wheat flour OR 1 cup spelt flour OR 2/3 cup whole wheat or all-purpose flour plus 1/3 cup finely ground almonds (see Almond Meal, page 390). Do not substitute more than 25% to 50% of the flour with ground almonds OR 1/2 cup all-purpose flour plus 1/2 cup finely ground rolled oats. (Also refer to "Soy Secrets" on page 375)
1 cup whole wheat pastry flour	3/4 cup all-purpose flour plus 1/4 cup wheat germ
gluten-free flour	2 parts brown rice flour, 1 part sweet sorghum flour plus 1 part tapioca starch (or buy gluten-free flour blend). Add 1 tsp xanthan gum for each cup of gluten-free flour in cakes and cookie recipes.
juice of 1 lemon	3 to 4 Tbsp lemon juice (fresh or bottled)
juice of 1 lime	2 Tbsp lime juice
juice of 1 orange	1/3 to 1/2 cup orange juice
1 cup milk	1 cup lactose-reduced milk/lactaid OR use soymilk, orange or apple juice, water, coffee, or rice milk for dairy-free baking or cooking. (Rice milk has a high GI value.)
1/2 cup nuts (for nut allergies)	1/2 cup seeds (e.g., pumpkin seeds) or crunchy cereal (e.g., Special K)
1/2 cup raisins	1/2 cup dried cranberries, dried cherries, dried blueberries, dried apricots, pitted prunes, or dates
1 cup sour cream	1 cup light or nonfat sour cream or yogurt OR 1 cup imitation sour cream such as Tofutti Sour Supreme
1 cup granulated sugar (in baking)	1/2 cup granulated sugar plus 1/2 cup granular Splenda

FOR:	USE: (Continued)
1 cup packed brown sugar	1 cup granulated sugar plus 2 Tbsp molasses
1 tsp pure vanilla extract	1 tsp orange, almond, or coffee-flavored liquor
1 cup whipped cream	1 cup frozen light whipped topping, Almost Whipped Cream (page 410) or Soft Yogurt Cheese (page 178). For non-dairy (pareve) desserts, you can use a non-dairy whipped topping but it's high in saturated fat.

NUTRITIONAL ANALYSIS

• The nutritional analysis was calculated using data from ESHA (*The Food Processor* SQL Edition 9.8) and when necessary, manufacturers' food labels.

• If a recipe indicated a range of servings (4 to 6 servings), it was analyzed for 4 servings.

• The first ingredient was analyzed when there was a choice of ingredients (e.g., skim milk was analyzed when a recipe called for 1 cup skim milk or orange juice).

• The smaller measure of an ingredient was analyzed when a range was given (e.g., 1/4 cup was analyzed when a recipe called for 1/4 to 1/3 cup).

• The nutrient values were not rounded off for carbohydrates, fiber, and fat, but they were rounded off for protein, iron, and calcium.

• Olive and canola oils were the oils of choice. Soft tub margarine was used in some baking recipes.

• When eggs were called for, the recipe was analyzed using large eggs.

• Recipes that gave an option of using sugar or granular Splenda were analyzed for sugar. An analysis with Splenda was also provided when there was a significant difference in carbohydrates and/or calories.

• Specific measurements of salt were included in the analysis (e.g., 1 tsp salt). When a recipe didn't give a specific measurement for salt, then salt wasn't included in the analysis.

• Optional ingredients weren't included in the analysis.

• Garnishes weren't calculated unless a specific quantity was indicated.

• Variations of a recipe weren't analyzed unless there was a significant nutritional difference between the main recipe and the variation(s).

• A serving of at least 2 grams of fiber is considered a moderate source, 4 grams is a high source, and 6 grams of fiber is considered a very high source of fiber.

appetizers
& starters

APPETIZERS AND STARTERS

Double Your Dip: Many of the dips in this chapter are multi-purpose and can do double-duty as a salad dressing when thinned with a little milk, yogurt, or broth.

Spread It Around: Some of the dips and spreads, such as Black Bean Dip (page 47) or Tapenade (page 52) can be used instead of butter, margarine, or mayonnaise as a spread for sandwiches and wraps (see Sandwich Savvy, page 276, for ideas). Others, such as Roasted Eggplant Spread (page 53) or Luscious Lentil Paté (page 55), make a terrific topping for salads.

Spread Yourself Thin: If you're pressed for time, buy prepared low-fat dips such as hummus, eggplant spread, red pepper dip, or tofu spread. Be sure to check labels for fat and calories.

Fill 'er Up! Fill hollowed-out yellow, orange, and red peppers, eggplant, or acorn squash with assorted dips or spreads. Perfect party fare!

Super Bowl: Cut off the top of a pumpernickel bread (store-bought or homemade, page 346). Hollow out the inside, leaving a wall about 1/2-inch thick around. Cut the bread you've removed into bite-sized chunks. Fill the hollowed-out bread with your favorite dip and surround with bread chunks and assorted veggies.

Veggie Heaven: Choose a variety of shapes and colors when preparing a vegetable platter. Serve broccoli and cauliflower florets, celery sticks, bell peppers cut in strips, baby carrots, cherry or grape tomatoes, lightly steamed asparagus spears, or sugar snap peas . . . the choice is yours.

Skinny Dip: Dip crunchy veggies such as baby carrots, celery sticks, bell pepper strips, broccoli florets, or grape tomatoes in your favorite low-cal dip.

Leftover Crudités? Transform them into soup! Sauté 1 onion over medium heat in 1 Tbsp olive oil until golden. Add leftover vegetables plus enough water, vegetable or chicken broth to cover the vegetables by 1 inch. Season with salt and pepper to taste. Simmer for 30 minutes, then purée using an immersion blender. Soup-er!

Stick 'em Up! Grilled chicken skewers make excellent appetizers for a party or barbecue. Try Chicken Satay (page 217) or Grilled Chicken Skewers (page 218). Marinate the chicken days in advance and store in the freezer in re-sealable freezer bags. When needed, thaw them overnight in the refrigerator, then thread them onto skewers. (Don't forget to soak wooden skewers in water for about 1 hour before using to prevent them from burning.) Allow 2 to 4 per person as an appetizer.

Bocconcini Skewers: Marinate miniature bocconcini (soft mozzarella) balls in Pesto (pages 109–11) for 30 minutes. Thread the marinated cheese onto wooden skewers, alternating each one with a grape tomato. For a pretty presentation, insert the skewers into a half melon, placed flat-side down, on a serving platter.

Ease up on Cheese: Those chunks of cheese can make you chunky too, and crackers aren't all they're cracked up to be—they can be high in calories, saturated fat, and trans-fat.

Make Room for Mushrooms: Marinated Mushrooms (page 301) are perfect party fare because they can be made 1 week ahead of time and they don't require any cooking or heating up.

Double Duty: Many appetizers can be served as a main dish and vice versa. A main dish for 4 people will usually serve 6 to 8 as an appetizer or starter.

Keep It Under 100: Choose high-fiber starters and appetizers under 100 calories that fill you up without filling you out! Some handy nibbles are cut-up veggies (cherry tomatoes, baby carrots, bell peppers), air-popped popcorn, or a handful of nuts.

Party Smart! When faced with temptation, your best choice is a veggie appetizer or starter. If you must indulge in high-fat fare, eat a small portion—very, very slowly. Adjust for added calories and fat by making lighter choices the rest of the day. Also, increase your activity level. Reaching for a second helping does not count as a stretching exercise!

🍎 AIOLI

This garlic-flavored mayonnaise is terrific with lightly steamed or raw vegetables, and delicious with grilled or baked fish. Use aioli as a replacement for mayonnaise in wraps and sandwiches. For a different twist, try the variations below.

1 cup light mayonnaise or
   No-Yolk Mayonnaise (page 113)
2 Tbsp lemon juice (preferably fresh)
2 tsp grated lemon rind
3 cloves garlic (about 1 Tbsp minced)

1. In a small bowl, combine the mayonnaise, lemon juice, rind, and garlic, and mix well.

2. Cover and refrigerate until ready to use. Serve chilled.

Yield: About 1 cup. Keeps up to 1 week in the refrigerator. Don't freeze.

44 calories per Tbsp, 1.4 g carbohydrate, 0.1 g fiber, 0 g protein, 4.2 g fat (0.6 g saturated), 5 mg cholesterol, 102 mg sodium, 11 mg potassium, 0 mg iron, 2 mg calcium

Variations
• Add your favorite fresh or dried herbs (e.g., basil, oregano, thyme, rosemary, or dill).

• For an Asian flavor, add a little wasabi paste, minced fresh ginger, and a dash of soy sauce.

• Transform Aioli into a delicious salad dressing by thinning it with a little water.

♦ BLACK BEAN DIP

This is skinny dipping at its finest. Serve with Baked Tortilla Chips (page 59) or assorted raw veggies. It's also delicious as a substitute for mayonnaise on wraps and sandwiches.

2 tsp extra virgin olive oil
1 small onion, chopped
2 to 3 cloves garlic, minced
1 can (19 oz/540 mL) black beans, drained and rinsed
1/3 cup water
1 tsp chili powder
1/4 tsp cumin
Salt and freshly ground black pepper
2 tsp lemon or lime juice (preferably fresh)
Finely minced fresh cilantro and red pepper, for garnish

1. Heat oil in a large nonstick skillet over medium heat. Add onion and garlic, and sauté for 3 to 4 minutes or until softened. Stir in the black beans, water, chili powder, cumin, salt, and pepper. Simmer uncovered for 5 minutes, stirring occasionally. Stir in lemon juice and remove pan from heat.

2. Using a potato masher, immersion blender, or food processor, mash the bean mixture to the desired consistency.

3. Transfer to a serving bowl, cover, and refrigerate until ready to use. Garnish with cilantro and red pepper and serve chilled.

Yield: About 2 cups. Leftovers keep 3 to 4 days in the refrigerator. Don't freeze.

10 calories per Tbsp, 2.0 g carbohydrate, 0.6 g fiber, 0 g protein, 0.2 g fat (0 g saturated), 0 mg cholesterol, 52 mg sodium, 40 mg potassium, 0 mg iron, 5 mg calcium

Chef's Secrets

• A-Salt with a Deadly Weapon! To reduce the sodium content of canned beans by half, rinse well. Organic brands are lower in sodium than regular brands but are usually more expensive.

• Using Your Bean! The versatile black bean is wonderful in dips, soups, salads, salsas, stews, casseroles, chili, fajitas, and burritos.

Nutrition Note

• Black beans are high in folate, fiber, protein, magnesium, and antioxidants. They have a low glycemic index, which helps to stabilize blood sugar levels. Many people find black beans easier to digest than other types of beans.

♦ WHITE BEAN DIP

This quick, versatile mixture is marvelous as a dip with assorted vegetables. Serve with red, green, and yellow pepper strips, sliced cucumbers, baby carrots, and celery sticks. It also makes a super spread on toasted wholegrain or pumpernickel bread.

2 cloves garlic
15 or 19 oz can (425 to 540 mL) white kidney beans (cannellini beans), drained and rinsed
2 Tbsp lemon juice (preferably fresh)
2 Tbsp extra virgin olive oil
1/2 tsp cumin
1/2 tsp salt (or to taste)
1/4 tsp freshly ground black pepper
5 to 6 drops hot pepper sauce or 1/4 tsp chili powder
Chopped fresh parsley, black olives, and paprika, for garnish

1. Drop the garlic through the feed tube of a food processor fitted with the steel blade while the motor is running. Process until minced, about 10 seconds. Add beans, lemon juice, olive oil, cumin, salt, pepper, and hot pepper sauce. Process until smooth and creamy, about 1 to 2 minutes, scraping down the sides of the bowl as needed. If the mixture is too thick, thin with 2 Tbsp water.

2. Transfer the white bean dip to a serving bowl. Cover and chill for 1 to 2 hours before serving. Garnish with parsley, olives, and paprika.

Yield: About 1½ cups. Keeps about 1 week in the refrigerator in a tightly sealed container. Don't freeze.

19 calories per Tbsp, 1.9 g carbohydrate, 0.5 g fiber, 1 g protein, 1.0 g fat (0.1 g saturated), 0 mg cholesterol, 57 mg sodium, 2 mg potassium, 0 mg iron, 5 mg calcium

Variations
• Prepare as directed, adding ½ cup well-drained Roasted Red Peppers (page 59).

• Omit the hot pepper sauce; add 1 Tbsp minced fresh dillweed.

Nutrition Note
• Beans are a rich source of dietary fiber and they have a low glycemic index. Lemon juice slows digestion, lowering the GI of foods.

● GARDEN VEGETABLE HUMMUS

This guilt-free hummus can be used as a spread on pita bread or as a filling for tortilla wraps. It's excellent as a dip with veggies, crisp flatbread, or Pita Chips (page 60). Dip "a-weigh" to your heart's delight!

1 can (19 oz/540 mL) chickpeas, drained and rinsed
3 to 4 cloves garlic (about 1 Tbsp minced)
½ green pepper, seeded and cut in chunks
½ red pepper, seeded and cut in chunks
4 green onions or 1 medium onion, cut in chunks
¼ cup fresh basil
2 Tbsp extra virgin olive oil
2 Tbsp lemon juice (preferably fresh)
2 to 3 Tbsp tahini (sesame paste)
Salt and freshly ground black pepper
Chopped fresh parsley, for garnish

1. Combine all the ingredients except the parsley in a food processor fitted with the steel blade. Process with quick on/offs to start, then let the motor run until the mixture is very smooth, about 2 minutes, scraping down the sides of the bowl as needed.

2. Transfer the hummus to a serving bowl and sprinkle with parsley. Cover and chill in the refrigerator for 1 to 2 hours before serving. (The hummus will thicken when refrigerated.)

Yield: About 2½ cups. Keeps about 1 week in the refrigerator. Don't freeze.

21 calories per Tbsp, 2.5 g carbohydrate, 0.5 g fiber, 1 g protein, 1.0 g fat (0.1 g saturated), 0 mg cholesterol, 28 mg sodium, 30 mg potassium, 0 mg iron, 6 mg calcium

Mediterranean Hummus
Add ½ cup well-drained Roasted Red Peppers (page 59) and a dash of cumin; blend well. For an Italian twist, substitute pesto for the tahini and cumin.

Quick Chickpea Salad

Instead of puréeing the chickpea mixture in a food processor, combine the drained chickpeas with garlic in a mixing bowl. Omit the tahini. Coarsely chop the peppers and green onions. Add to the chickpeas along with the remaining ingredients and mix well. Chill well. Makes 6 servings of ³/₄ cup each. One serving contains 150 calories, 21.1 g carbohydrate, 4.4 g fiber, 5 grams protein, and 5.7 g fat (0.8 g saturated).

🎃 PUMPKIN HUMMUS

They'll never know this scrumptious spread contains pumpkin. The inspiration for this recipe comes from cookbook author and dear friend Kathy Guttman. I added chickpeas to pump up the nutritional profile. It makes a big batch, but you can make half the recipe and use the leftover pumpkin to make Pumpkin Cranberry Muffins (page 369) or Pumpkin Cheesecake (page 413). Keep on pump-in!

6 cloves garlic (about 2 Tbsp minced)
¹/₄ cup fresh parsley or cilantro leaves
1 can (19 oz/540 mL) chickpeas, drained and rinsed
¹/₄ cup tahini (sesame paste)
¹/₄ cup lemon juice (preferably fresh)
2 Tbsp extra virgin olive oil
1 can (15 oz/425 mL) canned pumpkin (about 2 cups)
2 tsp cumin (or to taste)
1 tsp salt (or to taste)
¹/₄ tsp smoked or Hungarian paprika
¹/₄ tsp cayenne pepper
1 to 2 tsp pure maple syrup (or to taste)
Pumpkin seeds, for garnish

1. In a food processor fitted with the steel blade, process the garlic and parsley until finely minced, about 10 seconds. Add the chickpeas and process until puréed, about 18 to 20 seconds. Add remaining ingredients except the pumpkin seeds and process until very smooth, about 2 minutes. If the mixture is too thick, add a little water.

2. Transfer the puréed pumpkin mixture to a bowl, cover, and refrigerate overnight for maximum flavor. Garnish with pumpkin seeds at serving time.

Yield: About 4 cups. Keeps about 1 week in the refrigerator. Freezes well for up to a month.

19 calories per Tbsp, 2.4 g carbohydrate, 0.5 g fiber, 1 g protein, 0.9 g fat (0.1 g saturated), 0 mg cholesterol, 52 mg sodium, 30 mg potassium, 0 mg iron, 6 mg calcium

Chef's Secrets

• Skinny Dip! This hummus is delicious as a dip served with raw vegetables or toasted pita wedges. It's also scrumptious as a spread on grilled pita bread and sandwiches.

• Wrap-ture! When making wraps, spread tortillas with hummus instead of mayonnaise.

• Frozen Assets! Freeze in 1 cup containers. When needed, thaw overnight in the refrigerator and stir before serving.

🍎 GUACAMOLE WITH HEARTS OF PALM

The inspiration for this Venezuelan variation of guacamole, known as guasacaca, comes from my friend Elena Eder of Miami. Elena adds hearts of palm to reduce the calories and fat. It's traditionally served with grilled meats or fish, tortillas, pita bread, or flatbread.

1 can (14 oz/398 mL) hearts of palm, well-drained
2 Tbsp fresh cilantro and/or parsley
1 small onion
1 clove garlic (about 1 tsp minced)
1/2 red pepper, cut in chunks
1 medium tomato, cored and quartered
1 medium avocado, peeled and pitted
1 Tbsp extra virgin olive oil
1 Tbsp lemon juice (preferably fresh)
1/2 tsp salt
Freshly ground black pepper
1/4 tsp cayenne pepper or chili powder

1. In a food processor fitted with the steel blade, process the hearts of palm and cilantro, using quick on/off pulses, until finely chopped. Transfer to a medium mixing bowl—you should have about 1 cup.

2. Process the onion, garlic, and red pepper with quick on/off pulses, until coarsely chopped. Add the tomato, avocado, oil, lemon juice, salt, pepper, and cayenne. Continue processing with several quick on/offs pulses, until the vegetables are coarsely chopped. Add to the hearts of palm and mix well. Adjust seasonings to taste.

Yield: About 3 cups. Keeps 4 to 5 days, in a tightly sealed container, in the refrigerator. Don't freeze.

46 calories per 1/4 cup serving, 3.2 g carbohydrate, 1.6 g fiber, 1 g protein, 3.7 g fat (0.5 g saturated), 0 mg cholesterol, 127 mg sodium, 140 mg potassium, 0 mg iron, 9 mg calcium

Chef's Secrets
• Go for Green! You don't have to worry about the avocado turning brown in this recipe—the addition of hearts of palm solves the problem.

• Hot, hot, hot! This traditional South American dish is made with red and green chili peppers, but I used red pepper and kicked up the heat with cayenne.

🍎 SPINACH ARTICHOKE DIP

This delicious dip will get you all "choked up." It makes a large quantity, so it's ideal for entertaining.

2 cloves garlic (about 2 tsp minced)
1 small onion
1 jar (6 oz/170 mL) marinated artichoke hearts, well-drained and rinsed
1 pkg (10 oz/300 g) frozen spinach, thawed and squeezed dry
1 cup light mayonnaise
1 cup low-fat sour cream or yogurt
1/4 cup grated Parmesan cheese
Salt and freshly ground black pepper

1. In a food processor fitted with the steel blade, process the garlic and onion until minced, about 10 to 12 seconds. Add the remaining ingredients and process with several quick on/off pulses, until the mixture is smooth, scraping down the sides of the bowl as needed.

2. Transfer the dip to a serving bowl, cover,

and refrigerate for several hours or overnight to allow the flavors to blend.

Yield: About 3 cups. Leftovers keep 4 to 5 days in the refrigerator. Don't freeze.

24 calories per Tbsp, 1.1 g carbohydrate, 0.2 g fiber, 1 g protein, 1.9 g fat (0.5 g saturated), 3 mg cholesterol, 51 mg sodium, 24 mg potassium, 0 mg iron, 18 mg calcium

Spinach Wraps

Spread a thin layer of dip on 10-inch whole wheat flour tortilla(s), leaving a 1/2-inch border around the entire outside edge of each tortilla. Top with a layer of baby spinach leaves. Arrange a narrow band of Roasted Red Peppers (page 59) along one edge. Roll up tightly, cover with plastic wrap, and refrigerate for up to 24 hours. When ready to serve, slice each tortilla, on the diagonal, into 6 slices. Serve chilled. Wrap-sody!

Chef's Secrets

• Skinny Dipping: Serve with raw or lightly steamed veggies, toasted pita bread wedges, or Baked Tortilla Chips (page 59).

• Bowl Them Over: Cut one inch off the top of a round pumpernickel bread. Hollow out the inside, leaving a wall of bread about 1/2-inch thick around. Cut the bread you've removed into bite-sized cubes. Fill the hollowed loaf with dip and serve with veggies and bread cubes for dipping.

• Fishful Thinking: This dip also makes a super sauce for grilled or baked fish. Or add a spoonful or two of dip instead of mayonnaise to tuna or salmon salad.

• Leftover dip? Add a little skim milk to thin it down; use as a salad dressing.

❧ SUN-DRIED TOMATO DIP

Absolutely addictive! Serve this with assorted veggies or crisp flatbread.

1 clove garlic
2 green onions, cut in 1-inch pieces
1/3 cup oil-packed sun-dried tomatoes, well-drained
1 cup light or fat-free cream cheese, cut into chunks
1/2 cup light sour cream
1/2 cup light mayonnaise
1/2 tsp dried basil or 1 Tbsp fresh basil
Freshly ground black pepper

1. In a food processor fitted with the steel blade, process the garlic, green onions, and the sun-dried tomatoes until minced, about 6 to 8 seconds. Add the cream cheese, sour cream, mayonnaise, basil, and pepper to taste. Process until blended, about 10 seconds, scraping down the sides of the bowl as needed.

2. Transfer the mixture to a container, cover, and chill for at least 1 hour to allow the flavors to blend.

Yield: About 2 1/2 cups. Leftovers keep for 4 or 5 days in the refrigerator. Don't freeze.

32 calories per Tbsp, 1.3 g carbohydrate, 0.1 g fiber, 1 g protein, 2.6 g fat (1.1 g saturated), 6 mg cholesterol, 49 mg sodium, 38 mg potassium, 0 mg iron, 14 mg calcium

Variation

• Dairy-Free: Use an imitation sour cream and/or cream cheese, such as Tofutti.

appetizers & starters

TAPENADE

Tapenade is a thick paste made from olives, capers, and anchovies. Try it as a spread on bread or crackers, or add a dollop to cooked beans or pasta for a flavor boost. Olives, capers, and anchovies are all high in salt, so enjoy in moderation.

2 cups pitted kalamata or other brine-cured black olives such as Niçoise or Gaeta (1 lb/500 g)
5 to 6 oil-packed anchovy fillets (1/2 of a 2 oz/56 g can), drained and rinsed
3 to 4 cloves garlic (about 1 Tbsp minced)
2 Tbsp capers, drained and rinsed
2 Tbsp lemon juice (preferably fresh)
3 to 4 Tbsp extra virgin olive oil
1/2 tsp dried thyme
Freshly ground black pepper

1. In a food processor fitted with the steel blade, process the drained olives until coarsely chopped, about 10 to 12 seconds. Add the remaining ingredients and process with quick on/off pulses, until coarsely puréed.

2. Transfer to a container, cover, and refrigerate until ready to use.

Yield: About 1 1/2 cups. Keeps up to 1 month in the refrigerator. Don't freeze.

45 calories per Tbsp, 1.3 g carbohydrate, 0.1 g fiber, 0 g protein, 4.3 g fat (0.5 g saturated), 1 mg cholesterol, 228 mg sodium, 5 mg potassium, 0 mg iron, 6 mg calcium

Chef's Secrets
• True Wrap-ture! Spread a thin layer of tapenade on whole wheat flour tortillas. Top with thinly sliced turkey and grilled vegetables. Chicken or tuna salad also makes for delicious fillings.

• Bread Spread! Spread tapenade on crusty sourdough or a whole wheat baguette. Layer with thinly sliced tomatoes, hard-boiled egg, and red onion. Top with tuna salad.

TWO-WAY TZATZIKI

The dairy-free version (page 53) of this versatile cucumber sauce is terrific as a topping for grilled chicken, beef, or lamb. Either version goes great with fish, latkes, or roasted vegetables, and also makes a delicious dip for raw vegetables or pita bread wedges. Fresh mint adds an authentic Middle Eastern flavor.

1 medium English cucumber, peeled and grated
6 green onions, finely chopped
3 cloves garlic (about 1 Tbsp minced)
1/4 cup minced fresh dillweed or mint
1 1/2 cups light sour cream
Salt and freshly ground black pepper

1. Place cucumber in a strainer and press gently to drain excess liquid.

2. In a medium bowl, combine the cucumber, green onions, garlic, dillweed, sour cream, and salt and pepper to taste; mix well.

3. Cover and refrigerate until ready to use. Serve chilled.

Yield: 12 servings (about 1/4 cup each). Leftovers will keep 3 to 4 days in the refrigerator. Don't freeze.

48 calories per 1/4 cup serving, 3.7 g carbohydrate, 0.5 g fiber, 2 g protein, 2.6 g fat (2.0 g saturated), 10 mg cholesterol, 23 mg sodium, 138 mg potassium, 0 mg iron, 73 mg calcium

Dairy-Free Tzatziki

Instead of sour cream, substitute 1 tub (12 oz/340 g) imitation sour cream such as Tofutti Sour Supreme. One serving contains 58 calories, 2.7 g carbohydrate, 0.5 g fiber, 5.1 g fat (2.0 g saturated), and 14 mg calcium.

Chef's Secrets

• Lighten up! Instead of sour cream, you can use drained yogurt (also known as labeneh or yogurt cheese). To make it, just place 3 cups of plain low-fat yogurt in a strainer lined with cheesecloth or a coffee filter. Place the strainer over a bowl and transfer to the refrigerator; allow the yogurt to drain for 3 to 4 hours. Combine the drained yogurt with the remaining ingredients. The drained liquid (whey) is an excellent substitute in baking recipes for buttermilk or sour milk.

• Leftover Tzatziki? It's a delicious and healthy alternative to mayonnaise for egg, tuna, or salmon salad.

• Dairy Versatile! Tzatziki can also be thinned with a little milk, water, or soymilk and used as a salad dressing.

● ROASTED EGGPLANT SPREAD

This ruby-red spread comes from Penny Krowitz of Toronto, who got it from Melissa Adler. It's absolutely out of this world. I've nicknamed it "Penny's from Heaven!" Serve it on top of salad greens or with wholegrain crackers, flatbread, or toasted pita bread wedges.

1 eggplant (about 2 lb/1 kg), peeled and cut in 2-inch chunks
1 red onion, peeled and cut in 2-inch chunks
2 red peppers, seeded and cut in 2-inch chunks
2 Tbsp olive oil
1 tsp salt (or to taste)
1/4 tsp freshly ground black pepper
1 whole head garlic (trim and discard the top)
2 Tbsp tomato paste

1. Preheat the oven to 400°F. Line a 12- × 18- × 1-inch baking sheet with parchment paper or foil.

2. Combine the eggplant, onion, and peppers in a large bowl. Drizzle with oil and sprinkle with salt and pepper. Mix well. Spread out the vegetables in a single layer on the baking sheet.

3. Drizzle the cut side of the garlic with a few drops of oil, wrap in foil, and place on the baking sheet next to the vegetables.

4. Roast, uncovered and stirring occasionally, at 400°F for 40 to 45 minutes, or until the vegetables are tender but slightly blackened around the edges. Remove from the oven and cool slightly.

5. Transfer the vegetables to a food processor fitted with the steel blade. Squeeze the garlic cloves out of their skins and add to the processor along with the tomato paste. Process, using quick on/off pulses, until coarsely chopped. Transfer to a serving bowl, cover, and refrigerate to allow the flavors to blend.

Yield: About 2 1/4 cups. Keeps about two weeks in the refrigerator. Freezes well for up to 2 months.

73 calories per 1/4 cup, 10.8 g carbohydrate, 3.7 g fiber, 2 g protein, 3.3 g fat (0.5 g saturated), 0 mg cholesterol, 291 mg sodium, 322 mg potassium, 1 mg iron, 25 mg calcium

Roasted Eggplant and Peppers

For a delicious side dish, transfer the roasted vegetables to a serving bowl at the end of Step 4. Don't add the tomato paste or chop the vegetables. Delicious hot or at room temperature.

Chef's Secrets

• Frozen Assets! Drop tablespoonfuls of leftover tomato paste onto a parchment paper-lined baking sheet and freeze until solid. Transfer the frozen tomato-paste blobs to a re-sealable plastic bag. Store in the freezer and use as needed: add to soups, stews, and sauces—no need to defrost first.

• Instant Tomato Sauce! Another way to use up leftover tomato paste is to mix it with double the amount of water and turn it into tomato sauce.

● TURKISH EGGPLANT SALAD

This sweet and spicy eggplant dish is served in many Middle Eastern restaurants and everyone I know who tries it, loves it. It's absolutely addictive!

1 eggplant (about 1 1/2 lb/750 g)
Salt (for sprinkling on eggplant)
2 Tbsp olive oil
2 large onions, chopped
3 cloves garlic (about 1 Tbsp minced)
3 cups tomato sauce
2 Tbsp lemon juice (preferably fresh)
1/4 cup granulated sugar or granular Splenda
Salt and freshly ground black pepper
1/4 tsp cayenne pepper
1/2 tsp cumin
1/2 tsp dried thyme
2 Tbsp minced fresh cilantro or parsley

1. Cut off both ends from the eggplant but don't peel. Cut the eggplant into 1/2-inch chunks. (You should have about 8 cups.) Place the chunks in a colander and sprinkle with salt to drain out any bitter juices. Let stand for about 1/2 hour before rinsing and patting dry.

2. Heat oil in a large pot on medium heat. Sauté the onions and garlic for 5 minutes or until softened. Increase the heat to medium high, add the eggplant and sauté for 5 to 7 minutes longer or until softened.

3. Stir in the tomato sauce, lemon juice, sugar, salt, pepper, cayenne, cumin, thyme, and cilantro. Bring to a boil; reduce heat to low and cover partially. Simmer for 25 to 30 minutes, until sauce has thickened, stirring occasionally. Adjust seasonings to taste. When cool, cover and refrigerate. Serve chilled.

Yield: About 6 cups (12 servings of 1/2 cup each). Keeps 4 or 5 days in the refrigerator. Freezes well for up to 2 months.

75 calories per serving, 13.9 g carbohydrate, 3.0 g fiber, 2 g protein, 2.4 g fat (0.3 g saturated), 0 mg cholesterol, 322 mg sodium, 150 mg potassium, 1 mg iron, 3.0 g fiber, 13 mg calcium

Chef's Secrets

• Appe-Teasers! This spread makes a delicious addition to any Middle Eastern appetizer platter. Serve it along with Pumpkin Hummus (page 49), Two-Way Tzatziki (page 52), or Roasted Eggplant Spread (page 53).

• This also makes a terrific topping for Crostini (page 65). If desired, sprinkle with low-fat grated mozzarella and broil briefly until the cheese is melted.

• Phyll 'em up! Use this yummy mixture as a filling for Phyllo Nests (page 62), especially when topped with goat cheese.

• Using Your Noodle! Serve hot over pasta as a sauce. For a low-carb version, serve over strands of spaghetti squash instead of pasta.

• Sweet Choice: If made with Splenda instead of sugar, one serving contains 61 calories, 10.2 g carbohydrate, and 3.0 g fiber.

🍎 LUSCIOUS LENTIL PATE

When I was in Edmonton on a book tour a few years ago, Susan Binnington invited me to a dinner party, for which her friend Paula Globerman prepared this scrumptious spread. It was the hit of the evening—people thought it was chopped liver.

1 cup dried lentils (green or brown)
5 cups water
2 to 3 Tbsp olive or canola oil
2 medium onions, chopped
1 to 2 tsp Kosher salt
Freshly ground black pepper
1 cup toasted pecans (see Chef's Secrets)
4 hard-boiled eggs (discard 2 yolks)
1/2 cup fresh parsley leaves
1/4 cup fresh dillweed (or to taste)
2 tsp minced garlic or
   1 head Roasted Garlic (see Chef's Secrets)

1. Combine the lentils and water in a saucepan over medium-high heat, and bring to a boil. Reduce heat to low, cover, and simmer until the lentils reach the consistency of mushy oatmeal, about 1 hour. Let cool.

2. Heat oil in a large skillet on medium heat. Add the onions and sauté slowly until golden brown, about 10 to 15 minutes. Sprinkle lightly with salt and pepper to taste. If onions begin to stick, add a little water.

3. In a food processor fitted with the steel blade, combine the cooked lentils, sautéed onions, pecans, eggs, parsley, dillweed, and garlic. Process, using on/off pulses, until the mixture is smooth. Chill well and adjust seasoning to taste before serving.

Yield: About 4 1/2 cups. Keeps 3 or 4 days in the refrigerator. Freezes well for up to 2 months.

109 calories per 1/4 cup, 8.2 g carbohydrate, 3.1 g fiber, 5 g protein, 6.9 g fat (0.9 g saturated), 35 mg cholesterol, 120 mg sodium, 171 mg potassium, 1 mg iron, 19 mg calcium

Chef's Secrets

• How to Toast Nuts: Spread the nuts in a single layer in a glass pie plate. Bake at 325°F for 5 minutes (or microwave, uncovered, on high for 2 minutes). The nuts will continue to cook after being removed from the oven. When cool, store in the refrigerator. They'll keep for several weeks.

• Roasted Garlic: Trim and discard a 1/4-inch slice from the top of the garlic. Lightly brush the cut-side of the garlic with olive oil. Wrap the garlic in foil and bake in a preheated 375°F oven for 30 to 40 minutes or until tender. Remove from the oven and cool slightly. Squeeze the cloves out of the skin (like squeezing toothpaste out of a tube!) and spread on toasted whole wheat baguette slices. It's also excellent added to salad dressings.

Nutrition Notes
• Lentils are high in fiber and have a low glycemic index (30), making this dish diabetic-friendly.

• News in a Nutshell! Pecans are very high in antioxidants and contain vitamin E, calcium, magnesium, potassium, zinc, and fiber. Over 90% of the fat found in pecans is unsaturated, heart-healthy fat. One oz (about 20 pecan halves) contains 4 grams of carbohydrate and 3 g fiber, about the same amount of fiber as a medium-sized apple.

🐟 MUSHROOM MOCK CHOPPED LIVER

This is my favorite vegetarian version of chopped liver—it's perfect for Passover or all year round! I've updated it to make it more health-friendly, featuring an Omega-3 trio of olive oil, walnuts, and eggs. If you have a nut allergy, just omit the nuts.

2 cloves garlic
3 medium onions, quartered
1 Tbsp olive oil
8 oz (227 g) pkg sliced mushrooms
   (about 3 1/4 cups)
3 Tbsp walnuts
4 hard-boiled eggs (discard 2 yolks)
1/2 tsp salt (optional)
1/4 tsp freshly ground black pepper

1. Drop the garlic through the feed tube of a food processor fitted with the steel blade while the motor is running. Process until minced, about 10 seconds. Add the onions and process with several quick on/off pulses, until coarsely chopped.

2. Spray a large nonstick skillet with cooking spray. Add olive oil and heat on medium heat. Add the minced onions and garlic (don't bother washing the food processor bowl). Sauté until golden, about 6 to 8 minutes. If the garlic-onion mixture begins to stick, just add a little water. Add the mushrooms and cook for 6 to 8 minutes, stirring occasionally, until nicely browned. Remove the pan from heat and cool slightly.

3. In the food processor, add the walnuts and process until coarsely ground, about 10 to 12 seconds. Add the onion-mushroom mixture, eggs, salt, and pepper. Process with several quick on/off pulses, just until combined.

4. Transfer to a container and keep in the refrigerator, covered, until ready to serve. (Chilling enhances the flavor.)

Yield: About 2 1/4 cups (9 servings of 1/4 cup each). Keeps 3 or 4 days in the refrigerator. Don't freeze.

79 calories per 1/4 cup, 6.0 g carbohydrate, 1.2 g fiber, 4 g protein, 4.8 g fat (0.8 g saturated), 51 mg cholesterol, 30 mg sodium, 171 mg potassium, 1 mg iron, 21 mg calcium

Legume Lover's Liver
To boost the fiber and protein content, omit the mushrooms and substitute with 1 1/2 cups canned chickpeas or lentils, rinsed and drained. (If you are concerned about sodium, use a salt-free brand.) Sauté the onions and garlic for 8 to 10 minutes, or until well browned. One serving of 1/4 cup contains 115 calories, 13.6 g carbohydrate, 2.5 g fiber and 5 g protein. (Note: Legumes are not allowed for Ashkenazi Jews on Passover.)

Chef's Secrets
• Fill 'er Up! Serve in bibb lettuce leaves, hollowed-out bell pepper halves, or large tomatoes. Or stuff cherry tomatoes or mushroom caps with the mixture and serve as hors d'oeuvres.

• Spread It Around! Delicious with crisp vegetables, wholegrain crackers, Crostini (page 65), or Baked Tortilla Chips (page 59).

🍎 TRICOLOR CREAM CHEESE MOLD

The layered look is back! Thanks to my friend Eileen Mintz of Mercer Island, Washington, for inspiring this easy and colorful company dish. It's fairly high in calories and fat, so save this for special occasions. Serve with cut-up veggies or use as a spread for multi-grain crackers, pita bread, tortilla chips, or Crostini (page 65).

4 cups (2 lb/1 kg) light or fat-free
   cream cheese
1 cup Traditional Pesto (page 110)
1 cup Sun-Dried Tomato Pesto (page 109)
Baby spinach leaves, for garnish

1. Line the bottom and sides of a 6-cup deep glass bowl with plastic wrap. Spread 3/4 cup of cream cheese in a layer on the bottom of the bowl. Spread 1/2 cup of Traditional Pesto over the cream cheese. Gently spread another layer of cream cheese, then 1/2 cup of Sun-Dried Tomato Pesto. Top with another layer of cream cheese. Continue alternating layers, ending with a layer of cream cheese. You will have 5 layers of cream cheese and 4 layers of pesto. Cover and chill at least 2 hours or overnight.

2. When ready to serve, unmold the chilled layered cheese-pesto mold onto a large, round platter lined with baby spinach leaves. Carefully remove the plastic wrap and serve.

Yield: 6 cups. Keeps for 3 or 4 days in the refrigerator. Don't freeze.

42 calories per Tbsp, 1.0 g carbohydrate, 0.1 g fiber, 1 g protein, 3.4 g fat (1.4 g saturated), 5 mg cholesterol, 70 mg sodium, 38 mg potassium, 0 mg iron, 19 mg calcium

Variations
• Any flavored cream cheese, such as sun-dried tomato, vegetable, chive, or light boursin cheese can be used.

• Dairy-Free: Substitute a plain or herb-flavored imitation cream cheese (such as Tofutti) for the regular cream cheese.

• Power Pesto (page 109) or store-bought pesto can be substituted for the Traditional Pesto.

• Puréed sun-dried tomatoes packed in oil can be substituted for Sun-Dried Tomato Pesto.

🍎 SMOKED SALMON PINWHEELS

This easy, elegant low-carb appetizer is ideal for brunch or a cocktail party. Smoked salmon is usually high in sodium, so if you want to reduce your intake, compare brands and choose the one with the lowest sodium content.

1 cup light cream cheese
2 Tbsp non-fat plain yogurt
1 Tbsp minced fresh dillweed or 1/2 tsp dried
1/2 lb (250 g) smoked salmon (lox),
   thinly sliced
1 medium English cucumber, unpeeled

1. Combine cream cheese with yogurt and dillweed in a food processor fitted with the steel blade; process until smooth and blended, about 10 to 12 seconds.

2. Spread a thin layer on each slice of smoked salmon. Starting from one end, tightly roll up each slice. Slice the rolls with a sharp knife into 1/4-inch pinwheels (you should end up with about 24 pinwheels).

3. Trim and discard ends from the cucumber. Slice into 1/4-inch-thick rounds (you should have about 24 rounds). Pat dry with paper towels. Place a pinwheel on each cucumber round and arrange in a single layer on a serving platter. (Can be prepared several hours in advance; cover and refrigerate until needed.) Serve chilled.

Yield: About 2 dozen pinwheels. Keeps about 1 day in the refrigerator. Don't freeze.

37 calories each, 1.2 g carbohydrate, 0.1 g fiber, 3 g protein, 2.1 g fat (1.3 g saturated), 7 mg cholesterol, 243 mg sodium, 54 mg potassium, 0 mg iron, 18 mg calcium

Variations
• Say Cheese! Any flavored cream cheese (such as sun-dried tomato, veggie, chives), or light boursin cheese, can be substituted.

• Lighten Up! Low-fat pressed cottage cheese, moistened with a little skim milk, yogurt, or sour cream also works well. Another delicious option is Firm Yogurt Cheese (page 178).

• Dairy-Free Variation: Instead of cream cheese and yogurt, substitute Tofutti imitation cream cheese and omit the yogurt.

• Fill 'er Up! The cream cheese mixture can also be combined with minced lox trimmings and green onions to make a tasty low-carb filling for celery stalks.

• Skinny Dipping! For a delicious and tasty dip, thin the mixture with additional yogurt or skim milk.

TORTILLA SPIRALS

These pinwheels are so pretty if you use different-colored flour tortillas. Tortillas come in a variety of colors, such as red, green, and yellow, and flavors including sun-dried tomato, pesto, spinach, and whole wheat. Try the different fillings and combinations suggested as variations on page 59.

White Bean Dip (page 47)
4 10-inch whole wheat flour or corn tortillas
1 package (10 oz/300 g) baby spinach leaves (use half the package to line the serving platter)
1/2 cup roasted red peppers from a jar or homemade (page 59), patted dry and cut into narrow strips
1/2 cup grated carrots

1. Prepare Bean Dip as directed. Spread a thin layer of dip on each tortilla, leaving a 1/2-inch border around the entire outside edge of each tortilla. Place a row of spinach leaves across the middle of each tortilla. Top with roasted pepper strips and carrots. Roll up tightly. Cover the rolls with plastic wrap and refrigerate for 1 hour (or up to 24 hours).

2. When ready to serve, remove plastic wrap and trim ends. Slice each roll, on an angle, into 6 pieces. Arrange on a large platter lined with spinach leaves and serve chilled. (These spirals can be prepared up to a day

in advance. Cover tightly when storing in the refrigerator so they won't dry out.)

Yield: 2 dozen spirals. Keeps for 1 to 2 days in the refrigerator. Don't freeze.

63 calories per spiral, 8.3 g carbohydrate, 1.9 g fiber, 2 g protein, 2.0 g fat (0.3 g saturated), 0 mg cholesterol, 123 mg sodium, 43 mg potassium, 0 mg iron, 13 mg calcium

Variations

• Instead of White Bean Dip, substitute Black Bean Dip (page 47), Tapenade (page 52), or Hummus (pages 48–49).

• Use roasted or steamed asparagus spears instead of roasted red peppers or carrots. Different color bell peppers add flavor and eye appeal.

• Substitute bibb lettuce, mixed salad greens, or radicchio leaves for spinach.

• Thinly sliced grilled portobello mushrooms also make a marvelous addition.

• Dairy-Free Variations: Use various flavors of imitation cream cheese such as Tofutti. Other fillings include egg, tuna, or salmon salad, Curried Cranberry Chicken Salad (page 271), Tofu "Egg" Salad (page 161), or Great Grilled Vegetables (page 316).

• Lox De-Lite! Spread tortillas with light cream cheese (use plain or herb-flavored, or try Tofutti cream cheese), then top with strips of lox and baby spinach leaves.

Chef's Secrets

• Easy Rollers! If using corn tortillas, soften them by heating in the microwave oven, allowing about 10 seconds for each tortilla. This makes them easier to roll.

• Read Nutrition Notes (page 60).

Roasted Red Peppers

Preheat the broiler or grill. Broil or grill 4 red peppers until their skins have blackened and blistered, turning them occasionally, about 12 to 15 minutes. They will shrivel and collapse. Immediately place the hot peppers in a bowl, cover and let cool. Scrape off the skins using a paring knife. Cut each pepper in half and discard stems, cores, and seeds. Cut the peppers into long, narrow strips and place in a bowl; drizzle with 2 Tbsp extra virgin olive oil and season with salt and pepper. Cover and refrigerate up to 10 days, or freeze for up to 3 months. Drain before using.

BAKED TORTILLA CHIPS

Chip, chip hooray! These tasty triangles are delicious with your favorite dip, spread, or Tomato Salsa (page 63). Be sure to try the different variations suggested on page 60.

6 10-inch whole wheat flour or corn tortillas
2 egg whites, lightly beaten
6 Tbsp sesame seeds
Kosher salt
Italian seasoning

1. Preheat the oven to 400°F. Line a baking sheet with parchment paper or foil sprayed with cooking spray.

2. Using a pastry brush or paper towel, brush each tortilla with a light coating of egg white. Sprinkle with the sesame seeds, salt, and seasoning. Evenly stack the tortillas on top of each other and, using a sharp knife, cut into wedges (first cut the stack in

half, then into quarters, then into eighths, like cutting a pizza).

3. Arrange the tortilla wedges, sesame seed-side up, in a single layer on the prepared baking sheet. Bake uncovered for 8 to 10 minutes or until the tops are crisp and golden. Watch carefully to prevent burning.

Yield: 12 servings (48 triangles). Keeps 2 to 3 weeks at room temperature in a re-sealable plastic bag. If freezing, pack and store carefully in a freezer container as they are fragile. These freeze for 2 to 3 months.

65 calories per serving (4 triangles), 10.7 g carbohydrate, 1.4 g fiber, 4 g protein, 2.3 g fat (0 g saturated), 0 mg cholesterol, 103 mg sodium, 50 mg potassium, 1 mg iron, 20 mg calcium

Pita Chips
Use pita bread instead of tortillas. Split each pita into two rounds and prepare as directed.

Variations
• Use different flavored flour tortillas such as spinach, sun-dried tomato, or flaxseed.

• Instead of egg white, brush each tortilla lightly with extra virgin olive oil and sprinkle with minced garlic. Add a sprinkling of dried basil, thyme, oregano, rosemary or a barbecue seasoning mixture.

• Sprinkle with Parmesan cheese or sesame seeds, if desired.

Nutrition Notes
• The nutritional analysis was done using whole wheat flour tortillas, which have a GI value of 30. Corn tortillas (GI value 52) are an excellent alternative for those who are gluten-intolerant.

• Tortillas come in different sizes and contain different amounts of fat, calories, and fiber, so check the nutrient label when shopping and compare different brands.

• Don't use low-carb tortillas to make these chips—they'll have a cardboard-like texture. Low-carb tortillas taste best in their original soft state, so use them for wraps, or cut them in wedges and serve them lightly toasted with dips. One low-carb tortilla contains about 12 g of carbohydrates and 9 g of fiber.

🍎 SPANIKOPITA ROLL-UPS

These eye-catching hors d'oeuvres are truly a sight for sore eyes! Health experts believe that eating lutein-rich vegetables like spinach and broccoli at least twice a week may lower your risk of cataracts and/or macular degeneration. This recipe is dairy-free—for options made with dairy, refer to Dairy Good on page 61.

1 medium onion, chopped
1/2 red pepper, seeded and chopped
2 cloves garlic, minced
1 Tbsp olive oil
2 pkgs (10 oz/300 g each) frozen or
    fresh spinach, cooked and squeezed dry
1 package (8 oz/227 g) imitation cream
    cheese (such as Tofutti)
1 large egg
Salt and freshly ground black pepper
1 to 2 Tbsp minced fresh dillweed or
    1 tsp dried
8 sheets phyllo dough (see Phyllo Facts
    on page 61)
1/4 cup additional olive oil

1. Preheat the oven to 375°F. In a medium skillet, sauté the onion, red pepper, and garlic in the olive oil on medium-high heat for 3 to 4 minutes or until softened. (Or microwave in a glass bowl on high for 3 to 4 minutes.)

2. In a food processor fitted with the steel blade, process the cooked and drained spinach until finely chopped. Add the imitation cream cheese, egg, salt, pepper, and dillweed. Process just until mixed. Add the onion mixture and process with quick on/offs, just until mixed (scraping down the sides of the bowl as needed).

3. Line a baking sheet with parchment paper or foil sprayed with cooking spray.

4. Place 1 rectangular sheet of phyllo dough on a dry work surface, with the long side facing you. (Work with 1 sheet at a time and always keep the remaining phyllo dough covered with plastic wrap to prevent it from drying out.) Brush the phyllo sheet lightly with oil. Top with a second sheet of dough and brush lightly with oil. Spoon 1/4 of the spinach filling in a narrow band along the bottom edge of the phyllo; leave a 1-inch border on the bottom edge and on both sides. Fold both sides inwards and then roll up the dough into a long, narrow cylinder, starting from the edge closest to you. Place seam-side down on the prepared baking sheet. Repeat with the remaining phyllo sheets and filling. You should end up with 4 rolls.

5. Lightly brush the tops of each roll with oil. Using a sharp knife, mark 1-inch slices along the top of each roll, cutting partially through the dough but not through the filling. (This makes for easier slicing after baking. If you slice completely before baking, the filling will dry out.) You will get about 15 slices from each roll. (The rolls may be frozen at this point. There's no need to thaw before baking or reheating—just add 2 or 3 minutes to the baking time.)

6. Bake the rolls for 20 minutes or until golden. Slice and serve.

Yield: 5 dozen hors d'oeuvres. Reheats well. To reheat, bake uncovered at 325°F for 10 minutes. Slice and serve. Freezes well for up to 3 months.

34 calories each, 2.3 g carbohydrate, 0.5 g fiber, 1 g protein, 2.5 g fat (0.5 g saturated), 4 mg cholesterol, 41 mg sodium, 38 mg potassium, 0 mg iron, 16 mg calcium

Variations
• Dairy Good! Instead of Tofutti, substitute 1 cup light ricotta cheese. Or combine 1/2 cup light ricotta, 1/2 cup light feta, and 1/4 cup grated Parmesan cheese.

• Use broccoli instead of spinach. If desired, add 1/2 cup minced sun-dried tomatoes, rinsed and drained, to the filling.

• Leftover filling? Stuff large mushroom caps with the filling and sprinkle with sesame seeds. Bake uncovered at 350°F for 15 minutes.

Chef's Secrets—Phyllo Facts!
• Easy Dough's It! One package (1 lb/ 500 g) of phyllo dough contains 20 to 24 sheets. Phyllo dough packages are stored in the freezer. To thaw, place the package in the refrigerator overnight. Defrosted dough keeps 3 to 4 weeks in the refrigerator.

• Cover Up! When working with phyllo, keep it well covered with plastic wrap to prevent it from drying out. If you cover it with a damp cloth and the cloth is too wet, the dough will be soggy.

• A Tear-ific Tip! If phyllo dough tears, don't cry: just patch it together with a little oil or melted margarine.

• Leftovers? Store leftover phyllo in the refrigerator in a large re-sealable plastic bag for a few weeks. Don't refreeze dough that has been thawed.

PHYLLO NESTS

These phyllo nests are an excellent alternative to traditional pastry shells as they are much lower in fat and calories. But handle with care: they are delicate once baked. Fill the nests with a savory vegetable filling or sweet fruit filling to boost your intake of veggies and fruits.

3 sheets phyllo dough
2 Tbsp canola oil

1. Preheat the oven to 400°F. Lightly spray 24 mini muffin tins with cooking spray.

2. Take one sheet of phyllo dough and place it on a dry, flat surface. Brush lightly with oil. Repeat twice more with the remaining sheets, making three layers. Using a sharp knife, cut the dough lengthwise into 4 strips, then cut crosswise into 6 strips. You should have 24 squares. Press one square into each compartment of the prepared muffin tins.

3. Bake for 5 minutes or until crisp and golden. Remove from the oven and allow the phyllo nests to cool in the pans before removing them.

Yield: 2 dozen nests. Store in a loosely covered container at room temperature for 3 to 4 days. Freezes well for up to a month.

17 calories per serving, 1.2 g carbohydrate, 0 g fiber, 0 g protein, 1.3 g fat (0.1 g saturated), 0 mg cholesterol, 12 mg sodium, 2 mg potassium, 0 mg iron, 0 mg calcium

Chef's Secrets
• See Chef's Secrets—Phyllo Facts! (page 61).

• Super-Size It! For larger Phyllo Nests, cut the dough into 5- to 6-inch squares. Bake in standard muffin pans for 7 to 8 minutes or until golden.

• Be Prepared! These can be baked in advance and stored in an airtight container at room temperature for 3 to 4 days, or frozen.

• Fill 'er Up! Spoon the desired filling into the Phyllo Nests just before serving to prevent the nests from becoming soggy. If they were frozen, bake for 5 minutes at 350°F before filling them up.

• Chic Chick! Curried Cranberry Chicken Salad (page 271) makes an elegant main dish for guests.

• Vegetable Fillings: Fill with Caramelized Onions (page 303), Roasted Eggplant Spread (page 53), Turkish Eggplant Salad (page 54), Great Grilled Vegetables (page 316), or Stir-Fry Spinach with Garlic (page 310). If desired, top with cheese and bake briefly, just until the cheese melts.

• Dessert Fillings: Fill with Berry Mango Sherbet (page 418), Roasted Fruit Medley (page 426), Faster than Pumpkin Pie (page 414), or Chocolate Tofu Mousse (page 420).

• Speedy Sweets! Fill with low-calorie ice cream, frozen yogurt, or packaged pudding mix. Top with fresh berries or Warm Mixed Berry Sauce (page 430). Use your imagination!

BEST BRUSCHETTA

The terrific tomato topping on this bruschetta is so versatile and healthy. Tomatoes are packed with lycopene, a cancer-fighting antioxidant—and we like that! Lycopene is what gives tomatoes their red color. When tomatoes are cooked, more of the lycopene becomes available, so broil these beauties, for goodness sake!

2 cloves garlic (about 2 tsp minced)
6 firm, ripe plum tomatoes, cut into chunks
2 to 3 Tbsp chopped fresh basil or 1 tsp dried
1 Tbsp extra virgin olive oil
1 Tbsp lemon juice (preferably fresh)
Salt and freshly ground black pepper
Dash of cayenne pepper
Crostini (page 65)

1. Drop garlic through the feed tube of a food processor fitted with the steel blade while the motor is running. Process until minced, about 10 seconds. Add the tomatoes to the processor along with the basil, oil, lemon juice, salt, pepper, and cayenne. Process with 3 or 4 quick on/off pulses, until the tomatoes are coarsely chopped.

2. Shortly before serving, top each crostini with some of the tomato mixture and broil for 2 to 3 minutes.

Yield: About 18 bruschetta. Recipe doubles easily. Tomato mixture keeps for up to 2 to 3 days in the refrigerator. Don't freeze.

53 calories per serving, 6.1 g carbohydrate, 0.6 g fiber, 1 g protein, 2.7 g fat (0.4 g saturated), 0 mg cholesterol, 60 mg sodium, 65 mg potassium, 0 mg iron, 12 mg calcium

Tomato Salsa

Omit the crostini and you have salsa, a terrific topping—hot or cold—for grilled chicken, burgers, tofu, or mild-flavored fish such as halibut or sole. Or serve salsa as a dip with Baked Tortilla Chips (page 59) or toasted whole wheat pita bread wedges. This tastes much better than store-bought salsa!

Chef's Secrets

• Hot, Hot, Hot! Omit cayenne and add 1 fresh jalapeno chili pepper, seeded and minced. Instead of basil, add 1 tsp to 1 Tbsp minced fresh cilantro or parsley.

• Say Cheese! Bruschetta is also delicious topped with grated low-fat mozzarella, Swiss, Monterey Jack, or Parmesan cheese. Broil briefly before serving.

• To-mato, To-mahto: You can use any kind of tomatoes you have on hand. However, I prefer Italian plum tomatoes (romas) because they have less seeds and juice, making a thicker mixture. Choose tomatoes that are vine-ripened, firm, and heavy for their size.

• Ripe for the Eating: Place unripe tomatoes in a paper bag and let ripen at room temperature, about 2 to 4 days, or as needed.

• Chilling News! Don't refrigerate fresh tomatoes. Their texture will become mealy and they will taste watery.

🍎 BRUSCHETTI CONFETTI

Thanks to my friend and neighbor, Anne Per-relli, for these colorful corn-topped appetizers. She serves them on a large platter along with her Zucchini Appetizers (page 64) for a pretty presentation. Nibble away!

1 long, thin baguette (Italian, French,
   whole wheat, or sourdough)
1 can (12 oz/341 mL) corn kernels (about
   1¹/2 cups drained)
4 ripe roma (plum) tomatoes, chopped
4 green onions, chopped
¹/4 cup chopped fresh basil
2 cloves garlic, minced
2 Tbsp extra virgin olive oil
2 to 3 Tbsp balsamic vinegar
Salt and freshly ground black pepper
1 to 1¹/4 cups grated low-fat mozzarella
   cheese (or any cheese you like)

1. Preheat the oven to 400°F. Line a baking sheet with foil and spray with cooking spray. Slice bread thinly into ¹/2-inch slices. Arrange on the prepared baking sheet and bake 8 to 10 minutes or until slightly crispy but still chewy.

2. In a medium bowl, combine the corn, tomatoes, green onions, basil, garlic, oil, and vinegar. Season with salt and pepper to taste. (Steps 1 and 2 can be done a day in advance.)

3. Shortly before serving, top each bread slice with a spoonful of the corn-tomato mixture and sprinkle with cheese. Broil 4 inches from the heat for 2 to 3 minutes or just until the cheese melts.

Yield: About 18 bruschetta. Leftovers can be refrigerated for 1 to 2 days. If frozen, these will become soggy.

81 calories per serving, 10.3 g carbohydrate, 1.1 g fiber, 3 g protein, 3.0 g fat (0.9 g saturated), 4 mg cholesterol, 157 mg sodium, 70 mg potassium, 0 mg iron, 64 mg calcium

Chef's Secrets

• Frozen Assets! Instead of canned corn, use frozen corn kernels and microwave according to package directions.

• Be Prepared! Assemble these easy appetizers up to an hour before serving time so that the bread won't become soggy. Broil at serving time. They're delicious hot or at room temperature.

• Leftovers? You can reheat them briefly in the microwave oven for an easy lunch or snack, but they won't be as crispy. Place on a microwave oven-safe rack or paper towel to keep them from getting soggy. Alternatively, reheat the bruschetta in a 350°F oven for about 5 minutes.

🍎 ZUCCHINI APPETIZERS

My neighbor Anne Perrelli and I love to talk about recipes when we go for long walks. Everyone loves her excellent zucchini appetizers. I've modified her recipe slightly, using olive oil instead of butter and adding a red pepper for color. Pretty delicious, pretty healthy!

1 long, thin baguette (Italian, French,
   whole wheat, or sourdough)
1 Tbsp extra virgin olive oil
1¹/2 cups diced zucchini (do not peel)
¹/3 cup diced red onion
¹/2 cup diced red pepper
2 cloves garlic (about 2 tsp minced)
Salt and freshly ground black pepper

1 to 2 Tbsp chopped fresh basil or 1 tsp dried
1 to 1¼ cups grated low-fat Swiss cheese

1. Preheat the oven to 400°F. Line a baking sheet with foil and spray with cooking spray. Slice bread thinly into ½-inch slices. Arrange on the prepared baking sheet and bake for 8 to 10 minutes or until slightly crispy, but still chewy.

2. In a large skillet, heat the oil on medium heat. Add the zucchini, onion, bell pepper, and garlic; sauté for 3 to 4 minutes or until vegetables have softened. Remove from the heat and season with salt, pepper, and basil to taste. (Steps 1 and 2 can be done up to a day in advance.)

3. Shortly before serving, top each toasted bread slice with a tablespoon of the zucchini mixture and sprinkle with cheese. Broil 4 inches from the heat until golden, about 2 to 3 minutes. These appetizers are best if broiled just before serving.

Yield: About 18 appetizers. Leftovers can be refrigerated for 1 to 2 days. Don't freeze (if frozen, these will become soggy).

46 calories per serving, 5.6 g carbohydrate, 0.5 g fiber, 3 g protein, 1.4 g fat (0.4 g saturated), 2 mg cholesterol, 68 mg sodium, 50 mg potassium, 0 mg iron, 67 mg calcium

CROSTINI

Crostini is the Italian word for "little toasts." This upscale version of crispy garlic toast can be topped with a variety of savory toppings (see Chef's Secrets on page 66). Top notch—different every time!

2 Tbsp extra virgin olive oil
2 cloves garlic, minced
1 long, thin baguette (Italian, French, whole wheat, or sour dough)
Chopped fresh parsley or basil, for garnish

1. Preheat the oven to 375°F. Line a large baking sheet with parchment paper or foil. Do not grease.

2. Combine the oil and garlic in a small bowl. Slice the baguette thinly into ½-inch thick slices. Lightly brush both sides of each slice with oil and place on the baking sheet.

3. Bake for about 10 minutes or until the bread is slightly crispy but still chewy. Serve warm or at room temperature with desired toppings and garnished with parsley.

Yield: About 18 crostini, depending on the length of the loaf. These stay crisp for 2 to 3 days in a loosely covered container at room temperature. Don't freeze.

42 calories per piece, 5.1 g carbohydrate, 0.3 g fiber, 1 g protein, 1.9 g fat (0.3 g saturated), 0 mg cholesterol, 59 mg sodium, 12 mg potassium, 0 mg iron, 8 mg calcium

Variations
• Instead of the oil-garlic mixture, brush bread with your favorite homemade pesto (pages 109–11).

• Lighter Variation: Don't brush bread with olive oil. Bake, toast or grill the bread slices, then spray both slices with cooking spray and rub with garlic. One piece contains 28 calories and 0.4 g fat (0.1 g saturated).

• Instead of baking, either toast or grill the crostini on the barbecue for 2 to 3 minutes per side.

Chef's Secrets

• Upper Crost-ini! To "crisp up" Crostini if it gets soggy, bake in a preheated 300°F oven for 5 minutes.

• Top It Up! Here are some tasty toppings: Best Bruschetta (page 63), Caramelized Onions (page 303), Roasted Tomato Sauce (page 107), Roasted Eggplant Spread (page 53), Turkish Eggplant Salad (page 54), Guacamole with Hearts of Palm (page 50), Mushroom Duxelles (page 302), Mushroom Mock Chopped Liver (page 56), Pumpkin Hummus (page 49), Tapenade (page 52), Tricolor Cream Cheese Mold (page 57), Two-Way Tzatziki (page 52), White Bean Dip (page 47), Great Grilled Vegetables (page 316).

● MEDITERRANEAN STUFFED MUSHROOMS

These make excellent hors d'œuvres and are ideal as a low-carb side dish. A food processor makes quick work of preparing the stuffing. Children like to help stuff the mushroom caps and sprinkle them with cheese. For a dairy-free variation, see page 67.

2 dozen large mushrooms
1 Tbsp olive oil
1 medium onion, chopped
2 cloves garlic (about 2 tsp minced)
1/2 cup chopped, roasted red peppers
   (from a jar or homemade,
   page 59), drained
1/3 cup chopped sun-dried tomatoes,
   drained and rinsed (optional)
1 package (10 oz/300 g) frozen chopped
   spinach, thawed and squeezed dry
2 Tbsp chopped fresh basil or 1 tsp dried

Salt and freshly ground black pepper
1/2 cup grated low-fat mozzarella or
   Parmesan cheese

1. Wash mushrooms quickly and pat dry with paper towels. Remove stems and chop coarsely, reserving mushroom caps.

2. In a large nonstick skillet, heat oil on medium heat. Add the onion, garlic, and chopped mushroom stems. Sauté about 5 minutes or until tender. Stir in the roasted bell peppers, sun-dried tomatoes (if using), and spinach. Cook until most of the moisture has disappeared, about 3 to 4 minutes, stirring occasionally. If the mixture begins to stick, add a little water. Season with basil, salt, and pepper and let cool.

3. Stuff mushroom caps with the onion-garlic mixture, using a teaspoon to mound the filling slightly. Arrange the stuffed mushrooms in an oblong baking dish sprayed with cooking spray. Sprinkle the filling with cheese. (Can be prepared in advance and refrigerated, covered, overnight.)

4. Bake, uncovered, in a preheated 350°F oven for 15 minutes or until golden.

Yield: 2 dozen stuffed mushrooms. Keeps 2 days in the refrigerator; reheats well. Freezes well for up to a month.

24 calories each, 2.1 g carbohydrate, 0.7 g fiber, 2 g protein, 1.2 g fat (0.4 g saturated), 2 mg cholesterol, 26 mg sodium, 122 mg potassium, trace iron, 36 mg calcium

Variations

• Instead of roasted red peppers and sun-dried tomatoes, use 1/2 cup chopped red pepper and 1 stalk chopped celery. Instead of basil, use 1/2 tsp dried thyme.

• Dairy-Free: Omit the cheese and sprinkle with chopped almonds or seasoned breadcrumbs.

Chef's Secret

• Frozen Assets! Bake for 10 minutes. Let cool, then freeze in a single layer on a tray, wrapped tightly. When needed, bake the still-frozen mushrooms, covered loosely with foil, in a preheated 350°F oven for 15 minutes or until piping hot. Uncover and broil 2 to 3 minutes or until golden.

🍎 STUFFED MUSHROOMS FLORENTINE

These easy, delicious hors d'oeuvres are perfect party fare. They also make a scrumptious side dish with fish. Your guests will be "floored" when they taste these "teeny" treats.

24 large mushrooms
1 small onion
2 Tbsp fresh dillweed or 1 tsp dried
1 package (10 oz/300 g) frozen spinach, thawed and squeezed dry
1/2 cup light ricotta, feta, or cottage cheese
1/4 cup grated Parmesan cheese
1 egg white
Salt and freshly ground black pepper
2 Tbsp additional grated Parmesan cheese

1. Preheat the oven to 350°F. Wash the mushrooms quickly and pat dry with paper towels. Remove the stems and reserve them for another use.

2. In a food processor fitted with the steel blade, process the onion and dillweed until finely minced, about 10 seconds. Add the spinach, ricotta, 1/4 cup Parmesan cheese, egg white, salt, and pepper. Process just until mixed, scraping down the sides of the bowl as needed. Fill each mushroom cap with the spinach-ricotta mixture, mounding the filling slightly.

3. Arrange the mushroom caps in an oblong baking dish sprayed with cooking spray. Sprinkle with the remaining Parmesan cheese. (These can be prepared up to a day ahead and refrigerated.)

4. Bake, uncovered, for 15 to 18 minutes or until the cheese is golden on top.

Yield: 2 dozen stuffed mushrooms. Keeps 2 days in the refrigerator; reheats well. Freezes well for up to a month.

27 calories each, 1.9 g carbohydrate, 0.7 g fiber, 3 g protein, 1.2 g fat (0.7 g saturated), 3 mg cholesterol, 19 mg sodium, 137 mg potassium, trace iron, 47 mg calcium

Chef's Secret

• No Waste! Don't throw out the mushroom stems. Add them to soups, stir-fries, pasta dishes, or pilafs. Or use them to make Mushroom Duxelles (page 302).

🍎 MINI VEGGIE LATKES WITH SMOKED SALMON AND TZATZIKI

Dill-icious! When I demonstrated this recipe on TV, the crew inhaled them! You can peel the potato and sweet potato if you prefer, but I just scrub them well. That's more (or less?) a-peeling!

1 medium onion, cut in chunks
1 Idaho (russet) potato, cut in chunks
1 medium sweet potato, cut in chunks

1 carrot, cut in chunks
1 medium zucchini, cut in chunks
1 red pepper, cut in chunks
2 eggs (or 1 egg plus 2 egg whites)
1/3 cup matzo meal or dried breadcrumbs
   (preferably whole wheat)
1/2 tsp salt (or to taste)
Freshly ground black pepper
2 Tbsp fresh dillweed
3 Tbsp olive oil for frying (plus more
   as needed)
1 cup Two-Way Tzatziki (page 52)
1/4 lb/125 g smoked salmon, cut in
   bite-sized pieces
Additional dillweed, for garnish

1. In a food processor fitted with the steel blade, process the vegetables in batches until finely minced, about 8 to 10 seconds for each batch.

2. Transfer the minced vegetables to a large mixing bowl and add the eggs, matzo meal, salt, pepper, and dillweed; mix well.

3. Spray a large nonstick skillet with cooking spray. Add 1 Tbsp oil and heat over medium high heat. Drop the mixture from a teaspoon into the hot oil to form pancakes (latkes). Flatten each latke slightly with the back of the spoon. Reduce heat to medium and brown well on both sides, about 2 minutes per side. Remove latkes from the pan as ready and drain on paper towels. Add additional oil to the pan as needed and stir batter before cooking each new batch of latkes. (Can be made in advance and kept warm in a 250°F oven.)

4. When ready to serve, arrange the latkes on a platter and top each one with a dollop of tzatziki, smoked salmon, and a sprig of dillweed.

Yield: About 4 dozen miniature latkes. Keeps 2 days in the refrigerator; reheats well. Freezes well for up to a month.

38 calories per serving, 2.8 g carbohydrate, 0.3 g fiber, 1 g protein, 2.5 g fat (0.4 g saturated), 10 mg cholesterol, 78 mg sodium, 58 mg potassium, 0 mg iron, 10 mg calcium

Baked Mini Latkes
Place oven racks on the lowest and middle position in the oven and preheat oven to 450°F. Drop the latke mixture by teaspoonfuls onto well-oiled baking sheets; flatten slightly. Bake 10 minutes or until the bottoms are browned and crispy. Turn the latkes over and transfer the pan from the upper rack to the lower rack and vice versa. Bake 8 to 10 minutes longer.

Variation
• Dairy-Free: Use Dairy-Free Tzatziki (page 53), or use Aioli (page 46) mixed with 1/4 cup minced fresh dillweed.

Chef's Secrets
• Grate Tip! If you grate the onion and potato together, it prevents the potato from turning dark. I use Idaho (russet) potatoes as they are higher in starch and less watery when grated.

• No sweet potatoes? Use 2 Idaho or Yukon Gold potatoes.

• GI Go! Sweet potatoes with a purple peel and cream-colored flesh (such as Purple Sweeties) have a lower glycemic index value than regular potatoes and are less sweet than orange-fleshed sweet potatoes. Their taste and texture are similar to regular potatoes, but they are more nutritious.

• Green Cuisine! Instead of zucchini, use 1 package (10 oz/300 g) frozen spinach, thawed and squeezed dry.

CRUNCHY ROASTED CHICKPEAS (NAHIT)

This addictive snack comes from two "foodie" friends. Caryn Bloomberg of Columbus, Ohio, loves them because they satisfy her cravings when she has the munchies. Omi Cantor of Framingham, Massachusetts, remembers these being served at her synagogue after services. Crunch away!

1 can (19 oz/540 mL) chickpeas or 2 cups
   cooked chickpeas
Salt, pepper, and garlic powder
Sweet or smoked paprika

1. Preheat the oven to 350°F. Line a rimmed baking sheet with foil and spray with cooking spray.

2. If using canned chickpeas, drain, rinse, and pat dry with paper towels. Combine the chickpeas with salt, pepper, garlic powder, and paprika in a medium bowl and mix well.

3. Spread in a single layer on the prepared baking sheet. Roast, uncovered, for 50 to 60 minutes or until crisp and golden, stirring them every 15 minutes.

4. Remove from the oven and let cool. Store at room temperature in a loosely covered bowl or container. Serve at room temperature.

Yield: About 1 1/4 cups (5 servings of 1/4 cup each). We don't know how long they keep because they never last long enough! Don't freeze.

114 calories per serving, 21.7 g carbohydrate, 4.2 g fiber, 5 g protein, 1.1 g fat (0.1 g saturated), 0 mg cholesterol, 287 mg sodium, 165 mg potassium, 1 mg iron, 31 mg calcium

Cheater's Chickpeas
Season canned, drained chickpeas with salt and lots of pepper, but don't bother roasting them. Cover and refrigerate. Enjoy them as a snack.

Chef's Secrets
• Spice It Up! Chili powder, cumin, and/or curry powder add a spicy kick to these crunchy nibbles. Or use your favorite mixture of herbs and spices. Always different, always delicious!

• Soy Good! Omit the seasonings and lightly drizzle the chickpeas with tamari or soy sauce, then roast as directed.

• Easy-Peasy! Sprinkle on top of salads instead of nuts.

EDAMAME

Edamame (pronounced eh-dah-MAH-meh) means "beans on branches." It is the Japanese name for soybeans still in their pods. Available fresh or frozen, edamame makes a healthy snack or appetizer and is also delicious in salads and stir-fries. Al Jolson would probably have branched out his repertoire and sung about these for his Mammy if he had tasted them.

1 lb (454 g) frozen, unshelled edamame
2 cloves garlic (peeling isn't necessary)
Kosher or sea salt

1. In a large pot, bring 4 quarts of salted water to a boil on high heat. Add edamame and garlic. Bring water back to a boil, then cook uncovered for about 6 to 8 minutes or

until tender-crisp. Do not overcook or they will become mushy.

2. Drain well but don't rinse. Discard the garlic. Spread the edamame out on a baking sheet lined with paper towels and let cool.

3. Transfer to a platter or bowl and sprinkle with Kosher salt. Serve at room temperature.

Yield: 6 servings. Don't freeze.

133 calories per 100 g (edible portion), 12.0 g carbohydrate, 5.3 g fiber, 11 g protein, 4.0 g fat (0 g saturated), 0 mg cholesterol, 40 mg sodium, potassium (unavailable), 2 mg iron, 67 mg calcium

Variations
• Drizzle lightly with Asian Salad Dressing (page 274) or your favorite vinaigrette. Or omit Kosher salt and sprinkle with Montreal-Style Steak Spice (page 115).

Chef's Secrets
• Pod-cast the News! Pull the pods through your teeth to extract the soybeans, or squeeze the beans directly from the pods into your mouth with your fingers. Don't eat the pods. (Have an extra bowl for the discarded pods.)

• Fresh vs Frozen! Fresh edamame takes longer to cook than frozen. Cook fresh edamame, in the pod, in salted water for 20 minutes or until tender. (If frozen, edamame takes 6 to 8 minutes to cook.) Drain well, but don't rinse. The salt will cling to the outside of the pods.

Nutrition Note
• Edamame resembles sugar snap peas and are very easy to digest. This bright green vegetable is very high in protein and fiber.

One half cup of edamame contains 8 grams of soy protein, which helps reduce cholesterol. Oy, soy healthy!

TOMATO TIDBITS

Good things come in small packages. These tasty tidbits are very versatile. Enjoy them as a snack, add them to a vegetable tray, or use them in salads, pasta, or grains. Nibble a-weigh!

2 containers (about 4 cups) grape or
   cherry tomatoes
2 tsp extra virgin olive oil
Salt, freshly ground black pepper,
   and dried basil

1. Preheat the oven to 250°F. Line a baking sheet with foil and spray with cooking spray.

2. Cut the tomatoes in half and place, cut-side up, in a single layer on the baking sheet. Drizzle with oil and season with salt, pepper, and basil to taste. Bake, uncovered, for 2 to 3 hours or until the tomato halves are shriveled and somewhat chewy. Don't bother turning them over. Cooking time will vary depending on the size and moisture content of tomatoes.

3. Remove from the oven and cool completely before serving.

Yield: About 2 cups (8 servings of 1/4 cup each). Recipe doubles easily. These keep in the refrigerator for several weeks (but they're so good, they never last that long). Freezes well for up to 2 months.

23 calories per serving, 2.9 g carbohydrate, 0.9 g fiber, 1 g protein, 1.3 g fat (0.2 g saturated), 0 mg cholesterol, 4 mg sodium, 177 mg potassium, 0 mg iron, 8 mg calcium

Chef's Secret

• Chewy or Crispy? If you prefer them chewier, store in a tightly covered container in the refrigerator. If you prefer them more crispy, keep them uncovered at room temperature. The choice is yours.

🍏 TRAIL MIX

Keep this tasty mix handy for a quick fix when you get a snack attack. Dividing it into small, re-sealable bags ensures portion control. Now all you need is self-control!

1 cup toasted mixed nuts (walnuts, almonds, pecans, peanuts, and/or soy nuts)
1/2 cup semi-sweet chocolate chips (regular or miniature)
1/4 cup dried cranberries or raisins
1/4 cup toasted pumpkin seeds
2 cups toasted oat cereal (e.g., Cheerios) or other unsweetened breakfast cereal

1. Combine the nuts, chocolate chips, cranberries or raisins, pumpkin seeds, and cereal in a medium bowl and mix well.

2. Divide into 8 small re-sealable plastic bags.

Yield: 4 cups (8 servings of 1/2 cup each). Store in a cool, dry place. Keeps for 1 to 2 months, but it never lasts that long. Don't freeze.

181 calories per serving, 18.1 g carbohydrate, 2.7 g fiber, 4 g protein, 12.1 g fat (2.8 g saturated), 0 mg cholesterol, 55 mg sodium, 166 mg potassium, 3 mg iron, 47 mg calcium

Variations

• Nut Alert! If you have concerns about nut allergies, omit them and add any of the other suggested ingredients. Use your imagination. Calorie counts will vary.

• Kid Stuff: Instead of chocolate chips, substitute M&M's or miniature marshmallows.

• Tropical Fruit Mix: Instead of cranberries or raisins, substitute with slivered dried apricots, dried pineapple, or mango.

• Crunchy Munchies! Instead of toasted oat cereal, use bite-sized shredded wheat cereal or pretzels.

• Hop on Pop! Substitute popcorn for nuts and/or cereal.

super soups

SUPER SOUPS

Fill Up with Soup: Did you know that if you eat a bowl of vegetable soup, you will feel full for a longer period of time than if you drink a glass of water and eat the vegetables separately? Your body and brain actually recognize water differently when it's combined with food. So get smart and eat soup often to help control your appetite.

Eau so Good! The water content in soups ranges from 80 to 95 percent. The recipes in this book are packed with water-rich vegetables so you can enjoy a large portion of soup that's low in calories. My soups also contain low-to-medium glycemic index (GI) ingredients, are low in fat, and contain dietary fiber to help prevent rebound hunger.

Slow Down, You Eat Too Fast: It takes 20 minutes for your brain to know that your stomach is full, so starting a meal with soup helps fill you up and takes the edge off your hunger. Chunky soups take longer to eat and are more satisfying than clear, thin broths.

Homemade Is Best: You're in control when you make homemade soups. They're quick to make and are less expensive than commercial soups, which are usually loaded with sodium, fat, and calories.

Multivitamin in a Bowl: Soups with vegetables, grains, and legumes are a wonderful way to incorporate more protein, fiber, vitamins, minerals, and phytonutrients (potent antioxidants found in plants that strengthen the immune system) into your diet.

Bowl Them Over! To make soup, all you need are vegetables (fresh, frozen, or canned), lean protein (beans, lentils, chicken, beef, or tofu), grains (brown or basmati rice, whole wheat pasta, barley, or quinoa), chicken or vegetable broth (or water), plus herbs and spices.

Cut the Fat! One tablespoon of olive or canola oil is enough to sauté 3 to 4 cups of vegetables. Use nonstick cookware or spray the inside of your pot with cooking spray before adding veggies. If the vegetables start to stick, add a little water or broth instead of oil. You can also sauté vegetables in chicken or vegetable broth instead of fat.

Cook It Slow: A slow cooker is excellent for making large quantities of soup for people on the go. If your recipe calls for 15 to 30 minutes of cooking, slow-cook it for 4 to 8 hours on low, or $1\frac{1}{2}$ to 2 hours on high. If your recipe calls for 30 to 60 minutes of cooking, slow-cook it for 6 to 8 hours on low, or 3 to 4 hours on high. There will be little evaporation in a slow cooker, so adjust the seasonings accordingly.

Microwave Magic! Use a microwave oven for smaller, quick-cooking soups. An 8-cup glass batter bowl is a perfect size for soup. Cooking time is similar to cooking soups on top of the stove. Microwave soups on high power. Soups cooked in the microwave don't stick, so you don't need to add a lot of fat and clean-up is easy.

Dairy Good! Use skim or 1% milk, 2% evaporated milk, or light (5% or 10%) cream instead of heavy (35%) cream. Use nonfat or low-fat yogurt, or light sour cream instead of regular sour cream.

Whey to Go! Keep any leftover whey you have after making Homemade Cottage Cheese (page 177) or Yogurt Cheese (page 178): it makes a tasty addition to soups.

In the Thick of It! If your soup is too watery, simmer it, uncovered, to reduce some of the liquid. If it's still too thin, purée part of the cooked vegetables in a food processor, then stir them back into the soup: the puréed vegetables will give it a thicker consistency.

Bean Cuisine! Puréed canned white beans are a sneaky way to thicken your soup and add some fiber. About 1 cup of puréed vegetables or legumes will thicken 3 to 4 cups of broth.

Thin Is In: If your soup is too thick, thin it with a little water, vegetable or chicken broth, and adjust seasonings as needed.

Your Choice: If you don't have home-made chicken or vegetable broth on hand, use canned, bottled, or packaged broth (see Broth in a Box, below). You can also use bouillon cubes or instant powdered soup mix, although they are often high in sodium.

Quick Vegetable Broth: For each cup of vegetable broth, substitute with 1 tsp instant powdered soup mix and 1 cup water. To keep my recipes vegetarian and/or dairy-free, I use Kosher pareve chicken-flavored instant soup mix, which is vegetarian and contains absolutely no chicken.

Broth in a Box: Good quality brands of vegetable broth are available in most supermarkets. Imagine Organic No-Chicken Broth is Kosher, pareve, and fat-free. It comes in a Tetra Pak like the kind used for soymilk. One box contains about 4 cups (35 oz/1 L) and doesn't require refrigeration until it has been opened. One cup contains 10 calories, 2 g carbohydrate, and 470 mg sodium, so it's lower in sodium than canned broth but higher than homemade. It's great in a pinch.

A-Salt with a Deadly Weapon! One cup of canned vegetable broth contains about 1000 mg of sodium, almost 1/2 tsp salt. Bouillon cubes and instant soup mix are usually loaded with sodium. A quick trick to reduce the sodium is to add double the amount of water. Beware—some brands contain MSG and partially hydrogenated fats.

Don't be Fooled! Did you know that low-sodium instant soup mix contains sugar instead of salt? One teaspoonful contains about 3/4 tsp sugar.

Cold Facts: Make sure soups (or any cooked foods) are completely cooled before you transfer them to freezer-safe containers. Store the soup in 1- or 2-cup containers, leaving 2 inches at the top to allow for expansion. Cover and freeze. Square containers take up less space than round ones.

It's in the Bag! Not enough freezer containers? Remove frozen soup from the container(s) and transfer to a re-sealable freezer bag(s). A quick trick is to place the container in hot water briefly—the soup will slide right out.

Cube Cuisine: Freeze small quantities of chicken or vegetable broth in ice cube trays. One cube equals 2 Tbsp soup—very handy for adding to recipes when a small amount is needed.

Frozen Assets: Save the liquid from cooked vegetables and use it in recipes as a substitute for broth.

Hot Stock Tip: To reheat soup in the microwave, allow 2 to 3 minutes per cup on high, stirring once or twice during heating. If soup is frozen, there's no need to defrost it first. One cup of soup takes 4 minutes on high to defrost, then another 2 to 3 minutes on high to heat up.

AUTUMN VEGETABLE SOUP

This scrumptious low-cal, low-carb autumn soup is wonderful anytime of year. The recipe comes from Valerie Kanter of Chicago, editor of the Kosher cookbook, *Crowning Elegance*. Her family loves it, especially her children, who devour two or three bowlfuls at one sitting. Valerie often serves it from her slow cooker for the Sabbath lunch. It's a winner!

2 Tbsp olive oil
1 large onion, chopped
2 to 3 stalks celery, chopped
6 medium carrots (1 lb/500 g), peeled
    and chopped
3 medium sweet potatoes, peeled and
    cut in chunks
1 medium butternut or acorn squash,
    peeled and cut in chunks (about 5 cups)
1 cup sliced mushrooms
2 medium zucchini, cut in chunks
10 cups water
4 to 6 bay leaves
1 Tbsp salt (or to taste)
1/2 tsp freshly ground black pepper
2 Tbsp finely chopped fresh dillweed
2 Tbsp finely chopped fresh parsley
1 clove garlic (about 1 tsp minced)

1. Heat the oil in a large soup pot on medium heat. Sauté the onion, celery, and carrots for 5 minutes or until the vegetables are tender, stirring occasionally. Add the sweet potatoes, squash, mushrooms, and zucchini; mix well.

2. Add the water, bay leaves, salt, and pepper, and bring to a boil. Reduce heat to low and simmer, partially covered, for 2 hours, stirring occasionally. If the soup becomes too thick, add a little more water. Remove the bay leaves and discard.

3. Using a potato masher, coarsely mash the vegetables while still in the pot, leaving the soup somewhat chunky. Stir in the dillweed, parsley, and garlic. Serve hot.

Yield: 8 to 10 servings (about 15 cups). Keeps for up to 3 to 4 days in the refrigerator; re-heats well. Freezes well for up to 4 months.

78 calories per cup, 15.1 g carbohydrate, 3.8 g fiber, 1 g protein, 2.0 g fat (0.3 saturated), 0 mg cholesterol, 548 mg sodium, 443 mg potassium, 1 mg iron, 46 mg calcium

Chef's Secrets

• Short Cuts: To make it easier to cut a squash, slash the tough outer skin in several places with a sharp knife. Microwave, uncovered, on high for 4 to 5 minutes. Cool for 5 minutes, then cut in half or in large pieces. Remove the seeds and stringy fibers—an ice-cream scoop works perfectly.

• Love Me Tender! Summer squash varieties include zucchini, crookneck, and patty-pan squash—all have thin, edible skins and soft seeds. Summer squash cooks quickly because of the high water content.

• Bay Watch! Always remove and discard bay leaves after cooking. A bay leaf won't rehydrate even after boiling so, if left in the soup, someone could choke on it. Count how many you put in and how many you take out. Or, better yet, tie them up in a square of cheesecloth for easy removal after cooking.

🍎 BLACK BEAN AND CORN SOUP

Rabbi Robyn Fryer of Chicago transformed my black bean and corn casserole into a soup because she didn't realize that she was supposed to drain the canned beans! I modified her version slightly and this fiber-packed soup is the result. She likes to serve it chilled for Shabbat on a summer evening, but it's also delicious served hot. Pack some in a thermos for a healthy lunch.

4 cups (2 -19 oz/540 mL cans) canned
    black beans (don't drain)
2 cups (1 -14 oz/398 mL can) canned
    stewed tomatoes (don't drain)
3 cups tomato or vegetable juice
2 Tbsp maple syrup or honey (or to taste)
2 medium onions, chopped
2 green peppers, seeded and chopped
1 red pepper, seeded and chopped
2 cloves garlic (about 2 tsp minced)
1 cup corn kernels (frozen or canned)
1 tsp chili powder (or to taste)
1/2 to 1 tsp salt (or to taste)
1 tsp freshly ground black pepper
1 Tbsp olive oil

1. Preheat the oven to 350°F. Spray a 4- or 5-quart ovenproof casserole with cooking spray. Combine all the ingredients in the casserole and mix well (or combine all ingredients in a 6-quart slow cooker).

2. Bake, covered, for about 1 hour, stirring occasionally. If the soup is too thick after baking, add a little water. (If using a slow cooker, cook for 6 to 8 hours on low, or 3 to 4 hours on high.)

3. Once done, let stand for 1/2 hour to cool before refrigerating. Serve either chilled or hot.

Yield: 6 to 8 servings (about 12 cups). Keeps for 4 to 5 days in the refrigerator; reheats well. Freezes well for up to 4 months.

108 calories per cup, 23.6 g carbohydrate, 5.9 g fiber, 5 g protein, 1.4 g fat (0.2 g saturated), 0 mg cholesterol, 712 mg sodium, 561 mg potassium, 2 mg iron, 57 mg calcium

Nutrition Notes

• If sodium is a concern, choose an organic brand of canned black beans. They contain from 15 to 140 mg of sodium per serving, compared to 400 to 480 mg found in regular brands. Also, choose a low-sodium brand of canned stewed tomatoes and tomato or vegetable juice.

• GI Go! Pure maple syrup has a glycemic index value (GI) of 54, compared to maple-flavored syrup with a GI value of 68. Pure floral honey has an average GI value of 55, compared to mass market blended honeys from a variety of nectar sources, which have a GI value of more than 70. For those following a low GI diet, honey and pure maple syrup can be enjoyed in moderation. Or use a brown sugar substitute to lower the carbs by 2 grams per cup.

• The fiber from beans and vegetables lowers the glycemic load, making this soup diabetic-friendly.

• Cooked tomatoes provide the nutritional benefit of lycopene.

● BLACK BEAN, BARLEY AND VEGETABLE SOUP

Black beans are easier to digest than other beans, are very high in antioxidants, and are a good source of protein. This high-fiber soup is enhanced with fresh herbs—it's "soup-herb"! (Don't let the long list of ingredients deter you. To save prep time, use a food processor to chop the vegetables.)

1 to 2 Tbsp olive oil
3 cloves garlic (about 1 Tbsp minced)
2 medium onions, chopped
2 stalks celery, chopped
10 cups water, vegetable, or chicken broth
3 medium carrots, chopped
  (or 12 baby carrots)
1 1/2 cups mushrooms, chopped
1 medium sweet potato or 2 medium
  potatoes, peeled and chopped
1/2 cup pearl barley, rinsed and drained
1 cup dried red lentils, rinsed and drained
1 can (19 oz/540 mL) black beans, drained
  and rinsed
2 tsp salt (or to taste)
1 tsp freshly ground black pepper
  (or to taste)
1/4 cup minced fresh dillweed and/or
  finely chopped fresh basil
1/4 cup minced fresh parsley

1. Heat the oil in a large soup pot on medium heat. Add the garlic, onions, and celery, and sauté for 5 to 7 minutes or until golden. If the vegetables start to stick, add 2 to 3 Tbsp water.

2. Add the water or broth, carrots, mushrooms, sweet potato, barley, lentils, black beans, salt and pepper; bring to a boil. Reduce heat and simmer, partially covered, for 1 hour or until the vegetables are tender, stirring occasionally. If the soup becomes too thick, thin with a little water.

3. Add the dillweed and parsley, and adjust the seasonings to taste before serving.

Yield: 8 to 10 servings (about 15 cups). Leftovers keep 4 or 5 days in the refrigerator; reheats well. Freezes well for up to 4 months.

116 calories per cup, 22.0 g carbohydrate, 5.5 g fiber, 6 g protein, 1.3 g fat (0.2 g saturated), 0 mg cholesterol, 317 mg sodium, 340 mg potassium, 2 mg iron, 36 mg calcium

Nutrition Notes

• Black beans, barley, and lentils all have a low glycemic index, making this soup an excellent choice for diabetics or those who are insulin-resistant.

• Canned black beans are more convenient than dried because you don't need to soak and cook them, but they are higher in sodium. To lower the sodium, choose organic brands of canned black beans, which contain a fraction of the sodium of regular canned beans.

● BROCCOLI AND RED PEPPER SOUP

Broccoli rocks in this stalk-filled soup! This low-cal, low-carb soup is a light "weigh" to start a meal and curb your appetite.

1 Tbsp olive oil
1 medium onion, chopped
1 red pepper, seeded and chopped
2 cloves garlic (about 2 tsp minced)
2 carrots, coarsely chopped
  (or 12 baby carrots)
1 bunch broccoli, trimmed and
  coarsely chopped (about 4 cups)
6 cups vegetable broth
1 to 2 tsp salt (or to taste)
1/2 tsp freshly ground black pepper
1 tsp dried basil or 1 Tbsp chopped
  fresh basil
3 Tbsp chopped fresh dillweed
Light sour cream, nonfat yogurt,
  or skim milk (optional)

1. Heat the oil in a large saucepan on medium heat. Add the onion, red pepper, and garlic, and sauté for 3 to 4 minutes or until the vegetables are tender. Stir in the carrots and broccoli and mix well.

2. Add the broth, salt, pepper, basil, and dillweed, and bring to a boil. Reduce heat and simmer, partially covered, for 20 minutes or until the broccoli is tender. Remove from heat and cool slightly.

3. Using an immersion blender, purée the soup while still in the pot, or purée in batches in a blender or food processor. Adjust the seasonings to taste and serve with a dollop of sour cream, yogurt, or a little milk, if desired.

Yield: 4 to 6 servings (about 8 cups). Keeps 3 to 4 days in the refrigerator; reheats well. Freezes well for up to 4 months.

84 calories per cup, 13.7 g carbohydrate, 3.7 g fiber, 3 g protein, 2.4 g fat (0.3 g saturated), 0 mg cholesterol, 527 mg sodium, 354 mg potassium, 1 mg iron, 67 mg calcium

Nutrition Notes

• This scrumptious soup is high in fiber, potassium, beta carotene, and vitamins A and C.

• Frozen broccoli, which is mostly florets, may actually contain more beta carotene than fresh broccoli. Add fresh or frozen broccoli florets to this nutritious soup. The stems from fresh broccoli can be grated and used instead of cabbage when making stir-fries or coleslaw.

🍎 SECRET INGREDIENT CABBAGE BORSCHT

Bagged coleslaw mix is the secret ingredient to help speed up preparation for this scrumptious soup. Most of the ingredients are probably in your kitchen. Big soup, little effort!

2 Tbsp olive or canola oil
3 medium onions, chopped
1 pkg (16 oz/500 g) coleslaw mix
3 cloves garlic (about 1 Tbsp minced)
8 cups water, vegetable or chicken broth
1 cup tomato juice
1 can (28 oz/796 mL) diced
    or whole tomatoes, undrained
1 can (5¹/₂ oz/156 mL) tomato paste
1 cup dried green, brown,
    or red lentils, rinsed and drained
¹/₄ cup brown sugar or granular Splenda
    (or to taste)
¹/₂ tsp freshly ground black pepper
1 bay leaf
2 tsp salt (or to taste)
2 Tbsp lemon juice (preferably fresh)
2 Tbsp minced fresh dillweed

1. In a large soup pot, heat the oil on medium heat. Add the onions and sauté for 5 minutes or until tender. Add the coleslaw mix and garlic, and cook 5 to 7 minutes longer or until tender, stirring occasionally.

2. Stir in the water, tomato juice, tomatoes, tomato paste, lentils, brown sugar, pepper, and bay leaf, and bring to a boil. Reduce the heat and simmer, partially covered, for 1¹/₂ hours or until the lentils are tender. If the soup gets too thick, add a little water or broth.

3. Stir in the salt, lemon juice, and dillweed; simmer 5 minutes longer to blend the flavors. Remove and discard the bay leaf before serving.

Yield: 8 to 10 servings (about 16 cups). Keeps 3 to 4 days in the refrigerator; reheats well. Freezes well for up to 4 months.

103 calories per cup, 18.1 g carbohydrate, 3.6 g fiber, 4 g protein, 2.0 g fat (0.3 g saturated), 0 mg cholesterol, 539 mg sodium, 264 mg potassium, 1 mg iron, 33 mg calcium

Chef's Secrets

• Grate Idea! Instead of coleslaw mix, substitute 6 cups grated cabbage and 1 grated carrot. If you want to include more vegetables, add 2 stalks chopped celery and 1 chopped zucchini.

• Color Your World! Green or brown dried lentils will retain their shape, whereas red dried lentils will disintegrate during cooking and disappear into the soup.

• Juicy News: Always add salt and lemon juice at the end of the cooking time to soups containing beans or lentils. If you add them at the start of the cooking process, the lentils won't soften completely.

• Sodi-Yum! If you are concerned about sodium, use sodium-free tomato juice, canned tomatoes, and tomato paste.

🍎 CREAMY CARROT SOUP

This A-1 soup is packed with vitamin A and beta carotene. It's very quick to prepare and is great when you have guests—everyone loves it! Using baby carrots instead of regular carrots saves on preparation time and clean-up. Why not make a double batch and freeze some soup for a busy day?

1 Tbsp olive oil
1 large onion, chopped
1 to 2 cloves garlic (about 1 to 2 tsp minced)
4 cups baby carrots (or regular carrots, peeled, and cut in chunks)
6 cups vegetable broth
1/3 cup basmati or long-grain rice
Salt and freshly ground black pepper
1/4 cup minced fresh dillweed or basil (or 2 tsp dried)
Yogurt, for garnish (optional)

1. Heat the oil in a large saucepan on medium high heat. Add the onion and garlic, and sauté until tender, about 3 to 4 minutes. Stir in the carrots and cook 2 minutes longer.

2. Add the broth, rice, salt, and pepper (if using dried dillweed or basil, add it now), and bring to a boil. Reduce heat and simmer, partially covered, for 25 to 30 minutes or until the carrots are tender. Remove from heat and cool slightly.

3. Using an immersion blender, purée the soup while still in the pot, or purée in batches in a blender or food processor. If using fresh dillweed or basil, stir it in now. Adjust seasonings to taste. When serving, garnish with a dollop of yogurt, if desired.

Yield: 4 to 6 servings (about 8 cups). Keeps 3 to 4 days in the refrigerator; reheats well. Freezes well for up to 4 months. If soup is too thick, add a little extra broth when reheating.

101 calories per cup, 18.4 g carbohydrate, 2.5 g fiber, 2 g protein, 2.1 g fat (0.2 g saturated), 0 mg cholesterol, 376 mg sodium, 30 mg potassium, 0 mg iron, 38 mg calcium

Variations

• Add a 10 oz (300 g) package of frozen squash along with the carrots.

• Instead of rice, substitute red lentils or couscous.

• Instead of dillweed or basil, add a pinch of curry powder and ground cumin at the beginning of cooking. Add 2 Tbsp chopped fresh cilantro once the soup is done.

• Add 1 to 2 tsp minced fresh ginger to the cooked soup for a different flavor. A teaspoon of grated lemon rind will also add some zest.

Chef's Secrets

• Quick Tip: To save time and calories, omit the olive oil and don't bother sautéing the vegetables. Combine all the ingredients in a saucepan, bring to a boil, and simmer until tender. Purée with a blender or food processor until smooth.

• Dried or Fresh? Dried herbs should be added at the beginning of cooking. Fresh herbs are best added at the end of cooking.

CURRIED CARROT AND CASHEW SOUP

This scrumptious vegetarian soup will fill you up without filling you out! Jackie Toledano of Netanya, Israel, often makes this soup for her family for Friday night dinners. I love the curried version but Jackie prefers it with fresh dillweed (page 81). Her children go nuts over it!

1 Tbsp olive oil
1 large onion, chopped
1 large apple, peeled, cored, and chopped
1 medium sweet potato or 1 medium
  potato, peeled and chopped
2 lb (1 kg) baby carrots or frozen baby carrots
8 cups vegetable broth
1/3 cup roasted cashews
1 to 2 tsp salt (or to taste)
1/2 tsp freshly ground black pepper
1 to 2 tsp curry powder
1/4 tsp chili powder
Chopped cashews, for garnish (optional)

1. Heat the oil in a large soup pot on medium high heat. Add the onion, apple, sweet potato, and carrots, and sauté for 5 to 7 minutes or until the vegetables are tender.

2. Add the broth, cashews, salt, and pepper, and bring to a boil. Reduce heat to low and simmer, partially covered, for 30 minutes or until the vegetables are tender. Remove from heat and cool slightly.

3. Using an immersion blender, purée the soup while still in the pot, or purée in batches in a blender or food processor. If the soup is too thick, add a little extra broth or water. (Milk or soymilk are also good choices.) Stir in the curry powder and chili powder and serve hot. Sprinkle with chopped cashews, if desired.

Yield: 6 to 8 servings (about 12 cups). Keeps 3 to 4 days in the refrigerator; reheats well. Freezes well for up to 4 months.

112 calories per cup, 18.7 g carbohydrate, 3.6 g fiber, 3 g protein, 3.3 g fat (0.5 g saturated), 0 mg cholesterol, 546 mg sodium, 91 mg potassium, 1 mg iron, 41 mg calcium

Dill Carrot Cashew Soup

Instead of curry and chili powder, substitute with 2 Tbsp minced fresh dillweed, adding it at the end of the cooking process.

Nut-Free Variation

Replace cashews with 1 medium turnip or squash, peeled and coarsely chopped.

super
soups

Chef's Secrets

• A-Peeling News! Instead of using raw baby carrots or frozen carrots, use 2 lb (1 kg) regular carrots, peeled and coarsely chopped. (Jackie and I both prefer the lazy method—no peeling or cutting required.)

• Cash in on Cashews: Store cashews in a tightly sealed container in the refrigerator for up to 6 months or freeze them for up to a year. No cashews? Use blanched almonds.

🍅 CHICKEN SOUP FOR THE BOWL!

You don't have to be Jewish to love chicken soup—it's the ultimate comfort food. A steaming bowl of chicken soup, often called "Jewish penicillin," is thought to cure the common cold. Serve this golden broth with Matzo Balls (page 455), Notsa Balls (pages 455–56), noodles, rice, or quinoa.

3 lb (1.5 kg) chicken pieces, with skin and bones
1 Tbsp Kosher salt (or to taste)
2 medium onions
5 to 6 medium carrots
3 to 4 stalks celery
1 or 2 parsnips (optional)
2 cloves garlic
1 bunch fresh dillweed
1/2 tsp freshly ground black pepper

1. Trim excess fat from the chicken. Place the chicken in a large stockpot, preferably one with a pasta insert. Add enough cold water to cover the chicken completely by at least 1 inch. Add the salt and bring to a boil over high heat. Use a slotted spoon to skim off the foam that rises to the surface of the soup.

2. Add the onions, carrots, celery, and parsnip, if using, to the pot. Reduce heat and simmer, partly covered, for 1¼ to 1½ hours. Add the garlic and dillweed and simmer 15 to 20 minutes longer. Adjust the salt to taste and season with freshly ground pepper. Remove the pot from the heat and let cool for ½ hour.

3. Carefully strain the broth into a large bowl or container; reserve the chicken and vegetables. Store the broth, covered, in the refrigerator overnight.

4. Meanwhile, remove the skin and bones from the chicken and discard. Cut the chicken and vegetables into bite-sized pieces and place in a bowl or container. Cover and refrigerate the chicken and vegetables overnight.

5. When ready to serve, discard the hardened layer of fat from the surface of the broth. For a meal in a bowl, add the chicken and vegetables to the soup before reheating.

Yield: 5 to 6 servings (about 10 cups). Keeps 3 to 4 days in the refrigerator; reheats well. Freezes well for up to 6 months.

20 calories per cup of clear broth (without chicken or vegetables), 2 g carbohydrate, 0 g fiber, 1 g protein, 0.5 g fat (0 g saturated), 5 mg cholesterol, 570 mg sodium, 0 mg iron, 20 mg calcium

Chef's Secrets

• The Skinny on Skin! Chicken skin adds flavor to soup. I prefer to remove the skin after cooking and skim the chilled soup thoroughly.

• Lift and Separate! A stockpot with a pasta insert is fantastic for cooking chicken soup. No need to strain out the chicken, bones, and vegetables after cooking. Clearly a great idea!

• Sodi-Yum! Kosher salt has ⅓ less sodium than iodized salt and tastes much better. If you are on a restricted sodium diet, omit or reduce the salt, or use a salt substitute.

• To Salt or Not to Salt? If you want to use chicken broth as an ingredient in other dishes that contain salty ingredients, you may prefer to omit the salt from the soup.

• Chic Chick! Use leftover cooked chicken in stir-fries, casseroles, crepes, salads, and wraps.

🍎 EASY CORN CHOWDER

In the summertime, make this chunky soup with fresh corn and in the winter, use frozen. Corn and broccoli are excellent sources of lutein, which helps keep your eyes healthy . . . so, the "eyes" have it!

1 Tbsp extra virgin olive oil
2 medium onions, chopped
2 stalks celery, chopped
1 red pepper, seeded and chopped
4 cups fresh (about 6 ears)
    or frozen corn kernels
1 medium potato, peeled (about
    1 cup chopped)
2 cups broccoli florets

3 cups vegetable broth
1 tsp salt
1/2 tsp freshly ground black pepper
1/2 tsp dried thyme
1 tsp dried basil
    or 2 Tbsp chopped fresh basil
1 cup skim milk or soymilk

1. Heat the oil in a large saucepan on medium heat. Add the onions, celery, and red pepper, and sauté for 5 minutes or until the vegetables are tender. Add the corn and potato and cook 4 to 5 minutes longer, stirring often.

2. Add the broccoli, broth, salt, pepper, and thyme (if using dried basil, add it now), and bring to a boil. Reduce heat to low, cover, and simmer for 10 to 12 minutes or until the potatoes are tender. Remove from heat and cool slightly. If using fresh basil, add it now.

3. Using an immersion blender, partially purée the soup while still in the pot (or purée half the vegetables with a little of the cooking liquid in a food processor or blender and then return the purée to the pot). Add the milk and reheat gently on low heat. Don't bring to a boil or the soup may curdle.

Yield: 5 to 6 servings (about 7 cups). Keeps for up to 3 to 4 days in the refrigerator; reheats well. Freezes well for up to 3 months. If soup is too thick, add a little milk or soymilk.

112 calories per cup, 22.5 g carbohydrate, 3.5 g fiber, 4 g protein, 2.1 g fat (0.3 g saturated), 0 mg cholesterol, 339 mg sodium, 327 mg potassium, 1 mg iron, 49 mg calcium

Chef's Secrets

• Ears to You! If using fresh corn, remove the husks and silk. (A damp paper towel removes the silk quickly.) Cut the ears in half crosswise with a sharp knife, then stand each piece on its cut end and slice downward several times to cut off all the kernels. One ear yields about 3/4 cup corn kernels.

• Green Cuisine! Instead of broccoli, add 2 cups frozen green peas. Instead of onions, substitute 2 leeks, using the white and light green parts.

🍅 COOL AS A CUCUMBER SOUP

No cooking required for this low-cal, low-carb, calcium-packed summer cooler; it's really refreshing and perfect for Passover. When my mother tasted it, she said "Your grandmother would have been here first thing in the morning for lunch if she knew you had this in your refrigerator!"

1 1/2 cups grated unpeeled cucumber
    (1 English or 2 medium cucumbers)
2 green onions, chopped
3 cloves garlic (about 1 Tbsp minced)
2 cups nonfat or 1% plain yogurt
2 cups skim or 1% milk
1 tsp salt
1/2 tsp freshly ground black pepper
1/2 cup minced fresh parsley
3 to 4 Tbsp minced fresh dillweed
Additional minced fresh parsley
    and/or dillweed, for garnish

1. Combine all the ingredients in a large bowl and mix well.

2. Cover and chill for several hours or overnight. Garnish with additional minced fresh

parsley or dillweed and serve chilled.

Yield: 4 servings (about 6 cups). Keeps 4 to 5 days in the refrigerator. Don't freeze.

77 calories per cup, 13.6 g carbohydrate, 0.7 g fiber, 7 g protein, 0.3 g fat (0.1 g saturated), 3 mg cholesterol, 480 mg sodium, 270 mg potassium, 1 mg iron, 226 mg calcium

Variations
• 4 cups buttermilk can be used instead of yogurt and milk.

• Dairy-Free: Instead of yogurt and skim milk, combine 1/4 cup lemon juice plus 3 3/4 cups soymilk.

● CUCUMBER SWEET POTATO SOUP

Everyone thinks cucumbers can only be used in cold soups, but they're wrong! Sweet potato and carrots give this low-calorie, low-carb soup its orange color, so no one will know it contains cucumbers unless you tell them.

1 Tbsp olive oil
2 medium onions, chopped
1 red pepper, seeded and chopped
2 cloves garlic (about 2 tsp minced)
1 large English cucumber, peeled
  (about 1 lb/500 g)
1 large sweet potato, peeled and
  cut in chunks
2 medium carrots, cut in chunks
  (or 1 cup baby carrots)
4 cups vegetable broth
1 tsp salt (or to taste)
1/4 tsp freshly ground black pepper
1/2 tsp dried basil
1/4 cup chopped fresh dillweed

1. Heat the oil in a large saucepan on medium heat. Add the onions, red pepper, and garlic; sauté for 5 minutes or until tender. If the vegetables start to stick, add a little water.

2. Slice the cucumber in half lengthwise and scrape out the seeds with a spoon. Cut the cucumber in 1-inch chunks. You should have about 3 cups. Add the cucumber to the saucepan, along with the sweet potato, carrots, broth, salt, pepper, and basil; bring to a boil. Reduce heat to low and simmer, partially covered, for 30 minutes or until the vegetables are tender. Stir in the dillweed, remove from heat, and cool slightly.

3. Using an immersion blender, purée the soup while still in the pot, or purée in batches in a blender or food processor. Serve hot or cold.

Yield: 4 to 6 servings (about 8 cups). Keeps 3 to 4 days in the refrigerator; reheats well. Freezes well for up to 4 months. If soup becomes too thick, thin with a little milk or water. Adjust seasonings to taste.

77 calories per cup, 13.6 g carbohydrate, 2.2 g fiber, 2 g protein, 2.1 g fat (0.3 g saturated), 0 mg cholesterol, 536 mg sodium, 201 mg potassium, 1 mg iron, 39 mg calcium

Zucchini Sweet Potato Soup
Instead of cucumber, substitute with 3 or 4 medium zucchini, coarsely chopped (no peeling or seeding is necessary). This soup can also be made with regular potatoes instead of sweet potatoes. Serve hot.

SLOW COOKER VEGETABLE LENTIL SOUP

Quick prep, slow-cook! Chop the vegetables in the food processor, then put everything into the slow cooker and let this carefree soup cook all day while you are away at work or out doing errands. It's packed with fiber, phytochemicals (potent antioxidants found in plant foods that strengthen the immune system) and flavor—and it's virtually fat-free.

2 medium onions, cut in chunks
1 medium sweet potato, peeled and
    cut in chunks
3 stalks celery, cut in chunks
3 large carrots, cut in chunks
1 red pepper, seeded and cut in chunks
1/4 cup minced fresh dillweed
    or 1 Tbsp dried dillweed
3/4 cup pearl barley, rinsed and drained
1 cup dried red lentils, rinsed and drained
12 cups vegetable broth
Salt and freshly ground black pepper

1. In a food processor fitted with the steel blade, process the vegetables in batches, using quick on/off pulses, until finely chopped.

2. Transfer the finely chopped vegetables to a slow cooker, along with the dillweed, barley, red lentils, broth, salt, and pepper. Cover and cook on the low setting for 8 to 10 hours, until vegetables are tender. (The extra 2 hours of cooking time won't affect the finished dish if dinner is delayed.)

Yield: 10 to 12 servings (about 18 cups). Keeps 3 to 4 days in the refrigerator; reheats well. Freezes well for up to 4 months. This soup will thicken when refrigerated over-night, so thin it with a little water when reheating.

106 calories per cup, 20.4 g carbohydrate, 4.5 g fiber, 5 g protein, 0.7 g fat (0 g saturated), 0 mg cholesterol, 338 mg sodium, 237 mg potassium, 1 mg iron, 33 mg calcium

Everything but the Kitchen Sink Soup
I vary this soup depending on what I have on hand. Try it with chopped mushrooms, zucchini, or tomatoes. Instead of sweet potato, substitute with regular potato, turnip, or squash. Instead of lentils, use green or yellow split peas. Canned drained kidney beans are also a good addition. The main rule is to fill the pot halfway with vegetables. Add barley and legumes, then add enough vegetable broth or water to fill the pot to within 1 inch from the top. Sometimes I add a cup of leftover tomato sauce. Always different, always delicious.

Chef's Secrets
• Size Counts: I have a 6 quart slow cooker, but if yours is smaller, use less vegetables, seasonings. and water. As a guideline, fill the pot halfway with vegetables. Add 1/2 cup barley and 3/4 cup lentils then add enough vegetable broth or water to fill the pot to within 1 inch from the top.

• Quick Tip: The soup will cook faster if you add boiling water instead of tap water. Cook on high setting for 4 to 6 hours.

• Where's the Beef? For a meatier flavor, add a few soup bones. Cooking time will be the same.

• No Slow Cooker? You can also cook this soup on top of the stove. Combine all the ingredients in a large soup pot that has been sprayed with cooking spray. Bring to a boil, then cover partially and simmer for 2 to 2$^{1}/_2$ hours, stirring occasionally.

❀ LENTIL BARLEY SOUP

This simple and delicious soup is high in soluble fiber, which helps stabilize blood sugar. My mother's original version contained more starch but I omitted the potatoes and added lentils, bay leaves, and parsley. My Mom's mantra is "Eat some soup. It will fill you up!" Make half the recipe if you have a small family or don't have freezer space.

2 large onions, chopped
2 or 3 stalks celery, chopped
4 medium carrots, chopped
3 to 4 cloves garlic (about 1 Tbsp minced)
1 cup chopped mushrooms
1$^{1}/_2$ cups dried red lentils,
   rinsed and drained
1 cup pearl barley, rinsed and drained
14 cups water
2 Tbsp instant pareve chicken soup mix
2 bay leaves (optional)
2 tsp salt (or to taste)
1 tsp freshly ground black pepper
$^1/_4$ cup minced fresh dillweed
$^1/_4$ cup minced fresh parsley

1. Combine all the ingredients, except the dillweed and parsley, in a large soup pot and bring to a boil. Reduce heat to low and simmer, partially covered, for 1 hour or until the lentils are soft. Stir occasionally.

2. Once the lentils are fully cooked, stir in the dillweed and parsley and simmer 5 to 10 minutes longer. Discard the bay leaves and adjust the seasonings to taste. If the soup becomes too thick, add a little water.

Yield: 8 to 10 servings (about 18 cups). Keeps 3 to 4 days in the refrigerator; reheats well. Freezes well for up to 4 months.

112 calories per cup, 21.6 g carbohydrate, 4.9 g fiber, 6 g protein, 0.6 g fat (0 g saturated), 0 mg cholesterol, 279 mg sodium, 240 mg potassium, 1 mg iron, 26 mg calcium

Nutrition Note

• Lentils are an excellent source of folate and are filled with fiber. Red lentils melt into the soup and virtually disappear, making it an excellent way to sneak some fiber into your family's diet.

❀ LOVE THAT LENTIL SOUP!

This soup really lives up to its name—everyone who tastes it loves it! It reminds people of the popular soup served at a Middle Eastern restaurant in Toronto. This recipe makes a huge batch, but it won't last long, believe me! You can easily make half the recipe for a small family.

2 cups dried red lentils
$^2/_3$ cup rice (basmati or long-grain)
2 Tbsp olive oil
2 large onions, chopped
2 cloves garlic (about 2 tsp minced)
14 cups water
3 Tbsp instant pareve chicken soup mix
1 Tbsp ground cumin
1 tsp salt (or to taste)

1/2 tsp freshly ground black pepper
1 Tbsp lemon juice (preferably fresh)
1/4 cup minced fresh parsley or 1 Tbsp dried

1. Rinse the lentils and rice in a strainer. Drain well and set aside.

2. Heat the oil in a large soup pot on medium heat. Add the onions and garlic; sauté until golden, about 5 minutes. Add the water, soup mix, cumin, lentils, and rice. Bring to a boil. Reduce heat, cover partially and simmer for 20 to 25 minutes, stirring occasionally. Add the salt, pepper, lemon juice, and parsley. If too thick, thin with a little water.

Yield: 8 to 10 servings (about 14 cups). Keeps 3 to 4 days in the refrigerator; reheats well. Freezes well for up to 4 months.

126 calories per cup, 20.5 g carbohydrate, 3.7 g fiber, 7 g protein, 2.2 g fat (0.2 g saturated), 0 mg cholesterol, 323 mg sodium, 225 mg potassium, 1 mg iron, 26 mg calcium

Chef's Secrets

• Red to Green! Although this soup is made with red lentils, the color becomes yellowy-green when it is cooked.

• Freeze with Ease! If you freeze the soup, it will separate when you thaw it. Not to worry. Just stir it when reheating and it will be the same as if you had just made it.

🍎 MANGO GAZPACHO

Ladle up some sunshine with this colorful chilled soup, packed with vitamin A, beta carotene, and potassium: it's "mang"-nificent! Serve in wine glasses or champagne flutes for an elegant presentation.

3 to 4 cloves garlic (about 1 Tbsp minced)
1 medium red onion, cut in chunks
   (about 1 cup)
2 mangoes, peeled, pitted, and
   cut in chunks (about 2 cups)
2 Tbsp fresh basil
1/4 cup lightly packed fresh cilantro leaves
1 unpeeled English cucumber,
   cut in chunks
1 red pepper, seeded and cut in chunks
2 roma tomatoes, cut in chunks
1 Tbsp extra virgin olive oil
2 Tbsp lemon juice (preferably fresh)
2 Tbsp lime juice (preferably fresh)
1 tsp salt (or to taste)
1/4 tsp freshly ground black pepper
3/4 to 1 tsp chili powder
2 cups orange juice
   or 1 cup mango and 1 cup orange juice

1. Drop the garlic through the feed tube of the food processor while the motor is running; process until minced. Add the onion, mangoes, basil, and cilantro; process with quick on/off pulses, until finely chopped. Transfer to a large mixing bowl.

2. In the food processor, process the cucumber, red pepper, and tomatoes with quick on/off pulses, until finely chopped.

3. Add to the mango mixture along with the oil, lemon and lime juices, salt, pepper, and chili powder. Stir in the orange juice, cover and refrigerate until serving time.

Yield: 5 to 6 servings (about 7 cups). Keeps 2 days in the refrigerator. Don't freeze.

115 calories per cup, 23.8 g carbohydrate, 2.3 g fiber, 2 g protein, 2.6 g fat (0.4 g saturated), 0 mg cholesterol, 340 mg sodium, 416 mg potassium, 1 mg iron, 33 mg calcium

Watermelon Gazpacho
Instead of mango, substitute with 2 cups of seedless watermelon chunks.

Mango Cucumber Salsa
To transform this soup into a terrific fruit salsa, make half the recipe and omit the orange juice. It pairs perfectly with fish, chicken, or burgers.

● MIGHTY MINESTRONE

This quick and easy fiber-filled soup comes from my cousin Elsie Gorewich. It was a favorite of her late daughter Nancy, who included the recipe in her cookbook *Souperb!* Every year Nancy compiled a small cookbook that she sent to family and friends. I'm so glad I have my own copy, which is part of my treasured cookbook collection.

2 Tbsp olive oil
2 to 3 cloves garlic (about 2 to 3 tsp minced)
2 stalks celery, chopped
2 medium carrots, chopped
1 medium onion, chopped
1 can (28 oz/796 mL) whole tomatoes, undrained
1 can (19 oz/540 mL) red kidney beans, drained and rinsed
3 medium zucchini, chopped
2 cups vegetable or chicken broth
1 tsp dried oregano
Salt and freshly ground black pepper
Pinch of sugar (optional)
Chopped fresh basil, for garnish

1. Heat the oil in a large soup pot on medium heat. Add the garlic, celery, carrots, and onion; sauté until tender, about 5 minutes. Add the tomatoes, kidney beans, zucchini, broth, and oregano; bring to a boil. Reduce heat and simmer, partially covered, for 25 to 30 minutes. Stir occasionally. If the soup becomes too thick, thin with a little broth or water.

2. Season with salt and pepper. If necessary, add a pinch of sugar. (Some brands of canned tomatoes are more acidic than others; a small amount of sugar will counter that acidity.) Garnish with fresh basil and serve.

Yield: 6 to 8 servings (about 10 cups). Keeps 3 to 4 days in the refrigerator; reheats well. Freezes well for up to 4 months.

117 calories per cup, 19.2 g carbohydrate, 5.7 g fiber, 4 g protein, 3.2 g fat (0.4 g saturated), 0 mg cholesterol, 481 mg sodium, 500 mg potassium, 2 mg iron, 66 mg calcium

Variations
• Instead of zucchini, substitute with green or yellow beans, trimmed and cut in 1-inch pieces. For a calcium boost, add a sprinkling of grated Parmesan cheese or a dollop of Almost Sour Cream (page 114) at serving time.

Chef's Secrets
• Machine Cuisine! Chop the vegetables in batches in the food processor, using quick on/off pulses.

• Microwave Magic! Combine the oil, garlic, celery, carrots, and onion in a 3-quart microwaveable pot. Microwave, covered, on high for 5 minutes. Add the remaining ingredients and microwave, covered, on high for 20 minutes, stirring once or twice.

❦ MISO SOUP FOR ME!

This low-cal, low-carb soup is "good fast food" because it is high in protein, zinc, and antioxidants and may help lower cholesterol. If you can boil water, you can make this simple soup in no time. It makes for an easy portable snack or lunch if put in a thermos. A fermented soybean paste originating from Japan, miso paste is available in health food stores or the ethnic section of most supermarkets.

1 Tbsp miso paste
1 cup boiling water or vegetable broth
2 green onions, minced
2 to 3 Tbsp diced firm, medium or soft tofu
Dash of soy sauce, if desired

1. Place the miso paste in a measuring cup and gradually blend in about ¼ cup of boiling water. Stir in the remaining water, green onions, tofu, and soy sauce, if using. Serve immediately.

Yield: 1 serving. This recipe doubles or triples easily.

70 calories per serving, 10.3 g carbohydrate, 4.4 g fiber, 6 g protein, 1.6 g fat (0.2 g saturated), 0 mg cholesterol, 555 mg sodium, 176 mg potassium, 3 mg iron, 149 mg calcium

❦ QUICK PEA SOUP

This fabulous, fiber-filled soup, which uses frozen peas, is sure to "ap-pease" your hunger. The original recipe came from Sandra Gitlin, who is a superb cook. I substituted spinach for iceberg lettuce, added garlic and fresh basil, and reduced the cooking time from 1½ hours to just 30 minutes to retain more nutrients.

4 tsp olive oil
1 large onion, sliced
4 cups lightly packed baby spinach leaves
2 medium carrots, cut in chunks
1 medium potato, peeled and cut in chunks
1 pkg (2 lb/1 kg) frozen green sweet peas
   or baby peas (no need to defrost)
8 cups vegetable broth
3 to 4 cloves garlic (about 1 Tbsp minced)
2 tsp curry powder or 1 tsp ground cumin
1 tsp salt (or to taste)
½ tsp freshly ground black pepper
3 to 4 Tbsp minced fresh basil

1. Heat the oil in a large soup pot on medium heat. Add the onion and sauté for about 5 to 7 minutes or until golden.

2. Add the remaining ingredients, except the basil, to the soup pot and bring to a boil. Reduce heat to low and simmer, partially covered, for 30 minutes or until the vegetables are tender. Remove from heat and cool slightly.

3. Using an immersion blender, purée the soup while still in the pot, or purée in batches in a blender or food processor. Stir in the basil and adjust the seasonings to taste.

Yield: 6 to 8 servings (about 11 cups). Keeps 3 to 4 days in the refrigerator; reheats well. Freezes well for up to 4 months.

117 calories per cup, 19.3 g carbohydrate, 6.5 g fiber, 6 g protein, 2.3 g fat (0.3 g saturated), 0 mg cholesterol, 626 mg sodium, 217 mg potassium, 2 mg iron, 53 mg calcium

Chef's Secrets
• Frozen Assets: Most people keep green peas in their freezer. Frozen peas have

additional benefits besides acting as an ice pack. One-half cup of frozen peas contains 62 calories, 11.4 g carbohydrate, 4.4 g fiber, and 4 grams of protein, plus they're virtually fat-free.

• Sodi-Yum! If you are concerned about sodium, use a salt-free vegetable broth, or make your own Vegetable Broth (page 97), which is made without salt.

• Dairy Delicious! For a calcium boost, add a swirl of yogurt or a dollop of low-fat sour cream at serving time.

● RED PEPPER SOUP

This "soup-erb" soup is wonderful to make in the late summer when bell peppers are abundant and reasonably priced. Some like it hot, some like it cold. How cool is that!

2 Tbsp olive oil
2 cloves garlic (about 2 tsp minced)
2 leeks, trimmed, cleaned, and sliced
  or 2 medium onions, chopped
6 medium red peppers, halved, seeded,
  and chopped (about 2 lb/1 kg)
3 cups vegetable broth
1/2 tsp salt (or to taste)
Freshly ground black pepper
2 Tbsp fresh minced basil or 1 tsp dried
1/2 cup nonfat plain yogurt
1/2 cup skim milk

1. Heat the oil in a large soup pot over medium heat. Add the garlic, leeks, and red peppers; sauté for 8 to 10 minutes or until tender.

2. Add the broth, salt and pepper (if using the dried basil, add it now); bring to a boil. Reduce heat to low, cover and simmer for 20 to 25 minutes or until the vegetables are tender. Add the fresh basil, if using, remove from heat and cool completely.

3. Using an immersion blender, purée the soup while still in the pot, or purée in batches in a blender or food processor. Stir in the yogurt and milk and adjust the seasonings to taste. Serve hot or cold.

Yield: 4 to 5 servings (about 7 cups). Keeps for 2 to 3 days in the refrigerator; reheats well. Freezes well for up to 3 months. Don't boil when reheating or the soup may curdle.

112 calories per cup, 15.9 g carbohydrate, 2.4 g fiber, 3 g protein, 4.7 g fat (0.8 g saturated), 1 mg cholesterol, 408 mg sodium, 309 mg potassium, 1 mg iron, 78 mg calcium

Variations
• Instead of yogurt and skim milk, substitute with 1 cup buttermilk. To make this soup dairy-free, combine 1 Tbsp lemon juice with enough soymilk to make 1 cup.

Chef's Secrets
• Squeaky-Clean Leeks: To thoroughly clean leeks, first remove all but 2 or 3 inches of the green part. Make four lengthwise cuts to within 1 inch of the roots so that the leeks resemble a whisk broom. To remove sand and grit, swish leeks in a bowl of cold water. Remove and dry well, then slice off and discard the root end. (The dark green trimmings can be used when making vegetable broth.)

• Great Garnish! Garnish each serving with a red pepper ring, minced basil, green onions, or chives.

ROASTED TOMATO SOUP

Roasting brings out the full flavor of tomatoes and also increases the lycopene—and we like that! This low-cal soup tastes delicious hot or cold and is "weigh" tastier and healthier than canned tomato soup!

3 lb (1.5 kg) Italian plum tomatoes,
   halved lengthwise (12 to 14 tomatoes)
3 red peppers, seeded and
   cut in chunks
2 medium onions, cut in chunks
2 Tbsp olive oil
2 Tbsp balsamic vinegar
3/4 tsp salt
Freshly ground black pepper
2 Tbsp fresh minced basil (or 2 tsp dried)
1 Tbsp fresh minced thyme (or 1 tsp dried)
2 heads garlic (about 30 cloves of garlic)
4 cups vegetable broth or water
2 tsp sugar or granular Splenda (or to taste)

1. Preheat the oven to 400°F. Line a large baking tray with parchment paper.

2. Combine the tomatoes, red peppers, and onions in a large bowl. Drizzle with olive oil and balsamic vinegar. Sprinkle with salt, pepper, basil, and thyme; mix well. Spread the vegetables in a single layer on the baking tray, placing the tomatoes cut-side up. Cut a 1/4-inch slice from the top of each head of garlic, wrap each head in foil and place on the baking sheet. Roast vegetables, uncovered, for 35 to 45 minutes or until nicely browned, stirring occasionally.

3. Transfer the roasted tomatoes, peppers, and onions to a large pot. Squeeze the roasted garlic cloves into the pot. Add the broth and bring to a boil. Reduce heat to low and simmer, uncovered, for 10 minutes, stirring occasionally. Stir in the sugar. Remove from heat and cool slightly.

4. Using an immersion blender, purée the soup while still in the pot, or purée in batches in a blender or food processor. If too thick, add a little water or broth. Serve hot or cold.

Yield: 6 to 8 servings (about 10 cups). Keeps 4 to 5 days in the refrigerator; reheats well. Freezes well for up to 4 months.

98 calories per cup, 16.3 g carbohydrate, 3.0 g fiber, 3 g protein, 3.3 g fat (0.4 g saturated), 0 mg cholesterol, 369 mg sodium, 439 mg potassium, 1 mg iron, 48 mg calcium

Roasted Tomato Gazpacho

Prepare the soup as directed. When cool, cover and refrigerate. At serving time, stir in 1 chopped, unpeeled English cucumber, 1/2 cup chopped green pepper, 6 minced green onions, 1/2 tsp chili powder, 2 Tbsp minced fresh basil, and the juice of half a lemon. Serve chilled.

Chef's Secrets

• Can Do! If you don't have enough fresh tomatoes, canned ones will do. In Step 2, prepare and roast the tomatoes as directed, using 6 to 8 fresh tomatoes. In Step 3, add a can (28 oz/796 mL) of drained tomatoes to the roasted tomato mixture, along with the broth. Simmer for 10 to 15 minutes.

• Flavor Boost! Add a spoonful of pesto to each bowl of soup at serving time.

• Calci-Yum! Add 1/2 cup skim milk to each bowl of soup. Serve hot or cold.

ROOT SOUP

Include roots in your diet and you'll be on the "route" to good health! This recipe comes from Jackie Toledano of Netanya, Israel, whose own "roots" are from Glasgow, Scotland. She makes this low-cal soup with fresh pumpkin but I usually use butternut squash since it's more readily available in North America any time of year.

2 Tbsp olive oil
1 large onion, chopped
1 medium sweet potato, peeled
   and chopped
2 lb/1 kg carrots, peeled and chopped
   (frozen or baby carrots can be substituted)
2 cups peeled and chopped parsnips
2 to 3 cups chopped butternut squash
   or pumpkin
10 cups vegetable or chicken broth
1 to 2 tsp salt (or to taste)
1/2 tsp freshly ground black pepper
1 tsp ground cumin
1/4 cup minced fresh parsley or dillweed

1. Heat the oil in a large soup pot on medium high heat. Add the onion, sweet potato, carrots, turnip, and squash; sauté for 8 to 10 minutes, until golden.

2. Add the broth, salt, pepper, and cumin and bring to a boil. Reduce heat to low and simmer, partially covered, for 30 to 40 minutes or until all the vegetables are tender. Remove from heat and cool slightly.

3. Using an immersion blender, purée the soup while still in the pot, or purée in batches in a blender or food processor. If the soup is too thick, add a little extra broth or water. Before serving, add the parsley and adjust seasonings to taste.

Yield: 8 to 10 servings (about 15 cups). Keeps 3 to 4 days in the refrigerator; reheats well. Freezes well for up to 4 months.

105 calories per cup, 19.6 g carbohydrate, 4.0 g fiber, 2 g protein, 2.3 g fat (0.3 g saturated), 0 mg cholesterol, 502 mg sodium, 224 mg potassium, 1 mg iron, 59 mg calcium

Nutrition Notes
• Back to Your Roots! Carrots (GI 41) are rich in vitamin C and beta carotene. Sweet potatoes (GI 44) are packed with beta carotene, potassium, fiber, and vitamin A. Parsnips (GI 52) are high in potassium and fiber. Pumpkin and squash (GI 51) are high in Vitamin A and beta carotene.

SOUP OF SEVEN

This "mmm-masterpiece" comes from my friend Cheryl Goldberg, who often invites me for Friday night dinners. This low-cal meatless soup contains a medley of vegetables from A to Z, each one bringing their own nutritional benefit to this work of art. It's always a challenge to determine the correct quantities for the ingredients in her recipes because whenever I ask her how much, Cheryl either answers "A lot. A little. I don't know!"

1 bunch asparagus (about 1 lb/500 g),
   ends trimmed (or 1 bunch broccoli)
4 medium carrots, peeled and cut in chunks
3 stalks celery, cut in chunks
2 medium onions, cut in chunks
1 medium parsnip, peeled
4 medium potatoes, peeled and
   cut in chunks
1 medium zucchini, cut in chunks
9 cups water

2 Tbsp instant pareve chicken soup mix
1 to 2 tsp salt (or to taste)
1/2 tsp freshly ground black pepper
1/4 to 1/2 cup minced fresh parsley
  (Cheryl uses "a lot!")
1/4 cup minced fresh dillweed

1. Place the vegetables in a large soup pot.
Add the water, soup mix, salt, and pepper;
bring to a boil. Reduce heat to low and simmer, partially covered, for 25 to 30 minutes
or until the vegetables are tender. Remove
from heat and cool slightly. Add parsley and
dillweed. (Cheryl removes the parsnip at
this point, but I keep it in.)

2. Using an immersion blender, purée
the soup while still in the pot, or purée in
batches in a blender or food processor. If too
thick, add a little water or broth. Adjust the
seasonings to taste and serve.

Yield: 8 to 10 servings (about 13 cups).
Keeps 3 to 4 days in the refrigerator; reheats
well. Freezes well for up to 4 months.

87 calories per cup, 19.0 g carbohydrate, 3.5 g fiber, 3 g
protein, 0.5 g fat (0.1 g saturated), 0 mg cholesterol, 454 mg
sodium, 427 mg potassium, 1 mg iron, 43 mg calcium

● SPINACH, SWEET POTATO AND CARROT SOUP

*Popeye never had it so good! This satisfying
soup is quick to make and a good source of
fiber, folic acid, lutein, potassium, beta carotene, and Vitamin A. You'll "bowl" them
over with this smart-carb, low-cal soup.*

1 Tbsp olive oil
2 medium onions, chopped
2 cloves garlic (about 2 tsp minced)
1 pkg (10 oz/300 g) frozen spinach,

thawed and squeezed dry
3 cups sliced carrots (or 3 cups baby carrots)
1 large sweet potato, peeled and
  cut in chunks
1 tsp salt
1/4 tsp freshly ground black pepper
1 tsp dried basil
6 cups vegetable broth
1 cup skim or soymilk
1/4 cup minced fresh dillweed

1. Heat the oil in a large pot on medium
heat. Add the onions and garlic and sauté
about 5 minutes or until golden.

2. Add the spinach, carrots, sweet potato,
salt, pepper, basil, and broth; bring to a boil.
Reduce heat to low and simmer, partially
covered, for 25 to 30 minutes or until the
vegetables are tender. Remove from heat
and cool slightly.

3. Using an immersion blender, purée
the soup while still in the pot, or purée in
batches in a blender or food processor. Stir
in the milk and dill. If still too thick, thin
with a little broth, water or milk. Adjust
seasonings to taste and serve.

Yield: 5 to 6 servings (about 10 cups). Keeps
3 to 4 days in the refrigerator; reheats well.
Freezes well for up to 4 months. Don't boil
when reheating or the soup may curdle.

86 calories per cup, 14.8 g carbohydrate, 3.0 g fiber, 3 g
protein, 1.8 g fat (0.2 g saturated), 0 mg cholesterol, 563 mg
sodium, 182 mg potassium, 1 mg iron, 94 mg calcium

Variations
• Swiss chard can be substituted for
spinach. Wash the chard well but don't
dry. Chop the leaves and stems. Cover and
steam for 3 to 4 minutes (or microwave for

3 minutes on high). Let cool before gently squeezing to remove excess water.

• No sweet potato? Substitute with 2 medium potatoes.

• Great Garnishes! Top the soup with a dollop of yogurt or a sprinkling of grated Parmesan cheese. For a colorful garnish, add a spoonful or two of cooked spaghetti squash to each bowl of soup. The golden strands of squash will look like spaghetti.

● SPLIT PEA AND PORTOBELLO MUSHROOM SOUP

This decadent, velvety soup is full of fiber and flavor. My walking partner, Frieda Wishinsky, uses shallots rather than garlic in her cooking because they add another dimension of flavor. Frieda, a children's book author, refers to herself as "The Lady of Shallots." I'm sure Lord Tennyson would have poetic praise for her heavenly soup.

1 cup dried green split peas, rinsed
   and drained
5 cups water
1 cup vegetable or chicken broth
1 Tbsp canola or olive oil
1 large sweet onion, chopped
2 medium shallots (about 1/2 cup chopped)
2 cups sliced portobello mushrooms
   (about 5 mushrooms)
1 medium carrot, chopped
1/4 tsp paprika (sweet or smoked)
1 tsp salt
Freshly ground black pepper

1. Combine the split peas, water, and broth in a large pot. Bring to a boil. Reduce the heat to low, cover partially, and simmer for 35 minutes.

2. While the peas are cooking, heat the oil in a large skillet on medium-high heat. Add the onion, shallots, and mushrooms, and sauté until golden brown, about 5 minutes. Reduce the heat and cook slowly until the onion has caramelized, about 5 to 10 minutes.

3. Add the onion mixture to the peas. Add the carrot and simmer 15 minutes longer or until tender. Stir in the paprika and remove from heat to let cool slightly.

4. Using an immersion blender, purée the soup while still in the pot or purée in batches in a blender or food processor. If too thick, add a little water or broth. Season with salt and pepper to taste, and serve.

Yield: 4 to 5 servings (about 7 cups). Keeps 3 to 4 days in the refrigerator; reheats well. Freezes well for up to 4 months. If too thick, add a little water when reheating.

123 calories per cup, 19.6 g carbohydrate, 6.7 g fiber, 7 g protein, 2.4 g fat (0.2 g saturated), 0 mg cholesterol, 411 mg sodium, 376 mg potassium, 1 mg iron, 26 mg calcium

Variations
• Use a combination of split peas and lentils. You can use either green or yellow split peas.

• Cook 1/4 cup pearl barley, rinsed and drained, along with peas and/or lentils. Or substitute barley for half the peas. This makes a thicker soup, so thin as needed with additional broth.

• No shallots? Use 2 or 3 cloves garlic. Shallots look like small elongated onions, with a garlic flavor. When peeled, they divide into cloves like garlic.

• Instead of portobellos, try shiitake, oyster, or button mushrooms, or a combination of these.

Nutrition Notes

• Split peas are a nutritional powerhouse. Packed with protein, fiber, and vitamin C, they also contain iron, zinc, and B vitamins. Both green and yellow split peas have a low glycemic index (32). Soaking before cooking isn't necessary. A thorough rinsing in a colander is sufficient. When cooked, split peas break down to make a thick, satisfying soup.

☀ SQUASH, BROCCOLI AND SWEET POTATO SOUP

This scrumptious soup is packed with beta carotene and is very nourishing—it's like a multivitamin in a bowl.

2 lb (1 kg) acorn or butternut squash
1 Tbsp olive or canola oil
2 large onions, coarsely chopped
2 cloves garlic (about 2 tsp minced)
1 bunch broccoli, cut in chunks
   (about 4 cups)
2 medium sweet potatoes, peeled
   and cut in chunks
2 medium carrots, peeled and cut in chunks
   (or 8 baby carrots)
8 cups vegetable or chicken broth
1/4 cup chopped fresh dillweed
1 to 2 tsp salt (or to taste)
Freshly ground black pepper

1. Pierce the squash in several places with a sharp knife. Microwave, uncovered, on high for 6 to 8 minutes, turning the squash over halfway through cooking. Squash should be three-quarters cooked. When cool enough to handle, cut in half and discard the seeds. Scoop out the flesh and cut it in chunks. (An ice cream scoop does a great job.) You should have about 4 cups.

2. Heat the oil in a large soup pot on medium heat. Add the onions and garlic; sauté for 5 to 7 minutes or until golden. Add the broccoli, sweet potatoes, carrots, and squash and mix well.

3. Stir in the broth, dill, salt, and pepper; bring to a boil. Reduce heat to low and simmer, partially covered, for 30 minutes, stirring occasionally, or until vegetables are tender. Remove from heat and cool slightly.

4. Using an immersion blender, purée the soup while still in the pot, or purée in batches in a blender or food processor. If soup is too thick, add a little water or broth.

Yield: 7 to 8 servings (about 12 cups). Keeps 3 to 4 days in the refrigerator; reheats well. Freezes well for up to 4 months.

109 calories per cup, 21.8 g carbohydrate, 5.5 g fiber, 3 g protein, 1.8 g fat (0.2 g saturated), 0 mg cholesterol, 574 mg sodium, 547 mg potassium, 1 mg iron, 77 mg calcium

Chef's Secrets

• Squash Anyone? Winter varieties of squash include acorn, butternut, buttercup, hubbard, and spaghetti. All have deep yellow-to-orange flesh, seeds, and hard, thick skins. Choose squash that is heavy for its size, with a hard outer skin that is free of moldy spots or blemishes. Most squash is interchangeable in recipes.

super
soups

• Store It Right! Store squash and sweet potatoes in a cool, dark place. Squash will keep for 1 to 2 months and sweet potatoes will keep up to a month.

• Sweet News! Did you know that sweet potatoes are packed with more beta carotene than carrots or winter squash?

● SQUISH SQUASH SOUP

Squash, anyone? Thanks to my friend Jeff Goodman for this yummy, nutritious soup, which he often serves to guests. Everyone loves it, especially me!

1 medium butternut squash
   (about 3 lb/1.5 kg)
   (or 7 to 8 cups frozen squash cubes)
4 cups vegetable broth
6 large mushrooms (about 1 cup sliced)
2 Tbsp soy sauce (low-sodium or regular)
1/2 cup skim milk
1/2 cup light cream (10% or 5%)
Salt and freshly ground black pepper

1. If using fresh squash, cut in half with a sharp knife and scoop out the seeds (see Chef's Secrets, this page). Cut into cubes. Combine squash, broth, mushrooms, and soy sauce in a large saucepan; bring to a boil.

2. Reduce heat and simmer, partially covered or until the squash is tender, about 20 minutes. Remove from heat and cool slightly.

3. Using an immersion blender, purée the soup while still in the pot, or purée in batches in a blender or food processor. Stir in milk and cream. Season with salt and pepper to taste, and serve.

Yield: 6 servings (about 8 cups). Keeps 3 days in the refrigerator; reheats well. Freezes well for up to 3 months. Don't boil when reheating or the soup may curdle.

150 calories per cup, 32.3 g carbohydrate, 5.4 g fiber, 4 g protein, 2.1 g fat (1.0 g saturated), 5 mg cholesterol, 484 mg sodium, 913 mg potassium, 2 mg iron, 161 mg calcium

Dairy-Free Variation
• Instead of milk or cream, substitute soymilk.

Toasted Squash Seeds
Rinse the seeds to remove fibers; pat dry with paper towels. Spread in a single layer on a parchment-lined baking sheet, drizzle with a little olive oil, and sprinkle lightly with salt. Roast, uncovered, at 250°F for about 45 to 60 minutes or until they are toasted and golden, stirring every 20 minutes. The toasted seeds will keep for several months in a sealed container in a cool, dark place. They're ideal as a snack or garnish.

Chef's Secret
• Short Cuts! Score the outer skin of a squash with a sharp knife in several places. Microwave, uncovered, for 4 to 5 minutes on high; turn the squash over halfway through cooking. Let stand for 5 minutes or until cool enough to handle. The squash will be slightly softened and easier (and safer!) to cut in half. Scoop out the stringy fiber and seeds.

🍅 TOMATO, LENTIL AND VEGETABLE SOUP

This hearty soup comes together very quickly and is family-friendly. A food processor chops the fresh vegetables quickly, and using frozen vegetables cuts down on preparation time. Now that's my kind of recipe!

2 medium onions, chopped
2 stalks celery, chopped
2 carrots, chopped
1 to 2 Tbsp olive oil
2 to 3 cloves garlic (2 to 3 tsp minced)
4¼ cups vegetable or tomato juice
4¼ cups water
1 cup red lentils, rinsed and drained
1 tsp dried basil
2 cups frozen mixed vegetables (such as peas, carrots, corn, and green beans)
Salt and freshly ground black pepper

1. If using a food processor, chop the onions, celery, and carrots in batches, using quick on/off pulses.

2. Heat the oil in a large pot on medium heat. Add the chopped vegetables and sauté 5 to 7 minutes or until golden. Add the garlic and sauté 2 minutes longer.

3. Add the juice, water, lentils, and basil; bring to a boil. Reduce heat to low and simmer, partially covered, for about 45 minutes or until the lentils are soft and the vegetables are tender. Stir occasionally.

4. Add the frozen vegetables, salt, and pepper; simmer for 10 to 15 minutes longer. If the soup is too thick, thin with a little water or broth before serving.

Yield: 6 servings (about 10 cups). Keeps 3 to 4 days in the refrigerator; reheats well.

Freezes well for up to 4 months.

125 calories per cup, 21.3 g carbohydrate, 3.4 g fiber, 7 g protein, 1.4 g fat (0.2 g saturated), 0 mg cholesterol, 291 mg sodium, 361 mg potassium, 1 mg iron, 51 mg calcium

Chef's Secrets
• Quick Tip: One 46 oz/950 mL bottle contains 4¼ cups of juice, which makes for quick measuring of both the juice and water.

• Frozen Assets: Use any kind of frozen mixed vegetables you have on hand. Fresh vegetables also work well. Your soup will always be a little bit different, but it will always be delicious!

🍅 VEGETABLE BROTH

This could be called "chicken soup without the chicken!" Serve this low-sodium broth on its own or use it in recipes calling for vegetable broth.

2 large onions or leeks, cut in large chunks
3 cups (1 lb/500 g) baby carrots (or 6 medium carrots, peeled and cut in large chunks)
4 stalks celery, cut in large chunks
1 red pepper, seeded and cut in large chunks
1 medium parsnip, peeled and cut in large chunks
1 cup mushrooms
1 medium unpeeled zucchini, cut in large chunks
12 cups cold water
Salt (optional)
Freshly ground black pepper
6 cloves garlic
½ cup fresh dillweed
½ cup parsley stems, if desired (see Chef's Secrets)

1. Place all the ingredients into a large soup pot. The water should cover the vegetables by no more than 1 inch. Bring to a boil over high heat. Reduce heat to low and simmer, partially covered, for 45 minutes. Remove from heat and cool completely.

2. Using a colander, strain the liquid into a large bowl. Reserve the cooked vegetables (see Purée Power). Ladle the cooled broth into containers and cover tightly. Refrigerate or freeze until ready to use.

Yield: 5 to 6 servings (about 10 cups). Keeps 3 to 4 days in the refrigerator; reheats well. Freezes well for up to 4 months.

20 calories per cup, 3.0 g carbohydrate, 1.0 g fiber, 1 g protein, 0.5 g fat (0 g saturated), 0 mg cholesterol, 65 mg sodium, 50 mg potassium, 0 mg iron, 20 calcium

Chef's Secrets
• I Be Leaf! Parsley stems add flavor to the soup but the leaves can make your soup bitter. Use the leaves in salads such as Terrific Tabbouleh (page 261), or as a garnish.

• Veggie Power: Onion skins will add a rich, golden color to the broth. Add a cup or two of tomatoes, turnips, spinach, green onions, and/or celery tops. Don't add strong-flavored vegetables such as cabbage, broccoli, or cauliflower because their flavor will overwhelm the broth. Starchy vegetables (such as potatoes and sweet potatoes) will make the broth cloudy.

• Mushroom Magic! For a full, rich flavor, add a handful of reconstituted dried mushrooms that have been soaked in hot water for 20 minutes. Also add their soaking liquid to the broth and cook as directed.

• Purée Power: Purée the cooked vegetables from the broth in a food processor or blender, then return them to the clear broth. (If using onion skins and parsley stems, discard them.) The cooked vegetables contain valuable nutrients and flavor. Kids love this soup—it's a smart way to sneak nutrition into their tummies.

• Sodi-Yum! Nutrients for this broth are calculated without salt. Many chefs leave broth unsalted until they are ready to use it. You may not need to add salt if you use it in a recipe already containing salty ingredients. If serving this instead of chicken soup, season with salt and pepper.

✿ WHITE BEAN SOUP

Canned beans save on cooking time and the food processor makes quick work of preparing the ingredients. Lemon juice really adds a flavor boost. This recipe can be halved easily, but it's so delicious, why bother? Bean cuisine will keep you lean and healthy, and has a low glycemic index.

3 or 4 cloves garlic (about 1 Tbsp minced)
2 medium onions, cut in chunks
2 medium stalks celery, cut in chunks
2 medium carrots, cut in chunks
1 Tbsp olive or canola oil
2 cans (19 oz/540 mL each)
    white kidney beans, drained and rinsed
4 cups vegetable or chicken broth
1 can (28 oz/796 mL) tomatoes
    (don't drain)
1/2 tsp dried thyme
1 tsp ground cumin or dried basil
Salt and freshly ground black pepper
2 Tbsp lemon juice (preferably fresh)

1. Drop the garlic through the feed tube of a food processor while the motor is running; process until minced, about 10 seconds. Add the onions, celery, and carrots; process with several quick on/off pulses, or until the vegetables are coarsely chopped.

2. Heat the oil in a large soup pot on medium heat. Sauté the vegetables about 5 to 7 minutes or until tender. If they begin to stick, stir in a little water.

3. Working in batches, process the beans together with some of the broth in the food processor until puréed, about 30 seconds. Add to the soup pot. Purée the tomatoes in batches; add them to the pot, along with the seasonings. Bring to a boil; reduce heat to low and simmer, partially covered, for 20 minutes. Stir occasionally.

4. Add the lemon juice, adjust seasonings to taste, and serve.

Yield: 7 to 8 servings (about 12 cups). Keeps 3 to 4 days in the refrigerator; reheats well. Freezes well for up to 4 months.

109 calories per cup, 20.1 g carbohydrate, 4.0 g fiber, 5 g protein, 1.7 g fat (0.2 g saturated), 0 mg cholesterol, 334 mg sodium, 444 mg potassium, 3 mg iron, 79 mg calcium

Variation
• Instead of beans, substitute canned lentils.

sauces, marinades & seasonings

SAUCES, MARINADES AND SEASONINGS

Slim and Saucy: Fat-laden sauces are a source of calories, saturated fats, and trans-fats. Throughout this book, you'll find many delicious, "light-hearted" sauces and marinades that you can enjoy without guilt.

A-Salt with a Deadly Weapon! Most store-bought sauces, marinades, and seasonings are high in sodium. Making your own will help you control the sodium content.

Thick or Thin! Thicken sauces and gravies with leftover cooked vegetables, such as sweet potatoes or cauliflower. Purée cooked vegetables in a food processor or blender. Gradually add the hot broth or defatted pan juices through the feed tube in the processor or the opening in the top of the blender and process until smooth and silky. Season to taste.

Passover Tip: Instead of using cornstarch for thickening Passover sauces, use an equal amount of potato starch. One tablespoon of cornstarch or potato starch will thicken 1 cup liquid.

Dump those Lumps! Make sauces smooth and silky by processing them for a few seconds in a food processor fitted with the steel blade. You can also purée sauces in a blender.

Marin-Aides: Marinades enhance flavor and increase the tenderness of meats, poultry, and fish. Marinating food also protects it from forming harmful carcinogens during grilling.

Cheater's Marinade: Use low-calorie bottled salad dressing as a quick marinade.

Adore-a-Bowl: Because most marinades contain acidic ingredients, it's best to marinate foods in a non-reactive bowl or container made of glass, ceramic, or stainless steel; don't use an aluminum container. You can also use a heavy-duty re-sealable plastic bag.

It's in the Bag: Place marinade in a re-sealable freezer bag along with the chicken or meat. Seal well and refrigerate for up to 24 hours, or freeze. No fuss, no muss!

Timing's Everything: Raw meats and poultry can be marinated for up to 48 hours in the refrigerator whereas fish only needs to be marinated for 1 hour. Never marinate foods at room temperature for longer than one hour. If you don't have much time, even briefly marinating—for 10 or 15 minutes—adds flavor and tenderness.

Frozen Assets: You can freeze most marinades along with chicken or meat for up to 2 months. Thaw overnight in the refrigerator, then cook as directed. If you want to defrost in the microwave oven, always transfer the contents from the bag to a microwaveable bowl or dish.

The Raw Truth: If you want to continue using a marinade that has been in contact with raw meat or fish, simply boil the marinade for 5 minutes to kill any harmful bacteria. Then you can brush the boiled marinade on cooked food or use it as a sauce.

Safe at the Plate: Don't serve cooked food on the same plate that was used to transport the raw marinated meat or poultry from the kitchen to the grill. Cross-contamination can also occur when vegetables or other uncooked foods come into contact with cutting boards, plates, and utensils that were used for raw meat and poultry. Use separate plates, one for raw foods and one for cooked foods.

Clean Cuisine: Don't use the same utensils (e.g., pastry brush, spatula, fork, or tongs) for raw food, and then reuse the same, unwashed, utensils on the food after it's been cooked. The utensils could harbor and transfer bacteria to the cooked food. Either use two different sets of utensils (one for raw and one for cooked food), or wash utensils thoroughly before using them on the cooked food.

Rub-a-Dubba-Doo! Dry rubs are a blend of dried or fresh herbs and spices, salt, pepper, and, sometimes, sugar. If you add a little oil, your rub becomes a paste. When grilled or broiled, rubs form a flavorful crust on the food.

ALL-FRUIT CRANBERRY SAUCE

Thanks to Faygie Leshman of Boca Raton, Florida, for sharing this scrumptious, sugar-free sauce. It's "berry" versatile! Serve it as an accompaniment to turkey or chicken, or use it instead of jam on multi-grain toast, pancakes, or blintzes. You can either bake the sauce or cook it on top of the stove . . . your choice.

1 bag (12 oz/340 g) fresh or frozen
  cranberries, rinsed and drained
2 cups (16 oz/500 ml jar) all-fruit
  orange marmalade

Baked Method: Preheat the oven to 350°F. Combine the cranberries with marmalade in a 7- × 11-inch baking dish sprayed with cooking spray; mix well. Bake, uncovered, for 20 minutes. Stir well; continue baking for another 20 to 25 minutes longer or until the sauce thickens. Remove from the oven and cool before transferring to a serving dish. Cover and refrigerate until ready to use.

Stove-Top Method: Combine the cranberries and marmalade in a large saucepan. Cook on medium-high heat until mixture comes to a boil. Reduce the heat to medium and simmer uncovered, stirring occasionally, for 5 to 7 minutes or until all the berries have popped. Remove from the oven and cool before transferring to a serving dish. Cover and refrigerate until ready to use.

Yield: About 2³/₄ cups. Keeps for up to 3 to 4 weeks in the refrigerator. Freezes well for up to 3 months.

21 calories per Tbsp, 5.4 g carbohydrate, 0.3 g fiber, 0 g protein, 0 g fat (0 g saturated), 0 mg cholesterol, 0 mg sodium, 5 mg potassium, 0 mg iron, 0 mg calcium

Variations

• Other flavors of jam, such as apricot or peach, can be substituted.

• You can use sugar-free, low-sugar, or regular jam or marmalade in this recipe, but the nutrient content will differ.

Chef's Secrets

• Shop Talk! Buy fresh cranberries in season. Before storing, discard any soft, shriveled, or discolored berries. Store in the refrigerator for 2 to 3 weeks.

• Frozen Assets! Buy extra bags of berries to store in the freezer; they'll keep about 1 year. Cranberries don't need to be thawed before using.

• Berried Treasures! Fresh or frozen cranberries are terrific in salads, smoothies, homemade cranberry sauce, fruit crisps, cakes, scones, muffins, and quick breads.

Nutrition Notes

• Cranberries contain one of the highest concentrations of antioxidants. These shiny red jewels help protect against cancer, heart disease, and urinary tract infections.

• Cranberries may help prevent tooth decay and cavities. However, they're also loaded with natural acid that can strip away essential minerals from the teeth, so follow the old adage—everything in moderation.

🍎 CREAMY DILL SAUCE

This is "dill-icious" with fish! It also makes a terrific dip for raw vegetables.

1/4 cup light mayonnaise
1/4 cup fat-free plain yogurt
2 tsp lemon or lime juice (preferably fresh)
2 green onions, minced
2 Tbsp finely chopped fresh dillweed
Salt and freshly ground black pepper

1. In a small bowl, combine the mayonnaise, yogurt, lemon or lime juice, green onions, dillweed, and salt and pepper to taste.

2. Cover and refrigerate until ready to use. Serve chilled.

Yield: About 1/2 cup. Keeps for up to 2 to 3 days in the refrigerator. Don't freeze.

21 calories per Tbsp, 1.2 g carbohydrate, 0.1 g fiber, 0 g protein, 1.7 g fat (0.3 g saturated), 2 mg cholesterol, 44 mg sodium, 16 mg potassium, 0 mg iron, 10 mg calcium

Variations

• Instead of mayonnaise and yogurt, substitute with 1/2 cup Firm Yogurt Cheese (page 178).

• Dairy-Free: Instead of mayonnaise and yogurt, substitute 1/2 cup silken firm tofu. Blend well.

• Instead of dillweed, substitute your favorite fresh or dried herbs (such as basil, mint, rosemary, thyme).

🍎 MUSTARD DILL SAUCE

You must try this creamy, dairy-free sauce as an accompaniment to grilled chicken, poached salmon, or any other fish. It also makes a tasty spread for sandwiches.

¼ cup minced fresh dillweed
¼ cup light mayonnaise
3 Tbsp Dijon mustard
1 Tbsp honey
1½ Tbsp lemon juice (preferably fresh)
Freshly ground black pepper

1. In a small bowl, combine the dillweed, mayonnaise, mustard, honey, lemon juice, and pepper to taste; mix well.

2. Cover and refrigerate until ready to use. Serve chilled.

Yield: About ¾ cup. Keeps for up to 3 to 4 days in the refrigerator. Don't freeze.

32 calories per Tbsp, 2.9 g carbohydrate, 0.1 g fiber, 0 g protein, 2.3 g fat (0.3 g saturated), 2 mg cholesterol, 158 mg sodium, 14 mg potassium, 0 mg iron, 7 mg calcium

PEANUT SAUCE

This Szechuan-inspired sauce is scrumptious on chicken, beef, fish, or tofu. Try it in stir-fries or on steamed veggies such as broccoli, cauliflower, or carrots. It's wonderful as both a marinade and dipping sauce in Chicken Satay (page 217). You'll go nuts over it!

3 cloves garlic (about 1 Tbsp minced)
1 slice peeled fresh ginger
   (about 1 Tbsp minced)
3 Tbsp soy sauce (low-sodium or regular)
½ cup natural peanut butter
2 Tbsp honey (or to taste)
2 Tbsp rice vinegar
2 tsp Asian (toasted) sesame oil
¼ tsp cayenne pepper

1. In a food processor fitted with the steel blade, drop the garlic and ginger through the feed tube while the motor is running; process until minced, about 10 seconds.

2. Add the soy sauce, peanut butter, honey, vinegar, sesame oil, and cayenne; process until blended, about 15 seconds. Scrape down the sides of bowl if needed. If the sauce is too thick, thin with a little water.

Yield: About 1 cup. Keeps for up to 2 months in the refrigerator. Reheat gently but don't boil or the sauce may separate. Don't freeze.

58 calories per Tbsp, 3.9 g carbohydrate, 0.5 g fiber, 2 g protein, 4.0 g fat (0.5 g saturated), 0 mg cholesterol, 115 mg sodium, 10 mg potassium, 0 mg iron, 2 mg calcium

PINEAPPLE DIPPING SAUCE

You'll "pine" for this appealing sauce—it's delicious as a dipping sauce for skewered chicken, chicken fingers, or even grilled tofu. This is also excellent over white fish fillets such as tilapia or sole.

2 cups unsweetened pineapple juice
1 Tbsp rice vinegar or lemon juice
   (preferably fresh)
½ green pepper, seeded and minced
⅛ tsp red pepper flakes
1 Tbsp cornstarch
3 Tbsp cold water
1 cup finely chopped pineapple
   (fresh or canned)
2 green onions, minced
1 tsp minced fresh ginger

1. Combine the pineapple juice, rice vinegar, green pepper, and red pepper flakes in a small saucepan, and bring to a boil.

2. Blend the cornstarch with cold water in a small bowl until smooth. Add to the saucepan

and whisk the mixture over medium heat until thickened and smooth, about 2 to 3 minutes.

3. Remove the sauce from the heat and cool before stirring in the pineapple, green onions, and ginger.

Yield: About 3 cups. Keeps for up to 3 to 4 days, tightly sealed, in the refrigerator. Don't freeze.

9 calories per Tbsp, 2.1 g carbohydrate, 0.1 g fiber, 0 g protein, 0 g fat (0 g saturated), 0 mg cholesterol, 0 mg sodium, 23 mg potassium, 0 mg iron, 3 mg calcium

Passover Variation
• Use potato starch instead of cornstarch and lemon juice instead of rice vinegar. Omit the red pepper flakes.

🍎 PINEAPPLE SALSA

This flavorful salsa is scrumptious with grilled fish or chicken, and it's a colorful way to add vitamins and phytonutrients to your plate. A food processor will help you prepare this dish quickly, but use a chef's knife if you want to burn a few extra calories and get rid of some stress at the same time. Add the sugar or honey only if the salsa isn't sweet enough.

1 slice fresh peeled ginger
   (about 1 Tbsp minced)
1/4 cup fresh cilantro or parsley leaves
2 Tbsp fresh basil
1/4 medium red onion or 2 green onions
1 small jalapeno chili pepper,
   stem and seeds removed
1/4 red pepper, seeded
1 cup fresh pineapple, cut in 1-inch chunks
2 Tbsp lime juice (preferably fresh)

1 tsp sugar or honey (optional)
Salt and freshly ground black pepper

1. In a food processor fitted with the steel blade, process the ginger, cilantro, basil, onion, jalapeno, and red peppers until minced, about 10 seconds. Add the pineapple, lime juice, and sugar or honey, if using; season with salt and pepper to taste. Process with several quick on/off pulses, until coarsely chopped. Don't overprocess.

2. Transfer the mixture to a serving dish; cover and chill for several hours or overnight. Serve chilled.

Yield: 6 servings of about 1/4 cup each. Keeps for up to 1 to 2 days in the refrigerator. Don't freeze.

20 calories per serving, 5.1 g carbohydrate, 0.7 g fiber, trace protein, 0.1 g fat (0 g saturated), 0 mg cholesterol, 1 mg sodium, 72 mg potassium, 0 mg iron, 8 mg calcium

Mango or Papaya Salsa
Substitute mango or papaya for the pineapple.

Chef's Secrets
• Hot Stuff! No jalapeno pepper? Substitute a few drops of hot sauce or a dash of cayenne.

• Quick Tip: If you're grilling fish or chicken for dinner, prepare Grilled Pineapple (page 427) at the same time. Use some of the grilled pineapple in this scrumptious salsa.

Nutrition Notes
• Pineapple has a medium glycemic index (GI 58, plus/minus 8, the means of 2 studies). Combining it with vegetables and serving it with a protein dish such as fish or chicken lowers the glycemic load.

♦ PINEAPPLE TOMATO SALSA

I created this vibrant salsa using leftover canned pineapple and juicy, ripe tomatoes. Fresh dillweed complements the flavors perfectly. It's wonderful with fish or chicken and can be heated to make a tasty sauce for rice. Add a spoonful or two to your favorite vinaigrette salad dressing for a flavor boost.

2 Tbsp fresh dillweed
1/2 cup canned pineapple chunks, drained
1/2 green pepper, seeded and
   cut in chunks
2 medium plum tomatoes, cut in chunks
2 green onions, cut in 1-inch pieces
2 tsp extra virgin olive oil
2 tsp rice vinegar
Salt and freshly ground black pepper
1/8 tsp cayenne

1. In a food processor fitted with the steel blade, process the dillweed until minced.

2. Add the pineapple, bell pepper, tomatoes, green onions, oil, vinegar, salt, pepper, and cayenne. Process with several quick on/off pulses, just until coarsely chopped. Don't overprocess. Adjust seasonings to taste.

3. Transfer the mixture to a serving dish, cover, and chill for several hours or overnight. Serve chilled.

Yield: About 1 1/2 cups. Keeps for up to 2 to 3 days, tightly sealed, in the refrigerator. Don't freeze.

8 calories per Tbsp, 1.1 g carbohydrate, 0.2 g fiber, 0 g protein, 0.4 g fat (0.1 g saturated), 0 mg cholesterol, 1 mg sodium, 29 mg potassium, 0 mg iron, 3 mg calcium

♦ EMERGENCY TOMATO SAUCE

I created this quick, no-cook sauce when I unexpectedly ran out of tomato sauce while testing recipes, so don't panic if it ever happens to you. Easy and good!

1 can (5 1/2 oz/156 mL) tomato paste
3/4 cup water
   (or 2 tomato paste cans of water)
1 clove garlic, minced
   (or 1/2 tsp garlic powder)
1/2 tsp dried basil
1/4 tsp dried oregano
1/4 tsp dried thyme
Pinch of granulated sugar

1. Combine the tomato paste, water, garlic, basil, oregano, thyme, and sugar in a small bowl or food processor; mix or process until blended.

2. Transfer to a container, cover, and refrigerate until ready to use.

Yield: 2 cups. Keeps for up to 10 days in the refrigerator; reheats well. Freezes well for up to 3 months.

19 calories per 1/4 cup, 4.2 g carbohydrate, 1.0 g fiber, 1 g protein, 0.1 g fat (0 g saturated), 0 mg cholesterol, 168 mg sodium, 219 mg potassium, 1 mg iron, 11 mg calcium

♦ QUICK TOMATO SAUCE

This low-sodium tomato sauce comes together quickly with minimal ingredients. It's perfect over pasta, couscous, fish, or chicken. Use this in any recipe calling for tomato sauce.

1 Tbsp extra virgin olive oil
1 medium onion, finely chopped
2 cloves garlic (about 2 tsp minced)
1 can (28 oz/796 mL) whole tomatoes
 (don't drain)
1 can (5¹/2 oz/156 mL) tomato paste
Salt (optional)
Freshly ground black pepper
¹/4 tsp red pepper flakes
2 Tbsp chopped fresh basil or 1 tsp dried

1. Heat oil in a large pot over medium heat.
Add the onion and cook until tender, about
5 minutes. (If the onion begins to stick to
the pan, add 1 to 2 Tbsp water.) Stir in the
garlic and cook 2 minutes longer.

2. Add the tomatoes, breaking them up with
a wooden spoon. Stir in the tomato paste,
salt (if using), black pepper, and red pepper
flakes. If using dried basil, add it now. Bring
to a boil, reduce heat to low and simmer
partly covered for 15 minutes, stirring occasionally. If using fresh basil, add it now.

Yield: About 4 cups. Keeps for up to 1 week
in the refrigerator; reheats well. Freezes well
for up to 3 months.

59 calories per 1/2 cup serving, 10.0 g carbohydrate,
2.2 g fiber, 2 g protein, 2.0 g fat (0.3 g saturated), 0 mg
cholesterol, 30 mg sodium, 463 mg potassium, 1 mg iron,
44 mg calcium

Variations
• Add 1 can (19 oz/540 mL can) kidney or
black beans, drained and rinsed, to the sauce
along with tomato paste. If desired, add ¹/2 tsp
dried oregano and ¹/4 tsp dried thyme. Simmer uncovered for 15 minutes. Instead of
basil, stir in ¹/4 cup chopped fresh cilantro.

Chef's Secrets
• Microwave Method: Combine olive oil,
onion, and garlic in a 2-quart microwaveable bowl. Microwave uncovered on high
for 5 minutes. Add tomatoes, tomato paste,
and seasonings. Cover with parchment paper and microwave on high for 10 minutes,
stirring once or twice. Stir in fresh basil.

• Oat Cuisine! For a fiber boost, add 3 Tbsp
quick-cooking oats to the sauce 5 minutes
before it's done. If the sauce is too thick,
thin it down with a little water or wine.

Nutrition Note
• A-Salt with a Deadly Weapon! The analysis has been done using unsalted canned
tomatoes and tomato paste. Salt has not
been included in the nutrient analysis as it's
an optional ingredient. If you use regular
canned tomatoes and tomato paste, ¹/2 cup
sauce will contain 425 mg sodium.

ROASTED TOMATO SAUCE

This garden-fresh sauce is fabulous in the
summertime when tomatoes are sweet,
plentiful, and inexpensive. On a hot day,
roast them early in the morning so as not to
heat up the kitchen. Although you can roast
any kind of tomatoes, plum tomatoes work
best because of their thicker skins. This
scrumptious sauce is perfect on pasta, pizza,
crostini, chicken, or fish. Sauce it up!

12 to 14 ripe tomatoes (about 4 lb/2 kg)
2 medium onions, chopped
6 to 8 cloves garlic (about 6 to 8 tsp minced)
¹/2 tsp Kosher or sea salt
Coarsely ground black pepper
2 Tbsp extra virgin olive oil
¹/4 cup coarsely chopped fresh basil

1. Preheat the oven to 375°F. Spray a 9- × 13-inch baking dish with cooking spray.

2. Core the tomatoes; if the tomatoes are large, cut them in halves or quarters. Place in the baking dish with the onions and garlic. Sprinkle with salt and pepper to taste, and drizzle with oil. Mix well.

3. Roast, uncovered, about 1½ hours or until the vegetables are tender, stirring occasionally. When done, the tomatoes will collapse and reduce in size by half—their skins will be slightly brown and cracked.

4. Remove the baking dish from the oven and coarsely mash the tomato-onion mixture with the pan juices; the resulting texture should be chunky. Stir in the basil and serve warm or transfer to a container, seal tightly, and store in the refrigerator until ready to use.

Yield: About 3 cups (6 servings of ½ cup each). Keeps for up to a week in the refrigerator; reheats well. Freezes well for up to 3 months.

110 calories per serving, 15.6 g carbohydrate, 3.9 g fiber, 3 g protein, 5.1 g fat (0.7 g saturated), 0 mg cholesterol, 209 mg sodium, 725 mg potassium, 1 mg iron, 44 mg calcium

Chef's Secret
• Roast and Boast! Roast other vegetables along with the tomatoes (e.g., zucchini, mushrooms, peppers, and/or eggplant). Always delicious, always different!

● ROSY RED PEPPER SAUCE

This sauce is scrumptious with cheese tortellini, ravioli, or any stuffed pasta. Use it instead of tomato sauce in your favorite lasagna recipe. It's also delicious over baked or grilled fish.

1 Tbsp olive oil
2 cloves garlic (about 2 tsp minced)
1 medium onion, thinly sliced
3 red peppers, seeded and chopped
¾ cup vegetable broth
½ tsp salt (or to taste)
Freshly ground black pepper
Dash cayenne or red pepper flakes
2 Tbsp minced fresh basil or 1 tsp dried
¼ cup 10% table cream mixed
    with ¼ cup skim milk
    (or ½ cup 5% table cream)

1. Heat the oil in a large saucepan over medium high heat. Add the garlic, onion, and red peppers and sauté for 6 to 8 minutes or until tender.

2. Add the broth, salt, pepper, and cayenne; bring to a boil. Reduce heat to low, cover and simmer for 15 minutes, stirring occasionally.

3. Remove from heat and cool slightly. Purée in the saucepan with an immersion blender or use a food processor. Add the basil and cream/milk mixture; blend or process for a few seconds more to mix well. Adjust seasonings to taste. If the sauce is too thick, add a little more milk.

Yield: About 3 cups (4 servings of ¾ cup each). Keeps for up to 2 to 3 days in the refrigerator; reheats well. Freezes well for up to 2 months.

103 calories per serving, 12.9 g carbohydrate, 1.9 g fiber, 3 g protein, 5.3 g fat (1.5 g saturated), 5 mg cholesterol, 394 mg sodium, 275 mg potassium, 1 mg iron, 59 mg calcium

POWER PESTO

Spinach is the secret ingredient that gives this dairy-free pesto a powerful punch of phytonutrients. Even Popeye would be impressed! My grandson Maxie is a finicky eater, but he loves this pesto on noodles. (If you're allergic to nuts, you can omit the walnuts—it will still taste great.)

4 large cloves garlic
1 cup tightly packed fresh basil leaves
2 cups tightly packed baby spinach leaves
3 Tbsp chopped walnuts, almonds,
   or pine nuts
1/4 cup extra virgin olive oil
1/4 cup vegetable or chicken broth
Salt and freshly ground black pepper

1. In a food processor fitted with the steel blade, drop the garlic through the feed tube while the motor is running; process until minced, about 10 seconds.

2. Scrape down the sides of the bowl. Add the basil, spinach, and nuts; process until finely minced, about 15 seconds.

3. Combine the oil and broth in a glass measuring cup. Drizzle through the feed tube while the motor is running and process until well-blended and creamy. Season with salt and pepper to taste.

4. Transfer to a container and store, covered, in the refrigerator.

Yield: About 1 1/4 cups. Keeps for up to 1 week in the refrigerator. Freezes well for up to 3 months.

43 calories per Tbsp, 0.7 g carbohydrate, 0.3 g fiber, 0 g protein, 4.4 g fat (0.6 g saturated), 0 mg cholesterol, 51 mg sodium, 22 mg potassium, 0 mg iron, 10 mg calcium

Pesto Mushrooms

Remove stems from 2 dozen medium mushrooms. Brush caps lightly with olive oil. Place rounded-side down on a baking sheet sprayed with cooking spray and spoon a dollop of pesto into each cap. Sprinkle with grated cheese, if desired. Bake at 375°F for 8 to 10 minutes, or until golden brown.

SUN-DRIED TOMATO PESTO

This makes a terrific topping for grilled fish, vegetables, pasta, crostini, or bruschetta. Top of the day to you!

3/4 cup oil-packed sun-dried tomatoes,
   drained and well-rinsed
6 cloves garlic
1/2 cup tightly packed fresh basil leaves
1/2 cup tightly packed parsley leaves
3 Tbsp pine nuts, chopped walnuts,
   or almonds
3 Tbsp grated Parmesan cheese
1/4 cup extra virgin olive oil
1/4 cup tomato juice
1/4 tsp salt (or to taste)

1. Place sun-dried tomatoes in a single layer on paper towels and pat dry.

2. In a food processor fitted with the steel blade, drop the garlic through the feed tube while the motor is running. Process until minced, about 10 seconds.

3. Scrape down the sides of the bowl before adding the sun-dried tomatoes, basil, parsley, nuts, and Parmesan cheese. Process until finely minced, about 18 to 20 seconds.

4. Add the olive oil, tomato juice, and salt. Process the mixture until well blended, scraping down the sides of the bowl as needed.

5. Transfer to a container and store, covered, in the refrigerator.

Yield: About 2 cups. Keeps for up to 1 week in the refrigerator. Freezes well for up to 3 months.

47 calories per Tbsp, 1.7 g carbohydrate, 0.4 g fiber, 1 g protein, 4.3 g fat (0.6 g saturated), 1 mg cholesterol, 59 mg sodium, 94 mg potassium, 0 mg iron, 16 mg calcium

Variations

• Flavor Boost: Add a spoonful of pesto to salad dressing or dips.

• Pizza with Pizzaz! Spread pesto on pizza instead of tomato sauce.

• Wrap-ture! Add pesto to low-fat cream cheese or light mayonnaise and use as a spread when making wraps. Fill with grilled vegetables, tuna salad, smoked salmon . . . use your imagination.

• Dairy-Free Version: Omit the Parmesan cheese.

🍎 TRADITIONAL PESTO

This pesto is perfect in the summertime when basil is plentiful and inexpensive. It adds a burst of flavor to almost any vegetable, fish, or pasta dish.

4 large cloves garlic
2 cups tightly packed fresh basil leaves
1/2 cup tightly packed fresh parsley leaves (use the stems for soup)
3 to 4 Tbsp pine nuts, chopped walnuts, or almonds
1/3 to 1/2 cup grated Parmesan cheese
1/2 cup extra virgin olive oil
1/2 tsp salt (or to taste)
Freshly ground black pepper

1. In a food processor fitted with the steel blade, drop the garlic through the feed tube while the motor is running. Process until minced, about 10 seconds.

2. Scrape down the sides of the bowl before adding the basil, parsley, nuts, and cheese. Process until finely minced, about 15 seconds.

3. With the motor still running, drizzle the oil through the feed tube. Process the mixture until well blended and creamy; season with salt and pepper to taste.

4. Transfer to a glass jar and add a thin layer of olive oil to cover the pesto. Cover the jar, seal well, and refrigerate pesto until ready to use.

Yield: 2 cups. Keeps for up to 1 month in the refrigerator. Freezes well for up to 3 months.

69 calories per Tbsp, 0.7 g carbohydrate, 0.3 g fiber, 1 g protein, 7.0 g fat (1.1 g saturated), 1 mg cholesterol, 81 mg sodium, 40 mg potassium, 0 mg iron, 25 mg calcium

Chef's Secrets

• Frozen Assets! Freeze pesto in ice cube trays. Transfer frozen cubes to a heavy-duty freezer bag and store in the freezer. Each frozen cube contains about 2 Tbsp.

• Lazy-Freeze Method: Drop blobs of pesto on a foil-lined cookie sheet and place in the freezer. Transfer frozen blobs to a heavy-duty freezer bag and freeze for up to 3 months.

• Best-o Pesto! Pesto adds fabulous flavor to grilled or baked fish, chicken, vegetables, soups, salad dressings, or pasta sauces.

• Easy Appetizers: Combine 2 Tbsp of pesto with 1/2 cup low-fat cream cheese or ricotta cheese for a tasty filling for celery stalks. Or pipe it onto sliced cucumber rounds.

Nutrition Note
• To reduce the fat, reduce Parmesan cheese to 1/4 cup and use a combination of 1/4 cup extra virgin olive oil or walnut oil, and 1/4 cup vegetable broth.

❂ APRICOT HOISIN MARINADE

Oy, this hoisin-based marinade is soy sinful! It's wonderful on chicken, meat, fish, or tofu. A food processor speeds up preparation, so why not make a double batch?

1 small slice peeled fresh ginger
   (about 2 tsp minced)
3 cloves garlic
3 green onions, cut in 2-inch pieces
1/3 cup hoisin sauce
1/3 cup apricot jam (low-sugar or all-fruit)
2 Tbsp soy sauce (low-sodium or regular)
2 Tbsp rice vinegar or lemon juice
   (preferably fresh)
2 tsp Asian (toasted) sesame oil
1/8 tsp red pepper flakes or cayenne
1 tsp honey

1. In a food processor fitted with the steel blade, drop the ginger, garlic, and green onions through the feed tube while the motor is running. Process until minced, about 10 seconds.

2. Scrape down the sides of the bowl. Add hoisin sauce, jam, soy sauce, vinegar or lemon juice, sesame oil, pepper flakes, and honey; process for 8 to 10 seconds to blend.

3. Transfer to a container and store, covered, in the refrigerator until ready to use.

Yield: 1 1/4 cups. Keeps for up to 1 week in the refrigerator. Freezes well for up to 3 months.

23 calories per Tbsp, 4.1 g carbohydrate, 0.2 g fiber, 0 g protein, 0.6 g fat (0.1 g saturated), 0 mg cholesterol, 117 mg sodium, 17 mg potassium, 0 mg iron, 4 mg calcium

Variation
• Instead of apricot jam, substitute orange marmalade or peach jam.

Chef's Secrets
• Timing's Everything! Marinate poultry, meat, or tofu for at least 30 minutes at room temperature or up to 48 hours in the refrigerator. This marinade is also wonderful on fish, but don't marinate it for more than an hour. If it's marinated longer, it will start to "cook."

• Frozen Assets! Place boneless, skinless chicken breasts or lean beef in a re-sealable freezer bag. Add the marinade, seal the bag, and freeze for up to 3 months. Before grilling or baking, defrost overnight in the refrigerator.

• Spice It Up! Spice up tuna salad by mixing in a teaspoon or two of marinade.

sauces,
marinades &
seasonings

🍎 ASIAN MARINADE

This simple marinade is fabulous with fish, chicken, beef, or tofu. Use it to marinate grilled broccoli spears, green beans, asparagus, or portobello mushrooms. This also makes a terrific stir-fry sauce. Soy versatile!

2 cloves garlic
1 small slice peeled fresh ginger
  (about 2 tsp minced)
2 to 3 Tbsp soy sauce (low-sodium
  or regular)
2 Tbsp honey or granular Splenda
2 Tbsp orange juice (preferably fresh)
  or rice vinegar
1 tsp Asian (toasted) sesame oil
1/2 tsp dried basil
Freshly ground black pepper

1. In a food processor fitted with the steel blade, process the garlic and ginger until minced, about 10 seconds.

2. Scrape down the sides of the bowl. Add the soy sauce, honey, orange juice or vinegar, sesame oil, and basil. Season with pepper to taste. Process until combined, about 5 seconds.

3. Transfer to a container and store, covered, in the refrigerator until ready to use.

Yield: About 1/2 cup. Recipe can be doubled or tripled. Keeps for up to 1 week in the refrigerator. Freezes well for up to 3 months.

27 calories per Tbsp, 5.4 g carbohydrate, 0.1 g fiber, 0 g protein, 0.6 g fat (0.1 g saturated), 0 mg cholesterol, 133 mg sodium, 25 mg potassium, 0 mg iron, 4 mg calcium

Chef's Secret
• Ginger Tips: An easy way to peel fresh ginger is to scrape it with the tip of a spoon.

Nutrition Note
• Sweet Choice! If made with Splenda, 1 Tbsp contains 18 calories and 2.2 g carbohydrate.

🍎 TERIYAKI MARINADE

This terrific marinade is guaranteed to bring rave reviews from family and friends. It also does double-duty as a sauce and is delicious on meat, poultry, fish, tofu, or vegetables.

1/4 cup orange juice (preferably fresh)
  or mango juice
1/4 cup soy sauce (low-sodium or regular)
2 Tbsp lemon juice (preferably fresh)
3 cloves garlic (about 1 Tbsp minced)
1 slice peeled fresh ginger
  (about 1 Tbsp minced)
2 tsp Asian (toasted) sesame oil
2 Tbsp maple syrup or honey

1. Combine all the ingredients in a jar and shake well. (Or combine in a food processor and process for 8 to 10 seconds until blended.)

2. Store, covered, in the refrigerator, until ready to use.

Yield: About 3/4 cup, enough for 2 to 3 lb (1 to 1 1/2 kg) meat, fish, chicken, or tofu. Keeps for up to 1 week in the refrigerator. Freezes well for up to 3 months.

18 calories per Tbsp, 3.1 g carbohydrate, 0.1 g fiber, 0 g protein, 0.7 g fat (0.1 g saturated), 0 mg cholesterol, 146 mg sodium, 28 mg potassium, 0 mg iron, 4 mg calcium

Teriyaki Sauce
Prepare marinade as directed above. Place in a saucepan and heat until boiling. Dissolve 1 Tbsp cornstarch in 2 Tbsp water or

orange juice. Stir the cornstarch solution into the boiling marinade and cook, stirring constantly, until smooth and thickened, about 2 minutes. Serve as a sauce.

Chef's Secrets
• Timing's Everything! Marinate meat or poultry for 1 to 2 hours (or up to 48 hours) in the refrigerator. Marinate fish or tofu for 1 hour.

• Veggie Time! Marinate vegetables (e.g., asparagus, green beans, or broccoli) for 30 minutes to 2 hours. Drain, reserving the marinade. Grill, steam, or microwave the vegetables. Use the reserved marinade to make Teriyaki Sauce (above), and serve it over the grilled or cooked vegetables.

✿ LOW-CARB KETCHUP

Did you know that store-bought ketchup contains more sugar than ice cream? This yummy, sugar-free ketchup has half the calories and carbohydrates of the store-bought version and costs a fraction of the price. It takes just moments to make in a food processor or blender and is a perfect choice for people with diabetes or who are counting their carbs.

1/2 small onion
1 or 2 cloves garlic (about 1 tsp)
1 can (51/2 oz/156 mL) tomato paste
2/3 cup white or apple cider vinegar
3 Tbsp water
1/3 cup granular Splenda
1/4 tsp Italian seasoning
1/8 tsp freshly ground black pepper
1/8 tsp ground cloves
3 or 4 drops hot pepper sauce

1. In a food processor fitted with the steel blade, process the onion and garlic until minced, about 10 seconds.

2. Scrape down the sides of the bowl. Add the tomato paste, vinegar, water, Splenda, Italian seasoning, pepper, cloves, and hot pepper sauce. Process for 10 to 15 seconds or until blended. If too thick, add a few drops of water.

3. Transfer to a jar, cover tightly, and store in the refrigerator. Stir before using.

Yield: 11/2 cups. Recipe doubles easily. Keeps for up to a month in the refrigerator. Freezes well for up to 3 months.

8 calories per Tbsp, 1.8 g carbohydrate, 0.3 g fiber, 0 g protein, 0 g fat (0 g saturated), 0 mg cholesterol, 51 mg sodium, 68 mg potassium, 0 mg iron, 3 mg calcium

Variations
• Brown sugar substitute can be used instead of Splenda.

• Cayenne can be used instead of hot pepper sauce.

✿ NO-YOLK MAYONNAISE

No yolking! This cholesterol-free mayonnaise tastes much better than store-bought. Using pasteurized egg whites ensures food safety. The calorie count is the same as commercial mayonnaise but this version is made with heart-healthy fats.

3 Tbsp pasteurized liquid egg whites
1 Tbsp lemon juice (preferably fresh)
2 tsp Dijon mustard (or 1 tsp dried mustard)
1/4 tsp salt
Freshly ground black pepper
1/8 tsp cayenne
1 cup extra virgin olive oil or canola oil

1. In a food processor fitted with the steel blade, combine the egg whites, lemon juice, mustard, salt, pepper, and cayenne. Process for 5 seconds, until blended. While the machine is running, add the oil in a very slow, steady stream through the feed tube and process until the mixture has thickened, about 45 seconds.

2. Transfer to a clean container, cover, and refrigerate immediately.

Yield: About 1 cup. Keeps for up to 1 week in the refrigerator. Don't freeze.

102 calories per Tbsp, 0.3 g carbohydrate, 0 g fiber, 0 g protein, 11.0 g fat (1.5 g saturated), 0 mg cholesterol, 45 mg sodium, 7 mg potassium, 0 mg iron, 2 mg calcium

🍅 TOFU MAYONNAISE

This low-calorie alternative to mayonnaise may be egg-free, dairy-free, and cholesterol-free, but it's definitely not taste-free!

1 clove garlic (about 1 tsp minced)
1 pkg (10 oz/300 g) 1% silken tofu, drained
1 tsp Dijon mustard
2 tsp lemon juice (preferably fresh)
1/2 tsp salt
2 to 3 Tbsp extra virgin olive or canola oil

1. In a food processor fitted with the steel blade, process the garlic and tofu for 2 minutes or until well blended, scraping down the sides of the bowl as necessary.

2. Add the mustard, lemon juice, and salt, and process for a few seconds more. While the motor is still running, slowly drizzle the oil through the feed tube. Continue processing until well blended.

3. Transfer to a clean container, cover, and refrigerate immediately.

Yield: About 3/4 cup. Keeps for up to 1 week in the refrigerator. Don't freeze.

17 calories per Tbsp, 0.3 g carbohydrate, 0 g fiber, 1 g protein, 1.4 g fat (0.2 g saturated), 0 mg cholesterol, 69 mg sodium, 10 mg potassium, 0 mg iron, 5 mg calcium

Variation
• Add 1/4 packed cup fresh parsley or cilantro leaves, 2 Tbsp chopped fresh basil or mint, and 2 green onions at the end of Step 2. Process until blended.

🍅 ALMOST SOUR CREAM

This makes a terrific substitute for sour cream. Different brands of cottage cheese vary in their moisture content, so if the mixture is too thick after processing, add a little water to achieve the desired texture.

2 cups small-curd 1% cottage cheese

1. In a food processor fitted with the steel blade, process the cottage cheese for 2 to 3 minutes or until smooth and creamy. Scrape down the sides of the bowl as necessary.

2. Transfer to a container, cover, and refrigerate until ready to use.

Yield: 2 cups. Keeps for up to 1 week in the refrigerator. Don't freeze.

13 calories per Tbsp, 0.5 g carbohydrate, 0 g fiber, 2 g protein, 0.6 g fat (0.4 g saturated), 2 mg cholesterol, 50 mg sodium, 17 mg potassium, 0 mg iron, 13 mg calcium

Variation
• To serve with pancakes or cheese blintzes, blend in a dash of pure vanilla extract plus

1 to 2 Tbsp granulated sugar or granular Splenda.

🍎 CAJUN SPICE RUB

This spicy seasoning mixture is excellent on chicken, fish, or beef. Whether roasting, baking, or grilling, there's a whole lot of rubbing going on!

2 tsp Kosher or sea salt
1 tsp coarsely ground black pepper
1 Tbsp garlic powder
1 Tbsp onion powder
1 Tbsp sweet or smoked paprika
1 Tbsp brown sugar
1 tsp chili powder
1 tsp dried basil
1 tsp dried thyme
1 tsp dried oregano

1. Combine all ingredients in a spice bottle or small jar, cover, and shake well to combine.

2. Store, sealed, in a cool dark place. When needed, rub the mixture on both sides of the meat, chicken, or fish up to 1 hour before cooking.

Yield: About 6 tablespoons. Recipe can be doubled. Will keep for months.

7 calories per 1/2 teaspoon, 1.6 g carbohydrate, 0.3 g fiber, 0 g protein, 0.1 g fat (0 g saturated), 0 mg cholesterol, 127 mg sodium, 22 mg potassium, 2 mg iron, 5 mg calcium

🍎 MONTREAL-STYLE STEAK SPICE

Since Montreal steak spice isn't available everywhere, I've created my own version. Sprinkle it on steak, chicken, or salmon in-stead of salt—it adds a flavor boost to almost any dish.

1 Tbsp coarse salt (e.g., sea salt
   or Kosher salt)
2 tsp coarsely ground pepper
2 tsp garlic powder
2 tsp ground coriander
   or dried cilantro leaves
2 tsp dried dillweed
2 tsp Hungarian paprika
1 tsp cayenne pepper
Pinch of sugar

1. Combine all ingredients in a spice bottle or small jar, cover, and shake well to combine.

2. Store, sealed, in a cool dark place. When needed, rub the mixture on both sides of the meat, chicken, or fish up to 1 hour before cooking.

Yield: About 1/4 cup. Recipe can be doubled. Will keep for months.

4 calories per 1/2 teaspoon, 0.8 g carbohydrate, 0.2 g fiber, 0 g protein, 0 g fat (0 g saturated), 0 mg cholesterol, 314 mg sodium, 20 mg potassium, 4 mg iron, 6 mg calcium

Nutrition Notes

• Did you know that 1 tsp salt contains 2325 mg of sodium? Because of the addition of herbs and spices, 1 tsp of my steak spice mixture contains 628 mg sodium. Less salt, more flavor!

• My version of steak spice does not include partially hydrogenated soybean oil, but most commercial brands do.

• Refer to Shaking the Salt Habit! (page 27) for more information on sodium.

● SALT-FREE SEASONING

Use this salt-free seasoning if you're watching your sodium intake. (It may also be necessary to adjust or omit some of the other seasonings called for in your recipes.) Please note—salt-free does not mean sodium-free. Foods with no salt can still contain sodium.

1 Tbsp garlic powder
1 Tbsp onion powder
1 Tbsp sweet or smoked paprika
1 tsp coarsely ground black pepper
1 tsp granulated sugar or granular Splenda
1 tsp dried basil
1 tsp dried thyme
1 tsp dried oregano
1 tsp dried parsley

1. Combine all the ingredients in a spice bottle or small jar, cover, and shake well to combine.

2. Store, sealed, in a cool dark place. When needed, rub the mixture on both sides of the meat, chicken, or fish up to 1 hour before cooking.

Yield: About 5 tablespoons. Recipe can be doubled. Will keep for months.

8 calories per 1/2 tsp, 1.8 g carbohydrate, 0.5 g fiber, 0 g protein, 0.1 g fat (0 g saturated), 0 mg cholesterol, 1 mg sodium, 28 mg potassium, 2 mg iron, 8 mg calcium

Variations
• Add 1 tsp each of any of the following: celery seed, ground bay leaf, cayenne, coriander, cumin, chili powder, dried mustard, dried lemon rind, and/or crumbled, dried rosemary.

fish

FISH

When people ask me how I control my weight, I tell them that I am on a seafood diet—whenever I see food, I eat it! Kidding aside, fish is a wonderful way to bring many health benefits to your diet, so I try to eat it at least twice a week. My recipes are quick, easy and delicious, so I hope you'll take the bait and cook fish more often.

FISH FACTS

Fat Facts: Your body can make the most of the fats it needs from your diet. However, it can't produce the essential fats known as Omega-3 fatty acids, which need to come directly from certain foods. Firm-fleshed, fatty types of fish such as salmon, salmon trout, tuna, and sardines are excellent sources of Omega-3 fatty acids. They provide a defense against heart attacks and play a part in stroke prevention, depression, Alzheimer's, and a variety of other ailments. They also regulate blood clotting. The American Heart and Stroke Association advises eating two servings of fatty fish a week.

Fishful Thinking: Fish is an excellent source of protein, with salmon being the most popular choice. In addition to essential Omega-3 fatty acids, salmon also contains essential vitamins (A, B$_6$, and B$_{12}$) and minerals (potassium, selenium, and calcium).

SCHOOL OF FISH

The following are some helpful tips to guide you in selecting, storing, and cooking fish.

The Daily Catch: Visit the fish counter at your local supermarket and check what's available. Fresh is best, but frozen is also an excellent option. Choose from salmon, salmon trout, arctic char, halibut, tilapia, whitefish, sole, haddock, pickerel, snapper, orange roughy, or tuna.

Hook, Line, and Stinker! Fresh fish should smell sweet and vaguely like the ocean. If it has a strong, fishy, or ammonia-like smell, either it's not fresh or it may have been mishandled. The smell of ammonia usually occurs when frozen fish has been thawed and then refrozen.

Salmon Enchanted Evening: The American Institute of Cancer Research (AICR) recommends eating a variety of fish, but limiting consumption of farmed salmon to two 3-ounce servings per week to avoid PCBs (harmful toxins). Contaminant levels in salmon may vary, depending on where in the world it comes from.

Go Wild! Wild salmon is a better choice than farmed. Fresh wild salmon is readily available and is becoming more affordable. It is also available frozen. Canned sockeye salmon is usually wild salmon and is affordable, so enjoy it often. Farmed salmon is more affordable and available than wild. Wild salmon gets its Omega-3 fatty acids and color from eating natural prey, while farmed salmon gets its color from supplements in its feed. Without that added pigment, farmed salmon would be a pale grey. Pacific salmon is mostly wild, while Atlantic salmon is usually farmed.

Mercury's Rising! To reduce exposure to mercury, it is recommended that women of childbearing age should not eat fresh tuna more than once a month, or canned tuna more than once a week, especcially white (albacore) tuna. Canned tuna, which is generally produced from smaller species of fish, is lower in mercury and is safer to eat more often.

Store It Right: Store raw lean fish such as whitefish, tilapia or sole, in the coldest part of the refrigerator (40°F) for 2 to 3 days, or freeze for up to 6 months at 0°F. Fatty fish such as salmon can be stored in the refrigerator for 2 to 3 days, or freeze for 2 to 3 months at 0°F.

No Cooking Required: Canned salmon, tuna, sardines, anchovies, and herring are great choices for a no-cook meal, and the bones from sardines and salmon provide calcium. Add anchovies to salads or purée and add them to Caesar salad dressing.

Frosty Facts: To defrost fish quickly, unwrap it and place on a microwaveable plate. Allow 4 to 5 minutes per pound on the "defrost" setting (30% power), turning the fish over at half time. A few ice crystals should still remain: these will disappear after the fish stands at room temperature for a few minutes. If you plan to cook the fish in the microwave, defrost it completely before cooking so it will cook evenly.

Chill Out! You can also thaw the still-wrapped fish under cold running water, or thaw it overnight in the refrigerator. Don't thaw fish at room temperature. Never re-freeze fish after defrosting: once it has been cooked, it can then be frozen.

Marine-Aides: Marinating fish gives it great flavor. However, don't marinate fish longer than 1 hour or it will start to "cook."

If you are planning to cook fish on the barbecue, marinating it first will help protect it from forming cancer-causing substances while it is being grilled. (See Marin-Aides on page 36.)

The Skinny Truth: Fish fillets such as halibut and salmon are usually sold with the skin on, although fish fillets are also available skinless. It's fine to buy fish with the skin on. Just remove the skin and visible fat from cooked fish before eating it to reduce any trace amounts of PCBs (polychlorinated biphenyls). Bake, broil, or grill fish instead of frying it. You want to release as much fat as possible during cooking.

Timely Tips: Measure a fillet at its thickest point. Allow 10 minutes per inch of thickness and cook it at 425 to 450°F. If one end is thinner than another, fold it underneath so it is uniform in thickness. If the fillet is being cooked in a sauce or wrapped in foil, cook it five minutes longer. This rule applies to baking, broiling, grilling, poaching, and steaming. Cooking times for frying and microwaving are generally quicker. For frozen fish, double the cooking time, allowing 20 minutes per inch of thickness.

Microwave Magic: Calculate 4 minutes per pound on high. One serving of fish will cook in 2 to 3 minutes, depending on the wattage of your microwave. To "stop the pop" and save on clean-ups, cook fish between lettuce or spinach leaves, or wrap it in parchment paper.

Finny Grill! Preheat your electric grill according to the manufacturer's instructions. Season salmon fillets as desired. To save on clean-up, either spray the grill with cooking spray or line it with parchment paper, which is heatproof up to 400°F. Place the salmon in a single layer on the parchment paper, if using. Cover with another sheet of parchment paper. On a closed grill, cook 5 to 6 minutes per inch of thickness. On an open grill, cook 10 to 12 minutes per inch.

Skill at the Grill: Preheat your gas or charcoal grill. Season the salmon fillets as desired, oiling them lightly to prevent sticking. Place the fillets, flesh-side down, on the well-oiled grill. At the beginning, the fish will cling to the grate until it has cooked about 7 to 8 minutes. Turn the fish over carefully using a wide spatula and cook the second side 2 to 3 minutes longer or until the fish flakes. This is known as the 70/30 timing rule, which results in a beautiful presentation with great grill marks.

Is It Done Yet? Fish is done if it's opaque yet still moist in the center. It should just flake when gently pressed with a fork. On an instant-read thermometer, the interior temperature should reach 145°F. If overcooked, fish will become dry.

A Grate Tip: If you cook fish with the skin on, just slide a flexible metal spatula between the flesh and skin, leaving the skin behind on the cooking grate or pan. It's "E-fish-ent!"

● FAST FISH SALAD

Fast Fish Salad is a terrific way to use up any leftover cooked fish such as sole, tilapia, whitefish, or salmon. It's delicious as a filling for sandwiches or wraps, on top of salad greens, or as a stuffing for hollowed-out tomatoes or peppers. If you don't have enough fish, add one or two hard-boiled eggs to the mixture.

2 green onions
1 stalk celery
1 small carrot
2 or 3 radishes
2 cups leftover cooked fish
   (skin and bones removed)
1/4 to 1/3 cup light mayonnaise
   or Caesar salad dressing
Salt and freshly ground black pepper

1. In a food processor fitted with the steel blade, process the green onions, celery, carrot, and radishes for 8 to 10 seconds or until minced. Add the fish and mayonnaise. Process with quick on/off pulses, until combined. Season with salt and pepper to taste.

2. Transfer the mixture to a bowl, cover, and store in the refrigerator until ready to use. Serve chilled.

Yield: 4 servings. Recipe easily doubles or triples. Keeps for up to 2 days in the refrigerator. Don't freeze.

138 calories per serving, 4.0 g carbohydrate, 1.0 g fiber, 16 g protein, 6.0 g fat (1.0 g saturated), 45 mg cholesterol, 202 mg sodium, 377 mg potassium, 1 mg iron, 34 mg calcium

fish

Quick Crab Salad

Substitute 1 lb (500 g) flaked surimi (imitation crab) for cooked fish. Add ½ cup chopped red pepper, 2 Tbsp lemon juice, and 4 to 6 drops of hot pepper sauce.

🍎 ASIAN TUNA SALAD

Try this tasty tuna salad with an Asian twist. It's an excellent alternative to tuna in Grilled Tuna with Mango Salad (page 143) and is wonderful in wraps and sandwiches.

½ cup red onion, cut in 1-inch chunks
½ cup seeded red pepper,
   cut in 1-inch chunks
½ cup celery, cut in 1-inch chunks
1 apple, peeled, cored and
   cut in 1-inch chunks
2 cans (6½ oz/184 g each) water-packed
   tuna, drained
⅓ to ½ cup light mayonnaise
1 Tbsp lemon juice (preferably fresh)
   or rice vinegar
⅛ tsp wasabi powder
1 Tbsp low-sodium soy sauce (optional)

1. In a food processor fitted with the steel blade, combine the onion, bell pepper, celery, and apple; process for about 8 to 10 seconds, until finely chopped.

2. Transfer the mixture to a medium bowl. Add the tuna, mayonnaise, lemon juice, wasabi powder, and soy sauce, if using, and mix well.

3. Cover the bowl and store in the refrigerator until ready to use. Serve chilled.

Yield: 4 servings. Keeps for up to 2 to 3 days in the refrigerator. Don't freeze.

219 calories per serving, 12.4 g carbohydrate, 2.0 g fiber, 21 g protein, 9.3 g fat (1.7 g saturated), 43 mg cholesterol, 497 mg sodium, 366 mg potassium, 1 mg iron, 28 mg calcium

Variations

• Omit the apple and instead add ½ cup finely chopped jicama or water chestnuts. Instead of wasabi powder, substitute with 2 or 3 finely minced radishes.

🍎 SARDINE SPREAD (MOCK CHOPPED HERRING)

This is an updated version of an old favorite. Sardines are high in Omega-3 fatty acids and are a good source of protein and calcium. Omega-3 eggs and flaxseed bread make this a heart-healthy spread that won't make your hips spread!

1 medium onion, cut in chunks
1 apple, peeled, cored and cut in chunks
2 cans (3¼ oz/106 g each) sardines,
   well-drained
1 slice flaxseed, whole wheat, or rye bread
3 hard-boiled eggs, halved
3 Tbsp white or cider vinegar (or to taste)
1 tsp granulated sugar

1. In a food processor fitted with the steel blade, process the onion, apple, and sardines until finely minced, about 10 seconds.

2. Moisten the bread by placing it briefly under running water, squeeze out excess moisture, and tear the bread into chunks. Add the bread to the processor along with the eggs, vinegar, and sugar; process for 8 to 10 seconds longer or until combined.

3. Transfer to a medium bowl; cover well. Store in the refrigerator for 1 to 2 hours to blend the flavors.

Yield: 6 servings (about 2¹/₂ cups) Keeps for up to 10 days in the refrigerator. Don't freeze.

142 calories per serving, 9.7 g carbohydrate, 1.4 g fiber, 11 g protein, 6.4 g fat (1.3 g saturated), 150 mg cholesterol, 208 mg sodium, 226 mg potassium, 1 mg iron, 140 mg calcium

Chef's Secrets
• Spread It Around: This mixture makes a great filling for sandwiches or wraps. Serve a scoop on top of salad greens or use it to stuff hollowed-out tomatoes. Put it through a pastry bag and pipe onto cucumber rounds or wholegrain crackers. Your choice!

• Eggs-actly! Instead of 3 eggs, you can use 2 hard-boiled eggs plus 2 egg whites.

◖ THREE-COLOR GEFILTE FISH LOAF

Looks complicated—cooks easily! This layered loaf looks elegant and tastes terrific. You won't have to fish for compliments when you serve this to your guests. They'll fall for it—hook, line, and sinker!

Fish Mixture:

2 loaves frozen gefilte fish loaf, thawed
    (22 oz/623 g each)
2 large eggs, lightly beaten
¹/₂ tsp salt
¹/₂ tsp freshly ground black pepper
¹/₂ tsp garlic powder

First Layer:

¹/₃ of the Fish Mixture
¹/₂ cup seeded and diced red pepper

2 green onions, diced
2 Tbsp minced fresh dillweed

Second Layer:

¹/₃ of the Fish Mixture
1 pkg (10 oz/300 g) frozen spinach,
    thawed and squeezed dry
2 Tbsp minced fresh basil or parsley

Third Layer:

¹/₃ of the Fish Mixture
1 medium sweet potato, cooked and
    mashed (or 1 cup cooked mashed carrots)
1 Tbsp minced fresh dillweed or parsley

1. Preheat the oven to 350°F. Spray two 9- × 5-inch loaf pans with cooking spray.

2. Fish Mixture: In a large bowl, combine the gefilte fish mixture, eggs, salt, pepper, and garlic powder. Mix well. Divide the mixture in thirds and place in three separate bowls.

3. First Layer: Combine the fish mixture, red pepper, green onions, and dillweed; mix well. Divide in half and spread evenly in each prepared pan to make a first layer.

4. Second Layer: Combine the fish mixture, spinach, and basil; mix well. Divide in half and spread evenly in each pan to make a second layer.

5. Third Layer: Combine the fish mixture, sweet potato, and dillweed; mix well. Divide in half and spread evenly in each pan to make a third layer.

6. Bake, uncovered, for 1 hour. When done, the top layer should be firm to the touch and the edges should pull away from the sides of the pan. Remove from oven and cool for 20 to 30 minutes.

7. Loosen each loaf with a long flexible metal spatula and carefully invert onto an oblong serving dish. Cover and refrigerate until ready to serve. Serve chilled with horseradish, lettuce, sliced tomatoes, and cucumbers.

Yield: 16 to 20 servings. Keeps for up to 3 to 4 days in the refrigerator. Don't freeze.

157 calories per serving, 10.7 g carbohydrate, 1.1 g fiber, 9 g protein, 8.8 g fat (1.5 g saturated), 50 mg cholesterol, 508 mg sodium, 181 mg potassium, 1 mg iron, 48 mg calcium

Chef's Secret

• Fishful Thinking: Instead of using frozen gefilte fish loaves, eggs, and seasonings, you can prepare your own fish mixture with whatever fish fillets are available such as whitefish, pickerel, pike, or salmon.

HALIBUT WITH TINY ROASTED TOMATOES

This recipe makes a quick, delicious, and elegant meal that's perfect for entertaining.

4 halibut fillets (6 oz/180 g each)
Salt and freshly ground black pepper
2 cloves garlic (about 2 tsp minced)
2 Tbsp minced fresh basil or parsley
2 Tbsp grated Parmesan cheese
Tiny Roasted Tomatoes (page 312)

1. Preheat the oven to 400°F. Spray a 9- × 13-inch glass baking dish with cooking spray.

2. Place the fish in a single layer in the prepared baking dish and sprinkle lightly with salt and pepper. Top the fillets with garlic, basil, and cheese.

3. Prepare the Tiny Roasted Tomatoes as directed and bake in the lower third of the oven. After 6 to 8 minutes, place the fish in the upper third of the oven. Bake for 10 to 12 minutes or until the fish just flakes when gently pressed with a fork. By this time, the tomatoes should be tender. Top the fish with the roasted tomatoes and serve hot or at room temperature.

Yield: 4 servings. Keeps for up to 2 to 3 days in the refrigerator; reheats well. Don't freeze.

345 calories per serving, 7.3 g carbohydrate, 2.0 g fiber, 48 g protein, 13.0 g fat (2.2 g saturated), 72 mg cholesterol, 164 mg sodium, 1363 mg potassium, 2 mg iron, 156 mg calcium

Chef's Secrets

• It's About Time: Cooking time will depend on the thickness of the fish. Allow 10 minutes per inch of thickness, measured at the thickest point. If the fish is frozen, there's no need to thaw it before cooking. Allow 20 minutes per inch of thickness.

• Meal Deal: Serve with sweet potatoes that have been cooked in the microwave. Four sweet potatoes will take 8 to 10 minutes on high to microwave; pierce them in several places with a sharp knife before cooking. Steam 4 cups of cauliflower or broccoli florets for 6 minutes and you'll have a delicious, nutritious dinner.

🍎 PESTO HALIBUT WITH PISTACHIOS

Your guests will go nuts over this easy, elegant dish. It's really delicious.

4 halibut fillets (6 oz/180 g each)
4 Tbsp pesto (store-bought or homemade, pages 109–11)
Salt and freshly ground black pepper
1/2 cup shelled pistachios, coarsely chopped

1. Preheat the oven to 425°F. Line a baking sheet with foil and spray with cooking spray.

2. Arrange the fish in a single layer on the prepared baking sheet. Spread the top of each fillet evenly with pesto. Sprinkle with salt, pepper, and nuts.

3. Bake, uncovered, for 10 to 12 minutes or until the fish flakes when gently pressed with a fork. Serve immediately.

Yield: 4 servings. Recipe easily doubles or triples. Serve hot or cold. Keeps for up to 2 to 3 days in the refrigerator. Don't freeze: if frozen, the nuts won't be crispy after the fish thaws.

407 calories per serving, 5.3 g carbohydrate, 2.1 g fiber, 52 g protein, 19.5 g fat (3.5 g saturated), 75 mg cholesterol, 301 mg sodium, 1192 mg potassium, 3 mg iron, 230 mg calcium

Variations
• Substitute low-calorie bottled Caesar salad dressing for pesto.

• You can also make this with other white-fleshed fillets but if you do, reduce the baking time to 10 minutes.

🍎 PESTO SALMON OR HALIBUT

This elegant dish can be doubled or tripled easily for a crowd, yet it's quick to prepare if you're cooking for one or two. If you're short on time, substitute with store-bought pesto.

2 to 4 salmon or halibut fillets
   (6 to 8 oz/180 to 250 g each)
2 to 4 Tbsp Power Pesto (page 109)
2 to 4 Tbsp grated Parmesan cheese
   (1 Tbsp per fillet)
Salt and freshly ground black pepper

1. Preheat the oven to 425°F. Line a baking sheet with foil and spray with cooking spray.

2. Arrange the salmon fillets in a single layer on the prepared baking sheet. Spread evenly with pesto and then sprinkle with Parmesan cheese, salt, and pepper to taste.

3. Bake, uncovered, for 10 to 12 minutes or until the fish just flakes when gently pressed with a fork. Serve hot or cold.

Yield: 2 to 4 servings. Recipe easily doubles or triples. Keeps for up to 2 to 3 days in the refrigerator; reheats well. Freezes well for up to 2 months.

342 calories per serving, 0.9 g carbohydrate, 0.2 g fiber, 41 g protein, 18.3 g fat (3.3 g saturated), 112 mg cholesterol, 212 mg sodium, 982 mg potassium, 2 mg iron, 87 mg calcium

Pesto Salmon Salad
Add a spoonful of pesto to your favorite vinaigrette salad dressing (either store-bought or homemade). Drizzle over mixed salad greens or baby spinach leaves. Top the greens with chunks of salmon, a few olives, chopped sun-dried tomatoes, red or green onions, bell peppers, and a sprinkling of toasted slivered almonds or soy nuts.

fish

Chef's Secrets

• Pesto Power! This recipe is also delicious with Traditional Pesto (page 110) or Sun-Dried Tomato Pesto (page 109).

• Carb-Watching? Serve salmon with steamed cauliflower that has been tossed with a tablespoon or two of pesto.

• Leftovers? Flake leftover cooked fish and use it to make Fast Fish Salad (page 121). This makes a fabulous filling for tortilla wraps, along with baby spinach leaves and roasted red pepper strips. It's pure wrap-ture!

GRILLED SALMON PATTIES

For years I fried my salmon patties in a skillet because that's what my mother taught me to do, while my sister, Rhonda Matias, preferred to grill her patties on an indoor grill. Now I'm hooked on my sister's "weigh" of cooking salmon patties. Grilled patties taste terrific and you won't miss the extra fat.

2 cans (7^1/$_2$ oz/213 g) sockeye salmon
  (do not drain)
4 large eggs (preferably those with Omega-3)
1 to 2 tsp light mayonnaise or ranch-style
  salad dressing
1 tsp minced garlic
1 Tbsp minced dillweed (optional)
3 cups Special K cereal

1. Place the canned salmon (including the skin, bones, and liquid) in a large bowl and mash with a fork. Add the eggs, mayonnaise, garlic, dillweed, and cereal. Mix well. Mixture will be soft, but will hold together.

2. Preheat a two-sided indoor grill. Moisten your hands and form the salmon mixture into 10 patties about 3 inches in diameter. Carefully place the patties on the hot grill. (You may have to grill these in several batches, depending on the size of your grill.) Close the lid and cook for 6 to 7 minutes, until patties are golden brown, with grill marks.

Yield: 10 patties. Keeps for up to 3 to 4 days in the refrigerator; reheats well. Freezes well for up to 3 months.

137 calories per patty, 6.9 g carbohydrate, 0.2 g fiber, 12 g protein, 6.6 g fat (1.7 g saturated), 96 mg cholesterol, 276 mg sodium, 194 mg potassium, 3 mg iron, 111 mg calcium

Variations

• You can use leftover cooked salmon, but you'll need to add less cereal as there is no liquid from the salmon. Canned tuna can also be used. Add a finely chopped onion, if desired.

Nutrition Notes

• A-Salt with a Deadly Weapon: If sodium is a concern, use canned salmon with no added salt.

• Go Wild: Canned salmon is usually wild salmon.

AIOLI SALMON

Aioli is a garlic-flavored mayonnaise that, when spread on top, makes salmon taste awesome! For different taste sensations, try the suggested variations of Aioli (page 46).

4 to 6 salmon fillets (6 to 8 oz/
   180 to 250 g each)
Salt and freshly ground black pepper
4 to 6 Tbsp Aioli (page 46)
1/4 cup minced fresh dillweed
   or 1 Tbsp dried

1. Preheat the oven to 425°F. Line a baking sheet with foil and spray with cooking spray.

2. Arrange the salmon fillets in a single layer on the baking sheet and sprinkle with salt and pepper. Spread a thin layer of Aioli on top of the salmon and sprinkle with dillweed. (You can prepare the salmon up to this point, 1 hour in advance.)

3. Bake, uncovered, for 10 to 12 minutes or until the salmon is glazed and cooked through. The fish is done when it just flakes when gently pressed with a fork. Serve hot or cold.

Yield: 4 to 6 servings. Recipe easily doubles or triples. Keeps for up to 2 to 3 days in the refrigerator; reheats well. Freezes well for up to 2 months.

319 calories per serving, 1.4 g carbohydrate, 0.1 g fiber, 39 g protein, 16.5 g fat (2.5 g saturated), 112 mg cholesterol, 187 mg sodium, 966 mg potassium, 2 mg iron, 26 mg calcium.

Aioli Halibut
Instead of salmon, substitute with halibut fillets and sprinkle with minced fresh basil instead of dillweed. Bake at 400°F for 12 to 15 minutes.

Chef's Secret
• Short on Time? Make Garlic-Roasted Green Beans (page 299) as a side dish. You can roast the beans together with the fish at the same time.

APRICOT-GLAZED SALMON

It doesn't get much easier or better than this. If you're in a jam and out of apricot jam, substitute with marmalade, peach, or mango jam, or preserves.

4 salmon fillets (6 to 8 oz/180 to 250 g each)
1 Tbsp Dijon mustard
2 Tbsp apricot jam (low-sugar or all-fruit)
1 tsp dried basil or thyme
   or 1 Tbsp chopped fresh
Salt and freshly ground black pepper
Paprika

1. Preheat the oven to 425°F. Line a baking sheet with foil and spray with cooking spray.

2. Arrange the salmon fillets in a single layer on the prepared baking sheet. In a small bowl, combine the mustard, jam, and basil; mix well. Spread evenly on top of the fish. Sprinkle with salt, pepper, and paprika to taste. Let stand for 20 minutes.

3. Bake, uncovered, for 10 to 12 minutes or until the salmon is glazed and cooked through. The salmon is done when it just flakes when gently pressed with a fork. Serve hot or cold.

Yield: 4 servings. Recipe easily doubles or triples. Keeps for up to 2 to 3 days in the refrigerator; reheats well. Freezes well for up to 2 months.

293 calories per serving, 3.4 g carbohydrate, 0.1 g fiber, 39 g protein, 12.6 g fat (1.9 g saturated), 107 mg cholesterol, 179 mg sodium, 959 mg potassium, 2 mg iron, 28 mg calcium.

fish

Chef's Secrets

• Meal Deal: Oven-Roasted Asparagus (page 287) makes an excellent accompaniment and can be roasted in the oven with the salmon at the same time.

• Microwave Magic: Arrange the salmon fillets in a single layer in a microwaveable baking dish. Brush the mustard mixture evenly overtop of the salmon and sprinkle with seasonings. Cover the salmon with a sheet of parchment paper and microwave on high, allowing 4 to 5 minutes per pound. Four pieces of salmon will take 8 to 10 minutes on high.

🍎 MARMALADE-GLAZED SALMON

This salmon is simple enough for your family but festive enough for company. For variety, substitute apricot or peach jam for the marmalade. It's jam-good!

4 salmon fillets (6 to 8 oz/180 to 250 g each)
1/4 cup orange marmalade
   (preferably low-sugar or all-fruit)
2 Tbsp soy sauce (low-sodium or regular)
1 tsp Asian (toasted) sesame oil
Freshly ground black pepper

1. Preheat the oven to 425°F. Line a baking sheet with foil and spray with cooking spray.

2. Arrange the salmon fillets in a single layer on the prepared baking sheet. Combine the marmalade, soy sauce, and sesame oil in a bowl and mix well. Using a pastry or barbecue brush, spread the glaze evenly overtop of the fillets. Season with freshly ground pepper. Let stand for 20 to 30 minutes.

3. Bake, uncovered, for 10 to 12 minutes or until the salmon is glazed and just flakes when gently pressed with a fork. Serve hot or cold.

Yield: 4 servings. Recipe easily doubles or triples. Keeps for up to 2 to 3 days in the refrigerator; reheats well. Freezes well for up to 2 months.

316 calories per serving, 6.5 g carbohydrate, 0 g fiber, 39 g protein, 13.5 g fat (2.1 g saturated), 108 mg cholesterol, 387 mg sodium, 951 mg potassium, 2 mg iron, 23 mg calcium

Marmalade-Glazed Salmon with Mushrooms and Peppers

At one end of the prepared baking sheet, spread 2 to 3 cups of sliced mushrooms and 1 red pepper, sliced. Place the salmon fillets at the other end. Drizzle mushrooms and red pepper with 1 Tbsp olive oil and some of the marmalade-soy mixture. Sprinkle with salt and pepper and bake as directed above. Use the vegetables as a garnish for the salmon.

Chef's Secrets

• Meal Deal: This dish goes perfectly with steamed green beans or asparagus sprinkled with toasted slivered almonds.

• Leftovers? Break salmon into chunks and place on a bed of chilled salad greens, or add it to cooked pasta along with sliced onions and bell peppers. Drizzle with your favorite homemade or bottled Asian Salad Dressing (page 274).

• Wrap-ture! Leftover flaked cooked salmon makes an excellent filling for wraps.

• Eggs-Actly! Leftover flaked cooked salmon is also delicious in frittatas or omelets.

♠ CHUTNEY-GLAZED SALMON

This combination of flavors is amazing. It makes perfect fare for some "en-chutneyed" evening!

4 salmon fillets (6 to 8 oz/180 to 250 g each)
Salt and freshly ground black pepper
3/4 cup mango or apricot chutney
1 tsp curry powder
1 tsp ground cumin
1 tsp smoked or sweet paprika

1. Preheat the oven to 425°F. Line a baking sheet with foil and spray with cooking spray.

2. Arrange the salmon fillets in a single layer on the prepared baking sheet. Sprinkle lightly with salt and pepper. Spread about 3 Tbsp chutney evenly on top of each fillet, then sprinkle with curry powder, cumin, and paprika. Let stand for 15 to 20 minutes.

3. Bake, uncovered, for 10 to 12 minutes or until the salmon is glazed and golden. The salmon is done if it flakes when gently pressed with a fork. Serve hot or cold.

Yield: 4 servings. Recipe easily doubles or triples. Keeps for up to 2 to 3 days in the refrigerator; reheats well. Freezes well for up to 2 months.

359 calories per serving, 20.9 g carbohydrate, 1.7 g fiber, 39 g protein, 12.8 g fat (2.0 g saturated), 108 mg cholesterol, 96 mg sodium, 1179 mg potassium, 3 mg iron, 46 mg calcium

Chef's Secrets
• Skill at the Grill: When grilling salmon fillets, first preheat the barbecue or grill, setting it to medium high heat. If the salmon fillets are skinless, spread on both sides with chutney and then sprinkle with seasonings.

Otherwise, just spread the fleshy side with chutney. Spray the fillets lightly with cooking spray to prevent them from sticking and place, skin-side up, on the grill for 7 to 8 minutes. Turn the fillets over carefully and cook on the second side for 2 to 3 minutes longer, or until the fish flakes.

• Electric Grill: If using a two-sided contact grill, salmon fillets will take about 5 to 6 minutes total cooking time.

• Buffet Beauty: For a large crowd, buy a side of salmon that has been filleted (about 3 lb/1.4 kg). Use double the amount of remaining ingredients. Bake as directed above. Cooking time will take about 15 to 18 minutes at 425°F. Serve hot or at room temperature, garnished with parsley sprigs, and lemon and tomato wedges.

♠ HAIL CAESAR SALMON

This simple dish can be made for one person, a family, or a crowd. Seize the opportunity to cook some extra fillets then transform them into Caesar Salmon Salad (page 130). Cook once, eat twice. Everyone will think you've been slaving away!

4 salmon fillets (6 to 8 oz/180 to 250 g each)
6 Tbsp low-calorie Caesar salad dressing
   (store-bought or homemade,
   page 275)
1 tsp dried basil
Paprika
4 tsp sesame or pumpkin seeds

1. Preheat the oven to 425°F. Line a baking sheet with foil and spray with cooking spray.

2. Arrange the salmon fillets in a single layer on the prepared baking sheet. Top

each fillet with salad dressing and spread it evenly with the back of the spoon. Sprinkle with basil, paprika, and sesame seeds. Let marinate for 10 to 20 minutes.

3. Bake, uncovered, for 10 to 12 minutes or until the fish flakes when gently pressed with a fork.

Yield: 4 servings. Recipe easily doubles or triples. Keeps for 2 to 3 days in the refrigerator; reheats well. Freezes well for up to 2 months.

318 calories per serving, 4.7 g carbohydrate, 0.4 g fiber, 39 g protein, 14.7 g fat (2.1 g saturated), 108 mg cholesterol, 333 mg sodium, 965 mg potassium, 2 mg iron, 43 mg calcium

Caesar Salmon Salad
Flake the leftover salmon and add to a Caesar salad. Garnish with red pepper strips, thinly sliced red onions, cucumbers, sun-dried tomatoes, and capers.

Chef's Secrets
• Cooking for a Crowd? Use 1¹/₂ Tbsp salad dressing, ¹/₄ tsp basil, and 1 tsp sesame seeds for each fillet. This is also an excellent guideline to use when cooking for one or two.

• Meal Deal: Roasted Broccoli (page 289) makes a delicious side dish that can be roasted with the salmon at the same time. Cook the sweet potatoes in the microwave while the salmon and broccoli are in the oven.

● HONEY DIJON SALMON

This terrific salmon recipe comes from the files of Joy Kaufman of Toronto, who got it from Naomi Cohen. It's a honey of a dish!

4 salmon fillets (6 to 8 oz/180 to 250 g each)
2 Tbsp honey
2 Tbsp Dijon mustard
1 to 2 Tbsp toasted sesame seeds
1 Tbsp cumin seeds

1. Preheat the oven to 450°F. Line a baking sheet with foil and spray with cooking spray.

2. Arrange the salmon fillets in a single layer on the prepared baking sheet. In a small bowl, mix together the honey, mustard, sesame seeds, and cumin seeds. Drizzle evenly on top of the salmon and, using a pastry or barbecue brush, spread evenly.

3. Bake, uncovered, for 8 to 10 minutes. The salmon is done when it just flakes when gently pressed with a fork.

Yield: 4 servings. Recipe easily doubles or triples. Keeps for up to 2 to 3 days in the refrigerator; reheats well. Freezes well for up to 2 months.

336 calories per serving, 10.6 g carbohydrate, 0.5 g fiber, g protein, 14.4 g fat (2.0 g saturated), 108 mg cholesterol, 281 mg sodium, 998 mg potassium, 3 mg iron, 56 mg calcium

Chef's Secret
• Sauce It Up! In a medium bowl, mix together 1 cup Soft Yogurt Cheese (page 178), 2 Tbsp minced fresh parsley or dillweed, and a drizzle of honey. Transfer to a serving bowl, cover, and store in the refrigerator. Serve chilled as a sauce with salmon.

fish

🍎 LEMON DILL SALMON

Hot or cold, this dish is simply "dill-icious," especially when topped with Creamy Dill Sauce (page 103). You can prepare this so quickly that you won't have time to dilly-dally in the kitchen.

4 salmon fillets (6 to 8 oz/180 to 250 g each)
2 Tbsp lemon juice (preferably fresh)
1 tsp extra virgin olive oil
2 cloves garlic (about 2 tsp minced)
2 Tbsp minced fresh dillweed or 1 tsp dried
Salt and freshly ground black pepper

1. Preheat the oven to 425°F. Line a baking sheet with foil and spray with cooking spray.

2. Arrange the salmon fillets in a single layer on the prepared baking sheet. Drizzle with lemon juice and olive oil. Sprinkle with garlic, dillweed, salt, and pepper. Let marinate for 20 to 30 minutes.

3. Bake, uncovered, for 10 to 12 minutes or until cooked through. The salmon is done when it just flakes when gently pressed with a fork. Serve hot or cold.

Yield: 4 servings. Recipe easily doubles or triples. Keeps for up to 2 to 3 days in the refrigerator; reheats well. Freezes well for up to 2 months.

290 calories per serving, 1.2 g carbohydrate, 0.1 g fiber, 39 g protein, 13.5 g fat (2.1 g saturated), 107 mg cholesterol, 85 mg sodium, 968 mg potassium, 2 mg iron, 27 mg calcium

Chef's Secrets

• Flavor-Full! Substitute basil, mint, cilantro, or thyme for the dillweed. Use lime, orange, or grapefruit juice instead of lemon juice.

• Microwave Magic: Arrange the salmon fillets in a single layer in a microwaveable baking dish. Prepare as directed in Step 2. Cover with parchment paper (or a layer of lettuce leaves). Microwave on high, allowing 4 to 5 minutes per pound. Four pieces of salmon will take about 8 to 10 minutes on high.

• Bones Away! To check for bones, drape a salmon fillet over a drinking glass or the palm of your hand so that the ends extend and hang down. The layers of fish will spread, making it easy to see the bones and remove them. Eyebrow tweezers are a terrific tool for removing fish bones.

• Lemon Aid: When lemons are warmed, they yield more juice. Before squeezing, either soak lemons in hot water for a few minutes or microwave on high for 15 to 20 seconds. One lemon yields 3 to 4 Tbsp juice.

• Grate Idea! Don't throw away those hollowed-out lemons: freeze them in a re-sealable plastic bag. Using a microplane grater, grate the frozen lemon rind and add to baked goods, cooked vegetables, salad dressings, fish, or poultry.

🍎 PLANKED SALMON

"Wooden-it" be lovely! Grilling on a cedar plank imparts a deliciously smoky flavor to the salmon, as well as keeping it juicy. Marinating the salmon in a lemon-garlic-dill mixture before planking enhances the flavor even more so.

fish

2 (8- × 12-inch, or larger) untreated
  cedar planks (about 1-inch thick)
2 salmon fillets, with skin
  (about 2 lb/1 kg each)
¼ cup lemon or lime juice
  (preferably fresh)
2 Tbsp extra virgin olive oil
4 cloves garlic (about 4 tsp minced)
¼ cup minced fresh dillweed or basil
Salt and freshly ground black pepper
1 sliced lemon or lime, for garnish

1. Soak the cedar planks in cold water for
1 to 2 hours before grilling; use a couple of
unopened cans or other heavy objects on
top of the planks to keep them submerged.
While the cedar planks are soaking, season
each salmon fillet with lemon juice, olive
oil, garlic, dillweed, salt, and pepper.

2. When fully soaked, remove the planks
from the water and shake well to remove
any excess. Heat the planks on the grill's
grate over indirect medium heat until hot,
about 6 to 8 minutes. Carefully transfer the
salmon to the preheated planks (they will
be very hot!), placing the salmon skin-side
down. Grill for 12 to 15 minutes, until the
salmon is cooked through. Turning isn't
necessary. Keeping the lid closed will keep
the salmon grilling at an even heat.

3. Spray the lemon slices lightly with cooking spray and grill for about 2 minutes on
each side.

4. When the salmon is done, carefully
remove the hot planks from the grill and
place on a heatproof surface. Slide a wide
spatula between the skin and flesh of the
salmon, then transfer to serving platters.
Garnish with grilled lemon slices and serve
hot or cold.

Yield: 10 to 12 servings. Keeps for up to 2
to 3 days in the refrigerator; reheats well.
Freezes well for up to 2 months.

322 calories per serving, 0.9 g carbohydrate, 0.1 g fiber,
41 g protein, 15.9 g fat (2.4 g saturated), 115 mg cholesterol, 91 mg sodium, 1028 mg potassium, 2 mg iron,
27 mg calcium

Serving Suggestions

• To feed a smaller crowd, use one salmon
fillet and cut the other ingredients in half.

• If the salmon is seasoned with dillweed,
serve it with Two-Way Tzatziki (page 52).
Dill-icious!

• If salmon is seasoned with basil, serve
it with Oven-Roasted "Melted" Tomatoes
(page 311).

Chef's Secrets

• Where to Buy: You can buy untreated
cedar planks at many supermarkets during
grilling season. Or check with your local
building supply store as they will often cut
planks to the size you need.

• Grill It Right: If your grill has a thermo-
stat, the recommended temperature with
the lid closed is 350°F.

• No Smoking: Never leave planks unat-
tended on the grill! Keep an eye on the
planks while grilling; if they start to smoke,
spritz with water to stop the wood from
burning.

• Keep it Clean: Most planks get very
charred and can only be used once—soak
in water for 30 minutes to cool the planks
before discarding. If planks are reusable,
wash with warm running water and some

dishwashing detergent within an hour after using. Preheating the plank before use helps to sterilize it.

• No Plank? No Problem: Oil salmon well on both sides to prevent sticking. This also helps protect it from forming cancer-causing substances during grilling. Place the salmon, flesh-side down, on the grill. Cook on medium heat for 7 to 8 minutes. Turn the salmon over so that it's skin-side down and cook 3 to 4 minutes longer.

🍎 SHOW-STOPPING MAPLE-GLAZED SALMON

When I do my cooking demonstrations, I often require a show-stopping dish that will feed a crowd, can be made in advance, and tastes terrific either hot or cold. This dish fits the bill—it's a winner!

1 salmon fillet, with skin (about 3 lb/1.4 kg)
1/4 cup Dijon mustard
1/4 cup apricot jam or orange marmalade (low-sugar or all-fruit)
2 Tbsp maple syrup
1 Tbsp olive oil
2 Tbsp minced fresh rosemary or 1 tsp dried
Freshly ground black pepper
Sweet or smoked paprika
Baby spinach, lemon slices, and additional rosemary, for garnish

1. Line a large baking sheet (without sides) with foil and spray with cooking spray.

2. Place the salmon, skin-side down, on the prepared baking sheet. In a small bowl, combine the mustard, jam, maple syrup, oil, and rosemary; mix well. Using a pastry or barbecue brush, spread the mixture evenly on top of the salmon, reserving any extra glaze. Sprinkle the salmon with pepper and paprika. Transfer to the refrigerator and let marinate for 1 to 2 hours. Refrigerate the reserved glaze.

3. Preheat the oven to 425°F. Bake the marinated salmon, uncovered, for 15 to 18 minutes or until it's glazed and golden, basting occasionally with pan juices. Cool slightly.

4. Carefully transfer the salmon to a large serving platter lined with baby spinach leaves. Garnish with lemon slices and rosemary. Drizzle salmon with reserved glaze mixture and serve hot or cold.

Yield: 10 servings. Recipe easily doubles or triples. Keeps for up to 2 to 3 days in the refrigerator; reheats well. Freezes well for up to 2 months.

262 calories per serving, 5.8 g carbohydrate, 0.1 g fiber, 31 g protein, 11.8 g fat (1.8 g saturated), 86 mg cholesterol, 220 mg sodium, 783 mg potassium, 1 mg iron, 31 mg calcium

Chef's Secrets
• Fishing for Compliments? For a large party, calculate that each pound of salmon will feed 3 to 4 people. Allow 4 to 5 ounces per person for a buffet. Oven-Roasted Vegetables (page 316) make a perfect accompaniment. Both dishes are delicious served at room temperature.

• Buffet Beauty: When entertaining a large crowd, any of the salmon recipes in this book can be prepared using a large salmon fillet. Multiply the ingredients accordingly, depending on how many people you will be feeding. Line the platter with baby spinach leaves. Grape tomatoes or tomato roses, sliced cucumbers, and chopped green onions make for attractive garnishes.

• Pan-tastic! To transfer salmon to a serving platter, use a cookie sheet without sides as a giant spatula. You could also use two wide metal spatulas.

fish

🍎 SPICY SESAME SALMON

Open wide "sez-a-me!" Season a side of salmon with this exotic, aromatic blend of herbs and spices and then top it with sesame seeds and marinate briefly before roasting it. You can also make this with individual fillets. This scrumptious fish dish will definitely rub you the right way!

1 salmon fillet, skin removed
   (about 3 lb/1.4 kg)
2 to 3 Tbsp maple syrup or honey

Spice Rub:

2 cloves garlic (about 2 tsp minced)
2 tsp fresh minced ginger
   (or 1/2 tsp powdered ginger)
1 tsp Kosher or sea salt (to taste)
1 tsp coarsely ground black pepper
2 tsp sweet or smoked paprika
2 tsp crumbled dried cilantro leaves
   or thyme
2 tsp ground cumin
2 tsp ground cinnamon
2 Tbsp olive oil
2 Tbsp lemon juice (preferably fresh)
4 Tbsp sesame seeds (for sprinkling on top)

1. Line a large baking sheet with foil and spray with cooking spray.

2. Place the salmon on the prepared baking sheet and brush lightly on both sides with maple syrup. In a small bowl, combine the ingredients for the spice rub, except sesame seeds. Mix well. Spread spice rub over salmon, coating both sides. Sprinkle sesame seeds on top. Marinate for 30 minutes at room temperature or refrigerate for up to 2 hours.

3. Preheat the oven to 425°F. Bake uncovered for 15 to 18 minutes. The salmon is done when it just flakes when gently pressed with a fork. Cool slightly, then transfer to a serving platter using a wide spatula. Serve hot or cold. Garnish with parsley, lemon, and cucumber slices.

Yield: 10 servings. Keeps for up to 2 to 3 days in the refrigerator; reheats well. Freezes well for up to 2 months.

284 calories per serving, 4.6 g carbohydrate, 1.0 g fiber, 32 g protein, 14.5 g fat (1.9 g saturated), 86 mg cholesterol, 309 mg sodium, 783 mg potassium, 2 mg iron, 46 mg calcium

Spicy Sesame Chicken

Brush 10 boneless skinless single chicken breasts with maple syrup and coat with spice rub. Sprinkle with sesame seeds. Cover and refrigerate up to 24 hours. Bake uncovered at 400°F for 20 minutes or until firm but springy to the touch. (Or place on a hot grill and cook 5 to 6 minutes per side, depending on the thickness.) One serving contains 177 calories, 7.1 g fat, 1.1 g saturated fat and 59 mg cholesterol.

Chef's Secrets

• Fishful Thinking: Make half the recipe for a small family or multiply it for a large crowd. Allow 6 ounces of fish per person. Individual fillets take 8 to 12 minutes to cook, depending on the thickness.

• The Daily Catch: This aromatic rub is also excellent for grilled or baked salmon trout, red snapper, orange roughy, or any thick fish fillets. Rub-a-dub-dub!

SPICY STEAKHOUSE SALMON

My daughter-in-law, Cheryl Lis Gilletz, serves this scrumptious salmon at family gatherings, to rave reviews. She modified my original recipe by adding Worcestershire sauce to boost the flavor and it tastes terrific. Enjoy the fabulous flavor of Montreal.

1 salmon fillet, with skin (about 3 lb/1.4 kg)
4 cloves garlic (about 4 tsp minced)
2 Tbsp lemon juice (preferably fresh)
2 tsp Worcestershire sauce
2 Tbsp Montreal-Style Steak Spice
   (page 115)
   (or use store-bought steak spice)
2 tsp dried basil

1. Preheat the oven to 425°F. Line a large baking sheet with foil and spray with cooking spray.

2. Place the salmon skin-side down on the prepared baking sheet. Top with garlic, lemon juice, and Worcestershire sauce, then sprinkle with steak spice and basil. Let marinate at room temperature for 10 to 20 minutes (or refrigerate up to 2 hours).

3. Bake uncovered for 15 to 18 minutes or until the fish flakes when gently pressed with a fork. Serve hot or cold.

Yield: 8 servings. Keeps for up to 2 to 3 days in the refrigerator; reheats well. Freezes well for up to 2 months.

286 calories per serving, 2.3 g carbohydrate, 0.4 g fiber, 39 g protein, 12.4 g fat (1.9 g saturated), 108 mg cholesterol, 636 mg sodium, 1005 mg potassium, 8 mg iron, 41 mg calcium

Chef's Secrets

• Skill at the Grill: Preheat barbecue or electric grill. Cut salmon into individual portions and season as directed. Brush lightly on both sides with olive oil to prevent sticking. If using the barbecue, cook over indirect heat and close the lid to help retain heat; allow 5 to 6 minutes per side. If using a two-sided electric contact grill, total cooking time will be 5 to 6 minutes.

• Microwave Magic: Season 2 to 4 portions of salmon with a little minced garlic, lemon juice, and Worcestershire sauce. Sprinkle lightly with steak spice and basil. Place on a microwaveable dinner plate and cover with parchment paper or a layer of lettuce leaves. Two portions of salmon will take 4 minutes, on high, to microwave. Four portions will take about 7 to 8 minutes on high.

TERIYAKI SALMON WITH MUSHROOMS AND PEPPERS

Your guests won't stop yakking about this teriyaki dish once they taste it. Your culinary reputation will spread far and wide, but your hips won't!

4 cups sliced mushrooms
2 red peppers, seeded and cut in strips
1 yellow pepper, seeded and
   cut in strips
1 medium red onion, halved and
   thinly sliced
3 Tbsp extra virgin olive oil
1 salmon fillet, with skin (about 3 lb/1.4 kg)
Salt and freshly ground black pepper
Teriyaki Marinade (page 112)
Toasted slivered almonds, for garnish

1. Line a large baking sheet with foil and spray with cooking spray.

2. Spread the mushrooms, peppers, and onions in a single layer at one end of the prepared baking sheet and drizzle with oil. Place the salmon, skin-side down, at the other end of the baking sheet. Sprinkle the salmon and vegetables with salt and pepper to taste, then drizzle evenly with marinade. Cover and marinate for 1 to 2 hours in the refrigerator.

3. Preheat the oven to 425°F. Bake the marinated salmon, uncovered, for 15 to 18 minutes. The salmon will be glazed and golden and the vegetables will be tender-crisp when done.

4. Cool slightly, then transfer the salmon carefully to a large serving platter using a wide spatula. Surround the salmon with vegetables and sprinkle with almonds. Serve hot or cold.

Yield: 10 servings. Recipe easily doubles or triples. Keeps for up to 2 to 3 days in the refrigerator; reheats well. Freezes well for up to 2 months.

307 calories per serving, 9.4 g carbohydrate, 1.2 g fiber, 32 g protein, 15.2 g fat (2.3 g saturated), 86 mg cholesterol, 283 mg sodium, 964 mg potassium, 2 mg iron, 32 mg calcium

Variations

• The Daily Catch: This is also delicious with halibut, salmon trout, orange roughy, or red snapper fillets. Reduce temperature to 400°F and bake for 10 to 12 minutes, or until the fish flakes when gently pressed with a fork, and the vegetables are tender. The vegetables may require an extra few minutes of cooking.

• Veggie Heaven: Roast other quick-cooking vegetables, such as asparagus or broccoli spears, sliced zucchini, or baby bok choy cut in half, along with the fish. Portobello or other types of mushrooms are a tasty addition.

• Top It Up! Instead of almonds, use chopped cashews, walnuts, or sesame seeds as a garnish.

THYME FOR LIME SALMON

This takes very little time to prepare and tastes terrific. I love to use fresh lime juice because of its light, vibrant flavor, but you can easily substitute bottled juice. Did you know that limes don't contain any seeds? The pit stops here!

4 salmon fillets (6 to 8 oz/180 to 250 g each)
Salt and freshly ground black pepper
1 to 2 tsp minced fresh thyme or 1 tsp dried
Juice of 1/2 lime (about 1 Tbsp)
1 tsp extra virgin olive oil
2 tsp honey

1. Preheat the oven to 425°F. Line a baking sheet with foil and spray with cooking spray.

2. Place the salmon, skin-side down, on the prepared baking sheet. Season with salt, pepper, and thyme. In a small bowl, whisk together the lime juice, oil, and honey. Drizzle over the salmon and use the back of

a spoon to evenly spread the mixture.

3. Bake, uncovered, for 10 to 12 minutes or until the fish just flakes when gently pressed with a fork. Serve hot or cold.

Yield: 4 servings. Recipe easily doubles or triples. Keeps for up to 2 to 3 days in the refrigerator; reheats well. Freezes well for up to 2 months.

297 calories per serving, 3.3 g carbohydrate, 0.1 g fiber, 39 g protein, 13.4 g fat (2.1 g saturated), 108 mg cholesterol, 85 mg sodium, 958 mg potassium, 2 mg iron, 24 mg calcium

Variation
• Substitute orange or lemon juice for lime juice and/or substitute maple syrup for honey. For a spicy kick, sprinkle lightly with cayenne before baking.

Cindy Beer's Meal Deal
Cut 1 asparagus bunch into 2-inch pieces. Cut 12 to 16 baby new potatoes in quarters. Place the vegetables on a large baking sheet along with the salmon. Triple the amount of the seasonings, lime juice, oil, and honey to coat both the salmon and the vegetables. Bake as directed in Step 3. Thanks to Cindy Beer, my assistant and a wonderful friend, for this terrific time-saving tip!

🍎 PINEAPPLE SNAPPER FILLETS IN A SNAP

This colorful, potassium-packed dish takes very little time to prepare with the help of a food processor. The salsa makes a scrumptious sauce when it's heated and spooned over rice or other cooked grains. It's healthy, easy, and elegant.

1/4 cup tightly packed fresh parsley leaves
Pineapple Tomato Salsa (page 106)
6 to 8 red snapper fillets
   (about 8 oz/250 g each)
Salt, freshly ground black pepper,
   and paprika
2 Tbsp olive oil
3 to 4 cups hot cooked basmati rice, quinoa,
   or bulgar

1. Preheat the oven to 400°F. Line a baking sheet with foil and spray with cooking spray.

2. In a food processor fitted with the steel blade, process the parsley until minced. Transfer to a bowl and reserve to use as a garnish. Using the food processor, prepare the Pineapple Tomato Salsa according to directions. Transfer to a microwaveable bowl.

3. Place the fish fillets on the prepared baking sheet and season with salt, pepper, and paprika. Brush lightly with olive oil. (The fish can be prepared 30 to 60 minutes in advance.)

4. Bake, uncovered, for 10 minutes or until the fish just flakes when gently pressed with a fork. There's no need to turn over the fish.

5. Meanwhile, microwave the salsa for 2 minutes on high or until hot, stirring once or twice. Put 1/2 to 3/4 cup of cooked rice on each plate and top with a fish fillet. Spoon the salsa over the fish and rice. Sprinkle with the reserved minced parsley and serve immediately.

Yield: 6 to 8 servings. Keeps for up to 1 to 2 days in the refrigerator; reheats well. Don't freeze.

290 calories per serving (without rice), 4.4 g carbohydrate, 0.9 g fiber, 45 g protein, 9.1 g fat (1.5 g saturated), 80 mg cholesterol, 101 mg sodium, 1011 mg potassium, 1 mg iron, 83 mg calcium

Variations

• The Daily Catch: Instead of snapper fillets, substitute with salmon trout, halibut, whitefish, orange roughy, or sole. Baking time will vary slightly, depending on the thickness of the fish.

• Ready When You Are! Cook rice (or desired grain) while you are preparing the fish and salsa—that way everything will be ready at the same time.

◕ SNAPPER BALSAMICO WITH GRAPE TOMATOES AND MUSHROOMS

These snapper fillets are so scrumptious they'll get snapped up in a minute! Cooking the fish and vegetables together in one pan saves time and clean-up. This potassium-packed dish is also delicious made with tilapia, sole, or any other mild-flavored fish fillets.

6 red snapper fillets (about 8 oz/250 g each)
1 container (1 pint/550 mL) grape
   or cherry tomatoes (about 2 cups)
1/2 lb (250 g) mushrooms, coarsely chopped
   (about 2 1/2 cups)
6 to 8 cloves garlic, peeled and sliced
1 tsp dried thyme or 1 Tbsp fresh
Salt and freshly ground black pepper
2 Tbsp chopped fresh basil, for garnish

Marinade:

1/4 cup balsamic vinegar
2 Tbsp olive oil
1 to 2 Tbsp honey or maple syrup
1 Tbsp lemon juice (preferably fresh)

1. Line a large baking tray with foil and spray with cooking spray.

2. Arrange the fillets in a single layer on the prepared baking sheet. Scatter the tomatoes, mushrooms, and garlic around the fish. Season with thyme, salt, and pepper to taste.

3. In a measuring cup, combine the vinegar, oil, honey, and lemon juice; mix well. Drizzle the mixture over the fish and vegetables until all are well coated. Marinate for 30 to 60 minutes.

4. Preheat the oven to 425°F. Bake the fish and vegetables, uncovered, for 12 to 15 minutes. The fish is done when it just flakes when gently pressed with a fork. Garnish with basil and serve immediately.

Yield: 6 servings. Keeps for up to 2 days in the refrigerator; reheats well. Don't freeze: if frozen, vegetables will be watery when thawed.

298 calories per serving, 9.4 g carbohydrate, 1.1 g fiber, 46 g protein, 7.6 g fat (1.3 g saturated), 80 mg cholesterol, 105 mg sodium, 1206 mg potassium, 1 mg iron, 93 mg calcium

Chef's Secrets

• What's in Store: Red snapper is available fresh all year round. The peak season is in the summer months. Smaller sizes are often sold whole, while larger fish can be purchased as steaks or fillets. Red snapper gets its name because of its reddish-pink skin and flesh, and its red eyes. It has a mild, sweet flavor and its flesh is tender, firm, moist, and lean.

• Store It Right: Store fresh snapper in the refrigerator and use it within 2 days. It can be frozen for up to 6 months. If frozen, thaw overnight in the refrigerator or under cold running water.

• Cook It Right: Red snapper is delicious broiled, baked, grilled, poached, steamed, or pan-fried. Try it seasoned with pungent Cajun spices or with a delicate lemon, olive oil, and herb marinade. Red snapper's mild flavor matches well with mango, pineapple, or tomato and herb salsa.

🍎 FISH FILLETS IN PARCHMENT

Whether you're cooking for two or a crowd, this dish is true "wrap-ture!" Cooking in parchment paper saves on clean-up. If you don't have parchment paper, wrap fish in foil. Foiled again!

2 tilapia, sole, or whitefish fillets
   (about 6 oz/180 g each)
2 tsp extra virgin olive oil
2 tsp lemon or lime juice (preferably fresh)
1 clove garlic (about 1 tsp minced)
Salt, freshly ground black pepper, and
   paprika
2 tsp minced fresh basil, dillweed,
   or thyme (or 1/2 tsp dried)

1. Preheat the oven to 400°F. Cut 2 large squares of parchment paper. Place a fish fillet in the center of each piece of parchment.

2. In a small bowl, whisk together the oil and lemon juice. Drizzle each fillet with the oil-lemon mixture, then sprinkle with garlic and seasonings, coating the fish on both sides. Seal the parchment-paper packages by folding up the top, bottom, and sides, and crimping the edges closed with your fingers. Place the packages on a baking sheet and let the fillets marinate inside the parchment for 15 minutes.

3. Bake for 10 minutes. (Or microwave the parchment-paper packages on high for 3 1/2 to 4 minutes.) Place each package on a dinner plate and cut open at the table. Be careful not to scald yourself when the hot steam escapes once the packages are opened. Serve immediately.

Yield: 2 servings. Recipe easily doubles or triples. Keeps for up to 1 to 2 days in the refrigerator; reheats well. Freezes well for up to 2 months.

209 calories per serving, 1.0 g carbohydrate, 0.1 g fiber, 34 g protein, 7.6 g fat (1.6 g saturated), 85 mg cholesterol, 89 mg sodium, 530 mg potassium, 1 mg iron, 21 mg calcium

Fish and Vegetables in Parchment
Season fillets as directed in Step 2 but, before sealing the packages, top each fillet with broccoli or cauliflower florets, cherry tomatoes, chopped red pepper, sliced mushrooms, green onions, or zucchini. Sprinkle with a little white wine or salsa, then seal. Bake at 400°F for 12 to 15 minutes (or microwave on high for 5 minutes).

🍎 STUFFED SOLE DUXELLES

Heart and "sole" I fell in love with you . . . and you'll fall in love with this delicious fish dish! It's good for both your heart and your waistline. Stuffing fish and rolling the fillets is time consuming, but making them into "sandwiches" speeds up preparation. That's "sole-full" music!

8 sole fillets (about 2 lb/1 kg)
Salt, freshly ground black pepper
    and dried thyme
Mushroom Duxelles (page 302)
2 slices wholegrain bread, torn into chunks
2 tsp olive oil
1/2 tsp paprika
1/2 cup grated low-fat cheddar
    or Swiss cheese

1. Sprinkle fish lightly on both sides with salt, pepper, and thyme. Arrange half the fillets, in a single layer, in a sprayed 7- × 11-inch glass baking dish. Top each fillet with Mushroom Duxelles. Place the remaining fillets on top to make "fish sandwiches."

2. In a food processor fitted with the steel blade, drop the bread through the feed tube while the motor is running; process to make fine breadcrumbs. Add the oil, paprika, and additional salt and pepper. Process for a few seconds longer, until combined. Sprinkle the breadcrumb mixture over the fish. Sprinkle cheese over the breadcrumb topping. (You can prepare the dish up to this point and refrigerate for several hours until closer to serving time.)

3. Preheat the oven to 375°F. Bake, uncovered, for 25 to 30 minutes or until golden.

Yield: 4 servings. Recipe easily doubles or triples. Keeps for up to 2 days in the refrigerator; reheats well. Freezes well for up to 1 month.

365 calories per serving, 14.0 g carbohydrate, 2.4 g fiber, 47 g protein, 13.6 g fat (2.6 g saturated), 109 mg cholesterol, 322 mg sodium, 1005 mg potassium, 2 mg iron, 114 mg calcium

Variations

• Use any fish fillets you like. Try tilapia, whitefish, haddock, or halibut—the choice is yours!

• Spinach and Mushroom Stuffing (page 339) or Caramelized Onions (page 303) also make scrumptious fillings.

Chef's Secrets

• Crumb-ly News: One slice of bread yields about 1/2 cup soft breadcrumbs—the moisture will evaporate during baking. If you prefer, substitute with 1/4 cup dried breadcrumbs. If you make your own breadcrumbs, choose high-fiber wholegrain bread.

• Lighten Up! Without cheese, one serving contains 340 calories, 12.6 g fat, and 2.0 g saturated.

🍎 TILAPIA MEDITERRANIA

This luscious low-carb dish comes together very quickly to make a heart-healthy meal—and one that has a low glycemic index (GI). The tilapia in this recipe is topped with a garden-fresh tomato sauce that tastes like a trip to the Mediterranean!

Sauce:

3 medium roma tomatoes, quartered
3 green onions, cut in chunks
2 Tbsp fresh basil or 1 tsp dried
1 clove garlic (about 1 tsp minced)
1 Tbsp lemon juice (preferably fresh)
2 tsp extra virgin olive oil
Salt and freshly ground black pepper

fish

Fish:

6 tilapia fillets (about 2 lb/1 kg)
Salt and freshly ground black pepper
1 tsp dried thyme or basil
2 cloves garlic (about 2 tsp minced)
3 Tbsp lemon juice (preferably fresh)
2 Tbsp extra virgin olive oil
1/2 cup pitted and sliced black olives
2 Tbsp capers, rinsed and drained

1. In a food processor fitted with the steel blade, coarsely chop tomatoes, green onions, basil, and garlic, using quick on/off pulses. Add the lemon juice, oil, salt, and pepper. Transfer the sauce to a 2-cup glass measure; cover and refrigerate for up to 1 day.

2. Preheat the oven to 400°F. Line a baking sheet with parchment paper.

3. Arrange the tilapia fillets in a single layer on the prepared baking sheet. Season with salt, pepper, thyme, and garlic. Drizzle with lemon juice and olive oil, coating the fish on both sides. Let marinate for 10 minutes.

4. Bake, uncovered, for 10 minutes or until the fish flakes when lightly pressed with a fork.

5. Microwave the sauce, uncovered, on high for 1 to 2 minutes or until heated through. Spoon the sauce over the tilapia and sprinkle with olives and capers before serving.

Yield: 6 servings. Keeps for up to 2 days in the refrigerator; reheats well. Don't freeze.

230 calories per serving, 4.6 g carbohydrate, 1.4 g fiber, 31 g protein, 10.1 g fat (1.9 g saturated), 76 mg cholesterol, 265 mg sodium, 591 mg potassium, 2 mg iron, 46 mg calcium

Variations

• Substitute the tilapia with any fish fillets you like such as halibut, cod, sole, whitefish, or snapper.

• Meal Deal: To make a full meal, in Step 3, scatter 2 cups sliced mushrooms, zucchini, and/or asparagus spears around the fish. Sprinkle the vegetables with salt and pepper, and drizzle lightly with olive oil and lemon juice. Bake as directed and serve with couscous, bulgar, or boiled baby new potatoes.

🍎 PECAN-CRUSTED TILAPIA

You'll go nuts over this dish once you try it! The crusty coating is a terrific source of fiber.

4 tilapia fillets (6 oz/175 g each)
1/4 cup dried breadcrumbs
    (wholegrain is best)
1/4 cup wheat bran, oat bran,
    or whole wheat flour
1/4 cup finely chopped pecans
1/2 tsp salt (or to taste)
1/4 tsp freshly ground black pepper
1/4 tsp garlic powder
1/2 tsp paprika
1 Tbsp olive or canola oil
1 egg plus 1 Tbsp water
4 lemon wedges, for garnish

1. Preheat the oven to 425°F. Line a baking sheet with foil and spray with cooking spray.

2. Cut each fillet in half, lengthwise, making two long pieces. Cut the thicker piece in half crosswise (tilapia fillets have a thicker side and a thinner side). You should end up with three long pieces that are all the same thickness—this helps the fish to cook evenly.

3. Combine the breadcrumbs, bran, pecans, salt, pepper, garlic powder, paprika, and oil in a shallow dish and set aside. Whisk the egg and water together in a pie plate. Dip the fish first in the egg wash, making sure all sides are coated. Quickly dredge both sides of the dipped fish in the breadcrumb mixture.

4. Arrange the breadcrumb-coated fish in a single layer on the prepared baking sheet. (You can prepare the fish in advance up to this point and refrigerate for 3 to 4 hours.)

5. Bake, uncovered, for 10 minutes or until golden. (There's no need to turn the fish over while baking.) Serve hot, garnished with lemon wedges.

Yield: 4 to 6 servings. Keeps for up to 2 days in the refrigerator; reheats well. Don't freeze: if frozen, the coating won't be crispy.

300 calories per serving, 8.6 g carbohydrate, 2.7 g fiber, 38 g protein, 13.4 g fat (2.3 g saturated), 138 mg cholesterol, 449 mg sodium, 612 mg potassium, 2 mg iron, 43 mg calcium

Variations
• Any firm-fleshed fish fillets will work—try it with sole, snapper, flounder, or dore/pickerel.

• Substitute almonds, hazelnuts, or any nuts you like instead of pecans.

• Instead of dipping fish fillets in beaten egg, dip them in low-calorie honey mustard or Italian salad dressing, then in the crumb mixture.

Chef's Secrets
• What's in Store: Tilapia is a farm-raised fish that is low in fat and has a mild, delicious flavor. It is white-fleshed and often tinged with pink, with a fine texture.

• Cook It Right: Here's another technique to prevent overcooking. Cut each fillet in half lengthwise, making two long pieces. Coat each piece with the breadcrumb mixture as directed in Step 2. Thinner pieces take 10 minutes to bake and thicker pieces take 2 to 3 minutes longer.

• Pan-tastic! Don't add the oil to the breadcrumb mixture. Instead of baking, pan-fry the fish in a nonstick skillet in 1 to 2 Tbsp oil on medium-high heat for 2 to 3 minutes per side. Drain on paper towels.

🍎 CAJUN-STYLE WHITEFISH

You'll be hooked on fish when you try this dish. It's a great way to spice up your life.

6 whitefish or sole fillets
    (about 6 oz/180 g each)
2 Tbsp extra virgin olive oil
2 Tbsp lemon juice (preferably fresh)
1 tsp salt
1/4 tsp freshly ground black pepper
1 tsp chili powder
1/2 tsp sweet or smoked paprika
1/2 tsp cayenne
1/2 tsp dried thyme
2 cloves garlic (about 2 tsp minced)

1. Preheat the oven to 400°F. Place the fish fillets in a single layer in a sprayed 9- × 13-inch glass baking dish.

2. In a small bowl, combine the oil, lemon juice, salt, pepper, chili powder, paprika, cayenne, thyme, and garlic; mix well. Brush both sides of the fish with the oil-lemon

fish

juice mixture. Drizzle any remaining mixture over the fish and let it marinate for 15 to 20 minutes at room temperature.

3. Bake the marinated fish in the oven, uncovered, for 8 to 10 minutes or until the fish just flakes when lightly pressed with a fork. Serve immediately.

Yield: 6 servings. Recipe easily doubles or triples. Keeps for up to 2 days in the refrigerator; reheats well. Freezes well for up to 2 months.

193 calories per serving, 1.3 g carbohydrate, 0.3 g fiber, 31 g protein, 7.4 g fat (1.5 g saturated), 76 mg cholesterol, 471 mg sodium, 484 mg potassium, 1 mg iron, 21 mg calcium

Chef's Secrets

• A Fish Story! Did you know that whitefish is a member of the salmon family? It's called whitefish because its mild-flavored flesh is white and firm. Whitefish, available whole or in fillets year round, is delicious baked, broiled, grilled, pan-fried, or poached.

• Heart and Sole: Sole is slightly lower in fat and calories than whitefish. If you use sole fillets, a 6-ounce serving contains 185 calories, 29 g protein, 6.6 g fat (1.1 g sat) and 80 mg cholesterol.

• The Daily Catch: Substitute the whitefish with any white-fleshed mild fish fillets or steaks such as tilapia, snapper, halibut, or sea bass.

• Cook It Right: If fillets are very thin, it's better to broil rather than bake. When broiling, keep the fish about 4 inches from the heat to prevent overcooking—there's no need to turn them over! They'll be done in 3 or 4 minutes.

• Leftovers? They're excellent in Fast Fish Salad (page 121).

🍎 GRILLED TUNA WITH MANGO SALAD

The recipe for this impressive dish comes from the cookbook *Cooking Kindness*, compiled by my friend Gloria Guttman of Toronto. You can prepare the salad in advance and grill the tuna just before serving.

1 large mango, peeled, pitted, and
   cut into 1/4-inch wide strips
3/4 cup chopped red onion
1/2 cup chopped red pepper
3 Tbsp chopped fresh cilantro
2 Tbsp rice vinegar
2 Tbsp extra virgin olive oil
Salt and freshly ground black pepper
4 yellowfin tuna steaks, about 1-inch thick
   (5 to 6 oz/150 to 180 g each)
1 Tbsp canola oil

1. Mango Salad: Combine the mango, onion, red pepper, cilantro, rice vinegar, and olive oil in a medium bowl; season with salt and pepper. (Can be made several hours in advance and refrigerated.)

2. Grilled Tuna: Set the grill to medium-high heat (or preheat the broiler). Lightly brush both sides of the tuna steaks with oil. Grill or broil just until the tuna is opaque in the center, about 3 to 4 minutes per side. Don't overcook.

3. Divide the mango salad among 4 plates and top with the grilled tuna.

Yield: 4 servings. Keeps for up to 1 to 2 days in the refrigerator. Don't freeze.

298 calories per serving, 13.0 g carbohydrate, 1.7 g fiber, 34 g protein, 12.1 g fat (1.6 g saturated), 64 mg cholesterol, 55 mg sodium, 796 mg potassium, 1 mg iron, 36 mg calcium

307 calories per serving, 4.7 g carbohydrate, 2.6 g fiber, 37 g protein, 14.5 g fat (0.7 g saturated), 64 mg cholesterol, 87 mg sodium, 667 mg potassium, 2 mg iron, 93 mg calcium

Variations
• Instead of grilled tuna, top Mango Salad with Asian Tuna Salad (page 122) or Chicken Satay (page 217).

● PEPPER-CRUSTED TUNA

This looks absolutely fabulous served on a bed of mixed salad greens drizzled with your favorite salad dressing. It's definitely upper crust!

6 yellowfin tuna steaks, about 1-inch thick (5 to 6 oz/150 to 180 g each)
2 Tbsp canola oil
3/4 cup sesame seeds
3 Tbsp coarsely cracked black peppercorns or Montreal-Style Steak Spice (page 115)

1. Preheat the grill or broiler. Lightly brush both sides of the tuna steaks with oil. Combine the sesame seeds with the peppercorns. Press the sesame seed mixture onto both sides of the tuna. (Can be prepared up to 1 hour in advance and refrigerated.)

2. Grill or broil the tuna just until it is opaque in the center, about 3 to 4 minutes per side. Don't overcook. Slice diagonally across the grain into thin slices and serve immediately.

Yield: 6 servings. Keeps for up to 1 to 2 days in the refrigerator. Don't freeze.

Chef's Secrets
• Skillet or Grill It? Instead of grilling the tuna, use a heavy skillet and sear in hot oil for 2 to 3 minutes per side or until the outer edges are just cooked but the center is still rare.

• Company's Coming! Artfully arrange the slices of tuna on top of Apricot Hoisin Spinach Salad (page 254) or use the pepper-crusted tuna slices in Grilled Tuna with Mango Salad (page 143).

make it meatless

MAKE IT MEATLESS

Go Meatless: Whether you are a vegetarian or are just cutting back on meat for health, ethical, or environmental reasons, eating a plant-based diet offers many benefits, including making it easier to keep a Kosher kitchen.

The Garden of Eating: If you're looking for healthy, delicious ways to include more vegetarian dishes in your culinary repertoire, read on. Also check the chapters on appetizers, soups, salads, vegetables, grains, and side dishes for easy, healthy meatless recipes that will please both vegetarians and carnivores.

What's a Vegetarian? A vegetarian is often defined as someone who won't eat anything that has a face or a mother. Many people who call themselves vegetarians are actually semi-vegetarians. They may have eliminated red meat from their diet but might eat poultry or fish. Some vegetarians won't eat red meat, poultry, or fish but will eat dairy foods, eggs, and/or cheese. The major vegetarian categories include:

Vegan: Eat only food from plant sources. For instance, many vegans won't eat honey.

Lacto-Vegetarian: Eat dairy products, but no eggs, meat, poultry, or fish.

Ovo-Vegetarian: Eat eggs, but no dairy or meat, poultry, or fish.

Ovo-Lacto-Vegetarian: Eat eggs and dairy, but no meat, poultry, or fish.

Flexitarian: A vegetarian who occasionally eats meat or other proteins from animal sources.

Change Your Focus: Instead of focusing on meat and potatoes, why not make meatless side dishes the main part of your meal more often? Beans, grains, and vegetables can fill you up without filling you out.

Worried About Not Getting Enough Protein? Eating a plant-based diet of beans and legumes, soy products, grains, pasta, nuts, and seeds will provide you with plenty of protein. These foods also contain magnesium, folate, potassium, antioxidants, and phytochemicals (potent antioxidants found in plant foods that strengthen the immune system). They are also low in saturated fat, high in fiber, and are cholesterol-free. Protein from meat, fish, and dairy products contains saturated fat and cholesterol.

Say It Isn't Soy! Try different soy products such as tofu, soy meat crumbles, soy-based veggie deli slices, vegetable burgers, tempeh, seitan, and TVP (textured vegetable protein). Texture and taste, as well as protein, fat, and sodium content can vary among brands, so read the labels and experiment until you find a brand you like.

Firm Up: The firmer the tofu, the more nutritious it is. The calorie count is slightly higher, but firm tofu is also higher in protein. Its firmness depends on the amount of water that has been pressed out of it.

Cook It Right: For stir-fries, use extra-firm tofu or it will break up during cooking. Silken tofu is fragile and is better when puréed and used in salad dressings, desserts, and drinks.

To Soy or Not to Soy? Oy, it's soy confusing! Protein from soy foods, such as tofu and soymilk, is a good alternative to animal protein. Soy foods can lower cholesterol, but only if you consume very large quantities. Some studies suggest that a high intake of soy foods may increase the risk of breast and stomach cancer. What to do? It's best to eat soy foods in moderation, about 3 to 4 servings a week, until the research is definitive.

USING YOUR BEAN

Full of Beans: Explore the world of legumes such as beans, lentils, peanuts, and soybeans. They are a wonderful way to incorporate more fiber into your diet and are heart-healthy and a healthy choice for people with diabetes.

The Family Tree: Beans and other legumes are a family of plants that grow edible seeded pods. The most popular ones include black beans, chickpeas, kidney beans, lentils, pinto beans, split peas, soybeans, and peanuts.

Has-Beans: Here are some easy ways to sneak more legumes into your diet. Add mashed beans or chickpeas to meatloaf or spaghetti sauce. Spread multigrain bread or pita with natural peanut butter or hummus. Add canned chickpeas, beans, or lentils to soups, salads, pasta, rice, or other grains.

Bean Cuisine: Be adventurous—include beans and legumes in dips, soups, stews, sauces, casseroles, side dishes, and salads. Try Pumpkin Hummus (page 49), Black Bean, Barley, and Vegetable Soup (page 77), Kasha Chili (page 156), Almost Meat Lasagna (page 158) and Greek Chickpea Salad (page 260).

Bean Me Up! Beans and legumes are nutritional powerhouses. They are high in protein and fiber, low in fat, and cholesterol-free. They're also rich in B vitamins, calcium, iron, phosphorous, zinc, potassium, and magnesium. They are packed with folate, which helps prevent birth defects and reduces the risk of heart disease. In addition, legumes are gluten-free.

How Much Protein? You need 8 grams of protein for every 20 pounds of body weight. An average woman needs about 50 grams of protein a day and a man needs about 65 grams. A good guideline is to aim for 50% plant-based protein, coming from a variety of sources.

Complete or Incomplete? Some proteins are complete, containing all the amino acids your body needs. Other proteins are incomplete and lack one or more essential amino acids. Meat, poultry, fish, and cheese are complete proteins but contain saturated fat and cholesterol. Vegetable protein is often incomplete, so it's important to eat a mix of beans and legumes (including soy foods), nuts, whole grains, and vegetables to get your "fare share" of complete proteins, especially for vegetarians.

Bean Counter: Home-cooked or canned beans, lentils, or peas contain about 5 to 8 g protein per half cup, approximately the same amount as in 1 oz of meat, poultry, or fish. Legumes also contain 75 to 125 calories, 18 to 20 g carbohydrate and 6 to 8 g fiber per half cup. Low-calorie, fiber-full!

Fill up on Fiber: Beans and other legumes are high in fiber, which is what your body isn't able to digest—and that's a good thing. Fiber helps delay the absorption of sugars

make it meatless

and fats into the body, reducing spikes in insulin and decreasing the risk of heart attack and diabetes. This is a really good thing for people concerned with insulin-resistance, diabetes, and the glycemic index or for those who suffer from constipation, diverticulitis, and irritable bowel syndrome.

Filling Up with Gas: People who are accustomed to eating a low fiber diet and then switch to a high fiber one usually have a problem with flatulence. That's because their digestive tracts don't have enough of the necessary enzymes to digest the bean sugars. These sugars reach the colon intact, where bacteria cause them to ferment, producing fuel for energy, but also producing gas. Eventually your body will adapt by producing the necessary enzymes to digest them. Like many of life's problems, this too shall pass. Good news—black beans are easier to digest than most beans.

Go Slow: Shift slowly to a higher fiber diet by adding about 5 grams more fiber each week. Keep adding fiber each week until you reach 25 to 35 grams of fiber daily. Now isn't that sweet music to your ears?

Clean Those Beans: Check for small stones or debris before soaking or cooking beans and other legumes. Rinse thoroughly in a strainer under cold running water and discard any that are shriveled or discolored.

Time to Soak: Soaking dried beans and other legumes helps shortens the cooking time. Soaking also helps remove the indigestible sugars that cause gastric distress. I find it helpful to soak double or triple the amount so that I will have soaked beans ready when I need them. Lentils don't usually require soaking—rinsing is enough.

Overnight Soaking Method: Rinse dried beans. Soak overnight on the counter in triple the amount of cold water. In hot weather, it's best to soak them in the refrigerator. Discard any beans that are floating. Drain and rinse well. Beans will double in volume. Store them in the refrigerator for up to 2 days.

Quick Soak Method: Rinse dried beans. Place in a saucepan and cover with triple the amount of cold water. Bring to a boil and cook for 5 minutes. Remove from heat and let stand for 1 hour. Discard any beans that are floating. Drain and rinse well.

Freeze with Ease: Place soaked beans in re-sealable bags and freeze for up to 6 months—no need to cook them first. When needed, add them to boiling water, soups, or casseroles: no thawing required. Most of the expansion takes place during soaking, not cooking. One cup dried beans yields two cups when soaked.

Cook It Right: Cook soaked beans in triple the amount of fresh cold water (not the soaking water). Bring to a boil, then cover and simmer until tender. See Cooking Chart (page 150) for times. If beans are very old or dry, they can take longer to cook. To add flavor and help reduce gas, add 2 or 3 cloves garlic, a slice of fresh ginger, or a 3-inch piece of kombu (sea kelp).

Love Me Tender: Don't add salt or acidic ingredients such as lemon juice or vinegar until near the end of cooking as they prevent the beans from softening. When beans are almost tender, add these ingredients and cook 10 to 15 minutes longer. Lima beans are the exception—always cook them in salted water or they will become mushy.

Ready or Not? Beans are ready when you can crush them between your tongue and the roof of your mouth. For salads, cook them until just firm or they'll be too mushy. Check for doneness after the minimum suggested cooking time.

Frozen Assets: When you cook up a batch of beans, cook double or triple the quantity. Drain well. Freeze in re-sealable freezer bags. When needed, empty the frozen beans into your favorite soup or casserole: no thawing required. Cook for a few minutes, until just heated through.

Store It Right: Dried beans keep in a cool dry place in a tightly sealed container for up to a year. Cooked beans keep in the refrigerator for 3 to 4 days or can be frozen for 6 months.

Salt Alert! To reduce the sodium in canned beans and legumes by half, place them in a colander and rinse thoroughly under cold running water. Drain well. Choose low-sodium brands. Rinsing canned beans also helps reduce gas.

make it meatless

COOKING CHART FOR LEGUMES
(Use 3 cups unsalted water for each cup of presoaked beans. Yields are for 1 cup dried beans or legumes.)

BEANS AND LEGUMES	COOKING TIME	YIELD
Aduki beans	1 to 1½ hours	2 cups
Black (turtle) beans	1½ to 2 hours	2 cups
Black-eyed peas	1 to 1½ hours	2¼ cups
Cannellini (white kidney beans)	1 to 1½ hours	2 cups
Chickpeas (garbanzo beans)	2 to 3 hours	2½ cups
Cranberry (romano) beans	1½ to 2 hours	2¼ cups
Fava beans	1½ to 2 hours	2 cups
Flageolets	1 to 1½ hours	2 cups
Great Northern beans	1 to 1½ hours	2¼ cups
Kidney beans	1½ to 2 hours	2 cups
Lentils (don't presoak)	30 to 45 minutes	2 cups
Lima beans (cook with salt to keep skins from slipping off)	¾ to 1½ hours	2 cups
Navy or pea beans (white beans)	1½ to 2 hours	2 cups
Pinto beans	1½ to 2 hours	2¼ cups
Soybeans	3 to 4 hours	2¼ cups
Split peas (green/yellow—don't presoak)	45 minutes	2 cups

SAY CHEESE

Calci-Yum! Calcium is essential for strong bones and teeth, muscle contraction, blood clotting, nerve impulse transmission, regulating heartbeat, and fluid balance in cells. Dairy sources of calcium include milk, cheeses, and yogurt. Adults need between 1000 and 1300 mg of calcium in their daily diet.

Got Milk? An 8 oz glass of milk contains 300 mg of calcium. Skim, 1%, and 2% milk contain the same amount of calcium as whole milk. Lactose-free milk and sour cream are available for those who are lactose-intolerant. Yogurt with live cultures is usually tolerated by those who are lactose-intolerant.

D-Licious! Vitamin D is essential for calcium absorption. Milk contains vitamin D and many other foods are now fortified with it. Vitamin D can also be found in limited amounts in salmon, sardines, herring, egg yolks, margarine, fortified cereal, fortified orange juice, almonds, beans, broccoli, figs, and breads.

En-light-ening News: Our bodies manufacture vitamin D when our skin is exposed to sunlight without sunscreen. The amount of sunlight you need depends on age, gender, time of day, season, where you live, and how easily you burn. Aim for 10 to 15 minutes a day of direct sun several times a week, before 10 am or in late afternoon, when the sun is less damaging to your skin. (Wear sunscreen the rest of the time.) If you live in the northern US or Canada, your skin will not make vitamin D during winter when sunlight is weak. However your skin will actually store enough vitamin D to last the winter months. So take a walk in the sunshine, strengthen your bones and burn some calories.

D-Ficient? In Canada and the USA, the current recommended daily allowance for vitamin D for adults under 50 is 200 international units (IU), 400 IU for those age 50–70, and 600 IU for people over 70. Most scientists think women need significantly more—at least 1,000 IU a day. High risk groups such as the elderly (who often don't get adequate sun) probably require closer to 4,000 IU, which is well above the safe upper limit of 2,000 IU presently recommended. Vitamin D intake is currently under review and new recommendations will likely be forthcoming. Consider a multi-vitamin with vitamin D. Consult a health professional for more specific information.

Calcium Without Bothering the Cow: Many people are allergic to dairy products, while others may be lactose intolerant and cannot digest the milk sugar. Calcium is found in leafy dark green vegetables (cooked broccoli, collards, kale, bok choy), beans, and legumes (chickpeas, black beans, kidney beans), soy products (fortified soymilk, tofu processed with calcium), nuts and seeds (almonds, peanuts, walnuts, hazelnuts), figs, raisins, oranges, fortified orange juice, and seaweed. Eat canned salmon and sardines with the bones.

Boning Up: In Canada, contact the Osteoporosis Society of Canada at www.osteoporosis.ca. In the US, contact the National Osteoporosis Foundation at www.nof.org.

Cheese Please! Choose lower-fat or skim cheeses when possible. Compare labels for fat and calorie content. Lower fat cheeses are sometimes rubbery, so you may have to experiment and try different brands.

Light Is Right! Light cream cheese performs well in most recipes. Use small amounts of strong cheeses, such as Parmesan or strong cheddar, rather than mild cheeses, for maximum flavor and minimum calories. One tablespoon of grated Parmesan contains just 20 calories, so a little goes a long "weigh!"

A-peeling: A quick way to grate a small amount of cheese is to use a vegetable peeler. Cheese will grate more easily if it's chilled.

How Much Is Enough? One quarter pound of cheese (4 oz/125 g) yields 1 cup when grated.

Grate Idea! A food processor grates cheese quickly. Use medium pressure on the pusher when putting the cheese through the feed tube while grating/shredding. Cheese should be chilled for easier grating.

It's in the Bag! Grate or shred cheese and freeze it in heavy-duty re-sealable plastic bags. It can be frozen for 2 to 3 months. Press out excess air to prevent ice crystals from forming. No need to defrost it before using it in recipes. If cheese is lumpy and frozen into a clump, give it a few bangs on the counter to break it up.

So Dairy Good: Yogurt Cheese (page 178) and Homemade Cottage Cheese (page 177) make excellent alternatives to cream cheese. You can flavor either one with herbs and use as a spread in sandwiches and wraps. Or use in desserts such as cheesecakes and parfaits.

🍎 VEGETARIAN CHOLENT

A big thank you goes to American cookbook author Susie Fishbein for allowing me to use this delicious recipe from her bestselling cookbook, *Kosher by Design*. It's from a New Yorker friend of Susie's who is famous in his Upper West Side neighborhood for this vegetarian version of cholent. I've adapted his recipe slightly to lower its glycemic index by using sweet potatoes, and reduced the salt by one-third. If you make this heart-healthy dish, you'll be famous in your neighborhood, too!

1/2 cup dried red kidney beans
1/2 cup dried white navy beans
1 cup dried brown lentils
6 cups water
2 large sweet potatoes, peeled and
   cut in chunks (about 4 cups)
2 medium potatoes, peeled and
   cut in chunks (about 2 cups)
1 large or 2 medium onions, chopped
3 to 4 cloves garlic (about 1 Tbsp minced)
3 carrots, peeled and cut in chunks
   (or 1 1/2 cups baby carrots)
8 cups water (approximately)
1 cup old-fashioned oats
   (not the quick-cooking or 1-minute type)
1/2 cup pearl barley, rinsed and drained
1 Tbsp Kosher or coarse salt (or to taste)

1. Place the kidney beans, navy beans, and lentils in a large pot. Cover with 6 cups of water and bring to a boil; cover the pot and continue boiling for 5 minutes. Turn the heat off and let the bean mixture sit, covered, for 1 hour. When done, rinse thoroughly and drain.

2. Place the bean mixture in a 6-quart slow cooker that has been sprayed with cooking

spray. Add the sweet potatoes, potatoes, onions, garlic, and carrots. Pour in enough water to come to the top of the pot. Cover and cook on the high setting for 1 hour.

3. After 1 hour, remove the lid and add the oats; mix well. Add the barley, using a wooden spoon to push it just below the surface but not all the way to the bottom. If necessary, add more water so that it fills the slow cooker to the top. Sprinkle with salt. Cover, turn the heat to low, and cook overnight. Serve for Shabbat lunch, hot from the pot.

Yield: 10 servings (about 20 to 24 cups). Keeps for up to 2 days in the refrigerator. (Instead of freezing the leftovers, turn them into soup. See Chef's Secrets.)

264 calories per serving, 52.8 g carbohydrate, 13.1 g fiber, 13 g protein, 1.3 g fat (0.2 g saturated), 0 mg cholesterol, 566 mg sodium, 815 mg potassium, 10 mg iron, 69 mg calcium

Chef's Secrets
• It's in the Bag! Liners, which save on clean-up, are available to fit slow cookers in a variety of sizes. For a 6-quart slow cooker, use a 16- × 17½-inch liner or use a heatproof cooking bag (made by Reynolds). Once you've lined the slow cooker, fill with the ingredients and close the bag or liner. Make several slits in the top of the bag or liner to allow steam to escape. Don't add any water to the bottom of the slow cooker or your cooking bag or liner will bob up and down.

• Leftovers? Turn your leftover cholent into a scrumptious soup. Spray a large saucepan with cooking spray. Add leftover cholent and an equal amount of vegetable broth; mix well. Slowly simmer on medium-low

heat for 10 to 15 minutes, stirring occasionally. Freezes well for up to 3 months.

Nutrition Note
• This cholent is packed with folate, fiber, vitamins, minerals, and flavor. It's bean cuisine at its best.

SWEET POTATO, CAULIFLOWER AND BEAN TAGINE

This hearty and colorful vegetable stew is based on a recipe from Dianne Gold of Toronto. Although this Moroccan-style dish is usually served over couscous, it's also scrumptious over quinoa, barley, or wheat berries.

3 medium sweet potatoes
4 cups bite-sized cauliflower florets
2 Tbsp olive oil
2 medium onions, chopped
1 red or green pepper, seeded
   and chopped
3 cloves garlic (about 1 Tbsp minced)
1 can (19 oz/540 mL) white kidney beans,
   drained and rinsed
1 tsp salt (or to taste)
¼ tsp freshly ground black pepper
1 tsp ground cumin
1 tsp paprika
½ tsp ground cinnamon
¼ tsp cayenne pepper (or to taste)
3 cups tomato juice
2 cups frozen green peas (optional)
Minced fresh cilantro, for garnish

1. Pierce the sweet potatoes in several places with a sharp knife. Microwave, uncovered, on high for 8 to 10 minutes or until done but still firm. Cool slightly, then peel and cut into 1-inch chunks.

2. Rinse the cauliflower florets well but don't dry. Microwave in a covered casserole for 3 minutes on high or until nearly tender.

3. Heat the oil in a large pot on medium heat. Add the onions, red pepper, and garlic. Sauté for 2 to 3 minutes or until softened. Add the beans, reserved sweet potatoes, and cauliflower. Cook for 2 to 3 minutes longer, stirring often. Add the seasonings and tomato juice. Cover and simmer for 15 to 20 minutes or until the vegetables are tender. Stir in the frozen peas, if using. Adjust the seasonings and garnish with the minced cilantro before serving.

Yield: 10 servings of 1 cup each. Keeps for up to 3 to 4 days in the refrigerator; reheats well. Don't freeze: the vegetables will become mushy if frozen.

156 calories per serving, 27.4 g carbohydrate, 3.2 g fiber, 6 g protein, 3.2 g fat (0.5 g saturated), 0 mg cholesterol, 611 mg sodium, 694 mg potassium, 3 mg iron, 77 mg calcium

Variations
• Substitute broccoflower florets for the cauliflower, and chickpeas for the kidney beans. Instead of tomato juice, use vegetable juice or vegetable broth.

• To boost the protein content, add 2 cups cubed extra-firm tofu, or cubed leftover cooked chicken, during the last few minutes of cooking.

● LENTIL VEGETABLE MEDLEY

This nutritious dish is jam-packed with fiber and flavor. Delicious over bulgar, quinoa, rotini or rice, it makes a heart-healthy vegetarian main dish or side dish. Don't be turned off by the long list of ingredients. Just turn on your processor and give it a whirl, girl!

3 cloves garlic (about 1 Tbsp minced)
2 medium onions, cut in chunks
2 stalks celery, cut in chunks
3 medium carrots, cut in chunks
1 1/2 cups mushrooms
2 Tbsp olive oil
1 can (28 oz/796 mL) tomatoes
   (don't drain)
1 1/2 cups water
2 cups brown or green lentils,
   drained and rinsed
1 bay leaf
1 tsp Italian seasoning (or a mixture of
   oregano, basil, and thyme)
Salt and freshly ground black pepper
1 Tbsp lemon juice (preferably fresh)
2 Tbsp maple syrup or honey
1/4 cup minced fresh parsley

1. In a food processor fitted with the steel blade, process the garlic, onions, and celery until chopped, using quick on/off pulses. Transfer the chopped mixture to a bowl. Add the carrots and mushrooms to the food processor and repeat the process, transferring the chopped carrots and mushrooms to the bowl with the rest of the chopped vegetables.

2. In a large pot, heat the oil on medium heat. Add the chopped vegetables and sauté for about 6 to 8 minutes or until tender, stirring occasionally.

3. Add the tomatoes, water, lentils, bay leaf, and Italian seasoning; bring to a boil. Reduce heat to low, partly cover, and simmer for about 1 hour or until the lentils are tender, stirring occasionally. Add a little extra water if needed.

4. Add the salt, pepper, lemon juice, and maple syrup; simmer for 10 minutes longer. Remove the bay leaf, add the parsley, and serve.

Yield: 9 servings of 1 cup each. Tastes even better the next day. Keeps for up to 3 to 4 days in the refrigerator; reheats well. Freezes well for up to 3 months.

232 calories per serving, 39.7 g carbohydrate, 12.1 g fiber, 13 g protein, 3.8 g fat (0.5 g saturated), 0 mg cholesterol, 246 mg sodium, 840 mg potassium, 6 mg iron, 85 mg calcium

Variation

• Leftovers? Transform them into soup. In a saucepan, combine 4 cups of the cooked lentil mixture with 3 cups vegetable broth. Season with salt and pepper and bring to a boil. Reduce heat to low and simmer, partly covered, for 10 minutes. Makes 6 servings.

● WINTER VEGETABLE STEW

My cousin Carol Teichman, of Toronto, shared this recipe for her hearty vegetable stew, and I've modified it slightly to speed up the preparation. Don't stew over the long list of ingredients—this comes together very quickly. Chop the vegetables in batches in your food processor, and add them to the pot as they are ready. This scrumptious stew is sure to warm you up on a cold winter day.

2 Tbsp olive or canola oil
2 large onions, chopped
2 stalks celery, chopped
2 cloves garlic (about 2 tsp minced)
2 medium carrots, chopped
   (or 12 baby carrots)

2 parsnips, peeled and chopped
2 medium potatoes, cut into 1-inch cubes, or 6 small new potatoes
2 cups green beans, trimmed and sliced into 1-inch pieces
1 red pepper, seeded and coarsely chopped
2 cups sliced mushrooms
1 to 2 Tbsp chopped fresh dillweed or 1 tsp dried
1 tsp dried oregano
2 1/2 cups vegetable broth
1 Tbsp Dijon mustard
1 Tbsp maple syrup
Salt and freshly ground black pepper

make it meatless

1. Heat the oil in a large, heavy-bottomed pot over medium heat. Add the onions and celery, and sauté for 6 to 8 minutes or until golden.

2. Stir in the garlic, carrots, parsnips, potatoes, and green beans; mix well. Cook for 2 to 3 minutes. Add the red pepper and mushrooms and cook for 2 minutes before adding the dillweed, oregano, and broth; bring to a boil.

3. Reduce heat to low and stir in the mustard and maple syrup. Simmer for 10 to 12 minutes or until the potatoes are just tender. Season with salt and pepper to taste.

Yield: 6 servings. Keeps for up to 2 to 3 days in the refrigerator; reheats well. Don't freeze.

204 calories per serving, 37.4 g carbohydrate, 6.8 g fiber, 4 g protein, 5.5 g fat (0.7 g saturated), 0 mg cholesterol, 501 mg sodium, 712 mg potassium, 2 mg iron, 84 mg calcium

Nutrition Notes

• For additional protein, add 1 to 2 cups of black, navy, or red kidney beans (canned are fine, but drain and rinse well) in Step 2, along with the vegetables. Or add 1 cup diced, extra-firm tofu.

• For another protein boost, serve with an assortment of low-fat cheeses such as cheddar, Swiss, or havarti, and pumpernickel bread.

• Potatoes have a high glycemic index, so using smaller new potatoes are a better choice when you have them on hand—or substitute with sweet potatoes, which have a lower glycemic index than regular potatoes.

● KASHA CHILI

Wholegrain kasha provides a meaty texture to this meatless chili, which only takes 30 minutes to prepare and cook. Steaming hot, fiber-packed kasha chili is sure to take the chill out and warm you up on a cold winter day.

1 can (28 oz/796 mL) diced
   or stewed tomatoes
3½ cups vegetable broth
1 can (19 oz/540 mL) black
   or kidney beans, drained and rinsed
1 large onion, chopped
1 red bell or green pepper, chopped
1 cup sliced mushrooms
2 cloves garlic (about 2 tsp minced)
Salt and freshly ground black pepper
1 Tbsp chili powder (or to taste)
1 Tbsp unsweetened cocoa powder
1 tsp each paprika, cumin, and oregano
¾ cup wholegrain
   or medium-grain kasha (buckwheat groats)

1. In a large pot, combine all the ingredients except the kasha and mix well; bring to a boil. Reduce heat to low and simmer, uncovered, for 10 minutes.

2. Stir in the kasha. Cover and simmer for 15 minutes longer or until the kasha is tender, stirring occasionally. If the chili is too thick, thin with a little water. Serve immediately.

Yield: About 8 cups. Keeps for up to 3 to 4 days in the refrigerator; reheats well. Freezes well for up to 3 months.

141 calories per cup, 31.3 g carbohydrate, 7.8 g fiber, 6 g protein, 1.1 g fat (0.2 g saturated), 0 mg cholesterol, 601 mg sodium, 345 mg potassium, 2 mg iron, 63 mg calcium

Variation

• Substitute ½ cup uncooked green or brown lentils for the beans. In Step 1, increase the cooking time to 20 minutes before adding the kasha.

Chef's Secrets

• Can-Do: The can from the tomatoes holds 3½ cups, so measure the vegetable broth right in the empty can.

• No Yolk-ing! You don't need an egg to coat the kasha in this recipe. The thin seed coating will shield each kernel while it cooks, keeping it separate and fluffy.

Nutrition Notes

• Sodium Alert! If sodium is a concern, choose an organic brand of canned black beans, which usually contains anywhere from 15 to 140 mg of sodium per serving compared to 400 to 480 mg found in

make it
meatless

regular brands of canned beans. Also, choose low-sodium brands of canned tomatoes and vegetable broth.

• See the Nutrition Notes on page 327 for more info on kasha.

⏺ VEGETARIAN SHEPHERD'S PIE

The shepherd will be out of work if too many people discover this meatless version of shepherd's pie! This fiber-packed dish looks and tastes as if it was made with meat. Can you pull the wool over everyone's eyes?

Topping:

5 to 6 medium Yukon Gold potatoes, well-scrubbed (peeling is optional)
1/2 cup vegetable broth or soymilk
2 tsp extra virgin olive oil
2 Tbsp low-fat or imitation sour cream
Salt and freshly ground black pepper
Paprika, for garnish

Filling:

1 Tbsp olive oil
1 medium onion, chopped
1 red pepper, seeded and chopped
2 cups chopped mushrooms, or chopped zucchini
2 cloves garlic (about 2 tsp minced)
2 pkg (12 oz/340 g each) vegetarian ground beef substitute
1/3 cup tomato or barbecue sauce
1 cup corn kernels (frozen or canned)

1. In a medium saucepan, add the potatoes along with enough water to cover by 1 inch. Bring to a boil and continue boiling for about 25 minutes or until the potatoes are tender. Drain the potatoes well in a strainer, then return them to the pan and dry over medium heat for 1 minute. Transfer the dried potatoes to a medium bowl and mash well. Add the broth, olive oil, sour cream, salt, and pepper to the mashed potatoes; mix well and set aside.

2. Heat the oil in a large, deep nonstick skillet on medium high. Add the onion, red pepper, mushrooms, and garlic; sauté for 5 minutes or until the onion is soft and the garlic is golden. Stir in the ground beef substitute and tomato sauce. Cook, uncovered, for 3 or 4 minutes on medium high, until heated through.

3. Remove the mixture from the skillet and transfer it to a sprayed, 2-quart rectangular casserole dish. Spread evenly. Add a layer of corn kernels, then top with a layer of the reserved potato mixture. Sprinkle with paprika. (If desired, the recipe can be assembled in advance up to this point and refrigerated overnight.)

4. Bake, uncovered, in a preheated 350°F oven for 25 to 35 minutes or until the layers are heated through and the top is golden.

Yield: 6 servings. Keeps for up to 2 to 3 days in the refrigerator; reheats well. Freezes well for up to 2 months.

332 calories per serving, 46.7 g carbohydrate, 10.7 g fiber, 25 g protein, 4.9 g fat (0.9 g saturated), 2 mg cholesterol, 693 mg sodium, 1135 mg potassium, 7 mg iron, 113 mg calcium

Variation
• Instead of mashed potatoes, substitute with the topping used in Sweet Potato Shepherd's Pie (page 194).

make it meatless

Nutrition Note
• Salt Alert! If you have sodium concerns, choose a low-sodium brand of vegetable broth and tomato sauce—or make your own. Use frozen corn kernels instead of canned.

ALMOST MEAT LASAGNA

You'll have no "beefs" when you serve this delicious, fiber-packed dish. My friend Bev Binder of Winnipeg makes a marvelous meatless lasagna using ground beef substitute—it looks and tastes like it's made with meat. This adapted version is sure to please everyone, vegetarian or not.

9 or 10 lasagna noodles
  (preferably whole wheat)
1 to 2 Tbsp olive oil
1 medium onion, chopped
1 red pepper, seeded and chopped
1½ cups chopped mushrooms
2 cloves garlic (about 2 tsp minced)
1 pkg (12 oz/340 g) vegetarian
  ground beef substitute
3 cups chunky tomato sauce
1 tsp dried basil
½ tsp dried oregano
3 cups light ricotta cheese
1 pkg (10 oz/300 g) frozen chopped
  spinach, thawed and squeezed dry
1¼ cups grated low-fat mozzarella cheese

1. Cook the lasagna noodles according to package directions, but undercook them slightly so they are al dente, not too soft. Drain well and lay flat on a clean towel.

2. Meanwhile, heat the oil in a large, deep nonstick skillet on medium high heat. Add the onion, red pepper, mushrooms, and garlic and sauté for 5 minutes or until golden. Stir in the ground beef substitute, tomato sauce, basil, and oregano. Continue cooking, uncovered, on medium-high heat for 5 minutes or until the mixture is heated through, stirring occasionally. (If desired, the sauce can be prepared in advance, up to this point, and stored in the refrigerator overnight.)

3. In a large mixing bowl and using an electric mixer, or in a food processor fitted with the steel blade, combine the ricotta cheese and spinach; mix or process well.

4. Spray a 9- × 13-inch glass baking dish with cooking spray. Evenly spread about 1½ cups sauce in the bottom of the baking dish. Place 3 of the cooked lasagna noodles on top of the sauce and spread half the ricotta cheese mixture on top. Repeat with another layer of sauce, noodles, and ricotta. Top with the last 3 cooked lasagna noodles, sauce, and mozzarella. You'll have 3 layers of sauce and noodles, 2 layers of ricotta cheese, and a topping of mozzarella cheese. (If desired, the lasagna can be prepared in advance up to this point, covered, and refrigerated overnight.)

5. Bake, uncovered, in a preheated 375°F oven for 30 to 40 minutes or until bubbly and golden. Let stand for 10 minutes for easier slicing.

Yield: 8 to 10 servings. Keeps for up to 2 to 3 days; reheats well. Freezes well for up to 3 months.

389 calories per serving, 38.1 g carbohydrate, 9.3 g fiber, 30 g protein, 13.0 g fat (6.6 g saturated), 40 mg cholesterol, 701 mg sodium, 586 mg potassium, 5 mg iron, 468 mg calcium

Chef's Secrets

• Almost Meat Sauce: Prepare the sauce as directed in Step 2 and serve it over your favorite pasta.

• Where's the Beef? Soy meat crumbles (which are a ground beef substitute) make a great alternative to ground meat. (One soy brand, Yves Veggie Ground Round, is Kosher and dairy-free.) Soy is an excellent source of protein and fiber, is low in fat, and is cholesterol-free. Use soy ground beef substitutes in pasta sauces, stuffed peppers, casseroles, or chili. Do note, however, that some people may experience "gastric distress"—oy, that soy!

• Soy Good: Firm silken tofu can be used instead of ricotta cheese. Omit the mozzarella cheese if you want to make a dairy-free lasagna.

● FAKE 'N BAKE TOFU FINGERS

These fake chicken fingers are finger-lickin' good and they're kid-friendly too. (What a sneaky way to get your family to eat tofu!) They definitely won't say "to-phooey" once they taste them.

1¹/2 cups Special K or corn flakes
¹/3 cup wheat germ
¹/3 cup sesame seeds
¹/2 tsp salt (or to taste)
¹/8 tsp freshly ground black pepper
¹/4 tsp garlic powder
¹/2 tsp Italian seasoning
1 lb (500 g) extra-firm tofu
²/3 cup bottled barbecue sauce or duck sauce

1. Preheat the oven to 400°F. Line a large baking sheet with parchment paper or sprayed foil.

2. Combine the cereal, wheat germ, sesame seeds, and seasonings in a food processor fitted with the steel blade; process for 6 to 8 seconds to make coarse crumbs. Transfer to a wide, shallow bowl.

3. Slice the tofu into 1-inch slices, then cut each slice into strips about 1 inch wide. You should have about 20 strips. Pat the strips dry with paper towels. Dip each strip in a bowl of barbecue sauce and then in the crumb mixture. Arrange the breaded strips in a single layer on the prepared baking sheet. (If desired, the tofu strips can be prepared in advance up to this point and refrigerated for several hours or overnight.)

4. Bake, uncovered, for 7 to 8 minutes. Turn over the strips and bake for 7 to 8 minutes longer or until crisp and golden. (Or fry them in a little oil in a nonstick skillet for 3 or 4 minutes per side until golden.)

Yield: 20 tofu fingers. Keeps for up to 2 to 3 days in the refrigerator; reheats well. Freezing is not recommended.

56 calories each, 4.4 g carbohydrate, 0.7 g fiber, 4 g protein, 2.8 g fat (0.2 g saturated), 0 mg cholesterol, 149 mg sodium, 69 mg potassium, 1 mg iron, 51 mg calcium

Fake 'N Bake Fish Fingers
Substitute 1 lb (500 g) firm white fish fillets such as sole, tilapia, haddock, for the tofu. Total baking time will be 10 to 12 minutes. One fish finger contains 54 calories, 4.0 g carbohydrate, 0.6 g fiber, 6 g protein, and 1.7 g fat (0.1 g saturated).

make it
meatless

Variations

• Instead of cereal crumbs, use ¹/₂ cup dried breadcrumbs or cracker crumbs (preferably wholegrain). Instead of sesame seeds, use pumpkin seeds. You can also add 3 Tbsp finely chopped almonds or pecans to the crumb mixture.

Chef's Secret

• Chilling News: Refrigerate or freeze wheat germ or it may develop a musty flavor.

make it meatless

⚫ TERIYAKI TOFU

The marvelous marinade in this recipe boosts the flavor and doubles as a scrumptious sauce for the tofu.

Teriyaki Marinade (page 112)
1 lb (500 g) extra-firm tofu such as nigari
¹/₄ cup sesame seeds
1 Tbsp canola oil
2 tsp cornstarch dissolved in
   2 Tbsp orange juice (preferably fresh)

1. Prepare the marinade as directed.

2. Cut tofu into ¹/₂-inch-thick slices, then cut each slice in half on the diagonal to make triangles. Pat the tofu triangles dry with paper towels. Place the tofu in a shallow casserole, add the marinade, and turn the triangles to make sure both sides are well coated. Sprinkle both sides with sesame seeds and set aside to marinate for 20 to 30 minutes.

3. Heat oil in a large nonstick skillet over medium heat. Remove the tofu from the casserole dish and drain; reserve the marinade. Add the tofu to the hot skillet and cook for 3 to 4 minutes per side or until crisp and nicely browned.

4. Meanwhile, place the reserved marinade in a small saucepan and bring to a boil. Stir the cornstarch-juice mixture into the boiling marinade and cook, stirring constantly for 2 minutes or until the liquid is smooth and thick. Spoon the heated sauce over the tofu and serve.

Yield: 4 servings. Keeps for up to 3 or 4 days in the refrigerator. Reheats well in the microwave. Don't freeze.

261 calories per serving, 16.9 g carbohydrate, 1.6 g fiber, 14 g protein, 16.7 g fat (1.2 g saturated), 0 mg cholesterol, 561 mg sodium, 270 mg potassium, 3 mg iron, 244 mg calcium

Variations

• Instead of Teriyaki Marinade, use the Asian Marinade (page 112) or use bottled sauce. Instead of cutting the tofu in triangles, cut it in rectangles.

Grilled Teriyaki Tofu

Preheat the barbecue or electric grill. Marinate the drained tofu as directed. Grill 4 minutes per side over indirect heat. If using a two-sided electric contact grill, the total cooking time will be 4 to 5 minutes.

Chef's Secrets

• Store It Right: Once the tofu package has been opened, cover the unused tofu with water and refrigerate for up to a week, changing the water daily. Cooked tofu shouldn't be stored in water.

• Frozen Assets: To freeze tofu, slice it 1/2-inch thick and wrap each slice in plastic wrap. Place the tofu packages in an airtight container. Tofu can be frozen for about 3 months. If frozen, defrost at room temperature. (Freezing tofu will change the texture.) Crumble the thawed tofu and use it as a meat substitute in chili, lasagna, stews, or spaghetti sauce.

TOFU "EGG" SALAD

This is "tofu-rrific!" Excellent for sandwiches, wraps, and salads. It has the taste of chopped egg salad, minus the cholesterol.

1 pkg (10 oz/350 g) extra-firm tofu
3 green onions, cut in chunks
1 stalk celery, cut in chunks
2 Tbsp fresh dillweed
1/4 cup light mayonnaise
1/2 tsp salt
1/4 tsp freshly ground black pepper

1. Wrap the tofu in paper towels to absorb the excess moisture. Let stand for 5 minutes, then unwrap and cut into chunks.

2. Place the onions, celery, and dillweed in a food processor fitted with the steel blade; process until minced, about 8 to 10 seconds. Add the tofu and process with quick on/off pulses or until coarsely chopped. Add the mayonnaise, salt, and pepper; process briefly to combine.

3. Transfer to a storage container, cover, and refrigerate until using.

Yield: About 2 1/4 cups (4 servings). Keeps for up to 2 to 3 days in the refrigerator. Don't freeze.

138 calories per serving, 4.8 g carbohydrate, 1.0 g fiber, 9 g protein, 10.1 g fat (1.2 g saturated), 5 mg cholesterol, 428 mg sodium, 203 mg potassium, 2 mg iron, 173 mg calcium

Variations

• For a flavor boost, add 1 tsp Dijon mustard and 1/2 cup chopped red pepper.

• Instead of mayonnaise, use Low-Calorie Caesar Dressing (store-bought or homemade, page 275).

PASTA PRIMAVERA

This scrumptious, vegetable-packed dish is also packed with nutrients, including calcium, folate, and fiber. Use this recipe as a springboard for your favorite vegetables. Spring forward to good health!

1 pkg (12 oz/375 g) whole wheat pasta (such as rotini, penne, bow ties, or macaroni)
2 Tbsp olive oil
1 red onion, halved and thinly sliced
1 red pepper, halved, seeded and thinly sliced
3 cloves garlic (about 1 Tbsp minced)
1 medium zucchini, halved and thinly sliced
1 pound (500 g) thin asparagus, trimmed and cut in 1-inch pieces
6 plum tomatoes, coarsely chopped
2 tsp salt (or to taste)
1/4 tsp freshly ground black pepper
4 cups lightly packed fresh baby spinach
1/2 cup fresh chopped basil
6 Tbsp grated Parmesan cheese

1. Bring a large pot of salted water to a boil 15 to 20 minutes before cooking the pasta.

make it
meatless

2. Meanwhile, heat the oil in a large non-stick wok or deep skillet over medium. Add the onion, pepper, and garlic; sauté for 3 to 4 minutes or until tender-crisp. Add the zucchini, asparagus, and tomatoes, and mix well. Stir in the salt and pepper.

3. Reduce heat to low and simmer, uncovered, for 10 to 15 minutes, stirring occasionally. Stir in the spinach and fresh basil, and cook for 2 minutes longer. (If desired, the sauce can be prepared up to a day in advance and refrigerated overnight. Reheat it just before serving.)

4. While the sauce is simmering, cook the pasta in boiling water according to package directions or until al dente. Ladle out about ¹/₂ cup of cooking liquid and set aside. Drain the pasta.

5. Stir ¹/₃ to ¹/₂ cup of the reserved cooking liquid into the sauce. Divide the pasta among 6 bowls and top with the sauce. Sprinkle with cheese and serve immediately.

Yield: 6 servings. Keeps for up to 2 days in the refrigerator. Reheats well in the microwave. Don't freeze.

350 calories per serving, 59.1 g carbohydrate, 9.5 g fiber, 13 g protein, 8 g fat (1.6 g saturated), 4 mg cholesterol, 516 mg sodium, 699 mg potassium, 3 mg iron, 129 mg calcium

Variations
• Add 2 cups sliced mushrooms to the onions and bell peppers; use yellow, orange or purple bell peppers as well as red.

• Instead of asparagus, use green beans or snow peas. Sun-dried tomatoes and/or roasted red peppers also make a tasty addition.

• Use 1 tsp each of dried oregano and thyme instead of basil, or substitute with Italian seasoning.

• Instead of Parmesan cheese, top the pasta with ¹/₂ to 1 cup crumbled goat cheese or grated low-fat mozzarella cheese.

• Omit the Parmesan cheese. Add an 8 oz (250 g) package of smoked salmon, coarsely chopped, along with the spinach. Imitation flaked crabmeat is also an excellent option.

PENNE PESTO WITH TUNA AND VEGGIES

Presto—penne pesto! This versatile pasta dish is perfect when you're rushed for time. Pasta and veggies are cooked in the same pot and then the pot is used to combine all the ingredients, saving on clean-up.

1 pkg (16 oz/500 g) penne pasta
    (preferably whole wheat)
3 cups frozen mixed vegetables
¹/₃ cup Power Pesto (page 109)
    or store-bought pesto
2 cans (6 oz/170 g each) flaked,
    water-packed tuna, well-drained
Salt and freshly ground black pepper
1 cup grated low-fat mozzarella cheese

1. Preheat the oven to 375°F. Spray a 9- × 13-inch glass baking dish with cooking spray.

2. Bring a large pot of salted water to a boil. Add the pasta and cook for 7 to 8 minutes. Add the frozen vegetables and cook for 2 to 3 minutes longer or until the pasta is al dente.

3. Drain the pasta and vegetables and return to the pot. Stir in the pesto, tuna, salt, and pepper; mix well.

make it meatless

4. Spread the pasta-tuna mixture evenly in the prepared baking dish. Sprinkle evenly with cheese. (If desired, the dish can be prepared up to this point and refrigerated up to 24 hours.)

5. Bake, uncovered, for 20 to 25 minutes or until golden and piping hot.

Yield: 8 servings. Keeps for up to 2 to 3 days in the refrigerator; reheats well. Freezes well for up to 2 months.

384 calories per serving, 46.2 g carbohydrate, 6.4 g fiber, 32 g protein, 7.4 g fat (2.0 g saturated), 33 mg cholesterol, 412 mg sodium, 495 mg potassium, 3 mg iron, 156 mg calcium

Variations
• Using Your Noodle: Try different shapes and colors of pasta, such as rotini, macaroni, or bow ties and different combinations of frozen mixed vegetables such as broccoli, cauliflower, green beans, carrots, or green peas. Experiment with pasta made from different grains such as udon, soba, rice sticks, or cellophane noodles. It will taste different every time.

• Switch to Salmon: Although one can (6 oz/170 g) of drained tuna measures about 2/3 cup and one can (7½ oz/213 g) of drained salmon measures about 1 cup, using salmon instead of tuna won't affect the recipe.

• Using Your Bean: Instead of tuna or salmon, add 1 can (19 oz/540mL) kidney beans, drained and rinsed. Omit the cheese, if you want to lower the calorie, sodium, and fat content.

• The Choice Is Yours: Store-bought pesto is convenient but is higher in calories, fat, and sodium. Try Traditional Pesto (page 110) or Sun-Dried Tomato Pesto (page 109) in this recipe.

Chef's Secret
• Frozen Assets: Instead of a large baking dish, divide the mixture and spread evenly in individual foil containers that have been sprayed with cooking spray. Sprinkle with cheese. Wrap well and freeze for a future meal. There's no need to thaw before using; just bake, covered, for 15 minutes, then uncover and bake for 10 minutes more or until piping hot.

Nutrition Notes
• GI Go! Pasta has a lower glycemic index than bread because the starch is in a denser form and is digested more slowly. If pasta is cooked al dente, it has an even lower glycemic index. "Al dente" means that pasta is just cooked but still firm, not too soft or over-cooked.

• Turn Up the Volume: By adding vegetables and tuna to the pasta, you increase the portion size and lower the glycemic index.

⚫ SPAGHETTI SQUASH WITH ROASTED VEGETABLES

Squash, anyone? When spaghetti squash is cooked, the pale gold flesh turns into long, thin strands that resemble pasta. (Other varieties of squash don't work in this recipe.) Enjoy this fiber-packed delight for dinner tonight.

Spring Mix Vegetable Medley (page 317)
1 large spaghetti squash
   (about 3 to 4 lb/1.5 kg)
Salt and freshly ground black pepper
3 cups tomato sauce (preferably low-sodium)
Grated Parmesan cheese (optional)

make it
meatless

1. Prepare the Spring Mix Vegetable Medley as directed, using whatever vegetables are in season.

2. Pierce the spaghetti squash all over with the point of a sharp knife. Microwave, uncovered, on high, allowing about 5 minutes per pound. Turn the squash over halfway through the cooking process. An average squash cooks in about 15 to 18 minutes in the microwave. Let stand for 5 to 10 minutes.

3. Cut the squash in half. Using a spoon or melon baller, scrape out and discard the seeds and stringy fibers. With a fork, gently separate the cooked squash into spaghetti-like strands. Discard the shells. Season the squash with salt and pepper to taste.

4. Arrange a bed of cooked spaghetti squash on each serving plate. Top with tomato sauce and reserved roasted vegetables. Reheat briefly in the microwave before serving. Sprinkle with Parmesan cheese, if desired.

Yield: 6 servings. Keeps for up to 2 days in the refrigerator; reheats well. Don't freeze.

218 calories per serving, 36.2 g carbohydrate, 8.4 g fiber, 6 g protein, 8.2 g fat (1.2 g saturated), 0 mg cholesterol, 518 mg sodium, 1197 mg potassium, 3 mg iron, 101 mg calcium

Chef's Secrets
• What's in Store: Although spaghetti squash is considered a winter squash, it's available year-round. The peak season is early fall through winter. It has a smooth yellow skin and looks like an overgrown football. Store spaghetti squash in a cool, dark place for up to a month.

• Oven-Baked Squash: Pierce the squash all over with a sharp knife so steam can escape while it cooks. Place on a baking sheet and bake, uncovered, at 400°F for about 1 1/4 hours. When done, a skewer will glide easily through the flesh.

• Sauce It Up! Instead of commercial tomato sauce, make your own. Use Roasted Tomato Sauce (page 107), Quick Tomato Sauce (page 106), or Rosy Red Pepper Sauce (page 108).

• Pest-Oh! For a luscious, "smart-carb" dish, toss spaghetti squash with Pesto (pages 109–11) instead of tomato sauce.

• Say Cheese! Instead of Parmesan cheese, use grated low-fat mozzarella, cheddar, or havarti cheese.

🍎 EGGPLANT STACKS

These make an excellent vegetarian main dish. If you don't like spinach, just omit it. It's so easy to prepare, you can double the recipe and invite guests for dinner!

1 large eggplant, unpeeled
Salt and freshly ground black pepper
1/2 of a 10 oz/300 g pkg frozen chopped
    spinach, cooked, drained, and squeezed dry
2 green onions
1 1/4 cups nonfat dry cottage cheese
    or light ricotta cheese
2 Tbsp grated Parmesan cheese
1/2 tsp Italian seasoning
Salt and freshly ground black pepper
1 cup Italian-style tomato sauce
1 cup grated low-fat mozzarella or
    Monterey Jack cheese

1. Preheat the oven to 400°F. Line a baking sheet with foil and spray with cooking spray.

2. Slice the eggplant lengthwise into 8 slices, about ½-inch thick. Discard the end pieces that are mostly skin. Arrange the eggplant slices in a single layer on the prepared baking sheet; sprinkle with salt and pepper. Bake, uncovered, for 15 to 20 minutes or until tender. Cool slightly.

3. Combine the spinach, green onions, cottage cheese, Parmesan cheese, and Italian seasoning in a food processor fitted with the steel blade. Season with salt and pepper and process until combined, about 10 seconds.

4. Spread the spinach mixture on 4 of the eggplant slices. Top with the remaining eggplant slices to make 4 "sandwiches." Top each eggplant sandwich with tomato sauce and sprinkle with cheese. (If desired, the dish can be prepared up to this point, covered, and refrigerated for up to 24 hours.)

5. Bake, uncovered, for about 20 minutes or until the tops are golden and the eggplant is piping hot.

Yield: 4 servings. Recipe doubles and triples easily. Keeps for up to 2 days in the refrigerator; reheats well. Freezes well for up to 2 months.

197 calories per serving, 14.9 g carbohydrate, 6.1 g fiber, 23 g protein, 5.9 g fat (3.5 g saturated), 25 mg cholesterol, 569 mg sodium, 422 mg potassium, 2 mg iron, 329 mg calcium

Chef's Secrets
• Meal Deal: This dish pairs perfectly with a mixed green salad and whole wheat penne topped with tomato sauce and grated Parmesan cheese.

• Using Your Noodle: Watching your carbs? Serve with Zucchini "Pasta" (page 313) instead of penne.

● EGGPLANT MOCK PIZZAS

This makes a terrific low-carbohydrate vegetarian main dish. It's an excellent choice for people with diabetes.

1 large eggplant, unpeeled
2 Tbsp olive oil
Salt and freshly ground black pepper
Dried basil and oregano
¾ to 1 cup Italian-style tomato sauce
1 cup grated low-fat mozzarella
   or havarti cheese

make it
meatless

1. Preheat the oven to 400°F. Line a baking sheet with parchment paper or foil. If using foil, spray with cooking spray.

2. Cut off the top and bottom ends of the eggplant. Slice the eggplant into rounds about ½-inch thick and arrange on the prepared baking sheet. Lightly brush both sides of the eggplant slices with oil. Sprinkle on both sides with salt, pepper, basil, and oregano.

3. Bake, uncovered, for 8 to 10 minutes or until lightly browned. Remove the pan from the oven. Spread each eggplant slice with tomato sauce and top with cheese. (If desired, the recipe can be prepared up to this point and stored in the refrigerator for up to 24 hours.)

4. Bake for 12 to 15 minutes longer or until piping hot and the cheese is melted and golden. Serve immediately.

Yield: 8 to 10 slices. Recipe doubles and triples easily. Keeps for up to 2 days in the refrigerator; reheats well. Freezes well for up to 2 months.

85 calories per slice, 5.2 g carbohydrate, 2.3 g fiber, 4 g protein, 5.7 g fat (1.9 g saturated), 9 mg cholesterol, 209 mg sodium, 144 mg potassium, 0 mg iron, 116 mg calcium

make it meatless

🍎 PORTOBELLO MUSHROOM PIZZAS

Portobello mushroom caps make an excellent alternative to pizza crust if you are watching your carbohydrate intake. To remove excess moisture, I broil or bake the mushrooms before adding the toppings. These make a luscious vegetarian main dish and are also excellent as a side dish.

6 large portobello mushroom caps,
    stems removed
1 Tbsp olive oil
1 clove garlic (about 1 Tbsp minced)
Salt and freshly ground black pepper
Dried basil and oregano
1/2 cup chunky tomato sauce
3/4 to 1 cup grated low-fat mozzarella cheese

1. Preheat the broiler (or preheat the oven to 425°F). Rinse the mushroom caps briefly and pat dry with paper towels. Lightly brush mushroom caps on all sides with oil, then sprinkle with garlic and seasonings. Arrange on a broiler rack or baking sheet, rounded-side up. Broil until tender, 8 to 10 minutes (or bake, uncovered, at 425°F for 5 minutes).

2. Remove from the oven and turn the mushroom caps over. Fill each one with a tablespoonful of sauce. Sprinkle with cheese. Return the mushrooms to the oven and broil for 3 to 4 minutes longer or until the cheese is melted and golden (or bake 5 minutes longer).

Yield: 6 servings. As a main dish, serve 2 or 3 "pizzas" per person, along with a salad. Keeps for up to 2 days in the refrigerator; reheats well. Don't freeze.

91 calories per serving, 6.2 g carbohydrate, 1.6 g fiber, 6 g protein, 4.7 g fat (1.8 g saturated), 9 mg cholesterol, 146 mg sodium, 421 mg potassium, 1 mg iron, 118 mg calcium

Chef's Secrets

• Size Counts: Portobello mushrooms are just an oversized version of mushrooms. They can measure up to 6 inches in diameter and have a dense, meaty texture and a fabulous flavor.

• Weighing In: One portobello mushroom weighs about 3 oz (85 g), with just 27 calories, 4.3 g of carbohydrate, and 1.3 g of fiber.

• What's in Store: Choose mushrooms that have firm, smooth caps—avoid those that are bruised, wrinkled, or with a broken surface.

• Store It Right: To store, wrap unwashed mushrooms in paper towels or place them in a brown paper bag and refrigerate; they'll keep 7 to 10 days. Don't store them in plastic as they'll get wet and slimy.

• Cleaning Mushrooms: Clean mushrooms just before using, using a soft brush. Or rinse them quickly in cold water, then pat dry with paper towels.

• Save the Stems: The stems are very woody and should be removed. Don't throw them out—just chop them up and add them to soups and sauces. They add wonderful flavor.

• Mushroom Magic: Broiled or grilled portobello mushrooms are great served as a "burger" on a crusty multigrain roll, topped with sliced tomatoes, roasted red peppers, and onions. You can also slice them and use them as a side dish or add them to salads.

🍎 SHAKSHUKA

Shakshuka is a popular Israeli dish made with bell peppers, tomatoes, onions, and eggs. Thanks to Leah Perez of Montreal for sharing this excellent recipe. We're not "eggs-actly" sure of its origin, but Leah's great-aunt Rosa in Israel claims it's Turkish like she is, while others say it's from Tunisia! Leah makes a lot in the summer when tomatoes and peppers are in season.

4 cloves garlic (about 4 tsp minced)
2 medium onions, cut in chunks
2 Tbsp olive or canola oil
2 green peppers, cut in chunks
4 medium tomatoes, cut in chunks
1 cup water
1 tsp instant pareve soup mix
1/2 cup tomato paste (3/4 of a
    51/2 oz/156 mL can)
Salt and freshly ground black pepper
1/2 tsp ground cumin
1/8 tsp cayenne or chili powder
10 to 12 large eggs (preferably Omega-3)

1. In a food processor fitted with the steel blade, drop the garlic through the feed tube while the motor is running; process until minced. Add the onions and process, using quick on/off pulses, until coarsely chopped.

2. Heat the oil in a large pot on medium heat. Sauté the garlic and onions for about 5 minutes or until golden. Coarsely chop the peppers and tomatoes in batches in the processor, using quick on/off pulses. Transfer to the pot.

3. Cover and cook the vegetables on low heat for 10 minutes, stirring occasionally. Add the water, soup mix, tomato paste, salt, pepper, cumin, and cayenne. Simmer, covered, stirring occasionally, for 20 to 30 minutes, until the sauce is slightly thickened.

4. Break the eggs into the simmering sauce; cover, and cook until the eggs are firm, about 3 to 4 minutes. (If you prefer, you can scramble the eggs in the sauce instead of leaving them whole.) Serve immediately with plenty of good bread or pita to wipe up the sauce.

Yield: 6 servings. The sauce can be prepared up to the end of Step 3 and refrigerated for up to 2 days. When ready to serve, just heat the sauce over medium low heat, until simmering. Add the eggs, cover, and simmer for 3 to 4 minutes before serving.

221 calories per serving, 14.1 g carbohydrate, 2.6 g fiber, 13 g protein, 13.2 g fat (3.3 g saturated), 353 mg cholesterol, 389 mg sodium, 575 mg potassium, 3 mg iron, 74 mg calcium

Nutrition Note

• Yolk-ing Around: Fear of cholesterol has created considerable concern about eating whole eggs. Although 1 yolk contains about 200 mg of cholesterol, eggs are still very nutritious, low in saturated fat, and high in protein. They're also quick and easy to prepare, so enjoy them in moderation. Some health experts recommend up to 7 whole eggs a week, but people with diabetes should probably limit consumption to 2 whole eggs per week. Egg whites are

make it meatless

not a concern. Omega-3 eggs are an excellent choice. Check with your health professional for current guidelines.

● CRUSTLESS ZUCCHINI QUICHE

This treasured family recipe comes with "hugs and quiches" from Shani Bitan of Hong Kong. Her late grandmother, Ray Goldin, made this quiche for her family and now her two granddaughters make it for their children in Hong Kong and Lyon, France. Ray's recipe called for 1/2 cup oil, but I used half oil and half yogurt. I also used a combination of egg whites and eggs to lower the fat.

3 or 4 medium zucchini, cut in chunks
   (about 1 1/2 lb/750 g)
2 medium onions, cut in chunks
2 large eggs plus 4 egg whites (or 4 eggs)
1/2 cup canola oil
3/4 cup whole wheat flour
3/4 tsp baking powder
2 cloves garlic (about 2 tsp minced)
1/2 tsp salt
1/2 tsp dried oregano
1/2 tsp dried basil
1/2 tsp dried thyme
1 cup grated low-fat mozzarella cheese

1. Preheat the oven to 375°F. Spray a 10-inch ceramic quiche dish with cooking spray.

2. In a food processor fitted with the steel blade, process the zucchini in batches; chop coarsely, using 5 or 6 quick on/off pulses. Transfer the chopped zucchini to a large bowl. Add the onions to the food processor and process with quick on/off pulses, until coarsely chopped. Transfer to the bowl and mix together with the chopped zucchini; set aside.

3. In the food processor bowl, process the eggs and egg whites with the oil for 5 seconds or until combined. Add the flour, baking powder, garlic, salt, oregano, basil, and thyme; process for 10 to 12 seconds or until blended. Add the cheese and process 10 seconds longer.

4. Return the reserved zucchini and onion to the processor bowl and process with several on/off pulses or until combined, scraping down the sides of the bowl as needed. (If you have a small food processor, add the flour mixture to the zucchini mixture and stir with a wooden spoon to combine.)

5. Pour the mixture into the prepared dish and spread evenly. Bake, uncovered, for 45 to 50 minutes or until golden brown.

Yield: 8 servings. Keeps for up to 2 to 3 days in the refrigerator; reheats well. Freezes well for up to 2 months.

191 calories per serving, 15.5 g carbohydrate, 2.9 g fiber, 9 g protein, 10.8 g fat (2.4 g saturated), 62 mg cholesterol, 502 mg sodium, 331 mg potassium, 1 mg iron, 178 mg calcium

Chef's Secrets
• Timesaver: Grandma Ray sliced the zucchini, but her granddaughters chop it in the processor.

• Herbal Magic: Grandma used dried parsley, her granddaughters like to use Herbes de Provence, but I use basil and thyme because I always have them in my kitchen.

• Say Cheese! Shani Bitan increases the cheese to 1 1/2 cups and uses a mixture of cheeses. Experiment with Swiss, cheddar, havarti, etc.

make it meatless

❍ LOX AND BAGEL CHEESE STRATA

This do-ahead brunch dish is perfect fare for any special occasion. It's an excellent way to use up leftover bagels, or buy day-old bagels so that you can afford the lox. To save money, you can use lox bits and pieces. It's "dill-icious!"

5 to 6 whole wheat or sesame bagels,
    cut in bite-sized pieces (about 8 cups)
8 oz (250 g) lox (smoked salmon),
    cut in bite-sized pieces
8 oz low-fat Swiss and/or havarti cheese
    (about 2 cups grated)
2 green onions, chopped
2 to 3 Tbsp minced fresh dillweed
6 large eggs
    (or 4 eggs plus 4 egg whites)
1 cup light sour cream or plain yogurt
2 cups milk (skim or 1%)
1/2 tsp salt (optional)
1/4 tsp freshly ground black pepper

1. Spray the bottom and sides of a 9- × 13-inch glass baking dish with cooking spray. Spread the bagel pieces evenly in the dish. Top with lox and sprinkle with the grated cheese, green onions, and dillweed.

2. In a medium bowl, combine the eggs, sour cream, milk, and seasonings; blend well (you can use a blender, whisk, or large food processor). Pour evenly over the bagel-cheese mixture. Cover and refrigerate for at least 1 hour. (If desired, you can prepare the recipe up to this point and refrigerate for 24 hours.)

3. Preheat the oven to 350°F. Bake, uncovered, for about 1 hour or until the mixture is puffed and golden. Remove from the oven and let it stand for 10 minutes for easier cutting. Serve with a large Caesar or mixed garden salad.

Yield: 12 servings. Keeps for 2 to 3 days in the refrigerator; reheats well. Freezes well for up to 2 months.

277 calories per serving, 30.9 g carbohydrate, 2.2 g fiber, 20 g protein, 7.2 g fat (3.1 g saturated), 141 mg cholesterol, 761 mg sodium, 217 mg potassium, 2 mg iron, 308 mg calcium

Variations
• Use your favorite savory-flavored bagels such as sun-dried tomato, spinach, multigrain, or all-dressed. You can also make this using whole wheat or multigrain bread, cut in 1-inch pieces.

• Instead of lox, use 2 cans (71/2 oz/213 g each) of sockeye salmon, drained and flaked. You could also use 11/2 cups of leftover cooked salmon. This can also be made with canned tuna.

• Other cheeses can be substituted; try Monterey Jack, cheddar, Jarlsberg, or a mixture. For a different twist, add 1/2 cup crumbled feta or goat cheese.

❍ TERRIFIC TUNA BAKE

This recipe started off as a phone collaboration with my "persistent assistant." Shelley Sefton was missing five of the key ingredients she needed to make a crustless quiche for dinner. We came up with this light and fluffy dish and her family devoured it. I've added broccoli, but please don't tell her dad—he hates it!

make it meatless

1 medium onion, cut in chunks
1 clove garlic (about 1 tsp minced)
1 cup mushrooms
1 red pepper, seeded and cut in chunks
1 Tbsp olive oil
2 cups broccoli, cut in chunks
3 slices whole wheat or multigrain bread
2 large eggs plus 2 egg whites (or 3 eggs)
1 1/2 cups plain nonfat yogurt
1/2 cup milk (skim or 1%)
1 cup grated low-fat cheddar cheese
2 cans (6 1/2 oz/184 g each) water-packed
   tuna, drained
2 Tbsp minced fresh dillweed
   (or 2 tsp dried dill)

1. Preheat the oven to 350°F. Spray a 10-
inch deep glass quiche dish or 2 quart oval
casserole with cooking spray.

2. In a food processor fitted with the steel
blade, process the onion, garlic, mushrooms, and red pepper with several quick
on/off pulses, until the vegetables are
coarsely chopped.

3. Heat the oil in a large nonstick skillet
on medium high heat. Add the chopped
vegetables and sauté until golden, about 5
minutes. Meanwhile, microwave the broccoli in a covered microwaveable bowl on
high for 3 minutes or until tender-crisp.

4. Add the bread to the food processor and
process for about 20 seconds to make soft
crumbs. Add the eggs, egg whites, yogurt,
milk, and cheese; process with several quick
on/off pulses to combine. Add the sautéed
vegetables, broccoli, tuna, and dillweed.
Process with quick on/off pulses, just until
combined.

5. Spread the mixture evenly in the prepared dish. Bake, uncovered, for 1 hour or
until puffed and golden.

Yield: 6 to 8 servings. Keeps for 2 to 3 days
in the refrigerator; reheats well. Freezes well
for up to 2 months.

229 calories per serving, 17.7 g carbohydrate, 2.2 g fiber,
24 g protein, 7.4 g fat (2.2 g saturated), 95 mg cholesterol,
450 mg sodium, 406 mg potassium, 2 mg iron, 223 mg
calcium

● SPINACH BRUNCH BAKE

This scrumptious, calcium-packed casserole
was developed with the help of my nutrition student, Debbie Morson. It makes a
versatile brunch dish that's excellent as a
main dish, side dish, or as an hors d'oeuvre.
Who could ask for anything more—except
for another helping!

1 large onion, chopped
1/2 red pepper, seeded and chopped
2 cloves garlic (about 2 tsp minced)
1 Tbsp olive oil
6 large eggs (or 4 eggs plus 4 egg whites)
1 1/4 cups milk (skim or 1%)
2 tsp dry mustard
1 tsp salt (or to taste)
1/4 tsp freshly ground black pepper
1 pkg (10 oz/300 g) frozen chopped
   spinach, thawed and squeezed dry
3/4 cup dried breadcrumbs
   (preferably whole wheat)
1 1/2 cups grated low-fat cheddar cheese

1. Preheat the oven to 350°F. Spray a rectangular 2-quart baking dish with cooking
spray.

2. Sauté the onion, red pepper, and garlic in oil in a large skillet on medium heat for 5 minutes or until tender (or microwave, uncovered, on high for 5 minutes). Remove from heat and cool slightly.

3. In a large bowl, combine the eggs, milk, mustard, salt, and pepper; blend well. Add the spinach, breadcrumbs, cheese, and sautéed vegetables; mix well. Pour the mixture into the prepared casserole and spread evenly. (If desired, you can prepare the recipe in advance up to this point, and refrigerate, covered, for 24 hours.)

4. Bake, uncovered, for 40 to 50 minutes or until golden. A knife inserted into the center of the casserole should come out clean. Remove from the oven and let stand for a few minutes before serving.

Yield: 8 servings. Keeps for up to 2 days in the refrigerator; reheats well. Freezes well for up to 2 months.

185 calories per serving, 14.1 g carbohydrate, 1.8 g fiber, 15 g protein, 8.2 g fat (2.4 g saturated), 164 mg cholesterol, 596 mg sodium, 186 mg potassium, 2 mg iron, 209 mg calcium

Whole Wheat Breadcrumbs

One slice of bread makes $1/2$ cup soft breadcrumbs or $1/4$ cup dried breadcrumbs. For dried breadcrumbs, arrange slices of whole wheat bread in a single layer on a baking sheet. Bake, uncovered, for 20 to 30 minutes or until dry. Process in a food processor fitted with the steel blade to make fine crumbs. Refrigerate or freeze.

SPANIKOPITA PIE

This Greek spinach and cheese pie makes a wonderful vegetarian main dish. Serve it with a large garden salad and roasted vegetables for a vitamin-packed meal.

1 medium onion, chopped
2 cloves garlic (about 2 tsp minced)
1 Tbsp olive oil
1 pkg (10 oz/300 g) frozen chopped
  spinach, thawed and squeezed dry
$1/4$ cup fresh dillweed or 1 tsp dried
2 large eggs (or 1 egg plus 2 egg whites)
1 cup light feta cheese
1 cup light ricotta or cottage cheese
$1/4$ cup grated Parmesan cheese
Salt and freshly ground black pepper
8 sheets phyllo dough
4 Tbsp olive oil

1. In a medium skillet over medium heat, sauté the onion and garlic in olive oil for 3 or 4 minutes or until tender. Remove from heat and cool slightly.

2. In a food processor fitted with the steel blade, process the spinach and dillweed until minced, about 10 seconds. Add the sautéed onion, garlic, eggs, feta, ricotta, and Parmesan cheese. Season with salt and pepper to taste. Process just until mixed, scraping down the sides of the bowl as needed. (If desired, you can prepare the recipe up to this point, and refrigerate, covered, for 24 hours.)

3. Preheat the oven to 350°F. Spray a 9- × 13-inch glass baking dish with cooking spray.

4. Keep the phyllo dough covered with plastic wrap because it dries out quickly. Line the prepared baking dish with 4 sheets

of phyllo, brushing the top of each sheet lightly with oil as you layer it in the pan. Let the edges of the dough hang over the sides of the pan. Spread the filling evenly over the dough. Quickly layer with the remaining 4 sheets of phyllo, brushing each sheet lightly with oil. Fold the overhanging edges over the top and brush with oil once again. (The spanikopita can be prepared up to this point, covered, and refrigerated for up to 1 day or frozen for several months, until ready to use. If frozen, thaw before baking.)

5. Bake, uncovered, for 30 to 35 minutes or until puffed and golden.

Yield: 10 servings. Keeps for up to 2 to 3 days in the refrigerator; reheats well. Freezes well for up to 3 months.

219 calories per serving, 13.4 g carbohydrate, 1.7 g fiber, 12 g protein, 13.7 g fat (4.6 g saturated), 60 mg cholesterol, 473 mg sodium, 172 mg potassium, 1 g iron, 186 mg calcium.

Variation
• Dairy-Free: Use the filling mixture from Spanikopita Roll-Ups (page 60).

Chef's Secret
• Dough It Right: See Spanikopita Roll-Ups—Phyllo Facts (page 61) for tips.

CONFETTI VEGETABLE STRUDEL

Pretty as a picture! This elegant vegetarian main dish is also fabulous as an appetizer or side dish. To speed up preparation time, chop the vegetables in batches in the food processor. This recipe is quite flexible, so choose whatever vegetables you like. For a dairy-free variation, omit the cheese.

3 cups lightly packed fresh baby spinach leaves or chopped Swiss chard
2 Tbsp olive oil
1 medium onion, chopped
1 medium zucchini (about 1 cup chopped)
1 cup asparagus, sliced in 1-inch pieces
1 red pepper, seeded and chopped
1 yellow or green pepper, seeded and chopped
2 cups chopped mushrooms
3 cloves garlic (about 1 Tbsp minced)
1/4 cup chopped fresh dillweed or basil
1/2 tsp salt
1/4 tsp freshly ground black pepper
8 sheets phyllo dough
1 cup grated part-skim mozzarella, cheddar, or Swiss cheese
2 to 3 Tbsp additional olive oil, for brushing dough
1 Tbsp sesame seeds

1. Spray a large skillet with cooking spray and heat on high heat. Add the spinach and stir-fry for 1 minute or until slightly wilted. Transfer the wilted spinach to a small bowl and set aside.

2. Heat 1 Tbsp of oil in the same skillet on medium high heat. Add the onion, zucchini, and asparagus. Stir-fry for 4 to 5 minutes or until tender-crisp. Remove from the skillet and place in a large bowl. Heat the remaining 1 Tbsp oil in the skillet. Stir-fry the peppers, mushrooms, and garlic for 3 to 4 minutes or until tender-crisp. Add to the onion mixture and season with dillweed, salt, and pepper. Remove from the heat and let cool, draining any excess liquid. (If desired, you can prepare this recipe in advance up to this point, and refrigerate, covered, for 24 hours.)

3. Preheat the oven to 400°F. Line a large baking sheet with parchment paper.

make it meatless

4. Place one sheet of phyllo dough on a dry work surface with the short side facing you. Top with a second layer of dough. Lightly brush the top of the second layer with olive oil. Top with two more sheets of dough and brush lightly once again. You will have 4 layers of dough. (Keep the remaining phyllo dough covered with a tea towel or plastic wrap to prevent it from drying out.)

5. Spoon half the spinach in a line along the short end of the phyllo, leaving a 1½ inch border around the bottom and sides. Top with half the vegetable mixture and sprinkle with half the cheese. Fold the short edge of the phyllo layers over the filling, then fold in the long edges. Roll up the dough, starting from the bottom, to form a strudel roll. Place, seam-side down, on the prepared baking sheet. Repeat with remaining dough and filling. You will end up with two rolls.

6. Lightly brush the top of each roll with oil and sprinkle with sesame seeds. Using a sharp knife, partially cut through the top of the phyllo—but not through filling—to mark where you will slice it once it's baked (you will get 6 to 8 slices from each roll, depending on the size desired). Bake for 25 to 30 minutes or until the phyllo pastry is crisp and golden. Remove from the oven, slice, and serve warm.

Yield: 6 to 8 servings as a main dish, 12 to 16 servings as an appetizer or side dish. Keeps for up to 2 days in the refrigerator; re-heats well. Freezes well for up to 2 months.

251 calories per main dish serving, 23.0 g carbohydrate, 3.0 g fiber, 9 g protein, 14.5 g fat (3.6 g saturated), 12 mg cholesterol, 461 mg sodium, 299 mg potassium, 2 mg iron, 184 mg calcium

Chef's Secrets

• Freeze with Ease: If you plan to freeze this strudel, reduce the baking time by 8 to 10 minutes. Cool the strudel completely, then slice with a sharp knife. Transfer the slices carefully to a deep foil baking pan; wrap the pan well with heavy-duty foil and freeze. When needed, don't thaw first; just bake, uncovered, in a 350°F oven for about 20 minutes or until heated through. It will taste just-baked and won't be soggy.

• Phyllo Facts: See Spanikopita Roll-Ups— Phyllo Facts (page 61) for additional tips on working with phyllo dough.

make it meatless

CHEESE PANCAKES

You'll flip over these low-carb pancakes. The protein in the cottage cheese and eggs counteracts the flour, which makes these a low-glycemic index (low GI) pancake. Be sure to use a heavy nonstick skillet to prevent sticking. The batter can be quickly mixed up in a food processor, so give these a whirl.

1 cup low-fat (1%) cottage cheese
2 large eggs (or 1 egg plus 2 egg whites)
⅓ cup nonfat plain yogurt
1 Tbsp canola oil
2 Tbsp granular sugar or granular Splenda
½ tsp pure vanilla extract
⅓ cup flour (whole wheat or all-purpose)
2 Tbsp wheat germ or ground flaxseed
½ tsp baking powder
1 tsp ground cinnamon

1. Combine the cottage cheese, eggs, yogurt, oil, sugar, and vanilla in a food processor fitted with the steel blade. Process until smooth, about 20 seconds.

Scrape down the sides of the bowl. Add flour, wheat germ, baking powder, and cinnamon; process a few seconds longer or until blended.

2. Spray a large nonstick skillet or griddle with cooking spray. Heat over medium heat for 2 minutes or until a drop of water skips on its surface.

3. Drop the batter, using a scant 1/4 cup for each pancake, into the skillet. Brown on medium heat until golden, about 2 minutes per side. Transfer the cooked pancakes to a plate and keep warm. Repeat with the remaining batter, spraying the skillet between batches.

Yield: About 12 four-inch pancakes. Keeps for up to 2 days in the refrigerator; reheats well. Freezes well for up to 2 months.

63 calories per pancake, 6.4 g carbohydrate, 0.6 g fiber, 4 g protein, 2.4 g fat (0.5 g saturated), 36 mg cholesterol, 112 mg sodium, 54 mg potassium, 0 mg iron, 40 mg calcium

Chef's Secrets
• Berry Good: Sprinkle 3/4 cup blueberries, blackberries, or raspberries with 1 Tbsp flour. Gently stir into the batter in Step 1, using a rubber spatula.

• Top It Up: Serve these pancakes with nonfat yogurt and your favorite berries, or drizzle lightly with maple syrup (regular or light).

• Company's Coming! For a special treat, serve with Warm Mixed Berry Sauce (page 430).

Nutrition Notes
• GI Go! The addition of wheat germ, which contains soluble fiber, and serving these low-fat pancakes with berries and yogurt helps to make this a low-glycemic index dish.

• Spicy News! As little as 1/4 to 1/2 teaspoon of cinnamon a day may lower blood glucose, triglycerides, and LDL cholesterol levels in people with Type 2 diabetes. The active components do not seem to be affected by heat, so add ground cinnamon to pancakes, oatmeal, muffins, cookies, and cakes—or add a cinnamon stick to your cup of tea. "Cin-ful!"

● CHOCOLATE PANCAKES

Pancakes that taste like brownies—what a decadent combination! Serve them for breakfast, brunch, or dessert. These make a fabulous addition to your Chanukah repertoire. Everyone's face will light up when they taste them.

1/2 cup all-purpose flour
1/2 cup whole wheat flour
1/4 cup unsweetened cocoa powder
3 Tbsp granulated sugar or granular Splenda
2 tsp baking powder
1/8 tsp salt
2 large eggs
1 cup skim, 1%, or soymilk
2 Tbsp water
2 Tbsp canola oil
1/2 tsp pure vanilla extract
1/2 cup semi-sweet chocolate chips
Fresh or frozen strawberries
   or raspberries, for garnish
Vanilla yogurt, for garnish

1. In a large mixing bowl or food processor fitted with the steel blade, combine the flours, cocoa, sugar, baking powder, and salt; mix well. Add the eggs, milk, water, oil, and vanilla. Whisk together, or process for 8 to 10 seconds, until just smooth and blended. Stir in the chocolate chips with a rubber spatula.

2. Spray a large nonstick skillet or griddle with cooking spray. Heat over medium heat for 2 minutes or until a drop of water skips on its surface.

3. Drop the batter, using a scant 1/4 cup for each pancake, into the skillet. Cook the pancakes for 2 to 3 minutes or until bubbles appear on top. Turn the pancakes over with a spatula and lightly brown the other side for 2 to 3 minutes. Transfer the cooked pancakes to a plate and keep warm. Repeat with the remaining batter, spraying the skillet between batches. Serve warm with berries and yogurt.

Yield: About 16 three-inch pancakes. Keeps for up to 2 days in the refrigerator; reheats well. Freezes well for up to 2 months.

95 calories per pancake, 13.1 g carbohydrate, 1.3 g fiber, 3 g protein, 4.3 g fat (1.4 g saturated), 27 mg cholesterol, 97 mg sodium, 93 mg potassium, 1 mg iron, 61 mg calcium

Chef's Secrets
• Stir Crazy: Chocolate chips have a tendency to fall to the bottom of the bowl, so stir the batter often to make sure each pancake gets its fair share of chocolate chips.

• Feeling Desserted? If serving these for dessert, top with a small scoop of nonfat frozen yogurt or ice cream.

• Batter Up! Substitute 2 Tbsp soy flour or protein whey powder for part of the all-purpose flour in the batter to increase the protein content.

🍎 CINNAMON APPLE PANCAKES

These dairy-free pancakes are truly delicious. Make extra and freeze them—they'll reheat in seconds in the microwave. Check out the Variations on page 176.

2/3 cup whole wheat flour
2/3 cup all-purpose flour
2 Tbsp granular sugar or granular Splenda
1 tsp ground cinnamon
1/4 tsp salt
1 tsp baking powder
1/2 tsp baking soda
1 1/4 cups unsweetened apple juice
2 Tbsp canola oil
2 egg whites (or 1 large egg)
2 apples, peeled, cored, and grated

1. Combine the flours, sugar, cinnamon, salt, baking powder, and baking soda in a large mixing bowl or food processor fitted with the steel blade; mix well. Add the juice, oil, and egg whites. Whisk together, or process for 8 to 10 seconds, just until smooth and blended. Don't overmix. Gently stir in the grated apples with a rubber spatula.

2. Spray a large nonstick skillet or griddle with cooking spray. Heat over medium heat for 2 minutes or until a drop of water skips on its surface.

3. Drop the batter, using a scant 1/4 cup for each pancake, into the skillet. Cook the pancakes on medium heat for 2 to 3 minutes

or until bubbles appear on top. Turn the pancakes over with a spatula and lightly brown the other side for 2 to 3 minutes. Transfer to a plate and keep warm. Repeat with the remaining batter, spraying the skillet between batches. Serve warm.

Yield: About 20 three-inch pancakes. Keeps for 2 days in the refrigerator; reheats well. Freezes well for up to 2 months.

63 calories per pancake, 11.2 g carbohydrate, 1.0 g fiber, 1 g protein, 1.6 g fat (0.1 g saturated), 0 mg cholesterol, 91 mg sodium, 60 mg potassium, 0 mg iron, 19 mg calcium

make it meatless

Variations

• Top It Up: Top pancakes with yogurt and homemade chunky applesauce. Or drizzle pancakes lightly with honey, maple syrup, or sugar-free pancake syrup.

• Multiply Your Options: Fresh or frozen blueberries, blackberries, or strawberries add flavor and fiber to pancakes. If berries are frozen, you don't need to thaw them first. Instead of apples, add 1 1/2 cups berries to batter. Or add chopped pears, peaches, or nectarines for a twist.

• Pom Power: Use pomegranate juice instead of apple juice.

• Go for Protein: To add a protein boost to the pancake batter, add 1 to 2 Tbsp protein whey powder and reduce the amount of flour accordingly.

• Soy Good: To increase your intake of soy, use soymilk instead of apple juice.

• Dairy Good: Combine equal parts of nonfat yogurt and skim milk, and mix well. Use instead of apple juice.

• Lighten Up! For light, fluffy pancakes, substitute club soda for up to half of the liquid.

◖ BLUEBERRY CORNMEAL PANCAKES

These pancakes are light and luscious. If you're using frozen blueberries, there's no need to defrost them: just stir the frozen blueberries into the batter and cook. Berry smart!

1/2 cup whole wheat or all-purpose flour
3/4 cup cornmeal
2 Tbsp granulated sugar or granular Splenda
1 tsp baking powder
1/2 tsp baking soda
1/8 tsp salt
1 cup buttermilk (or 1 Tbsp lemon juice plus enough skim milk to make 1 cup)
2 Tbsp canola oil
2 large eggs (or 6 Tbsp liquid egg whites)
1 cup blueberries (fresh or frozen)

1. Combine the flour, cornmeal, sugar, baking powder, baking soda, and salt in a large mixing bowl or food processor fitted with the steel blade; mix well. Add the buttermilk, oil, and eggs. Whisk together, or process for 8 to 10 seconds, until just smooth and blended. Gently stir in the blueberries with a rubber spatula.

2. Spray a large nonstick skillet or griddle with cooking spray. Heat over medium heat for 2 minutes or until a drop of water skips on its surface.

3. Drop the batter, using a scant 1/4 cup for each pancake, into the skillet. Cook on medium heat for 2 to 3 minutes, until bubbles appear on top. Turn the pancakes over with

a spatula and lightly brown the other side for 2 to 3 minutes. Transfer to a plate and keep warm. Repeat with the remaining batter, spraying the skillet between batches.

Yield: About 20 three-inch pancakes. Keeps for 2 days in the refrigerator; reheats well. Freezes well for up to 2 months. Delicious topped with additional berries, yogurt, or maple syrup (regular or light).

63 calories per pancake, 9.2 g carbohydrate, 0.9 g fiber, 2 g protein, 2.2 g fat (0.4 g saturated), 22 mg cholesterol, 91 mg sodium, 33 mg potassium, 0 mg iron, 30 mg calcium

Variations
• Omit the blueberries and instead add $1/2$ cup semi-sweet chocolate chips, dried cranberries, or dried blueberries to the batter.

• Dairy-Free: Instead of buttermilk, use orange juice. Or combine 1 Tbsp lemon juice with enough soymilk to equal 1 cup.

• Alphabet Pancakes: Children love when you write their initials with pancake batter. Put the batter into a re-sealable plastic bag and cut an opening in the bottom corner. Carefully drizzle the batter into the hot skillet to form the desired letters of the alphabet. It's as easy as ABC!

• Happy Face Pancakes: Kids love to make "happy faces" on their pancakes using chocolate chips for the eyes, a cherry for the nose, and dried cranberries for the smile.

Chef's Secrets
• Batter Up! Substitute 2 Tbsp soy flour or protein whey powder for part of the flour in the batter to boost the protein content. You can also add 2 Tbsp wheat germ or ground flaxseed.

• Ready or Not? To test if a skillet or griddle is hot enough, sprinkle with a few drops of water. If the water sizzles and bounces off, your pan is hot enough. If it evaporates, your pan is too hot.

• Hot Stuff! Place cooked pancakes in a 250°F oven to keep warm. Or reheat pancakes in the microwave, allowing 15 seconds per pancake on high.

• Frozen Assets: Microwave frozen pancakes on high for 20 to 25 seconds per pancake, until hot. (There's no need to thaw first!)

🍎 HOMEMADE COTTAGE CHEESE

This old Russian recipe is also known as Tvarog. It's a wonderful homemade cottage cheese that's low in fat and high in taste, and without added salt. Use it in cheesecakes, frostings, and blintzes or as a spread on wholegrain bread. Everyone will say "More cheese, please!"

4 cups (1 L) buttermilk
8 cups (2 L) skim or 1% milk

1. Combine the buttermilk and skim milk in a large, ovenproof stainless steel pot or casserole dish. Cover and let stand at room temperature for 24 hours. The mixture will curdle and thicken over time.

2. Preheat the oven to 350°F. Place the covered pot in the oven and bake for 40 to 45 minutes. As it bakes, the curdled milk will separate into curds and whey. When fully baked, remove from the oven and let cool until lukewarm.

3. Pour the mixture into a cheesecloth-lined colander set over a very large bowl. Tie the

ends of the cheesecloth together and let it sit for several hours. (You can also hang the tied cheesecloth over the faucet of your sink and place a bowl underneath to catch the whey as it drains through the cloth.) For a firmer cheese, squeeze out most of the liquid. When the liquid is fully drained, you should have about 3 cups of cheese and 9 cups of whey. Wrap the cheese well in plastic wrap and refrigerate. Transfer the whey to a large, covered container and refrigerate until ready to use.

Yield: About 3 cups cottage cheese. Keeps for up to a week in the refrigerator. Don't freeze.

43 calories per ¼ cup, 1.6 g carbohydrate, 0 g fiber, 7 g protein, 0.6 g fat (0.4 g saturated), 2 mg cholesterol, 30 mg sodium, 52 mg potassium, 0 mg iron, 37 mg calcium

Chef's Secrets
• No cheesecloth? Line a large colander with strong paper towels before placing it over a large bowl.

• Whey to Go! Use the drained whey to replace buttermilk or sour milk in muffins, quick breads, and cakes. You can also use it as the liquid in soups or add it to smoothies.

• Safe Whey: Although the milk mixture is left at room temperature for 24 hours, heating it in the oven makes the cheese and whey safe for consumption.

☙ YOGURT CHEESE

So easy! To make yogurt cheese, all you need is yogurt, a strainer, some cheesecloth, and a bowl. The longer the yogurt is drained through the cheesecloth, the firmer the cheese. Be sure to use yogurt without added gelatin, starches, or stabilizers.

3 cups nonfat plain yogurt

1. Line a strainer with a double layer of cheesecloth, leaving the edges hanging over slightly. Place the strainer over a large measuring cup or bowl. Spoon the yogurt into the strainer, wrap with cheesecloth, and refrigerate. (You can weigh down the yogurt with a heavy can to help it drain faster.) Let yogurt drain for 2 to 24 hours, depending on the desired firmness. Don't discard the drained liquid or whey; reserve it to use in other recipes (see Chef's Secrets).

Soft Yogurt Cheese
After 2 to 3 hours of draining, you'll have 2 cups soft yogurt cheese and 1 cup whey. Soft yogurt cheese is ideal as a substitute for whipped cream (no whipping necessary). If desired, add a little vanilla extract or liqueur and a bit of sweetener.

Firm Yogurt Cheese
After 24 hours of draining, you'll have 1½ cups firm yogurt cheese and 1½ cups whey. Firm yogurt cheese is ideal as a substitute for cream cheese or cottage cheese in sweet or savory dishes such as dips, spreads, cheesecakes, or desserts.

Yield: About 1½ to 2 cups, depending on draining time. Cover and refrigerate for up to a week. Don't freeze.

50 calories per $1/4$ cup, 9.5 g carbohydrate, 0 g fiber, 5 g
protein, 0 g fat (0 g saturated), 2 mg cholesterol, 67 mg
sodium, 160 mg potassium, 0 mg iron, 150 mg calcium

Chef's Secrets

• No cheesecloth? Place a paper coffee filter in the cone-shaped holder of a coffee maker. Place the holder over a measuring cup. Spoon in 1 cup yogurt, cover, and refrigerate for 24 hours. You will have $1/2$ cup Firm Yogurt Cheese and $1/2$ cup whey. (You can only make a small quantity at a time with this method.)

• Feeling Drained? If you drain too much whey out of the yogurt and it's too firm for your needs, don't worry. Just stir some whey back in.

• Whey to Go! Don't throw out the drained whey. It's an excellent replacement for buttermilk or yogurt in smoothies, cakes, and muffins. You can also add it to soups or use it for a facial! Keeps for up to a week in the refrigerator.

make it
meatless

meat & poultry

MEAT AND POULTRY

WHAT'S YOUR BEEF?

Reduce the Red: The American Institute of Cancer Research recommends limiting intake of red meat to 3 ounces (cooked) a day, about the size of a deck of cards. To lower your risk of colorectal cancer, limit red meat, especially processed ones such as deli meats, hot dogs, salami.

Size Counts: Reduce portion sizes by cutting meat into thin slices or pieces and cooking them with hearty helpings of vegetables in stir-fries, stews, and chili. Add grated vegetables such as zucchini, onions, carrots, or mashed beans to replace a portion of the ground meat in recipes. Whole grain breadcrumbs or rolled oats are also excellent alternatives.

The Canadian Numbers Game: In Canada, the regulated maximum fat content for whole cuts (stewing beef, roasts, steak) is 7% for extra-lean beef and 10% for lean beef. For ground beef, it is 10% for extra-lean ground beef and 17% for lean.

The American Numbers Game: In the USA, the guidelines are different. For both whole cuts and ground beef, extra-lean contains less than 5 g total fat, 2 g or less saturated fat, and less than 95 mg cholesterol per 3.5 ounce serving. Lean beef has less than 10 g total fat, 4.5 g or less saturated fat, and 95 mg cholesterol per 3.5 ounce serving.

The Daily Grind: When buying ground beef, look for packages with the lowest percentages of fat—10% or lower. Lean cuts of Kosher ground beef are usually ground chuck, shoulder steak, or chuck shoulder.

The Shrink Tank: Meats with a higher percentage of fat will shrink more when cooked, so take this into consideration when purchasing ground beef.

Switch A-Ground: You can use lean ground turkey, chicken, or veal in any recipe calling for extra-lean ground beef, such as burgers, meatballs, and meat loaf. Ground bison is another lean option, although I've never used it. Ground turkey breast is a leaner choice than ground turkey, which often includes dark meat and has an average fat content of 8%. Ask your butcher to grind well-trimmed, boneless beef, veal, chicken breast, or turkey breast or grind it yourself in your food processor.

Grind Your Own: Use lean boneless beef, veal, chicken breast, or turkey breast. Cut into 1-inch chunks. Chill thoroughly for best results. Process in batches, filling the processor bowl 1/4 to 1/3 full. Use several quick on/off pulses, just until the desired texture is reached, about 12 to 15 seconds. Don't overprocess. Scrape down the sides of the processor bowl as needed.

Clean Cuisine: Always wash your hands when handling raw meat or poultry. Use separate dishes and utensils for raw and cooked meat or poultry.

Safe Storage: Use or freeze raw ground beef, veal, or poultry within 1 day of purchase.

Thaw It Right: Ground meat takes 6 hours per pound to thaw in the refrigerator. Never thaw it on the counter. You can also defrost it in the microwave—check your manual for times. Once it has thawed, cook it as soon as possible.

meat & poultry

Salt Alert! Kosher meat has already been salted, so take this into account when adding seasonings.

Rare Findings: Don't eat burgers that are rare. They should be cooked to a minimum internal temperature of 165°F (71°C) on an instant-read thermometer.

Refer to Grill It Right (page 34) and Marin-Aides (page 36) for important information on grilling.

CHICK-INFORMATION

The Skinny Truth: Did you know that chicken skin contains mostly unsaturated fat? If calories and fat intake are not a major concern, you can enjoy the skin in moderation. I prefer to cook chicken with the skin on to keep it moist and flavorful, then I remove the skin after cooking to save on calories and fat.

Breast Is Best: One roasted single chicken breast (without skin), contains 142 calories, 3.1 g fat (0.9 g saturated), and 73 mg cholesterol. With the skin, it contains 193 calories, 7.6 g fat (2.2 g saturated), and 82 mg cholesterol.

Drum It Up: One roasted drumstick (without skin), contains 76 calories, 2.5 g fat (0.6 g saturated), and 41 mg cholesterol. With the skin, it contains 112 calories, 5.8 g fat (1.6 g saturated), and 47 mg cholesterol.

Thighs of Regret: Dark meat has more calories and fat than white meat, but it is juicier. One roasted chicken thigh (without skin) contains 109 calories, 5.7 g fat (1.6 g saturated), and 50 mg cholesterol. With the skin, it contains 154 calories, 9.6 g fat (2.7 g saturated), and 58 mg cholesterol.

Winging It: One roasted chicken wing (with skin) contains 99 calories, 6.6 g fat (1.9 g saturated), and 29 mg cholesterol. Watch those portions!

Salute to Salt: Kosher chicken has already been salted, so consider this when adding seasonings. The salting process adds flavor to the chicken and also greatly reduces the incidence of salmonella in Kosher poultry.

Salt Alert! If sodium intake is a concern, soak raw chicken or turkey in cold water, changing the water every half hour, for up to 2 hours. Since most of the salt is in the skin, removing it helps to reduce the salt levels.

Grounds for Concern: When buying Kosher ground poultry, be aware that ground chicken contains more salt than ground turkey. One pound of Kosher ground chicken contains about 1/4 teaspoon (500 mg) sodium. One pound of Kosher ground turkey contains about 1/8 teaspoon (200 mg) sodium.

To Cover or Not to Cover? If the skin has been removed, cook chicken covered to prevent it from drying out. Uncover it for the last 15 to 20 minutes to thicken any pan juices, basting occasionally. If the skin is on, you can cook it covered or uncovered. The choice is yours!

Skinny Secrets: When cooking chicken in a sauce, remove the skin before cooking if you plan to serve it immediately. Otherwise, the fat from the skin melts and drains into the sauce. If you plan to serve the chicken the next day, you can cook it with the skin on, and then refrigerate it overnight. Discard congealed fat before reheating. Remove the skin before eating.

meat & poultry

No Bones About It: Boncless, skinless single chicken breasts that have been marinated should be cooked, uncovered, at 400°F for 20 to 25 minutes or until juices run clear. Cooking time will depend on the thickness. If you are grilling them, allow 4 to 6 minutes per side, on medium high over indirect heat, depending on the thickness.

Crispy Chicken: If the chicken has the skin on or it has a crumb coating, cook it uncovered until golden and crispy.

Is It Done Yet? Use an instant read thermometer to check the chick! Chicken must reach a safe minimum internal temperature of 165°F throughout. If you prefer it more well done, cook it a little longer.

Pink Poultry? Cooked poultry sometimes has a pink tinge, but don't worry, it's safe to eat—the color may be due to the salting process, or from grilling or smoking it. Always check the temperature by inserting an instant-read thermometer into the thickest part of the meat to ensure that poultry is thoroughly cooked.

Dark Secrets: Darkening around the bones sometimes occurs in young broiler-fryers. Pigment from the bone marrow can seep through the porous bones. Freezing can also cause this seepage, so when the chicken is cooked, the pigment turns dark. Not to worry—the chicken is safe to eat.

Store It Right: Store raw chicken as soon as possible after purchase. Store it in the coldest part of the refrigerator for 1 to 2 days or freeze it. Chicken cooked in a sauce keeps for up to 2 to 3 days in the refrigerator. Chicken without a sauce keeps for up to 3 to 4 days in the refrigerator. Cooked ground poultry keeps for up to 1 to 2 days in the refrigerator. Reheat to 165°F or until piping hot. Refrigerate or freeze cooked chicken as soon as possible after cooking or serving it.

Frozen Assets: Raw chicken can be frozen 6 to 9 months—wrap it very well to prevent freezer burn. Frozen chicken takes 6 hours per pound to thaw in the refrigerator. Don't thaw it on the counter. You can also defrost it in the microwave—check your manual for times. Once thawed, cook it as soon as possible.

Freeze with Ease: Cooked poultry freezes very well, but for best texture and flavor, use it within 4 months.

LET'S TALK TURKEY

Unfreeze with Ease: If turkey is frozen, defrost it in its original plastic wrapper in the refrigerator. Place it on a tray or in a large bowl to catch any drippings and prevent cross-contamination. Calculate 5 lb per day—a 10 lb (4.5 kg) turkey will take about 2 days to defrost. Thaw it completely to ensure that it cooks evenly.

Water Works: To thaw frozen turkey in cold water, immerse it completely in its original wrapper, changing the water every 30 minutes to be sure it stays cold. Allow 1 hour per lb (2 hours per kg).

Prep Time: Rinse the turkey thoroughly inside and out; remove the giblets and neck. Season the turkey at least a day in advance for best flavor. Refrigerate, covered, until ready to cook.

Pan-tastic! Place a rack in the bottom of a large roasting pan. Place the seasoned turkey on the rack, breast-side up. A disposable heavy-duty roasting pan helps save on clean-up. Place the disposable pan on a large rimmed baking sheet to help support it when you remove the turkey from the oven.

Cover Up: Cover turkey loosely with a tent of foil for the first 1 to 1½ hours, then remove the foil so that the turkey will brown.

Time It Right: Roast turkey in a preheated 325°F oven. Cooking times indicated below are for an unstuffed turkey. Times are approximate and should be used in conjunction with an instant-read thermometer.

WEIGHT	COOKING TIME
8 to 12 lb (3.6–5.4 kg)	2¾–3 hours
12 to 14 lb (5.4–6.4 kg)	3½–3¾ hours
14 to 18 lb (6.4–8.2 kg)	3¾–4¼ hours

Is It Done Yet? The turkey is done when a drumstick moves easily and juices run clear when it is pierced. An instant-read thermometer inserted into the innermost portion of the thigh and the thickest part of the breast should register a safe minimum internal temperature of 165°F. If you prefer it more well-done (as I do), cook it slightly longer or until it reaches an internal temperature of 170 to 175°F.

The Right Stuff: Never stuff poultry ahead of time. You can prepare the stuffing up to 24 hours in advance and refrigerate it separately. Health professionals now recommend not stuffing a whole turkey. Instead, bake the stuffing separately in a large sprayed casserole dish in a preheated 325°F oven for 45 to 60 minutes (the same temperature for roasting the turkey). For a crusty top, bake stuffing uncovered. Stuffing is done when the center registers 165°F.

No Bones About It: Instead of roasting a whole turkey, why not make a boneless rolled turkey breast? See Honey 'n Herb Turkey Breast (page 461). Calculate 25 to 30 minutes per pound at 350°F. An unrolled boneless turkey breast takes 20 to 25 minutes per pound at 350°F. If you can't find one large turkey breast, use 2 smaller ones.

Bone In: If roasting a turkey breast with the bone and skin, loosen the skin from the turkey but don't remove it. Season the turkey under the skin. Calculate 20 minutes per pound as your cooking time. Roast, uncovered, at 350°F, basting every 20 minutes. Let stand for 10 to 15 minutes after cooking for easier carving. Remove the skin and slice the turkey on an angle off the bone.

Store It Right: Refrigerate or freeze cooked turkey as soon as possible after cooking or serving it.

Leftovers? Cooked turkey keeps for up to 3 to 4 days in the refrigerator, or will freeze for up to 4 months. Use cooked turkey in soups, salads, sandwiches, wraps, stir-fries, or shepherd's pie. Or combine the turkey with vegetables and pasta or grains for a quick meal. They'll gobble it up!

meat & poultry

Turkey Soup: Don't throw out the turkey carcass—make soup. Place the carcass in a large pot and cover with water. Add 2 onions, 3 stalks celery, and 4 carrots. Simmer, partially covered, for 1 to 2 hours. When cool, strain, then transfer to containers and refrigerate or freeze. Use turkey broth in recipes calling for chicken or vegetable broth.

🍎 BEEF, BEAN AND BARLEY CHOLENT

Cholent, a traditional Jewish dish served on the Sabbath, is a slow-cooked casserole that gets its name from the French "chaud" (hot) and "lent" (slow). Because observant Jews are forbidden from turning on an oven or lighting a fire on the Sabbath (from sunset on Friday until sunset on Saturday), cholent must be almost completely cooked before Shabbat begins. This highly nutritious meal-in-a-pot is true comfort food.

1 cup mixed dried beans such as kidney
   beans, white navy beans, or chickpeas
3 cups cold water (for soaking)
2 Tbsp olive or canola oil
3 medium onions, chopped
2 stalks celery, chopped
4 to 6 cloves garlic, coarsely chopped
2 lb (1 kg) lean stewing beef,
   cut into 1-inch cubes
1 cup pearl barley, rinsed and drained
1 Tbsp sweet or Hungarian paprika
2 large sweet potatoes, peeled and
   cut into chunks (about 4 cups)
4 medium carrots, peeled and
   cut into chunks (or 2 cups baby carrots)
1/2 cup ketchup or Low-Carb Ketchup
   (page 113)
8 cups water (approximately)
1 Tbsp sea salt or Kosher salt (or to taste)
1/2 tsp freshly ground black pepper

1. Place the beans in a colander and rinse well under cold running water. Transfer to a bowl and add 3 cups water. Soak for 8 hours or preferably overnight. When fully soaked, drain the beans and rinse well. (Or see Quick-Soak Method on page 149).

2. Preheat the oven to 250°F. Heat the oil on medium high heat in a large pot or

meat & poultry

Dutch oven. Add the onions, celery, and garlic, and brown for 5 minutes. Toss in the stewing beef and cook for 5 minutes longer, stirring often, until the meat is no longer pink.

3. Add the drained beans, barley, paprika, sweet potatoes, carrots, and ketchup to the pot. Pour in enough water to cover the beef-and-vegetable mixture completely (the water should nearly reach the top of the pot). Season with salt and pepper and bring to a boil. Cover the pot tightly and immediately transfer to the oven. Cook overnight and serve for Shabbat lunch.

Yield: 10 servings. Although leftovers can be refrigerated for a day or two, it's best to transform them into soup. (See Chef's Secrets.)

353 calories per serving, 42.7 g carbohydrate, 8.7 g fiber, 25 g protein, 9.7 g fat (2.8 g saturated), 56 mg cholesterol, 691 mg sodium, 773 mg potassium, 10 mg iron, 65 mg calcium

Slow Cooker Cholent

Soak and drain the beans as directed in Step 1. Reduce the oil to 1 Tbsp. Place all the ingredients in a slow cooker that has been sprayed with cooking spray, adding the ingredients in the order listed. Water should come almost to the top of the slow cooker. Cover and cook on the high setting for 6 hours. Before Shabbat, turn the heat setting to low and cook overnight or until ready to serve. Slow cooker disposable liners help save on clean-up and there's no need to spray with cooking spray. For more information, refer to Slow Cookers (page 33).

Variation

• Add 1 or 2 parsnips or turnips, cut in chunks. Omit the ketchup and add dried thyme and/or basil, 1 can (28 oz/796 mL) tomatoes, and 1/2 to 1 cup dry red wine. Pour in enough water (approximately 4 cups) to nearly reach the top of the pot.

Chef's Secrets

• Leftovers? Transform leftover cholent into soup! Just combine with an equal amount of water or broth and simmer for 10 minutes. A soup-er idea!

• Salt Alert! If sodium is a concern, use low-sodium ketchup and replace salt with a salt substitute.

CRANBERRY BRISKET WITH CARAMELIZED ONIONS

This dish is excellent for a large crowd, making it perfect for any of the major Jewish holidays. Be sure to check out the variations on page 187. This brisket is tender and tasty—it's sure to become a family favorite.

2 large onions, sliced
1 beef brisket (4 1/2 to 5 lb/2 kg), well-trimmed
3 to 4 cloves garlic, minced (or 1 tsp garlic powder)
Salt and freshly ground black pepper
1 cup whole cranberry sauce or All-Fruit Cranberry Sauce (page 102)
1/2 cup tomato sauce
1/2 cup water

1. Spray a large roasting pan with cooking spray. Spread the onions in the bottom of

the pan and place the brisket on top. Season both sides of the brisket with garlic, salt, and pepper. In a small bowl, combine the cranberry sauce and tomato sauce. Mix well; spread over the brisket. Pour the water around and underneath the brisket and cover the pan tightly with foil. (If desired, marinate for an hour at room temperature or up to 48 hours in the refrigerator.)

2. Preheat the oven to 325°F. Cook the brisket, covered, about 4 hours or until the meat is fork-tender and the onions are caramelized. (Calculate 45 minutes per pound as your cooking time.) For the last hour of cooking, slightly loosen the foil and baste the meat occasionally.

3. When done, remove the pan from the oven and cool completely. Cover the pan and refrigerate overnight. Remove the congealed fat from the surface. Slice the brisket thinly across the grain, trimming away the fat. Reheat the slices in the pan gravy for 25 to 30 minutes in a covered casserole at 350°F.

Yield: 12 servings. Keeps for up to 3 to 4 days in the refrigerator; reheats well. Freezes well for up to 4 months.

264 calories per serving, 12.2 g carbohydrate, 0.9 g fiber, 35 g protein, 7.4 g fat (2.8 g saturated), 73 mg cholesterol, 116 mg sodium, 353 mg potassium, 3 mg iron, 25 mg calcium

Cranberry Veal Brisket

Instead of beef, use a veal brisket. Cooking time will be the same. If desired, have the butcher cut a pocket in the roast; insert your favorite stuffing into the pocket and increase the cooking time by 1/2 hour.

Variations

• Replace the onions with 1 package of dried onion soup mix and omit the salt. Rub the soup mix, garlic, and pepper evenly over the brisket. Instead of water, use dry red wine, diet ginger ale, or cola.

• Barbecue or chili sauce can be used instead of tomato sauce.

Chef's Secrets

• Flat or Fat? Beef brisket is divided into two sections. The flat cut has less fat and is usually more expensive than the point, which is much fattier and also more flavorful. A double brisket has a thick layer of fat between the two sections. Ask your butcher to trim the brisket well. Cook it a day in advance so you can remove the congealed fat before slicing and reheating.

• Double Brisket? Don't double the time! If your brisket is very large (8 to 10 lb), cut it crosswise into two smaller briskets (4 to 5 lb each). Cook them in a large roaster for 3 to 4 hours, until fork-tender.

• Overnight Method: Cook, lightly covered, in a 225°F oven for 7 to 8 hours. (Put the brisket into the oven just before going to bed and remove it first thing in the morning.)

• Meal Deal: Serve with Pretend Potato Kugel (page 335) and Spring Mix Vegetable Medley (page 317).

● SAUCY BRISKET

This saucy brisket is perfect for any Jewish holiday or Friday night dinner. For extra-tender brisket, use beer instead of water (but not for Passover). This sauce mixture is also excellent for veal brisket or stewing beef.

2 large onions, sliced
1 beef brisket (about 5 lb/2.3 kg),
 well-trimmed
3 cloves garlic (about 1 Tbsp minced)
1 tsp dried basil
Salt, freshly ground black pepper,
 and paprika
1 cup duck sauce (try Szechuan spicy
 duck sauce)
3/4 cup tomato sauce
2 Tbsp balsamic vinegar or orange juice
 (preferably fresh)
3/4 cup water

1. Spray a large roasting pan with cooking spray. Spread the onions in the bottom of the pan and place the brisket on top. Season both sides of the brisket with the garlic, basil, salt, pepper, and paprika to taste.

2. In a medium bowl, combine the duck sauce, tomato sauce, and balsamic vinegar; mix well. Spread the sauce evenly on top of the brisket. Pour the water around and underneath the brisket and cover the pan tightly with foil. (If you have time, marinate the brisket for an hour at room temperature, or up to 48 hours in the refrigerator.)

3. Preheat the oven to 325°F. Cook the brisket, covered, for about 4 hours (calculate 45 minutes per pound), until fork tender. During the last hour of cooking, loosen the foil slightly and baste the meat occasionally.

4. When done, remove the pan from the oven and cool completely. Cover the pan and refrigerate overnight. Remove the congealed fat from the surface. Slice the brisket thinly across the grain, trimming away any fat. Place the slices and gravy in a covered casserole and reheat in a 350°F oven for 25 to 30 minutes before serving.

Yield: 12 servings. Keeps for up to 3 to 4 days in the refrigerator; reheats well. Freezes well for up to 4 months.

289 calories per serving, 12.0 g carbohydrate, 0.6 g fiber, 39 g protein, 8.2 g fat (3.1 g saturated), 81 mg cholesterol, 210 mg sodium, 406 mg potassium, 4 mg iron, 30 mg calcium

Variations
• Substitute jellied cranberry sauce for duck sauce and/or ketchup or chili sauce for tomato sauce. Instead of water, use red wine or beer. And for a sweet-and-sour flavor, add 2 Tbsp honey or granular Splenda.

Slow Cooker Brisket
Spray the slow cooker with cooking spray. Reduce water to 1/3 cup—you need less water in the slow cooker as there is little evaporation. Place a sheet of parchment paper on top of the meat to hold in the steam. Cook on the high setting for 1 hour, then on the low setting until tender, about 8 to 10 hours. Some briskets may take up to 12 hours to cook. You can make any brisket recipe or pot roast in the slow cooker using this method.

ROASTED VEAL CHOPS WITH RICE

It's no big deal to make this scrumptious one-dish meal, which requires almost no attention once it's in the oven—veal-ly!

1 cup brown basmati or long-grain rice
1 large onion, sliced
1 red pepper, seeded and sliced
6 lean veal chops (about 3 lb/1.4 kg)
2 cloves garlic (about 2 tsp minced)
1 tsp salt

Norene's Healthy Kitchen

1/4 tsp freshly ground black pepper
1/2 tsp sweet paprika
1/2 tsp dried basil
1/2 tsp dried oregano
2 cups chicken or vegetable broth
    (preferably low-sodium)
1/2 cup Italian-style tomato sauce

1. Preheat the oven to 350°F. Spray a 9- × 13-inch casserole dish with cooking spray.

2. Place the rice in bottom of the prepared casserole dish. Sprinkle with onion and red pepper. Arrange the veal chops on top of the rice and sprinkle with garlic, salt, pepper, paprika, basil, and oregano. Combine the broth and tomato sauce, and add to the dish.

3. Cover with foil. Bake for 1 1/4 to 1 1/2 hours or until the veal is fork-tender and the rice is cooked through. Uncover and cook for 15 minutes longer before serving.

Yield: 6 servings. Keeps for up to 2 days in the refrigerator; reheats well. Freezes for up to 3 months.

307 calories per serving, 28.8 g carbohydrate, 2.6 g fiber, 32 g protein, 7.7 g fat (2.2.g saturated), 113 mg cholesterol, 598 mg sodium, 420 mg potassium, 2 mg iron, 38 mg calcium

Variation
• Instead of rice, use 1 cup bulgar, rinsed and drained.

🍎 BETTER BURGERS

Everyone loves burgers. These are a healthier alternative to commercial frozen burgers, which are loaded with fat and sodium. Make these with ground beef, turkey, chicken, or veal, or a combination. It's okay to "switch a-ground!" Rolled oats have a lower glycemic index value than breadcrumbs.

1 lb (500 g) extra-lean ground beef
1 large egg (or 2 egg whites)
1/2 tsp Kosher salt (or to taste)
1/4 tsp freshly ground black pepper
1 clove garlic (or 1/4 tsp garlic powder)
3 Tbsp rolled oats or matzo meal
    (preferably whole wheat)
3 Tbsp water or ketchup

1. In a large bowl, combine all the ingredients and mix lightly.

2. Preheat the grill to medium-high. Wet your hands for easier handling; shape the mixture into 4 equal-sized patties. Place the patties on the hot grill and close the lid. Grill for 5 to 6 minutes per side over indirect heat. (On a 2-sided grill, total cooking time will be about 5 to 6 minutes.) When done, an instant-read thermometer inserted into the center of the burger, should read at least 160°F (71°C).

Yield: 4 burgers. Recipe doubles or triples easily. Keeps for up to 1 to 2 days in the refrigerator; reheats well. Freezes well for up to 3 months.

235 calories per burger, 3.1 g carbohydrate, 0.5 g fiber, 25 g protein, 12.9 g fat (5.0 g saturated), 127 mg cholesterol, 252 mg sodium, 385 mg potassium, 5 mg iron, 25 mg calcium

Variations
• Use 1/4 cup low-cholesterol liquid egg substitute or pasteurized liquid egg whites for 1 large egg.

• For the kids, make miniature burgers and serve them on small whole wheat buns. Let the kids choose their own toppings. (Ketchup does not count as a vegetable!)

• Add grated onion or leftover mashed cooked vegetables to the meat mixture for a flavor boost. A nutritious addition is 1/2 cup canned chickpeas, rinsed, drained, and finely mashed. Instead of water, use salsa, chutney, barbecue, or chili sauce. Add mustard and your favorite herbs such as basil, oregano, and thyme.

• Tasty Toppings: Add lettuce, sliced tomatoes, onions, pickles, roasted red peppers, grilled mushrooms, chutney, ketchup, salsa, or your favorite condiments. Caramelized Onions (page 303), Mushroom Duxelles (page 302) or Great Grilled Vegetables (page 316) also add flavor.

Chef's Secrets

• Size Matters: Burgers should be uniform in size and thickness so they will cook evenly and in the same amount of time. If you use ground meat with a higher fat content, your burgers will shrink more during cooking.

• Frozen Assets: Shape the raw meat into burgers and place in a single layer on a parchment paper-lined baking tray. Cover loosely with parchment and freeze until firm, 1 to 2 hours. Store them in re-sealable freezer bags for up to 3 months. When needed, thaw overnight in the refrigerator and grill as usual.

• Turkey Time: With lean ground turkey (8% fat), one burger contains 205 calories and 10.9 g fat (2.9 saturated). With ground

veal or chicken, the nutrient content will be similar to using beef.

• Mushroom Magic: Add 1/4 to 1/2 cup minced, raw mushrooms per pound of ground meat for moist, juicy burgers (especially turkey burgers). Mushrooms boost the flavor and give you a bigger burger.

• Tip-Top Burgers: See What's Your Beef? (page 181) and Grill It Right (page 34) for more tips.

● MIGHTY GOOD MEATBALLS

They'll never guess that the sauce for these scrumptious meatballs is made with diet cola and barbecue sauce. These do double-duty as a main dish or appetizer. If you don't have time to roll meatballs (or are feeling lazy), then make the meat loaf version on page 191.

Meatballs:

1 lb (500 g) extra-lean ground beef
   (or lean ground veal, chicken, or turkey)
1 large egg (or 2 egg whites)
Salt and freshly ground black pepper
1 clove garlic (about 1 tsp minced)
1/4 cup rolled oats or matzo meal
2 Tbsp barbecue sauce
3 to 4 Tbsp water

Sauce:

1/2 green pepper, seeded and sliced
1 medium onion, sliced
1 cup sliced mushrooms
1 cup barbecue sauce
3/4 cup diet cola

1. Preheat the oven to 350°F. Spray a 9- × 13-inch baking dish with cooking spray.

2. In a large bowl, combine all the ingredients for the meatballs and mix lightly. Wet your hands and shape the mixture into 1-inch balls. Arrange in a single layer in the prepared baking dish.

3. In another bowl, combine the peppers, onion, mushrooms, barbecue sauce, and cola; mix well. Pour the sauce mixture over and around the meatballs.

4 Bake, uncovered, for about 1 hour or until the sauce is bubbly and the meatballs are cooked through.

Yield: About 40 meatballs (4 servings as a main dish, 8 to 10 servings as hors d'oeuvres.) Keeps for up to 2 days in the refrigerator; reheats well. Freezes well for up to 3 months.

297 calories per serving, 14.7 g carbohydrate, 1.8 g fiber, 27 g protein, 14.1 g fat (5.2 g saturated), 127 mg cholesterol, 667 mg sodium, 618 mg potassium, 4 mg iron, 42 mg calcium

Mighty Good Meat Loaf

Shape the meat mixture into an oval-shaped loaf and place in the prepared baking dish. For the sauce, use 1/2 cup barbecue sauce and 1/3 cup diet cola; combine with the vegetables and mix well. Pour the sauce over and around the meat loaf. Bake, uncovered, at 350°F for about 1 hour, or until it is cooked through. Let stand a few minutes, then slice and serve.

Chef's Secrets

• No Barbecue Sauce? If you don't have barbecue sauce, use ketchup and add 2 tsp low-sodium soy sauce to the sauce mixture.

• Pick a Pop: Instead of diet cola, use ginger ale, 7Up, or other lemon-lime carbonated beverage. If made with regular pop instead of sugar-free, one serving will contain 316 calories and 19.7 g carbohydrate.

• Double Without Trouble: If doubling the recipe, make the meatballs in a large pot on top of the stove over medium-high heat. Prepare the sauce mixture and heat until bubbly. Add the meatballs to the sauce and reduce heat to low. Simmer, partially covered, for about 1 hour, stirring occasionally.

✦ BARBECUE MEAT LOAF

Make it big, make it small, make it any way at all! Meat loaf is a comfort food, no matter how you slice it.

2 lb (1 kg) extra-lean ground beef
1 large egg plus 2 egg whites
  (or 2 large eggs)
1/3 cup barbecue sauce
1/3 cup rolled oats or matzo meal
1/2 tsp salt (or to taste)
Freshly ground black pepper
2 cloves garlic (about 2 tsp minced)
1 tsp dried basil

1. Preheat the oven to 350°F. Spray a 9- × 13-inch baking dish with cooking spray.

2. In a large bowl, combine the ground beef, egg, egg whites, barbecue sauce, rolled oats, salt, pepper, garlic, and basil; mix lightly. Don't overmix or the meat will get tough.

3. Transfer the meat mixture to the prepared baking dish and form into an oval-shaped loaf, wetting your hands for easier handling. Bake, uncovered, for 1 hour. Slice and serve.

Yield: 6 servings. Keeps for up to 2 days in the refrigerator; reheats well. Freezes well for up to 3 months.

315 calories per serving, 5.5 g carbohydrate, 0.8 g fiber, 34 g protein, 16.6 g fat (6.4 g saturated), 134 mg cholesterol, 437 mg sodium, 548 mg potassium, 4 mg iron, 35 mg calcium

Mini Meat Loaves

Shape the mixture into 4 mini loaves. Bake, uncovered, at 375°F for 35 to 40 minutes.

Meat Loaf Muffins

Spoon the meat mixture into sprayed compartments of a muffin pan. Top each one with some mashed potatoes (or sweet potatoes) and sprinkle lightly with paprika. Bake at 375°F for 25 to 30 minutes or until golden. Great for kids!

Variations

• Instead of ground beef, use lean ground turkey, chicken, or veal. Instead of barbecue sauce, use chili sauce, spicy tomato sauce, or salsa.

● MUSHROOM TURKEY LOAF

This moist and flavorful loaf is made with dried shiitake mushrooms instead of breadcrumbs. It's packed with fiber and is an excellent source of iron. Although you can make half the recipe for a small family, I prefer to freeze the extra loaf for another day. Cook once, eat twice!

2 cups dried shiitake mushrooms
2 medium onions, cut in chunks
3 to 4 cloves garlic (3 to 4 tsp minced)

2 lb (1 kg) lean ground turkey
1 large egg plus 2 egg whites
   (or 2 large eggs)
1/3 cup hoisin, barbecue, or duck sauce
3/4 tsp salt (or to taste)
1/2 tsp freshly ground black pepper
1 tsp dried basil
1 tsp dried oregano

1. Preheat the oven to 350°F. Line a baking sheet with foil and spray with cooking spray.

2. In a food processor fitted with the steel blade, process the dried mushrooms until finely ground, about 45 to 60 seconds. Transfer the ground mushrooms to a large mixing bowl.

3. Add the onions and garlic to the food processor and process with several quick on/off pulses, until minced. Transfer to the bowl with the mushrooms and add the ground turkey, egg, egg whites, hoisin sauce, and seasonings; mix lightly to combine.

4. Divide and shape the mixture into two loaves on the prepared baking sheet, wetting your hands for easier handling. (If desired, the turkey-vegetable mixture can be prepared in advance up to this point, covered and refrigerated overnight.)

5. Bake, uncovered, for 1 hour. Slice and serve.

Yield: 2 loaves (8 servings). Keeps for up to 2 days in the refrigerator; reheats well. Freezes well for up to 3 months.

341 calories per serving, 26.8 g carbohydrate, 5.4 g fiber, 32 g protein, 11.4 g fat (2.9 g saturated), 117 mg cholesterol, 551 mg sodium, 350 mg potassium, 8 mg iron, 50 mg calcium

Passover Variation

• If Passover dried mushrooms aren't available, use 2 cups minced fresh mushrooms. Sauté the mushrooms on medium-high heat in 1 Tbsp oil for 6 to 8 minutes or until golden. Add 1/4 to 1/3 cup matzo meal to the ground turkey to act as a binder. Instead of hoisin sauce, use Passover barbecue sauce, ketchup, or duck sauce.

Chef's Secrets

• Mushroom Magic: Substitute ground dried mushrooms for matzo meal or breadcrumbs in recipes—it adds flavor and moisture, especially to ground turkey, which can be bland because of its low fat content. One cup of dried shiitake mushrooms yields 1/2 cup when ground. Make an extra batch or two and store it in a cool dry place, or freeze it.

• Switching A-Ground: Instead of turkey, use extra-lean ground beef, veal, or chicken.

• Meal Deal: Serve with Pretend Potato Kugel (page 335), which can be baked at the same temperature for almost the same amount of time.

BOBOTIE

Bobotie (pronounced boh-BOO-tee) is a traditional South African dish made from spiced ground beef. This curry-flavored rectangular meat loaf is topped with a custard-like egg mixture. My assistant Shelley makes this lighter, healthier version and serves it with sliced bananas, coconut, raisins, chutney, diced tomatoes, and onions. I prefer mine plain. Either way, it's divine.

2 Tbsp olive oil
2 medium onions, chopped
2 to 3 tsp ground turmeric (or to taste)
2 to 3 Tbsp curry powder (or to taste)
1/2 tsp salt
1/4 tsp freshly ground black pepper
1/2 cup apricot or peach chutney
2 lb (1 kg) lean ground turkey or chicken
  (or a combination)
4 slices whole wheat or multigrain bread
2 Tbsp cider or white vinegar
2 large eggs beaten with 1/4 cup water

1. Preheat the oven to 350°F. Spray a 9- × 13-inch casserole dish with cooking spray.

2. Heat the oil in a large pot on medium heat. Add the onions and sauté for 5 minutes or until golden. Add the turmeric, curry powder, salt, pepper, and chutney; mix well and cook for 2 to 3 minutes longer. Stir in the ground turkey and brown for 8 to 10 minutes, stirring often.

3. In a food processor fitted with the steel blade, process the bread for about 10 seconds to make fine crumbs. Add the breadcrumbs and vinegar to the turkey mixture and mix well.

4. Spread the turkey mixture evenly into the prepared casserole dish. Drizzle the egg mixture on top and spread evenly with a pastry brush. Bake, uncovered, for 1 hour or until golden.

Yield: 8 servings. Keeps for up to 2 days in the refrigerator; reheats well. Freezes well for up to 3 months.

294 calories per serving, 16.8 g carbohydrate, 2.0 g fiber, 23 g protein, 14.8 g fat (3.6 g saturated), 142 mg cholesterol, 348 mg sodium, 450 mg potassium, 3 mg iron, 47 mg calcium

Nutrition Note

• The Spice is Right: Turmeric, an Indian spice used to season curry dishes, is an ingredient in curry powder and prepared mustard. It's sometimes used as a cheaper alternative to saffron, but the flavor is totally different. Turmeric's deep yellow-orange color comes from curcumin, which is believed to have strong anti-inflammatory and anti-cancer properties. Regular use of turmeric and ginger can help reduce symptoms of osteoarthritis. Beware—turmeric and curry will stain everything they come into contact with!

❧ SWEET POTATO SHEPHERD'S PIE

My assistant, Shelley Sefton, served this award-winning dish for dinner the night of the Academy Awards and we all went back for more helpings than we should have. (Her dad nabbed the last corner piece to freeze for a future meal!) This is perfect for Passover or all-year round, accompanied by a big garden salad and roasted vegetables.

Topping:

4 medium sweet potatoes, peeled and
  cut into chunks
1/2 cup water
2 tsp olive oil
Salt and freshly ground black pepper
Paprika, for garnish

Chicken Mixture:

2 medium onions, cut in chunks
1 cup baby carrots (about 12)
2 to 3 cloves garlic (1 to 2 tsp minced)
1 Tbsp olive oil
2 lb (1 kg) lean ground chicken, beef,
  or veal (or a combination)

1/2 tsp salt (or to taste)
1/8 tsp freshly ground black pepper
1/2 tsp each dried basil and dried oregano
2 egg whites
1/4 cup ketchup
1/3 cup matzo meal (preferably whole wheat)

1. Place the sweet potatoes and water in a large microwaveable bowl. Microwave, covered, on high for 18 to 20 minutes or until tender. (Or cook the sweet potatoes in a medium saucepan on top of the stove for 20 minutes over high heat.) Drain well. Add the oil, salt, and pepper, and mash until very smooth. Set aside.

2. Preheat the oven to 350°F. Spray a 9- × 13-inch baking dish with cooking spray.

3. In a food processor using the steel blade, process the onions, carrots, and garlic until finely chopped, about 6 to 8 seconds. Heat the oil in a large pot on medium heat. Sauté the onions, carrots, and garlic for 2 to 3 minutes or until soft. Add the ground chicken and brown for 6 to 8 minutes, stirring often. Remove from the heat. Add the salt, pepper, basil, oregano, egg whites, ketchup, and matzo meal; mix well.

4. Spread the meat mixture evenly in the prepared baking dish. Top with the sweet potato mixture and sprinkle with paprika. (If desired, the shepherd's pie can be prepared in advance up to this point and refrigerated overnight.)

5. Bake, uncovered, for 50 to 60 minutes or until golden. Cut into squares and serve.

Yield: 8 servings. Keeps for up to 2 days in the refrigerator; reheats well. Freezes for up to 3 months.

280 calories per serving, 23.0 g carbohydrate, 2.6 g fiber, 21 g protein, 12.1 g fat (2.9 g saturated), 75 mg cholesterol, 336 mg sodium, 256 mg potassium, 1 mg iron, 33 mg calcium

Nutrition Notes

• Sweet potatoes have a lower glycemic index value than regular potatoes and are packed with fiber and potassium.

• One cup of mashed sweet potato contains 180 calories, 41.4 g carbohydrate, 6.6 grams of fiber, and 4 grams protein. Sweet potatoes are also packed with beta carotene and vitamins A and C.

• I often use a purple-peel sweet potato with a creamy-white flesh (Purple Sweeties), as they closely resemble regular potatoes when cooked but are far more nutritious.

● UNSTUFFED CABBAGE

My friend, Lela Kornberg of Toronto, used to make stuffed cabbage rolls but her kids always unrolled the leaves and ate only the meat. This recipe solved that problem. I've modified it to lower the calories and glycemic index value. I also used coleslaw mix, which almost disappears in the sauce when cooked. What a "grate" idea for fussy eaters!

Meatballs:

2 lb (1 kg) extra-lean ground beef
   or lean ground turkey, chicken, or veal
1 large egg plus 2 egg whites
   (or 2 large eggs)
1/4 cup tomato sauce or tomato juice
1 tsp salt (or to taste)
1/4 tsp freshly ground black pepper
1 tsp dried basil

2 cloves minced garlic
   (or 1 tsp garlic powder)
1/2 cup rolled oats
1/3 cup raw rice (basmati or long-grain)

Sauce and Vegetables:

5 cups tomato juice or tomato sauce
1/2 cup brown sugar or granular Splenda
2 Tbsp lemon juice (preferably fresh)
   or white vinegar
2 onions, thinly sliced
2 cloves garlic (about 2 tsp minced)
1 pkg (16 oz/454 g) coleslaw mix
   (or 6 to 8 cups thinly sliced cabbage)
3 to 4 bay leaves

1. Preheat the oven to 350°F. Spray a large roasting pan with cooking spray.

2. In a large mixing bowl, combine all the ingredients for the meatballs and mix lightly. Wet your hands and shape the mixture into meatballs about 1 1/2 inches in diameter. Place them on a parchment paper-lined tray. You should have about 5 dozen meatballs.

3. In the same mixing bowl (why wash extra dishes?) combine the tomato juice, brown sugar, and lemon juice; mix well.

4. Layer half the onions, garlic, and coleslaw mix in the prepared roasting pan. Add half the meatballs and top with half the sauce. Repeat to make a second layer. Add the bay leaves and cover the pan tightly with foil.

5. Bake for 1 1/2 hours. Uncover and bake for 1/2 hour longer to thicken the sauce. Remove the bay leaves before serving.

Yield: 10 servings. Keeps for up to 3 days in the refrigerator; reheats well. This tastes even better the second or third day. Freezes for up to 3 months.

285 calories per serving, 26.5 g carbohydrate, 2.6 g fiber, 22 g protein, 10.1 g fat (3.9 g saturated), 80 mg cholesterol, 682 mg sodium, 796 mg potassium, 3 mg iron, 68 mg calcium

Slow Cooker Method

Use tomato sauce instead of tomato juice; tomato juice will make the sauce too liquidy as there is little evaporation when cooking in a slow cooker. Layer the ingredients in a sprayed 6-quart slow cooker as directed in Step 4. Cook on the low setting for 6 to 8 hours (or on the high setting for 3 to 4 hours).

Nutrition Notes

• Salt Alert! If salt is a concern to you, use low-sodium tomato sauce and juice, and omit the salt when preparing the meatballs.

• Sweet Choice: If you use granular Splenda instead of brown sugar, one serving will contain 262 calories and 20.7 g carbohydrates.

● STUFFED CABBAGE, SLOW COOKER STYLE

Children's author Rona Arato, of Toronto, shared her stuffed cabbage recipe with me, along with this story and an invitation for dinner: "I really loved my mother's stuffed cabbage so I set out to duplicate it when I moved into my first apartment. I didn't have her recipe, so I made it from memory. The results were a hit, and the dish became a staple in my culinary repertoire. Years later, when I made stuffed cabbage for my husband, he was delighted that I'd cooked a dish from Hungary, his native land. That was how I learned that stuffed cabbage was a Hungarian dish!"

1 large cabbage, frozen (see Freeze
    with Ease on page 197) and then thawed
2 lb (1 kg) lean ground turkey
    or ground chicken, veal, or beef
2 large eggs (or 1 large egg
    plus 2 egg whites)
1/2 cup uncooked brown rice
1 tsp salt (or to taste)
Freshly ground black pepper
    and sweet paprika
1 tsp dried basil
1 large onion, diced
1 can (28 oz/796 mL) crushed tomatoes
3/4 cup water (approximately)
1/2 cup cider vinegar (or to taste)
2 to 3 Tbsp granulated sugar (or to taste)
1 tsp caraway seeds
1 tsp dried basil
Dash of Worcestershire sauce
Salt, freshly ground black pepper,
    and paprika

1. Remove the leaves from the thawed cabbage and squeeze out any excess water. In a large bowl, combine the ground turkey, eggs, rice, and seasonings; mix well. Place a large spoonful of filling on one end of each cabbage leaf. Starting at the end with the filling, tightly roll up the leaves, folding in the sides. Place the cabbage rolls, seam-side down, in the slow cooker. Slice any leftover cabbage and add it to the slow cooker along with the onion.

2. In a large bowl, mix together the diced onions, the crushed tomatoes, water, cider vinegar, sugar, caraway seeds, basil, Worcestershire sauce, and the salt, pepper, and paprika to taste. If the mixture is too thick, add a little water to thin. Taste the mixture and adjust the vinegar/sugar ratio to get the right sweet-and-sour flavor. Pour the sauce over the cabbage rolls.

3. Cover and cook on the high setting for about 4 hours or until the cabbage is soft. If you prefer, cook on the low setting for 8 hours.

Yield: 24 cabbage rolls. Keeps for up to 3 days in the refrigerator; reheats well. Freezes well for up to 3 months.

107 calories per cabbage roll, 9.6 g carbohydrate, 2.0 g fiber, 9 g protein, 4.0 g fat (1.0 g saturated), 47 mg cholesterol, 188 mg sodium, 264 mg potassium, 1 mg iron, 40 mg calcium

Chef's Secrets

• Freeze with Ease: Place the whole cabbage in a plastic bag in the freezer for up to 2 days. Remove it from the freezer the night before using and thaw at room temperature overnight. When fully thawed, use a sharp knife to remove the core. The wilted leaves will separate easily.

• Easy Roller: To roll the cabbage leaves easily, pare the thick rib portion with a sharp paring knife. Larger leaves are best for stuffing.

• Saucy Secret: Most brands of Worcestershire sauce contain anchovies, so check the label if this is a concern.

🍎 CAN-CAN CHICKEN

This recipe, sometimes called Beer-Can Chicken or Beer-Butt Chicken, is fun to cook. Each chicken sits, like can-can dancers, on beer, coke, or even ginger ale cans. One thing you can count on—you'll end up with crispy, tender, oven-baked and beer-steamed chicken that will win rave reviews from family and friends.

2 whole chickens (about 3 lb/1.4 kg each)
1 Tbsp Kosher or sea salt (or to taste)
2 Tbsp freshly ground black pepper
2 Tbsp brown sugar
2 Tbsp garlic powder
2 Tbsp sweet paprika
2 tsp dried basil
2 cans (12oz/341 mL each) beer

1. Rinse the chickens well and then pat each one dry, inside and out, with paper towels. Trim the excess fat.

2. In a small bowl, combine the seasonings. Rub each chicken inside, outside, and under the skin with seasonings. (If desired, the chicken can be prepared in advance up to this point and refrigerated for up to 2 days.)

3. Remove the upper oven rack from the oven and place the remaining oven rack in the lowest position. Preheat the oven to 350°F.

4. Open the beer cans and remove about $1/2$ of the liquid so it won't boil over while in the oven. (Either drink the beer or discard it—the rest is the chicken's share!) Line a large baking sheet with foil, or use a disposable foil pan for easy clean-up. Place the opened beer cans on the baking sheet. Spray the top and sides of the cans well with cooking spray. Carefully place the cavity of each chicken on top of each of the opened beer cans and push down so that most of the can is inside the chicken. Be careful not to tip the cans and spill the beer. (Pull the chicken's legs forward so they almost form a tripod with the cans—this prevents the chickens from getting "tipsy" and toppling over!)

5. Carefully transfer the baking sheet to the oven. Roast, uncovered, on the lowest rack for $1 1/2$ hours or until the skin is

well-browned. If the top of the chickens start to brown too much, shield with foil. The chickens are done when an instant read thermometer, inserted into the thickest part of the breast, registers a minimum temperature of 165°F.

6. Carefully transfer the baking sheet from the oven to a heatproof surface and cool the chickens for 10 minutes before removing the cans. Take care not to burn yourself: the cans will still be very hot! Slice the chickens into serving pieces. (I usually cut the chicken into pieces while it's still sitting on the can!) Discard the cans and any remaining beer.

Yield: 8 servings. Keeps for up to 3 days in the refrigerator; reheats well. Freezes well for up to 4 months.

269 calories per serving (without skin), 4.8 g carbohydrate, 0.6 g fiber, 38 g protein, 9.7 g fat (2.7 g saturated), 116 mg cholesterol, 594 mg sodium, 353 mg potassium, 17 mg iron, 30 mg calcium

Steak-Spiced Chicken
Replace the salt, pepper, and garlic with 2 Tbsp Montreal-Style Steak Spice (page 115).

Honey Thyme Chicken
Rub each chicken with a mixture of 1 tsp each of salt, pepper, minced garlic, paprika, dry mustard, and thyme. Drizzle each chicken with 1 Tbsp honey, then 2 tsp low-sodium soy sauce, and rub to coat well.

Grilled Can-Can Chicken
Turn on a gas grill and set to medium. Season 2 whole chickens with your favorite spice mixture. Carefully place the cavity of each chicken on top of an opened, 1/2-full beer can and push down so that most of the can is inside the chicken. Transfer the upright, beer-can-stuffed chickens to the preheated grill, on the side without any flame underneath (be careful that the cans and chickens are properly balanced so they won't tip over). Close the lid and grill over indirect, medium heat for 1 1/4 to 1 1/2 hours, until the skin is well-browned. The chickens are done when an instant-read thermometer, inserted into the thickest part of the breast, registers a minimum temperature of 165°F. Carefully remove the chickens from the grill. (Silicone oven mitts are ideal for this step.) Let the chickens stand for 10 minutes before removing the cans. Slice chickens into pieces and serve.

🍐 CHEATER CHICKEN

I make variations of this dish using an assortment of bottled sauces—the chicken tastes different every time! It's a perfect recipe when you're in a hurry and it doubles or triples easily if you're serving a crowd. When your guests tell you how tasty it is, just smile serenely, gently wipe your brow, and say: "You're worth it."

1 barbecued chicken (store-bought)
1/4 cup barbecue sauce
   (try a hickory-flavored sauce)
1/4 cup duck sauce or chutney
   (see Chef's Secret on page 199)

1. Preheat the oven to 375°F. Cut the chicken into serving pieces. Arrange in a single layer in a sprayed, 2-quart casserole dish. Pour the barbecue sauce and duck sauce into a measuring cup; stir well. Spread

meat & poultry

evenly over the chicken pieces. (The chicken can be prepared in advance up to this point and refrigerated overnight.)

2. Transfer the casserole dish to the oven and roast, uncovered, for 25 to 30 minutes or until the chicken is glazed and heated through.

Yield: 4 servings. Recipe doubles or triples easily. Keeps for up to 2 days in the refrigerator; reheats well. Freezes well for up to 3 months.

284 calories per serving (without skin), 8.1 g carbohydrate, 0.2 g fiber, 38 g protein, 10.0 g fat (2.7 g saturated), 116 mg cholesterol, 291 mg sodium, 344 mg potassium, 2 mg iron, 23 mg calcium

Chef's Secrets
• **The Raw Truth:** If using raw chicken, roast uncovered at 400°F for 1 hour, basting occasionally. Freezes and reheats well.

• **No Duck Sauce or Chutney?** Substitute with 3 Tbsp Chinese plum sauce and 1 Tbsp orange marmalade.

Nutrition Note
• For my nutrient analysis, I used whole chicken with a raw weight of 3 pounds (1.4 kg). Chicken shrinks about 25% to 29% during cooking, so the cooked weight will be about 2 to 2¼ pounds (about 1 kg).

🍎 CHICKEN IN THE BAG

Stumped on what to make for dinner? It's chicken to the rescue! Combine all the ingredients in a re-sealable plastic bag and store in the freezer. When needed, transfer the bag to the refrigerator and let it thaw overnight. Once thawed, empty the contents into a

pan and cook. This recipe works well with chicken pieces of all shapes and sizes.

1 whole chicken (4 lb/1.8 kg),
  cut into pieces
½ cup white wine
¼ cup apricot jam (low-sugar or all-fruit)
2 Tbsp maple syrup or honey
2 Tbsp Dijon mustard
2 Tbsp low-sodium soy sauce
½ tsp salt
½ tsp freshly ground black pepper
1 tsp paprika
3 cloves garlic (about 1 Tbsp minced)
¼ cup sesame seeds, for sprinkling
  at cooking time

1. Rinse the chicken well and trim the excess fat. If desired, remove the skin. In a large re-sealable plastic bag, combine the chicken with the remaining ingredients except sesame seeds; seal tightly. Press on the bag to spread out the chicken pieces so they are in a single layer. Marinate for up to 2 days in the refrigerator or freeze for up to 4 months for a future meal.

2. When needed, place the bag of frozen chicken and sauce in the refrigerator and thaw for 24 hours.

3. Preheat the oven to 350°F. Spray a large baking dish with cooking spray. Empty contents of bag into the prepared baking dish and spread out in a single layer. Sprinkle with sesame seeds.

4. Bake, covered, for 1¼ hours, until tender. Uncover and bake 30 minutes longer, until the skin is golden, basting occasionally.

Yield: 8 servings. Keeps for up to 3 days in the refrigerator; reheats well. Freezes well for up to 4 months.

238 calories per serving (without skin), 8.8 g carbohydrate, 0.6 g fiber, 27 g protein, 8.9 g fat (1.8 g saturated), 77 mg cholesterol, 457 mg sodium, 246 mg potassium, 2 mg iron, 40 mg calcium

Boneless Breasts in the Bag

Use 10 boneless, skinless single chicken breasts. Bake, uncovered, at 375°F for 25 to 30 minutes, basting occasionally. Juices should run clear when the chicken is pierced with a fork. One serving contains 201 calories and 4.9 g fat (0.8 g saturated).

Chef's Secrets

• Time It Right: It takes 6 hours per pound to thaw frozen chicken in the refrigerator. To speed things up, place the sealed plastic bag of frozen chicken under hot water for 30 seconds to warm and loosen contents from the bag. Transfer the chicken to a microwaveable bowl. Set the microwave oven to defrost (30% power), calculating 5 to 7 minutes per pound: it will take about 25 to 30 minutes to thaw. If thawing chicken in the microwave oven, cook it as soon as it has thawed.

CHICKEN MARVELOSA

This elegant chicken dish is marvelous for any special occasion, especially the Jewish High Holidays as it contains honey, wine, and dried fruit. This recipe is a triple blessing—it's easy, can be doubled for a large crowd, and can be prepared in advance. It's guaranteed to inspire rave reviews.

2 whole chickens (3 lb/1.4 kg each), cut into pieces
Salt and freshly ground black pepper
2 Tbsp Italian seasoning (or a mixture of basil, oregano, thyme, and rosemary)
6 to 8 cloves garlic (about 2 to 3 Tbsp minced)
3/4 to 1 cup chopped dried apricots
1/2 cup pitted black olives
1/2 cup dry-packed, sun-dried tomatoes, halved or coarsely chopped
1/4 cup balsamic vinegar
1/4 cup honey
2 Tbsp olive oil
1/2 cup white wine
2 bay leaves
Chopped fresh parsley, for garnish

1. Rinse the chickens well and pat dry with paper towels. Trim the excess fat. Place the chickens in a large roasting pan sprayed with cooking spray. Season the chickens inside, outside, and under the skin with salt, pepper, Italian seasoning, and garlic. Add the apricots, olives, and sun-dried tomatoes to the pan. (The dried apricots and sun-dried tomatoes will plump up during marinating and cooking.)

2. In a measuring cup, combine the balsamic vinegar, honey, and olive oil. Drizzle evenly over the chicken mixture; mix well so that the chicken is thoroughly coated. Pour the wine around the chicken and add the bay leaves. Cover the pan and refrigerate for several hours or for as long as 2 days.

3. When the chicken is marinated, remove from the refrigerator, uncover, and bake in a 350°F oven for 1 1/4 to 1 1/2 hours, basting often. When done, the skin will be golden and the juices will run clear when pierced

with a fork. Remove the bay leaves and discard.

4. Using a slotted spoon, transfer the chicken mixture to a serving platter. Drizzle with some of the pan juices and sprinkle with chopped fresh parsley. Place the remaining pan juices in a gravy bowl, skim off the fat, and serve alongside the chicken.

Yield: 10 to 12 servings. Keeps for up to 2 to 3 days in the refrigerator; reheats well. Freezes well for up to 4 months.

307 calories per serving (without skin), 17.4 g carbohydrate, 1.3 g fiber, 31 g protein, 11.7 g fat (2.6 g saturated), 93 mg cholesterol, 245 mg sodium, 477 mg potassium, 2 mg iron, 36 mg calcium

Chef's Secrets

• Cover Up? If you prefer to remove the skin, cover the skinless chicken while cooking so it won't dry out.

• Keep A-Breast of the Times: Use chicken breasts to lower the calorie, fat, and cholesterol content. Use 10 to 12 breasts; remove the skin either before or after cooking. Cooking time will be about an hour for chicken breasts on the bone. Boneless, skinless breasts will take about 35 to 45 minutes. Cook, covered, to prevent the chicken from drying out. One serving (without skin) contains 263 calories, 7.1 g fat (1.4 g saturated), and 73 mg cholesterol.

🍎 CHICKEN YUM-YUM

The name says it all! This delicious dish can be doubled easily and works equally well with chicken breasts or legs. Your guests will agree that this dish is yum-yum, not ho-hum.

1 whole chicken (4 lb/1.8 kg),
 cut into pieces
2 cloves garlic (about 2 tsp minced)
Salt and freshly ground black pepper
1 medium onion, coarsely chopped
1/2 cup ketchup
3 Tbsp brown sugar or granular Splenda
1 Tbsp lemon juice (preferably fresh)
1 Tbsp soy sauce (low-sodium or regular)
1/2 tsp dried basil

1. Preheat the oven to 400°F. Rinse the chicken well and pat dry with paper towels. Trim the excess fat. Arrange the chicken in a single layer in a sprayed 9- × 13-inch casserole dish. Rub with garlic and lightly sprinkle with salt and pepper to taste. Scatter onions around the chicken.

2. In a small bowl, combine the ketchup, brown sugar, lemon juice, soy sauce, and dried basil; mix well. Spoon the mixture over the chicken pieces and spread evenly. (If desired, the chicken can be prepared in advance up to this point and refrigerated for as long as 2 days.)

3. Roast the chicken, uncovered, basting occasionally, for about 1 hour. Juices should run clear when the chicken is pierced with a fork.

Yield: 8 servings. Recipe doubles or triples easily. Keeps for up to 2 to 3 days in the refrigerator; reheats well. Freezes well for up to 4 months.

201 calories per serving (without skin), 9.0 g carbohydrate, 0.3 g fiber, 26 g protein, 6.5 g fat (1.8 g saturated), 77 mg cholesterol, 311 mg sodium, 311 mg potassium, 1 mg iron, 25 mg calcium

Chef's Secret

• The Naked Truth: For maximum flavor without the guilt, leave the skin on the chicken and cook it a day ahead, according to the instructions above. When the fully baked chicken is cool, cover, and refrigerate overnight. About 20 minutes before serving, remove any congealed fat, cover, and reheat. Remove the skin from the chicken before you eat it. (That's the way I like to make this dish!)

Nutrition Note

• Sweet Choice: To reduce the calories and carbs, use Low-Carb Ketchup (page 113) and granular Splenda. One serving contains 183 calories and 4.1 grams carbohydrate (0.5 g fiber).

● SLOW COOKER GARLICKY CHICKEN STEW

Your kitchen will smell absolutely wonderful when you make this scrumptious dish! The garlic becomes mild and mellow from the long, slow cooking. You can use less (or more) garlic if you wish and add whatever vegetables you have on hand. This is perfect for a chilly winter day. No slow cooker? Make it in the oven as directed below.

1 whole chicken (4 lb/1.8 kg),
   cut into pieces
2 medium onions, sliced
8 cloves garlic (don't chop)
2 stalks celery, cut into chunks
1 green pepper, seeded and
   cut into chunks
2 cups sliced mushrooms
2 cups baby carrots (or 4 medium carrots,
   peeled and cut into chunks)
4 medium potatoes, peeled and
   cut into chunks
4 medium sweet potatoes, peeled and
   cut into chunks
1 tsp each dried basil, oregano, and thyme
1/2 tsp cayenne pepper
Salt and freshly ground black pepper
3/4 cup ketchup or barbecue sauce
3/4 cup water
2 Tbsp lemon juice (preferably fresh)

1. Rinse the chicken well and pat dry with paper towels. Trim the excess fat and remove the skin, if desired.

2. Place the chicken into the slow cooker. Add the onions, garlic, celery, bell pepper, mushrooms, carrots, potatoes, and sweet potatoes. Sprinkle with basil, oregano, thyme, cayenne pepper, and salt and pepper to taste. In a small bowl, combine the ketchup, water, and lemon juice. Pour the mixture over the chicken and vegetables; mix well.

3. Cover and cook on the high setting for 4 to 6 hours, or on the low setting for 8 to 10 hours, until the chicken and vegetables are tender.

Yield: 8 servings. Keeps for up to 3 days in the refrigerator; reheats well. Chicken and vegetables can be frozen for up to 3 months, but don't freeze the potatoes or sweet potatoes or they will become mushy when thawed.

298 calories per serving (without skin), 32.2 g carbohydrate, 6.0 g fiber, 28 g protein, 6.3 g fat (1.7 g saturated), 73 mg cholesterol, 363 mg sodium, 912 mg potassium, 3 mg iron, 79 mg calcium

Oven Method

Combine all the ingredients in a large roasting pan sprayed with cooking spray. Cover and bake in a preheated 350°F oven for 1 1/2 to 2 hours. If desired, uncover and baste occasionally for the last half hour of baking.

DAPHNE'S FAMOUS CHUTNEY CHICKEN

My assistant, Shelley Sefton, shared this treasured recipe from her late mom's recipe collection. Daphne Zarenda's friends have been waiting impatiently for it so they could savor the special memories of this special lady who loved to cook and bake for her friends and family. Daphne—this one's for them—and you!

1 whole chicken (3½ lb/1.6 kg),
   cut into pieces
1 tsp garlic salt (or to taste)
½ tsp freshly ground black pepper
½ tsp paprika
¾ cup apricot or peach chutney
2 Tbsp lemon juice (preferably fresh)
1 Tbsp brown sugar
2 to 3 tsp curry powder
1 tsp ground ginger

1. Rinse the chicken well and pat dry with paper towels. Trim the excess fat. Spray a large casserole dish with cooking spray. Season the chicken pieces with garlic salt, pepper, and paprika. Place in a single layer in the prepared casserole.

2. In a small bowl, combine the chutney, lemon juice, brown sugar, curry powder, and ginger; mix well. Pour the mixture over the chicken and mix well, coating it on all sides. (If desired, the chicken can be prepared in advance up to this point and refrigerated for as long as 2 days.)

3. Preheat the oven to 350°F. Bake the chicken, covered, for 1 hour, basting with the sauce every 20 minutes. Uncover and bake for 15 to 20 minutes longer or until the chicken is glazed and golden.

Yield: 6 servings. Recipe doubles or triples easily. Keeps for up to 3 days in the refrigerator; reheats well. Freezes well for up to 4 months.

218 calories per serving (without skin), 16.2 g carbohydrate, 1.0 g fiber, 19 g protein, 8.8 g fat (2.4 g saturated), 58 mg cholesterol, 216 mg sodium, 322 mg potassium, 2 mg iron, 32 mg calcium

Shelley's Lighter Variation
• Use 8 boneless, skinless, single chicken breasts. Bake uncovered, basting occasionally, at 400°F for 20 to 25 minutes. Juices should run clear when chicken is pierced with a fork. One breast contains 190 calories, 12.1 g carbohydrate, 0.8 g fiber, and 3.3 g fat (0.9 g saturated).

NUTTY-BAKED CHICKEN

The inspiration for this crispy, high-fiber dish comes from Natasha Goldberg of Chicago. She likes to use a mixture of nuts, so choose whatever kind you like. You'll go nuts when you taste this!

1 whole chicken (3½ lb/1.6 kg),
   cut into pieces
Salt and freshly ground black pepper
2 Tbsp light mayonnaise
1 Tbsp Dijon mustard
¾ cup finely chopped nuts (almonds,
   walnuts, pecans, filberts, and/or peanuts)
¾ cup wheat or oat bran
1 Tbsp garlic powder
1 Tbsp onion powder

1. Preheat the oven to 375°F. Line a large baking sheet with foil and spray with cooking spray.

2. Rinse the chicken well and pat dry with paper towels. Trim the excess fat and remove the skin. Season the chicken with salt and pepper to taste.

3. In a small bowl, combine the mayonnaise and mustard. Combine the nuts, wheat bran, garlic powder, and onion powder in a re-sealable plastic bag. Lightly brush the seasoned chicken pieces with the mayonnaise mixture, then place in the bag, one or two pieces at a time, and shake to thoroughly coat with the nut mixture. Transfer the coated chicken pieces to the prepared baking sheet, arranging them in a single layer.

4. Bake the chicken, uncovered, for about 1 1/4 hours or until the coating is crispy and golden. Juices should run clear when the chicken is pierced with a fork.

Yield: 6 servings. Keeps for up to 3 days in the refrigerator; reheats well. Freezes well for up to 4 months. Don't cover when reheating or the chicken coating won't be crisp.

339 calories per serving (without skin), 9.3 g carbohydrate, 4.8 g fiber, 32 g protein, 20.4 g fat (3.3. g saturated), 92 mg cholesterol, 191 mg sodium, 426 mg potassium, 3 mg iron, 40 mg calcium

"Nut"-rition Notes

• Although nuts are high in fat and calories, they contain mostly unsaturated fat that helps protect your heart. Nuts are cholesterol-free and provide good sources of protein, phosphorus, zinc, and magnesium, along with vitamin E and selenium.

• Go Nuts! Different nuts have different benefits, so enjoy a variety. Almonds are high in calcium, vitamin E, magnesium, potassium, and fiber. Walnuts are the best source of Omega-3 fats, but it's best to eat them raw as heat diminishes their Omega-3 content; they're also high in polyunsaturated fats, antioxidants, protein, and fiber. Pecans are the highest of all nuts in antioxidants, and contain vitamin E, potassium, zinc, and fiber. Filberts (hazelnuts) are high in potassium, monounsaturated fats, vitamin E, and antioxidants. Peanuts are high in protein and are a good source of folate. Nuts to you!

• Unsalted nuts are usually found in the baking aisle, while salted nuts are found with the snack foods. Nuts help satisfy hunger, so eat a small serving of nuts (about a handful) 5 times a week.

• Store nuts in a sealed container in the refrigerator, or freeze them. They'll keep for up to a year if stored properly.

PEANUT BUTTER CHICKEN

Peanut butter isn't just a spread for sandwiches. Try it on chicken and don't worry —your "butt" won't spread. Peanut butter chicken is delicious over brown basmati rice or whole grain pasta and stir-fried vegetables.

1 whole chicken (3 lb/1.4 kg),
   cut into pieces
1/3 cup natural peanut butter
1 to 2 Tbsp honey
3 Tbsp lime juice (preferably fresh)
2 Tbsp low-sodium soy sauce
2 cloves garlic (about 2 tsp minced)
1/2 tsp ground cumin
1/2 tsp ground coriander
1/4 tsp hot pepper sauce

1. Rinse the chicken well and pat dry with paper towels. Remove the skin and trim the excess fat. Spray a large baking dish with cooking spray; place the chicken in a single layer in the sprayed dish.

2. In a small bowl, combine the peanut butter, honey, lime juice, soy sauce, garlic, cumin, coriander, and pepper sauce; mix well. Pour over the chicken in the baking dish. Cover and marinate in the refrigerator for 2 hours, or for as long as 2 days.

3. When the chicken is marinated, preheat the oven to 375°F. Bake the chicken, covered, for 45 minutes. Turn the chicken over; baste with the sauce in the dish, and bake, uncovered, for 30 minutes longer. Remove from the oven and let cool before refrigerating overnight.

4. About 30 minutes before serving, remove and discard any congealed fat from the top of the sauce. Reheat, covered, at 350°F for 20 to 25 minutes, until heated through. Serve immediately.

Yield: 6 servings. Keeps for up to 3 days in the refrigerator; reheats well. Freezes well for up to 4 months.

283 calories per serving (without skin), 10.5 g carbohydrate, 1.1 g fiber, 29 g protein, 13.6 g fat (2.7 g saturated), 77 mg cholesterol, 312 mg sodium, 240 mg potassium, 1 mg iron, 19 mg calcium

"Nut"-rition Note

• Spreading the News: Whether peanut butter is smooth, chunky, or crunchy doesn't affect the nutritional content. Sometimes salt or small amounts of sugar may be added for flavor. Reduced-fat varieties of peanut butter often have added sugars, or the natural oils may be hydrogenated to make them more spreadable, which also makes them somewhat more saturated. The best kind of peanut butter is one that lists nothing but peanuts on the label. Stir it well before using—and store it in the refrigerator to prevent rancidity.

● POMEGRANATE CHICKEN

According to ancient lore, the amount of seeds in the pomegranate is exactly the same number (613) as the mitzvot (good deeds) found in the Torah (the Jewish Bible). If you're curious, count away! This fragrant dish also contains honey, carrots, and apricots—traditional foods served with hope for a sweet and fruitful New Year.

2 medium onions, sliced
2 cups baby carrots (or 2 cups peeled and
   sliced regular carrots)
2 whole chickens (3 1/2 lb/1.6 kg each),
   cut into pieces
1 tsp dried thyme
Kosher salt and freshly ground black pepper
1 cup dried whole apricots, loosely packed
1 cup pitted whole prunes, loosely packed
2 tsp sweet paprika

Marinade:

1/2 cup pomegranate juice
   (or juice of 1 pomegranate)
2 cloves garlic (about 2 tsp minced)
Juice and rind of 1 lemon
1/3 cup balsamic vinegar
2 Tbsp extra virgin olive oil
2 Tbsp honey

1. Spray a large roasting pan with cooking spray. Scatter the onions and carrots in the bottom of the pan. Rinse the chicken well

and pat dry with paper towels. Trim the excess fat. Place the chicken on top of the vegetables and sprinkle—under the skin and on top—with thyme, and salt and pepper to taste. Tuck the apricots and prunes between the chicken pieces.

2. Whisk the ingredients for the marinade together in a bowl. (If using the juice of a whole pomegranate, reserve some of the seeds for garnish.) Pour over the chicken and sprinkle with paprika. Cover and marinate in the refrigerator for at least 1 hour or for as long as 2 days.

3. When the chicken is marinated, preheat the oven to 350°F. Cook the chicken, covered, for 1½ hours or until tender. Uncover and cook for 30 minutes longer, basting occasionally, or until the skin is golden. Remove from the pan from the oven and let cool before refrigerating overnight.

4. About 30 minutes before serving, remove and discard any congealed fat from the chicken. Reheat, covered, for 25 to 30 minutes at 350°F. Transfer the heated chicken to a large serving platter and sprinkle with pomegranate seeds. Serve immediately.

Yield: 12 servings. Keeps for up to 3 days in the refrigerator; reheats well. Freezes well for up to 4 months.

315 calories per serving (without skin), 25.9 g carbohydrate, 2.8 g fiber, 31 g protein, 10.0 g fat (2.4 g saturated), 90 mg cholesterol, 103 mg sodium, 526 mg potassium, 2 mg iron, 43 mg calcium

Chef's Secrets

• Pomegranate Power: See Pomegranate Power Smoothie (page 434) for information on pomegranates. One pomegranate contains about 3/4 cup seeds and yields ½ cup juice.

• No Pomegranates? Substitute either bottled pomegranate or cranberry juice. If desired, sprinkle with toasted pumpkin or sesame seeds at serving time.

ROSEMARY MAPLE CHICKEN

This delicious dish is quick to assemble, can be doubled easily, and makes an excellent main dish for family or friends. Chunks of potatoes or sweet potatoes can be roasted together with the chicken for a dinner-in-a-dish.

1 whole chicken (3½ lb/1.6 kg),
    cut into pieces
1 medium onion, sliced
1 tsp Kosher or sea salt (or to taste)
Freshly ground black pepper and paprika
2 cloves garlic (about 2 tsp minced)
2 Tbsp lemon juice (preferably fresh)
1 Tbsp olive oil
¼ cup pure maple syrup
1 tsp dried rosemary, crumbled

1. Rinse the chicken pieces well and pat dry with paper towels. Trim off the fat. Scatter the onions in a sprayed 9- × 13-inch baking dish. Arrange the chicken in a single layer on top of the onions. Season the chicken and onions with salt, pepper, and paprika to taste.

2. In a small bowl, combine the garlic, lemon juice, oil, maple syrup, and rosemary; mix well. Drizzle the mixture on top of the chicken and onions and toss to thoroughly coat. Sprinkle with additional paprika. Cover and marinate in the refrigerator for at least 1 hour or as long as 2 days.

3. Preheat the oven to 375°F. Roast the chicken, uncovered and basting occasionally, for about 1¼ hours or until the skin is golden.

Yield: 6 servings. Keeps for up to 3 days in the refrigerator; reheats well. Freezes well for up to 4 months.

259 calories per serving (without skin), 11.7 g carbohydrate, 0.4 g fiber, 30 g protein, 9.8 g fat (2.4 g saturated), 90 mg cholesterol, 303 mg sodium, 314 mg potassium, 4 mg iron, 33 mg calcium

Variations
• Instead of lemon juice, use balsamic vinegar. To reduce the carbs and calories, reduce maple syrup to 2 Tbsp or use ¼ cup sugar-free pancake syrup. Instead of rosemary, use dried tarragon, thyme, or basil.

Chef's Secret
• Freeze with Ease: Combine all the ingredients in a large re-sealable plastic bag. Seal well. Press on the bag to spread out the uncooked chicken pieces so they are in a single layer. Freeze for up to 4 months. When needed, thaw the chicken in the refrigerator—it will take about 24 hours. Transfer the chicken and marinade to a sprayed baking dish and roast as directed.

� TIPSY APRICOT CHICKEN

You'll flip over this sweet and juicy chicken—it's tip-top! This scrumptious dish was a favorite of my friend, the late Bev Gordon, of Richmond Hill. In the winter, make it with dried apricots or canned peaches, and in the summer, use fresh nectarines or peaches.

1 whole chicken (3½ lb/1.6 kg), cut into pieces
1 cup baby carrots (or 2 medium carrots, peeled and cut into chunks)
1 cup dried whole apricots (or canned sliced peaches, rinsed and drained)
Salt, freshly ground black pepper, and paprika

Sauce:

¼ cup peach schnapps or orange liqueur
¼ cup orange marmalade (low-sugar or all-fruit)
½ cup orange juice (preferably fresh)
1 Tbsp hoisin sauce

1. Preheat the oven to 350°F. Spray a 9- × 13-inch glass baking dish with cooking spray.

2. Rinse the chicken pieces and pat dry with paper towels. Trim the excess fat. Place the carrots and apricots in the bottom of the baking dish. Arrange the chicken pieces on top. Season the chicken on all sides with salt, pepper, and paprika to taste.

3. In a medium saucepan over high heat, combine the schnapps, marmalade, orange juice, and hoisin sauce; stir to mix well and bring to a boil. Pour the hot sauce evenly over the chicken, carrots, and apricots.

4. Roast, uncovered, basting frequently, for about 1 to 1¼ hours or until the chicken is glazed and golden.

Yield: 6 servings. Keeps for up to 3 days in the refrigerator; reheats well. Freezes well for up to 4 months.

316 calories per serving (without skin), 26.2 g carbohydrate, 2.1 g fiber, 30 g protein, 7.8 g fat (2.1 g saturated), 90 mg cholesterol, 143 mg sodium, 524 mg potassium, 2 mg iron, 34 mg calcium

Tipsy Nectarine Chicken

Instead of dried apricots, add 6 nectarines (peeled, pitted, and sliced) to the baking dish. One serving contains 324 calories, 27.0 g carbohydrate, and 2.9 fiber.

Chef's Secrets

• The Skinny on Skin: Roast the chicken with the skin on to prevent it from drying out, then remove the skin before eating to reduce your calorie and fat intake. You can substitute any chicken parts you like for this recipe.

• Multiple Pleasures: This elegant dish is a real crowd-pleaser, so why not double or triple the recipe for guests. Even if tripling the recipe, you only need to double the sauce ingredients.

● OVEN-FRIED CHICKEN

This recipe tastes best if made with dark meat, which is higher in fat. You can use chicken breasts, but it won't be as moist. Your choice!

6 chicken drumsticks and 6 thighs
1 large egg (or 2 egg whites)
2 tsp Dijon mustard
24 wholegrain crackers, crushed
   (preferably reduced-fat)
Salt and freshly ground black pepper
1/2 tsp dried basil
1/2 tsp dried thyme
Paprika

1. Preheat the oven to 400°F. Line a large baking sheet with foil; spray with cooking spray. (For extra-crispy chicken, see Chef's Secret.)

2. Rinse the chicken well and pat dry with paper towels. Remove the skin, and trim the excess fat. In a pie plate, whisk together the egg and mustard; mix well. In a re-sealable plastic bag, combine the crushed crackers and seasonings. Dip both sides of the chicken pieces in the egg mixture, then place in the bag, one or two pieces at a time, and shake to thoroughly coat with the crumb mixture. Arrange the crumb-coated chicken pieces in a single layer on the prepared baking sheet.

3. Bake the chicken, uncovered, for 45 to 50 minutes or until the coating is crispy and golden. Juices should run clear when the chicken is pierced with a fork.

Yield: 6 servings. Keeps for up to 3 days in the refrigerator; reheats well. Freezes well for up to 4 months. Don't cover when reheating or the chicken coating will not be crisp.

372 calories per serving (1 leg and 1 thigh, without skin), 12.3 g carbohydrate, 1.8 g fiber, 42 g protein, 16.2 g fat (4.0. g saturated), 174 mg cholesterol, 429 mg sodium, 368 mg potassium, 3 mg iron, 26 mg calcium

Passover Variation

• Omit the mustard. Instead of crushed crackers, use 1 cup whole wheat matzo meal or finely chopped nuts such as almonds or pecans.

Chef's Secret

• Rack It Up! For extra-crispy chicken, bake it on a rack. Spray the slotted rack from a broiling pan with cooking spray. Line the pan underneath with foil for easy clean-up. The air will circulate freely, producing crispier chicken.

Nutrition Notes

• Chick Pick: Use 6 single skinless chicken breasts (with bone in) and increase the cooking time to 1 hour. One breast contains 224 calories and 5.6 g fat (1.1 g saturated).

• Going Crackers: You need about 3/4 to 1 cup cracker crumbs for this recipe. Choose wisely—look for the words "whole grain" at the top of the ingredient list, with a maximum of 130 calories per serving and no trans-fats or hydrogenated oils.

◖ ALMOND MANDARIN CHICKEN BREASTS

Thanks to Sandy Glazier of St. Louis, Missouri, for sharing one of her favorite dishes. Sandy arranges the chicken breasts like the spokes of a wheel on a bed of basmati rice. To cut the fat, I baked the chicken instead of sautéing it. I also used less sugar and honey, and balsamic vinegar instead of sherry. It's a winner!

1/4 cup slivered almonds
6 boneless, skinless single chicken breasts
1 cup orange juice (preferably fresh)
2 to 4 Tbsp lemon juice (preferably fresh)
1 Tbsp soy sauce (low-sodium or regular)
2 Tbsp olive oil
2 Tbsp balsamic vinegar
3 to 4 Tbsp brown sugar
2 Tbsp honey
2 cloves garlic (about 2 tsp minced)
1/2 tsp ground ginger
1 Tbsp cornstarch
Salt and freshly ground black pepper
1 can (10 oz/284 mL) mandarin oranges
   (about 3/4 cup drained)
1/4 cup minced fresh parsley

1. Scatter the almonds onto a baking tray and toast in a 350°F oven for 6 to 8 minutes until lightly browned (or microwave on high for 2 minutes). Set aside.

2. Rinse the chicken well and pat dry with paper towels. Trim the excess fat. In a large bowl, combine the orange juice, lemon juice, soy sauce, oil, vinegar, brown sugar, honey, garlic, and ginger. Add the chicken breasts and toss to coat well. Cover and marinate in the refrigerator for 1 hour or for as long as 2 days.

3. Preheat the oven to 400°F. Line a baking sheet with foil and spray with cooking spray. Remove the chicken from the marinade; reserve the marinade and set aside. Arrange the chicken in a single layer on the prepared baking sheet. Bake, uncovered, for 20 minutes, or until the juices run clear.

4. Meanwhile, pour the reserved marinade into a saucepan and stir in the cornstarch. Heat over medium high heat until boiling, stirring often; continue cooking for 1 to 2 minutes or until thickened. Season with salt and pepper to taste.

5. Pour half the sauce into the bottom of a large casserole dish. Place the chicken breasts in the dish and pour the remaining sauce over the chicken. Top with the oranges and bake for 10 minutes or until piping hot. Transfer the chicken to a platter, garnish with parsley and the reserved toasted almonds, and serve.

Yield: 6 servings. Recipe doubles or triples easily. Keeps for up to 3 days in the refrigerator; reheats well. Freezes well for up to 4 months.

292 calories per serving, 21.7 g carbohydrate, 0.8 g fiber, 28 g protein, 10.0 g fat (1.7 g saturated), 73 mg cholesterol, 150 mg sodium, 390 mg potassium, 2 mg iron, 44 mg calcium

meat & poultry

Variations

• To add color and fiber, sauté 1 seeded and chopped red pepper, 1 cup snow peas, and 6 sliced green onions in 1 Tbsp olive oil for 3 to 4 minutes. Add to the chicken in Step 5.

• Instead of mandarin oranges, use canned lychees or sliced kiwis. Instead of almonds, use cashews.

CHIMICHURRI CHICKEN

Chimichurri is a bold-flavored herb sauce that is as common in Argentina as ketchup is in North America. Everyone will be swept off their feet and singing "Chim-Chim-Churri" when you serve this delicious dish. You'll never know who will "Popp-in" for this "merry" meal!

6 boneless, skinless single chicken breasts
Salt and freshly ground black pepper
3 cloves garlic
1 medium onion, cut in chunks
2/3 cup packed fresh parsley leaves
1/3 cup extra virgin olive oil
1/3 cup red wine vinegar (or sherry
   or rice vinegar)
1/2 tsp dried oregano
1/2 tsp cayenne pepper
1 tsp salt
1/2 tsp freshly ground black pepper

1. Rinse the chicken breasts and pat dry with paper towels. Trim the excess fat. Lightly sprinkle the chicken with salt and pepper to taste, then place in a large, re-sealable plastic bag.

2. In a food processor fitted with the steel blade, process the garlic, onion, and parsley until minced, about 8 to 10 seconds. Add the olive oil, vinegar, oregano, cayenne, salt, and pepper; process for about 5 seconds to blend. Transfer the sauce to a large glass measuring cup.

3. Pour half the sauce over the chicken in the plastic bag. Seal the bag tightly and shake well to thoroughly coat the chicken in the sauce. Let the chicken marinate in the sauce for 30 to 60 minutes at room temperature or for up to 48 hours in the refrigerator. Place the remaining sauce in a gravy boat or serving bowl; cover and refrigerate to serve with the cooked chicken.

4. When the chicken is marinated, preheat the grill and set to medium high. Remove the chicken from the marinade in the bag; discard the marinade. Grill the chicken over indirect heat for 5 to 6 minutes per side, until grill marks appear and juices run clear. Serve immediately with the reserved sauce.

Yield: 6 servings. Keeps for up to 3 days in the refrigerator; reheats well. Freezes well for up to 3 months. Sauce may discolor slightly if frozen.

262 calories per serving, 3.1 g carbohydrate, 0.6 g fiber, 27 g protein, 15.2 g fat (2.5 g saturated), 73 mg cholesterol, 456 mg sodium, 295 mg potassium, 2 mg iron, 32 mg calcium

Chimichurri Beef
Instead of chicken, use 2 lb (1 kg) lean London broil. In Step 3, grill the meat over indirect heat for 8 to 10 minutes per side or until medium (pink juices will come to the surface of meat). Remove from the grill and let rest for 5 to 10 minutes. Slice thinly across the grain and serve with reserved

sauce. One serving contains 302 calories and 18.1 g fat (5.0 g saturated).

Chef's Secret
• Refer to Grill It Right (page 34) and Marin-Aides (page 36) for important information on grilling.

CRUNCHY CHUTNEY CHICKEN

This is so quick and easy you'll probably have it done before you can say, "Crunchy Chutney Chicken," ten times in a row!

6 boneless, skinless single chicken breasts
   (2 lb/1 kg)
Salt and freshly ground black pepper
Paprika
1 tsp dried basil
1 tsp curry powder
2 cloves garlic (about 2 tsp minced)
1/2 cup mango or apricot chutney
2 cups coarsely crushed Special K
   or corn flakes

1. Rinse the chicken well and pat dry with paper towels. Trim the excess fat. Place the chicken in a large bowl and season with salt, pepper, paprika, basil, curry powder, and garlic. Brush both sides of the chicken with chutney. Let marinate for 30 minutes at room temperature or for up to 48 hours, covered, in the refrigerator.

2. Preheat the oven to 375°F. Line a large baking sheet with parchment paper or sprayed foil.

3. Combine the cereal with additional salt and pepper in a re-sealable plastic bag. Add the marinated chicken pieces to the bag, a few at a time; shake well to coat with the crumb mix-

ture. Arrange the coated chicken in a single layer on the prepared baking sheet.

4. Bake, uncovered, for 30 minutes or until golden brown, turning the chicken over halfway through baking.

Yield: 6 servings. Recipe doubles or triples easily. Keeps for up to 3 days in the refrigerator; reheats well. Freezes well for up to 4 months.

219 calories per serving, 16.9 g carbohydrate, 0.9 g fiber, 29 g protein, 3.4 g fat (0.9 g saturated), 73 mg cholesterol, 143 mg sodium, 348 mg potassium, 4 mg iron, 30 mg calcium

Variation
• Instead of chicken breasts, use 12 boneless, skinless chicken thighs. One serving (2 thighs) contains 294 calories and 11.6 g fat (3.2 g saturated).

GRILLED MOROCCAN CHICKEN BREASTS

Grill-y delicious! Use your outdoor grill in the summertime or an electric indoor grill the rest of the year. Couscous, Moroccan-Style (page 325) and Terrific Tabbouleh (page 261) make perfect accompaniments. You'll feel like a well-seasoned traveler.

6 boneless, skinless single chicken breasts
   (2 lb/1 kg)
Salt and freshly ground black pepper
2 cloves garlic (about 2 tsp minced)
3 Tbsp minced fresh mint or cilantro
1 Tbsp minced fresh thyme or 1 tsp dried
1 tsp ground cumin
1 tsp sweet paprika
2 Tbsp extra virgin olive oil
2 Tbsp lemon juice (preferably fresh)

1. Rinse the chicken well and trim the excess fat. Lightly sprinkle the chicken with salt and pepper to taste; place in a re-sealable plastic bag.

2. In a small bowl, combine the garlic, mint, thyme, cumin, paprika, olive oil, and lemon juice; mix well. Pour the marinade over the chicken in the plastic bag, seal tightly, and shake to coat all sides. (If desired, the chicken can be prepared in advance up to this point and marinated for as long as 2 days in the refrigerator.)

3. Preheat the grill to medium-high. Remove the chicken from the marinade and drain well; discard the marinade. Grill the chicken over indirect heat about 5 to 6 minutes per side, until grill marks appear and juices run clear. (If using a two-sided indoor grill, spray with cooking spray. Place the chicken breasts on the grill, close lid, and grill for 5 to 6 minutes total cooking time.) Don't overcook or the chicken will be dry.

Yield: 6 servings. Recipe doubles or triples easily. Keeps for up to 3 days in the refrigerator; reheats well. Freezes for up to 4 months.

188 calories per serving, 1.3 g carbohydrate, 0.3 g fiber, 27 g protein, 7.7 g fat (1.5 g saturated), 73 mg cholesterol, 65 mg sodium, 252 mg potassium, 1 mg iron, 22 mg calcium

Variations
• Instead of mint, use basil or parsley. If using dried herbs, substitute 1 tsp dried for 1 Tbsp fresh herbs.

• Instead of lemon juice, use orange, lime, or pomegranate juice.

• For a slightly sweet flavor, add 1 Tbsp honey or apricot jam to the marinade.

Chef's Secrets
• Leftovers? Slice the chicken thinly and serve on salad greens or use to fill pita pockets or wraps.

• Frozen Assets: I like to marinate several batches of chicken in re-sealable freezer bags and freeze for a future meal. I just thaw the chicken in the refrigerator the night before serving, then grill as directed.

● HOISIN SESAME CHICKEN

Enjoy this chicken baked or grilled, hot or cold—it's sinfully good! It can be doubled easily, so why not make extra for another day?

4 boneless, skinless single chicken breasts
Salt and freshly ground black pepper
3 Tbsp hoisin sauce
1 Tbsp apricot preserves or orange marmalade (reduced-sugar or all-fruit)
2 tsp minced garlic
2 tsp lemon or lime juice (preferably fresh)
2 Tbsp sesame seeds

1. Spray a foil-lined baking sheet with cooking spray. Rinse the chicken and pat dry with paper towels. Trim the excess fat. Place the chicken on the prepared baking sheet and lightly sprinkle with salt and pepper to taste.

2. In a small bowl, combine the hoisin sauce, apricot preserves, garlic, and juice; mix well. Brush the sauce evenly over the chicken. Sprinkle with sesame seeds and let marinate for 30 minutes or refrigerate, covered, for as long as 2 days.

3. Preheat the oven to 400°F. Bake, uncovered, for 18 to 20 minutes, or until the juices run clear when pierced with a fork.

Yield: 4 servings. Recipe doubles or triples easily. Keeps for up to 3 days in the refrigerator; reheats well. Freezes well for up to 4 months.

203 calories per serving, 8.1 g carbohydrate, 0.8 g fiber, 28 g protein, 5.6 g fat (0.9 g saturated), 73 mg cholesterol, 266 mg sodium, 243 mg potassium, 1 mg iron, 34 mg calcium

Grilled Hoisin Sesame Chicken

Prepare the chicken and marinate as directed. Preheat the barbecue to medium-high. Grill the chicken over indirect heat, 5 to 6 minutes per side or until the juices run clear and grill marks appear. If using a two-sided indoor grill, spray with cooking spray. Place the chicken on the grill and close the lid. Total cooking time will be 5 to 6 minutes.

Hoisin Sesame Chicken with Vegetables

Make an extra batch of the sauce, or use 1/3 cup of your favorite bottled Asian-style sauce. Mix the sauce with assorted sliced vegetables such as 2 onions, 1 red pepper, 1 green pepper, 1 zucchini, and 2 cups mushrooms. Spread the vegetables in a single layer on the same baking sheet as the chicken. Bake at 400°F for 20 minutes, stirring the vegetables once or twice. Everything will be ready at the same time.

Hoisin Chicken Salad

Thinly slice the cooked chicken breasts and place on a bed of mixed salad greens. Drizzle with Asian Salad Dressing (page 274) or your favorite vinaigrette dressing. Garnish with mandarin oranges or pineapple chunks and toasted slivered almonds.

Chef's Secret

• Time-Saver: While the oven or barbecue is preheating, cook up a batch of rice. (Brown basmati is one of my favorites.) If you cook double the amount of rice, leftovers can be used for another meal. Twice the rice with half the work!

● NO-FRY ALMOND SCHNITZEL

You'll go nuts for these crispy, crunchy chicken breasts. The coating is healthy because of the good fat in the almonds and sesame seeds. These go smashingly well with Smashed Potato "Latkes" (page 306).

1 cup Special K cereal
   (1/3 cup when coarsely crushed)
1/3 cup wheat germ
1/4 cup almonds
3 Tbsp sesame seeds
1/2 tsp salt (or to taste)
1/2 tsp freshly ground black pepper
1/2 tsp garlic powder
1/2 tsp dried basil
1/2 tsp paprika
2 egg whites (or 1 large egg)
4 boneless, skinless single chicken breasts
   (1 1/2 lb/750 g)

1. Preheat the oven to 400°F. Line a baking sheet with parchment paper or foil sprayed with cooking spray.

2. In a food processor fitted with the steel blade, combine the cereal, wheat germ, almonds, sesame seeds, and seasonings; process for 15 to 20 seconds to make coarse crumbs. Transfer to a plate.

3. In a pie plate, lightly whisk the egg whites; set aside.

4. Rinse the chicken well and pat dry with paper towels. Trim the excess fat. Dip the chicken breasts first in the egg whites, then dredge both sides in the crumb mixture to thoroughly coat. Arrange the chicken in a single layer on the prepared baking sheet. (If desired, the chicken can be prepared in advance up to this point, covered, and refrigerated overnight.)

5. Bake, uncovered, for 20 to 25 minutes or until crisp and golden, turning chicken over after 10 minutes.

Yield: 4 servings. Recipe doubles or triples easily. Keeps for up to 3 days in the refrigerator; reheats well. Freezes well for up to 4 months.

346 calories per serving, 13.3 g carbohydrate, 3.1 g fiber, 44 g protein, 12.7 g fat (1.6 g saturated), 94 mg cholesterol, 472 mg sodium, 497 mg potassium, 5 mg iron, 70 mg calcium

Almond-Crusted Chicken Fingers
Cut each chicken breast into 4 or 5 long strips. Coat as directed. Bake for 10 minutes, then flip and bake 6 to 8 minutes longer.

Chef's Secrets
• Be Prepared: Make several batches of the crumb mixture and store in re-sealable plastic bags in your refrigerator or freezer for up to 6 months.

• Nut Allergies? Omit the almonds and increase the amount of Special K cereal to 1³/4 cups.

• GI Go! Special K cereal has a lower glycemic index value than corn flakes, making it a healthier choice as a crispy coating.

◉ STUFFED CHICKEN BREASTS

Elegant and luscious, this wonderful low-carb dish can be prepared in advance. It's easy to make half the recipe for a small family or double the recipe for a crowd.

Spinach and Mushroom Stuffing
  (page 339)
8 skinless, boneless single chicken breasts
Salt and freshly ground black pepper
1/4 cup orange juice (preferably fresh)
4 tsp olive oil
1 tsp honey
1/2 tsp dried basil or 1 Tbsp chopped fresh
Paprika

1. Prepare the stuffing as directed. Rinse the chicken well and pat dry with paper towels. Trim the excess fat. Butterfly the chicken breasts by cutting, horizontally, through the middle of each breast, leaving it hinged on one side, so that it opens flat like a book. Season both sides with salt and pepper to taste. Spread about 3 to 4 Tbsp filling on one side, then fold the other side over to cover the filling. Repeat with the remaining chicken breasts and filling.

2. Place the stuffed chicken breasts in a single layer in a 9- × 13-inch baking dish sprayed with cooking spray.

3. Combine the orange juice, olive oil, honey, and basil in a measuring cup; mix well. Drizzle the mixture over the chicken breasts. Sprinkle with paprika and marinate for at least 1/2 hour. (If desired, the chicken can be prepared up to this point and refrigerated up to 24 hours, basting once or twice. Remove the chicken from the refrigerator about 30 minutes before cooking.)

meat & poultry

4. Preheat the oven to 375°F. Roast the chicken, uncovered and basting occasionally, for 30 to 35 minutes. Juices should run clear when the chicken is pierced with a fork.

Yield: 8 servings. Recipe doubles or triples easily. Keeps for up to 2 days in the refrigerator; reheats well. Freezes well for up to 2 months.

208 calories per serving, 6.5 g carbohydrate, 1.7 g fiber, 28 g protein, 7.3 g fat (1.5 g saturated), 73 mg cholesterol, 88 mg sodium, 397 mg potassium, 2 mg iron, 60 mg calcium

● CHICKEN FAJITAS

This easy, nutrition-packed dish is a fun way for a family to enjoy a meal together. It gives everyone a chance to be creative, adding the ingredients that they like. Let the good times roll!

4 boneless, skinless single chicken breasts, cut into thin strips (about 1 1/2 lb/750 g)
Salt and freshly ground black pepper
2 cloves garlic (about 2 tsp minced)
1 tsp ground cumin
Juice of 1 lime (about 2 Tbsp)
2 Tbsp olive oil
1 large onion, thinly sliced
1 green and 1 red pepper, seeded and cut into strips
1 jalapeno chili pepper, seeded and cut into strips
6 10-inch flour tortillas (preferably whole-wheat), warmed

Additional Fillings:

2 cups shredded romaine lettuce
1 cup chunky salsa (bottled or homemade)
Optional: Refried Black Beans (page 331), guacamole, chopped tomatoes, cilantro

1. Rinse the chicken well and trim the excess fat. Place chicken in a medium bowl. Season it with salt, pepper, garlic, and cumin. Add the lime juice and 1 Tbsp of the olive oil; mix well. Cover and marinate for 1 hour (or for up to 2 days in the refrigerator).

2. Heat the remaining 1 Tbsp oil in a large nonstick skillet over medium high heat. Add the onion and peppers and sauté until tender, about 6 to 8 minutes. Transfer to a plate and set aside.

3. Pour the marinade from the chicken into the skillet and heat over medium high heat. (No need to wash the skillet first.) Add the chicken strips and sauté in the marinade until lightly browned, about 3 to 4 minutes. Using a slotted spoon, transfer the chicken to a plate.

4. Assembly: Spoon the chicken onto the warm tortillas, leaving a 1-inch border on the bottom and the sides. Top with the sautéed vegetables and desired fillings. Fold in the sides and the bottom of the tortilla, and roll up tightly into a cylinder. Serve immediately.

Yield: 6 servings. Recipe doubles or triples easily. Chicken freezes well for up to 3 months; reheats well. The vegetables will get soggy if frozen, then thawed.

401 calories per serving, 46.1 g carbohydrate, 4.1 g fiber, 25 g protein, 12.5 g fat (2.6 g saturated), 49 mg cholesterol, 718 mg sodium, 435 mg potassium, 4 mg iron, 131 mg calcium

Variation
• Instead of chicken, substitute thinly sliced lean beef such as London broil or extra-firm tofu.

Fast Fajitas

Instead of marinating and cooking chicken strips, substitute 3 cups of cooked chicken or beef strips. A great way to use up leftovers!

Vegetarian Burritos

Omit the chicken. Fill warm tortillas with Refried Black Beans (page 331) and 2 cups of low-fat grated cheese such as mozzarella or Monterey Jack.

Chef's Secrets

• Roll Your Own: Place chicken, vegetables, and tortillas in separate mounds on a large platter. Place desired toppings in separate bowls. Let everyone help themselves.

• Be Prepared: Chicken strips can be marinated and/or cooked in advance and frozen until needed, then heated at serving time.

● HIGH-FIVE CHICKEN FINGERS

Kids and adults agree that this versatile dish deserves two-thumbs up! Try all five flavors and you'll also give them a high-five rating. These make terrific party appetizers and are excellent as an after-school snack for kids.

1 1/2 cups Frosted Flakes cereal
1 cup Special K cereal
1/2 cup wheat germ
1/2 cup sesame seeds
1 tsp salt (or to taste)
1/2 tsp freshly ground black pepper
1/2 tsp garlic powder
1/2 tsp dried basil
1/2 tsp paprika
4 boneless, skinless single chicken breasts
3/4 to 1 cup barbecue sauce

1. Preheat the oven to 400°F. Line a large baking sheet with parchment paper or sprayed foil.

2. Combine the cereals, wheat germ, sesame seeds, and seasonings in the processor fitted with the steel blade. Process 6 to 8 seconds to make coarse crumbs. Transfer to a pie plate.

3. Rinse the chicken breasts and trim the excess fat. Cut each breast into 5 long strips. Dip in barbecue sauce, then in crumb mixture. Arrange them in a single layer on the prepared baking sheet. (Can be prepared in advance and refrigerated up to 24 hours.)

4. Preheat the oven to 400°F. Bake, uncovered, for 10 minutes. Turn chicken fingers over and bake 6 to 8 minutes longer or until crisp and golden.

Yield: 20 chicken fingers. Keeps for up to 2 days in the refrigerator; reheats well. Freezes well for up to 3 months.

83 calories each, 7.0 g carbohydrate, 1.0 g fiber, 8 g protein, 2.8 g fat (0.3 g saturated), 15 mg cholesterol, 238 mg sodium, 97 mg potassium, 2 mg iron, 19 mg calcium

Variations

• Instead of chicken, substitute firm fish fillets such as sole or tilapia, or use extra-firm tofu.

• Instead of using barbecue sauce, use any of the following:

· 3/4 cup light mayonnaise plus 1 Tbsp honey mustard
· 1/2 cup Italian or French salad dressing (low-calorie)
· 1/2 cup Vidalia onion salad dressing
· 1/2 cup Asian honey garlic sauce

Norene's Healthy Kitchen

Nutrition Notes
• Crumb-y News: Surprisingly, Frosted Flakes cereal is quite GI-friendly, with a glycemic index of 55 and Special K has a glycemic index of 56. Believe it or not, the GI for corn flakes is 77 and the GI for Rice Krispies is 82!

• Saucy Thoughts: When shopping for bottled barbecue sauce, avoid brands that contain trans-fats or partially hydrogenated, palm and/or coconut oil. Watch for hidden sugars such as dextrose, sucrose, or anything ending with "ose." Avoid sauces that include high-fructose corn syrup in the first 5 ingredients. Otherwise, choose marinara or tomato sauce and boost the flavor with a dash of cayenne pepper, garlic, ground cinnamon, and cloves.

◔ CHICKEN SATAY

This Indonesian favorite is delicious as a main dish or appetizer. These make perfect party fare, so double the recipe for a crowd. The peanut sauce is used both as a marinade and a dipping sauce. If you don't want to bother with skewers, see No Skewing Around (on page 218)!

6 skinless, boneless single chicken breasts
1 cup Peanut Sauce (page 104)
30 wooden skewers (about 8 inches long)
Sesame seeds (optional)

1. Rinse the chicken well and trim the excess fat. Cut each chicken breast lengthwise into 5 long strips. Place in a large bowl or re-sealable plastic bag. Add 1/2 cup of sauce and mix well. Reserve the remaining sauce. Marinate chicken for at least 1/2 hour (or up to 2 days in the refrigerator).

2. Soak the skewers in cold water for 20 minutes. Remove the chicken from marinade; discard marinade. Thread the chicken onto the fully soaked skewers; sprinkle with sesame seeds, if using. (If desired, the chicken can be prepared up to this point and refrigerated for several hours until ready to use.)

3. Preheat the grill to medium-high. (If using an indoor grill, spray with cooking spray.) Grill the skewers for 3 to 4 minutes per side over indirect heat. Don't overcook or the chicken will be dry.

4. Arrange the skewers attractively on a serving platter and serve with remaining sauce. Delicious hot or cold.

Yield: 30 skewers. Recipe doubles or triples easily. Keeps for up to 3 days in the refrigerator; reheats well. Freezes well for up to 3 months. You don't need to remove the wooden skewers if freezing.

58 calories per skewer, 2.6 g carbohydrate, 0.2 g fiber, 6 g protein, 2.2 g fat (0.4 g saturated), 15 mg cholesterol, 71 mg sodium, 49 mg potassium, 0 mg iron, 3 mg calcium

Variations
• Instead of chicken breasts, substitute well-trimmed steak. Extra-firm tofu makes a delicious vegetarian option. If desired, add pineapple chunks and green peppers.

Chef's Secrets
• "Wood" You Believe This? Denise Levin of Toronto soaks the whole package of wooden skewers in cold water for 20 minutes. She transfers them to a re-sealable freezer bag and stores them in the freezer for future use. What a terrific timesaver!

• No Skewing Around: Instead of cutting chicken breasts into strips, marinate them whole. Grill 5 to 6 minutes per side over indirect heat. (Or place chicken on a parchment paper-lined baking sheet, sprinkle with sesame seeds and bake, uncovered, at 400°F about 20 minutes.) Slice across the grain and serve with reserved sauce.

GRILLED CHICKEN SKEWERS

These scrumptious skewers are ideal as an appetizer or main dish. They're delicious with Pineapple Dipping Sauce (page 104) or Dairy-Free Tzatziki (page 53). Go grill, go!

6 boneless, skinless, single chicken breasts
1 medium red onion
1 medium red pepper
1 medium green or yellow pepper
3 Tbsp olive oil
2 Tbsp lemon juice (preferably fresh)
3 cloves garlic (about 1 Tbsp minced)
1 Tbsp minced fresh basil or rosemary
 (or 1 tsp dried)
2 Tbsp minced fresh parsley (or 2 tsp dried)
Salt and freshly ground black pepper
30 wooden skewers (about 8 inches long)

1. Rinse the chicken well and trim the excess fat. Cut each chicken breast lengthwise into 5 long strips. Cut the onion and peppers into 1-inch chunks.

2. In a large glass bowl, mix together the olive oil, lemon juice, garlic, basil, parsley, salt, and pepper. Add the chicken and vegetables; mix well. Marinate for at least 1/2 hour (or up to 2 days in the refrigerator). Soak wooden skewers in cold water for 20 minutes.

3. Remove the chicken from marinade; discard marinade. Place a piece of red or green pepper on one end of a wooden skewer. Then weave on a chicken strip and end with a piece of onion. Repeat with remaining skewers. (If desired, the skewers can be assembled a few hours in advance and refrigerated until you're ready to use.)

4. Preheat the grill to medium-high. (If using an indoor grill, spray with cooking spray.) Grill the skewers 3 to 4 minutes per side over indirect heat. Don't overcook.

5. Arrange the skewers attractively on a serving platter and serve with desired sauce.

Yield: 30 skewers. Recipe doubles or triples easily. Best served hot from the grill, but leftovers can be refrigerated for 2 days; reheats well. The vegetables will get soggy if frozen, then thawed.

45 calories per skewer, 1.2 g carbohydrate, 0.2 g fiber, 5 g protein, 2.0 g fat (0.4 g saturated), 15 mg cholesterol, 13 mg sodium, 62 mg potassium, 0 mg iron, 5 mg calcium

Chef's Secrets

• No grill? No problem! Bake or broil them. Place skewers on a sprayed foil-lined baking sheet and bake at 400°F for 8 to 10 minutes. Or broil them 5 inches from the heat for 4 minutes per side.

• Skewing Around: Instead of cutting chicken into strips, cut into 1-inch cubes and marinate as directed. Alternate the chicken on the skewers with onions and peppers. Grill or broil over indirect heat, turning to cook them evenly.

meat & poultry

QUICK CHICKEN CACCIATORE

Dinner's done in 30 minutes! This is perfect when you're short on time and need something wonderful for dinner. It is elegant enough for guests or makes a perfect family meal. Serve it over noodles or rice, or for carb-watchers, spoon it over golden strands of spaghetti squash.

6 boneless, skinless single chicken breasts, cut into thin strips
Salt and freshly ground black pepper
2 Tbsp olive oil
3 cloves garlic (1 Tbsp minced)
2 medium onions, sliced
1 green pepper, seeded and sliced
1 red pepper, seeded and sliced
3 cups sliced mushrooms
3 cups tomato basil sauce
1/2 cup red wine
1 tsp dried basil
1/2 tsp dried oregano
1/4 tsp red pepper flakes (optional)
2 Tbsp minced fresh basil and/or parsley

1. Rinse the chicken strips and pat dry. Trim the excess fat. Sprinkle chicken with salt and pepper.

2. Heat 1 Tbsp oil in a large, deep nonstick skillet or Dutch oven on medium high heat. Add the chicken strips and garlic; stir-fry until the chicken is no longer pink, about 3 to 4 minutes. Transfer to a bowl.

3. Heat the remaining oil in the pan. Add the onions, peppers, and mushrooms; stir-fry for 4 to 5 minutes or until golden.

4. Return the chicken to the pan. Add the tomato sauce, wine, basil, oregano, and red pepper flakes, if using; mix well. Bring to a simmer, then reduce heat and cover partially.

Simmer for 20 minutes or until tender, stirring occasionally. Season with additional salt and pepper. Sprinkle with fresh basil and/or parsley.

Yield: 6 servings. Recipe doubles or triples easily. Keeps for up to 2 days in the refrigerator; reheats well. Freezes well for up to 3 months, but the veggies won't be as crisp when thawed.

317 calories per serving, 19.3 g carbohydrate, 2.1 g fiber, 31 g protein, 10.3 g fat (1.5 g saturated), 73 mg cholesterol, 538 mg sodium, 492 mg potassium, 3 mg iron, 138 mg calcium

Variation

• Substitute 2 lb (1 kg) boneless, skinless chicken thighs for breasts. One serving contains 393 calories and 18.6 g fat (3.8 g saturated).

HOISIN CHICKEN AND BROCCOLI STIR-FRY

Hoy-sinful! Hoisin sauce, also known as Chinese ketchup, is a thick, reddish-brown sauce with a sweet and spicy taste. It is made from a mixture of soybeans, garlic, chili peppers, and spices. This is delicious over cooked soba noodles (Japanese buckwheat noodles) or rice.

1/2 cup hoisin sauce
2 Tbsp orange marmalade or apricot jam (preferably low-sugar or all-fruit)
2 Tbsp lemon juice (preferably fresh)
1 lb (500 g) boneless, skinless single chicken breasts, cut into thin strips
2 Tbsp canola oil
2 tsp minced garlic
2 tsp minced fresh ginger

1 red onion, thinly sliced
1 red pepper, thinly sliced
2 cups broccoli florets
2 cups mushrooms, sliced
2 cups bean sprouts
2 tsp cornstarch dissolved in
   2 Tbsp cold water or chicken broth

1. Combine the hoisin sauce, marmalade, and lemon juice in a large glass bowl; mix well.

2. Rinse the chicken well and pat dry. Trim the excess fat. Add the chicken and marinate for 30 minutes at room temperature (or refrigerate for up to 2 days). Drain the chicken, reserving marinade.

3. Heat 1 Tbsp oil on medium high heat in a large nonstick wok. Add the drained chicken, garlic, and ginger. Stir-fry for 2 to 3 minutes or until the chicken is no longer pink. Remove from the wok.

4. Heat remaining oil. Stir-fry the onion, red pepper, broccoli, mushrooms, and bean sprouts on high heat for 2 minutes. Add the chicken, reserved marinade, and cornstarch mixture. Stir-fry 1 to 2 minutes longer or until bubbly and thickened. This is best served immediately.

Yield: 4 servings. Leftovers can be reheated in the microwave or a wok, but won't be as crunchy. Don't freeze.

361 calories per serving, 35.8 g carbohydrate, 4.7 g fiber, 32 g protein, 11.2 g fat (1.5 g saturated), 68 mg cholesterol, 590 mg sodium, 680 mg potassium, 3 mg iron, 64 mg calcium

Variations
• Substitute lean boneless beef or firm tofu, cut into strips, for the chicken breasts.

• Add 2 cups sliced water chestnuts or bamboo shoots to the wok along with reserved marinade.

• Garnish with 1/2 cup toasted cashews or slivered almonds.

Chef's Secrets
• It's a Keeper: Bottled hoisin sauce can be refrigerated for at least a year.

• Saucy Secret: Hoisin sauce adds body to stir-fries, so less cornstarch is needed to thicken the sauce.

STIR-FRY CHICKEN WITH MANGO AND VEGETABLES

Don't go stir-crazy when you read the list of ingredients for this simple stir-fry. Have everything prepared in advance and ready to cook as this comes together very quickly. Experiment with the variations suggested and enjoy a different dinner every time. Serve with brown or basmati rice.

Marinade and Chicken:

1 Tbsp soy sauce (low-sodium or regular)
2 Tbsp hoisin sauce
1 tsp rice vinegar or lemon juice
   (preferably fresh)
1 to 2 tsp honey or maple syrup (to taste)
1 clove garlic (about 1 tsp minced)
1 tsp Asian (toasted) sesame oil
1/8 tsp cayenne pepper or red pepper flakes
4 boneless, skinless single chicken breasts,
   cut into thin strips

Vegetable Mixture:

1 red pepper, cut into thin strips
1 green pepper, seeded and
   cut into thin strips
1 medium onion, halved and thinly sliced
2 baby bok choy (about 2 cups thinly sliced)
1/4 lb (125 g) snow peas, ends trimmed
   (about 1 1/2 cups)
2 cloves garlic (about 2 tsp minced)
1 mango, peeled and cut into chunks
   (or 1 cup frozen mango chunks)
1 Tbsp canola or peanut oil
1 Tbsp cornstarch dissolved in
   1/4 cup orange juice (preferably fresh)
   or mango juice

1. For the marinade, combine the soy sauce, hoisin sauce, vinegar, honey, garlic, sesame oil, and cayenne pepper in a large bowl. Rinse the chicken breasts and pat dry. Trim the excess fat. Add the chicken breasts to the marinade and mix well. (Can be prepared in advance and marinated up to 2 days in the refrigerator, stirring occasionally.)

2. Prepare the peppers, onion, bok choy, snow peas, and garlic; place on a large platter. Place mango on a separate plate. (If desired, prepare in advance up to this point and refrigerate overnight.)

3. Heat the oil in a nonstick wok or large skillet over high heat. Drain the chicken, reserving the marinade, and stir-fry for 2 minutes, or until chicken is white. Add the vegetables and stir-fry for 2 minutes longer. Stir in the mango and reserved marinade and bring to a boil. Stir in the cornstarch mixture and cook for 1 to 2 minutes longer or until the sauce is bubbly and thickened. This is best served immediately.

Yield: 4 to 6 servings. Can be reheated in the microwave or in a wok, but vegetables won't be as crunchy. If frozen, vegetables will become soggy when thawed.

296 calories per serving, 26.2 g carbohydrate, 2.9 g fiber, 30 g protein, 8.2 g fat (1.3 g saturated), 73 mg cholesterol, 338 mg sodium, 599 mg potassium, 2 mg iron, 70 mg calcium

Variations
• Go Nuts: Stir-fry 1 can (8 oz/250 mL) sliced water chestnuts, rinsed and drained, along with vegetables. Garnish with 1/4 cup toasted chopped walnuts, sliced almonds, or sesame seeds.

• Beef Variation: Substitute 1 1/2 lb (750 g) lean boneless beef, cut into strips, for the chicken.

• Vegetarian Variation: Substitute 1 lb (500 g) extra-firm tofu, cut into strips, for the chicken.

As You Like It Stir-Fry
Instead of bok choy, substitute thinly sliced cabbage. Instead of bell peppers, substitute 2 cups sliced mushrooms. Instead of snow peas, use pea pods or green peas. Instead of mango, substitute 1 cup pineapple tidbits or mandarin orange segments.

● CITRUS ROAST TURKEY

It's turkey thyme! The zesty blend of citrus fruit, garlic, and herbs will impart a fabulous flavor to your turkey. This is excellent with cranberry sauce for Thanksgiving, Passover, or any holiday celebration!

Marinade:

4 cloves garlic
1/4 cup orange or mixed fruit marmalade
    (preferably all-fruit)
Juice of 1 large orange, about 1/4 cup
    (reserve the rind)
Juice of 1/2 a large lemon, about 2 Tbsp
    (reserve the rind)
1 Tbsp extra virgin olive oil
1 Tbsp honey
2 tsp Kosher salt
1 tsp freshly ground black pepper
1 Tbsp paprika
1 tsp dried thyme

12 to 14 lb (5.4 to 6.4 kg) turkey
4 stalks celery, cut into chunks

1. In a food processor fitted with the steel blade, drop the garlic through the feed tube while the motor is running; process until minced. Add the marmalade, orange juice, lemon juice, olive oil, honey, salt, pepper, paprika, and thyme; process until blended, about 8 to 10 seconds. (The marinade can be prepared in advance and refrigerated, covered, for up to 2 days.)

2. Rinse the turkey well and pat dry. Trim excess fat and remove the giblets from the cavity. Place the turkey, breast-side up, on a rack in a large roasting pan. Loosen the skin but don't remove it. Rub the marinade over the turkey, inside the cavity, and under the skin. Pour any of the remaining marinade into the pan. Place the celery and reserved orange and lemon rinds inside the cavity of the turkey.

3. Cover the pan and refrigerate the turkey overnight (or up to 2 days), basting occasionally. Remove the turkey from the refrigerator about 30 minutes before cooking.

4. Preheat the oven to 325°F. The turkey will take a total of 3 1/2 to 3 3/4 hours to cook. Cover the pan loosely with foil and roast the turkey for 1 1/2 hours. Remove the foil and continue cooking the turkey for 2 to 2 1/4 hours longer, basting occasionally. If it gets too brown, cover loosely with foil. When done, the juices will run clear when pierced and a meat thermometer, inserted into the thickest part of the breast, should register 165 to 170°F.

5. Let turkey stand for 20 minutes before carving. Discard the celery, and orange and lemon rinds. Serve the turkey with defatted pan juices and All-Fruit Cranberry Sauce (page 102).

Yield: 16 servings. Keeps for up to 3 to 4 days in the refrigerator; reheats well. Freezes well for up to 4 months.

282 calories per serving (without skin), 4.8 g carbohydrate, 3.5 g fiber, 50 g protein, 5.4 g fat (1.6 g saturated), 166 mg cholesterol, 274 mg sodium, 472 mg potassium, 5 mg iron, 38 mg calcium

Chef's Secrets
• How Much is Enough? Calculate 3/4 lb (350 g) per serving. An average turkey will serve 12 hungry people, plus leftovers if you are lucky!

• Good Stuff: For Thanksgiving, see Cornbread Stuffing Mounds (page 338). For Passover, see Matzo and Vegetable Stuffing (page 469). Bake the stuffing separately so it does not absorb the fatty drippings from the turkey.

• Let's Talk Turkey: For more helpful tips, including how to check when the turkey is done, see pages 183–85.

● MAPLE GLAZED TURKEY BREAST

If you don't want to cook a whole turkey, this is a terrific option. Stuff it or not, depending on your mood. You can also add sliced onions, mushrooms, and red peppers to the roasting pan. Great for guests!

1 turkey breast, bone in (about 4 1/2 lb/2 kg)
Salt, freshly ground black pepper,
  and paprika
2 Tbsp soy sauce (low-sodium or regular)
2 Tbsp maple syrup
2 cloves garlic (about 2 tsp minced)
2 tsp peeled, minced fresh ginger
1/2 cup water

1. Spray a roasting pan with cooking spray. Rinse the turkey well and pat dry. Place skin-side up in the pan. Loosen turkey skin, but don't remove it. Season the turkey under the skin with salt, pepper, and paprika. Combine the soy sauce, maple syrup, garlic, and ginger in a measuring cup and stir to combine. Drizzle the mixture over the turkey breast, including under the skin. Marinate for 1 hour at room temperature or for up to 2 days, covered, in the refrigerator.

2. Preheat the oven to 350°F. Pour the water into the bottom of the roasting pan and cover loosely with foil. Roast the turkey for 30 minutes. Remove the foil and roast turkey about 1 hour longer, basting occasionally. Calculate 20 minutes per pound as your cooking time. When done the juices will run clear when pierced with a fork, and a meat thermometer, inserted into the thickest part of the turkey, should register an internal temperature of 165 to 170°F.

3. Remove the turkey from the oven and cover loosely with foil to keep warm. Let stand for 10 to 15 minutes before slicing the turkey meat on an angle off the bone.

Yield: 8 servings. Keeps for up to 3 days in the refrigerator; reheats well. Freezes well for up to 4 months.

232 calories per serving (without skin), 4.0 g carbohydrate, 0.1 g fiber, 48 g protein, 1.2 g fat (0.4 g saturated), 0 mg cholesterol, 217 mg sodium, 487 mg potassium, 3 mg iron, 25 mg calcium

Stuffed Turkey Breast

Using a sharp knife, cut horizontally through the middle of the turkey breast, but not all the way through, making a pocket. Rub turkey inside and out with salt, pepper, and paprika. Stuff loosely with Matzo and Vegetable Stuffing (page 469) or Spinach and Mushroom Stuffing (page 339). Fasten with skewers. (If you don't have metal skewers, use wooden skewers that have been soaked in cold water for at least 20 minutes.) Roast, uncovered, increasing the cooking time slightly—calculate 25 to 30 minutes per pound.

Chef's Secrets

• Weight-ing for Dinner: Calculate 8 ounces per person for turkey breast on the bone.

• The Skinny on Skin: Cooking turkey with the skin on will keep it moist and prevent it from drying out. Remove the skin before serving to reduce calorie and fat content.

• A Neat Way to Reheat: Place sliced cooked turkey into a casserole dish and cover with lettuce leaves to prevent it from drying out. Reheat at 350°F about 20 to 25 minutes, until heated through. Discard the lettuce afterwards.

🍎 ROLLED STUFFED TURKEY BREAST

This rolled-up roast tastes terrific and can be made a day ahead. It makes a beautiful pinwheel effect that will surely dazzle your guests. It makes a beautiful addition to your Passover or Thanksgiving table.

Spinach and Mushroom Stuffing (page 339)
2 medium onions, chopped
1 boneless, skinless turkey breast
 (about 4 lb/1.8 kg)
2 cloves garlic, minced
Salt, freshly ground black pepper and paprika
1/2 tsp each dried basil and thyme
3 Tbsp orange juice (preferably fresh)
3 Tbsp balsamic vinegar
2 Tbsp extra virgin olive oil

1. Prepare desired stuffing as directed. Spray a large roasting pan with cooking spray. Spread chopped onions in the bottom of pan.

2. Rinse the turkey breast well and pat dry. Butterfly the turkey breast by slicing it almost in half horizontally, leaving it hinged on one side so that it opens flat like a book. Cover with plastic wrap; pound lightly and flatten to 1/2 inch thick. Rub on both sides with garlic and seasonings. Spread with stuffing mixture to within 1 inch of the edges. Starting at the narrow end, roll up tightly. Tie with string in several places, about 3 inches apart. Place in the prepared pan.

3. In a measuring cup, combine the orange juice, balsamic vinegar, and olive oil with additional salt and pepper to taste; mix well. Pour the mixture over the turkey, turning to coat it on all sides. Cover the casserole with foil and marinate the turkey in the refrigerator for at least 1 hour or up to 2 days, basting occasionally. Remove from the refrigerator about 1/2 hour before cooking.

4. Preheat the oven to 350°F. Roast turkey covered, calculating 25 to 30 minutes per pound. Total cooking time will be about 2 hours. Uncover the last 1/2 hour of cooking and baste occasionally. When done, a meat thermometer should register an internal temperature of 165 to 170°F and juices will run clear when turkey is pierced. Let stand covered loosely with foil for 15 minutes for easier slicing. Slice the turkey thinly, making a pinwheel effect. Serve with pan juices.

Yield: 10 servings. Keeps for up to 2 days in the refrigerator; reheats well. Freezes well for up to 2 months.

263 calories per serving, 7.3 g carbohydrate, 1.6 g fiber, 45 g protein, 5.4 g fat (0.9 g saturated), 119 mg cholesterol, 96 mg sodium, 597 mg potassium, 3 mg iron, 62 mg calcium

Stuffed Turkey London Broil

Instead of rolling turkey breast with the stuffing, buy a boneless turkey breast with the skin attached. (This is called Turkey London Broil.) Spread stuffing just under the skin. Cooking time will be about 25 minutes per pound. If cooking turkey breast that is still on the bone, check the temperature to make sure it is fully cooked. Turkey breast will stay tender and juicy when the internal temperature does not exceed 170°F. When eating, skip the skin to reduce calories and fat.

Chef's Secrets

• Weigh-ting for Dinner: Calculate 6 ounces raw boneless turkey breast per person.

• Be Prepared: Prepare and cook the turkey as directed. Wrap in foil and refrigerate overnight. Reheat loosely covered at 350°F for 25 to 30 minutes. Carve into 1/2-inch slices and arrange the overlapping slices on a serving platter. Drizzle with pan juices.

Romaine, Avocado and Mango Salad with Citrus Dressing (page 253)

Show-Stopping Maple-Glazed Salmon (page 133)

Luscious Lemon Berry Mousse (page 416)

Pumpkin Cranberry Muffins (page 369)
Blueberry Corn Muffins (page 362)

Mini Veggie Latkes with Smoked Salmon and Tzatziki (page 67)

Pomegranate Chicken (page 205)

Roasted Tomato Sauce (page 107)

Curried Carrot and Cashew Soup (page 80)

Confetti Vegetable Strudel (page 172)

Spaghetti Squash with Roasted Vegetables (page 163)

Couscous, Mediterranean-Style (page 326)

Cinnamon Tortilla Triangles (page 393)
Trail Mix Biscotti (page 400)
Cranberry Oatmeal Flax Cookies (page 396)

Three-Color Gefilte Fish Loaf (page 123)

Decadent Marbled Cheesecake (page 475)

Broccoli Salad for a Crowd (page 246)

Whole Wheat Braided Challah (page 347)

salads, dressings & sandwiches

SALADS, DRESSINGS AND SANDWICHES

SUPER SALADS

I Be Leaf: Did you know that the most popular lettuce consumed is iceberg? It's time to broaden your horizons and narrow your hips—experiment with different varieties of salad greens. Try arugula (rocket), bibb, Boston, endive, leafy field greens (mesclun), radicchio, romaine, spinach, or watercress. The darker the greens, the better! Add some thinly sliced red or green cabbage for color and flavor.

It's in the Bag! When buying pre-washed packaged salad greens, even though the instructions on the bag say they don't need to be washed, I always wash the greens well in cold water and dry in a lettuce spinner. Just wash and give it a whirl. Wrap them in paper towels and store in a re-sealable plastic bag in the refrigerator; squeeze out the air and seal well. They'll keep for a few days and be ready when you are.

Color Your World: Insert splashes of color into your salad greens by adding brightly colored vegetables such as beets, carrots, red and yellow peppers, broccoli florets, red cabbage, cauliflower florets, celery, corn, cucumbers, fennel, red, green or sweet onions, peas, radishes, and tomatoes of all sizes. These vegetables provide a feast for your eyes as well as health benefits for your body.

Sweet News: Add some chopped fresh or dried fruits to sweeten up your salad. Include apples, avocados, assorted berries, figs, grapefruit, grapes, kiwifruit, mangoes, oranges, pears, plums, nectarines, or dried fruits such as cranberries, apricots, or raisins.

Bean Me Up! Add ½ cup of any kind of canned or cooked beans, lentils, or chickpeas to your salad. Legumes add fiber, folate, flavor, protein, as well as volume. If using canned beans, be sure to drain and rinse them well to lower the sodium content.

Grain Power: If you have leftover cooked grains such as barley, bulgar, quinoa, or rice, add them to your salad greens—they provide fiber, vitamins, and minerals.

Go for Protein: In addition to beans and legumes, to add lean protein to your salad you can include tuna, salmon, low-fat cheese, hard-boiled eggs or egg whites, or extra-firm tofu. Or add chicken, turkey, or lean beef for an additional protein (and energy) boost.

Crispy Toppings: Top your salad with a handful of roasted pumpkin or sunflower seeds, or toasted nuts such as almonds, walnuts, pecans, pistachios, or pine nuts.

Homemade Croutons: You can make croutons yourself from whole wheat or multigrain bread instead of using packaged croutons. Cut bread in small squares, drizzle lightly with olive oil, and sprinkle with salt, pepper, and some herbs. Spread the cubed bread out on a cookie sheet and bake, uncovered, at 375°F for 15 minutes or until crispy.

Dress Lightly: Use a small amount of healthy, flavorful fat such as extra virgin olive oil, walnut oil, canola oil, or Asian (toasted) sesame oil. Mix with lemon, lime, or orange juice, or vinegar (choose between balsamic, rice, red, cider, or white vinegar for variety). Add some green herbs and spices for additional phytochemicals and flavor.

Dress Right at the Last Minute: Add the dressing to the salad greens and toss together just before serving. Be sure that the salad greens are dry or the dressing won't cling to the greens. Serve salads on chilled plates to preserve crispness.

Bowl Them Over: Prepare your favorite salad dressing and put it in the bottom of the salad bowl. Place a long-handled salad fork and spoon in the bowl, in the shape of a cross, above the dressing so that the salad greens won't come in contact with the dressing. Pile the prepared salad greens on top of the salad utensils, cover the bowl with plastic wrap, and refrigerate until serving time. When needed, remove the plastic wrap, reach down and retrieve the utensils, and toss the salad. "Bowl-lievably" easy!

Pesto Power: Add a spoonful of pesto (pages 109–11) to your favorite Italian dressing for a powerful flavor punch.

Skinny Dipping: When eating in a restaurant, ask for the salad dressing on the side. First dip your fork into the dressing, then into your salad. Every bite of salad you take will have some dressing and you'll consume a fraction of the fat you'd normally eat.

Dip A-Weigh: Leftover dips can be thinned down with a little skim milk or buttermilk and used as a salad dressing.

Tomatoes Are Tops: Don't store tomatoes in the refrigerator—they'll lose their flavor. Instead, let them ripen on the counter or on a window ledge and eat them as soon as they are ripe. Red tomatoes have more lycopene than yellow ones. You can choose from a variety of sizes, from baby tomatoes to super-sized.

What's in Store: When choosing store-bought salad dressings, look for those that contain 4 grams of sugar or less per serving. Choose salad dressings made with good fats (extra virgin olive oil, or canola, grapeseed, walnut, or flaxseed oil). Avoid salad dressings made with hydrogenated oils as they contain trans-fats. Choose low-calorie dressings rather than low-fat dressings, which often contain high-fructose corn syrup—it tricks your body into staying hungry.

Well-Dressed: It takes very little time to make your own salad dressing and you can control what goes in it—and what goes in you! Forget about the old formula of "3 parts oil to 1 part acid." Use 2 parts oil to 1 part acid such as vinegar or lemon juice. A drizzle of honey, maple syrup, or sugar will lower the acidity and round out the flavor. Mustard adds a nice punch but isn't essential. Add your favorite dried or fresh herbs.

Seeing Is Be-Leafing! Help protect your eyes against cataracts and macular degeneration by eating a diet rich in lutein and zeaxanthin, found in corn, egg yolks, and dark green vegetables such as spinach, green beans, broccoli, and zucchini. Kiwifruit contains more vision-saving lutein than any other fruit or vegetable except corn. Now you'll clearly see why salads are so beneficial for your eyes—and other parts of your body as well.

Portable Salads: Many salads make scrumptious fillings for sandwiches. Refer to Sandwich Savvy (pages 276–78).

ROASTED BEET SALAD

Roasting beets enhances the flavor, producing beets that are moist and tender. You can't "beet" that!

2 lb (1 kg) fresh beets
1/2 cup thinly sliced red onions
3 Tbsp orange juice (preferably fresh)
3 Tbsp extra virgin olive oil
1 tsp Dijon mustard
1 tsp honey
Salt and freshly ground black pepper

1. Preheat the oven to 400°F. Scrub the beets well and then trim the stems and roots to within 1 inch. Spray a large piece of heavy-duty foil with cooking spray. Place the beets in the center and wrap tightly, pinching the edges of foil together. Bake for about 1 to 1 1/4 hours or until tender.

2. When fully roasted, remove from the oven, carefully open up the foil packet and let the beets stand until cool enough to handle. Using paper towels, rub off the skins and then cut the beets into 1/4-inch-thick rounds. Arrange the beet slices on a platter and scatter with the onion slices.

3. Whisk together the orange juice, olive oil, mustard, and honey in a small bowl. Drizzle the mixture over the beets and onions, then sprinkle with salt and pepper to taste. Serve warm or at room temperature.

Yield: 8 servings. Keeps for up to 2 or 3 days in the refrigerator.

90 calories per serving, 9.7 g carbohydrate, 2.3 g fiber, 1 g protein, 5.5 g fat (0.8 g saturated), 0 mg cholesterol, 75 mg sodium, 275 mg potassium, 1 mg iron, 16 mg calcium

Variations
• Instead of orange juice, use balsamic or raspberry vinegar. Instead of red onion, use shallots.

• Top with 1 cup crumbled goat cheese and 1/2 cup toasted walnuts.

Sauteed Beet Greens
If you buy beets with the greens still attached, cook the greens as you would cook spinach. Wash well and chop into 1-inch pieces. Stir-fry the beet greens in 1 Tbsp olive oil for 2 to 3 minutes on medium high heat. Stir in 1 tsp minced garlic. Season with salt and pepper to taste before serving. Can't "beet" those greens!

Chef's Secrets
• Beet Me Up, Scotty! Choose fresh beets that are roughly the same size for even cooking. Large beets tend to be tough, so small-to-medium-sized are best, about 4 oz (125 g) each.

• Roast and Boast: Roasting concentrates the flavor of beets while boiling only lessens its flavor—once you try roasting, you won't prepare them any other way.

• Skewing Around: Beets are done when a metal skewer glides easily through them.

• Buffet Beauty: For a beautiful presentation, use both red and golden beets. Arrange them in separate piles on a platter so that the colors don't bleed into each other. If golden beets aren't available, alternate the beets with orange slices.

Nutrition Notes

• Beet-iful news: Beets are a colorful source of anthocyanins, the purple pigments which are also found in blueberries, red cabbage, cherries, and red grapes. Anthocyanins are powerful antioxidants that may help protect against cancer and heart disease. As a general rule, the deeper the color, the higher the level of anthocyanins.

• GI Go! The glycemic index for beets is 64, making them a medium GI food, but they're packed with antioxidants, so enjoy them often.

◖ BROCCOLI SALAD FOR A CROWD

My friend Judy Mandel, of Toronto, shared her recipe for this scrumptious, colorful salad, which I've modified slightly. It has made the rounds among our friends and is always a hit, especially on a buffet table. It makes a large quantity but can be halved easily. Be sure to try the variations below.

2 or 3 bunches broccoli (about 3 lb/1.4 kg)
1 large red onion, chopped
   (about 2 cups chopped)
1 red pepper, seeded and chopped (optional)
1 cup light mayonnaise
2 Tbsp vinegar or lemon juice
   (preferably fresh)
2 tsp granulated sugar or granular Splenda
1 cup dried cranberries, raisins,
   or dried apricots
1 cup toasted pine nuts, sunflower seeds,
   and/or slivered almonds
1/2 tsp salt (or to taste)
1 cup grated low-fat cheddar cheese
   (optional)

1. Rinse the broccoli thoroughly and drain well. If desired, blanch in boiling water as directed in Chef's Secrets on page 247. (I don't bother.)

2. Cut off and discard the woody ends of the broccoli stalks. Using a paring knife, trim away 1/8-inch of the outer peel from the remaining stalks. Chop the broccoli into bite-sized pieces. Place in a large bowl and combine with the remaining ingredients; mix well.

3. Transfer the salad to a serving bowl, cover, and refrigerate until needed. If desired, top with grated cheese just before serving.

Yield: About 12 cups. Can be made up to a day in advance. Keeps for up to 3 to 4 days in the refrigerator.

106 calories per 1/2 cup serving, 9.4 g carbohydrate, 1.6 g fiber, 2 g protein, 7.3 g fat (0.8 g saturated), 4 mg cholesterol, 140 mg sodium, 170 mg potassium, <1 mg iron, 21 mg calcium

Broccoli Salad with Feta
Bev Binder of Winnipeg makes a delicious dairy version of this scrumptious salad. She uses only 1/2 cup light mayonnaise and adds 1/2 cup low-fat yogurt. She increases the sugar to 2 Tbsp, and adds 1/2 to 3/4 cup feta cheese. Bev makes her version with lemon juice, raisins, and sunflower seeds. It's a winner!

Broccoli Salad Vinaigrette
Omit the mayonnaise and vinegar. Add 1/2 cup of Shake-It-Up Vinaigrette (page 273) or your favorite low-calorie vinaigrette.

Chef's Secrets

• Eater's Digest: To make broccoli easier to digest, blanch it in boiling water for 1 minute, then rinse with cold water and drain well.

• What's in Store: Choose broccoli with tightly closed florets. Broccoli should be dark green or purplish-green: if the florets are discolored or open, broccoli is past its prime. Refrigerate unwashed broccoli in a loosely sealed plastic bag; it will keep for up to 1 to 2 weeks.

• Weighing In: One large bunch of broccoli weighs 1½ lb/750 g and yields about 4 cups chopped.

⬤ RED CABBAGE SLAW

Red cabbage dyes anything it touches purple. It's culinary magic—pour the hot dressing over the salad, and the cabbage will turn a brilliant magenta color!

1 medium head red cabbage, cored and
   thinly sliced (about 6 cups sliced)
2 medium carrots, peeled and grated
¾ cup chopped red onion
1 red or green pepper, seeded and
   chopped
2 cloves garlic (about 2 tsp minced)
¼ cup balsamic vinegar
¼ cup extra virgin olive oil
¼ cup granulated sugar
   or granular Splenda
2 Tbsp minced fresh dillweed
½ tsp celery seed (optional)
Salt and freshly ground black pepper

1. Combine the cabbage, carrots, onion, red pepper, and garlic in a large mixing bowl.

2. In a 2-cup glass measure, combine the vinegar, oil, and sugar. Microwave, uncovered, on high for 45 seconds or until almost boiling. Pour the hot dressing over the vegetables and toss to mix well. Add the dillweed, celery seed (if using), and the salt, and pepper to taste; mix well.

3. Cover and refrigerate for at least 1 hour, or overnight, to blend the flavors. Adjust seasonings before serving.

Yield: 8 to 10 servings. Keeps for up to 1 week in the refrigerator.

154 calories per serving, 22.0 g carbohydrate, 3.9 g fiber, 3 g protein, 7.3 g fat (1.0 g saturated), 0 mg cholesterol, 52 mg sodium, 456 mg potassium, 1 mg iron, 77 mg calcium

Passover Variation

• Omit the celery seed. Splenda isn't allowed for Passover, so use a sweetener that is approved for Passover use and is heat-stable. Otherwise, add the sweetener to the hot vinegar/oil mixture; mix well before pouring it over the vegetables.

Chef's Secrets

• It's a Slice: To properly slice a cabbage, first peel off and discard any tough or dry outer leaves. Using a large sharp knife, cut the cabbage through the stem end into 4 pieces, then cut out and discard the hard white core attached at the base of each quarter. Cut each piece crosswise into very thin slices.

• Processor Power: You can also use your food processor (fitted with the slicing blade) to slice the cabbage; just cut the cabbage into wedges small enough to fit through the feed tube. Slice the cabbage wedges, using very light pressure on the pusher.

• Quicky Slaw: Substitute a bag of coleslaw mix or broccoli slaw (shredded broccoli stems) for the red cabbage.

Nutrition Note
• Sweet Choice: With Splenda, one serving contains 132 calories and 16.5 g carbohydrate.

🍎 CHINESE COLESLAW

The recipe for this quick and scrumptious slaw came from Bev Corber of Vancouver. She likes to make it with ramen noodles but to make it healthful, we omitted the noodles and added a red pepper plus another bag of coleslaw mix. Now that's a "grate" idea!

1 tsp dried mustard
3 Tbsp granulated sugar or granular Splenda
1/4 cup canola oil
1 tsp minced peeled fresh ginger
   (or 1/4 tsp ground)
1/4 cup soy sauce (low-sodium or regular)
2 Tbsp Asian (toasted) sesame oil
6 Tbsp rice vinegar
2 bags (16 oz/454 g each) coleslaw mix
4 green onions (about 1/2 cup chopped)
1 red pepper, seeded and chopped
1 1/2 cup toasted slivered almonds (optional)

1. In a large bowl, combine the mustard, sugar, oil, ginger, soy sauce, sesame oil, and rice vinegar. Mix well. Add the coleslaw mix, green onions, and red pepper. Toss to combine.

2. Cover and store in the refrigerator to chill before serving. (If desired, this salad can be prepared up to this point, and stored in the refrigerator for a day or two.) At serving time, garnish with toasted almonds, if using.

Yield: 10 servings of 1 cup each. Keeps for up to 3 to 4 days in the refrigerator.

126 calories per serving, 11.2 g carbohydrate, 2.7 g fiber, 2 g protein, 8.6 g fat (0.8 g saturated), 0 mg cholesterol, 242 mg sodium, 67 mg potassium, 0 mg iron, 54 mg calcium

Variations
• Make-Your-Own Coleslaw Mix: Use 8 cups finely grated cabbage plus 2 grated carrots.

• Use your Noodle: Use only 1 bag of coleslaw mix. Just before serving, add 1/2 of a package of ramen noodles, broken up. (Discard the seasoning packet that comes inside the package: it's high in sodium and packed with bad fat.)

• Bev Corber likes to make this with 1 bag of broccoli slaw and 1 bag of coleslaw mix. She serves it with smoked turkey and Winter Vegetable Latkes (page 337) for an easy and elegant buffet dinner. She also adds bean sprouts and/or sliced water chestnuts for added crunch.

Nutrition Note
• Sweet Choice: With Splenda, one serving contains 113 calories and 7.9 g carbohydrate.

🍎 CARROT ALMOND SALAD

This quick-to-make, tasty, and brightly colored salad has eye-appeal—now you see it, but soon you won't!

1 bag (10 oz/283 g) grated carrots
   (about 3 cups)
2 green onions, thinly sliced
1/2 cup dried cranberries or raisins
1/2 cup toasted slivered almonds
2 Tbsp extra virgin olive oil
2 Tbsp lemon juice (preferably fresh)
   or vinegar
1 Tbsp honey or granular Splenda
1 tsp Dijon mustard
2 Tbsp minced fresh dillweed or parsley
1/2 tsp salt

1. In a large bowl, combine the carrots, green onions, cranberries, and almonds.

2. In a small bowl, whisk together the oil, lemon juice, honey, mustard, dillweed, and salt. Drizzle over the carrot mixture and mix well. Cover and refrigerate for up to 1 to 2 hours or overnight, before serving.

Yield: 6 servings. Recipe doubles and triples easily. Keeps for up to 2 to 3 days in the refrigerator.

162 calories per serving, 18.7 g carbohydrate, 3.1 g fiber, 3 g protein, 9.4 g fat (1.0 g saturated), 0 mg cholesterol, 249 mg sodium, 255 mg potassium, 1 mg iron, 46 mg calcium

Passover Variation
• Omit the Dijon mustard. Splenda isn't allowed for Passover, so use honey or a Passover sugar substitute.

Nutrition Note
• Sweet Choice! With Splenda, one serving contains 152 calories and 16.0 g carbohydrate.

◉ BEST GREEN BEAN SALAD

This outstanding salad is served in many popular Greek restaurants. It's become my favorite way to eat green beans because it's absolutely delicious! This recipe also works well with yellow wax beans.

1 lb (500 g) green beans
8 cups water
Salt
1/2 red pepper, chopped
2 green onions, chopped
1/4 cup minced fresh dillweed
2 Tbsp lemon juice (preferably fresh)
2 Tbsp extra virgin olive oil
Coarse salt and freshly ground black pepper

1. Snap off both ends from each green bean; rinse well. Meanwhile, bring the water, sprinkled with salt, to a boil in a large pot. Add the beans and cook, uncovered, for 3 to 4 minutes or just until tender-crisp and bright green. Drain immediately. Rinse the beans under cold water to stop the cooking process. Drain well and set aside to cool completely.

2. Combine the cooled green beans with the red pepper, green onions, and dillweed in a large bowl, cover, and refrigerate until serving time.

3. When ready to serve, add the lemon juice and olive oil to the green beans. Season with salt and pepper to taste and toss to combine. Serve immediately.

Yield: 4 to 6 servings. Leftovers keep for up to 1 to 2 days in the refrigerator, but the color won't be as vibrant.

110 calories per serving, 10.9 g carbohydrate, 4.1 g fiber, 2 g protein, 7.4 g fat (1.1 g saturated), 0 mg cholesterol, 268 mg sodium, 228 mg potassium, 1 mg iron, 57 mg calcium

Chef's Secrets

• Less-Than-7 Rule: To preserve their bright color, cook green beans and other green vegetables for no more than 7 minutes. Plunging green vegetables in ice cold water immediately after cooking them stops the cooking process and preserves their color.

• Buffet Beauty: For a large crowd, double or triple the recipe and serve it on a large serving platter. Top with crumbled feta cheese.

• No dillweed? Substitute with chopped fresh basil.

● HEARTS OF PALM AND AVOCADO SALAD

My neighbor Vivian Felsen of Toronto shared this delicious recipe she got from her daughter-in-law Sarah. I've modified it slightly to reduce the calories. It's guaranteed to win your heart.

1 can (14 oz/398 mL) hearts of palm, drained and rinsed
1 jar (6 oz/170 g) marinated artichoke hearts, drained
1 Vidalia or red onion (about 1 cup chopped)
1 container (550 g/2 cups) cherry tomatoes
1 medium avocado, diced (see Chef's Secrets)
Juice of 1 lemon (about 3 Tbsp)
2 tsp light mayonnaise
1 clove garlic (about 1 tsp minced)
1/2 tsp dried basil
Salt and freshly ground black pepper

1. Slice the hearts of palm into 1/2-inch coins and cut the artichokes into bite-sized pieces.

2. Combine the hearts of palm and artichokes in a large bowl along with the onion and cherry tomatoes. Add the avocado and sprinkle with lemon juice. Add the mayonnaise, garlic, and seasonings; mix gently. Chill, covered, for at least 1 hour before serving.

Yield: 6 cups (8 servings of 3/4 cup each). Keeps for up to 1 to 2 days in the refrigerator. The avocado may discolor slightly.

73 calories per serving, 8.5 g carbohydrate, 3.1 g fiber, 2 g protein, 4.3 g fat (0.6 g saturated), 0 mg cholesterol, 139 mg sodium, 275 mg potassium, 1 mg iron, 21 mg calcium

Hearts of Palm Salad
Instead of avocado, add 1 green or red pepper, seeded and chopped. Instead of mayonnaise, add 1 to 2 Tbsp of your favorite low-calorie salad dressing.

Chef's Secrets

• Fruity News: Avocados are a fruit, not a vegetable. They come in different sizes and shapes, from oval to pear-shaped. My favorite variety is the Haas, with a pebbly skin that is almost black when it's ripe. For immediate use, choose avocados that yield to gentle pressure. If you plan to use them in a few days, buy firm ones; they'll ripen in several days if left out on the counter.

• Is It Ready Yet? Put unripe avocados in a brown paper bag and let ripen at room temperature for 2 to 5 days. (If you add an apple or banana to the bag, it will speed up the ripening process—don't seal the bag.) Transfer ripe avocados to the refrigerator— they'll keep for several days.

• Nice Dice! Cut avocado in half lengthwise. Gently twist the 2 halves back and forth until you can separate them. Stick the tip of a sharp knife into the pit and move it back and forth until it loosens, then remove the pit. Dice the avocado flesh right in its shell without cutting through the skin. Scoop out the diced avocado flesh with a spoon.

• Weighing In: One medium avocado yields about 1 to 1¼ cups diced or 1 cup mashed.

• Discoloration: Avocado tends to discolor once the flesh has been cut and exposed to the air, so it's best to add it to a dish at the last moment. Sprinkling lemon or lime juice on the avocado helps prevent discoloration.

• It's the Pits! To avoid discoloration when storing a cut avocado, leave the pit in the cavity and place plastic wrap directly on the cut flesh. Refrigerate for up to 2 days.

Nutrition Notes
• Although avocados are high in fat, it's a heart-healthy monounsaturated fat. One medium avocado contains about 322 calories, 17 g carbohydrate, 13 g fiber, and 29 g fat (4 g saturated), so watch your portion size.

• Avocados are a good source of folate (a B vitamin), vitamin C, beta carotene (which forms vitamin A), and potassium.

🍅 MUSHROOM TARRAGON SALAD

Brenda Borzykowski of Winnipeg is always asked to make a mushroom-tarragon salad for family gatherings. This old family favorite originally came from her aunt, Lil Slonim, and through the years Brenda modified it to make it her own. Vroom!—this mushroom tarragon salad will be "gone" before you know it.

Tarragon Dressing:

2 cloves garlic
1 bunch fresh parsley, leaves only
¼ cup tarragon vinegar
¾ cup extra virgin olive oil
1½ tsp salt

Salad:

1 lb (500 g) mushrooms, sliced
1 bag (1 lb/500 g) romaine lettuce (about 8 cups, packed)
½ English cucumber, unpeeled and thinly sliced
1 container (550 g/2 cups) grape or cherry tomatoes, halved
1 red pepper, seeded and diced
1 can (14 oz/398 mL) baby corn, drained and cut in pieces
1 jar (6 oz/170 g) marinated artichoke hearts, drained and sliced

salads, dressings & sandwiches

1. In a food processor fitted with the steel blade, drop the garlic and parsley through the feed tube while the motor is running; process until minced, about 10 seconds. Add the vinegar, oil, and salt to the bowl and process until well mixed, about another 10 seconds.

2. Place the mushrooms in a large bowl. Pour the dressing over the mushrooms and toss lightly. Cover and marinate in the refrigerator for up to 24 hours. (See Chef's Secret: Be a Mushroom Maven on page 252.)

3. When the mushrooms are marinated, wash and dry the lettuce thoroughly; transfer to a large salad bowl. (If desired, you can prepare the lettuce several hours in advance and refrigerate until ready to use.)

4. Just before serving, add the cucumber, tomatoes, red pepper, baby corn, and artichoke hearts to the lettuce. Toss in the marinated mushrooms with the marinade; mix well. Serve immediately.

Yield: 12 servings.

104 calories per serving, 10.9 g carbohydrate, 2.8 g fiber, 3 g protein, 5.8 g fat (0.7 g saturated), 0 mg cholesterol, 330 mg sodium, 404 mg potassium, 1 mg iron, 25 mg calcium

Chef's Secrets

• No tarragon vinegar? Use white wine or rice vinegar plus 1/4 tsp dried tarragon.

• Heads Up! You can substitute 1 1/2 to 2 medium heads of romaine lettuce or 2 to 3 medium romaine hearts. A medium head of romaine yields about 6 cups torn.

• Mushroom Myth: Mushrooms don't become waterlogged if you immerse them in water when cleaning. However, mushrooms can discolor and become slimy shortly after washing unless wiped clean with a damp paper towel.

• Be a Mushroom Maven: If you prefer not to eat raw mushrooms, follow this method of preparation instead: Combine the vinegar, oil, and salt in a 2-cup glass measure and microwave on high for 2 minutes, until piping hot. Pour the hot oil/vinegar mixture over the sliced mushrooms and toss well. Stir in the minced garlic and parsley. When cool, cover and marinate in the refrigerator for up to 24 hours. Continue with Step 3.

• Clean Greens: Even though the packaging may indicate that lettuce and other greens are ready-to-eat or pre-washed, I always wash and dry thoroughly before using.

✿ MIXED GREENS WITH MANDARINS, BERRIES AND PEARS

This scrumptious salad, with its crunchy topping of pistachios, is a perfect pairing of fruits and salad greens. The fat is mainly heart-healthy monounsaturated. Your guests will be green with envy when they taste it.

Raspberry Vinaigrette (page 272)
4 cups packed baby spinach
   or mixed salad greens
1 head romaine lettuce, torn into
   bite-sized pieces (about 6 cups)
1/2 cup red onion, thinly sliced
1 can (10 oz/284 mL) mandarin oranges,
   drained (about 1 cup)
1 cup fresh strawberries and/or raspberries,
   hulled and halved
1/2 cup dried cranberries
2 firm ripe pears, peeled, cored, and sliced
2 tsp lemon juice (preferably fresh)
1/2 cup toasted pistachios or pine nuts,
   for garnish

1. Prepare the Raspberry Vinaigrette as directed and chill until serving time.

2. Combine the spinach, romaine, onion, oranges, strawberries, and cranberries in a large salad bowl but don't toss. (If desired, the salad can be prepared up to this point several hours in advance and refrigerated.)

3. At serving time, sprinkle the pears with lemon juice to prevent discoloration, and add to the salad. Drizzle the chilled vinaigrette over the salad and toss gently. Garnish with pistachios and serve immediately.

Yield: 8 servings.

221 calories per serving, 25.5 g carbohydrate, 4.4 g fiber, 3 g protein, 13.2 g fat (1.8 g saturated), 0 mg cholesterol, 41 mg sodium, 222 mg potassium, 1 mg iron, 48 mg calcium

Variations

• Instead of pears, use sliced mango or apples. Instead of mandarin oranges, add 1 cup of grapefruit segments. If desired, top the salad with 1/2 cup crumbled goat cheese just before serving.

🍎 ROMAINE, AVOCADO AND MANGO SALAD WITH CITRUS DRESSING

I love to serve this elegant salad on a large platter—it's perfect for a crowd and pretty as a picture. This tastes best using fresh citrus juices, but use bottled juices if you're in a tight squeeze!

Citrus Dressing:

1/4 cup lemon juice (preferably fresh)
1/4 cup orange juice (preferably fresh)
1/2 cup extra virgin olive oil
2 cloves garlic (about 2 tsp minced)
2 tsp Dijon mustard
1 tsp honey
Salt and freshly ground black pepper
Rind of 1/2 a lemon and 1/2 an orange
   (optional)

3 large romaine lettuce hearts, trimmed
2 ripe medium avocados, pitted, peeled, and
   diced
2 mangoes, pitted, peeled, and diced
1 English cucumber, unpeeled, quartered
   and thinly sliced
1/2 red onion, thinly sliced
   (about 1 cup chopped)
1/2 cup thinly sliced radishes
1 red pepper, seeded and thinly sliced
1/4 cup chopped fresh basil or parsley
1 pkg (4 oz/113 g) goat cheese, crumbled
   (optional)

1. Combine the ingredients for the salad dressing in a glass jar, seal tightly, and shake well. Refrigerate until serving time.

2. Wash the romaine leaves well and tear into bite-sized pieces. Dry, in batches, in a lettuce spinner. (Can be prepared up to a day in advance, wrapped in towels and refrigerated.)

3. Arrange the lettuce on a large oval platter. Scatter the avocado, mango, cucumber, onion, and radishes over the lettuce. Top with the red pepper and basil. Just before serving, drizzle the dressing on top and garnish with crumbled goat cheese, if using.

Yield: 16 to 20 servings. Recipe can be halved easily for a smaller crowd.

141 calories per serving, 11.2 g carbohydrate, 3.1 g fiber, 2 g protein, 10.9 g fat (1.5 g saturated), 0 mg cholesterol, 23 mg sodium, 243 mg potassium, 1 mg iron, 33 mg calcium

Variation

• Instead of goat cheese, garnish with 1 cup toasted sliced almonds for a dairy-free calcium boost.

Chef's Secrets

• Go for Green! Other greens, such as baby spinach, arugula, mesclun mix, or Boston lettuce can be added or substituted.

• Meal Deal: To turn it into a main dish, top with sliced grilled chicken breasts or poached salmon.

• Avocado Info: See the Hearts of Palm and Avocado Salad recipe's Chef's Secrets on page 250, for more information on avocados.

APRICOT HOISIN SPINACH SALAD

Apricot Hoisin Marinade, an Asian delight, is reinvented as a salad dressing with the addition of orange juice and oil, then is served over a fiber-packed combination of almonds, apricots, snow peas, and spinach or mixed greens. You can transform this marvelous Asian salad into a main dish by simply adding a scoop of chicken, tuna, or salmon salad.

Dressing:

1/2 cup Apricot Hoisin Marinade
   (page 111)
1/4 cup orange juice (preferably fresh)
1 tsp canola oil

Salad:

1 bag (10 oz/300 g) baby spinach leaves
   or mixed salad greens
1 red pepper, seeded and cut into strips
1/2 red onion, thinly sliced
1/2 cup grated carrots
2 cups snow peas, trimmed
1 cup sliced dried apricots
1/2 cup toasted sliced almonds
   or sesame seeds, for garnish

1. In a small bowl, whisk together ingredients for the dressing and blend well. Set aside.

2. In a large bowl, combine the spinach, red pepper, onion, carrots, snow peas, and apricots. (If desired, the vegetables and dressing can be prepared in advance up to this point and refrigerated separately for several hours.)

3. At serving time, combine the salad ingredients with the dressing and toss gently to mix. Top with almonds and serve immediately.

Yield: 6 servings. Dressing keeps for up to a week in the refrigerator.

180 calories per serving, 31.2 g carbohydrate, 6.3 g fiber, 5 g protein, 5.8 g fat (0.5 g saturated), 0 mg cholesterol, 242 mg sodium, 477 mg potassium, 3 mg iron, 86 mg calcium

Apricot Hoisin Chicken and Spinach Salad

Marinate 4 to 6 boneless, skinless chicken breasts in 1/2 to 3/4 cup Apricot Hoisin Marinade for 30 minutes; grill for 5 to 6 minutes per side. When cool, slice chicken thinly and arrange attractively on top of salad. So chic!

WATERMELON AND FETA SALAD

This refreshing summer salad will be a "feta" in your cap! The recipe was inspired by Monty Joffin, of Toronto, who wanted my opinion on this unusual combination of sweet watermelon and salty feta cheese. I told him it was a perfect pairing because in Middle Eastern countries, eating watermelon with salt was quite common.

6 cups mache, arugula,
   or baby spinach leaves
6 cups cubed seedless watermelon,
   (about 1/4 of a small watermelon
   cut into 1-inch cubes)
1/2 cup thinly sliced red onion
3/4 cup crumbled low-fat feta cheese
6 to 8 Tbsp Raspberry Vinaigrette (page 272)

1. Place the greens in a shallow oval or round bowl, or an oblong serving dish. Tuck the watermelon cubes among the greens. Scatter the sliced onion on top and sprinkle with crumbled feta cheese. Cover and refrigerate until serving time.

2. Prepare Raspberry Vinaigrette as directed and refrigerate for up to a day.

3. At serving time, drizzle the vinaigrette over the salad but don't toss. Serve immediately.

Yield: 8 servings.

135 calories per serving, 13.7 g carbohydrate, 0.8 g fiber, 6 g protein, 7.5 g fat (2.2 g saturated), 7 mg cholesterol, 289 mg sodium, 338 mg potassium, 1 mg iron, 65 mg calcium

Chef's Secrets
• Green Power: Mache (pronounced "mosh") is also known as field salad, lamb's lettuce, or corn salad. It has a mild, nutty flavor. Instead of mache, substitute with arugula, Boston, bibb, or red leaf lettuce.

• Here's the Scoop: If you have time and patience, use a mini ice-cream scoop or melon baller and make small watermelon balls. You'll have a ball with this field of greens!

• Shake It Up! Instead of Raspberry Vinaigrette, use Shake-It-Up Vinaigrette (page 273).

VIDALIA ONION SALAD

Cookbook author Sue Epstein, formerly of Atlanta, now lives in Efrat, Israel. Whenever she makes this dish, at least 5 people ask for the recipe including one friend's husband, who took one taste and told his wife to hide it from the other guests so that the two of them could enjoy it later! My taste testers loved it and said it reminded them of creamy coleslaw.

3 or 4 Vidalia onions
1 cup granular Splenda
2 cups water
1/2 cup white vinegar
1/2 cup light mayonnaise
1 tsp celery salt (or to taste)

1. Peel and dice the onions; you should have about 6 cups. (To save time, you can cut the onions in chunks and then chop, in batches, in a food processor fitted with the steel blade, using quick on/off pulses.)

2. In a large bowl, whisk together the Splenda, water, and vinegar. Add the onions and toss to mix well. Cover and refrigerate for 1 to 2 days. While marinating, the onions will reduce slightly in volume.

3. Once fully marinated, drain the onions using a fine mesh strainer. Add the drained onions, mayonnaise, and celery salt to a large bowl and mix well. Transfer to a serving bowl, cover, and refrigerate before serving. Serve chilled.

Yield: About 4 1/2 cups. Keeps for up to 1 week in the refrigerator (if it lasts that long).

100 calories per 1/2 cup serving, 14.6 g carbohydrate, 1.5 g fiber, 1 g protein, 4.5 g fat (0.7 g saturated), 5 mg cholesterol, 221 mg sodium, 161 mg potassium, 0 mg iron, 24 mg calcium

Serving Suggestions
• Serve as a side dish with fish, chicken, or meat. To use as an hors d'oeuvre, serve with wholegrain crackers or Baked Tortilla Chips (page 59).

salads, dressings & sandwiches

Chef's Secrets

• On-yums! Vidalia and other sweet onions are not available in Israel, so Sue uses regular or red onions.

• No More Tears: Sue's eyes are very sensitive, so when she has a lot of onions to peel and chop, she puts on the gas mask they issued to her family during the first Gulf War. She's armed and ready!

• Fight Onion Breath: Eat a couple of sprigs of fresh parsley, chew on citrus peel, or rinse your mouth with lemon juice and water to eliminate onion breath. (The odor comes from eating raw onions, not cooked ones.)

• Lemon Aid: Lemon juice removes onion odors from your hands, knives, and cutting boards.

• Sodi-Yum! Celery salt adds wonderful flavor to coleslaw and other marinated salads.

• See Chef's Secrets on page 304 following the Caramelized Onions recipe.

Nutrition Notes

• Sweet Choice: Sue got the recipe from her friend Gloria Glusman, who makes it with sugar and regular mayonnaise. Sue modified the recipe by using granular Splenda and light mayonnaise to make it more carb-friendly. Gloria's version contains 220 calories, 33.0 g carbohydrate, 9.9 g fat (1.4 g saturated) per serving.

• Raw onions have more health benefits than cooked ones—the sulphur compounds in raw onions help combat heart disease by raising good HDL levels and thinning the blood, which helps prevent blood clots—but any way you slice them, onions are good for you.

• Raw onions contain anti-inflammatory flavonoids, which help prevent cancer, as well as anti-bacterial flavonoids, which help protect against ulcers.

⚫ NEW POTATO SALAD

Some like it warm, some like it cold—here's a new spin on something old. If you have any leftover potato salad, pan-fry it in a sprayed nonstick skillet until crispy—kids love this!

2¹/₂ lb (1.2 kg) small new potatoes,
    well-scrubbed (red-skinned are excellent)
Salted water
2 to 3 Tbsp extra virgin olive oil
2 Tbsp balsamic or apple cider vinegar
1 Tbsp Dijon mustard
4 green onions, thinly sliced
¹/₂ red pepper, seeded and chopped
2 Tbsp chopped fresh dillweed
¹/₂ tsp salt
¹/₄ tsp freshly ground black pepper

1. Place the potatoes in a large pot and add enough water to cover, plus 2 inches more. Add a dash of salt and bring to a boil over high heat. Reduce heat to medium and cook for 15 to 20 minutes or until the potatoes are tender.

2. Drain well and return the cooked potatoes to the pot to dry over medium heat for a minute or two. Remove the potatoes and cut into bite-sized chunks while still warm.

3. In a large bowl, combine the chopped potatoes with the remaining ingredients and mix well. Transfer to a serving bowl and serve warm, or cover and refrigerate overnight.

Yield: 8 servings. Keeps for up to 2 to 3 days in the refrigerator. Don't freeze.

146 calories per serving, 26.4 g carbohydrate, 2.6 g fiber, 3 g protein, 3.7 g fat (0.5 g saturated), 0 mg cholesterol, 201 mg sodium, 511 mg potassium, 1 mg iron, 20 mg calcium

Variations
• Instead of vinegar, substitute fresh lemon juice and add 1 tsp grated lemon rind. Instead of dillweed, substitute 1 Tbsp minced fresh rosemary.

• Add 2 cups of steamed green beans, cut in 1-inch pieces, if desired.

Nutrition Notes
• GI Go! To lower the glycemic index of potato salad, don't eat it hot. Make it the day before, mix with vinaigrette dressing, and refrigerate. The cold temperature will increase the resistant starch content of the potatoes by more than a third, while the acid from the vinegar will help to slow down the stomach-emptying process. Check out www.glycemicindex.com for additional information.

• Using new potatoes for this potato salad helps lower the glycemic index. If you add some steamed green beans to the potatoes, it will help to lower the glycemic load.

🍎 ROASTED SWEET POTATO SALAD

This fiber-filled dish is absolutely addictive. The sweet potatoes become glazed during the roasting process and have a scrumptious candied taste, even though there's only one tablespoon of maple syrup in this recipe.

You can double the recipe for a crowd, but if you do, use two baking trays to be sure to spread out the potatoes in a single layer when roasting.

4 medium sweet potatoes, peeled and
   cut into 1-inch pieces (about 6 cups)
1 red pepper, seeded and cut into
   1-inch pieces
2 Tbsp balsamic vinegar
4 tsp extra virgin olive oil
1 tsp dried basil
1/2 tsp salt
1/4 tsp freshly ground black pepper

Dressing:

1 Tbsp balsamic vinegar
1 Tbsp extra virgin olive oil
1 tsp Dijon mustard
1 Tbsp pure maple syrup
1 tsp minced garlic
4 green onions, thinly sliced (about 3/4 cup)

1. Preheat the oven to 425°F. Line a large baking tray with foil and spray with cooking spray.

2. In a large bowl, combine the sweet potatoes, red pepper, vinegar, oil, basil, salt, and pepper; mix well. Spread out in a single layer on the prepared baking sheet. Bake for 25 to 30 minutes or until golden. Remove from the oven and let cool.

3. Meanwhile, in a large bowl, combine the vinegar, oil, mustard, maple syrup, and garlic. Add the roasted sweet potato mixture and green onions to the dressing; toss to mix well. Serve at room temperature or chilled.

Yield: 8 servings of 1/2 cup each. Keeps for up to 2 to 3 days in the refrigerator.

126 calories per serving, 20.8 g carbohydrate, 3.1 g fiber, 2 g protein, 4.2 g fat (0.6 g saturated), 0 mg cholesterol, 193 mg sodium, 440 mg potassium, 1 mg iron, 45 mg calcium

Passover Variation
• Omit the mustard and, instead of maple syrup, use honey.

○ LUSCIOUS LAYERED SALAD

This colorful, nutrition-packed salad tastes just as good as it looks. Thanks to my friend Bella Borts, of Toronto, for sharing this super recipe, which I modified slightly. It's a real crowd-pleaser!

Dressing:

1/4 cup rice or cider vinegar
1/4 cup extra virgin olive oil
2 cloves garlic (about 2 tsp minced)
1 tsp sea or Kosher salt
1/4 tsp freshly ground black pepper
1 tsp dried basil or 2 Tbsp chopped fresh
1 tsp dried oregano or 1 Tbsp chopped fresh

Salad:

1 can (19 oz/540 mL) black beans,
   drained and rinsed
1 can (12 oz/341 mL) corn kernels, drained
1 red pepper, halved, seeded, and sliced
1/2 red onion, halved and sliced
2 cups broccoli or cauliflower florets
1 can (19 oz/540 mL) red kidney beans
   or chickpeas, drained and rinsed
2 cups chopped tomatoes or 1 container
   (550 g/1 pint) grape tomatoes
4 cups packed baby spinach leaves
   or mixed salad greens
1/2 cup dried cranberries or raisins
1/2 cup toasted sliced almonds

1. Combine the ingredients for salad dressing in a jar; cover tightly and shake well. Refrigerate until serving time.

2. In a large glass salad bowl, arrange the ingredients in layers, starting with the black beans and ending with the spinach. Top with the cranberries and almonds. Cover and refrigerate for up to 24 hours before serving.

3. At serving time, drizzle the salad dressing over the salad and toss gently to combine. Serve chilled.

Yield: 16 servings (about 1 cup per serving)

137 calories per serving, 19.8 g carbohydrate, 5.7 g fiber, 5 g protein, 5.3 g fat (0.6 g saturated), 0 mg cholesterol, 399 mg sodium, 307 mg potassium, 3 mg iron, 40 mg calcium

Variations
• Add 1/2 cup thinly sliced or grated carrots, zucchini and/or sliced mushrooms. Instead of dried cranberries or raisins, substitute with dried blueberries. Instead of almonds, top with chopped pistachios or roasted soy nuts.

Chef's Secrets
• I Be Leaf! If using flat-leaf spinach, wash it well, dry thoroughly, and tear into bite-sized pieces.

• Shake It Up Baby! Mix ingredients for the dressing right in the salad bowl, then layer the salad ingredients as directed. Cover tightly with plastic wrap. Use elastic bands around the edge of the bowl to keep the plastic wrap in place. Salad bowl must be tightly covered or you will be wearing your salad instead of eating it! At serving time, shake bowl to combine all the ingredients. Now that's exercising your options, and your body, too!

♦ LAUREN'S BLACK BEAN SALAD

My 12-year-old granddaughter Lauren chose her favorite ingredients to create this version of her mother Jodi's bean salad. Lauren adds feta cheese "because I like it!" You can easily substitute chickpeas or kidney beans for the black beans. For more color and fiber, make Tex-Mex Bean Salad.

1 can (19 oz/540 mL) black beans,
   drained and rinsed
1/2 cup chopped red onion
2 Tbsp extra virgin olive oil
2 Tbsp balsamic vinegar
1 tsp minced garlic
Salt and freshly ground black pepper
1/2 cup crumbled feta cheese

1. Combine the beans, onion, oil, vinegar, garlic, salt, and pepper in a large bowl; mix well. Sprinkle with feta cheese and serve immediately.

Yield: About 3 cups (6 servings of 1/2 cup each). Recipe can be doubled. Keeps for up to 3 to 4 days in the refrigerator.

131 calories per serving, 14.1 g carbohydrate, 4.2 g fiber, 5 g protein, 7.3 g fat (2.5 g saturated), 11 mg cholesterol, 488 mg sodium, 273 mg potassium, 1 mg iron, 94 mg calcium

Tex-Mex Bean Salad
Omit feta cheese. Add 1 cup drained corn kernels, 1 red pepper, chopped, and 1/4 cup minced fresh cilantro or parsley. Makes about 4 cups. One serving contains 104 calories, 16.8 g carbohydrate, 4.2 g fiber, 4 g protein, 3.6 g fat (0.5 g saturated), and 349 mg sodium.

♦ MEDITERRANEAN KIDNEY BEAN SALAD

This Mediterranean delight is packed with fiber and protein. Serve it with a grain such as bulgar, rice, or quinoa to make it a complete protein dish. This makes a satisfying, nutritious, and delicious salad that's an excellent addition to your lunch box.

1 can (19 oz/540 mL) red
   or white kidney beans, drained and rinsed
3 green onions, minced
2 cloves garlic (about 2 tsp minced)
1/2 cup minced fresh parsley
1/2 red pepper, seeded and chopped
1 cup grape or cherry tomatoes
2 Tbsp extra virgin olive oil
2 Tbsp lemon juice (preferably fresh)
Salt and freshly ground black pepper
1/2 tsp dried oregano, basil, thyme,
   or rosemary, or 1 Tbsp minced fresh

1. Combine all the ingredients in a large bowl and toss to mix well. Set aside and let marinate for 10 to 15 minutes before serving.

Yield: 4 servings. Recipe doubles and triples easily. Keeps for up to 3 or 4 days in the refrigerator.

196 calories per serving, 25.4 g carbohydrate, 9.8 g fiber, 8 g protein, 7.7 g fat (1.1 g saturated), 0 mg cholesterol, 446 mg sodium, 561 mg potassium, 3 mg iron, 65 mg calcium

Mediterrranean Chickpea Salad
Substitute chickpeas for kidney beans. Add a handful of pitted black olives and use different-colored peppers such as a combination of red, green, orange, and yellow. Sun-dried tomatoes also make a delicious addition.

**salads,
dressings &
sandwiches**

Mediterranean Bean and Pasta Salad
Add 2 cups of cooked pasta such as whole wheat rotini, shells, or macaroni. Don't overcook the pasta: it should be al dente (just cooked but still firm to the bite) to give it a lower glycemic index. Increase the olive oil and lemon juice to 3 Tbsp each and use 1 tsp oregano or desired herbs.

Mediterranean Mixed Bean Salad
Double or triple the recipe for a crowd, using a mixture of red or white kidney beans, black beans, and chickpeas. If desired, sprinkle with 1 cup crumbled feta or goat cheese. For an elegant presentation, serve it on a large platter instead of using a salad bowl.

◉ GREEK CHICKPEA SALAD

This tasty salad comes from Debbie Morson, of Toronto, who assisted with some of the recipe testing for this book. It's full of fiber, flavor, and phytochemicals, making it an excellent vegetarian dish.

1 can (19 oz/540 mL) chickpeas,
   drained and rinsed
1 red or yellow pepper, seeded and chopped
1 green pepper, seeded and chopped
1 cup chopped sweet onion (try Vidalia)
3/4 of an English cucumber, unpeeled,
   halved, seeded, and chopped
1 medium tomato, chopped
1/4 cup minced fresh basil
2 Tbsp minced fresh dillweed
1 clove garlic (about 1 tsp minced)
Juice of 1 lemon (about 3 Tbsp)
3 Tbsp extra virgin olive oil
1/2 to 3/4 cup pitted and halved black olives
Salt and freshly ground black pepper
1/2 cup crumbled light feta cheese

1. Place the drained chickpeas in a large bowl. Add the peppers, onion, cucumber, tomato, basil, dillweed, and garlic; mix well. Add the lemon juice, olive oil, olives, salt, and pepper to taste; toss gently to mix. Crumble the feta cheese over the top, cover, and chill before serving.

2. When ready to serve, adjust seasonings and drain off any excess liquid.

Yield: 8 servings. Keeps for up to 2 to 3 days in the refrigerator.

177 calories per serving, 20.2 g carbohydrate, 4.1 g fiber, 7 g protein, 8.5 g fat (2.0 g saturated), 5 mg cholesterol, 440 mg sodium, 266 mg potassium, 1 mg iron, 67 mg calcium

◉ BRING ON THE BULGAR SALAD

This colorful, fiber-packed dish is excellent for a buffet. Experiment with other grains and nuts. Dried cherries or dried blueberries add color, fiber, and flavor.

1 cup bulgar
1 cup boiling water
1/2 cup slivered almonds
1/4 cup raw sunflower seeds
4 green onions, thinly sliced
1 red pepper, seeded and chopped
1 yellow pepper, chopped
2 stalks celery, chopped
3/4 cup dried cranberries or raisins
3/4 cup slivered dried apricots

Dressing:

1/4 cup extra virgin olive oil
2 Tbsp honey (or to taste)
2 Tbsp lemon or orange juice (preferably fresh)
1 tsp salt (or to taste)
Freshly ground black pepper
1/2 tsp ground cumin
1/2 tsp ground cinnamon

1. Place the bulgar in a large bowl and add the boiling water. Cover and let stand for 20 minutes or until the water is absorbed. Fluff with a fork and set aside.

2. Meanwhile, toast the almonds and sunflower seeds in a 350°F oven for 5 to 10 minutes. Watch carefully to prevent burning. Add to the bulgar along with the green onions, peppers, celery, cranberries, and apricots.

3. In a measuring cup, combine the olive oil, honey, lemon juice, and seasonings. Add to the bulgar and mix well. Cover and refrigerate for up to 24 hours. Serve chilled or at room temperature.

Yield: 12 servings (about 1/2 cup each). Keeps for up to 2 to 3 days in the refrigerator.

188 calories per serving, 27.0 g carbohydrate, 4.6 g fiber, 4 g protein, 8.6 g fat (1.0 g saturated), 0 mg cholesterol, 205 mg sodium, 288 mg potassium, 1 mg iron, 35 mg calcium

Variations

• Instead of bulgar, soak 1 cup couscous in 1 1/2 cups boiling water for 10 minutes.

• Instead of bulgar, cook 1 cup brown basmati rice in 2 cups boiling water for 40 to 45 minutes.

Quinoa Salad

Instead of bulgar, use 1 cup quinoa. Rinse well, then cook in 2 cups boiling water for 15 minutes. Let stand, covered, for 15 minutes, then fluff with a fork and let cool. Omit the sunflower seeds and cumin for Passover.

❧ TERRIFIC TABBOULEH

Everyone will shout "yahoo!" when they taste this terrific tabbouleh. Most recipes call for soaking the bulgar in water, but I prefer the Lebanese method which I learned from Vivianne Barzel, of Israel. She rinses the bulgar, drains it well, and then mixes it with olive oil before adding the other ingredients. This produces a vibrant-green tabbouleh that isn't watery. Vivi chops the parsley and herbs by hand, but I use my food processor. I like to layer the ingredients, which helps the bulgar absorb the other flavors.

1/3 cup bulgar (cracked wheat)
2 Tbsp extra virgin olive oil
1/2 tsp salt (or to taste)
4 plum (Italian) tomatoes, coarsely chopped
2 cloves garlic (about 2 tsp minced)
2 cups tightly packed fresh parsley
   (washed and well-dried)
1/2 cup tightly packed fresh mint leaves
   (washed and well-dried)
1/4 cup tightly packed fresh cilantro
1/2 cup chopped red or green onions
3 Tbsp lemon juice (preferably fresh)
1 tsp grated lemon rind
Freshly ground black pepper

1. Place the bulgar in a fine-mesh strainer and rinse under cold running water for 1 to 2 minutes. Press down firmly to remove excess moisture. Transfer to a bowl and add the olive oil and salt; mix well. Cover and refrigerate for 1 to 2 hours (or even overnight).

2. Top the bulgar with a layer of chopped tomatoes. Mince the garlic, parsley, mint, cilantro, and onion. (This takes 10 to 12 seconds in a food processor fitted with the steel blade.) Spread the minced herbs and onions on top of the tomato layer. Add the lemon

juice, rind, and pepper but don't mix. Cover and refrigerate for 2 to 3 hours to allow the flavors to blend. Mix well. Taste and adjust seasonings if needed. This tastes even better the next day!

Yield: About 4 cups (8 servings). Recipe doubles and triples easily. Keeps for up to 2 to 3 days in the refrigerator.

69 calories per serving, 8.3 g carbohydrate, 1.7 g fiber, 2 g protein, 3.8 g fat (0.5 g saturated), 0 mg cholesterol, 157 mg sodium, 212 mg potassium, 1 mg iron, 34 mg calcium

Confetti Tabbouleh
For a more colorful salad, add any of the following: 1/2 cup chopped English cucumber, 1/2 cup chopped red pepper, 1/2 to 1 cup corn kernels, or baby green peas. Basil can be used instead of cilantro. Add an extra drizzle of lemon juice and olive oil.

Couscous Tabbouleh
Omit the bulgar. Combine 1/3 cup couscous with 2/3 cup boiling water. Cover and let stand 10 minutes, until the water is absorbed. Transfer to a bowl and add the olive oil and salt; mix well. Continue as directed in Step 2.

Barley Tabbouleh
Omit the bulgar and add 1 cup cooked barley (page 323).

Quinoa Tabbouleh
Substitute 1 cup cooked quinoa (page 323) for the bulgar. Excellent for Passover.

🍎 COUSCOUS, CRANBERRY AND MANGO SALAD

This colorful, low-fat salad comes together quickly—no cooking required!

1 1/2 cups hot vegetable or chicken broth
1 cup couscous (whole wheat or plain)
1/2 cup fresh parsley or 1/4 cup fresh mint
2 Tbsp chopped fresh basil
1 slice fresh ginger, peeled
  (about 1 Tbsp minced)
2 cloves garlic (about 2 tsp minced)
3 green onions or 1/2 cup chopped red onion
1 red pepper
1/2 cup dried cranberries
1 large ripe mango, peeled and diced
  (see Nice Dice, on page 270)

Dressing:

2 Tbsp soy sauce (low-sodium or regular)
2 Tbsp rice vinegar
1 Tbsp Asian (toasted) sesame oil
1 Tbsp orange juice (preferably fresh)
Freshly ground black pepper

1. Combine the hot broth with couscous in a large bowl. Cover and let stand 10 minutes, until the liquid is absorbed. Fluff with a fork.

2. In a food processor fitted with the steel blade, process the parsley, basil, ginger, and garlic until minced, about 10 seconds. Add to the couscous. Cut the green onions and red pepper into chunks. Process with quick on/off pulses, until coarsely chopped. Add to the couscous along with the dried cranberries and mango.

3. Add the soy sauce, vinegar, sesame oil, orange juice, and pepper to couscous; mix gently to combine. (If desired, this salad can

be prepared a day in advance and refrigerated.) Adjust the seasonings to taste before serving.

Yield: 8 servings (about 1/2 cup each). Recipe doubles and triples easily. Keeps for up to 2 to 3 days in the refrigerator.

128 calories per serving, 25.8 g carbohydrate, 3.4 g fiber, 3 g protein, 2.3 g fat (0.3 g saturated), 0 mg cholesterol, 211 mg sodium, 131 mg potassium, 1 mg iron, 25 mg calcium

Variations
• Instead of mango, use 1 cup fresh pineapple or oranges, cut into bite-sized pieces. Add some diced celery, water chestnuts, and/or bamboo shoots for extra crunch. Garnish with toasted sliced almonds or chopped pistachios.

KASHA AND VEGETABLE SALAD

This is a wonderful grain-based salad that my Mom made for me while I was writing this book. Kasha is one of my comfort foods, so this salad makes me very happy. It nourishes the body as well as the soul! You can use either coarse or medium kasha in this recipe.

3 cups cooked kasha (page 327)
1 English cucumber, unpeeled and
  chopped
1 red pepper, seeded and chopped
1 medium onion, chopped
1 stalk celery, chopped
1/4 cup minced fresh dillweed
1/4 cup bottled salad dressing
  such as honey mustard, Vidalia onion,
  or vinaigrette
Salt and freshly ground black pepper

1. Cook the kasha as directed; cool completely. (Kasha can be prepared in advance and refrigerated overnight.)

2. In a large bowl, combine the cooked kasha with the cucumber, red pepper, onion, celery, and dillweed. Add the salad dressing. Season with salt and pepper to taste; mix well. Serve chilled.

Yield: 6 servings (about 1 cup each). Keeps for up to 3 to 4 days in the refrigerator.

131 calories per serving, 26.1 g carbohydrate, 3.2 g fiber, 4 g protein, 2.5 g fat (0.4 g saturated), 0 mg cholesterol, 35 mg sodium, 227 mg potassium, 1 mg iron, 24 mg calcium

Barley and Vegetable Salad
Use 3 to 4 cups cooked pearl barley instead of kasha. One cup contains approximately 150 calories, 31.5 carbs (3.9 g fiber). Delicious!

Chef's Secrets
• Switch Around: One cup kasha yields 3 cups when cooked. One cup pearl barley yields 4 cups when cooked. To prepare barley, cook 1 cup in 3 cups boiling water for 40 to 45 minutes.

• Go with the Grain! Other cooked grains excel in this easy salad: try quinoa, couscous, millet, wheat berries, wild rice, bulgar (cracked wheat), or amaranth—the choice is yours. See Cooking Chart for Grains (page 323).

• Dress Right: When choosing bottled salad dressings, look for those that don't contain high-fructose corn syrup, hydrogenated oils, or trans-fats. Choose brands that contain less than 4 grams of saturated fat and less than 4 grams of sugar per serving.

salads, dressings & sandwiches

Choose low-calorie dressings, not low-fat, which usually contain high-fructose corn syrup and are high in carbs. Or make your own dressing—use Balsamic Vinaigrette (page 272) or Shake-It Up Vinaigrette (page 273).

♠ QUINOA, BLACK BEAN AND CORN SALAD

Quinoa (KEEN-wah) has a delicate, nutty flavor and chewy texture. It looks similar to raw sesame seeds. This nutritious salad is a fabulous dish for a buffet and can be expanded into a main course easily. Everyone will be keen on quinoa once they taste this!

2 cups vegetable or chicken broth
1 cup quinoa
1 can (19 oz/540 mL) black beans,
    drained and rinsed
1 cup corn kernels
1 medium red pepper,
    seeded and chopped
4 green onions, chopped
1/4 cup chopped fresh cilantro or parsley
2 cloves garlic (about 1 tsp minced)
1/2 tsp ground cumin
1/4 to 1/2 tsp cayenne pepper (or to taste)
3 to 4 Tbsp lime or lemon juice
    (preferably fresh)
3 to 4 Tbsp extra virgin olive oil
Salt and freshly ground black pepper

1. Bring the broth to a boil in a medium saucepan over high heat. Place the quinoa in a fine-mesh strainer and rinse under cold running water for 1 to 2 minutes; drain well. (Rinsing removes the bitter coating.)

2. Add the quinoa to the boiling liquid. Reduce heat to low and simmer, covered, for 15 minutes. Don't overcook. Remove from heat and let stand, covered, for 5 minutes. Fluff with a fork, transfer to a large bowl and let cool.

3. Add the beans, corn, red pepper, green onions, cilantro, garlic, cumin, and cayenne to the quinoa. Drizzle the lime juice and olive oil over the salad. Season with salt and pepper; toss well. Can be made a day ahead, covered and refrigerated. Adjust seasonings to taste before serving.

Yield: 12 servings of about 3/4 cup. Keeps for up to 3 to 4 days in the refrigerator.

137 calories per serving, 21.5 g carbohydrate, 3.9 g fiber, 4 g protein, 4.5 g fat (0.6 g saturated), 0 mg cholesterol, 313 mg sodium, 267 mg potassium, 2 mg iron, 32 mg calcium

Chicken, Spinach and Quinoa Salad
Arrange a bed of baby spinach leaves on a large platter; top with the quinoa salad. Arrange thinly sliced grilled chicken breasts (warm or cold), roasted red pepper strips, and sliced avocado on top. Pretty delicious!

Couscous and Black Bean Salad
Substitute couscous for quinoa, but reduce broth to 1 1/2 cups. (No need to rinse or cook the couscous.) Combine the couscous with hot broth in a large bowl, cover and let stand for 10 minutes, until liquid is absorbed. Continue as directed in Step 3.

Chef's Secrets
• Switch Around: Quinoa can replace rice or couscous in many recipes and is delicious as a breakfast cereal instead of oatmeal.

• What's in Store: Quinoa can be found in natural food stores and many supermarkets. At home, store it in the refrigerator for 3 to 4 months, or freeze for up to 6 months.

Nutrition Notes

• Go with the Grain: Quinoa is lower in carbohydrates than most grains and is considered a complete protein because it contains all eight essential amino acids.

• GI Go! The glycemic index value for quinoa is 51. It's packed with fiber and is a great source of B vitamins and minerals, including, iron, magnesium, phosphorus, and zinc.

● WHEAT BERRY SALAD

This hearty, high-fiber salad is based on a recipe that comes from Lee Ann Gallant, a Toronto pediatrician. Lee Ann, a vegetarian, uses organic foods whenever possible to optimize good nutritional health. Use your food processor to speed up the preparation time.

1 cup wheat berries (white or red)
3 cups lightly salted water (for cooking)
1 red pepper, seeded and chopped
4 green onions, thinly sliced
1/2 cup chopped fresh parsley
1/2 cup dried cranberries
2 green apples, cored and chopped
  (don't peel)
1/2 cup thinly sliced fennel bulb or celery
2/3 cup Raspberry Vinaigrette
  (page 272)
1 tsp salt
Freshly ground black pepper

1. Place the wheat berries in a colander and rinse with cold water; drain well. Transfer the rinsed wheat berries to a bowl, cover with at least triple the amount of water and soak overnight. Drain well.

2. Combine the wheat berries with lightly salted water in a saucepan and bring to a boil. Reduce heat to low, cover, and simmer for 1 to 1 1/2 hours or until tender. Drain if necessary and let cool.

3. In a large bowl, combine the wheat berries, red pepper, green onions, parsley, cranberries, apples, and fennel. Add the vinaigrette, salt, and pepper; mix well. Refrigerate for at least 1 hour to blend the flavors.

Yield: 6 cups (12 servings of 1/2 cup each). Keeps for up to 2 to 3 days in the refrigerator.

162 calories per serving, 24.5 g carbohydrate, 4.1 g fiber, 3 g protein, 6.7 g fat (0.9 g saturated), 0 mg cholesterol, 213 mg sodium, 142 mg potassium, 1 mg iron, 26 mg calcium

Variations

• Grain Power: No wheat berries? Use barley, bulgar, couscous, kasha, millet, quinoa, or rice. See pages 319–23 for more information and cooking times.

• Herb Magic: Instead of parsley, use cilantro. Add additional herbs such as basil, oregano, thyme, or rosemary to vary the flavor.

• Tutti-Fruity: Instead of dried cranberries, use raisins, dried cherries, dried blueberries or sliced dried apricots. Instead of apples, use firm plums, peaches, nectarines, or Asian pears.

• Mix It Up! Instead of fennel, use jicama, water chestnuts, or hearts of palm.

salads,
dressings &
sandwiches

• Dress it Up! Experiment with different salad dressings. Fruity dressings are especially nice.

• Go Nuts! Garnish with toasted walnuts, pine nuts, slivered almonds, or pumpkin seeds.

Chef's Secrets

• Shop Talk! Wheat berries are available in many supermarkets and health food stores. They come in soft and hard varieties, but this doesn't refer to tenderness. Soft wheat berries are low in gluten and hard wheat berries are high in gluten. Wheat berries will triple in volume when cooked.

• Chews Right! Wheat berries have a chewy texture, so be prepared to chew! Choose them to use in salads, as a substitute for rice, pasta or other grains, or as a breakfast cereal.

• Mix and Match: Combine wheat berries with other cooked grains in salads and pilafs. Cooked wheat berries will keep for up to a week in the refrigerator or can be frozen for 3 or 4 months, so cook up a big batch and use them throughout the week in different recipes. Now that's using your grain!

ASIAN RICE SALAD WITH CASHEWS

This exotic salad comes from food writer Felisa Billet of Lawrence, NY. When she made it for a party in honor of her daughter's birth, it was a huge hit and the recipe spread like wildfire! I've modified it slightly by reducing the sesame oil and adding orange juice. "Rice" to the occasion!

Dressing:

$^1/_3$ cup soy sauce (low-sodium or regular)
$^1/_4$ cup Asian (toasted) sesame oil
3 Tbsp rice vinegar
2 Tbsp orange juice (preferably fresh)
2 Tbsp granulated sugar
2 cloves garlic (about 2 tsp minced)

4 cups cooked brown or white rice
  (see Chef's Secrets, page 267)
6 green onions, sliced
2 red peppers, seeded and diced
1 cup chopped toasted cashews
1 cup dried cranberries or raisins
Salt and freshly ground black pepper

1. In a small bowl, combine the soy sauce, sesame oil, vinegar, orange juice, sugar, and garlic; blend well. (If desired, the dressing can be prepared in advance up to this point and refrigerated overnight.)

2. In a large bowl, combine the cooked rice with the dressing. Add the green onions, bell peppers, cashews, and cranberries; mix well. Season with salt and pepper to taste. Cover and refrigerate. Best prepared at least 1 hour in advance to allow flavors to blend.

Yield: About 8 cups (16 servings of $^1/_2$ cup each). Keeps for up to 3 to 4 days in the refrigerator.

175 calories per serving, 24.1 g carbohydrate, 2.1 g fiber, 3 g protein, 8.0 g fat (1.4 g saturated), 0 mg cholesterol, 167 mg sodium, 144 mg potassium, 1 mg iron, 18 mg calcium

Chef's Secrets

• Double Up! Make double the amount of dressing. You can use it as a dressing for coleslaw or other salads. It's also excellent as a marinade for fish, chicken, beef, or tofu.

• Triple Hitter! Rice triples in volume when cooked, so if you need 4 cups of cooked rice, cook 1¹/₃ cups brown or white rice in 2²/₃ cups lightly salted water. Experiment with different types of rice (e.g., basmati or a mixture of brown, white, red, and wild rice).

• Grain Power! Other grains can be substituted. Try this with cooked kasha, quinoa, bulgar, millet, wheat berries, or couscous. Read pages 319–23 for more information.

• Go Nuts! Instead of cashews, substitute toasted chopped almonds or pecan halves.

• Easy-Peasy! Add 1 cup lightly steamed snow peas, cut in pieces, and 1 can (10 oz/300 mL) of drained mandarin oranges.

• Asian Twist! Add 1 Tbsp minced fresh ginger and ¹/₂ tsp Chinese five-spice powder.

🍎 ROTINI SALAD WITH ARTICHOKES, FETA AND DILL

My friend Debbie Diament, who teaches cooking classes in Toronto, created this "dill-ectible" pasta salad because she loved the combination of bold flavors. This is ideal for a large gathering or makes an excellent side dish. It's best made in advance for maximum flavor. Take this to your next potluck dinner and you'll be welcomed with open arms.

Salad:

1 pkg (1 lb/500 g) tri-colored rotini, fusilli or bow-shaped pasta
2 jars (6 oz/170g each) marinated artichoke hearts, drained and coarsely chopped
1 container (7 oz/200 g) feta cheese, crumbled
1 cup Kalamata olives
1 cup roasted red peppers, cut in strips or pieces
1 cup chopped fresh dillweed, packed

Dressing:

2 to 3 Tbsp extra virgin olive oil
1 Tbsp red wine or balsamic vinegar
1 tsp dried oregano
1 clove garlic (about 1 tsp minced)
³/₄ tsp Kosher salt (or to taste)
¹/₄ tsp freshly ground black pepper

1. Salad: Cook the pasta according to package directions. Drain well. Place in a large mixing bowl. Add the artichokes, feta cheese, olives, red peppers, and dillweed.

2. Dressing: Combine the dressing ingredients in a small bowl; whisk to blend. Add to the pasta mixture and toss lightly. Cover and chill for at least 2 hours (or up to a day) to blend flavors.

Yield: About 12 cups. Keeps for up to 2 to 3 days in the refrigerator.

144 calories per 1/2 cup serving, 17.4 g carbohydrate, 1.6 g fiber, 4 g protein, 6.9 g fat (1.8 g saturated), 7 mg cholesterol, 398 mg sodium, 84 mg potassium, 1 mg iron, 59 mg calcium

Chef's Secrets

• Be Firm! Pasta in any shape or form has a relatively low glycemic index if it is cooked al dente (firm to the bite). Start checking for doneness about 2 to 3 minutes before the end of the time indicated on the package. It should be slightly firm and offer some resistance when you chew it. Overcooking will boost the glycemic index.

• Keep It Low! Even though pasta has a fairly low glycemic index, eating too much will affect your blood glucose. Watch your portion size if this is a concern. If you add lots of vegetables and some protein (e.g., chicken or fish), you can easily stretch 1 cup of cooked pasta into a 3 cup serving. So fill up without filling out!

• Shop Smart: Your healthiest choice is 100% whole wheat pasta, such as rotini or bow ties. The vegetables and herbs will still add lots of color to this salad.

🍎 ASIAN CHICKEN & NOODLE SALAD

This aromatic Asian salad is a favorite of Judy Gruen of Los Angeles, author of *Till We Eat Again: Confessions of a Diet Dropout.* Thank goodness laughing burns calories—I lost three pounds reading about her weight-loss adventures!

Asian Dressing:

3 Tbsp low-sodium soy sauce
3 Tbsp rice vinegar
2 Tbsp Asian (toasted) sesame oil
2 Tbsp canola oil
1 Tbsp minced fresh ginger
2 cloves garlic (about 2 tsp minced)

1/2 tsp granulated sugar
1/4 tsp freshly ground black pepper
1/4 tsp Chinese five-spice powder

Noodle Salad:

2 cups cooked slivered chicken breasts
1 pkg (16 oz/500 g) soba noodles, cooked (or substitute your favorite whole wheat pasta)
1 cup sliced celery
2 cups bean sprouts
1/2 cup sliced green onions
1/4 lb (125 g/2 cups) snow peas, blanched for 1 minute, then sliced diagonally into 1-inch pieces
1 to 2 Tbsp toasted sesame seeds
3 cups baby spinach or mixed salad greens, well-packed

1. Dressing: Combine all ingredients for the dressing in a large bowl and mix well. (Can be made in advance; it will keep for 1 to 2 weeks in the refrigerator in a tightly closed container.)

2. Add the cooked chicken to the dressing and let marinate at least 30 minutes. Add all the other salad ingredients except for the spinach and toss to combine. Refrigerate until serving time. Add the spinach and toss to combine.

Yield: 6 servings as a main dish.

483 calories per serving, 68.4 g carbohydrate, 5.4 g fiber, 32 g protein, 12.2 g fat (1.7 g saturated), 40 mg cholesterol, 510 mg sodium, 411 mg potassium, 4 mg iron, 74 mg calcium

Chef's Secrets

• Get Dressed! This Asian dressing is also delicious on coleslaw, salad greens, pasta, or couscous. One Tbsp contains 49 calories, 0.9 g carbohydrate, 0.1 g fiber, and 5.1 g fat (0.5 g saturated).

• Spice It Up! Chinese five-spice powder consists of equal parts of cinnamon, cloves, fennel seed, star anise, and Szechuan peppercorns. It adds fabulous flavor to almost any Asian dish. You can find it in Asian markets and most supermarkets.

• Pass the Buck-Wheat! Soba are spaghetti-shaped noodles made from buckwheat flour and wheat flour. These Japanese noodles, available in health food stores, are brownish-grey and cook in 5 minutes. They are an excellent whole-grain alternative to refined wheat flour noodles or pasta.

• Using Your Noodle! Adding chicken and vegetables to pasta dishes lowers the glycemic index. To lower the carbs and GI value, use double the amount of chicken, half the amount of noodles and add more vegetables. Judy often adds diced red pepper, jicama, and baby corn for color and flavor.

• Squash, Anyone? You can cut the carbs by two-thirds if you substitute cooked spaghetti squash for the noodles. Refer to Spaghetti Squash with Roasted Vegetables (page 163) for cooking method. One serving of salad will contain 265 calories, 22.6 g carbohydrate, 5.5 g fiber, and 19 g protein.

🍎 CHICKEN MANGO SALAD WITH PEANUT DRESSING

I've transformed my recipe for Peanut Sauce into a sensational salad dressing by adding fruit juice to thin it down. You'll go nuts when you try it! Roasted or grilled chicken turns this into a main dish salad. How "chick" is that?

Peanut Dressing:

Peanut Sauce (page 104)
1/4 cup pineapple, mango,
   or freshly squeezed orange juice

Salad:

1 pkg (10 oz/300 g) mixed salad greens
1 red pepper, cut in strips
4 green onions, sliced on the diagonal
1 cup snow peas, ends trimmed
1 can (8 oz/227 g) sliced water chestnuts,
   drained
4 roasted or grilled boneless, skinless single
   chicken breasts, thinly sliced
1 mango, peeled, pitted, and diced
   (see Chef's Secrets on page 270)
Chopped peanuts, for garnish

1. In a small bowl, combine the peanut sauce with juice and mix well. Reserve 1/2 cup dressing to drizzle over the salad. Cover and refrigerate the remaining dressing for another time.

2. In a large bowl, combine the salad greens, red pepper, onions, snow peas, and water chestnuts. (Dressing and salad mixture can be prepared in advance and refrigerated separately.)

3. At serving time, transfer the salad mixture to a serving platter. Arrange the chicken slices and mango on top. Drizzle with reserved dressing and garnish with chopped peanuts.

Yield: 4 servings as a main dish. Recipe doubles and triples easily.

330 calories per serving, 31.7 g carbohydrate, 6.4 g fiber, 34 g protein, 7.9 g fat (1.7 g saturated), 73 mg cholesterol, 456 mg sodium, 816 mg potassium, 4 mg iron, 98 mg calcium

salads, dressings & sandwiches

Chef's Secrets

• Nuts to You! Peanut Dressing is also excellent over mixed salad greens or in pasta salads. One Tbsp contains 42 calories, 3.7 g carbohydrate, 0.3 g fiber, 2 g protein, 2.2 g fat (0.4 g saturated), and 181 mg sodium.

• Quick Chick! Use leftover cooked chicken or store-bought barbecued chicken, but remove the skin.

• Nice Dice! Using a sharp knife, cut down one side of the flesh of the mango, feeling for the pit with your knife. Repeat on the other side. You will have 2 large pieces. Dice the mango flesh, but don't cut right through to the skin. Bend it backwards and cut mango flesh away from the skin.

salads, dressings & sandwiches

🍎 TUSCAN GRILLED CHICKEN SALAD

This scrumptious meal-in-one salad is packed with vitamins, minerals, and phytonutrients. If you don't like rosemary, substitute other dried or fresh herbs such as oregano, basil, or thyme. This dish multiplies easily and can be prepared in advance, so it's ideal for entertaining.

Dressing:

1/2 cup extra virgin olive oil
3 Tbsp balsamic vinegar
3 cloves garlic, minced
1 Tbsp minced fresh rosemary
   (or 1 tsp dried rosemary)
1/2 tsp salt
Freshly ground black pepper

6 skinless, boneless, single chicken breasts
3 red peppers, cut in quarters

6 large portobello mushrooms,
   stems discarded
1 pkg (10 oz/300 g) fresh baby spinach
   or mixed salad greens
1 medium red onion, quartered and
   thinly sliced
Salt and freshly ground black pepper
1/4 to 1/3 cup toasted sliced almonds,
   for garnish

1. Dressing: In a small bowl, whisk together oil, vinegar, garlic, rosemary, salt, and pepper.

2. Place chicken breasts in a re-sealable plastic bag and add 1/4 cup of the dressing. (Reserve remaining dressing.) Marinate chicken for at least 30 minutes or up to 48 hours in the refrigerator. Turn bag over occasionally to coat chicken on all sides.

3. Preheat grill. Brush peppers and mushrooms with 3 Tbsp of reserved dressing. Grill them over indirect medium-high heat, turning once, about 8 to 10 minutes. Grill chicken breasts over indirect heat until juices run clear and meat is no longer pink in the center, about 8 to 10 minutes (4 to 5 minutes per side). Discard any leftover marinade from the chicken.

4. Remove chicken, peppers, and mushrooms from the grill and transfer them to a cutting board. Cut into 1/2-inch wide strips. (Can be prepared up to a day in advance and refrigerated until serving time.)

5. At serving time, combine the spinach and onion in a large bowl. Drizzle with reserved salad dressing and toss well. Season with salt and pepper. Transfer spinach mixture to a large serving platter or individual serving plates. Add the grilled peppers and

mushrooms. Top with sliced chicken and sprinkle with almonds.

Yield: 6 servings as a main dish.

405 calories per serving, 15.9 g carbohydrate, 5.0 g fiber, 31 g protein, 24.0 g fat (3.2 g saturated), 73 mg cholesterol, 342 mg sodium, 770 mg potassium, 3 mg iron, 77 mg calcium.

Chef's Secrets
• Save Time, Save Calories! Replace marinade with 2/3 cup commercial low-calorie balsamic or Italian vinaigrette. One serving contains 247 calories, and 6.6 g fat (1.2 g saturated).

● CURRIED CRANBERRY CHICKEN SALAD

This colorful chicken salad is a wonderful way to use up leftover cooked chicken. For convenience, you can use store-bought barbecued chicken—however, it's usually higher in sodium and fat. A food processor chops the vegetables quickly.

Chicken Mixture:

2 1/2 cups diced cooked chicken
   (white or dark meat)
1 stalk celery, chopped
3 green onions, chopped
1/2 red pepper, seeded and chopped
1/2 cup dried cranberries
1/2 cup light mayonnaise
1/2 tsp smoked or sweet paprika
1 tsp curry powder
Salt and freshly ground black pepper
Cherry tomatoes and cucumbers,
   for garnish

Salad:

1 bag (10 oz/300 g) mixed salad greens
1/2 cup Italian low-calorie salad dressing
   (or your favorite homemade dressing)
Cherry tomatoes and cucumber slices,
   for garnish

1. In a large mixing bowl, combine the chicken, celery, green onions, and red pepper. Add the cranberries, mayonnaise, paprika, curry powder, salt, and pepper; mix well. Cover and chill for 1 to 2 hours (or overnight).

2. At serving time, place the mixed salad greens on 4 individual serving plates; drizzle lightly with salad dressing and top with a scoop of chicken salad. Garnish with cherry tomatoes and cucumbers.

Yield: 4 servings. Recipe doubles and triples easily. Chicken mixture keeps for up to 2 days in the refrigerator.

335 calories per serving, 22.3 g carbohydrate, 3.6 g fiber, 29 g protein, 14.3 g fat (2.5 g saturated), 87 mg cholesterol, 756 mg sodium, 609 mg potassium, 3 mg iron, 76 mg calcium

Variations
• Instead of cranberries, use dried apricots and cut them up with a scissors. Instead of curry powder, use dried basil. Instead of chicken, use leftover cooked turkey.

• Garnish with 1/2 cup chopped toasted pecans or almonds. Pumpkin or sunflower seeds also add a nice crunch.

Chef's Secrets
• Eggs-actly! If you don't have enough chicken, add 2 diced hard-boiled eggs.

• Fill 'em Up! This mixture can be used to fill Phyllo Nests (page 62), or hollowed-out bell peppers or tomatoes. It also makes a delicious filling for wraps or sandwiches.

• A-Salt with a Deadly Weapon! When a recipe calls for salad dressing, using the bottled variety will do in a pinch, but this boosts the sodium count. If you want to lower the amount of salt, substitute with homemade dressing.

● BALSAMIC VINAIGRETTE

This simple, versatile dressing is scrumptious on salads or can be used to marinate chicken, fish, or roasted vegetables. When you make your own salad dressings, you can control the sodium content and also choose healthier fats such as extra virgin olive oil. You won't regret making this vinaigrette.

1 clove garlic (about 1 tsp minced)
1/4 cup balsamic vinegar
1/2 cup extra virgin olive oil
2 tsp maple syrup or honey
1/4 tsp salt
Freshly ground black pepper
1/4 tsp each dried basil and thyme

1. Combine all the ingredients in a jar, cover tightly, and shake well. Store in the refrigerator until ready to use. Shake well before using.

Yield: About 3/4 cup. Keeps for up to 2 to 3 months in the refrigerator.

86 calories per Tbsp, 1.5 g carbohydrate, 0 g fiber, 0 g protein, 8.8 g fat (1.2 g saturated), 0 mg cholesterol, 47 mg sodium, 8 mg potassium, 0 mg iron, 3 mg calcium

Passover Variation
• For Passover, use honey. If desired, use lemon or orange juice (preferably fresh) instead of balsamic vinegar. If made with fresh juice, the dressing will keep up to a week in the refrigerator.

● RASPBERRY VINAIGRETTE

If you keep frozen raspberries on hand, you can whip up this fruity dressing in about 30 seconds. It's excellent over grains or greens. For a real taste sensation, drizzle it over grilled asparagus. You'll razzle-dazzle them!

1/3 cup fresh or frozen raspberries
   (no need to defrost)
1/3 cup extra virgin olive oil
1 tsp Dijon mustard
2 Tbsp balsamic vinegar
   (or 1 Tbsp balsamic vinegar and
   1 Tbsp orange juice)
1 Tbsp honey
Salt and freshly ground black pepper

1. In a food processor fitted with the steel blade, process raspberries for 8 to 10 seconds. Add the remaining ingredients and process 10 seconds longer to combine. Transfer to a jar and store in the refrigerator. Shake well before using.

Yield: About 2/3 cup. Recipe doubles and triples easily. Keeps for up to a week to 10 days in the refrigerator.

68 calories per Tbsp, 2.5 g carbohydrate, 0.2 g fiber, 0 g protein, 6.5 g fat (0.9 g saturated), 0 mg cholesterol, 12 mg sodium, 4 mg potassium, 0 mg iron, 2 mg calcium

salads, dressings & sandwiches

SHAKE-IT-UP VINAIGRETTE

This luscious, low-calorie salad dressing also does double-duty as a quick marinade for chicken, beef, fish, or vegetables. Dress it up, dress it down, it's a winner all around!

1/3 cup extra virgin olive oil
1/3 cup red wine vinegar
1/3 cup orange juice, preferably fresh
  (or 3 Tbsp orange juice and
  2 Tbsp lemon juice)
1/2 Tbsp Dijon mustard
1 Tbsp honey
2 cloves garlic (about 2 tsp minced)
1/2 tsp salt
1/4 tsp freshly ground black pepper

1. Combine the all ingredients in a jar, cover tightly and shake very well. Mixture will thicken as you shake it. Store it in the refrigerator. Remove from the refrigerator a few minutes before you need it, then shake well.

Yield: About 1 cup. Keeps for up to a week in the refrigerator.

42 calories per Tbsp, 1.6 g carbohydrate, 0 g fiber, 0 g protein, 4.0 g fat (0.6 g saturated), 0 mg cholesterol, 72 mg sodium, 11 mg potassium, 0 mg iron, 2 mg calcium

Quick Greek Salad
Add 1 Tbsp chopped fresh oregano (or 1 tsp dried) to the salad dressing. Drizzle over tomato wedges, black olives, chopped red onions, cucumbers, and green peppers. Top with crumbled feta cheese.

Variations
• Substitute canola, walnut, or grapeseed oil for olive oil.

• Use rice, balsamic, or white wine vinegar instead of red wine vinegar.

• Instead of orange juice, use mango or pineapple juice.

• Instead of honey, use maple syrup, brown sugar, or granular Splenda.

• Add 1/2 tsp dried thyme, basil, or rosemary for a herb-flavored version. If desired, add 2 Tbsp minced fresh parsley or coriander. Add 1 minced shallot as a flavor booster.

Chef's Secrets
• Quick Trick! Add the oil, then vinegar, then orange juice to a 2-cup glass measuring cup—no need to empty between additions! You'll have 1 cup of liquid. Add the remaining ingredients and whisk well, using a mini whisk or fork.

• Chill Out! Olive oil congeals when refrigerated but will become liquid again when it stands at room temperature for a few minutes.

MAPLE BALSAMIC DRIZZLE

A drizzle goes a long way. This dressing goes beautifully with mixed salad greens, baby spinach, or romaine lettuce, especially when paired with fruit such as strawberries or mandarin oranges.

1/4 cup balsamic vinegar
1/4 cup orange juice (preferably fresh)
  or mango juice
1/4 cup maple syrup
1 Tbsp extra virgin olive oil
1 tsp Worcestershire sauce
1 clove garlic (about 1 tsp minced)
1 tsp minced fresh ginger (optional)

1. Combine all the ingredients in a jar, cover tightly, and shake well. Store in the refrigerator until ready to use. Shake well before using.

Yield: About 3/4 cup. Keeps for up to a week in the refrigerator.

27 calories per Tbsp, 4.8 g carbohydrate, 0 g fiber, 0 g protein, 1.0 g fat (0.1 g saturated), 0 mg cholesterol, 5 mg sodium, 26 mg potassium, 0 mg iron, 6 mg calcium

POMEGRANATE HONEY SPLASH

This is the perfect salad dressing for the Jewish High Holidays because it combines pomegranate juice and honey, two traditional holiday foods. Worcestershire sauce contains anchovies, so if this is a concern, look for a brand that is anchovy-free or omit it from the recipe.

1/4 cup balsamic vinegar
1/4 cup pomegranate juice
1/4 cup honey
1 Tbsp extra virgin olive oil
1 tsp Worcestershire sauce (optional)
1 clove garlic (about 1 tsp minced)

1. Combine all the ingredients in a jar, cover tightly, and shake well. Store in the refrigerator until ready to use. Shake well before using.

Yield: About 3/4 cup. Keeps for up to 2 weeks in the refrigerator.

31 calories per Tbsp, 5.9 g carbohydrate, 0 g fiber, 0 g protein, 0.9 g fat (0.1 g saturated), 0 mg cholesterol, 2 mg sodium, 7 mg potassium, 0 mg iron, 3 mg calcium

ASIAN SALAD DRESSING

This Asian-inspired dressing is scrumptious on baby spinach leaves or your favorite blend of salad greens. It also makes a terrific marinade for chicken, fish, or beef.

2 cloves garlic (about 2 tsp minced)
1/4 cup extra virgin olive oil or canola oil
1 Tbsp Asian (toasted) sesame oil
3 Tbsp rice vinegar
2 Tbsp orange juice (preferably fresh)
2 Tbsp soy sauce (low-sodium or regular)
2 Tbsp honey or maple syrup (or to taste)
1 tsp Dijon mustard
2 Tbsp toasted sesame seeds

1. Combine all the ingredients in a glass jar, cover tightly, and shake well. Store in the refrigerator until ready to use. Shake well before using.

Yield: About 1 cup. Keeps for up to a week in the refrigerator.

55 calories per Tbsp, 2.8 g carbohydrate, 0.1 g fiber, 0 g protein, 4.8 g fat (0.6 g saturated), 0 mg cholesterol, 75 mg sodium, 11 mg potassium, 0 mg iron, 5 mg calcium

POPPY SEED DRESSING

This light dressing is delectable on mixed salad greens or baby spinach leaves, especially when topped with mandarin oranges, sliced mangoes, or kiwis, and thinly sliced red onions.

1/4 cup canola oil
1/4 cup rice vinegar
2 Tbsp orange juice (preferably fresh)
2 Tbsp lemon juice (preferably fresh)
2 to 3 Tbsp honey (or to taste)
1 Tbsp poppy seeds

salads, dressings & sandwiches

1 tsp Dijon mustard

1/4 tsp salt

Freshly ground black pepper

1. Combine all the ingredients in a jar, cover tightly, and shake well. Store in the refrigerator until ready to use. Shake before using.

Yield: About 1 cup. Keeps for up to a week in the refrigerator.

45 calories per Tbsp, 1.8 g carbohydrate, 0.1 g fiber, 0 g protein, 3.9 g fat (0.3 g saturated), 0 mg cholesterol, 45 mg sodium, 8 mg potassium, 0 mg iron, 10 mg calcium

🍎 LOW-CALORIE CAESAR DRESSING

This creamy salad dressing also makes an excellent coating for Hail Caesar Salmon (page 129) or any baked fish fillets.

1/4 cup extra virgin olive oil

1/4 cup nonfat plain yogurt
  or light sour cream

1/4 cup light mayonnaise

1/4 cup grated Parmesan cheese

2 Tbsp lemon juice (preferably fresh)
  or wine vinegar

2 Tbsp water

1/2 tsp salt

1/2 tsp granulated sugar

Freshly ground black pepper

1/2 to 1 tsp Worcestershire sauce

2 cloves garlic (about 2 tsp minced)

3 or 4 anchovies, rinsed, drained, and
  mashed (optional)

1. In a 2-cup glass measure, add the oil, then yogurt, then mayonnaise, then the Parmesan cheese—no need to empty the cup between additions. You should have 1 cup total. Add the lemon juice, water, salt, sugar, pepper, Worcestershire sauce, and

garlic. Add the anchovies, if using. Whisk well, using a mini whisk or fork.

2. Cover and refrigerate for 1 to 2 hours before using to allow the flavors to blend.

Yield: About 1 1/4 cups. Keeps for up to a week in the refrigerator.

47 calories per Tbsp, 1.0 g carbohydrate, 0 g fiber, 1 g protein, 4.6 g fat (0.8 g saturated), 2 mg cholesterol, 114 mg sodium, 7 mg potassium, 0 mg iron, 18 mg calcium

Lighter Caesar Salad

Wash the romaine lettuce hearts and dry well. Tear into bite-sized pieces. Calculate 1 cup lettuce per person. Wrap in paper towels, place in a re-sealable plastic bag and chill. At serving time, transfer to a salad bowl. Add 1/4 cup Whole Wheat Croutons (see below) and 2 Tbsp Caesar dressing and toss gently to combine. Sprinkle with 2 tsp grated Parmesan cheese. One serving contains 147 calories, 9.1 g carbohydrate, 0.9 g fiber, 4 g protein, and 10.7 g fat (2.3 g saturated).

Whole Wheat Croutons

Cut half of a 16-oz (500-g) whole wheat baguette into bite-sized pieces. Toss with 2 Tbsp olive oil and 1 Tbsp minced garlic. Spread on a baking tray. Bake in a preheated oven at 350°F for 15 minutes or until dry and crisp. Makes about 6 cups croutons. One serving (1/4 cup) contains 58 calories, 8.8 g carbohydrate, 1.3 g fiber, 2 g protein, and 2.0 g fat (0.3 g saturated).

CREAMY YOGURT DRESSING

This light and creamy dressing is perfect on a steamy summer day. Serve it over mixed salad greens or baby spinach leaves.

2 cloves garlic (about 2 tsp minced)
2 green onions
1/4 cup packed parsley (or 1 Tbsp dried)
1 cup nonfat or 1% plain yogurt
2 Tbsp extra virgin olive oil
1 1/2 Tbsp lemon or lime juice
   (preferably fresh)
1/2 tsp salt
Freshly ground black pepper
1 tsp dried basil or dillweed
   (or 1 Tbsp chopped fresh)
1/2 tsp dried thyme (or 2 tsp fresh)

1. In a food processor fitted with the steel blade, process the garlic, green onions, and parsley until minced. Add the remaining ingredients and process for 10 to 12 seconds longer.

2. Transfer the dressing to a container, cover, and refrigerate for 1 to 2 hours before using, to blend flavors.

Yield: About 1 1/3 cups. Keeps for up to a week in the refrigerator.

17 calories per Tbsp, 1.2 g carbohydrate, 0.1 g fiber, 1 g protein, 1.2 g fat (0.2 g saturated), 0 mg cholesterol, 56 mg sodium, 13 mg potassium, 0 mg iron, 17 mg calcium

Farmer's Salad
Combine chopped lettuce, thinly sliced cucumbers, green or red onions, green peppers, and thinly sliced radishes on a platter. Top with cottage cheese and drizzle with this refreshing dressing. So dairy-good!

SANDWICH SAVVY

• **Wrap Stars!** If you stuff whole wheat tortillas or pita bread with lots of veggies, you can consider them as "portable salads." Tortillas and pita bread do double-duty as edible containers.

• **Wrap It Up:** Although sandwiches have gotten a bad "wrap," here's how to fill up, not fill out, on sandwiches. Start with whole-grain bread, add a lean protein choice, and pile on those veggies to enjoy a satisfying, guilt-free, nutrition-packed sandwich.

• **The Whole Story:** A good rule of thumb is to look for the phrase "100% whole wheat" or "100% wholegrain" on the label. If wheat flour, not whole wheat flour, is listed as the first ingredient, it means that the bread is made from refined white flour. Avoid breads made with added sugars, such as high-fructose corn syrup or honey. Choose those that contain less than 4 grams of sugar per serving.

• **Grain Power:** For sandwiches, choose 100% wholegrain, stone ground, or multi-grain breads, or pumpernickel, rye, or sour-dough breads and rolls. For wraps, choose whole wheat pitas or corn tortillas. These breads contain more fiber and have a lower glycemic index (GI) than white bread, so you will feel full longer.

• **Best Bets:** Choose breads that include some soluble fiber, such as oats, oat bran, or wheat germ. Flaxseed, sesame, caraway, and sunflower seeds are healthy, tasty additions.

• **Browned Off!** Breads that are brown in color are not necessarily healthy—the color sometimes comes from molasses (a hidden sugar), or even from coffee.

salads, dressings & sandwiches

• **White Stuff:** Manufacturers are now making "improved" white bread with whole grains for people who crave white bread. An average slice contains 75 calories, 1.5 grams fiber, and 3 grams protein.

• **The Numbers Game:** Read the label carefully. Best bets are breads that contain 90 to 120 calories per slice, 3 or more grams protein, 3 or more grams fiber, and 15 to 20 grams carbohydrate. Avoid breads that contain trans-fats.

• **GI Go!** Choose lower GI varieties of breads, preferably those with visible grainy bits (but not just sprinkled on the top for decoration)! Here are some average numbers as a guideline: multi-grain breads (43 to 54), pumpernickel (50), seeded rye (51), sourdough (54), pita bread (57), stone-ground whole wheat bread (59) white or enriched whole wheat bread (70), white bagel (72).

• **Thin Is In:** Choose thinly sliced breads to keep the carb and calorie count down.

• **The Hole Truth:** Did you know that an average bagel contains the same amount of carbs and calories as 4 to 5 slices of bread? Dark bagels are not necessarily healthier than white, so don't be deceived by color. Bialies are usually smaller than bagels and contain less calories and carbs.

• **Go Topless:** Leave off the top when eating bagels or sandwiches but heap on the toppings.

• **The Dough Must Go:** Cut a bagel in half and pull out most of the dough. Spread the shell lightly with light cream cheese or Homemade Cottage Cheese (page 177), then pile it high with smoked salmon (lox), tomatoes, onions, and cucumbers.

• **Say Cheese!** Firm Yogurt Cheese (page 178) or Homemade Cottage Cheese (page 177) make excellent alternatives to cream cheese. Boost the flavor by adding minced green onions, dillweed, and/or basil. Roasted red peppers or sun-dried tomatoes also add flavor and fiber.

• **It's a Slice!** Sliced cheese adds calcium and protein, but it also adds saturated fat, so enjoy in moderation. Hard white cheeses such as Swiss are generally lower in calories than yellow cheeses such as cheddar. Choose lower-fat or light brands of cheese.

• **Rule of Thumb:** Your thumb is about the same size as one ounce of cheese, so measure up!

• **Hold the Mayo:** For a lighter spread, combine low-fat or fat-free mayonnaise with equal parts of Dijon mustard or your favorite chutney. Or replace mayo on sandwiches with Aioli (page 46), grainy mustard, chutney, low-calorie salad dressing, or salsa.

• **Avocado Advantage:** Mashed avocado makes a tasty alternative to mayonnaise and adds healthy fats, but be aware that it also packs a caloric load. One medium avocado has approximately 322 calories. Spread it thin so you won't spread!

• **Bean There:** Bean spreads (e.g., Black Bean Dip, page 47) and Hummus (pages 48–49) are an excellent way to add protein and fiber. Spread on pita bread or tortillas and top with shredded lettuce, tomatoes, avocado, and pepper strips for a healthy handful.

• **Go for Tofu:** Try Tofu "Egg" Salad (page 161) as a sandwich filling, with lettuce, sliced tomatoes, and cucumbers.

salads, dressings & sandwiches

• Meatless Burgers: Use Roasted Portobello Mushrooms (page 303) or veggie burgers instead of burgers or meat loaf for a heart-healthy sandwich.

• Veggie Deli: Use soy-based veggie deli slices (e.g., turkey, bologna, salami) as an alternative to sliced luncheon meats. They are low in fat, cholesterol-free, and a good source of protein. They're great in sandwiches, salads, and wraps.

• Go for Protein: Choose sandwich fillings that come from a lean protein source. When making tuna, salmon, or egg salad, use low-fat or fat-free mayonnaise. Use natural peanut butter with no added sugar. If you eat meat or poultry, your best bets are skinless chicken breast, turkey, or lean roast beef.

• Deli Dilemma: If you buy deli meat products, choose lower sodium brands. A diet high in pickled or salt-cured foods is associated with an increased risk of certain cancers, especially because of the nitrates. Add tomato slices to deli sandwiches, or drink a glass of tomato or orange juice with your meal to counteract the risks of eating cured foods.

• Chick Pick: Instead of processed deli meats, try this healthier alternative: when cooking boneless chicken or turkey breasts, cook a few extra. Refrigerate until needed, then slice thinly across the grain. You can also freeze them after slicing—so convenient!

• Fishful Thinking: Transform leftover cooked fish, such as salmon, into a scrumptious sandwich filling. See recipe for Fast Fish Salad on page 121.

• Fill 'em Up! Load up your sandwiches with lots of veggies. Add lettuce, spinach, tomatoes, onions, peppers, cucumbers, and/or grated carrots. Roasted red peppers, sun-dried tomatoes, or marinated artichokes add color and flavor. Open wide!

• The Right Stuff: Great Grilled Vegetables (page 316) or Spring Mix Vegetable Medley (page 317) make fantastic fillings for wraps, pita pockets, or open-face sandwiches. Or stuff Terrific Tabbouleh (page 261) into pita pockets that have been spread with hummus.

• Hot Stuff: Spread wholegrain bread lightly with Aioli (page 46), top with roasted veggies and sprinkle with grated low-fat cheese. Broil until golden and the cheese has melted.

• Wrap-ture! Spread flour tortillas with mango chutney, then add a layer of thinly sliced cooked chicken or turkey breast. Top with mango slices or roasted red peppers. Place a row of baby spinach leaves along one edge. Roll up tightly and enjoy these edible envelopes!

• Fajita Fun: Chicken Fajitas (page 215) can be filled with extra-firm tofu instead of chicken, or transform them into Vegetarian Burritos (page 216).

• Crunch Power: Instead of serving potato chips with your sandwich, serve cut-up vegetables such as baby carrots, celery, or red pepper strips along with a low-fat dip. Dip, dip a-weigh!

🍎 STUFFED PITA POCKETS

Pita bread makes a perfect holder for these tasty pockets—they're packed with phytonutrients, fiber, and flavor. Pack your pockets with any of the tasty variations for lunch or use miniature pitas for perfect appetizers. It's like eating a salad without the fork!

1 cup Black Bean Dip (page 47)
4 medium whole wheat pitas
1 cup packed baby spinach leaves
    or mixed salad greens
1/2 cup diced green pepper
1 cup diced red pepper
2 plum tomatoes, cored and diced
1/2 English cucumber, unpeeled and diced
2 green onions, thinly sliced
1 Tbsp extra virgin olive oil
1 Tbsp lemon juice (preferably fresh)
Salt and freshly ground black pepper
4 tsp roasted sunflower seeds (optional)

1. Prepare the dip as directed. Measure 1 cup and reserve the remainder for another use.

2. Slice each pita open along one edge. Spread the inside of the pita evenly with the dip.

3. Combine the spinach, bell peppers, tomatoes, cucumber, and green onions in a large bowl. Add the olive oil, lemon juice, salt, and pepper; mix well. Spoon some of the vegetable mixture into each pita pocket. Sprinkle with sunflower seeds, if desired.

Yield: 4 servings. Recipe doubles and triples easily. Can be prepared up to 24 hours in advance. Don't freeze.

91 calories per serving, 16.8 g carbohydrate, 3.1 g fiber, 3 g protein, 2.1 g fat (0.3 g saturated), 0 mg cholesterol, 188 mg sodium, 178 mg potassium, 1 mg iron, 18 mg calcium

Variations

• Use White Bean Dip (page 47), Garden Vegetable Hummus (page 48), Pumpkin Hummus (page 49), Tapenade (page 52), or Roasted Eggplant Spread (page 53). What a spread!

• Chopped egg, tuna, salmon, or chicken salad make excellent fillings. Sliced chicken or turkey breast are also delicious fillings. For a vegan option, use Tofu "Egg" Salad (page 161).

🍎 VEGETABLE WRAPS

This versatile recipe comes from my friend Gloria Guttman, of Toronto. It appears in her heartwarming cookbook, *Cooking Kindness*, which benefits the Israel Cancer Research Fund. Because of the concern with eating raw bean sprouts (uncooked and unwashed sprouts can carry salmonella and E-coli), I've suggested using other greens in this recipe. Overall, these delicious "envelopes" of vegetables and greens deliver healthy, handy meals. See Variations on page 280 for more ideas.

1/3 cup light mayonnaise
2 tsp Dijon mustard
6 large (10-inches) flour tortillas
    (whole wheat and/or flavored)
1 English cucumber, trimmed and
    thinly sliced (unpeeled)
1 small red onion, thinly sliced
1 large tomato, finely chopped
1 1/2 cups packed watercress, baby spinach
    leaves, or mixed salad greens
1 avocado, peeled, pitted, and thinly sliced
1 1/2 cups shredded, low-fat
    mozzarella cheese

1. Mix the mayonnaise with mustard in a small bowl. Lightly spread 1 side of each tortilla with the mayonnaise mixture, leaving 1/2-inch border around the edges of each tortilla.

2. Place an overlapping row of cucumber slices along the bottom edge of each tortilla, leaving a 1/2-inch border around the bottom and sides. Place an overlapping row of onion slices on top of the cucumber. Then top with chopped tomato, then watercress, then avocado, ending with cheese. Tightly roll each tortilla: starting from the filling end, roll up part-way, fold in both sides, then finish rolling.

Yield: 6 servings. Best served immediately, but can be made a few hours in advance.

403 calories per serving, 40.2 g carbohydrate, 9.0 g fiber, 14 g protein, 18.0 g fat (5.3 g saturated), 23 mg cholesterol, 724 mg sodium, 349 mg potassium, 1 mg iron, 251 mg calcium

salads, dressings & sandwiches

Variations

• Spread It Around: Instead of mayonnaise, use Garden Vegetable Hummus (page 48) or Aioli (page 46). White Bean Dip (page 47) or Tapenade (page 52) also make tasty spreads. Instead of sliced avocado, spread some mashed avocado on these wraps for a heart-healthy spread.

• Veggie Heaven: Fill wraps with raw or roasted pepper strips, grated carrots, or green onions. Roasted or grilled vegetables, such as mushrooms, peppers, onions, eggplant, and asparagus also make fantastic additions to a wrap.

• Go for Protein: Instead of cheese, fill the wraps with tuna, egg, or salmon salad, or thinly sliced grilled chicken or turkey breast. For a fabulous flavor, fill wraps with Curried Cranberry Chicken Salad (page 271). Tofu "Egg" Salad (page 161) is a delicious vegan option.

• Dill-icious Delight: Spread tortillas with light cream cheese. Fill with smoked salmon, sliced cucumbers, onions, and tomatoes. Sprinkle with minced fresh dillweed and roll up.

vegetables

VEGETABLES

Eat Your Veggies: Mom was right! From asparagus to zucchini, vegetables provide a variety of nutrients for optimal health. They're low in calories and high in vitamins, minerals, fiber, antioxidants, and phytonutrients. Vegetables come in a rainbow of colors, so follow the yellow, red, orange, and green "path-weigh" to good health.

The Garden of Eating: Most people keep buying and eating the same vegetables in the same way. Don't be afraid to try something different. There are hundreds of choices in the produce aisle, so experiment and enjoy. It's time to expand your horizons and shrink your waistline. The healthy recipes and tips in this book will help you make them in easy and tasty ways.

Are You Getting Enough? Aim for 5 to 9 servings of vegetables and fruits a day. Adults need more than children, men need more than women. A serving is about 1 cup raw (the size of a baseball) or 1/2 cup cooked (the size of a tennis ball).

"Bene-Fits!" Vegetables and fruits are the most important and effective choices for good health, disease prevention, and weight management. They can help you reduce your risk of heart disease, stroke, diabetes, cancer, cataracts, and macular degeneration. Their colorful pigments give them their antioxidant, disease-fighting power, so fill your plate with a kaleidoscope of color and health.

High Satiety: Vegetables contain about 80 to 95 percent water, so they will help fill you up and control your hunger. People tend to eat the same volume of food each day so if you replace high-calorie foods with low-calorie vegetables, you can eat bigger portions for the same number of calories.

GI Go! Most vegetables have a low glycemic index, especially those that are green. Some vegetables (such as asparagus, broccoli, cauliflower, and leafy greens), contain little or no carbohydrate, so their GI can't be tested by standard methods. For updated GI values, visit www.glycemicindex.com. Here's a quick overview:

Low GI (GI 55 or less): Green vegetables include artichokes, asparagus, green beans, bok choy, broccoli, Brussels sprouts, cabbage, celery, collard greens, cucumber, kale, lettuce, peas, salad greens, snow peas, and Swiss chard. Also enjoy colored peppers, carrots, cauliflower, corn, eggplant, fennel, garlic, jicama, leeks, mushrooms, onions, parsnips, pumpkin, radishes, radicchio, squash, sweet potatoes, tomatoes, yellow beans, and zucchini.

Medium GI (GI from 56 to 69): These vegetables include Jerusalem artichokes, beets, and small new potatoes.

High GI (GI of 70 or more): These vegetables include broad beans, rutabaga, and turnips. Most spuds are duds when it comes to GI because they are mostly starch and are quickly digested. These include French fries, baked, mashed, boiled, or instant potatoes.

The Numbers Game: Don't exclude medium or high GI veggies just because they have a higher glycemic index. Most are rich in nutrients and also boost your fiber intake. Either combine them with lower GI foods or exercise portion control. A little physical exercise also helps.

vegetables

Calling All Cruciferous Veggies! Broccoli, cauliflower, cabbage, kale, collard greens, and Brussels sprouts contain special phytonutrients that fight inflammation as well as cancer, especially breast cancer. They also contain sulphur-containing compounds: folate, calcium, iron, and vitamin K. Aim for 3 to 4 servings a week.

The Allure of Allium: Garlic, onions, leeks, and chives belong to the allium family. They provide similar benefits to the cruciferous veggies due to their powerful phytonutrients. Garlic, onions, and leeks stimulate the immune system and fight cancer. They also boost flavor, so enjoy them often.

Garlic Is Rich in Allicin! It gives raw garlic its distinctive odor and pungent taste. Garlic acts as a natural antibiotic and an antifungal medication. To optimize garlic's benefits, let it sit 10 to 15 minutes after it is cut. It's worth the wait!

Go for Green: Dark leafy greens include spinach, Swiss chard, kale, and collard greens. Spinach and Swiss chard are interchangeable in most recipes and their cooking time is similar. The darker the green, the higher the nutritional value and disease-fighting potential. Greens are high in folate and rich in lutein and zeaxanthin, which help reduce the risk of cataracts and macular degeneration.

Pepper Power: Bell peppers add color, fiber, and flavor to recipes. They are high in vitamins A and C, as well as lycopene. (Red peppers are higher in vitamin C than green ones and are easier to digest.) Peppers contain powerful antioxidants and promote heart and eye health.

Step Up to the Plate: The American Institute of Cancer Research recommends that your plate should contain 2 vegetables, 1 serving of whole grains, and a smaller portion of protein.

Try, Try Again: Introduce vegetables to young children at an early age. Research has shown that you have to offer new foods up to 10 times before kids really like them. Serve them in fun and creative ways. Cut vegetables into attractive shapes and offer a variety of textures, flavors, and colors.

Sneaky Cuisine: Sneak vegetables into puréed soups, casseroles, pasta dishes, and grains, meat loaf, and burgers. Add them to stir-fries, dips, and spreads. Use your food processor to mince carrots, celery, onions, and garlic; then add the minced vegetables to chicken, salmon, or tuna salad or to burgers.

A-Peeling Shortcuts: There are so many vegetables that require minimal effort to get to the table, with no cutting or peeling required. Try baby carrots, grape tomatoes, baby spinach, broccoli and cauliflower florets, coleslaw mix, jarred roasted peppers, sun-dried tomatoes, minced garlic, ginger, basil, and other herbs. Try precut vegetables (broccoli and cauliflower florets, sliced peppers, stir-fry mix). Although they are a bit more expensive, you can buy just the amount you need—no waste.

Clean Cuisine: Although many packages indicate that leafy greens are pre-washed, I still prefer to wash them. A quick rinse is usually adequate for most vegetables. Add a drop or two of liquid dish detergent to the washing water, then rinse thoroughly. Shake to remove excess water, or dry in a salad spinner. Pat dry with paper towels if necessary. For root vegetables, scrub them with a vegetable brush.

Cool Tools: You need a good vegetable peeler, a paring knife for trimming vegetables, a chef's knife to chop, mince or slice, several cutting boards (color-coded if possible), and a salad spinner. A food processor is like an extra pair of hands and makes chopping, mincing, puréeing, slicing, and shredding a breeze. A miniature food processor is helpful for mincing herbs and small quantities of foods. For cooking, I use a steamer, wok, nonstick skillet, indoor and outdoor grills, and my microwave oven. I have two kitchens—lucky me (except when it comes to clean-ups).

Cook It Right: Vegetables can be blanched, boiled, steamed, sautéed, stir-fried, roasted, grilled, or microwaved to preserve their flavor and texture.

Time to Cook: The nutritional value is affected by the cooking time and method. Cooking time depends on the type of vegetable and whether it is whole, sliced, chopped, or grated. For most methods (except roasting or grilling), estimate 3 to 4 minutes for grated vegetables, 5 to 6 minutes for chopped or sliced vegetables, and 10 to 15 minutes for whole veggies.

Less Than Seven Rule: Cook green vegetables no longer than 7 minutes to preserve their bright green color and texture. If necessary, cut them into small pieces to ensure they'll be done in this time frame. Cut broccoli into small florets and slice the stems thinly. Some veggies take longer to become tender, so if you cook them longer than 7 minutes, their color won't be as bright.

Caterer's Secret: Prepare a variety of vegetables ahead of time. Wash, trim, and cut them up. Blanch them quickly by plunging them into a large pot of boiling salted water. Cook uncovered until nearly tender, about 2 minutes, then drain and rinse with cold water. Let cool, then store in the refrigerator in re-sealable plastic bags for 3 or 4 days. When needed, just sauté or stir-fry them quickly in a little olive oil and garlic, or microwave them. You can also serve them as crudités with a dip. Quick cuisine!

Roast and Boast: Roasting vegetables concentrates their flavor and brings out their natural sweetness. They're delicious hot, cold, or at room temperature as an accompaniment to chicken, beef, fish, or tofu. Or add them to pasta, rice, quinoa, bulgar, or other grains. Try them in salads, wraps, casseroles, omelets, and frittatas, or enjoy them as a snack. Veggie time is any time.

The Spice Is Right: Kosher salt or sea salt and freshly ground black pepper will add terrific flavor. Fresh herbs are best, but dried will do in a pinch. Citrus juices such as orange, lemon or lime, should be fresh, if possible. A sprinkling of Parmesan or some crumbled feta or goat cheese will add calcium and flavor. Sliced or slivered nuts add healthy fats and crunch.

Cold Storage: Most vegetables should be stored in the vegetable crisper of your refrigerator in a loosely sealed plastic bag. This helps prevent moisture from being trapped, causing softening or spoilage. Wrap unwashed leafy greens in paper towels and store them in a re-sealable plastic bag.

Store It Right: Store root vegetables in a cool, well-ventilated pantry, away from light. Good keepers are onions, potatoes, sweet potatoes, and winter squash. I store my garlic, uncovered, in a small basket for easy access.

Frozen Assets: Frozen vegetables are handy and economical. The nutrient content is usually as good as, or sometimes better than, fresh. Although the texture of fresh veggies is better, if you forget about them and they vegetate in your vegetable bin until they rot, frozen is often a better option. Frozen vegetables are usually picked and frozen within hours, so they can often be a better choice than fresh veggies that have been shipped long distances and have been in storage for a long time before they reach your kitchen.

What's in Store: Buy locally grown and in season produce when possible. Choose organic produce to avoid pesticides.

Microwave Magic: One pound of fresh vegetables (about 2 cups) takes about 5 minutes on high to microwave, depending on the density and water content of the vegetable. There's no need to add extra water—the water from washing is usually sufficient. One 10 oz/300 g pkg (about 1½ cups) of frozen vegetables defrosts and cooks in 5 minutes on high. It's not necessary to add water as the ice crystals will create enough steam to cook them. It takes 2 to 3 minutes to defrost (but not cook) on high power.

Color Your World: No single vegetable contains all of the nutrients you need, so eat a variety of vegetables and let color be your guide. Paint your plate (and your palate) with juicy red tomatoes, crunchy orange carrots, emerald-green spinach, and other dark leafy greens, and all the colors in between. Including more fruits and vegetables each day is a great "weigh" to achieve better health.

GRILL 'N CHILL ASPARAGUS

My assistant Cindy Beer makes this simple and delicious dish ahead of time on her two-sided indoor grill. Her guests and family love it. Cindy insists on using thin asparagus spears because she thinks they taste better. If you munch a bunch of fiber-packed grilled asparagus rather than nosh on noodles or other starchy side dishes, over time you'll be be pencil-thin too.

2 bunches fresh asparagus (about 2 lb/1 kg)
2 Tbsp extra virgin olive oil
1/2 cup Raspberry Vinaigrette
   (page 272)

1. Preheat an indoor grill. Soak the asparagus in cold water for a few minutes. Drain thoroughly and pat dry. Bend asparagus and snap off the tough ends at the point where they break off naturally; discard the ends. Place the trimmed asparagus in a loaf pan or shallow dish and drizzle with olive oil. Roll the asparagus around to coat all sides with oil.

2. Transfer the spears to the hot grill, close the lid and grill for 5 minutes or until the asparagus is tender-crisp. Remove from the grill and let cool. Cover and refrigerate for several hours or overnight.

3. When ready to serve, transfer the asparagus to a serving platter and drizzle with Raspberry Vinaigrette.

Yield: 8 servings. Serve hot or at room temperature. Will keep for up to 2 days in the refrigerator. Don't freeze.

122 calories per serving, 6.8 g carbohydrate, 2.3 g fiber, 3 g protein, 10.3 g fat (1.5 g saturated), 0 mg cholesterol, 26 mg sodium, 240 mg potassium, 1 mg iron, 26 mg calcium

Chef's Secrets
• Grilling Tip: If grilling asparagus spears on an outdoor grill, lay them crosswise to prevent them from falling through the cracks or place them in a grill basket.

• Size Counts: Some cooks prefer large asparagus spears but these tend to be somewhat stringy and usually require peeling. Thin and medium-sized spears don't require peeling. Try to buy spears that are all the same thickness so that they will cook evenly.

• Weighing In: One bunch of asparagus weighs about 1 lb (500 g). There are 16 to 20 spears in a pound, yielding 2 1/2 cups cooked. Calculate 4 to 6 spears per person as a serving.

• It's in the Bag: Store asparagus in the refrigerator in a loosely sealed plastic bag. To keep it moist, first wrap it in a damp paper towel. It will keep for up to 2 weeks.

Nutrition Note
• Asparagus is high in vitamins A, B, and C, and it's high in folate, which is important for pregnant women and for cardiovascular health. Asparagus is also a good source of potassium and iron.

OVEN-ROASTED ASPARAGUS

This fiber-packed dish is a snap to prepare. Roasting concentrates the flavor of the asparagus and the tips will get very crispy. Warning—this is addictive.

1 1/2 lb (750 g) asparagus spears
2 Tbsp extra virgin olive oil
2 Tbsp lemon juice (preferably fresh)
   or balsamic vinegar
2 cloves garlic (about 2 tsp minced)
Sea salt or Kosher salt

1. Preheat the oven to 425°F. Line a large baking tray with foil; spray with cooking spray.

2. Soak asparagus thoroughly in cold water; drain well. Bend asparagus and snap off the tough ends at the point where they break off naturally. Place in a single layer on the prepared baking sheet. Drizzle with olive oil, lemon juice, and garlic. Roll the asparagus to coat all sides.

3. Roast, uncovered, in the lower third of the oven for 12 to 15 minutes or until the spears are tender-crisp and lightly browned. Using tongs, turn the asparagus once or twice during roasting for even browning. Transfer to a platter, lightly sprinkle with salt, and serve.

Yield: 4 to 6 servings. Recipe doubles or triples easily. Serve hot or at room temperature. Don't freeze.

102 calories per serving, 7.7 g carbohydrate, 3.2 g fiber, 4 g protein, 7.4 g fat (1.1 g saturated), 0 mg cholesterol, 22 mg sodium, 370 mg potassium, 1 mg iron, 40 mg calcium

Caesar's Spears

Omit the oil, lemon juice and garlic, and instead coat the asparagus with 1/4 cup low-calorie Caesar dressing. Sprinkle with 2 Tbsp sesame seeds and 2 Tbsp grated Parmesan cheese. Roast as directed above. Romans, seize your spears!

Grilled Asparagus

Preheat the grill. Prepare the asparagus as directed in Step 2. Transfer to the hot grill, laying spears crosswise to prevent them from falling through the cracks in the grate, or place in a grill basket. Grill over medium-high heat for 7 to 8 minutes or until the spears are lightly browned and somewhat crispy.

Herb-Roasted Asparagus

Add 1 tsp minced fresh rosemary, thyme, tarragon, or dried Italian seasoning to the olive oil, lemon juice, and garlic. Roast or grill.

Chef's Secrets

• Juicy Secrets: The zest from citrus fruits such as lemons adds a fresh citrus flavor to asparagus without discoloring it. So instead of adding lemon juice to asparagus, add finely grated lemon zest. Lemon aid, without the juice!

❥ MICROWAVED ORIENTAL BROCCOLI

Broccoli is an Italian word that means "little arms." Your guests are sure to welcome this nutritious, delicious dish with open arms.

1 clove garlic (about 1 tsp minced)
1 small slice peeled fresh ginger
    (about 1 Tbsp)
2 Tbsp orange juice (preferably fresh)
1 Tbsp soy sauce (low-sodium or regular)
2 tsp honey
1 tsp Asian (toasted) sesame oil
1 large bunch broccoli
    (about 1 1/2 lb/750 g)
1/2 cup seeded and finely chopped
    red pepper, for garnish
1/4 cup toasted slivered almonds, for garnish

1. In a food processor fitted with the steel blade, process the garlic and ginger until finely minced. Add the orange juice, soy sauce, honey, and sesame oil; process for 6 to 8 seconds or until blended. (If desired,

the sauce can be prepared in advance and refrigerated for 1 to 2 days.)

2. Rinse the broccoli thoroughly in cold water, shaking off any excess. Trim the woody ends and cut the broccoli into florets. Slice the thick parts of the stems into 1 inch pieces. Place the broccoli in a large microwaveable bowl. Cover and microwave on high for about 5 minutes or until tender-crisp and bright green. Don't overcook. Drain well.

3. Drizzle the sauce over the broccoli and mix gently. Transfer to a serving dish and garnish with the red pepper and toasted almonds.

Yield: 4 servings. Recipe doubles or triples easily. Serve hot or at room temperature. Don't freeze.

123 calories per serving, 16.8 g carbohydrate, 5.7 g fiber, 6 g protein, 5.2 g fat (0.5 g saturated), 0 mg cholesterol, 184 mg sodium, 593 mg potassium, 2 mg iron, 92 mg calcium

Variations
• This sauce also tastes marvelous over asparagus, cauliflower, or green beans. Try it with broccoli raab, which is similar to broccoli but has fewer florets and more stems.

• Substitute 1/4 cup bottled Asian salad dressing or sauce instead of making your own.

Chef's Secrets
• Microwave Magic: When you microwave broccoli, there's no need to add additional water. The residual moisture from washing the broccoli is sufficient to create steam for cooking. Use parchment paper that has been rinsed under cold water to cover the cooking dish—wetting the paper makes it flexible so you can mold it easily around the dish.

• Time It Right: Microwave broccoli, covered, on high, allowing 4 to 5 minutes per pound. Microwave ovens vary in wattage, so some experimentation might be necessary.

• Nuts to You! To toast almonds, microwave, uncovered, on high for 2 minutes.

• Steam Power: Instead of microwaving broccoli, cook it in a vegetable steamer for 5 minutes.

ROASTED BROCCOLI

Roasting broccoli transforms it, enhancing the flavor. If you use fresh herbs instead of dried, add them the last few minutes of cooking; always add dried herbs at the beginning of cooking. Broccoli, like all vegetables, will shrink in volume during roasting, so I like to make a lot. It's a perfect low-carb snack. Addictive!

1 large bunch broccoli (about 1 1/2 lb/750 g)
2 Tbsp olive oil
2 Tbsp lemon or orange juice
   (preferably fresh)
2 to 3 cloves garlic (about 2 to 3 tsp minced)
1 tsp Italian seasoning or a mixture of
   basil, oregano, and thyme
Salt and freshly ground black pepper
Toasted sesame seeds, for garnish

1. Preheat the oven to 400°F. Line a baking sheet with foil; spray with cooking spray.

2. Trim the woody ends from the broccoli; discard ends. Peel the broccoli stems with a vegetable peeler and then cut the broccoli into spears or large pieces. Soak thoroughly in cold, salted water for a few minutes; drain well. Spread the broccoli out in a single layer on the prepared baking sheet and

drizzle with olive oil and juice. Sprinkle with garlic, Italian seasoning, and salt and pepper to taste. Toss the broccoli gently with your hands to coat all sides.

3. Roast, uncovered, in the lower third of the oven for 15 to 20 minutes or until the broccoli is tender-crisp and lightly browned. (Cooking time depends on the thickness of the pieces.) Use tongs to turn the broccoli once or twice during roasting for even browning. Garnish with sesame seeds.

Yield: 4 to 6 servings. Serve hot or at room temperature. Don't freeze.

100 calories per serving, 8.3 g carbohydrate, 2.9 g fiber, 3 g protein, 7.2 g fat (0.9 g saturated), 0 mg cholesterol, 35 mg sodium, 346 mg potassium, 1 mg iron, 59 mg calcium

Variations
• Strips of red pepper can be roasted along with the broccoli. Instead of sesame seeds, sprinkle with toasted almonds, pine nuts, or walnuts.

Grilled Broccoli
Prepare the broccoli as directed in Step 2. Preheat a two-sided electric grill. Arrange the broccoli in a single layer on the grill, close the lid, and cook for 5 to 6 minutes. If using an outdoor grill, cook over indirect heat for 3 to 4 minutes per side.

🍎 STEAMED BROCCOLI WITH OLIVE OIL AND GARLIC

If you cook broccoli too long, it develops an unpleasant, sulfur-like odor and loses valuable nutrients. Steaming retains maximum nutrients because little water is used. Full steam ahead!

1 large bunch broccoli (about 1 1/2 lb/750 g)
4 tsp extra virgin olive oil
2 cloves garlic (about 2 tsp minced)
1/2 tsp dried basil
1/4 tsp dried thyme
Kosher salt and freshly ground black pepper

1. Trim the woody ends from the broccoli; discard ends. Peel the broccoli stems with a vegetable peeler and cut the broccoli into bite-sized pieces. Soak the broccoli thoroughly in cold salted water for a few minutes; drain well. Place in a steamer basket.

2. Bring 1 inch of water to a boil in a large saucepan. Place the steamer in the saucepan, making sure it doesn't touch the water. Cover and simmer the broccoli for 5 to 6 minutes or until it is tender-crisp and bright green. Drain well. Transfer to a bowl. (See Do-Ahead Trick below.)

3. Add the oil, garlic, and seasonings, and gently mix with the broccoli. Serve immediately.

Yield: 4 servings. Recipe doubles or triples easily. Don't freeze.

74 calories per serving, 6.1 g carbohydrate, 3.3 g fiber, 3 g protein, 5.0 g fat (0.7 g saturated), 0 mg cholesterol, 28 mg sodium, 351 mg potassium, 1 mg iron, 58 mg calcium

Chef's Secrets
• Do-Ahead Trick: Steam broccoli for 4 to 5 minutes. Rinse thoroughly in cold water to stop the cooking. Drain well, cover, and refrigerate. At serving time, combine the broccoli with the oil, garlic, and seasonings. Reheat briefly in a large skillet over medium heat; serve immediately.

• Quick Broccoli for One: Rinse 1 or 2 spears of broccoli; drain well. Place in a 2-cup glass measure with the stems downward. Microwave, covered, on high for 1 to 2 minutes or until tender-crisp. Drizzle with freshly squeezed lemon juice, low-calorie salad dressing, or finely grated lemon zest; garnish with sesame seeds.

• Less-Than-7 Rule: Cook the broccoli less than 7 minutes to preserve its bright green color. For even cooking, cut the florets no larger than 1 1/2 inches and cut the stems into 1/2-inch slices.

• Flower Power: Broccoli is excellent in dips, soups, casseroles, salads, stir-fries, pasta dishes, quiches, or omelets. It's so versatile—you can steam, sauté, stir-fry, roast, grill, or microwave it.

• It's in the Bag: Wrap unwashed broccoli in dry paper towels and place in a re-sealable plastic bag. It will stay fresh in the refrigerator for up to 2 weeks.

Nutrition Notes
• What's in Store: Choose broccoli with tightly closed florets and firm stalks. The florets contain more beta carotene than the stalks. Also, florets that are dark green or purplish green contain more beta carotene and vitamin C than paler or yellowing florets.

• Fresh or Frozen? Frozen broccoli contains more beta carotene than fresh. However, it contains twice as much sodium and less iron, thiamin, riboflavin, calcium, and vitamin C.

• Worth Stalking About: A member of the cruciferous family, broccoli is high in vitamins C, A, and K, fiber, folate, calcium, and potassium. It contains powerful anti-cancer compounds including sulforaphane. Its antibacterial properties kill H-pylori, the bacteria which cause ulcers and are implicated in stomach cancer. Broccoli also helps reduce heart disease risk and helps protect eyes from cataracts and macular degeneration.

ROASTED BRUSSELS SPROUTS

The fresher the sprouts are, the finer the flavor. This method of preparing Brussels sprouts was shared by my friend Risa Golding of Oxford, New Jersey. People who say they hate this vegetable will be pleasantly surprised when they try it roasted. They'll shout for more sprouts!

1 1/2 lb (750 g) Brussels sprouts
   (about 30 to 36)
2 to 3 Tbsp olive oil
3/4 tsp Kosher salt (or to taste)
Freshly ground black pepper

1. Preheat the oven to 425°F. Line a large baking tray with foil and spray with cooking spray.

2. Trim the ends from the Brussels sprouts and pull off any yellow leaves. Cut the sprouts in half and soak in salted lukewarm water for 10 minutes to rid them of any hidden insects; drain well.

3. Transfer the pre-soaked sprouts to a bowl and mix with olive oil, salt, and pepper to taste. Spread the sprouts in a single layer on the prepared baking sheet.

4. Place the pan in the lower third of the oven and roast, uncovered, for 20 to 30 minutes or until crispy and well-browned

outside and tender inside. Halfway through the cooking process, turn the Brussels sprouts over for even browning. Sprinkle with additional salt and serve immediately.

Yield: 6 servings. Recipe doubles or triples easily. Serve hot or at room temperature. Don't freeze.

84 calories per serving, 9.1 g carbohydrate, 3.9 g fiber, 3 g protein, 4.8 g fat (0.7 g saturated), 0 mg cholesterol, 261 mg sodium, 397 mg potassium, 1 mg iron, 45 mg calcium

Variations
• Brussels sprouts are also fabulous drizzled with freshly squeezed lemon juice or sprinkled with finely minced lemon or lime zest. Experiment with various seasonings such as minced garlic, thyme, or barbecue spice—the choice is yours.

Chef's Secrets
• What's in Store: Brussels sprouts look like miniature cabbages. Smaller sprouts are more tender than larger ones; larger sprouts tend to be bitter and woody in the center. Choose small, dark green sprouts that are tightly closed, about 1 to 1½ inches in diameter. Wilted or yellowing leaves are a sign that the sprouts are past their prime. One pound (500 g) contains 3 cups or about 20 to 24 sprouts.

• It's in the Bag: Store unwashed sprouts in a re-sealable plastic bag in the refrigerator for up to 4 or 5 days. If stored longer, they may develop a strong, unpleasant odor.

Nutrition Note
• Brussels sprouts are a good source of vitamins A and C, are high in fiber, low in calories, have a low glycemic index, and have anti-cancer properties.

🍎 GARLIC-ROASTED CARROTS

These are absolutely addictive! Roasting brings out the natural sweetness of carrots.

1 large onion, sliced
2 lb (1 kg) carrots, peeled and
   cut in 2-inch lengths
3 to 4 cloves garlic (about 3 to 4 tsp minced)
2 to 3 Tbsp olive oil
Kosher salt and freshly ground black pepper

1. Preheat the oven to 375°F. Spray a 9- × 13-inch glass baking dish with cooking spray.

2. Place the onion, carrots, and garlic in the prepared baking dish. Drizzle with olive oil and sprinkle with salt and pepper to taste; mix well. For best results, the carrots should be in a single layer in the dish.

3. Roast, uncovered, for 45 to 60 minutes or until golden and tender, stirring the carrots occasionally. Serve hot or at room temperature.

Yield: 6 servings. Keeps for up to 2 days in the refrigerator; reheats well. Don't freeze.

115 calories per serving, 17.5 g carbohydrate, 4.6 g fiber, 2 g protein, 4.9 g fat (0.7 g saturated), 0 mg cholesterol, 105 mg sodium, 526 mg potassium, 1 mg iron, 58 mg calcium

Garlic-Roasted Carrots and Potatoes
Use 1 lb carrots and 3 medium potatoes, peeled and sliced. Add ½ cup water and roast as directed. One serving contains 164 calories, 28.5 g carb, and 4.4 g fiber.

Garlic-Roasted Parsnips

Use 2 lb parsnips instead of carrots. One serving contains 165 calories, 29.8 g carbohydrates, and 6.2 g fiber. Parsnips (GI 52) are a terrific source of Vitamins C and E and folate.

Variations

• Use half carrots and half parsnips. Add a drizzle of balsamic vinegar or freshly squeezed lemon juice. Add your favorite herbs (try cumin, minced basil, oregano, dillweed, thyme, or rosemary). If using fresh herbs, add them during the last 5 minutes of roasting.

• Lazy Day Carrots: Substitute with bagged baby carrots, which require no peeling or cutting.

Chef's Secrets

• What's in Store: Choose carrots that are firm and smooth, without cracks. Hairy white fibers are a sign of age. If carrots still have the greens attached, twist them off and discard as soon as possible or the carrots will spoil quickly.

• Size Counts: Small-to-medium carrots are best. Although large carrots take less time to peel, they usually have tough, tasteless, woody cores and are less sweet. One lb (500 g) contains 6 medium carrots and yields about 3 cups.

• How A-Peeling: Here's an easy way to peel carrots, which I learned from a chef after I finished peeling 50 pounds of carrots in his kitchen! Holding the end in one hand, place the point of the carrot on a cutting surface. With a vegetable peeler, use long strokes, rotating the carrot until all the peel is removed; trim the ends. Get the point?

Nutrition Notes

• Myth-Information: Many people who are on a low-carb diet are afraid to eat carrots because they think they have a high glycemic index value, but their GI is 41, which makes them a low GI food. It's important to note that the glycemic index is based on eating 50 grams of carbohydrate—that's about 9 carrots or 1 1/2 pounds! One medium carrot contains 5.8 g carbohydrate, 1.7 g fiber, and 25 calories—how's that for a "root awakening"? Munching on a crunchy carrot will have minimal effect on blood sugar, so munch without guilt. For more information, visit www.glycemicindex.com.

• What's Up, Doc? Carrots are loaded with fiber, vitamin A, some vitamin C, plus beta carotene, which helps promote eye health. Look at the whole picture and don't just choose foods based on their glycemic index value. Hopefully, now everyone will see eye to eye on this point.

🍴 HONEY-GLAZED CARROTS

This is a honey of a dish because you don't need to peel or cut the carrots, which is so a-peeling! These glazed carrots are perfect for the Jewish High Holidays, Passover, or any time of year.

2 lb (1 kg) baby carrots
2 Tbsp extra virgin olive oil
2 Tbsp lemon juice (preferably fresh)
2 Tbsp honey
2 Tbsp apricot or mango preserves
   (preferably low-sugar or all-fruit)
Salt and freshly ground black pepper
1/2 tsp dried thyme
1/4 cup chopped fresh parsley
   or dillweed, for garnish

1. Place the carrots in a medium saucepan and add enough water to cover by 1 inch; bring to a boil. Reduce heat to low and simmer, covered, for 12 to 15 minutes or until tender. Drain well and return the carrots to the saucepan.

2. Add the oil, lemon juice, honey, jam, salt, pepper, and thyme. Cook for 2 or 3 minutes longer, stirring to prevent sticking, until the carrots are nicely glazed. Garnish with parsley and serve.

Yield: 6 servings. Recipe doubles or triples easily. Keeps for up to 3 days in the refrigerator; reheats well. Don't freeze.

127 calories per serving, 21.0 g carbohydrate, 2.9 g fiber, 1 g protein, 4.9 g fat (0.7 g saturated), 0 mg cholesterol, 120 mg sodium, 383 mg potassium, 2 mg iron, 54 mg calcium

Maple Balsamic Carrots
Replace the lemon juice and honey with balsamic vinegar and maple syrup.

Variations
• Instead of using baby carrots, substitute with 3 bags (10 oz/300 g each) of grated carrots: the carrots will cook in about 10 minutes. Instead of lemon juice and apricot jam, use orange juice and orange marmalade.

Chef's Secrets
• Baby Bonus: Baby carrots are a terrific time-saver because they don't require peeling. They are actually regular carrots that have been cut by a machine into mini carrots. It takes 1 medium carrot to make 4 or 5 baby carrots. Bagged baby carrots are not fresh if they have a white tinge on the outside.

• Carrot Cuisine: Carrots are also delicious in soups, salads, stews, casseroles, grain dishes, side dishes, cakes, muffins, and quick breads. Enjoy them raw, roasted, steamed or stir-fried, or add them raw to salads. Very versatile.

CARROT AND SWEET POTATO TZIMMES

My late friend Bev Gordon, of Richmond Hill, loved to cook and often helped me test recipes. She shared this family favorite with me that she got from a cousin years ago. Bev told me: "I associate September with Rosh Hashanah, Yom Kippur, and new beginnings. This wonderful dish is a sweet blend of root vegetables, plentiful at this time of the year."

3 medium sweet potatoes, peeled
1 acorn squash, peeled and seeded
4 large carrots, peeled
24 pitted prunes, halved
1 cup orange juice (preferably fresh)
1 tsp grated orange rind
1/4 cup packed brown sugar
   or granular Splenda
1 tsp ground cinnamon (optional)
Salt and freshly ground black pepper

1. Preheat the oven to 375°F. Spray a 9- × 13-inch baking dish with cooking spray.

2. Cut the sweet potatoes and squash into a 1-inch dice. Slice the carrots into 1/2-inch slices. Place the sweet potatoes, squash, and carrots in a large bowl and add the prunes, orange juice, orange rind, brown sugar, cinnamon, salt, and pepper; toss to combine. Transfer the vegetable mixture to the prepared baking dish and cover with foil.

3. Bake, covered, for 40 minutes. Uncover and bake for 20 minutes longer, stirring occasionally. Serve hot.

Yield: 10 servings. Keeps for up to 3 days in the refrigerator; reheats well. Freezes well for up to 2 months.

152 calories per serving, 38.4 g carbohydrate, 5.8 g fiber, 2 g protein, 0.3 g fat (0.1 g saturated), 0 mg cholesterol, 36 mg sodium, 628 mg potassium, 1 mg iron, 61 mg calcium

Nutrition Notes
• This dish is loaded with vitamin A, beta carotene, potassium, and fiber.

• Sweet Choice: To reduce the calories and carbs in this dish, replace half the orange juice with water and use Splenda instead of brown sugar. One serving contains 135 calories, 34.1 g carbohydrate, and 5.8 g fiber.

🍴 CREAMY GARLIC MASHED FAUX-TATOES

Cauliflower is a sneaky substitute for potatoes in this creamy alternative to mashed potatoes. The potato version contains more than triple the carbs and double the calories.

1 medium cauliflower
6 cloves garlic, peeled
Salted water
1 Tbsp soft tub margarine
  or extra virgin olive oil
1/4 to 1/3 cup light cream cheese
  (or imitation cream cheese such as Tofutti)
Salt and freshly ground black pepper
2 Tbsp chopped green onions, for garnish

1. Wash the cauliflower well and cut into florets. Place the cauliflower florets and garlic in a large saucepan. Add enough water to cover and add a dash of salt; bring to a boil. Reduce heat to low and simmer for 15 to 20 minutes or until very tender. Remove from heat and drain well.

2. Transfer the cooked cauliflower to a food processor fitted with the steel blade; process for 25 to 30 seconds or until very smooth. Scrape down the sides of the bowl as needed. Add the margarine, cream cheese, salt and pepper; process for a few seconds longer to combine.

3. Transfer to a serving dish and garnish with green onions.

Yield: 4 servings. Recipe doubles or triples easily. Reheats well in the microwave. Don't freeze.

104 calories per serving, 10.4 g carbohydrate, 3.8 g fiber, 5 g protein, 5.5. g fat (2.2 g saturated), 8 mg cholesterol, 158 mg sodium, 491 mg potassium, 1 mg iron, 63 mg calcium

Variation
• Instead of cream cheese, use light sour cream and add 2 Tbsp grated Parmesan cheese.

Creamy Garlic Mashed Potatoes
Substitute 4 medium potatoes for the cauliflower; cook with garlic until tender. Drain thoroughly and mash well, using a potato masher. (A food processor will create a gluey mess.) Blend in margarine, cream cheese, salt, and pepper. One serving contains 212 calories, 36.1 g carbohydrate, and 3.6 g fiber.

Chef's Secrets

• Size It Up: A medium cauliflower (6 to 7 inches in diameter) yields about 8 cups of florets.

• Steps to Prep: Cut off the leaves and woody base of the stem. Break the cauliflower into florets. Soak in cold salted water for 10 minutes to help remove any hidden insects; drain well.

• Steam Cuisine: Pour 1 inch of water into a large saucepan. Place the florets in a steamer basket and place in the saucepan, making sure the florets don't come into contact with the water. Cover and bring to a boil. Reduce heat to low, and steam for 12 to 15 minutes or until very tender. Drain well and pat dry with paper towels.

• Microwave Magic: Don't cut up the cauliflower; place it whole in a microwaveable casserole. Sprinkle with 2 Tbsp water, cover, and microwave on high until very tender, about 10 to 12 minutes. Drain well and pat dry with paper towels. (If your casserole doesn't have a lid, cover it with parchment paper that has been placed under running water so you can mold it around the dish.)

• Im-press-ive! A terrific way to remove excess water from cooked cauliflower is to mash it with a potato masher. Just place the cauliflower into a colander and lightly press down with the masher. (Using a potato masher is also a great way to remove excess water from cooked spinach.)

CURRY ROASTED CAULIFLOWER

Whenever my assistant Shelley Sefton makes this high-fiber, high-flavor dish for family and friends, everyone asks when she's going to make it again. If making this for a crowd, double the recipe or make one of the variations. Shelley says that she can eat the whole thing by herself. So can I!

1 large cauliflower
1 red pepper, seeded and
   cut into long, narrow strips
2 Tbsp olive oil
2 tsp curry powder
1/2 tsp salt (or to taste)
1/4 cup sliced fresh chives
   or green onions, for garnish

1. Preheat the oven to 400°F. Line a large baking tray with parchment paper or sprayed foil.

2. Wash the cauliflower well and cut into large florets. Place in a large bowl along with the red pepper strips. Drizzle with oil and sprinkle with curry powder and salt; toss to mix. Spread in a single layer on the prepared baking tray. (If desired, the vegetables can be prepared a few hours in advance and set aside.)

3. Roast, uncovered, for 40 to 45 minutes until golden and crispy; halfway through the cooking process, stir the vegetables around. When roasted, some of the vegetables will be blackened around the edges—that's okay. Remove the vegetables from oven and sprinkle with chives. Serve immediately.

Yield: 4 to 6 servings. Leftovers, if any, are best served at room temperature. Don't freeze.

124 calories per serving, 13.6 g carbohydrate, 6.2 g fiber, 5 g protein, 7.2 g fat (1.0 g saturated), 0 mg cholesterol, 355 mg sodium, 724 mg potassium, 1 mg iron, 56 mg calcium

Rosemary Roasted Cauliflower

Instead of curry powder, use 2 tsp dried rosemary and 2 to 3 cloves minced garlic.

Roasted Cauliflower Medley

Add 1 to 2 cups of sliced mushrooms, sliced Japanese eggplant, and zucchini (don't peel). Red peppers and baby carrots are also delicious. If you add more vegetables, you'll need 3 to 4 Tbsp olive oil and 1 Tbsp curry powder. If desired, add a little ground cumin and turmeric for extra flavor.

Chef's Secrets

• Leftovers? Top with crumbled goat cheese and slivered sun-dried tomatoes. You can also add leftover roasted vegetables to an omelet, pasta, or soup.

🍎 POPCORN CAULIFLOWER

Cauliflower shrinks a lot when roasted, so be sure to make a lot. This makes a fabulous snack or side dish, and it's delicious at any temperature with just about anything.

1 large cauliflower
2 Tbsp olive oil
4 cloves garlic (about 4 tsp minced)
Salt and freshly ground black pepper
1 tsp dried basil
1 tsp dried oregano

1. Preheat the oven to 425°F. Line a large baking tray with foil and spray with cooking spray.

2. Wash the cauliflower well and break into very small florets. Place the florets, oil, garlic, and seasonings in a large bowl and toss well. Spread in a single layer on the prepared baking tray.

3. Roast, uncovered stirring occasionally, in the lower third of the oven for 30 to 35 minutes or until well-browned and tender-crisp.

Yield: 6 servings (or less!) Keeps for up to 3 days in the refrigerator. Don't freeze.

80 calories per serving, 8.4 g carbohydrate, 3.8 g fiber, 3 g protein, 4.7 g fat (0.6 g saturated), 0 mg cholesterol, 43 mg sodium, 43 mg potassium, 1 mg iron, 43 mg calcium

Variation

• Instead of Italian seasoning, use chili powder and sprinkle with paprika for a spicy kick. Seasoning salt and lemon pepper also taste terrific in this dish.

Chef's Secrets

• What's in Store: White cauliflower is the most popular, but you can also buy yellow, green, and purple cauliflower. Choose firm cauliflower with compact florets and no brown spots. The leaves should be crisp and green, without any signs of yellowing.

• It's in the Bag: Store cauliflower in a plastic or perforated paper bag in the refrigerator. It will keep for about a week to 10 days. It's best to store cauliflower stem-side down.

• Smash Hit! When making mashed potatoes, a good trick is to replace half the potatoes with well-cooked cauliflower.

Nutrition Notes

• Cauliflower is an excellent source of vitamins C and K, folate, and fiber. A member of the cabbage family, it has many of the same health benefits as broccoli. Since it's low in carbs and has no noticeable effect on blood sugar, it's considered a low glycemic index food (GI 0) and can replace potatoes in many recipes.

vegetables

CURRIED CHUNKY EGGPLANT AND CHICKPEAS

My friend Maurice Borts of Ottawa re-named this dish "Seven-Time Winner" because he's served it seven times and each time the guests asked for the recipe. This makes a big batch but leftovers freeze well. If you have vegetarians at your table, they'll devour this dish.

2 medium eggplants
Salt
1 Tbsp olive oil
1 large red onion (about 2 cups chopped)
1 can (19 oz/540 ml) chickpeas,
    drained and rinsed
3 to 4 tsp curry powder
1/2 tsp ground cumin
1/2 cup cold water
6 Tbsp lemon juice (preferably fresh)
2 to 3 Tbsp honey (or to taste)
2 Tbsp ketchup
Salt and freshly ground black pepper

1. Peel the eggplant if desired. Cut into 1/2-inch chunks and measure 8 cups. Place the chopped eggplant into a colander and lightly sprinkle with salt. Let stand for 20 to 30 minutes; rinse well and squeeze gently to remove any excess liquid and bitter juices from the eggplant.

2. Steam the eggplant in a vegetable steamer until tender, about 10 to 12 minutes. (Or cover and microwave in a large microwaveable bowl for 10 minutes, stirring at half time.) Don't overcook.

3. Heat the oil in a large pot on medium high heat. Add the onion and sauté until tender-crisp, about 6 to 8 minutes. Transfer the steamed eggplant along with the drained chickpeas to the pot; mix well. Add the curry powder, cumin, water, lemon juice, honey, and ketchup; stir to combine and bring to a boil. Reduce heat to low and simmer, uncovered, stirring occasionally, for 8 to 10 minutes. Season with salt and pepper to taste and serve.

Yield: About 6 cups (12 servings of 1/2 cup each as a side dish). Keeps for up to 3 days in the refrigerator; reheats well. Freezes well for up to 2 months.

104 calories per 1/2 cup serving, 20.8 g carbohydrate, 3.7 g fiber, 3 g protein, 1.8 g fat (0.2 g saturated), 0 mg cholesterol, 272 mg sodium, 199 mg potassium, 1 mg iron, 26 mg calcium

Chef's Secrets
• What's in Store: Eggplants come in all shapes, sizes, colors, and varieties. Choose shiny, smooth, firm eggplants with no soft spots. Avoid those with spongy or brown spots.

• Size Counts: Large eggplants tend to be bitter and are often full of seeds. Small, slender eggplants have smaller seeds and are usually more tender. Choose small or medium eggplants for grilling or broiling. Larger ones are fine for making an eggplant spread, but remove the seeds after cooking.

• To Peel or not to Peel? That is the question! Peel eggplant when making an eggplant spread or if the skin is tough. Otherwise, the choice is yours. (I usually don't bother.)

• Sponge-Blob Eggplant: Eggplant acts like a sponge, soaking up as much oil as you give it. Salting eggplant before cooking draws out the bitter juices and excess moisture, so it needs less oil and you won't turn into a blob! Smaller varieties usually don't need to be salted before cooking.

vegetables

🍎 FAUX FRIED RICE

This fiber-packed dish tastes just like fried rice but contains a fraction of the carbs. I got the recipe from Carolyn Blackman, of Toronto. She got it from Ella Burakowski, who got it from her cousin, and so on. I modified the original recipe and added some variations, including one for Passover, when rice is not allowed for Ashkenaz Jews. It's faux-tastic!

1/2 large cauliflower
1 Tbsp olive oil
4 to 6 garlic cloves
   (about 1 to 2 Tbsp minced)
1 tsp minced fresh ginger
6 green onions, chopped
1 cup sliced mushrooms
1 cup snow peas or sugar snap peas,
   trimmed
2 to 3 Tbsp soy sauce (low-sodium or regular)
1 tsp Asian (toasted) sesame oil
1/2 cup frozen green peas
2 large eggs, lightly beaten
Freshly ground black pepper

1. Wash the cauliflower thoroughly and cut it into large chunks. Grate the cauliflower in the food processor fitted with the grater. Use medium-firm pressure on the pusher when putting the cauliflower through the feed tube to grate it; set aside. (The grated cauliflower is the "rice.")

2. Heat the oil in a large nonstick wok or skillet on medium high. Stir-fry the garlic, ginger, and green onions for 1 minute. Add the mushrooms and snow peas; stir-fry for 2 to 3 minutes. Add the grated cauliflower and stir-fry for 4 to 5 minutes longer or until tender-crisp. Pour in the soy sauce and sesame oil and stir-fry for another 1 to 2 minutes

before adding the frozen peas; mix well.

3. Push the entire mixture to one side of the wok. On the empty side, add the beaten eggs and scramble for about 2 minutes or until they are just set. Mix the eggs into the "rice" and season with pepper to taste. Remove from heat and serve immediately.

Yield: 6 servings. Keeps for up to 2 days in the refrigerator; reheats well in the microwave. Don't freeze.

99 calories per serving, 9.7 g carbohydrate, 3.6 g fiber, 5 g protein, 5.0 g fat (0.8 g saturated), 70 mg cholesterol, 235 mg sodium, 385 mg potassium, 2 mg iron, 54 mg calcium

Passover Faux Fried Rice
Omit the snow peas, soy sauce, sesame oil, and green peas. In Step 2, sauté the mushrooms with 1 cup chopped red pepper and 1 cup chopped celery. Add salt, pepper, and 1 tsp instant chicken soup mix. Garnish with 1/2 cup toasted sliced almonds.

Variations
• For more volume and crunch, add 1 to 2 cups bean sprouts and 1/2 cup canned water chestnuts with peas in Step 3 (but not for Passover). To make this a main dish, add strips of cooked chicken, lean beef, or extra-firm tofu.

🍎 GARLIC-ROASTED GREEN BEANS

Green beans are transformed when roasted at high heat—thicker green beans are best for this dish. For those of you who love French fries, these are an awesome alternative! They're good at any temperature and are very addictive, so make lots.

1 lb (500 g) green beans, trimmed
4 cloves garlic (about 4 tsp minced)
2 tsp peeled and minced fresh ginger
2 Tbsp extra virgin olive oil
3 to 4 Tbsp orange juice (preferably fresh)
Salt and freshly ground black pepper

1. Preheat the oven to 425°F. Line a large baking tray with foil and spray with cooking spray.

2. In a large bowl, toss the green beans with garlic, ginger, oil, and orange juice. Season with salt and pepper to taste. Spread out in a single layer on the prepared baking tray.

3. Roast, uncovered, for 10 to 12 minutes or until lightly browned, slightly shriveled, and tender-crisp.

Yield: 4 servings. Leftovers (if any!) keep for up to 2 days in the refrigerator. Don't freeze.

112 calories per serving, 11.1 g carbohydrate, 3.7 g fiber, 2 g protein, 7.4 g fat (1.1 g saturated), 0 mg cholesterol, 266 mg sodium, 372 mg potassium, 2 mg iron, 58 mg calcium

Nutrition Notes
• Green beans are an excellent source of vitamin K, which is important for maintaining strong bones. They also contain a variety of nutrients, including vitamins C and A, potassium, folate, magnesium, iron, and fiber. One cup of green beans contains about 38 calories, 8.5 g carbohydrate, and 3.4 g fiber.

☙ SESAME GREEN BEANS

For a colorful presentation, use a combination of green and yellow wax beans. Cut the red peppers into strips about the same size as the beans. Prepare all the ingredients in advance and cook just before serving. It will be ready to eat in minutes.

1/4 cup water, or chicken or vegetable broth
2 Tbsp soy sauce (low-sodium or regular)
1 tsp granulated sugar or granular Splenda
1 Tbsp canola oil
2 green onions, trimmed and chopped
3 to 4 cloves garlic (about 3 to 4 tsp minced)
2 tsp peeled and minced fresh ginger
1 lb (500 g) green beans, trimmed
1 red pepper, seeded and
    cut into long, narrow strips
Salt and freshly ground black pepper
2 tsp Asian (toasted) sesame oil
2 Tbsp sesame seeds

1. In a small bowl, combine the water, soy sauce, and sugar; set aside.

2. Heat the oil in a wok or large nonstick skillet on medium high heat. Add the green onions, garlic and ginger, and stir-fry for 1 minute. Add the green beans and red pepper strips; stir to coat well. Cook for 1 minute longer.

3. Add the reserved soy sauce mixture and bring to a boil. Cover, reduce heat to low, and simmer for 4 to 5 minutes or until tender-crisp. Season with salt and pepper to taste and toss with the sesame oil.

4. Transfer the cooked beans to a platter. Sprinkle with sesame seeds and serve immediately.

Yield: 4 servings. Can be reheated briefly in the microwave. Don't freeze.

142 calories per serving, 15.4 g carbohydrate, 4.9 g fiber, 4 g protein, 8.4 g fat (0.7 g saturated), 0 mg cholesterol, 544 mg sodium, 284 mg potassium, 2 mg iron, 81 mg calcium

Almond Green Beans

Instead of soy sauce, use teriyaki sauce. Instead of sesame seeds, sprinkle with 1/4 cup toasted sliced almonds.

Sesame Asparagus

Substitute asparagus for green beans.

Chef's Secrets

• No Strings Attached: Green beans used to be called string beans because they had an inedible string that ran along the length of the pod, but modern hybrids are stringless and much less work! Either snap off the tough ends by hand or use a paring knife to trim them.

• Thin Is In: Avoid thicker beans for this dish. Thinner beans tend to be more tender and sweeter.

• It's a Snap! To test for freshness when buying beans, snap one in half and taste it for sweetness. They should snap, not bend.

🍎 MARINATED MUSHROOMS

Make room for these versatile 'shrooms. They're delicious as a side dish or can be used as an appetizer or salad. When you've used up at least half of them, you can add more blanched mushrooms to the refrigerated marinade.

1 lb (500 g) small button mushrooms (white or cremini)
1/4 cup red wine vinegar
1/4 cup olive oil
1 medium onion, chopped
2 Tbsp maple syrup or honey
1 Tbsp Dijon mustard

1/2 tsp dried thyme
Salt and freshly ground black pepper

1. Bring a large pot of water to a boil. Plunge the mushrooms into the boiling water and blanch for 2 to 3 minutes. Remove and immediately rinse under cold water to stop the cooking process. Set aside to drain on paper towels.

2. In a medium saucepan, combine the vinegar, oil, onion, maple syrup, and mustard. Bring to a boil and cook for 2 to 3 minutes. Remove from the heat. Add mushrooms, thyme, salt, and pepper; stir well.

3. When cool, transfer the mushrooms to a container. Cover and refrigerate for at least 1 day before serving. Serve chilled.

Yield: 30 to 36 mushrooms, depending on size. Recipe doubles or triples easily. Keeps for up to 7 to 10 days in the refrigerator. Don't freeze.

25 calories per mushroom, 1.9 g carbohydrate, 0.3 g fiber, 0 g protein, 1.9 g fat (0.3 g saturated), 0 mg cholesterol, 13 mg sodium, 48 mg potassium, 0 mg iron, 3 mg calcium

Chef's Secrets

• Be a Mushroom Maven: There are three types of button mushrooms—white (the most common), cremini (coffee-colored, with a meaty flavor), and portobello (which are grown-up cremini mushrooms). Shiitake mushrooms have a smoky flavor and a meaty texture, but tend to be expensive. Dried shiitakes are an excellent and affordable alternative, will give your immune system a boost, and have anti-cancer and cholesterol-lowering properties. Oyster mushrooms are cheaper than shiitake and also offer protection from cancer. Maitake mushrooms, a newer arrival on the market, are meaty and very tasty, with immune-enhancing properties. All mushrooms are a good source of selenium, which may help reduce the risk of prostate cancer.

• It's in the Bag: Store mushrooms in a loosely closed paper bag in the refrigerator for up to a week.

• Raw or Cooked? Although many people love to eat raw mushrooms, they should be cooked thoroughly as most types are carcinogenic if eaten raw. Heat destroys many toxins, makes mushrooms more digestible, and improves their taste and texture, so cook them, for goodness sake.

• Wash or Not? Fresh mushrooms are 90% water and, surprisingly, don't absorb much water when rinsed. Rinse them quickly before cooking, then wrap them in a towel to absorb the moisture. Any excess moisture will evaporate during cooking. You can also clean mushrooms by wiping them with a damp cloth or using a mushroom brush.

• Dried Mushrooms: Rehydrate dried mushrooms by soaking them in warm water in a small bowl for at least 15 minutes, then add them to your favorite recipe. Save the soaking liquid, after straining, and add it to soups and sauces for extra flavor.

● MUSHROOM DUXELLES

Duxelles are a perfect way to use up leftover mushroom stems from recipes that use just the caps, or if mushrooms are nearly past their prime. Caps off to the chef!

2 to 3 shallots or 1 small onion
  (about 1/2 cup minced)
2 Tbsp olive oil
1 lb (500 g) mushrooms
1 tsp dried thyme or rosemary
1 Tbsp lemon juice (preferably fresh)
Kosher salt and freshly ground black pepper

1. In a food processor fitted with the steel blade, process the shallots until finely minced, about 6 seconds. Heat the oil in a large nonstick skillet on medium heat. Sauté the shallots until softened, about 3 minutes.

2. Process the mushrooms until finely minced, about 8 to 10 seconds. Add to the skillet and sprinkle with thyme and lemon juice. Sauté for about 15 minutes, stirring occasionally or until the mixture is dry and has reduced to about 1 1/2 cups. Season with salt and pepper to taste. Use immediately or refrigerate.

Yield: About 1 1/2 cups. Keeps for up to a week in the refrigerator; reheats well. Freezes well for up to 3 months.

17 calories per Tbsp, 1.3 g carbohydrate, 0.2 g fiber, 1 g protein, 1.2 g fat (0.2 g saturated), 0 mg cholesterol, 1 mg sodium, 71 mg potassium, 0 mg iron, 3 mg calcium

Chicken Duxelles
Stuff 4 seasoned chicken breasts (on the bone) with a layer of Duxelles under the skin. Roast, uncovered, at 375 °F for 1 hour or until juices run clear. For boneless, skinless breasts, cut a pocket horizontally in each breast. Stuff with Duxelles. Roast, uncovered, for 30 to 35 minutes.

Chef's Secrets

• Fishful Thinking: Duxelles make a fabulous filling for fish fillets. See Stuffed Sole Duxelles (page 139).

• Bread Spread: Use Duxelles as a topping for Crostini (page 65).

• Frozen Assets: Spoon Duxelles into ice cube trays. When frozen, transfer to a plastic re-sealable bag. Add frozen cubes to soups, stews, pasta sauce, stuffings, omelets, or grain dishes for a fabulous flavor boost.

🍎 ROASTED PORTOBELLO MUSHROOMS

These large, meaty mushrooms are delicious with chicken, fish, or steak. They also make an excellent vegetarian alternative to burgers. Add roasted portobello mushrooms to salads and wraps, or use them as part of a mixed vegetable platter.

6 large portobello mushrooms
    (about 1 lb/500 g)
2 Tbsp extra virgin olive oil
2 tsp balsamic vinegar
2 cloves garlic (about 2 tsp minced)
1 tsp Kosher salt (or to taste)
Freshly ground black pepper
2 Tbsp chopped fresh parsley, for garnish

1. Preheat the oven to 400°F. Line a large baking tray with parchment paper.

2. Wash the mushrooms and dry well. Trim the stems and cut the mushrooms into $1/2$-inch thick slices; spread the slices in a single layer on the prepared baking sheet. Drizzle with oil and vinegar and sprinkle with garlic, salt, and pepper to taste. Using your hands, toss the mushroom slices to coat all sides with the oil and seasoning.

3. Roast, uncovered, stirring the mushrooms occasionally, for 20 to 25 minutes or until nicely browned. Transfer to a platter, garnish with parsley, and serve.

Yield: 6 servings. Keeps for up to 3 days in the refrigerator; reheats well in the microwave. Don't freeze.

64 calories per serving, 4.8 g fat (0.7 g saturated), 0 mg cholesterol, 2 g protein, 4.4 g carbohydrate, 319 mg sodium, 367 mg potassium, 1 mg iron, 1.2 g fiber, 10 mg calcium

Grilled Portobello Mushrooms
Preheat the grill. Leave the mushrooms whole and place them in a medium bowl; season as directed. Grill over medium-high heat until tender, about 5 minutes per side.

🍎 CARAMELIZED ONIONS

Maxine Wolfson, of Rhode Island, likes to make caramelized onions in her slow cooker. She uses 6 cups of sliced onions, but my slow cooker has a 6-quart capacity, so I've doubled her recipe. Once you taste these, you'll cry for more! No slow cooker? Use the Stovetop Method on page 304.

12 large onions (about 12 cups sliced)
3 to 4 Tbsp olive oil
1 to 2 tsp granulated sugar (optional)

1. Peel the onions and slice thinly (a food processor does this quickly). Place in a slow cooker and drizzle with olive oil.

2. Cook, covered, on the high setting for 8 to 10 hours or until the onions have reduced and caramelized. If the onions are too strongly flavored, stir in a little sugar at

the end of the cooking process. (You can also cook them on the low setting for 12 to 14 hours.)

Yield: About 6 cups. Keeps for up to 4 to 5 days in the refrigerator; reheats well. Freezes well for up to 3 months.

43 calories per $1/4$ cup, 6.5 g carbohydrate, 0.9 g fiber, 1 g protein, 1.8 g fat (0.2 g saturated), 0 mg cholesterol, 2 mg sodium, 106 mg potassium, 0 mg iron, 14 mg calcium

Stovetop Method

Thinly slice 6 large onions. Heat 2 Tbsp olive oil in a large, heavy-bottomed pot. Add onions and cook, uncovered, on medium heat for 8 to 10 minutes or until tender. Sprinkle with sugar and stir in $1/2$ cup vegetable broth or water. Reduce heat to low, cover, and simmer for about 30 minutes or until golden. Uncover and cook for 20 to 30 minutes longer or until well-browned, stirring often. Season with salt and pepper to taste.

Variations

• Add a splash of balsamic vinegar to the onions at the end of the cooking process for a rich, delicious flavor. You can add dried thyme, basil, oregano, garlic, salt, and pepper.

Chef's Secrets

• Size Matters: If you have a smaller slow cooker, use enough onions to fill the pot, then cover with parchment paper to keep the steam in. The onions will shrink in volume by about half.

• Frozen Assets: To freeze, divide the caramelized onions into 1-cup portions and store in plastic re-sealable bags in the freezer. There's no need to thaw before using.

• Serving Suggestions: Caramelized onions are delicious with chicken or beef, or in mashed potatoes, sweet potatoes, or mashed squash. As an appetizer, top slices of whole-grain baguette with caramelized onions, sprinkle with grated cheese, and broil for 2 to 3 minutes. They also make a terrific pizza topping.

• Weigh-ing In: One small onion yields $1/4$ to $1/3$ cup, one medium onion yields $1/2$ to $3/4$ cup, and one large onion yields 1 to $11/4$ cups.

• Tears to You: The sulphuric compounds in onions cause your eyes to tear. To help minimize tears, refrigerate or freeze onions for 15 minutes. Cut off the tops first, then peel downwards. Trim the roots at the last moment. Some people put onions under water and peel them. Others hold a burnt-out match between their teeth or light a candle. A food processor, contact lenses, glasses, swimming goggles, or even a gas mask help act as a barrier to onion fumes.

• Storage Tips: If you store onions in a cool, dry place with good air circulation, they'll keep for months. Never store onions and potatoes together—they cause each other to spoil quickly. Don't store raw onions in the refrigerator or in plastic bags. Raw sliced or chopped onions can be stored in the refrigerator for up to a week or can be frozen for 3 to 4 months.

Nutrition Notes

• Enjoy onions often, either raw or cooked. Onions have sulphur-containing compounds that give them their powerful odor. The variety and method of preparation affect their benefits. The stronger, the better. Onions help reduce the risk of heart disease and a wide ranger of cancers, and help to lower cholesterol levels and blood pressure. They are rich in chromium, a mineral that helps cells respond to insulin, as well as vitamin C and many flavonoids. While raw onions are the most beneficial, cooked onions also offer excellent health benefits. Start chopping!

🍎 ROASTED NEW POTATOES

Everyone loves potatoes. Small new potatoes have lower starch content than larger, more mature potatoes. Enjoy them occasionally and in small amounts. Yukon golds, red, or baby fingerling potatoes are interchangeable in this recipe. Sweet potatoes and purple-skinned sweet potatoes are also lower glycemic options. Potato Fans (on this page) are made the same way and will impress your guests—they'll be fans forever!

2 lb (1 kg) small new potatoes
  (about 24 to 30)
2 Tbsp extra virgin olive oil
3 or 4 cloves garlic, sliced
2 Tbsp minced fresh dillweed
2 tsp Kosher salt (or to taste)
Freshly ground black pepper
  and sweet paprika

1. Preheat the oven to 400°F. Spray a shallow 3-quart casserole with cooking spray.

2. Scrub the potatoes but don't peel. Pat dry and arrange in a single layer in the prepared casserole dish. Don't overlap the potatoes or they will steam rather than roast. Drizzle with olive oil and sprinkle with garlic,

dillweed, salt, pepper, and paprika to taste. Using your hands, toss the potatoes to coat all sides evenly.

3. Roast, uncovered, for 50 to 60 minutes or until tender and crispy, shaking the pan several times during roasting. Cooking time will depend on the size of the potatoes. To test for doneness, use a sharp knife.

Yield: 6 servings. Recipe doubles or triples easily. If reheating, don't cover the potatoes so they will stay crispy. Don't freeze.

158 calories per serving, 26.4 g carbohydrate, 2.7 g fiber, 3 g protein, 4.8 g fat (0.7 g saturated), 0 mg cholesterol, 400 mg sodium, 663 mg potassium, 1 mg iron, 22 mg calcium

Potato Fans

Substitute 6 medium Idaho (russet) potatoes. Slice each potato three-quarters of the way through, being careful not to cut all the way through. Cuts should be about 1/4 inch apart. Place potatoes in casserole, separating the slices slightly. Prepare as directed in Step 2. Roast uncovered at 400°F about 1 hour or until crisp and golden.

Roasted Sweet Potatoes

Substitute 3 to 4 large sweet potatoes, unpeeled but well scrubbed and cut into chunks. Instead of fresh dillweed, you can use 1 tsp dried rosemary, basil, and/or thyme. Roast, uncovered, at 400°F for about 1 hour, until tender.

☙ SMASHED POTATO "LATKES"

A no-grate alternative to potato latkes, these are a wonderful way to get rid of your frustration—just smash away. Baby red-skinned new potatoes have a lower glycemic index than baking potatoes. Small potatoes—big potassium count.

8 baby red-skinned potatoes
   (2 to 2¹/₂ inches in diameter)
Salted water
1 Tbsp extra virgin olive or canola oil
¹/₂ tsp salt or Montreal-Style Steak Spice
   (page 115)
¹/₄ tsp lemon pepper (or to taste)
Dried basil, garlic powder, onion powder,
   and/or paprika

1. Boil the potatoes in salted water to cover for 15 to 20 minutes or until fork tender. Drain well. (If desired, the potatoes can be prepared in advance up to this point and refrigerated for a day or two.)

2. Preheat the oven to 400°F. Line a large baking sheet with parchment paper or sprayed foil.

3. Place the potatoes in a single layer about 3 inches apart on the prepared baking sheet. Cover one potato with a piece of parchment paper. Smash it once or twice with the flat part of the palm of your hand, making a flat disc about 4 inches in diameter. Round off any ragged edges by pushing them together with your fingers. Repeat with the remaining potatoes.

4. Brush the tops of of the smashed potatoes lightly with olive oil and sprinkle with seasonings. Bake, uncovered, for 20 to 25 minutes or until golden and crispy. If desired, turn over the potatoes halfway through the cooking process.

Yield: 8 potatoes. Recipe doubles or triples easily. Reheats well. Don't freeze.

139 calories per potato, 27.0 g carbohydrate, 2.5 g fiber, 3 g protein, 2.0 g fat (0.3 g saturated), 0 mg cholesterol, 156 mg sodium, 752 mg potassium, 1 mg iron, 13 mg calcium

All Season Smashers
Sprinkle potatoes lightly with your favorite seasonings such as seasoning salt or coarse salt, rosemary, dillweed, or thyme. Bake as directed.

Go-Goat Smashers
My assistant, Shelley Sefton, loves to top these smashed potatoes with goat cheese when they come out of the oven. Not baah-d!

Easy Cheesy Smashers
During the last 5 minutes of baking, sprinkle each potato with 2 Tbsp grated low-fat Swiss, cheddar, or mozzarella cheese, finely chopped red pepper, and minced parsley.

Loxy "Latkes"
Buy the smallest baby potatoes you can find; prepare and bake as directed. To serve, arrange on a serving platter and top each "latke" with a dollop of light sour cream, a slice of smoked salmon, and a sprig of dillweed. Dill-icious!

☙ MASHED SWEET POTATOES

Sweet potatoes have a velvety texture, superb flavor, and are nutrition-packed, so enjoy them often. For very little work, this recipe gives such big benefits!

vegetables

6 medium sweet potatoes, peeled and
    cut into chunks
Salted water
1/4 cup vegetable broth or water
2 tsp extra virgin olive oil
Salt and freshly ground black pepper

1. Place the sweet potatoes in a large saucepan with salted water to cover and bring to a boil. Reduce heat to low and simmer for about 20 minutes or until very tender. Drain well.

2. Return the drained, cooked sweet potatoes to the saucepan over low heat. Add the broth and olive oil, and season with salt and pepper to taste. Mash until they are smooth and lump-free. Serve immediately.

Yield: 6 servings. Recipe doubles or triples easily. Keeps for up to 3 or 4 days in the refrigerator; reheats well in the microwave. Don't freeze.

130 calories per serving, 27.0 g carbohydrate, 3.8 g fiber, 2 g protein, 1.8 g fat (0.3 g saturated), 0 mg cholesterol, 60 mg sodium, 347 mg potassium, 1 mg iron, 42 mg calcium

Maple Mashed Sweet Potatoes
Instead of vegetable broth, use orange juice. Add a drizzle of maple syrup and a dash of cinnamon. Mash well.

Variations
• Replace 3 of the sweet potatoes with 2 cups of cooked mashed squash or carrots. Or use a mixture of sweet potatoes and regular potatoes. Sautéed onions make a delicious topping.

• Microwave Magic: Instead of peeling and boiling the sweet potatoes, slash the skin in several places with a sharp knife. Microwave, uncovered, on high for 12 to 14 minutes or until tender, turning them over halfway through the cooking process. When the sweet potatoes are cool enough to handle, cut in half. Scoop out the flesh and mash. Discard peel.

Chef's Secrets
• What's in Store: The orange-fleshed variety of sweet potato with a reddish-brown skin is the most common kind found in our markets. The darker the flesh, the sweeter and moister the sweet potato will be. Other varieties include purple-peel sweeties with creamy flesh, and purple-flesh sweet potatoes.

• Store It Right: Never refrigerate raw sweet potatoes; store in a cool dark place with adequate ventilation. They'll keep for up to a month.

• Skinny Secret! The skin of sweet potatoes, unlike regular potatoes, doesn't develop green patches when exposed to light. These green patches (solanine) in regular potatoes are toxic, and should not be eaten, unless you completely cut away the green part.

• Cook Them Right: Sweet potatoes are delicious baked, boiled, steamed, grilled, or roasted. Slice them, dice them, shred them, or cut into chunks—so many choices! Use them as an ingredient in a variety of dishes, from dips to desserts.

Nutrition Notes
• Sweet potatoes are packed with beta carotene and antioxidants. In fact, they contain more beta carotene than carrots. They also contain vitamins C, E, folate, thiamine,

riboflavin, fiber, and several minerals in-cluding copper, magnesium, and potassium. Because of their lower glycemic index (GI 44), they are a carbohydrate-friendly choice for people with diabetes as well as people with insulin resistance.

❍ SWEET POTATO "FRIES"

Everyone loves sweet potato fries. These make a delicious and much healthier alternative to traditional French fries made from regular potatoes. If you like, sprinkle sweet potato fries with your favorite vinegar at serving time. Yam good!

3 medium sweet potatoes, well-scrubbed
   or peeled
2 Tbsp extra virgin olive oil
1 tsp Kosher or sea salt
Freshly ground black black pepper
1 tsp sweet paprika
1 tsp garlic powder

1. Preheat the oven to 425°F. Line a large baking sheet with foil—this makes for easier clean-up. Place the baking sheet in the lower third of the oven to heat up.

2. Meanwhile, cut the sweet potatoes into 1/4-inch strips or wedges. Combine in a large bowl with oil, salt, pepper, paprika, and garlic powder. Using your hands, toss the sweet potatoes in the oil and spices to coat well on all sides.

3. When the oven is fully heated, spread out the sweet potatoes onto the hot baking sheet so that they will brown well.

4. Bake in the lower third of the oven for 20 minutes. Turn the sweet potato pieces over with a spatula and continue baking until brown and crispy, about 20 to 25 minutes longer. Serve immediately.

Yield: 4 servings. Freezes well for up to 2 months. Reheats well.

180 calories per serving, 27.3 g carbohydrate, 3.8 g fiber, 2 g protein, 7.2 g fat (1.0 g saturated), 0 mg cholesterol, 361 mg sodium, 358 mg potassium, 5 mg iron, 41 mg calcium

Variations
• Season with salt and pepper; omit the paprika and garlic powder. Sprinkle with ground cinnamon and nutmeg, or sprinkle with seasoning salt, chili powder, Cajun spices, basil, curry powder, or any spices you like.

Chef's Secrets
• Frozen Assets: Sweet potatoes freeze well, unlike white potatoes. If you do freeze, there's no need to thaw when reheating: just spread the frozen "fries" on a foil-lined baking sheet and bake, uncovered, at 400°F for about 10 to 12 minutes.

• Confused? Sweet potatoes are not yams, although they are often marketed that way. Sweet potatoes usually have an orange flesh, but can also be yellow, white, or even purple. The darker the flesh, the moister and sweeter they are. Sweet potatoes with dark orange flesh have more vitamin A than those with lighter color flesh. The skin can be different colors, including red-orange, brown, and purple. Yams are bigger, usually have white flesh, thick, dark-brown skin and tend to be bland, floury, and starchy; they are never sweet.

🍎 PUMPKIN PUREE

Small pumpkins are the best ones for eating as they are sweet and tasty. Jack O'Lantern pumpkins are too large and stringy for cooking. Pumpkin purée can be enjoyed as an alternative to squash as a side dish, or it can also be used instead of canned pumpkin in recipes. Peek-a-boo, this recipe's for you!

1 small sugar or pie pumpkin
  (about 4 lb/2 kg)

1. Preheat oven to 350°F. Line a baking sheet with foil and spray with cooking spray.

2. Cut the pumpkin in half with a very sharp knife. Scoop out the seeds and fibers. Save the seeds for roasting (see Toasted Pumpkin Seeds on this page). Place the pumpkin halves, cut-side down, on the prepared baking sheet and cover with additional foil. Bake for about 1 hour. When done, the pumpkin should be tender and easily pierced with a knife. Set aside to cool.

3. Once cooled, scoop out the pulp and discard the shell. Purée the pulp in a food processor fitted with the steel blade, about 30 to 45 seconds, or mash with a potato masher.

Yield: 1½ cups purée (3 half-cup servings). Keeps for up to 3 days in the refrigerator; reheats well in the microwave. Freezes well for up to 2 months.

25 calories per serving, 6.0 g carbohydrate, 1.3 g fiber, 1 g protein, 0.1 g fat (0 g saturated), 0 mg cholesterol, 1 mg sodium, 282 mg potassium, 1 mg iron, 18 mg calcium

Variations
• Add 2 Tbsp freshly squeezed orange or lime juice, ½ tsp ground cinnamon, 1 Tbsp extra virgin olive oil, and salt and pepper to taste, to the puréed pumpkin. A drizzle of pure maple syrup is also delicious. Serve hot as a side dish.

• For a dairy version, add 2 Tbsp skim milk, 1 Tbsp extra virgin olive oil or soft tub margarine, and ½ cup grated Parmesan cheese to the puréed pumpkin. Season with salt and pepper to taste.

Toasted Pumpkin Seeds
Scoop out the seeds and rinse to remove the fibers; pat dry with paper towels. Spread the seeds on a parchment paper-lined baking sheet and toss with a little olive oil and salt. Roast, uncovered, at 250°F for 45 to 60 minutes or until toasted and golden, tossing every 20 minutes. These will keep for several months. An average pumpkin contains about 1 cup of seeds.

Chef's Secrets
• Microwave Magic: Microwave the whole pumpkin on high for 5 minutes—this makes it easier to slice up. (Since the cooking time is so brief, it's not necessary to pierce the skin first.) Next, cut the pumpkin into large pieces and place in a large microwaveable casserole dish. Microwave, covered, on high, allowing 5 to 6 minutes per pound.

• Processor Power: The food processor produces pumpkin purée that is perfectly creamy and smooth, and will eliminate any small strings and fibers.

• Pumpkin Power: Pumpkin belongs to the squash family and is interchangeable with sweet potatoes or squash in recipes. Pumpkin can be baked, roasted, boiled, or microwaved.

vegetables

Nutrition Notes

• Cooked pumpkin has a low glycemic index (GI 51). Pumpkin is rich in lutein, potassium, alpha and beta carotene, and vitamin A.

• Pumpkin seeds are high in zinc. One-quarter cup of seeds contains 71 calories, 8.6 g carbohydrate, 3 g protein, and 3.1 g fat (0.6 g saturated).

● STIR-FRY SPINACH WITH GARLIC

This quick and garlicky stir-fry tastes terrific and is healthy, too. Spinach shrinks a lot when cooked—eat spinach more often and your waistline will also shrink!

1 bag (10 oz/300 g) baby spinach
2 to 3 Tbsp slivered almonds or pine nuts
1 Tbsp olive oil
1 medium onion (or 2 shallots), sliced
1/2 red pepper, seeded and sliced
2 to 3 cloves garlic (about 1 Tbsp minced)
1 Tbsp lemon juice (preferably fresh)
Salt and freshly ground black pepper

1. Wash the spinach, dry well, and set aside.

2. Heat a nonstick wok or large skillet on medium heat. Add the nuts and dry-roast them for 2 to 3 minutes or until golden, stirring frequently. Remove from the wok and set aside.

3. Add the oil to the wok and increase the heat to medium high. Add the onion and red pepper; stir-fry for 2 minutes. Add the garlic and spinach (you may have to add the spinach in batches) and stir-fry for about 2 to 3 minutes or until the spinach has wilted and all the liquid has evaporated. Season with lemon juice, salt, and pepper. Garnish with the reserved nuts and serve immediately.

Yield: 4 servings. Don't freeze.

83 calories per serving, 7.7 g carbohydrate, 2.4 g fiber, 3 g protein, 5.3 g fat (0.6 g saturated), 0 mg cholesterol, 40 mg sodium, 361 mg potassium, 2 mg iron, 94 mg calcium

Swiss Chard with Garlic

Instead of spinach, use 1 1/2 lb (750 g) Swiss chard. Cut the leaves into 1-inch pieces and the tender part of the stems into 1/2-inch pieces. If desired, sauté 2 cups sliced mushrooms along with chopped onion and red pepper.

Chef's Secrets

• I Be Leaf: Large, curly-leaf spinach has thick leaves often filled with grit and fibrous stems that need removal. Baby spinach has flat, tender, dark green leaves that only require a quick rinse and virtually no stems, which don't need to be removed. It's the ultimate fast food.

• True Grit: To clean large leaf spinach, remove and discard the tough stems. Fill the sink with cold water, add the spinach and swish it around for a minute or two. Lift the spinach leaves out and drain the water from the sink, rinsing away the dirt. Repeat several times until there is no dirt left after rinsing. Dry the spinach in a salad spinner.

• Cook It Right: There's no need to dry spinach well if you're boiling, steaming, or microwaving it. However, if you're sautéing or stir-frying the spinach in oil, dry the leaves well to avoid splattering during cooking. And remember, the shorter the cooking time, the higher the nutrient content.

• Go for Green: Because of its nutrient content, spinach is excellent raw or lightly cooked. It's also perfect as an ingredient in salads, dips, soups, stuffings, grains, or even as a pizza topping. Use spinach instead of lettuce in sandwiches and wraps.

• Weighing In: Cello bags of spinach usually contain 10 oz (300 g) and yield about 1 1/2 cups when cooked. A bunch of fresh spinach weighs about 12 oz (340 g) and yields 1 1/2 to 1 3/4 cups cooked. Greens shrink a lot during cooking, so calculate that 3 cups raw will yield 1 cup cooked.

• It's in the Bag: Store spinach in the vegetable compartment of the refrigerator for 4 to 5 days. If there's moisture in the bag, place a few paper towels inside the bag to absorb it.

• Frozen Assets: Frozen spinach is so convenient. When ready to use, quickly defrost in the microwave by slashing the package in several places with a sharp knife and placing it in a microwaveable bowl. Microwave on high for 3 minutes. Let cool, then squeeze dry. Spinach will reduce to about 1/3 of its original volume. If there's foil on the package, be sure to remove the spinach from its package first before microwaving.

• Green Cuisine: Swiss chard can be substituted for spinach in most recipes; cooking time is about the same. Bok choy also works well in this dish.

• Kale Cuisine: If you want to try kale instead of spinach, you must steam the kale first for 5 minutes, then stir-fry as directed. O-kale?

Nutrition Notes

• Eye Spy: Spinach is high in many antioxidants, especially lutein, which is beneficial for eye health. It's also rich in folate, which reduces the risk of heart disease and is important for pregnant women or those who might become pregnant.

• Spinach is very high in beta carotene and iron. It is rich in vitamins A, C, and K, and in calcium, potassium, zinc, and fiber. Citrus maximizes the benefit of iron, so pair spinach with orange, lemon, or grapefruit.

• Trade-Off: Raw spinach provides more lutein, but cooking makes its beta carotene more available. The choice is yours.

☙ OVEN-ROASTED "MELTED" TOMATOES

Don't have a meltdown if you have too many tomatoes that ripen at the same time. This recipe transforms your ripe tomatoes into a wonderful dish that's packed with lycopene. It's a melt-in-your mouth medley that's marvelous with fish, chicken, pasta, or other grains.

6 to 8 large tomatoes (about 3 lb/1.5 kg)
6 to 8 cloves garlic
2 medium onions
1 red or yellow pepper
2 to 3 Tbsp olive oil
2 to 3 Tbsp balsamic vinegar
Salt and freshly ground black pepper
1 tsp dried basil (or 2 Tbsp chopped
    fresh basil)
1 tsp dried oregano (or 1 Tbsp chopped
    fresh oregano)

1. Preheat the oven to 375°F. Spray a 9- × 13-inch glass baking dish with cooking spray.

2. Cut the tomatoes into quarters or wedges (depending on the size) and spread out in a

single layer in the prepared baking dish. Cut each clove of garlic in half lengthwise and scatter over the tomatoes. Slice the onions and bell pepper; spread over the tomatoes. Drizzle the vegetables with oil and vinegar, then sprinkle with salt and pepper. If using dried herbs, add them now and mix well. If using fresh herbs, add them at the end of the cooking process.

3. Bake, uncovered, and stirring occasionally, 45 to 60 minutes or until the vegetables are very tender. Serve hot or at room temperature.

Yield: 4 cups (6 servings of 3/4 cup each). Keeps for up to a week in the refrigerator; reheats well in the microwave. Freezes well for up to 3 months.

117 calories per serving, 17.5 g carbohydrate, 3.5 g fiber, 3 g protein, 5.4 g fat (0.7 g saturated), 0 mg cholesterol, 24 mg sodium, 618 mg potassium, 2 mg iron, 34 mg calcium

vegetables

Chef's Secrets
• Chilling News: When storing tomatoes, don't refrigerate because temperatures below 55°F destroy their flavor. Keep them on a kitchen counter or on a rack, out of direct sunlight, until ready to use.

• It's in the Bag: To speed up the ripening process, place unripe tomatoes in a brown paper bag, along with an apple. The ethylene gas emitted by the apple will help ripen the tomatoes. Once they are ripe, put them in the refrigerator for a day or two. Bring them to room temperature before using for maximum flavor.

● TINY ROASTED TOMATOES

These roasted tomatoes are a snap to prepare and make a mouth-watering accompaniment to fish or poultry. If you don't want to turn on the oven, make the sautéed variation below.

4 cups (about 2 pints) cherry
   or grape tomatoes
3 to 4 cloves garlic (about 3 to 4 tsp minced)
2 Tbsp extra virgin olive oil
Kosher salt and freshly ground black pepper
2 Tbsp chopped fresh basil

1. Preheat the oven to 400°F. Place the oven rack in the lower third of the oven. Line a large baking tray with parchment paper or foil sprayed with cooking spray.

2. Place the tomatoes on the prepared baking tray and sprinkle the garlic on top. Drizzle with olive oil and, using your hands, mix the tomatoes well to coat all sides. Spread out evenly in a single layer and season with salt and pepper.

3. Roast, uncovered, for 15 to 20 minutes or until tender. Transfer the roasted tomatoes to a serving platter and sprinkle with basil, and salt and pepper to taste.

Yield: 4 servings. Serve hot or at room temperature. Keeps for up to 4 to 5 days in the refrigerator. Don't freeze.

94 calories per serving, 6.6 g carbohydrate, 1.9 g fiber, 1 g protein, 7.3 g fat (1.0 g saturated), 0 mg cholesterol, 8 mg sodium, 368 mg potassium, 0 mg iron, 21 mg calcium

Sautéed Tiny Tomatoes
Heat the olive oil in a large skillet over medium heat. Add the tomatoes and cook for 2 to 3 minutes, stirring often. The tomatoes will be heated through and the skins will

begin to brown in spots. Add the garlic and cook for 1 minute longer. Season with salt, pepper, and chopped basil before serving.

Variations
• Sprinkle cooked tomatoes with grated Parmesan cheese while still piping hot. The heat of the tomatoes will melt the cheese. The tomatoes can also be used as a topping for Crostini (page 65).

• If desired, add a pinch of oregano and 1/2 cup crumbled feta cheese for a Greek flavor.

Nutrition Notes
• We Like Lycopene: Tomatoes are rich in lycopene, a powerful antioxidant that has been linked with lower rates of a variety of cancers, particularly lung, stomach, and prostate cancer. Only red tomatoes contain lycopene—yellow and orange tomatoes don't.

• Cooked tomatoes (as well as canned tomatoes, tomato paste, juice, and even ketchup) contain more lycopene than raw ones. Fat is necessary for proper absorption of the lycopene, so adding a little olive oil not only makes tomatoes tastier but also healthier.

• The Skinny on Tomatoes: The skin of tomatoes contains more antioxidants than the flesh. Since cherry and grape tomatoes contain more skin than larger ones, they may contain more antioxidants. Small but mighty!

• Power Pack: Tomatoes are packed with potassium and contain vitamins A and C, plus fiber.

• Snack Attack! Cherry, grape, and teardrop tomatoes make a handy low-calorie snack.

Try to eat them every day. One cup contains 27 calories and 2 grams of fiber.

ZUCCHINI "PASTA"

This calcium-rich dish is a wonderful low-carb alternative to pasta. It's fabulous with fish and also makes a protein-packed dish if you have vegetarians at your table.

4 to 6 small-to-medium zucchini
    (about 1 1/2 lb/750 g), ends trimmed
2 cups tomato sauce (bottled or homemade)
1 cup grated low-fat mozzarella
    or Parmesan cheese

1. Cut the zucchini into pieces small enough to fit through the food processor's feed tube horizontally. (Feeding it in horizontally will produce longer shreds of zucchini.) Insert the grater into the food processor and grate the zucchini using medium pressure on the pusher. (If you have the time, you can make "fettucine" by using a vegetable peeler to cut the zucchini into lengthwise strips.)

2. Bring a large saucepan of salted water to a boil. Add the zucchini shreds or strips to the boiling water and cook for 2 minutes, stirring 2 or 3 times, just until tender. Drain well and transfer to a platter.

3. In a small saucepan, heat the tomato sauce and pour it over the cooked zucchini. Sprinkle with cheese and serve immediately.

Yield: 4 servings. Keeps for up to 2 days in the refrigerator; reheats well in the microwave. Don't freeze.

125 calories per serving, 14.5 g carbohydrate, 4 g fiber, 10 g protein, 4.6 g fat (2.9 g saturated), 16 mg cholesterol, 776 mg sodium, 390 mg potassium, 1 mg iron, 206 mg calcium

vegetables

• Salt Alert! If sodium is a concern, choose a brand of tomato sauce that is low in sodium, or make your own.

🍎 GRILLED ZUCCHINI

This is delicious hot off the grill or at room temperature. It makes a wonderful addition to a platter of grilled mixed vegetables.

4 to 6 small to medium zucchini
 (about 1½ lb/750 g), ends trimmed
2 Tbsp extra virgin olive oil
2 cloves garlic (about 2 tsp minced)
Salt and freshly ground black pepper
Paprika
2 Tbsp balsamic vinegar

1. Preheat the grill to medium high. Cut the zucchini lengthwise into ½-inch thick slices and arrange in a single layer on a large platter or baking pan. In a small bowl, whisk together the oil and garlic; brush lightly on both sides of the zucchini slices. Sprinkle both sides with salt, pepper, and paprika to taste.

2. Transfer the seasoned zucchini slices to the preheated grill. Grill the zucchini over direct heat for about 4 to 5 minutes per side. Grill marks should appear on both sides. Transfer to a serving platter and drizzle with balsamic vinegar before serving.

Yield: 4 to 6 servings. Don't freeze.

99 calories per serving, 8.8 g carbohydrate, 2.1 g fiber, 1 g protein, 7.1 g fat (1 g saturated), 0 mg cholesterol, 347 mg sodium, 377 mg potassium, 1 mg iron, 22 mg calcium

Chef's Secrets

• Leftovers? Cut the grilled zucchini slices into strips and add to salads.

• It's a Wrap! Leftover grilled zucchini is delicious in a tortilla with crumbled goat cheese, roasted red peppers, and/or tomato slices. Pure wrap-ture.

• Using Your Noodle: Substitute grilled zucchini slices for lasagna noodles in your favorite lasagna recipe.

Nutrition Notes

• Zucchini, which is a summer squash, is part of the melon family. The entire zucchini, including the flesh, skin, and seeds, is edible. It's a good source of vitamins A and C, magnesium, fiber, potassium, folate, lutein, and more. Because of its high water content, raw zucchini keeps for up to a week in the refrigerator. It's "grate" in zucchini bread, muffins, soups, quiches, and casseroles.

🍎 SHREDDED ZUCCHINI WITH GARLIC

Here is a quick, delicious way to enjoy the bumper crop of zucchini from your garden. This makes an excellent alternative to pasta if you are watching your carb intake. For a pretty presentation, use both green and yellow zucchini.

4 to 6 medium zucchini
 (about 1½ lb/750 g), ends trimmed
2 Tbsp extra virgin olive oil
3 cloves garlic (about 1 Tbsp minced)
½ cup chopped red pepper
2 Tbsp minced fresh basil
Salt and freshly ground black pepper
Juice of ½ lemon

vegetables

1. Cut the zucchini into pieces that will fit through the feed tube of the food processor. In the food processor fitted with the grater, shred the zucchini, using medium pressure on the pusher. Transfer the shredded zucchini onto several layers of paper towels and squeeze gently to remove excess moisture. (Or place the zucchini in a colander, sprinkle with salt, and let drain for 20 to 30 minutes.)

2. Heat the oil in a large skillet on medium high heat. Add the shredded zucchini, garlic, and red pepper. Sauté for 5 to 6 minutes, stirring occasionally, until tender. Stir in the basil, salt, pepper and lemon juice, and serve immediately.

Yield: 4 to 6 servings. Don't freeze.

96 calories per serving, 8.2 g carbohydrate, 2.4 g fiber, 1 g protein, 7.1 g fat (1 g saturated), 0 mg cholesterol, 346 mg sodium, 418 mg potassium, 1 mg iron, 27 mg calcium

Variations
• Instead of basil, use dillweed, oregano, or thyme. Sprinkle a little Parmesan cheese over the zucchini just before serving. Leftovers can be used in omelets, quiches, or even lasagna.

ZUCCHINI TOMATO TIAN

A tian is a Provençal dish of baked vegetables topped with breadcrumbs or grated cheese. It's a wonderful way to use up the bounty of the fall harvest. If yellow zucchini isn't available, use baby new potatoes or fingerlings (thumb-size potatoes), which are lower in starch than regular potatoes. This dish can be halved easily. See the cheese-topped (au gratin) version on page 316.

2 Tbsp olive oil
2 large onions
4 cloves garlic (about 4 tsp minced)
2 large green zucchini, ends trimmed
2 large yellow zucchini, ends trimmed
6 plum tomatoes, cored
Salt and freshly ground black pepper
1/4 cup lightly packed fresh basil
    (or 2 tsp dried basil)

Topping:

3 slices rye or multigrain bread
2 Tbsp olive oil
Salt and freshly ground black pepper

1. Preheat the oven to 375°F. Spray a 3-quart oval or oblong casserole with cooking spray.

2. Heat the oil in a large skillet on medium heat. Add the onions and garlic, and sauté for 8 to 10 minutes or until golden.

3. Slice the zucchini and tomatoes on the diagonal, about 1/2-inch thick. Alternate slices of green zucchini, tomatoes, and yellow zucchini in the baking dish, forming concentric circles or rows. Season with salt and pepper to taste. Tear up the fresh basil and tuck in between the vegetable slices. Top with sautéed onions and garlic, spreading evenly. Cover with foil. (The vegetables can be prepared in advance up to this point and refrigerated overnight.)

4. Tear the bread into chunks and process in a food processor fitted with the steel blade until crumbs form, about 10 seconds. Add the oil to the crumbs, and season with salt and pepper. Process for a few seconds longer to combine. Set aside.

5. Bake the covered casserole for 20 minutes. Remove the foil and sprinkle the

crumb topping over the vegetables. Bake, uncovered, for another 20 to 25 minutes or until golden and crispy.

Yield: 10 to 12 servings. Keeps for 1 to 2 days in the refrigerator; reheats well. Don't freeze.

102 calories per serving, 11.3 g carbohydrate, 2.1 g fiber, 2 g protein, 5.9 g fat (0.8 g saturated), 0 mg cholesterol, 56 mg sodium, 286 mg potassium, 1 mg iron, 26 mg calcium

Zucchini Tomato Tian au Gratin

Omit the crumb topping and bake, covered, for 20 minutes. Uncover and sprinkle with 1 1/2 cups grated low-fat Swiss, cheddar, or Monterey Jack cheese. Bake for 20 to 25 minutes longer or until the cheese is melted and golden. One serving contains 83 calories, 7.6 g carbohydrate, and 3.7 g fat (0.9 g saturated).

● GREAT GRILLED VEGETABLES

"Veg-out" at your next barbecue with this easy Mediterranean-style dish. When the weather is bad, you can roast the vegetables in a hot oven. This dish is a winner at any temperature.

1 large red onion, sliced in rings
3 bell peppers (red, orange and/or yellow), cut in chunks
8 medium portobello mushrooms, halved
1 small eggplant, ends trimmed, sliced into 1/2-inch thick rounds
2 zucchini, sliced diagonally 1/2-inch thick
4 cloves garlic (about 4 tsp minced)
1/4 cup extra virgin olive oil
1/4 cup balsamic vinegar
2 tsp Kosher or sea salt
Freshly ground black pepper

1/4 cup lightly packed chopped fresh basil or 2 tsp dried
1 Tbsp chopped fresh oregano or 1 tsp dried
1 cup crumbled feta or goat cheese (optional)

1. In a large bowl, combine the onion, bell peppers, mushrooms, eggplant, and zucchini. Add the garlic, oil, balsamic vinegar, and salt and pepper to taste; mix well. Marinate for at least 30 minutes (or cover and refrigerate overnight).

2. Transfer the marinated vegetables to a perforated grilling basket, reserving any leftover marinade. (If you don't have a grilling basket, use heavy-duty foil that has been slashed in several places.) Grill over medium-high heat, stirring 2 or 3 times, for 18 to 20 minutes or until the vegetables are golden brown and tender-crisp.

3. Transfer the vegetables from the grill to a large serving platter. Add the reserved marinade, basil, and oregano; mix well. Top with cheese, if using, at serving time.

Yield: 8 servings. Keeps for up to 2 to 3 days in the refrigerator. Don't freeze.

134 calories per serving, 14.6 g carbohydrate, 4.5 g fiber, 4 g protein, 7.4 g fat (1.0 g saturated), 0 mg cholesterol, 331 mg sodium, 738 mg potassium, 1 mg iron, 33 mg calcium

Oven-Roasted Vegetables

Instead of grilling vegetables, spread them in a single layer on a large baking tray that has been lined with sprayed foil. Roast, uncovered and stir occasionally, for 20 to 25 minutes at 425°F, or until golden brown and tender-crisp.

Variations

• Omit the eggplant and cheese and add 2 Belgian endives, trimmed and halved lengthwise. Add 1 Tbsp honey along with oil, vinegar, and seasonings. Serve with grilled chicken breasts or salmon on a bed of salad greens.

Chef's Secrets

• Herb Magic: If using dried herbs, add them at the beginning of the cooking process. Thyme or rosemary also make flavorful seasonings.

• Leftovers? Use in wraps, as a filling for Phyllo Nests (page 62) or as a topping for Crostini (page 65). Or brighten up any pasta, rice, or grain dish with these colorful vegetables.

SPRING MIX VEGETABLE MEDLEY

This colorful vegetable medley is delicious as a side dish or served over pasta. The recipe can be halved easily, but I always make a big batch because it's so versatile. Leftovers make a delicious snack right from the refrigerator.

2 medium onions, halved and sliced
2 red peppers, seeded and cut in strips
2 cups sliced mushrooms
1 lb (500 g) asparagus (tough ends trimmed), cut diagonally into 2-inch pieces
1 large zucchini or yellow squash, unpeeled and cut into strips
3 to 4 cloves garlic (about 3 to 4 tsp minced)
3 Tbsp extra virgin olive oil
3 Tbsp lemon juice (preferably fresh) or rice vinegar
2 tsp sea salt or Kosher salt
Freshly ground black pepper

2 Tbsp minced fresh dillweed (plus additional for garnish)
1 Tbsp minced fresh thyme or 1 tsp dried
1/2 cup sesame seeds

1. Place the prepared vegetables in a large bowl. Add the garlic, olive oil, lemon juice, salt, pepper, dillweed, and thyme; mix well. (If desired, the vegetables can be prepared in advance up to this point and refrigerated, covered, for several hours or overnight.)

2. Preheat the oven to 425°F. Line a large baking tray with foil and spray with cooking spray.

3. Spread the vegetables in a single layer on the prepared baking tray and sprinkle with sesame seeds. Roast, uncovered, for 15 to 18 minutes or until golden brown and tender-crisp, stirring once or twice. Transfer to a serving platter and garnish with additional dillweed. Serve hot or at room temperature.

Yield: 6 servings. Keeps for up to 3 days in the refrigerator. To reheat, bake uncovered at 375°F for 10 to 12 minutes. Don't freeze.

122 calories per serving, 13.2 g carbohydrate, 3.5 g fiber, 3 g protein, 7.4 g fat (1.1 g saturated), 0 mg cholesterol, 440 mg sodium, 452 mg potassium, 7 mg iron, 40 mg calcium

Variations

• Substitute trimmed green beans for asparagus. This recipe is also tasty with small cauliflower florets. For a spicy kick, add 1 tsp red pepper flakes or smoked paprika to the seasoning mixture in Step 1.

• This versatile combination makes a delicious topping for chicken, fish, pasta, or grains. To turn this into a vegetarian main dish, make Spaghetti Squash with Roasted Vegetables (page 163).

vegetables

grains &
side dishes

GRAINS AND SIDE DISHES

The Grain Train: Hop on board and include more whole grains in your diet. A great way to get on track is to aim for three servings a day. Experiment with barley, bulgar, cornmeal, couscous, kasha, millet, quinoa, rice, and wheat berries. To sneak more whole grains into your diet, add them to vegetables, soups, salads, side dishes, casseroles, and breads.

Gluten-Alert! Many people are gluten intolerant and/or suffer from celiac disease. Grains that contain gluten are wheat, rye, oats, barley, and spelt. Gluten-free grains include barley, corn, quinoa, kasha/buckwheat, and rice.

The Whole Truth: Whole grains tend to be darker, chewier, and more flavorful because all three layers of the kernel are included, which make them nutritionally superior to refined grains. Whole grains provide protein, antioxidants, fatty acids, and many phytochemicals (natural compounds found in plants which contain antioxidant properties that strengthen the immune system). Fiber is one of the major benefits of whole grains—up to quadruple the amount found in refined grains.

A Salute to the Kernel: Most of the fiber in kernels is found in the bran, which is the outer layer of the kernel. The germ is in the center, where many of the vitamins, minerals, and fatty acids are found. The endosperm is in the core and contains most of the starch plus a few vitamins and minerals. When grains are refined, the germ and the bran are discarded, resulting in starchy and fluffy white foods with little fiber or nutritional value.

What's in Store: Look for the words "whole" or "100% whole" before the name of the grain when buying grains, pastas, cereals, breads, and crackers.

Health Gains from Grains: Whole grains offer protection against diabetes, heart disease, cancer, and many digestive problems because of their fiber content (food with more fiber takes longer to digest, which is a good thing). On the other hand, refined grains are quickly digested, resulting in higher levels of blood sugar, insulin, and triglycerides and lower levels of HDL (good cholesterol).

GI Go! Whole grain foods can have either a high or low glycemic index (GI) value. The larger the particle size, the lower the GI value. Soluble fiber helps lower your body's glycemic response to a food. Grains that are digested slowly and have a lower GI value include barley (GI 25), buckwheat (GI 54), bulgar (GI 48), quinoa (GI 51), and rolled oats (GI 42).

No-Brain Grains: Grains are very simple to cook and are very versatile. If you can boil water, you'll have no problem cooking grains. Bulgar and couscous don't require cooking—soaking is sufficient. See the Cooking Chart for Grains on page 323 for cooking times.

Cook It Right: Place the grains in a strainer, rinse and drain well. Transfer to a saucepan and add water as directed, along with a pinch of salt. You can also cook grains in vegetable or chicken broth. A clove of garlic in the cooking liquid won't hurt either (but not for breakfast). Bring to a boil; reduce heat to low and simmer, covered tightly, until all the water is absorbed. No peeking allowed! If any water remains, just drain it off.

grains & side dishes

Ready or Not? If grains aren't cooked to your liking, add a little more water, cover, and cook for a few minutes longer. Fluff with a fork before serving.

Staying Power: Since grains are so easy to prepare, why not cook extra? Grains can be cooked in advance, cooled, and stored in a covered container in the refrigerator for up to 4 to 5 days. To reheat in the microwave, allow 1 minute per cup on high. Cook once, eat twice!

Frozen Assets: Most grains freeze well. Some people like to freeze rice while others don't like the texture once it's been thawed. Wheat berries will become mushy when frozen. Pack cooked grains in small airtight containers or re-sealable plastic bags for quick convenience. Thaw overnight in the refrigerator or transfer to a microwaveable container. Microwave for 2 minutes per cup on high to defrost and heat. If you want to heat defrosted grains, microwave for 1 minute per cup on high.

Pump Up the Volume: Add raw or cooked veggies such as onions, green onions, bell peppers, celery, carrots, tomatoes or zucchini, to grains. Vegetables will increase the volume and help lower the glycemic load.

Protein Power: Add some protein such as chicken, fish, tofu, cheese, chickpeas, or cooked beans, to turn grains into a main dish.

Boost the Flavor: To jazz up the flavor of grains, add a drizzle of extra virgin olive oil and some lemon, orange, or lime juice—fresh is best. Balsamic, red wine, or rice vinegar can be used instead of citrus juices. For an additional flavor boost, add some minced garlic, dillweed, basil, thyme, parsley, rosemary, or other herbs. Toasted (Asian) sesame oil and soy sauce work well in Asian-inspired dishes. Use your imagination.

Hidden Treasures: Cooked grains are ideal as a stuffing for poultry or meat and can also be used to stuff vegetables such as cabbage rolls, bell peppers, squash, or zucchini.

RICE IS NICE

Rice Around the World: Rice is a staple food for over half the world's population. Soup, salad, or a stir-fry based around rice, with the addition of some lean protein such as chicken, lean meat, fish, or tofu, plus lots of colorful vegetables will provide a healthy balance of carbs, fat, and protein, plus some fiber, vitamins, and minerals.

Best Bets: Make the switch from white rice to brown. I love brown basmati rice, which has a wonderful, nutty flavor and doesn't taste "brown." Brown rice is extremely nutritious and contains several B vitamins, minerals, dietary fiber, and protein. White rice has had its husk, bran, and germ removed, so it's less nutritious than brown rice.

GI Go! If you are a big rice eater, choose varieties with a lower glycemic index (GI) value and with a higher amylose content, such as basmati (GI 58) or Uncle Ben's converted long-grain rice (GI 38). Amylose is a kind of starch that is digested more slowly, so the grains stay firm and separate when cooked, rather than becoming soft and sticky. Wild rice (GI 57) isn't actually rice but a type of grass seed.

Pump up the Volume: Combine $\frac{1}{2}$ cup of cooked rice with 2 cups of vegetables that have a low GI value, such as chopped red peppers, onions, garlic, ginger, mushrooms, and zucchini. Add a dash of soy sauce and toasted (Asian) sesame oil for a satisfying rice dish that also has a lower GI value.

Rice in the Microwave: Combine 1 cup rice (basmati or long-grain) with 2 cups water or broth and a pinch of salt in a 3-quart microwaveable casserole. Microwave, covered, on high for 5 to 6 minutes or until boiling. Reduce power to defrost (30%) and microwave for 10 minutes longer. Let stand, covered, for 10 minutes or until the liquid is absorbed. If the rice is kept covered, it will stay warm for about 30 minutes. Fluff with a fork before serving.

Twice the Rice: Combine 2 cups rice (basmati or long-grain), 4 cups liquid, and a pinch of salt. Microwave on high for 6 to 7 minutes, then on defrost (30%) for 12 to 14 minutes; let stand, covered, for 10 minutes before serving. Fluff with a fork before serving.

Brown Rice in the Microwave: Brown rice takes longer to cook in the microwave than white rice. Microwave brown rice on high for 5 to 6 minutes, then on defrost (30%) for 25 to 30 minutes; let stand covered for 10 minutes before serving. Fluff with a fork before serving.

Brown Rice in Half the Time: For each cup of brown rice, add 2 cups of water and a pinch of salt. Place in a saucepan and soak at room temperature for several hours or overnight. (Do this in the morning, then cook it at mealtime.) When ready to cook, bring the liquid to a boil over high heat. Reduce heat to low and simmer, tightly covered, for just 22 minutes. Turn off the heat and let stand, covered, for 10 minutes. Fluff with a fork before serving.

PASTA-BILITIES

Don't Pass Up Pasta: Like people, pasta comes in different shapes, sizes, and colors. Experiment with spaghetti, fettuccine, bowties, fusilli, penne, ziti, or tortellini. Pasta is quick to prepare, inexpensive, nourishing, and satisfying. Here are some helpful guidelines on "healthy weighs" to enjoy pasta.

What's in Store: Whole wheat pasta, made from durum whole wheat semolina, is higher in fiber and chewier than traditional wheat pasta. It comes in a variety of shapes and goes well with heartier pasta sauces. High-quality pasta made with hard/durum wheat contains more protein and less starch. Regular pasta contains little fiber.

Oodles of Noodles: Chinese cellophane noodles are made from mung beans rather than grain, so they are higher in protein and lower in starch. Udon are delicious, thick, light-colored Japanese noodles made from wheat. Japanese soba noodles, made from buckwheat and wheat flour, have a dark-brownish color. Reduced-carbohydrates noodles work well in kugels and casseroles. Stuffed pastas, such as tortellini and ravioli, are another way to get a hearty meal on the table quickly.

GI Go! Pasta in any shape or form has a relatively low GI value (30 to 60), but always keep the portion size moderate. Packaged macaroni and cheese dinners have medium-to-high GI values. Cook pasta until al dente (firm to the bite)—don't overcook it or you will boost the GI value. Start testing for doneness about 2 minutes before the cooking time indicated on the package directions.

Portion Distortion: Did you know that a serving of cooked pasta is only 1/2 a cup and contains about 100 calories? Most people can easily eat 2 to 3 cups of pasta at a meal. That's the equivalent of 4 to 6 slices of bread.

Sizing Up: Noodles swell slightly when cooked. Spaghetti and macaroni double in volume. Calculate 3 oz (85 g) dried pasta as a main dish or 2 oz (55 g) as a side dish.

Expand without Expanding: By adding lots of vegetables to pasta, you'll consume fewer calories and will still be able to enjoy a full plate. Add asparagus, broccoli, carrots, cauliflower, eggplant, spinach, or zucchini. Sauté vegetables in olive oil instead of butter; add garlic, onions, and herbs for flavor. Add some lean protein such as chicken, fish, tofu cubes, or grated reduced-fat cheese. Avoid creamy, calorie-packed sauces.

Fiber Up: Adding 1 cup of puréed kidney beans or lentils to any pasta sauce will thicken it and increase the fiber content. They'll never know!

Saucy Secrets: Bottled and canned sauces are convenient when you're rushed for time. Check nutrition labels for fat, calories, and sodium content. Also, check what is indicated as a serving size—you may be surprised.

Frozen Assets: Cook extra pasta, rinse, drain, and let cool. Freeze portions in re-sealable plastic bags. When needed, remove pasta from the bag, place in a strainer, and rinse with boiling water. It's ready when you are.

BREAKFAST

Breakfast Bonanza: Cooked whole grains make an excellent breakfast—they're pure comfort food. Breakfast provides an easy way to eat one of the three daily servings of whole grains recommended by many health professionals.

GI Go! Hot cereals with a lower glycemic index (GI) value include large flake rolled oats, oat bran, 7-grain cereal, steel-cut oats, and Red River cereal. Cold cereals with a lower GI value include All-Bran, Bran Buds, Fiber First, Kashi Go Lean, Red River cereal, and natural muesli made with rolled oats, dried fruit, nuts, and seeds.

More GI Go! Many breakfast cereals are made from fine flours and tend to have a high GI value. If your favorite breakfast cereal such as corn flakes (GI 77), Rice Krispies (GI 82), or Cheerios (GI 74) has a high or moderate GI value, combine it with yogurt, berries, and nuts to reduce the glycemic load.

Cook It Right: Prepare cooked cereal according to package directions, using water, nonfat milk, soymilk, or apple juice as the cooking liquid. If microwaving, use a bowl that's large enough (about triple the size) to prevent boil-overs. Top each serving with 1/2 to 1 cup mixed berries or sliced apple and 1/2 cup nonfat yogurt or milk. Add a dash of cinnamon and sugar, honey, or sweetener to taste. Sprinkle with toasted nuts, seeds, and/or ground flaxseed, if desired.

Label Lingo: A serving size of hot or cold cereal is approximately 30 grams, which can vary from 1/3 to 1 1/4 cups, depending on the type of cereal and the manufacturer. One serving should contain 150 calories or less, 4 or more grams of protein, and 3 or more grams of fiber.

Some Like It Cold: When buying cold cereals, whole grains should be at the top of the ingredient list on the label.

Cereal Killers: Beware of sugar-packed cereals in wild, colorful packages that are marketed for children. Look for a reduced-sugar or sugar-free cereal and combine it with a whole grain, unsweetened variety. Mix it up!

grains & side dishes

COOKING CHART FOR GRAINS

Rinse grains in a fine-mesh strainer; drain well. Transfer the grains to a saucepan with water or broth and a pinch of salt, and bring to a boil. Reduce heat to low and simmer, covered, according to the cooking times below. If any liquid remains after cooking, drain.

GRAINS (1 CUP)	LIQUID	COOKING TIME	YIELD
Amaranth	1¾ cups	25 minutes	2 cups
Barley, pearl	3 cups	40 to 45 minutes	4 cups
Bulgar/Precooked cracked wheat	1 cup	Soak 30 minutes in 2 cups boiling water/broth (no cooking required)	2 cups
Cornmeal, yellow/white	4 cups	20 minutes	4 cups
Couscous	1½ cups	Soak 5 to 10 minutes in boiling water/broth (no cooking required)	2 cups
Cracked wheat	2 cups	10 minutes	3 cups
Kasha/Buckwheat groats (mix with egg white before cooking, page 327)	2 cups	10 to 12 minutes for medium grain 15 to 18 minutes for coarse grain	3 cups
Millet	2 cups	20 to 25 minutes	3 cups
Oats, rolled (preferably large flake or steel-cut)	3 cups	10 to 20 minutes	4 cups
Quinoa (rinsed well)	2 cups	15 minutes	3 cups
Rice, basmati or long grain	2 cups	20 minutes	3 cups
Rice, brown	2 cups	40 to 45 minutes	3 cups
Rice, wild	2½ cups	45 to 60 minutes	3 to 4 cups
Wheat berries (soak overnight in 3 cups water)	3 cups	1 to 1½ hours	3 cups

grains & side dishes

◖ BARLEY RISOTTO WITH PORTO-BELLO MUSHROOMS & SUN-DRIED TOMATOES

Pearl barley makes a terrific substitute for Arborio rice in this creamy, non-traditional risotto—it's less expensive and has a lower glycemic index value, making this fiber-packed dish very "smart-carb." The portobello mushrooms and sun-dried tomatoes add a rich elegance to this humble grain. There will barely be any barley once they taste this!

$^1/_2$ cup (about 8 to 10) sun-dried tomatoes
   (if packed in oil, rinse well)
1 cup boiling water
$4^1/_2$ cups vegetable or chicken broth
$1^1/_2$ Tbsp olive oil
$^1/_2$ red onion (about 1 cup chopped)
2 cups chopped portobello mushrooms
2 cloves garlic (about 2 tsp minced)
$1^1/_2$ cups pearl barley, rinsed and drained
1 tsp minced fresh thyme or $^1/_2$ tsp dried
2 Tbsp minced fresh basil or 1 tsp dried
Salt and freshly ground black pepper

1. Combine the sun-dried tomatoes with boiling water in a small bowl. Let stand for 10 minutes to rehydrate. Drain, cut into bite-sized pieces, and set aside. (Scissors work well.) Heat the broth to simmering (either in the microwave or in a saucepan over medium-low heat), about 8 to 10 minutes.

2. Meanwhile, heat the oil in a large pot on medium high heat. Add the onion, mushrooms, and garlic; sauté for 5 minutes or until tender. If necessary, add a little water to prevent sticking or burning. Stir in the barley and cook for 2 to 3 minutes or until lightly toasted, stirring to thoroughly coat the grains.

3. Reduce heat to low and slowly stir in $^1/_2$ cup of hot broth. Cook and stir for about 2 minutes or until the broth evaporates. Add another $^1/_2$ cup of broth and continue stirring until you can drag a spoon along the bottom of the pot and almost no liquid remains. Repeat twice more, adding $^1/_2$ cup of broth each time and stirring constantly.

4. Pour in the remaining $2^1/_2$ cups of broth. Cover and simmer for 40 to 45 minutes, stirring occasionally, until the barley is tender. Add the sun-dried tomatoes, thyme, basil, salt, and pepper; mix well. Remove from the heat, cover, and let stand 5 minutes longer.

Yield: 12 servings of $^1/_2$ cup each. Keeps for up to 3 days in the refrigerator; reheats well, especially in the microwave. Freezes well for up to 2 months.

133 calories per serving, 25.1 g carbohydrate, 5.1 g fiber, 4 g protein, 2.3 g fat (0.3 g saturated), 0 mg cholesterol, 224 mg sodium, 262 mg potassium, 1 mg iron, 24 mg calcium

Variations

• You can substitute up to 1 cup dry white wine for part of the broth.

• Instead of mushrooms, substitute with 1 bunch asparagus, ends trimmed. Cut on the diagonal into 1-inch slices and lightly steam for 3 to 4 minutes before adding to the barley in Step 4. Frozen peas also make a great "green" option.

grains & side dishes

🍎 BULGAR WITH ALMONDS AND RAISINS

Bulgar is actually precooked cracked wheat so it doesn't require cooking, just soaking. While the bulgar soaks in water, take a soak in your bathtub and you'll both be ready at the same time.

1½ cups medium bulgar
1½ cups boiling water or vegetable broth
½ cup slivered almonds
2 Tbsp extra virgin olive oil
3 Tbsp lemon or orange juice
   (preferably fresh)
¼ cup chopped fresh basil or 1 tsp dried
½ cup raisins
1 tsp salt (or to taste)
¼ tsp freshly ground black pepper

1. Place the bulgar in a heat-resistant bowl and add boiling water or broth. Cover the bowl with a large plate and let stand for about 30 minutes or until the liquid is absorbed and the bulgar is tender.

2. Meanwhile, toast the almonds in a toaster oven for 5 to 7 minutes at 350°F or until golden and fragrant. (Or toast in a skillet on medium heat, stirring frequently, about 5 minutes.) Watch carefully to prevent the almonds from burning.

3. Stir the olive oil, lemon juice, basil, and raisins into the bulgar. Season with salt and pepper, and top with toasted almonds. Serve hot or at room temperature.

Yield: 6 servings. Keeps for up to 3 days in the refrigerator; reheats well. Freezes well for up to 2 months. Add the toasted almonds only at serving time.

253 calories per serving, 38.7 g carbohydrate, 8.1 g fiber, 7 g protein, 9.8 g fat (1.1 g saturated), 0 mg cholesterol, 395 mg sodium, 317 mg potassium, 2 mg iron, 45 mg calcium

Variations
• Instead of raisins, add dried cranberries, sliced dried apricots, or dried mango. Instead of almonds, substitute with toasted walnuts, pecans, or pine nuts. Instead of bulgar, substitute with 3 cups of cooked rice, millet, quinoa, or kasha.

Chef's Secrets
• Love Me Tender: Bulgar has a tender, chewy texture and makes a nice alternative to rice. Although this dish is best made with medium bulgar, you can use fine bulgar as well. If you use coarse bulgar, you will have to cook it first. Bulgar is delicious in pilafs, salads, meat, poultry, and vegetable dishes. Try Terrific Tabbouleh (page 261).

🍎 COUSCOUS, MOROCCAN-STYLE

This delicious one-pot dish, with its blend of exotic Moroccan flavors, is a favorite of Shayla Goldstein of Toronto. It's great for busy families.

1½ cups chicken broth (or a mixture
   of half orange juice and half water)
⅛ tsp ground cumin
⅛ tsp ground coriander
⅛ tsp ground ginger (optional)
1 cup couscous (whole wheat or regular)
2 green onions, finely chopped
⅓ cup dried cranberries or chopped
   dried apricots
¼ cup shelled pistachios or pine nuts

grains & side dishes

1. In a small saucepan over high heat, bring the broth, cumin, coriander, and ginger, if using, to a boil. Stir in the couscous, green onions, cranberries, and pistachios.

2. Remove the pan from the heat; cover and let stand for 5 minutes. Fluff with a fork and serve.

Yield: 4 servings. Recipe doubles or triples easily. Keeps for up to 3 days in the refrigerator; reheats well. Freezes well for up to 2 months.

190 calories per serving, 34.1 g carbohydrate, 5.2 g fiber, 6 g protein, 4.3 g fat (0.4 g saturated), 0 mg cholesterol, 187 mg sodium, 137 mg potassium, 2 mg iron, 30 mg calcium

● COUSCOUS, MEDITERRANEAN-STYLE

Experience the fabulous flavors of the Mediterranean with this colorful dish. You can use regular or whole wheat couscous, or try the pearl-shaped grains of pasta known as Israeli couscous (or maftoul), which are much larger and more versatile than the typical Moroccan couscous. You can substitute the couscous with orzo (a rice-shaped pasta), bulgar, or quinoa.

2 Tbsp olive oil
2 medium onions, chopped
1 red pepper, seeded and chopped
2 cloves garlic (about 2 tsp minced)
1 1/2 cups couscous
1 tsp ground cumin
3 cups hot vegetable or chicken broth
1/2 cup raisins or currants
1/2 cup chopped dried apricots or dates
Salt and freshly ground black pepper
1/2 cup chopped fresh parsley or mint
1/3 cup toasted pine nuts
    or slivered almonds

1. Heat the oil in a large, deep skillet on medium heat. Add the onions, red pepper, and garlic; sauté for 6 to 7 minutes or until golden.

2. Stir in the couscous and cumin and cook for 2 minutes longer or until golden. Slowly add the hot broth and bring to a boil. Reduce heat to low, cover, and simmer for 10 to 12 minutes or until the couscous is tender.

3. Stir in the raisins, apricots, salt, and pepper. Sprinkle with parsley and pine nuts and serve.

Yield: 8 servings. Keeps for up to 3 days in the refrigerator; reheats well. Freezes well for up to 2 months.

264 calories per serving, 43.7 g carbohydrate, 3.9 g fiber, 6 g protein, 7.9 g fat (0.8 g saturated), 0 mg cholesterol, 182 mg sodium, 345 mg potassium, 2 mg iron, 42 mg calcium

Couscous with Mushrooms and Chickpeas

Sauté 2 cups of sliced mushrooms with the onions, pepper, and garlic. Instead of cumin, add 1 tsp dried basil or thyme. Replace the dried fruit and nuts with 1 1/2 cups of cooked or canned chickpeas, rinsed and well-drained. One serving contains 242 calories, 40.6 g carbohydrate, 4.5 g fiber, 5.6 g fat (0.7 g saturated).

Couscous with Sun-Dried Tomatoes

Omit the cumin, dried fruit, and nuts. In Step 3, stir in 1 tsp Italian seasoning and 1/2 cup chopped sun-dried tomatoes, rinsed and drained. If desired, add 1/2 cup sliced pitted black olives. One serving contains 192 calories, 32.2 g carbohydrate, 3.1 g fiber, 4.8 g fat (0.6 g saturated).

grains & side dishes

🍎 KASHA (BUCKWHEAT GROATS)

Kasha is extremely versatile. It's excellent hot as a breakfast cereal, ideal in casseroles, or super as a side dish. Use kasha instead of rice or other grains in salads and pilafs. Kasha has a toasty, nutty flavor and triples in volume when cooked. Some people use a whole egg to toast it but I only use the white. White on!

1 cup medium or wholegrain kasha
1 egg white
2 cups hot vegetable broth
Salt and freshly ground black pepper

1. In a large, heavy-bottomed skillet, mix the kasha together with the egg white. Cook on medium heat, stirring constantly for about 5 minutes or until the kasha is dry and toasted.

2. Remove the pan from the heat and slowly add the broth to the kasha. Be careful—it splatters. Return the pan to the heat, cover, and simmer on low until most of the liquid is absorbed. The cooking time is 10 to 12 minutes for medium kasha and 15 to 18 minutes for wholegrain kasha. When done, holes will appear on the surface and the kasha will be tender.

3. Remove the pan from the heat and let stand, covered, for 10 minutes or until the remaining liquid is absorbed. Fluff with a fork and season with salt and pepper to taste.

Yield: 3 cups. Keeps for up to 3 days in the refrigerator; reheats well. Freezes well for up to 3 months.

112 calories per 1/2 cup, 23.0 g carbohydrate, 3.3 g fiber, 4 g protein, 1.0 g fat (0.2 g saturated), 0 mg cholesterol, 242 mg sodium, 97 mg potassium, 1 mg iron, 15 mg calcium

Kasha and Bowties

Combine 3 cups of cooked kasha with 2 cups of cooked bowtie pasta. Sauté 2 chopped onions and 2 cups of sliced mushrooms in 2 Tbsp olive oil until golden. Combine all the ingredients and stir in 1/4 cup chopped fresh dill, salt, and pepper. This is true comfort food.

Chef's Secrets

• No Yolk-ing! Toasting kasha with an egg white before adding the liquid keeps the grains separate and prevents them from becoming sticky.

• Double Without Trouble: If you want to double the recipe, use the whole egg instead of just the egg white. The extra cooked kasha can be used to make Kasha and Vegetable Salad (page 263). Easy and delicious.

• Chick-Information: Use chicken soup instead of vegetable broth for a richer flavor. Cooked kasha is delicious in chicken soup as a substitute for rice or noodles.

Nutrition Notes

• Kasha is actually a fruit, not a grain. It's available in whole (coarse), medium, and fine grains.

• Kasha is a wonderful source of plant protein and is 20% higher in fiber than oatmeal; it's mostly soluble fiber, which helps lower cholesterol. This satisfying, heart-healthy food is an excellent choice for people with diabetes. Kasha is also wheat-free and gluten-free, making it ideal for people with celiac disease.

grains & side dishes

❧ KASHA AND SQUASH CASSEROLE

Don't be deterred by the length of this recipe—it's a winner! Although it takes a little time to prepare, the time-saving tips on page 329 will help speed things up. Once you taste it, you'll agree it's well worth it—we all did. This makes a wonderful side dish, but vegetarians can enjoy it as a main dish.

Onion Mixture:

1 Tbsp olive oil
3 medium onions, chopped

Kasha Mixture:

1 cup medium or wholegrain kasha
1 large egg, separated
2 cups hot vegetable broth
$1/2$ tsp salt (or to taste)
$1/4$ tsp freshly ground black pepper
1 large egg

Squash Mixture:

3 lb (1.4 kg) butternut squash
2 large eggs
3 Tbsp olive oil
$1/4$ cup crushed wholegrain crackers
1 Tbsp brown sugar or granular Splenda
$1/2$ tsp salt
$1/4$ tsp freshly ground black pepper

Topping:

$1/2$ cup crushed wholegrain crackers
1 Tbsp granulated sugar or granular Splenda
1 tsp olive oil
$1/2$ tsp ground cinnamon

1. Onion Mixture: Heat the oil in a large nonstick skillet on medium heat. Add the onions and sauté for 8 to 10 minutes or until golden. Remove the onions from the skillet and reserve half for the kasha, and half for the squash mixture.

2. Kasha Mixture: In the same skillet (no need to wash it), combine the kasha with the egg white. Reserve the yolk. Cook on medium heat, stirring constantly, for about 5 minutes or until the kasha is dry and toasted. Remove the skillet from the heat. Slowly add the hot broth to the kasha. Be careful—it splatters. Return the skillet to the heat, cover, and simmer for 12 to 15 minutes or until most of liquid is absorbed and holes appear on the surface. (Wholegrain kasha takes a few minutes longer than medium grain.) Remove the kasha from the heat and let stand covered for 5 minutes or until the liquid is absorbed. Fluff with a fork and cool slightly.

3. Combine the kasha with half the sautéed onions. Add the salt, pepper, egg, and reserved egg yolk; mix well. Spread the kasha mixture in the bottom of a 9- × 13-inch glass baking dish sprayed with cooking spray. Press down lightly and into the corners to form a base for the casserole.

4. Squash Mixture: Pierce the squash in several places with a sharp knife. Microwave, uncovered, on high for 15 minutes or until tender, turning it over at half time. Cool slightly before cutting the squash in half and removing the seeds. Scoop out the flesh into a bowl and mash. You should end up with $2^{1}/2$ to 3 cups of mashed squash. Add the remaining sautéed onions, eggs, oil, cracker crumbs, brown sugar, salt, and pepper to the mashed squash; mix well. Spread evenly over the kasha layer.

5. Topping: Combine the cracker crumbs, sugar, oil, and cinnamon in a medium bowl; mix well. Sprinkle evenly over the squash

grains & side dishes

layer. (The casserole can be assembled up to this point, covered, and refrigerated for up to 24 hours.)

6. Bake, uncovered, in a preheated 350°F oven for 45 minutes, or until golden. The casserole is done if, when a knife is inserted, it comes out clean. Cool slightly before cutting into squares.

Yield: 12 servings. Keeps for up to 3 days in the refrigerator; reheats well. Freezes well for up to 2 months.

185 calories per serving, 25.2 g carbohydrate, 4.0 g fiber, 5 g protein, 8.1 g fat (1.5 g saturated), 71 mg cholesterol, 336 mg sodium, 190 mg potassium, 1 mg iron, 35 mg calcium

Chef's Secrets
• Timesaving Tips: Prepare the squash while the kasha is cooking. Instead of cooking the squash, you can substitute with 2 packages (10 oz/300 g each) of frozen squash, thawed, and well-drained.

• Crumb-ly News: Place the wholegrain crackers in a re-sealable plastic bag and seal well. Let your kids pound away with their fists to make crumbs, or use a rolling pin. You need a total of 3/4 cup crumbs for this recipe.

• Read the Nutrition Notes on page 327 for more on kasha.

❦ ORZO WITH SPINACH AND ASPARAGUS

Although Sheilah Kaufman lives in Potomac, Maryland, and I live in Toronto, we are connected with a culinary umbilical cord that reaches over the miles. Sheilah is the author of several wonderful cookbooks, including *Simply Irresistible*, which includes a version of this delicious, rice-shaped pasta dish. Some like it hot, some like it cold—either way, it's ideal for entertaining.

1/2 cup pine nuts
Salted water
1 pkg (1 lb/500 g) orzo
1 lb (500 g) fresh asparagus,
    ends trimmed, sliced in 1-inch pieces
6 Tbsp olive oil, divided use
1 medium onion, thinly sliced
1 pkg (10 oz/300 g) fresh baby spinach,
    washed and well-drained
2 Tbsp chopped garlic
1/2 tsp ground nutmeg
Salt and freshly ground black pepper
1 Tbsp Dijon mustard
1/4 cup lemon juice (preferably fresh)
1/4 cup white wine
1 tsp dried oregano
    or 1 Tbsp minced fresh oregano
1/2 cup chopped fresh parsley
3/4 to 1 cup dried cranberries

1. Preheat the oven or toaster oven to 350°F. Toast the nuts for 5 to 7 minutes, until golden; set aside.

2. Bring a large pot of salted water to a boil. Add the orzo and cook for 3 minutes. Add asparagus to the pot and cook for 2 minutes longer or until tender-crisp. Transfer the orzo and asparagus to a colander, rinse in cold water several times, and drain well. Set aside.

3. Heat 2 Tbsp oil in a large skillet over medium heat. Sauté the onion for 8 to 10 minutes or until golden brown. Add the spinach, garlic, nutmeg, salt, and pepper. Cook for about 3 minutes, turning it carefully with a spatula, until the spinach is just wilted. Remove the spinach mixture, drain well, and set aside.

4. In a large glass bowl, whisk together the mustard, lemon juice, and white wine. Whisk in the remaining 4 Tbsp of olive oil. Add the cooked orzo, asparagus, and spinach mixture to the bowl. Add the oregano, parsley, and dried cranberries; toss well. Season with salt and pepper to taste and top with reserved pine nuts before serving. Serve hot or cold.

5. To serve hot, cover and microwave on high for 10 to 12 minutes, or bake, covered, for 20 to 25 minutes in a 350°F oven.

Yield: 12 cups. Can be made up to a day in advance then stored, covered, in the refrigerator for up to 2 days. Freezes well for up to 2 months.

191 calories per 3/4 cup serving, 26.5 g carbohydrate, 2.2 g fiber, 5 g protein, 7.6 g fat (1.0 g saturated), 0 mg cholesterol, 165 mg sodium, 199 mg potassium, 2 mg iron, 35 mg calcium

Passover Variation with Quinoa
• Omit the mustard and use sliced almonds for the pine nuts, quinoa for the orzo, and raisins for the dried cranberries. Rinse 2 cups quinoa in a fine-meshed strainer under cold water. Bring 4 cups salted water to a boil and add the quinoa. Cover and cook for 15 minutes. Remove from heat and let stand for 5 minutes before combining with the remaining ingredients. Toss well and serve.

Chef's Secrets
• Grain Power: Orzo is a dried pasta that is shaped like rice. One pound (454 to 500 g) yields 6 cups cooked. You can substitute cooked pasta, rice, wheat berries, or quinoa for orzo. Now that's using your grain!

• Tips on Asparagus: Using your fingers, snap off the ends from the asparagus, just at the point where they break off easily. Add the asparagus to boiling water and cook for 2 minutes or until al dente. Drain, then rinse in cold water several times. Green beans can be substituted for asparagus.

● POLENTA

Polenta, also known as cornmeal mush, is served instead of rice or pasta in Northern Italy. European Jews have their own version, called mamaliga, which is served as a main dish. There are "plenta" of wonderful ways to eat polenta. Serve it for breakfast or as a main or side dish—it's delicious!

4 cups water
1 tsp salt
1 cup yellow or white cornmeal
  (medium grind)

1. Combine the water and salt in a large, heavy-bottomed saucepan and bring to a boil. Add the cornmeal in a thin stream (like falling rain), stirring constantly.

2. Reduce the heat to low and cook for 20 minutes, stirring constantly with a long-handled spoon. As it cooks, the mixture will become a thick mass and pull away from the sides of the pan. For lump-free polenta, don't stop stirring the polenta until it is done. Serve immediately.

Yield: 6 servings. Keeps for up to 3 days in the refrigerator. Reheats well in the microwave—no sticking! Freezes well for up to 2 months.

73 calories per serving, 15.3 g carbohydrate, 1.3 g fiber, 1 g protein, 0.7 g fat (0 g saturated), 0 mg cholesterol, 394 mg sodium, 0 mg potassium, 1 mg iron, 7 mg calcium

Mamaliga

Cook cornmeal as directed above. Once the polenta is cooked, stir in 1/2 cup skim milk and 1 Tbsp extra virgin olive oil. Scoop out the polenta with an ice cream scoop onto serving plates. Top each serving with 1/2 cup of nonfat cottage cheese and 1/4 cup nonfat yogurt. One serving contains 211 calories, 28.3 g carbohydrate, 16 g protein, and 175 mg calcium. So dairy good!

Polenta Pizza

Evenly spread hot polenta into a sprayed 10-inch pie plate and top with 3/4 cup tomato sauce. Add any of the following: sliced tomatoes, mushrooms, bell peppers, roasted peppers, sun-dried tomatoes, onions, marinated artichoke hearts, basil, or other herbs. Drizzle lightly with extra virgin olive oil and sprinkle with salt and pepper. Top with 3/4 to 1 cup grated low-fat mozzarella, Monterey Jack, or Swiss cheese. Bake, uncovered, in a preheated 375°F oven for 15 minutes or until the cheese is melted and golden. Cut into 6 wedges and serve.

Polenta with Refried Black Beans

For a fiber-packed vegetarian main dish, top cooked polenta with Refried Black Beans on this page.

Variations

• For a tasty side dish, serve polenta topped with sautéed mushrooms, onions, and peppers.

• For breakfast, serve polenta with a drizzle of honey or maple syrup and a pinch of ground cinnamon.

Chef's Secret

• Microwave Magic: In a 4-cup glass measure, combine 1/4 cup cornmeal with 1 cup water and a pinch of salt. Microwave, covered, on high for 5 minutes, stirring at half time. Serves 1 or 2.

REFRIED BLACK BEANS

My friend Kathy Guttman, of Toronto, who loves food with an extra spicy kick, shared this tasty dish with me. If you do too, add even more cumin, chili powder, and/or hot sauce than what's called for in this recipe. These refried black beans makes for a zesty side dish with grilled salmon, beef, or chicken. For a vegetarian meal, serve these over Polenta (page 330). Kathy likes to serve these frijoles (beans) in burritos, as a dip, or as a topping for Chicken Fajitas (page 215).

1 tsp olive oil
1 small onion, chopped
1 can (19 oz/540 mL) black beans,
    drained (do not rinse)
2 cloves garlic (about 2 tsp minced)
1/4 tsp ground cumin (or to taste)
1/2 tsp chili powder (or to taste)
Salt and freshly ground black pepper
1 small tomato, chopped
1/4 cup minced fresh cilantro
4 to 6 drops hot sauce (optional)

1. Heat oil in a large nonstick skillet over medium heat. Add the onion and sauté for 3 to 4 minutes or until softened. Stir in the black beans, garlic, cumin, chili powder, salt, and pepper; continue sautéing for 3 to 4 minutes to blend the flavors. Add the tomato, cilantro, and hot sauce, if using.

2. Remove the pan from the heat and, using a potato masher, immersion blender or fork, mash until the mixture is somewhat creamy, but with some beans still whole or partially mashed. Serve warm.

Yield: About 2 cups (6 servings of 1/3 cup). Keeps for up to 3 days in the refrigerator. Reheats well in the microwave. Don't freeze.

64 calories per serving, 13.7 g carbohydrate, 4.5 g fiber, 4 g protein, 0.9 g fat (0.1 g saturated), 0 mg cholesterol, 351 mg sodium, 302 mg potassium, 1 mg iron, 34 mg calcium

Chef's Secrets

• Using Your Bean: For maximum flavor, drain the black beans but don't rinse them. Reserve some of the drained canned bean liquid and add it to soups and stews for a flavor boost.

• Bean Cuisine: Black beans are so versatile—use them in appetizers, spreads, soups, sauces, stews, chili, burritos, or salads.

Nutrition Notes

• Lean Beans: Most canned refried black beans are made with lard—this homemade version is much healthier.

• Salt Alert! Organic brands of canned beans are lower in sodium than regular brands.

• Black Beans Are Best: Black beans are easier to digest than most beans, making them a top choice when it comes to legumes. They're packed with antioxidants and fiber and are high in protein. Eating black beans helps to lower cholesterol, stabilizes blood sugar, and reduces your cancer risk. Black beans also have a lower glycemic index (GI 42), and they're high in folate, an essential nutrient for pregnant women.

● BASIC RICE PILAF

Rice is a staple food for almost half the world's population. There are over 7,000 varieties of rice—that's really grain power! Rice is gluten-free and cholesterol-free. I love brown basmati rice, which has a nutty flavor and gives off a wonderful aroma as it cooks. This basic pilaf comes together quickly and tastes terrific.

1 Tbsp olive or canola oil
1 medium onion or 4 green onions, chopped
1 red pepper, seeded and chopped
1 cup sliced mushrooms
2 cloves garlic (about 2 tsp minced)
1 cup brown basmati rice, rinsed and drained
2 cups water, or vegetable or chicken broth
1 tsp salt
1/4 tsp freshly ground black pepper

1. Heat the oil in a large nonstick skillet on medium high heat. Add the onion, red pepper, mushrooms, and garlic; sauté for 4 to 5 minutes or until softened.

2. Add the rice, water or broth, salt, and pepper; stir well and bring to a boil. Reduce heat to low and simmer, covered, for 40 minutes—no peeking allowed!

3. Remove the pan from the heat and let stand, covered, for 10 minutes. When ready, fluff with a fork and serve.

Yield: 6 servings. Recipe doubles or triples easily. Keeps for up to 3 days in the refrigerator. Reheats well in the microwave. Can be frozen but the texture may be compromised slightly.

131 calories per serving, 24.9 g carbohydrate, 2.1 g fiber, 3 g protein, 3.4 g fat (0.3 g saturated), 0 mg cholesterol, 389 mg sodium, 100 mg potassium, 1 mg iron, 9 mg calcium

Variations

• Instead of brown rice, use white basmati or Uncle Ben's converted long-grain rice, and reduce the cooking time to 20 minutes. Other types of rice can be substituted—use cooking times on the package directions. Try a brown and wild rice blend, or check for interesting rice blends at the supermarket. Experiment!

Vegetable Rice Pilaf

Add 2 stalks celery in Step 1. At the beginning of Step 3, add 1 cup of any of the following: grated carrots, chopped zucchini, bean sprouts, and/or snow peas. Vegetables will cook during standing time. Mix well and garnish with 1/4 cup fresh chopped parsley before serving.

Mixed Vegetable Rice

At the beginning of Step 3, add 2 cups of frozen mixed vegetables. Cover and let stand for 10 minutes: the vegetables will cook during standing time. Season with basil, oregano, and thyme (or add 2 to 3 Tbsp soy sauce and 1 tsp Asian (toasted) sesame oil).

Oven Method

Sauté vegetables as directed in Step 1. Combine all the ingredients in an oven-proof casserole, cover tightly, and bake in a preheated 350°F oven for 50 to 60 minutes or until all the liquid is absorbed. If adding additional vegetables, add them at the end of the cooking time and let stand, covered, for 10 minutes.

◐ MANDARIN RICE PILAF

Basmati rice is known for its aromatic, nutty flavor, but with the addition of fragrant ingredients, this dish is elevated to a new taste level. It's nutritious and delicious.

1 cup basmati rice
2 cups water
1/2 cup tightly packed parsley
2 Tbsp fresh basil
2 cloves garlic (about 2 tsp minced)
1 slice peeled fresh ginger (about 1 Tbsp)
1 red pepper, seeded and cut in chunks
4 green onions or 1 medium onion,
    cut in chunks
1 Tbsp canola oil
3 cups packed baby spinach,
    rinsed and dried
1 cup snow peas, trimmed and cut in half
2 Tbsp soy sauce (low-sodium or regular)
2 Tbsp orange juice (preferably fresh)
1 tsp Asian (toasted) sesame oil
Salt and freshly ground black pepper
1 can (10 oz/284 mL) mandarin oranges,
    drained

1. Place the rice in a strainer; rinse and drain well. Bring the water to a boil in a medium saucepan over high heat. Add the rice, cover, and simmer for 15 minutes. Remove from the heat and let stand, covered, for 10 minutes. Fluff with a fork.

2. In a food processor fitted with the steel blade, process the parsley with the basil until minced, about 10 seconds. Transfer to a bowl and set aside.

grains & side dishes

3. Drop the garlic and ginger through the feed tube while the motor is running; process until minced. Add the red pepper and green onions; process with quick on/off pulses or until coarsely chopped.

4. Heat oil in a large nonstick wok or skillet on medium high heat. Add the garlic, ginger, pepper, and onions. Stir in the spinach and pea pods; stir-fry for 2 to 3 minutes or until tender-crisp.

5. Add the soy sauce, orange juice, and sesame oil to the wok along with the cooked rice, salt, and pepper. Add the reserved parsley and basil. Stir in the mandarin oranges and serve.

Yield: 6 servings. Recipe doubles or triples easily. Keeps for up to 3 days in the refrigerator; reheats well. Don't freeze.

186 calories per serving, 36.4 g carbohydrate, 3.0 g fiber, 4 g protein, 3.3 g fat (0.3 g saturated), 0 mg cholesterol, 206 mg sodium, 219 mg potassium, 2 mg iron, 57 mg calcium

Mandarin Quinoa Pilaf

Instead of rice, substitute with quinoa. Cook the quinoa, covered, in boiling water for 15 minutes. Remove from heat and let stand, covered, for 5 minutes. Substitute green beans for pea pods. One serving contains 181 calories, 30.6 g carbohydrate, 4.3 g fiber, and 6 g protein.

✪ BARLEY AND MUSHROOM KUGEL

This makes an excellent alternative to noodle kugel (pudding). Even though there are several steps, this healthy kugel is quite quick to assemble. There will "barley" be any left once your family or guests try it.

1 cup pearl barley
3 cups water
Salt
1 Tbsp olive oil
2 medium onions, chopped
2 cups chopped mushrooms
1 red pepper, seeded and chopped
2 large eggs plus 2 egg whites
   (or 3 large eggs)
Salt and freshly ground black pepper
1 cup vegetable or chicken broth
1/4 cup minced fresh dillweed or parsley

1. Place the barley in a strainer; rinse and drain well. In a large saucepan over high heat, bring salted water to a boil. Stir in the barley and return to a boil. Cover, reduce heat to low, and simmer for about 40 minutes or until the barley is tender. Remove from heat and let cool. (The barley can be prepared in advance and refrigerated for a day or two.)

2. Preheat the oven to 375°F. Spray a 7- × 11-inch casserole with cooking spray.

3. Heat the oil in a large nonstick skillet on medium heat. Add the onions, mushrooms, and red pepper; sauté for 5 to 7 minutes or until the onions are golden.

4. In a large bowl, combine the cooked barley with the sautéed vegetables. Add eggs, salt, pepper, broth, and dillweed; mix well. Spread the barley mixture evenly in the prepared casserole. Bake for 45 to 55 minutes or until the top is golden. Remove from the oven, let cool slightly, and cut in squares before serving.

Yield: 8 servings. Keeps 3 days in the refrigerator; reheats well. Freezes well for up to 2 months.

175 calories per serving, 28.6 g carbohydrate, 4.3 g fiber, 6 g protein, 4.5 g fat (0.9 g saturated), 71 mg cholesterol, 123 mg sodium, 256 mg potassium, 2 mg iron, 32 mg calcium

Barley and Mushroom Pilaf

Omit the eggs and bake, covered, for 15 to 20 minutes.

Chef's Secrets

• Bountiful Barley: One cup of pearl barley yields 4 cups when cooked. Cooked barley will keep for up to 4 to 5 days in the refrigerator. Barley is excellent in soups, stews, pilafs, casseroles, and salads.

• Timesaving Tip: If you love barley as much as I do, it's a good idea to cook double the amount. Cook 2 cups pearl barley in 6 cups boiling salted water as directed in Step 1. Use half to make Barley and Vegetable Salad (page 263). One pot, two delicious dishes!

Nutrition Notes

• Barley is a nutty-flavored whole grain with a chewy texture. It's high in soluble fiber and is a good source of protein and iron. This nutritious grain has the lowest glycemic index (GI) of any grain, making it a good choice for people with diabetes. The average GI of pearl barley is 25. Pearl barley cooks more quickly than pot barley.

◓ PRETEND POTATO KUGEL

I brought this yummy kugel to a dinner party and never admitted that I made it with cauliflower and packaged products. The guests thought it was potato kugel made from scratch. It was devoured in moments.

5 cups frozen chopped cauliflower
 or 1 small fresh cauliflower
3 large eggs (or 2 large eggs plus 2 egg whites)
1/3 cup light mayonnaise
3 Tbsp onion soup mix
 (about 1/2 of an envelope)
1 Tbsp all-purpose or whole wheat flour
 (or potato starch)

1. Thaw the frozen cauliflower; drain thoroughly. (If using fresh cauliflower, steam until tender, about 12 to 15 minutes; drain well.) In a large bowl, mash the cauliflower well. Add the eggs, mayonnaise, onion soup mix, and flour; mix until well combined. (The mashing and combining of ingredients can be done quickly in a food processor fitted with the steel blade.)

2. Preheat oven to 350°F. Spray a 10-inch ceramic quiche dish or 7- × 11-inch oblong glass dish with cooking spray.

3. Spread the cauliflower mixture evenly in the prepared dish. Bake, uncovered, for 40 to 45 minutes or until firm and golden. Remove from the oven and let the kugel stand a few minutes to firm up before serving.

Yield: 8 servings. Keeps 2 days in the refrigerator; reheats well. Freezes well for up to 2 months. (See Chef's Secret on page 336.)

93 calories per serving, 7.6 g carbohydrate, 3.2 g fiber, 5 g protein, 5.5 g fat (1.1 g saturated), 83 mg cholesterol, 355 mg sodium, 188 mg potassium, 1 mg iron, 35 mg calcium

Broccoli Spinach Kugel

Substitute 1 package (10 oz/300 g) frozen broccoli and 1 package (10 oz/300 g) frozen spinach for the cauliflower. (You can also make this kugel with 2 packages of either broccoli or spinach.) Defrost completely and squeeze well to remove any excess water before preparing as directed above.

Chef's Secret

• Frozen Assets: To reheat the frozen kugel, remove it from the freezer, unwrap, and transfer it to a preheated 375°F oven. Don't defrost it first or it will be too soft. Reheat, uncovered, for 20 to 25 minutes or until piping hot. If the kugel begins to brown too much, cover loosely with foil.

● EASIEST NOODLE KUGEL

With this recipe, there's no need to cook the noodles first—now that's using your noodle! If you don't feel like grating an apple, leave it out. If you have high cholesterol or diabetes, see the lighter variation.

1 pkg (10 oz/300 g) medium egg noodles
1/2 cup dried cranberries or raisins
1 large apple, peeled and grated
4 large eggs (or 2 large eggs plus
    4 egg whites)
2 Tbsp melted soft tub margarine
    or canola oil
3/4 cup nonfat yogurt or light sour cream
3/4 cup cottage cheese (nonfat or 1%)
3 to 4 Tbsp sugar (or to taste)
4 cups skim or 1% milk

Topping:

2 cups bran flakes or Special K cereal
1 Tbsp brown sugar
1/2 tsp ground cinnamon

1. Preheat the oven to 350°F. Spray a 9- × 13-inch glass baking dish with cooking spray.

2. Spread the uncooked noodles on the bottom of the baking dish. Sprinkle with the cranberries and grated apple. In a large bowl, whisk together the eggs, margarine, yogurt, cottage cheese, and sugar. Add the milk and mix well. Pour over the noodles and let stand 5 to 10 minutes.

3. For the topping, combine the bran flakes, brown sugar, and cinnamon in a re-sealable plastic bag. Crush coarsely and sprinkle over the noodle mixture.

4. Bake, uncovered, for 1 hour or until golden. Serve it warm with berries and nonfat yogurt or light sour cream.

Yield: 12 servings. Keeps for up to 2 to 3 days in the refrigerator; reheats well. Freezes well for up to 2 months.

230 calories per serving, 36.0 g carbohydrate, 2.6 g fiber, 11 g protein, 5.1 g fat (1.2 g saturated), 90 mg cholesterol, 153 mg sodium, 250 mg potassium, 3 mg iron, 147 mg calcium

Lighter Variation

• Omit the cranberries and apple and, instead of eggs, add 1 cup low-cholesterol liquid eggs. Use Splenda instead of sugar and omit the topping. One serving contains 162 calories, 20.4 g carbohydrate, 0.7 g fiber, 4.0 g fat (0.8 g saturated), and 20 mg cholesterol.

● SOY GOOD NOODLE KUGEL

This sugar-free, dairy-free noodle pudding uses soy products instead of dairy, making it an excellent non-dairy "whey" to incorporate soy into your diet. Some brands of soymilk are fortified with calcium, so check the label.

grains &
side dishes

1 pkg (10 oz/300 g) medium egg noodles
Boiling salted water
4 large eggs (or 1 cup low-cholesterol
 liquid eggs)
1^1/$_3$ cups plain soymilk
1 tub (12 oz/340 g) imitation sour cream
 such as Tofutti Sour Supreme
1 tub (8 oz/227 g) imitation plain cream
 cheese such as Tofutti
1^1/$_2$ tsp salt (or to taste)
^{1}/$_2$ tsp freshly ground black pepper
^{1}/$_2$ tsp onion powder

1. Preheat the oven to 375°F. Spray a 9- ×
13-inch glass baking dish with cooking spray.

2. Cook the noodles in boiling salted water
according to package directions. Drain and
rinse well.

3. In a large mixing bowl, blend the eggs
with soymilk, sour cream, cream cheese,
salt, pepper, and onion powder. Add the
drained noodles and mix well. Pour the
mixture into the prepared baking dish and
bake for 45 to 55 minutes or until set and
golden on top.

Yield: 12 servings. Keeps 2 to 3 days in the
refrigerator; reheats well. Freezes well for up
to 2 months.

219 calories per serving, 17.6 g carbohydrate, 1.0 g
fiber, 8 g protein, 13.4 g fat (4.1 g saturated), 90 mg
cholesterol, 634 mg sodium, 73 mg potassium, 2 mg
iron, 27 mg calcium

Variations
• Sweet Variation: Reduce the salt to ^{1}/$_2$ tsp
and omit the pepper and onion powder. Add
3 Tbsp sugar or granular Splenda and 1 tsp
ground cinnamon to the noodle mixture. If
desired, add ^{1}/$_2$ cup dried cranberries or raisins.

• Dairy Variation: Use skim or 1% milk,
light sour cream, and light cream cheese.
One serving contains 191 calories, 19.1 g
carbohydrate, 8.5 g fat (4.7 g saturated), and
114 mg calcium.

🍎 WINTER VEGETABLE LATKES

Everyone loves latkes! This luscious recipe
from Beverley Corber, of Vancouver, B.C.,
makes a big batch so it's perfect for a crowd.
While baking, it was tricky to keep track of
how many latkes the recipe actually made
because we kept tasting them to make sure
they were perfect—and they were.

2 medium sweet potatoes, peeled
2 large carrots or 12 baby carrots
2 large parsnips
2 large Idaho potatoes
^{1}/$_2$ Vidalia or sweet onion
4 to 5 green onions
^{1}/$_4$ cup fresh dillweed
6 large eggs
1 cup whole wheat flour or matzo meal
2 tsp salt
^{1}/$_2$ tsp freshly ground black pepper
^{1}/$_4$ cup grapeseed or canola oil
 (plus more as needed)

1. Peel the vegetables and cut into chunks.
In a food processor fitted with the grater,
grate the sweet potatoes, carrots, and parsnips in batches through the feed tube, using
medium pressure on the pusher. Transfer
to a large bowl and set aside. Next, grate
the potatoes in batches through the feed
tube, using medium pressure on the pusher.
Transfer to the bowl of grated vegetables.

2. Remove the grater and insert the steel
blade in the food processor. Process the

Vidalia onion, green onions, and dillweed until finely minced, about 8 to 10 seconds. Add the eggs to the processor bowl and process for 5 seconds longer. Transfer the mixture to the grated vegetables along with the flour, salt, and pepper; mix well.

3. Spray a large nonstick skillet with cooking spray. Add 2 Tbsp oil and heat over medium high heat. Using a tablespoon, drop the mixture by rounded spoonfuls into the hot oil and brown well on both sides, about 2 to 3 minutes per side. Remove the browned latkes from the pan and drain well on paper towels. Add additional oil to the pan as needed and stir the batter before cooking each new batch.

Yield: 48 latkes. Keeps for up to 2 to 3 days in the refrigerator; reheats well. Freezes well for up to 2 months.

58 calories per latke, 6.5 g carbohydrate, 1.0 g fiber, 2 g protein, 3.0 g fat (0.4 g saturated), 26 mg cholesterol, 127 mg sodium, 103 mg potassium, 0 mg iron, 12 mg calcium

Chef's Secrets

• Eggs-Actly! Instead of 6 eggs, substitute with 4 eggs and 4 egg whites or 1¼ cups liquid egg substitute.

• Grate Tips: Beverley rinses the grated potatoes and then squeezes out the excess moisture—I don't bother. She likes to use grapeseed oil as it has a high smoking point, so you can cook at higher temperatures without burning the latkes.

• Warm It Up: To keep cooked latkes warm, arrange in a single layer on a large baking sheet and place in 250°F oven. Do not cover.

• Frozen Assets: To save space when freezing or reheating latkes, stand them upright in

loaf pans. Reheat, uncovered, in a preheated 400°F oven for about 10 minutes or until crispy. There's no need to defrost them first.

❤ CORNBREAD STUFFING MOUNDS

Instead of stuffing a turkey, veal brisket, or chicken, shape this cornbread mixture into mounds. It "a-mounds" to a superb side dish! Use your food processor to speed up preparation.

Confetti Corn Muffins (page 363)
   or Cornbread (page 364)
2 Tbsp olive oil
2 medium onions, chopped
2 stalks celery, chopped
1 red pepper, seeded and chopped
3 cups chopped zucchini
   (about 1 large zucchini)
2 cloves garlic (about 2 tsp minced)
2 large eggs, lightly beaten
1 tsp salt
¼ tsp freshly ground black pepper
½ tsp dried thyme
½ cup chopped fresh parsley or 2 Tbsp dried

1. Bake the muffins or cornbread as directed. Cut into ½-inch cubes and place in a large mixing bowl.

2. Heat the oil in a large nonstick skillet on medium high. Sauté the onions, celery, red pepper, zucchini, and garlic for 6 to 8 minutes or until softened. Remove from the heat and cool slightly before adding to the cornbread; mix well. Add the eggs, salt, pepper, thyme, and parsley; mix well.

3. Preheat the oven to 375°F. Line a large baking sheet with parchment paper.

4. With an ice cream scoop or a $1/3$ cup dry measure, scoop the stuffing mixture into mounds onto the prepared baking sheet, leaving about 2 inches between each mound. Bake, uncovered, for 25 to 30 minutes or until the stuffing is golden and crusty.

Yield: 18 servings. Keeps for up to 2 days in the refrigerator; reheats well. Freezes well for up to 2 months.

133 calories per serving, 15.7 g carbohydrate, 2.7 g fiber, 4 g protein, 6.4 g fat (0.8 g saturated), 47 mg cholesterol, 332 mg sodium, 158 mg potassium, 1 mg iron, 66 mg calcium

Multi-Grain Stuffing Mounds
Instead of cornbread, substitute with 6 cups multi-grain, whole wheat, or rye bread, cut in cubes.

Chef's Secrets
• Bread-y When You Are! Make cornbread or muffins in advance and freeze until needed. You can even cut the cornbread in cubes in advance before freezing in re-sealable plastic bags.

● SPINACH AND MUSHROOM STUFFING

This versatile mixture is packed with phytonutrients, vitamins, and flavor. It makes a super stuffing for boneless chicken breasts, meat loaf, butterflied turkey breast, or salmon fillet. Leftovers make a terrific omelet filling.

1 Tbsp olive oil
1 large or 2 medium onions, chopped
$1/2$ cup seeded and chopped red pepper
$2^{1}/2$ cups coarsely chopped mushrooms
2 to 3 cloves garlic (about 2 tsp minced)

1 pkg (10 oz/300 g) frozen chopped
    spinach, thawed, and squeezed dry
    or 2 cups packed fresh baby spinach
1 tsp grated orange rind
1 Tbsp orange juice (preferably fresh)
3 Tbsp fresh chopped basil or 1 tsp dried
Salt and freshly ground black pepper

1. In a large nonstick skillet, heat the oil on medium heat. Add the onions and sauté for 4 to 5 minutes or until tender. Stir in the red pepper, mushrooms, and garlic; sauté for 5 minutes longer, stirring occasionally. If the mixture begins to stick, add a little water.

2. Stir in the spinach and cook for about 2 to 3 minutes or until most of the moisture has disappeared. Remove from heat and add the orange rind, juice, basil, salt, and pepper. Let the mixture cool before using.

Yield: 8 servings (3 to 4 Tbsp per serving). Stuffing can be made up to a day in advance and refrigerated. Freezing is not recommended.

39 calories per serving, 4.8 g carbohydrate, 1.6 g fiber, 2 g protein, 1.9 g fat (0.3 g saturated), 0 mg cholesterol, 24 mg sodium, 177 mg potassium, 1 mg iron, 43 mg calcium

Mushroom and Sun-Dried Tomato Stuffing
Instead of red pepper, substitute with sun-dried tomatoes. Omit the spinach, orange rind, and juice; substitute 1 tsp dried thyme for the basil.

Broccoli Stuffing
Instead of spinach, substitute with $1^{1}/2$ cups chopped broccoli.

breads & muffins

BREADS AND MUFFINS

LOAFING AROUND WITH BREAD MACHINES

Temperature's Rising! All ingredients, including liquids, should be at room temperature when making yeast dough in a bread machine. Measure carefully.

Bread Machine Method: Add liquids, oil, and salt to the bread machine first, then sugar (or desired sweetener), and flour(s). Add yeast last and make certain that the yeast doesn't come in direct contact with liquids or salt.

No Bread Machine Yeast? Substitute $2^{1}/4$ tsp (1 envelope) active dry yeast for 2 tsp bread machine yeast. Always check the expiry date!

Flour Power: In the USA, use bread flour for best results. In Canada, use either all-purpose or bread flour. The protein content of Canadian all-purpose flour is higher than American flour. Spelt flour works well in yeast breads, quick breads, and muffins.

Dough It Right! Check the consistency of the dough during the first few minutes of the kneading cycle. If it's too wet, add some flour. If too dry, add some water to make a soft dough. It should feel like a baby's bottom.

Weather Changes: The amount of flour needed in yeast dough varies according to the weather and humidity. Hot, humid weather requires more flour. I like my yeast dough to be slightly sticky, resulting in baked yeast products that are moist rather than dry.

How Sweet It Is: Sugar and honey add flavor to bread and enhance the browning process. If you use sugar substitutes, your bread will be lighter in color.

Easy Dough's It! Mix up the dough in the bread machine and let it rise until doubled, about 2 hours. Although you can bake bread in the bread machine, I prefer the results when it is baked in a conventional oven. Remove the dough, punch it down, and shape as directed. Place on a parchment-lined baking sheet or in a sprayed loaf pan. Cover and let rise until slightly more than doubled, about 1 hour. Bake as directed in a conventional oven.

Warming Up: Heat water to 120°F. Use either bread machine yeast or instant yeast. Then proceed as directed in any of the methods described below, using a large mixing bowl, electric mixer, or a food processor.

NO BREAD MACHINE?

Mixing Bowl Method: Combine the dry ingredients (such as yeast, flour, sugar, and salt) in a large mixing bowl (just read the ingredient list backwards). Then stir in the liquid ingredients such as water, oil, and eggs. Mix with a wooden spoon to make a soft dough, then transfer to a floured surface and knead by hand for 8 to 10 minutes, until smooth and elastic. Transfer to a large, greased bowl, cover, and let rise until the dough has slightly more than doubled. Punch down and shape as directed.

Electric Mixer Method: Use a heavy-duty standing mixer fitted with the dough hook. Add the dry ingredients (such as yeast, flour, sugar, salt) and mix on low speed for

breads &
muffins

1 to 2 minutes (just read the ingredient list backwards). Then add the liquid ingredients. Mix on low speed for 2 minutes, until combined, then on medium speed for 6 to 8 minutes, until smooth and elastic. Transfer to a large greased bowl, cover, and let rise until doubled. Punch down and shape as directed.

Processor Power: In a heavy-duty food processor fitted with the steel blade, add the dry ingredients and process for 10 seconds (just read the ingredient list backwards). Then add the liquid ingredients. Process until the dough gathers together and forms a mass around the blades, then process for 45 seconds longer, or until smooth and elastic. If the processor begins to slow down, add a little extra flour through the feed tube. The processor will return to normal speed and knead the dough perfectly. Dough should be somewhat sticky. Knead by hand on a floured surface for 1 to 2 minutes, then transfer to a greased bowl, cover, and let rise until doubled. Punch down and shape as directed.

BREAD-Y OR NOT?

The Hole Truth! To test if yeast dough has doubled in bulk before shaping it, do the finger test: poke your finger fairly deep into the dough. If the hole remains, the dough is ready to shape. If it fills in, wait a little longer and test it again.

Chilling News! After preparing yeast dough, place it in a large greased bowl, cover, and refrigerate until you have time to shape and bake it, up to 4 to 5 days. When needed, remove dough from the refrigerator and punch it down. Shape the dough, cover with a towel, and let rise until slightly more

than doubled. Then bake as directed in the middle or lower third of a preheated oven. Dough can be refrigerated at any point after mixing it up, even after you shape it.

Spray Away! Spray a little water on the oven floor before closing the door. Repeat once or twice during baking. This creates steam and produces breads with a crisp crust.

Ready or Not? When done, the baked yeast dough will be evenly browned and sound hollow when the crust is tapped lightly. If the dough is browning too quickly, cover it loosely with foil. Remove the baked bread from the pan immediately after baking and cool on a wire rack away from drafts.

Freeze with Ease: Cool bread or rolls completely after baking. Place in a heavy-duty re-sealable freezer bag, and squeeze out any excess air. Baked breads and rolls can be frozen for up to 3 months if well wrapped. One slice takes about 10 seconds on high to defrost in the microwave.

MUFFIN-FORMATION

It's in the Bag! If you use the same baking recipes (e.g., muffins, quick breads, cakes) on a regular basis, try this terrific timesaver: combine the dry ingredients in a re-sealable plastic bag. Label the bag with the recipe name and tape a copy of the recipe to the bag. Store it in a cool dry place. When needed, transfer the contents to a bowl and mix with the other ingredients. Bake and enjoy!

Going Bananas! Place ripe bananas in a re-sealable plastic bag (no peeling or mashing required—just freeze them whole). When needed, place the frozen bananas under hot water for 20 to 30 seconds. Remove the peel with a sharp paring knife, then mash. Two medium bananas makes 1 cup mashed.

Frozen Assets: Instead of fresh berries, you can use frozen ones in muffins and quick breads. No need to defrost them first.

Fruit-full Thinking: When muffins and quick breads call for chocolate chips, you can substitute with raisins or dried cranberries. Why not try fresh, frozen, or dried blueberries or cherries? Chopped apricots, pitted prunes, and/or dates are delicious, too. And chopped or sliced nuts such as almonds, walnuts, pecans, and pistachios add a satisfying crunch.

To Line or Not to Line? Baked muffins may stick to paper liners if your batter is very low in fat. It's better to forgo the liners and spray the muffin pan compartments with cooking spray if your batter contains less than 1/4 cup oil or margarine for 12 muffins.

Here's the Scoop: For even-sized muffins, use an ice cream scoop or a 1/3-cup or 1/2-cup measure, mounding the batter slightly.

Freeze with Ease: Store cooled muffins and quick breads in a re-sealable plastic bag in the freezer for up to 3 months. You can defrost them in the microwave in moments. Or add frozen muffins to the lunch box—they thaw in 20 to 30 minutes at room temperature.

Microwave Magic: If you like warm muffins, microwave on high just until heated through, about 12 to 15 seconds per muffin. If muffins are frozen, microwave on high, allowing 25 to 30 seconds per muffin.

Mini Muffins Make Super Snacks: Any of the muffin recipes can be baked in sprayed mini muffin pans at 375°F for 15 to 18 minutes. Three minis equal one regular-sized muffin.

Muffin Tops are Tip-Top: Many people like only the crusty top of the muffin. Invest in muffin-top pans, available in kitchen specialty stores. These pans produce flat, round circles that look like giant cookies with a cake-like texture. The amount of batter used for one muffin is the same amount needed to make one muffin top. Bake muffin tops for 15 minutes at 375°F.

breads & muffins

🍎 BEST BROWN BREAD

My friend Sydell Waxman made this wonderful bread when a group of authors met for a birthday lunch. The summer sun was shining, so after enjoying a wonderful lunch, we all went swimming and loafed around her pool, becoming as brown and toasted as this wonderful loaf.

1/2 cup skim milk (at room temperature)
1/2 cup water (at room temperature)
1 Tbsp soft tub margarine
   (at room temperature)
1 1/2 tsp salt
1/4 cup molasses
2 1/4 cups all-purpose flour
1 cup rye flour
1 Tbsp unsweetened cocoa powder
2 1/4 tsp bread machine yeast

1. Place all the ingredients in the baking pan of a bread machine in the order given. Make sure the yeast does not come in contact with the salt or liquids. Select the Whole Grain or Basic Bread setting. Times vary, depending on your bread machine, so check your instruction manual.

2. Using oven mitts, remove the bread immediately after the bake cycle is finished to prevent the crust from becoming soggy. Cool the bread on a rack.

Yield: One 2 lb loaf (18 servings). Freezes well for up to 3 months.

103 calories per serving, 20.9 g carbohydrate, 2.2 g fiber, 3 g protein, 1.1 g fat (0.2 g saturated), 0 mg cholesterol, 208 mg sodium, 162 mg potassium, 2 mg iron, 25 mg calcium

Chef's Secrets

• Free-Style! If you have a small bread machine, mix the dough in the bread machine and let it rise until doubled in size. Remove the dough from machine and shape into a loaf. Place seam-side down in a sprayed 9- × 5-inch loaf pan, cover and let rise. When doubled, bake in a preheated conventional oven at 375°F for 30 minutes. When the bread is done, it will sound hollow when tapped with your fingertips.

• Portion Distortion! Because breads baked in a bread machine come in various shapes, it's difficult to determine how many slices a loaf actually yields. Most machines make bread in the shape of a tall, square column. Some machines make breads that more closely resemble the traditional rectangular loaf. Sydell cuts the bread into thick slices, and then cuts each slice in half. (We all had second helpings, of course!)

• Soy Good! Soymilk can be used instead of skim milk to make this bread dairy-free.

• Crust Me! If you prefer to use water instead of milk, increase the margarine to 2 Tbsp. When bread is made with water, the crust will be thicker and crispier but it also dries out more quickly than bread made with milk, so it's best eaten the day it's made, or you can freeze it.

🍎 HIGH FIBER BREAD

Thanks to Sharon Kravetsky of Winnipeg for sharing her recipe for this tasty, fiber-packed bread. Her bread machine has a super-rapid cycle that makes bread from start to finish in 59 minutes, so she uses water that is 110°F and increases the yeast to 2 1/2 tablespoons. I prefer to mix the dough in my bread machine, then shape and bake it conventionally, so I use room temperature water and less yeast.

8 to 9 oz water (at room temperature)
1 tsp salt
1 Tbsp honey
1 Tbsp canola oil
1/4 cup rolled oats
1/2 cup ground 100% bran cereal,
   (about 1 cup whole cereal)
1 1/2 cups all-purpose flour
2 1/4 tsp bread machine yeast

1. Place all the ingredients in the baking pan of a bread machine in the order given. Select the dough cycle. If the dough seems too sticky during the kneading cycle, add 1 to 2 Tbsp additional flour. When the dough cycle is complete (it will take about 2 hours), the dough should reach to the top of the pan. If it doesn't, let the dough rise a few minutes longer in the machine.

2. Remove the dough from the machine and transfer it to a lightly floured surface. Knead for 1 to 2 minutes or until smooth and elastic. Pat out the dough into a 9- × 12-inch rectangle and then roll up into a cylinder from the longer side. Seal the ends by pressing down with the edge of your hand. Lengthen it into a long loaf by rolling it back and forth with your hands. Place seam-side down on a parchment paper-lined baking sheet, cover with a towel, and let rise for 1 to 1 1/2 hours or until slightly more than doubled.

3. Heat the oven to 375°F. Bake for 30 minutes. When the bread is done, it should sound hollow when tapped with your fingers.

Yield: 1 long loaf (about 18 slices). Freezes well for up to 3 months.

70 calories per slice, 13.9 g carbohydrate, 2.0 g fiber, 2 g protein, 1.1 g fat (0.1 g saturated), 0 mg cholesterol, 151 mg sodium, 74 mg potassium, 2 mg iron, 7 mg calcium

Chef's Secret
• Bran Power! Use a food processor or blender to grind the bran cereal to a flour-like consistency. It will yield a little more than 1/2 cup bran flour when ground.

🍎 OATS 'N HONEY BREAD

This versatile bread is a healthier alternative to most store-bought breads. Mix up the dough in a bread machine or food processor, then bake it free-form in a regular oven. Dough baby, dough!

1 cup water (at room temperature)
1 Tbsp canola oil
2 Tbsp honey
1 tsp salt
1 1/2 cups all-purpose flour
1 cup whole wheat flour
1/2 cup rolled oats
2 tsp bread machine yeast

1. Place all the ingredients in the baking pan of a bread machine in the order given. Choose the dough cycle. If the dough seems too sticky during the kneading cycle, add 1 to 2 Tbsp additional flour. When the dough cycle is complete (it will take about 2 hours), the dough should reach to the top of the pan. If it doesn't, let the dough rise a few minutes longer in the machine.

2. Remove the dough from the machine and transfer it to a lightly floured surface. Knead for 1 to 2 minutes or until smooth and elastic. Pat out the dough into a

9- × 12-inch rectangle, and then roll up into a cylinder from the longer side. Seal the ends by pressing down with the edge of your hand. Lengthen into a long loaf by rolling it back and forth with your hands. Place seam-side down on a parchment paper-lined baking sheet, cover with a towel and let rise for about 1 to 1½ hours or until it has slightly more than doubled.

3. Heat the oven to 375°F. Bake for 30 minutes or until golden brown. When the bread is done, it should sound hollow when tapped with your fingers.

Yield: 1 long loaf (about 16 slices). Freezes well for up to 3 months.

96 calories per slice, 18.6 g carbohydrate, 1.6 g fiber, 3 g protein, 1.3 g fat (0.1 g saturated), 0 mg cholesterol, 146 mg sodium, 54 mg potassium, 1 mg iron, 7 mg calcium

Food Processor Method

Heat the water to 120°F. You can use either bread machine yeast or instant yeast. Add the dry ingredients to the processor bowl first, then the wet ingredients. (Read ingredient list backwards!) First process the yeast, oats, flours, and salt on the steel blade for 10 seconds. Then add the honey, oil, and hot water. Process until the dough gathers together and forms a mass around the blade. If the motor slows down because the dough is too sticky, add 1 to 2 Tbsp additional flour. Let the machine knead dough for 45 seconds; the dough will be somewhat sticky. Turn out the dough onto a lightly floured surface and knead by hand for 1 to 2 minutes. Transfer to a large greased bowl, cover, and let rise until it has doubled in size. Shape and bake as directed.

Herbed Foccaccia

Prepare the dough as directed. In Step 2, pat the dough out into a large rectangle about ½-inch thick. Transfer to a parchment paper-lined baking sheet, cover and let rise until doubled, about 1 hour. Preheat the oven to 375°F. Poke your fingers into the surface of the dough to give it a dimpled appearance. Brush the top of the dough with 2 Tbsp olive oil. Top with 4 cloves minced garlic and 1 Tbsp each of dried rosemary and thyme. Sprinkle with ¼ cup dried onion flakes and a little Kosher salt. If desired, you can also top with thinly sliced onions, red peppers, and tomatoes, then sprinkle lightly with grated Parmesan cheese. Bake at 375°F for 25 to 30 minutes or until crisp and golden. Makes 8 servings.

🍎 PUMPERNICKEL LOAVES

Looks like bread but tastes like cake, so control yourself. Sharon Kravetsky of Winnipeg shared this yummy bread machine recipe with me. She wrote "Even though this recipe has sugar, it has healthy flours, very little fat, and no eggs. Sounds healthy to me!"

1⅔ cups warm water (about 105°F)
2 Tbsp canola oil
¼ cup granulated sugar
3 Tbsp molasses
2 tsp salt
2⅓ cups all-purpose flour
1 cup whole wheat flour
¾ cup rye flour
3 Tbsp unsweetened cocoa powder
2 tsp instant coffee granules
2 Tbsp caraway seeds
⅓ cup dried onion flakes
2 tsp bread machine yeast
1 to 2 Tbsp cornmeal
   (for dusting baking sheet)

1. Place all the ingredients except the corn-meal in the baking pan of a bread machine in the order given. Choose the dough cycle. If the dough seems too sticky during the kneading cycle, add 1 to 2 Tbsp additional flour. When the dough cycle is complete (it will take about 2 hours), the dough should reach to the top of the pan. If it doesn't, let the dough rise a few minutes longer in the machine.

2. Remove the dough from the machine and shape it into 2 round loaves. Place the loaves a few inches apart on a parchment paper-lined baking sheet that has been sprinkled lightly with cornmeal. Cover with a towel and let rise for about 1 hour or until slightly more than doubled.

3. Heat the oven to 350°F. Bake about 35 minutes; when the loaves are done, they should sound hollow when tapped with your fingers. Remove from the baking sheet and let cool on a wire rack.

Yield: 2 loaves (about 24 slices). Freezes well for up to 3 months.

108 calories per slice, 21.1 g carbohydrate, 2.4 g fiber, 3 g protein, 1.7 g fat (0.2 g saturated), 0 mg cholesterol, 196 mg sodium, 143 mg potassium, 1 mg iron, 19 mg calcium

Pumpernickel Rolls

In Step 2, shape the dough into 24 rolls. (You can also shape them into football-shaped logs, placing some fried onions in the middle of each roll.) Cover and let rise for 45 to 60 minutes. Bake at 325°F for 25 minutes.

Chef's Secrets

• Refer to Loafing Around with Bread Machines (page 341) for helpful hints on baking breads.

• Sweet Treat: Sharon uses 1/2 cup granulated sugar as her family loves sweeter bread. Everyone inhales it!

• Timing Tip: Add dried onions and caraway seeds when the machine beeps, which indicates when more ingredients can be added. The onions and seeds will retain more of their distinct flavor when added later.

• Super Bowl! Cut 1 inch off the top of the baked pumpernickel. Hollow out the inside, leaving a wall of bread about 1/2-inch thick around. Cut the bread you've removed into bite-sized cubes. Fill the hollowed-out bread with dip. Serve with crudités and bread cubes. You'll bowl them over!

🍎 WHOLE WHEAT BRAIDED CHALLAH

Maxine Wolfson of Rhode Island wrote, "All week long, I eat whole wheat bread, brown rice, wholegrain, everything. Since challah should be special and different, there had to be a way to make it healthy as well as tasty. I took a little bit from a few different recipes plus some advice from the local bakery. My version turned out to be light, delicious, and healthy. No matter how large or small we make the loaves, they disappear before the dousing of the havdallah candle."

2 cups whole wheat flour

2 1/4 cups all-purpose flour (reserve an
    additional 1/4 cup flour to use if needed)

3 Tbsp granulated sugar

1 1/2 tsp Kosher salt

6 to 8 threads saffron, crumbled (optional)

1 tsp ground cinnamon

2 Tbsp instant yeast

2 large eggs plus 1 egg white

2 Tbsp olive oil

1 1/4 to 1 1/3 cups hot water (120°F)

Glaze and Topping:

1 egg yolk plus 1 Tbsp water
    and 1 tsp granulated sugar

2 to 4 Tbsp poppy or sesame seeds

1. Sift the flours, sugar, salt, saffron, and cinnamon into a large bowl. Make a well in the center and add the yeast. In a medium bowl, whisk together the eggs, egg white, and oil. Slowly whisk in the hot water. Add to the dry ingredients and mix until the dough peels away from the sides of the bowl. If necessary, add up to 1/4 cup of the reserved all-purpose flour.

2. Turn the dough out onto an oiled surface and knead for about 5 to 7 minutes or until smooth and elastic, oiling your hands lightly for easier kneading.

3. Cover with a towel and let rise for about 1 to 1 1/2 hours in a warm place or until the dough has doubled in size. Punch down the dough, cover, and let rise for 1 hour to double in size once again.

4. Divide the dough into 3, 6, or 9 equal pieces. Roll into long strands, making the strands thicker in the middle and tapering the ends. Braid into 1 large, 2 medium or 3 small loaves. Place on an oiled or parchment paper-lined baking sheet. Cover and let rise until slightly more than double in size.

5. Preheat the oven to 375°F. In a small bowl, mix the egg yolk with water and sugar until the sugar is dissolved. Gently brush the mixture on top of the loaves; reserve any unused egg mixture. Place the loaves in the oven and bake for 20 minutes. Remove from the oven and brush with the remaining egg mixture, sprinkling with poppy or sesame seeds at this time. Continue baking for 20 to 30 minutes longer or until the loaves are evenly browned and sound hollow when tapped with your fingers.

Yield: 1 large, 2 medium, or 3 small loaves (24 slices). Freezes well for up to 3 months.

100 calories per slice, 18.6 g carbohydrate, 1.9 g fiber, 4 g protein, 1.4 g fat (0.3 g saturated), 26 mg cholesterol, 155 mg sodium, 82 mg potassium, 1 mg iron, 22 mg calcium

Bread Machine Method

1. Add the water (which should be at room temperature), olive oil, eggs, and egg white to the baking pan of a bread machine. Then add the salt, flours, sugar, saffron, cinnamon, and yeast: make sure the yeast does not come in direct contact with the salt or the liquid. Select the dough cycle. If the dough seems too sticky during the kneading cycle, add 1 to 2 Tbsp additional flour.

2. Once the bread machine has finished kneading the dough, remove it from the machine and transfer to a large greased bowl, turning the dough over so that all sides are lightly greased. Cover the bowl with a towel and let the dough rise for 1 to 1 1/2 hours or until it has doubled in size. Punch down the dough, cover, and let rise until it has

doubled once again, about 1 hour. Then continue with Steps 4 and 5 to shape, rise, and bake the loaves.

Chef's Secrets
• Machine Cuisine! You can mix up this dough effortlessly in a bread machine, but the quantity is too large to let it rise to completion, so transfer it to a greased bowl once it has completed the kneading cycle. Most loaves made in a bread machine are made with 3 cups of flour.

• Tip-Top Shape: Refer to Shaping Suggestions and Topping Tips for Whole Wheat Challah Crown on pages 350–51.

❧ WHOLE WHEAT CHALLAH CROWN

This is not your traditional challah! The balls of dough join together and form a magnificent golden crown when baked. Pass the challah around the table and let each person pull off a ball (or two)! In a bread machine, the liquid ingredients are added first, then the dry ingredients. In a food processor, the order is reversed. See Loafing Around with Bread Machines on page 341.

Dough:

1 cup water (at room temperature)
1 large egg plus 2 egg whites
   (reserve 1 egg yolk for glazing challah)
3 Tbsp canola oil
1 Tbsp granulated sugar
   plus 3 Tbsp granular Splenda
   (or 1/4 cup granulated sugar)
1 tsp salt
1 3/4 cups all-purpose flour
   (plus additional for forming the dough)

1 1/2 cups whole wheat flour
2 tsp bread machine yeast

Topping:

1 egg yolk plus 1 tsp water
   (for glazing challah)
2 to 3 Tbsp sesame or poppy seeds
   (for sprinkling on top)

Bread Machine Method

1. Place all the ingredients for the dough in the baking pan of a bread machine, beginning with the liquids. (Check the instructions in your bread machine manual.) Don't let the yeast come in direct contact with the salt or liquids. Select the dough cycle. If the dough seems too sticky during the kneading cycle, add 1 to 2 Tbsp additional flour. When the dough cycle is complete (it will take about 2 hours), the dough should reach to the top of the pan. If it doesn't, let it rise for a few minutes longer in the machine.

2. Transfer the dough to a lightly floured surface. Punch down the dough before forming into 26 golf ball-sized balls, flouring your hands occasionally for easier handling. Arrange 12 balls on a parchment paper-lined baking sheet, in a large circle; the balls should be barely touching. Fill in the circle with 5 more balls, then place 1 ball in the center of the circle. (This first layer will have 18 balls.) Top with a smaller circle of 7 balls, then place 1 ball in the center (The second layer will have 8 balls). Cover with a towel and let rise for 1 to 1 1/2 hours or until slightly more than doubled in size.

3. Preheat the oven to 375°F. Gently brush the egg yolk mixture on the challah. Sprinkle with sesame seeds. Bake for 30 to 35 minutes

or until golden brown. When it's done, the bread should sound hollow when tapped with your fingers. Keep away from drafts.

Yield: 1 challah (26 balls). Freezes well for up to 3 months.

82 calories per ball, 12.4 g carbohydrate, 1.2 g fiber, 3 g protein, 2.5 g fat (0.3 g saturated), 16 mg cholesterol, 99 mg sodium, 51 mg potassium, 1 mg iron, 8 mg calcium

Food Processor Method

1. Heat water to 120°F. Use either bread machine or instant/quick-rise yeast. Add the dry ingredients to the processor bowl first, then the wet ingredients. (Follow the order of the ingredient list backwards.) First process the yeast, flours, salt, sugar, and Splenda on the steel blade for 10 seconds. Then add the oil, egg, egg whites, and hot water; process until the dough gathers together and forms a mass around the blade. Have an extra 1/4 cup flour handy in case the motor slows down because the dough is too sticky. If it slows down, add flour, a tablespoon at a time, through the feed tube while the motor is running. When you have added enough flour, the motor will return to its normal speed. Let the bread machine knead the dough for 45 seconds; when kneaded, the dough will be somewhat sticky.

2. Transfer the dough onto a lightly floured board. Knead by hand for 1 to 2 minutes or until smooth and elastic. Transfer to a large, greased bowl. Turn the dough over so that all surfaces are lightly greased. Cover the bowl with plastic wrap and let rise in a warm place for 1 1/2 to 2 hours or until doubled. Shape and bake as directed.

Shaping Suggestions

• Mushroom-Shaped Challah: Arrange balls of dough, barely touching, in a well-sprayed 9- or 10-inch springform pan. Cover and let rise until the dough has slightly more than doubled in size. Brush with egg glaze, sprinkle with sesame seeds, and bake. Cool for 10 minutes and then carefully remove the sides of the springform pan. Remove the challah from the base and transfer to a serving platter.

• Challah Ring: Arrange the balls of dough, barely touching, in a well-sprayed 10-inch Bundt or ring-shaped pan. Cover with a towel and let rise until the dough has slightly more than doubled in size. Brush with egg glaze, sprinkle with seeds, and bake. Cool for 10 minutes before loosening the edges with a flexible spatula. Invert the pan and carefully remove the bread.

• Challah Bubble Loaves: Arrange the balls of dough, barely touching, in two well-sprayed loaf pans. Cover with a towel and let rise until the loaves are slightly more than double in size. Brush with egg glaze and sprinkle with seeds. Baking time will be 25 to 30 minutes. Cool for 10 minutes before removing from pans.

• Braided Challah: Divide the dough into 3 equal portions. Roll into 3 long strands, making the strands thicker in the middle and tapering the ends. Braid loosely and tuck the ends under. Cover with a towel and let rise until it is slightly more than double in size. Brush with egg glaze, sprinkle with seeds, and bake. (For 2 smaller braided loaves, divide the dough into 6 strands; shape into 2 smaller braids. Baking time will be 25 to 30 minutes for smaller loaves.)

breads & muffins

• Coiled Loaf (Feigel): To shape, roll the dough into a long, thin rope, tapering one end. Place on a sprayed baking sheet. Starting with the thick end, coil the rope like a snail, tucking the tapered end under. Cover with a towel, and let rise until it is slightly more than double in size. Brush with egg glaze, sprinkle with seeds, and bake.

• Challah Rolls: Divide the dough into 26 equal pieces. Roll each piece between your palms into a 6-inch strand and tie up in a knot. Cover with a towel and let rise until they are slightly more than double in size. Brush with egg glaze and sprinkle with seeds. Bake for 18 to 20 minutes.

Topping Tips

• Top with slivered almonds, pumpkin seeds, sunflower seeds, black sesame seeds, flaxseed, za'aatar, or your favorite herb mixture.

• For a magnificent presentation, sprinkle each ball with a different topping before baking.

Nutrition Notes

• Did you know that a slice of regular challah (5- × 3- × 1/2- inches) contains 287 calories, 47.8 grams carbohydrate, and 6 grams of fat? That's because it's triple the size of sliced bread.

• Forming the dough into balls helps control portion size. Now all you need to do is control your appetite!

• For a more nutritious loaf, add 2 Tbsp ground flaxseed to the dough.

• For a more festive loaf, omit the whole wheat flour and use 3 1/4 cups all-purpose flour.

❤ WHOLE WHEAT PITAS

Mix up the dough in your bread machine, then shape into pitas and bake them in your conventional oven—easy dough's it! Pitas puff up during baking, producing a pocket that is perfect for filling. Make a slit along one edge and stuff with your favorite heart-healthy fillings.

1 1/4 cups water (room temperature)
1 Tbsp canola or olive oil
1 tsp salt
1 Tbsp granulated sugar or honey
2 cups whole wheat flour
1 cup all-purpose flour
2 Tbsp ground flaxseed or wheat germ
    (optional)
2 tsp bread machine yeast
2 to 3 Tbsp cornmeal
    (for dusting the baking sheet)

1. In the order given, add the water, oil, salt, sugar, flours, flaxeed (if using), and yeast to the baking pan of a bread machine. If the dough seems too sticky during the kneading cycle, add 1 to 2 Tbsp additional all-purpose flour. When the dough cycle is complete (this will take about 2 hours), the dough should reach to the top of the pan—if it doesn't, let it rise a few minutes longer.

2. Remove the dough from the machine and transfer to a lightly floured surface. Knead for 1 to 2 minutes by hand or until the dough is smooth.

3. Divide the dough into 15 pieces and roll each piece into a flat circle about 1/4-inch thick. Cover with a towel and let rise for about 45 minutes or until nearly doubled.

breads & muffins

4. Preheat the oven to 500°F. Line a large baking sheet with parchment paper and sprinkle lightly with cornmeal.

5. Working in batches, place the pitas on the baking sheet about 3 inches apart. Bake for 6 to 8 minutes or until puffed and golden; the insides will be hollow. Remove from the baking sheet and cool on a rack.

Yield: 15 pitas. Freezes well for up to 3 months.

101 calories per pita, 19.7 g carbohydrate, 2.5 g fiber, 3 g protein, 1.4 g fat (0.1 g saturated), 0 mg cholesterol, 157 mg sodium, 80 mg potassium, 1 mg iron, 8 mg calcium

Mini Pitas
Divide the dough into 30 small pieces. Roll each piece into a thin, flat circle. Then continue with Steps 3, 4, and 5 to shape, rise, and bake the pitas. Baking time will be about 5 minutes.

♦ WHOLE WHEAT CINNAMON BUNS

You'll "dough" crazy when you taste these! Using a bread machine speeds up the prep time. You can also use a food processor, or even mix up the dough in a big bowl.

Dough:

1 cup water (at room temperature)
1 large egg plus 2 egg whites
   (reserve 1 egg yolk for glazing)
1/4 cup canola oil
3 Tbsp granulated sugar
1/2 tsp salt
1 3/4 cups all-purpose flour (plus additional
   for forming the dough)
1 1/2 cups whole wheat flour
2 tsp bread machine yeast

Filling:

2 Tbsp soft tub margarine
1/2 cup lightly packed brown sugar
   or granular Splenda
2 tsp ground cinnamon
1/2 cup raisins or chocolate chips

Bread Machine Method
1. Place the water, egg, egg whites, oil, sugar, salt, flours, and yeast in the baking pan of a bread machine. (Check instructions in your bread machine manual.) Don't let the yeast come in direct contact with the salt or liquids. Select the dough cycle. When the dough cycle is complete (it will take about 2 hours), the dough should reach top of pan. If not, let it rise a few minutes longer in the machine.

2. Transfer the dough to a lightly floured surface. Punch down the dough. Divide in half and roll out on a floured surface. Spread each piece of dough lightly with margarine, then sprinkle with brown sugar, cinnamon, and raisins. Roll up and then slice in 1/2-inch slices. Place about 2 inches apart on a parchment paper-lined baking sheet, cover with a towel, and let rise for about 1 1/2 to 2 hours or until the buns are slightly more than double in size.

3. Preheat the oven to 375°F. Combine the reserved egg yolk with 1 tsp water and gently brush on the buns. Bake for 20 to 25 minutes or until golden brown. The buns should sound hollow when tapped with your fingers.

Yield: 2 dozen. Freezes well for up to 3 months.

124 calories per bun, 20.0 g carbohydrate, 1.5 g fiber, 3 g protein, 4.0 g fat (0.5 g saturated), 18 mg cholesterol, 72 mg sodium, 92 mg potassium, 1 mg iron, 14 mg calcium

Food Processor Method

1. Heat the water to 120°F. Use either bread machine or instant/quick-rise yeast. Add the dry ingredients to the food processor bowl first, then the wet ingredients. First process the yeast, flours, salt, and sugar using the steel blade, for 10 seconds. Then add the oil, egg, egg whites, and hot water; process until the dough gathers together and forms a mass around the blade. Have an extra 1/4 cup flour handy in case the motor slows down because the dough is too sticky. If necessary, add flour, 1 Tbsp at a time, through the feed tube while the motor is running. When you have added enough flour, the motor will return to normal speed. Let the machine knead dough for 45 seconds; the dough will be somewhat sticky.

2. Turn out the dough onto a lightly floured surface. Knead by hand for 1 to 2 minutes or until smooth and elastic. Transfer to a large greased bowl, turning the dough over so that all sides are lightly greased. Cover the bowl with plastic wrap and let the dough rise for about 1 1/2 to 2 hours in a warm place until it has doubled in size. Shape and bake as directed in Steps 2 and 3 of the Bread Machine Method.

Nutrition Note

• Sweet Choice: With Splenda, one serving contains 114 calories and 17.5 g carbohydrate.

Chef's Secrets

• Bowl Me Over! Follow the Bread Machine Method, using a large bowl to mix the ingredients. Add half the flour to the liquids, and then mix well. Gradually work in the remaining flour, and then knead by hand for 8 to 10 minutes to make a soft dough. Let rise, shape, and bake as directed.

• Rise to the Occasion! Although most yeast recipes call for shaped buns or breads to rise until double in size, I usually let them rise a little longer so they will be light and airy. However, if you let them rise too much, they could collapse.

♠ APRICOT PRUNE LOAVES

Prunes are being marketed as dried plums so they will seem more elegant. No matter what they're called, you'll go plum-crazy when you taste this recipe. It came from my late friend Bev Gordon, who loved to make mini loaves to give as hostess gifts. I've modified her recipe to lower the fat and sugar. These luscious loaves are sure to become a regular at your house.

Topping:

1 Tbsp soft tub margarine or canola oil
1/4 cup lightly packed brown sugar
1/3 cup pecans or walnuts
1 tsp ground cinnamon

Batter:

1 large egg
1/4 cup canola oil
1/4 cup unsweetened applesauce
1 1/4 cups lightly packed brown sugar
2 tsp pure vanilla extract
1 1/2 cups whole wheat flour
1 cup all-purpose flour
1 Tbsp baking powder
3/4 tsp baking soda
1 tsp ground cinnamon
1/8 tsp salt
1 cup buttermilk (or 1 Tbsp lemon juice
    plus skim or soymilk to equal 1 cup)
3/4 cup dried apricots
3/4 cup pitted prunes

1. Preheat the oven to 350°F. Spray two 9- × 5-inch loaf pans with cooking spray.

2. In a food processor fitted with the steel blade, process the topping ingredients for 6 to 8 seconds or until crumbly. Transfer to a small bowl and reserve.

3. Process the egg, oil, applesauce, brown sugar, and vanilla for 2 minutes or until light in color. Add the flours, baking powder, baking soda, cinnamon, salt, and buttermilk; process with 6 to 8 quick on/off pulses, just until combined. Add the apricots and prunes and process with several more on/off pulses or until coarsely chopped. Pour the batter into the prepared loaf pans and spread evenly. Sprinkle with the reserved topping.

4. Bake for 45 to 55 minutes. The loaves should spring back when lightly pressed. Cool for 10 to 15 minutes before removing from the pans.

Yield: 2 loaves (20 to 24 slices). Freezes well for up to 3 months.

178 calories per slice, 30.5 g carbohydrate, 2.2 g fiber, 3 g protein, 5.4 g fat (0.6 g saturated), 11 mg cholesterol, 147 mg sodium, 215 mg potassium, 1 mg iron, 87 mg calcium

Mini Loaves

Pour the batter into 4 disposable loaf pans (5³/4 × 3¹/4-inches) sprayed with cooking spray. Bake for about 35 to 40 minutes. Don't remove the loaves from the pans. When cool, wrap the loaves in cellophane and tie with a ribbon. Great for gifts!

Apricot Prune Cake

Not enough loaf pans? Spread the batter in a sprayed 9- × 13-inch or 12 cup fluted baking pan and sprinkle with topping. Bake at 350°F for 45 to 55 minutes.

Apricot Prune Muffins

Bake in sprayed muffin pans at 375°F for 20 to 25 minutes.

🍎 BERRY MANGO LOAF

Barry Manilow (or Berry Mango-low!) would definitely sing "This loaf is a many-splendored thing!"

1 cup rolled oats
³/4 cup lightly packed brown sugar
¹/4 cup canola oil
1 large egg
1 tsp pure vanilla extract
³/4 cup all-purpose flour
¹/2 tsp baking soda
¹/2 tsp baking powder
¹/4 tsp salt
¹/2 cup buttermilk (or 1 Tbsp lemon juice plus skim or soymilk to make ¹/2 cup)
³/4 cup fresh blueberries
³/4 cup chopped mango mixed with 1 Tbsp flour

1. Preheat the oven to 350°F. Spray a 9- × 5-inch loaf pan with cooking spray.

2. In a food processor fitted with the steel blade, process the oats until finely ground, about 30 seconds. Transfer to a small bowl and set aside.

3. In the food processor, add the brown sugar, oil, egg, and vanilla; process for 2 minutes or until well-blended. Add the

reserved ground oats, flour, baking soda, baking powder, salt, and buttermilk. Process with several quick on/off pulses, just until combined. Add the blueberries and mango, folding them in gently with a rubber spatula. Pour the batter into the prepared loaf pan and spread evenly.

4. Bake for 50 to 55 minutes or until golden brown; the top will spring back when touched. Let cool for 10 to 15 minutes, and then remove from pan.

Yield: 1 loaf (10 to 12 slices). Freezes well for up to 3 months.

189 calories per slice, 28.6 g carbohydrate, 1.7 g fiber, 3 g protein, 7.0 g fat (0.7 g saturated), 22 mg cholesterol, 165 mg sodium, 84 mg potassium, 1 mg iron, 51 mg calcium

Chef's Secrets
• Oat Flour: Process rolled oats in your food processor to keep on hand and store in a sealed container in a cool dry place. One cup rolled oats will yield 1 cup less 2 Tbsp of oat flour.

• Oat Flour Power! Use 25% to 50% oat flour instead of whole wheat or all-purpose flour in muffins, quick breads, cakes, and cookies. Oat flour is high in soluble fiber and helps lower the glycemic index (GI) of baked goods when combined with all-purpose or whole wheat flour.

• Frozen Assets: You can make this with frozen mango chunks and frozen wild blueberries. Because frozen fruit is moister than fresh fruit, toss the frozen blueberries and mango with 2 Tbsp all-purpose or oat flour before gently folding into the batter.

🍎 BRAN-ANA SOUR CREAM LOAF

This loaf is low-fat and fiber-full. I modified my original recipe by replacing half the sugar with Splenda, substituting light sour cream for some of the bananas and increasing the amount of whole wheat flour. Everyone loves it!

1 large egg plus 2 egg whites
  (or 2 large eggs)
1/2 cup granulated sugar
1/2 cup granular Splenda
2 Tbsp canola oil
1 Tbsp molasses
1 tsp pure vanilla extract
1 cup All-Bran cereal
2 very ripe medium bananas
  (about 1 cup mashed)
1/2 cup light sour cream
2 Tbsp lemon juice (preferably fresh)
1 cup whole wheat flour
1/2 cup all-purpose flour
1/8 tsp salt
2 tsp baking powder
1/2 tsp baking soda

1. Preheat the oven to 350°F. Spray a 9- × 5-inch loaf pan with cooking spray.

2. In a food processor fitted with the steel blade (or in a large bowl and using an electric mixer), process (or beat) the egg, egg whites, sugar, Splenda, oil, molasses, and vanilla until light in color, about 1 minute. Add the bran cereal and process to mix well. Add the bananas, sour cream, and lemon juice and process just until smooth. Add the flours, salt, baking powder, and baking soda; mix just until blended. Don't overprocess or the loaf will be tough.

breads & muffins

3. Pour the batter into the prepared pan and spread evenly. Bake for 50 to 55 minutes or until golden brown. A cake tester or toothpick, when inserted in the middle, should come out clean.

Yield: 1 loaf (12 slices). Freezes well for up to 3 months.

169 calories per slice, 31.0 g carbohydrate, 3.3 g fiber, 5 g protein, 4.1 g fat (0.9 g saturated), 21 mg cholesterol, 194 mg sodium, 231 mg potassium, 2 mg iron, 96 mg calcium

Bran-ana Sour Cream Muffins
Scoop the batter into sprayed muffin pans, filling each compartment three-quarters full. You will have enough batter for about 15 muffins. Bake at 375°F for about 20 to 25 minutes. (Fill any empty compartments of muffin pans three-quarters full with water to prevent discoloration during baking.) One muffin contains 135 calories, 24.8 g carbs, 2.7 g fiber, and 3.3 g fat (0.7 g saturated).

Chef's Secret
• Going Bananas? When I have ripe bananas on hand and no time to bake, I make Banana Purée (see page 373).

Nutrition Note
• Sweet Choice! If you replace Splenda with sugar, one slice contains 197 calories and 38.3 g carbohydrate and one muffin contains 158 calories and 30.7 g carbohydrate.

● STRAWBERRY CHOCOLATE LOAF

Chocolate and strawberries team up to make this luscious, dairy-free loaf. The original recipe came from my walking buddy, cookbook author Kathy Guttman. Her recipe contained more than double the fat, so I reduced the fat and also used less sugar. For a heart-healthy treat for your sweetheart, serve this with Chocolate Dipped Strawberries (page 428).

2 large eggs (or 1 large egg
    plus 2 egg whites)
3/4 cup granulated sugar
1/3 cup canola oil
1/2 cup unsweetened applesauce
3/4 tsp pure vanilla extract
3/4 cup whole wheat flour
3/4 cup all-purpose flour
1 tsp baking powder
1/2 tsp baking soda
1 1/2 tsp ground cinnamon
1/8 tsp salt
1 1/2 cups fresh strawberries,
    hulled and sliced
1/2 cup (3 oz) coarsely chopped
    dark chocolate (or chocolate chips)

1. Preheat the oven to 350°F. Spray a 9- × 5-inch loaf pan with cooking spray.

2. In a food processor fitted with the steel blade, process the eggs, sugar, oil, applesauce, and vanilla until light in color, about 2 minutes. Add the flours, baking powder, baking soda, cinnamon, and salt; process with several quick on/off pulses, just until blended. Add the strawberries and chocolate and fold in gently with a rubber spatula.

3. Pour the batter into the prepared loaf pan and spread evenly. Bake for 50 to 55 min-

utes. When done, a cake tester or toothpick inserted into the center should come out with melted chocolate clinging to it, but no batter. Let cool for 10 minutes before removing from pan.

Yield: 1 loaf (12 slices). Freezes well for up to 3 months.

218 calories per slice, 30.6 g carbohydrate, 2.3 g fiber, 4 g protein, 10.4 g fat (2.3 g saturated), 35 mg cholesterol, 130 mg sodium, 91 mg potassium, 1 mg iron, 38 mg calcium

Strawberry Chocolate Muffins
Scoop the batter into a paper-lined or sprayed muffin pan. You'll have enough batter for 12 muffins. Bake at 350°F for 20 to 25 minutes.

Variations
• Berry Good! Frozen whole strawberries can be substituted for fresh. Thaw slightly, then slice and pat dry with paper towels. You can also substitute 1 cup pitted chopped cherries (either fresh or canned and drained).

• Go Nuts: Instead of chopped chocolate, fold in 1/2 cup chopped almonds, pecans, or walnuts.

• Go Bananas: Coarsely chopped dried banana chips are another yummy option.

• Top It Up! After spreading batter in loaf pan, sprinkle with 1 Tbsp sugar or granular Splenda mixed with 1/2 tsp ground cinnamon; bake as directed. Or drizzle the baked, cooled loaf with melted dark chocolate, making a zig-zag design.

● APPLE MUFFINS

"App-solutely" addictive! Thanks to my friend Sue Devor, former owner of Sweet Sue's Pastries in Toronto, for sharing her yummy recipe. Sue is involved in an Out of the Cold program, feeding 100 homeless people each week. I modified her recipe by lowering the fat, adding whole wheat flour, and making a lighter topping. These are moist and marvelous.

Topping:

1 Tbsp oil or melted tub margarine
2 Tbsp brown sugar
2 Tbsp flour (whole wheat or all-purpose)
1/2 tsp ground cinnamon

Batter:

3/4 cup lightly packed brown sugar
1/4 cup canola oil
1 large egg
1/2 tsp pure vanilla extract
2/3 cup whole wheat flour
2/3 cup all-purpose flour
1/2 tsp baking soda
1/2 tsp baking powder
1/4 tsp salt
1/2 cup plain nonfat yogurt, sour cream, or buttermilk
1 large or 2 small apples, peeled, cored, and chopped

1. Preheat the oven to 325°F. Line the compartments of a muffin pan with paper liners (or spray with cooking spray).

2. In a medium bowl or a food processor fitted with the steel blade, combine the ingredients for the topping. Mix until crumbly; transfer to a small bowl and set aside.

3. In a large bowl or a food processor fitted with the steel blade, combine the brown

sugar, oil, egg, and vanilla; mix well or process for 1 minute, until well blended. Combine the flours, baking soda, baking powder, and salt; add to the egg mixture along with the yogurt. Just stir together—don't beat. (Or process with quick on/off pulses, just until combined.) Stir in the apples with a rubber spatula.

4. Scoop the batter into the prepared muffin pan, filling each compartment about two-thirds full. Sprinkle evenly with reserved topping. Bake at 325°F for 25 to 30 minutes or until golden brown and the tops spring back when touched.

Yield: 12 muffins. Freezes well for up to 3 months (if you're quick enough)!

164 calories per muffin, 24.7 g carbohydrate, 1.6 g fiber, 3 g protein, 6.5 g fat (0.6 g saturated), 18 mg cholesterol, 133 mg sodium, 101 mg potassium, 1 mg iron, 44 mg calcium

APRIC-OAT ALMOND MUFFINS

"Oat cuisine" at its best! This combination of apricots and almonds make these muffins A-okay.

1/2 cup whole wheat flour
1/2 cup all-purpose flour
1 cup rolled oats
1 tsp baking powder
1/2 tsp baking soda
1 large egg (or 2 egg whites)
1/4 cup soft tub margarine or canola oil
1/2 cup lightly packed brown sugar
1 cup plain nonfat yogurt
1/2 tsp almond or pure vanilla extract
2/3 cup dried apricots, cut in small pieces
12 whole almonds

1. Preheat the oven to 400°F. Line the compartments of a muffin pan with paper liners (or spray with cooking spray).

2. In a food processor fitted with the steel blade, combine the flours, oats, baking powder, and baking soda; process for 5 seconds to combine. Add the egg, margarine, brown sugar, yogurt, and almond extract; process for 25 to 30 seconds or until smooth and blended. Stir in the apricots with a rubber spatula.

3. Scoop the batter into the prepared muffin pan, filling each compartment about two-thirds full. Top each muffin with 1 almond. Bake for 20 to 25 minutes or until the tops are golden brown and spring back when lightly touched.

Yield: 12 muffins. Freezes well for up to 3 months.

160 calories per muffin, 24.8 g carbohydrate, 2.2 g fiber, 4 g protein, 5.5 g fat (0.7 g saturated), 18 mg cholesterol, 155 mg sodium, 147 mg potassium, 1 mg iron, 77 mg calcium

Chef's Secrets
• Brown Sugar Substitute: Use 1/2 cup granulated sugar plus 1 Tbsp molasses.

• No Yogurt? Substitute 1 Tbsp lemon juice plus skim or soymilk to make 1 cup.

• Sharp Thinking! To cut up apricots easily, use scissors.

• Nuts to You! Almonds are high in protein, fiber, calcium, vitamin E, and magnesium. Ground almonds can replace part of the flour in baked goods. See Almond Meal, page 390.

◝ BERRY CHOCOLATE MUFFINS

These muffins make a terrific snack or breakfast treat. Dried cranberries come in a variety of flavors including cherry-flavored, which are tart and delicious. You can also make these muffins with dried cherries or dried blueberries, which are available at bulk food stores.

1 large egg plus 2 egg whites (or 2 large eggs)
2/3 cup granulated sugar
1/4 cup canola oil
1/2 cup unsweetened applesauce
2 Tbsp water or orange juice (preferably fresh)
3/4 tsp pure vanilla extract
1 cup whole wheat flour
1/2 cup all-purpose flour
1 tsp baking powder
1/2 tsp baking soda
11/2 tsp ground cinnamon
1/8 tsp salt
1/2 cup dried cranberries
    (or dried cherries, blueberries, or raisins)
1/2 cup chocolate chips

1. Preheat the oven to 375°F. Line the compartments of a muffin pan with paper liners (or spray with cooking spray).

2. In a food processor fitted with the steel blade, combine the egg, egg whites, sugar, oil, applesauce, water, and vanilla; process until light in color, about 2 minutes. Add the flours, baking powder, baking soda, cinnamon, and salt. Process with several quick on/off pulses, just until blended. Add the cranberries and chocolate chips; stir in gently with a rubber spatula.

3. Scoop the batter into the prepared muffin pan, filling each compartment about two-thirds full. Bake for 20 to 25 minutes or until the tops are golden brown and spring back when lightly touched. When done, a cake tester or toothpick inserted into the center will come out with melted chocolate clinging to it, but no batter.

Yield: 12 muffins. Freezes well for up to 3 months.

204 calories per muffin, 31.6 g carbohydrate, 2.4 g fiber, 4 g protein, 8.4 g fat (2.0 g saturated), 18 mg cholesterol, 133 mg sodium, 73 mg potassium, 1 mg iron, 33 mg calcium

◝ REFRIGERATOR BRAN MUFFINS

If you like freshly baked healthy muffins, this fiber-packed recipe is perfect for you! Prepare the batter and bake as few or as many muffins as you like. Refrigerate the leftover batter in an airtight container for up to 3 weeks so you can enjoy fresh-from-the-oven muffins in less time than it takes to visit the bakery. Brew a big pot of tea, use one cup in the batter and pour a cup to sip while mixing up the batter. Tea-licious!

3 cups bran buds with psyllium (or natural bran, All-Bran cereal, or bran flakes)
1/3 cup canola oil
1/3 cup unsweetened applesauce
1 cup raisins
1 cup dried cranberries
1 cup hot tea (green tea is a great choice)
2 large eggs (or 1/2 cup liquid egg substitute)
2 cups buttermilk (or 2 Tbsp lemon juice plus skim or soymilk to equal 2 cups)
1/2 cup lightly packed brown sugar
1/2 cup molasses or honey
21/2 cups whole wheat or all-purpose flour
2 tsp ground cinnamon
2 tsp baking soda
1 tsp baking powder

breads & muffins

1. Preheat the oven to 375°F. Line the compartments of muffin pan(s) with paper liners (or spray with cooking spray).

2. Combine the bran, oil, applesauce, raisins, and cranberries in a large mixing bowl. Pour the hot tea over mixture and let stand for 5 minutes. Stir in the eggs, buttermilk, brown sugar, and molasses. Add the flour, cinnamon, baking soda, and baking powder. Stir briefly, just until combined. Let the batter stand for 20 minutes.

3. Scoop the batter into the prepared muffin pan(s), filling each compartment about three-quarters full. (Refrigerate any remaining batter in an airtight container for up to 3 weeks.)

4. Bake for 20 to 22 minutes or until golden brown. Tops will spring back when lightly touched.

Yield: 24 muffins. Recipe easily doubles or triples. Freezes well for up to 3 months.

183 calories per muffin, 37.4 g carbohydrate, 7.1 g fiber, 4 g protein, 4.2 g fat (0.6 g saturated), 18 mg cholesterol, 235 mg sodium, 369 mg potassium, 3 mg iron, 71 mg calcium

Nutrition Notes
• Bran Baby, Bran! One cup of All-Bran buds with psyllium contains 39 grams of fiber whereas one cup of bran flakes contain just 7 grams. Natural wheat bran contains 28 grams of fiber and original All-Bran cereal contains 17.6 grams of fiber per cup. Although all are interchangeable in this recipe, go for the maximum amount of fiber for maximum health.

• Here's the Scoop! For even-sized muffins, use an ice cream scoop or a 1/3-cup measure, mounding the batter slightly.

• Soy Good! Replace 1/2 cup of the flour with soy flour.

🍎 BLUEBERRY BANANA OATMEAL MUFFINS

Blueberries are packed with health-protecting antioxidants and vitamins and are "berry" good for your memory—if you remember to eat them. Best of all, you never have to peel blueberries!

Topping:

1/4 cup rolled oats
2 tsp granulated sugar or granular Splenda
1/2 tsp ground cinnamon

Batter:

1/2 cup skim or 1% milk
2/3 cup rolled oats
2 large eggs (or 1 large egg
    plus 2 egg whites)
1/3 cup canola oil
2/3 cup granulated sugar
2 very ripe medium bananas
3/4 cup whole wheat flour
1/2 cup all-purpose flour
2 tsp baking powder
1/4 tsp baking soda
1/8 tsp salt
1 cup frozen or fresh blueberries
    (don't defrost if frozen)

1. Preheat the oven to 375°F. Line the compartments of a muffin pan with paper liners (or spray with cooking spray).

2. Combine the topping ingredients in a small bowl, mix well, and set aside.

breads & muffins

3. In a large bowl, combine the milk with oats. Let stand for 3 to 4 minutes or until the oats have softened.

4. In a food processor fitted with the steel blade, process the eggs, oil, and sugar for 2 minutes or until light in color. Add the bananas and process with several quick on/off pulses, until coarsely mashed but not puréed. Transfer the banana mixture to the milk-oat mixture and stir to combine. Add the flours, baking powder, baking soda, and salt to the bowl; mix just until combined. Using a rubber spatula, carefully fold in the blueberries.

5. Scoop the batter into the prepared muffin pan, filling each compartment about two-thirds full; sprinkle with the reserved topping. Bake for 25 minutes or until golden brown. When done, a cake tester or toothpick inserted into the center will come out clean.

Yield: 12 muffins. Freezes well for up to 3 months.

208 calories per muffin, 32.3 g carbohydrate, 2.5 g fiber, 4 g protein, 7.8 g fat (0.8 g saturated), 36 mg cholesterol, 150 mg sodium, 163 mg potassium, 1 mg iron, 71 mg calcium

Muffin Tops
Scoop the batter into sprayed muffin-top pans (available in kitchen specialty stores). Bake at 375°F for about 15 minutes.

Chef's Secrets
• Go Topless! Without the topping, one muffin contains 199 calories, 30.4 g carbohydrate, and 2.3 g fiber.

• Chilling News! Don't defrost frozen blueberries before folding them into cake or muffin batters. Using frozen berries helps to prevent the batter around the berries from turning blue. You'll notice that when you do add frozen blueberries, the batter gets thicker—that's because the berries are actually freezing the batter! Don't worry, they'll bake up perfectly.

🍎 BLUEBERRY MUFFIN TOPS

Muffin tops are the best part of the muffin. You can find special pans to make just the tops in kitchen specialty stores. Any muffin recipe can be adapted when using the shallower muffin-top pans; just reduce the baking time to 15 minutes. These muffin tops are tip-top!

3/4 cup granulated sugar
1/4 cup canola oil
1 large egg
1 tsp pure vanilla extract
2/3 cup whole wheat flour
2/3 cup all-purpose flour
1/2 tsp baking soda
1/2 tsp baking powder
1/8 tsp salt
1/2 cup plain nonfat yogurt
1 cup fresh or frozen blueberries
  (don't defrost if frozen)

1. Preheat the oven to 375°F. Spray each compartment of a muffin-top pan with cooking spray. You will need 2 pans.

2. In a food processor fitted with the steel blade (or in a large bowl and using an electric mixer), combine the sugar, oil, egg, and vanilla. Process (or beat) until well mixed.

3. In a small bowl, sift together the flours, baking soda, baking powder, and salt. Add to the egg mixture along with the yogurt. Process with quick on/off pulses (or stir), just until combined; don't overprocess. Using a rubber spatula, gently stir in the blueberries.

4. Scoop the batter into the prepared muffin-top pans, filling each compartment about three-quarters full. Bake for about 15 minutes or until golden brown and the tops spring back when lightly touched.

Yield: 12 muffin tops. Freezes well for up to 3 months.

156 calories per muffin top, 25.3 g carbohydrate, 1.3 g fiber, 3 g protein, 5.3 g fat (0.5 g saturated), 18 mg cholesterol, 104 mg sodium, 50 mg potassium, 1 mg iron, 33 mg calcium

Chef's Secrets
• Fill 'em Up! Instead of fresh or frozen blueberries, use dried blueberries, cranberries, raisins, chopped dried apricots, prunes, dates, or fresh mango. Chocolate chips or chopped nuts are other delicious options.

• Pan-tastic! If you don't have muffin top pans, line the compartments of a regular muffin pan with paper liners (or spray with cooking spray). Bake at 375°F for 20 to 25 minutes. Mini muffins take 15 to 18 minutes to bake.

Nutrition Notes
• So Blue-tiful! Blueberries contain the most health-protecting antioxidants of all fruits because of their high level of anthocyanin, the pigment that makes blueberries blue. Like cranberries, blueberries provide protection against bladder infections as they contain compounds that prevent bacteria from adhering to the walls of the bladder. Researchers believe that blueberries play an important role in preventing cancer, diabetes, and cardiovascular diseases. Blueberries are an excellent source of fiber, with almost 3 grams in a half-cup serving. A cup of blueberries contains about 1/3 of your daily requirement for vitamin C.

BLUEBERRY CORN MUFFINS

Berry photogenic! Are you wild about blueberries? Bite into these yummy muffins and say goodbye to the blues. Blueberries are supposed to improve your memory, so remember to add them to your shopping list!

1 cup cornmeal
1 cup whole wheat or all-purpose flour
2 tsp baking powder
3/4 tsp baking soda
1/8 tsp salt
1/2 cup plain nonfat yogurt
1/2 cup orange juice (preferably fresh)
1/4 cup canola oil
1/2 cup granulated sugar
2 large eggs (or 1 large egg
   plus 2 egg whites)
1 tsp ground cinnamon
1 cup fresh or frozen blueberries
   (don't defrost if frozen)

1. Preheat the oven to 375°F. Line the compartments of a muffin pan with paper liners (or spray with cooking spray).

2. In a food processor fitted with the steel blade (or in a large bowl and using an electric mixer), combine the cornmeal, flour, baking powder, baking soda, and salt; process until well mixed. Add the yogurt,

orange juice, oil, sugar, eggs, and cinnamon; process, using quick on/off pulses, just until smooth. Stir in the blueberries with a rubber spatula.

3. Scoop the batter into the prepared muffin pan, filling each compartment about three-quarters full. Bake for 20 to 25 minutes or until golden brown and the tops spring back when lightly touched. Cool slightly before removing from the pan.

Yield: 12 muffins. Freezes well for up to 3 months.

173 calories per muffin, 27.1 g carbohydrate, 3.4 g fiber, 4 g protein, 6.1 g fat (0.6 g saturated), 35 mg cholesterol, 206 mg sodium, 81 mg potassium, 1 mg iron, 73 mg calcium

Cranberry Orange Muffins
Instead of blueberries, substitute with frozen cranberries or dried cranberries. Instead of cinnamon, substitute with 1 tsp grated orange zest.

Chef's Secrets
• Frozen Assets: Freeze fresh unwashed blueberries in a single layer on a baking tray, and then transfer to re-sealable plastic freezer bags for up to 3 months. Keep frozen blueberries on hand so you can make these muffins at a moment's notice.

• Fresh, Frozen or Dried? Dried blueberries are also delicious in these muffins, so keep some on hand in your pantry. Dried blueberries are a better source of antioxidants than fresh or frozen. They're available dried in bulk food stores and can be stored in the pantry for several months. One-half cup of fresh or frozen blueberries is the equivalent of 1/4 cup dried blueberries.

CONFETTI CORN MUFFINS

Thanks to my mom, Belle Rykiss, for sharing her scrumptious recipe for these colorful, savory muffins. With no added sugar, these muffins are much lower in carbs and calories than most muffins and make for a healthy, diabetic-friendly snack or breakfast choice. "Nibble-it" away!

1/2 red pepper, seeded
2 green onions or 1/4 cup chopped onion
1 cup cornmeal
1/2 cup all-purpose flour
1/2 cup whole wheat flour
2 1/2 tsp baking powder
3/4 tsp baking soda
1/4 tsp red pepper flakes or cayenne
1/4 tsp salt
1/4 cup canola oil
2 large eggs (or 1/2 cup egg substitute)
1 cup buttermilk (or 1 Tbsp lemon juice plus skim or soymilk to equal 1 cup)
1/2 cup canned corn kernels, well-drained
2 Tbsp fresh dillweed or 1 tsp dried

1. Preheat the oven to 400°F. Line the compartments of a muffin pan with paper liners (or spray with cooking spray).

2. Finely chop the red pepper and green onions (either in a food processor fitted with the steel blade, using quick on/off pulses, or by hand). Place in a small bowl.

3. In a food processor fitted with the steel blade (or in a large bowl and using an electric mixer), combine the cornmeal, flours, baking powder, baking soda, red pepper flakes, and salt; process (or mix) until well mixed. Add the oil, eggs, and buttermilk; continue processing until smooth. Add the corn, dillweed, reserved red peppers, and

onions; process with quick on/off pulses, just until combined.

4. Scoop the batter into the prepared muffin pan, filling each compartment about three-quarters full. Bake for 20 to 25 minutes or until golden.

Yield: 12 muffins. Freezes well for up to 3 months.

146 calories per muffin, 19.3 g carbohydrate, 2.9 g fiber, 4 g protein, 6.0 g fat (0.6 g saturated), 36 mg cholesterol, 284 mg sodium, 93 mg potassium, 1 mg iron, 94 mg calcium

Confetti Cornbread

Spray a 9- × 5-inch loaf pan with cooking spray. Spread the batter evenly in the pan. Bake at 350°F for 45 to 55 minutes. When done, a cake tester or toothpick inserted into the center should come out clean. If using this cornbread to make Cornbread Stuffing Mounds (page 338), replace the buttermilk with the lemon juice/soymilk mixture (or chicken or vegetable broth).

Variations

• Instead of red peppers, use 1/2 cup drained and chopped bottled roasted red peppers. You can also substitute with 1/2 cup drained and chopped bottled sun-dried tomatoes.

CHOCOLATE BRAN-ANA MUFFINS —TWO WAYS!

These guilt-free, dairy-free muffins are "oat of this world!" Enjoy these fiber-packed delights instead of cereal and a banana for breakfast.

1/4 cup canola oil
1/2 cup granulated sugar
1/3 cup plus 1 Tbsp water
1 large egg (or 2 egg whites)
1 cup mashed ripe bananas
   (about 2 medium)
1 cup oat bran cereal
1/4 cup unsweetened cocoa powder
1 1/4 cups whole wheat flour
2 tsp baking powder
1/2 tsp baking soda
Dash of salt
1/2 cup chocolate chips or chopped pecans
   (optional)

1. Preheat the oven to 375°F. Line the compartments of a muffin pan with paper liners (or spray with cooking spray).

2. In a food processor fitted with the steel blade, combine the oil, sugar, water, and egg; process for 1 minute. Add the bananas and process just until blended. Add the oat bran and process 20 seconds longer to combine. Add the cocoa, flour, baking powder, baking soda, and salt; process with several quick on/off pulses, just until blended. If adding chocolate chips or pecans, fold them in with a rubber spatula.

3. Scoop the batter into the prepared muffin pan, filling each compartment three-quarters full. Bake for about 20 minutes or until a cake tester or toothpick inserted into the center of a muffin comes out clean.

Yield: 12 muffins. Freezes well for up to 3 months.

163 calories per muffin, 28.1 g carbohydrate, 3.8 g fiber, 4 g protein, 6.2 g fat (0.8 g saturated), 18 mg cholesterol, 165 mg sodium, 195 mg potassium, 1 mg iron, 60 mg calcium

Variations

• Instead of oat bran, use 1 cup natural wheat bran or lightly crushed bran flakes and increase the amount of oil to 1/3 cup. If desired, fold in 1/2 cup chopped walnuts or pecans at the end of Step 2. One muffin (without nuts) contains 163 calories, 24.8 g carbohydrate, 3.9 g fiber, and 7.3 g fat (0.8 saturated).

Nutrition Notes

• Oat bran is high in soluble fiber, making these muffins an excellent choice if you want to lower your blood cholesterol. Oat bran also helps lower the glycemic index.

• The wheat bran variation is ideal for those who want to increase their intake of insoluble fiber. Natural wheat bran is higher in fiber than bran flakes, but you can use whatever kind you have on hand.

• Dark chocolate and cocoa powder contain compounds called flavonoids that help protect against heart disease, cancer, and diabetes.

• If you add chocolate chips, one muffin contains 196 calories, 32.5 g carbohydrate, 4.2 g fiber, and 5.7 g fat (2 g saturated). We think it's worth it!

◉ CHOCOLATE ZUCCHINI WALNUT MUFFINS

Chocoholics will adore these light and luscious muffins. Whole wheat flour provides insoluble fiber but has a high glycemic index. Oats are high in soluble fiber, which helps to reduce the glycemic index of baked goods made with whole wheat or all-purpose flour. Balance is the key!

1/2 medium zucchini
  (about 1 cup chopped)
1 cup rolled oats
1/2 cup whole wheat or all-purpose flour
1 cup granulated sugar
3 Tbsp unsweetened cocoa powder
1 tsp ground cinnamon
1 tsp baking soda
1/2 tsp baking powder
1 large egg
1/4 cup orange juice (preferably fresh),
  or soy or skim milk
1/4 cup canola oil
1/2 tsp pure vanilla extract
1/2 cup chopped walnuts

1. Preheat the oven to 375°F. Spray the compartments of a muffin pan with cooking spray.

2. Grate the zucchini and set aside. (If you used the processor to grate the zucchini, wipe out the bowl with a paper towel. No washing required!)

3. Process the rolled oats, flour, sugar, cocoa, cinnamon, baking soda, and baking powder until the oats are finely ground, about 30 seconds. Add the egg, juice, oil, and vanilla. Process 15 to 20 seconds or until blended. Add the reserved zucchini and process 10 seconds longer or until combined. Add the nuts and process with several quick on/off pulses to combine.

4. Scoop the batter into the prepared muffin pan, filling each compartment three-quarters full. Bake for 20 to 25 minutes or until the tops are golden brown and spring back when lightly touched.

Yield: 12 muffins. Freezes well for up to 3 months.

197 calories per muffin, 27.6 g carbohydrate, 2.3 g fiber, 3 g protein, 9.2 g fat (0.9 g saturated), 18 mg cholesterol, 133 mg sodium, 106 mg potassium, 1 mg iron, 31 mg calcium

"Nut"-rition Notes

• "Wal-nut-rition:" Walnuts provide protein, essential fats, fiber, folate, and magnesium. When eaten as part of a healthy diet, walnuts may help reduce the risk of heart disease. Walnuts contain the highest level of Omega-3 and Omega-6 fatty acids of any nut. Evidence suggests that Omega-3s and Omega-6s help lower blood cholesterol. Walnuts also contain ellagic acid, a compound that supports the immune system and that appears to have anti-cancer properties.

• Nuts to Hunger! About 6 walnut halves, eaten 20 minutes before a meal, along with a glass of vegetable juice or a bowl of soup, can help to curb appetite.

• More "Nut"-rition! Different nuts have different benefits, so it's a good idea to eat a variety. Read Nut-rition Notes (page 204). Frequent consumption of nuts has been linked with a lower risk of heart disease. The type of fat they contain does not seem to raise heart or cancer risk. However, nuts are a concentrated source of calories, so limit yourself to a handful (about 1/4 cup)!

🍎 COTTAGE CHEESE AND DILL MUFFINS

These moist muffins have no added sugar, and both the cottage cheese and oats counteract the high glycemic index of the flours—making these muffins low glycemic, with half the carbs of most muffins. They're perfect for people with diabetes or anyone watching their carb intake. Consider using these muffins as a side dish with fish instead of potatoes or rice. Dairy dill-icious!

1/2 cup all-purpose flour
1/2 cup whole wheat flour
1 cup rolled oats
1 tsp baking powder
1/2 tsp baking soda
1/4 tsp salt
1/4 tsp freshly ground black pepper
1 cup low-fat (1%) cottage cheese
1 large egg (or 2 egg whites)
1/4 cup canola oil
    or melted soft tub margarine
1/4 cup skim milk
1/4 cup light sour cream
    or plain nonfat yogurt
2 Tbsp chopped fresh dillweed
    or 1/2 tsp dried

1. Preheat the oven to 375°F. Spray the compartments of a muffin pan with cooking spray.

2. In a large bowl, whisk together the flours, oats, baking powder, baking soda, salt, and pepper. In another bowl, combine the cottage cheese, egg, oil, milk, sour cream, and dillweed; mix well. Add the wet mixture to the flour mixture, and stir just until combined.

3. Scoop the batter into the prepared muffin pan, filling each compartment three-quarters full. Bake for 20 to 25 minutes or until the tops are golden brown and spring back when lightly touched.

Yield: 12 muffins. Freezes well for up to 3 months; reheats well.

131 calories per muffin, 13.3 g carbohydrate, 1.5 g fiber, 6 g protein, 6.3 g fat (0.9 g saturated), 20 mg cholesterol, 231 mg sodium, 92 mg potassium, 1 mg iron, 59 mg calcium

Chef's Secret

• What's Your Liner? Don't use paper liners because the muffins will stick and you'll waste some of the muffin. You'll want to savor every crumb once you taste these!

🍎 DOUBLE OATS CRANBERRY MUFFINS

Double oats, double good! This recipe is adapted from one that my mom often makes. She uses all-purpose flour because that's what she keeps on hand. She also likes to make her own yogurt as she prefers it to store-bought. I like to use whole wheat flour, store-bought yogurt, and add dried cranberries or raisins. Both versions taste terrific.

1 cup whole wheat or all-purpose flour
   (or a mixture of both)
3/4 cup rolled oats
1/4 cup oat bran cereal
11/4 tsp baking powder
1/2 tsp baking soda
1 tsp ground cinnamon
1 large egg (or 2 egg whites)
1/3 cup canola oil
1/2 cup lightly packed brown sugar
1 cup plain nonfat yogurt
1/2 cup dried cranberries or raisins

1. Preheat the oven to 400°F. Line the compartments of a muffin pan with paper liners (or spray with cooking spray).

2. In a food processor fitted with the steel blade, combine the flour, oats, oat bran, baking powder, baking soda, and cinnamon; process for 5 seconds to blend. Add the egg, oil, brown sugar, and yogurt; process for 25 to 30 seconds or until smooth and blended. Stir in the cranberries with a rubber spatula.

3. Scoop the batter into the prepared muffin pan, filling each compartment three-quarters full. Bake for 20 to 25 minutes or until the tops are golden brown and spring back when lightly touched.

Yield: 12 muffins. Freezes well for up to 3 months.

169 calories per muffin, 24.1 g carbohydrate, 2.4 g fiber, 4 g protein, 7.3 g fat (0.6 g saturated), 18 mg cholesterol, 11 mg sodium, 81 mg potassium, 1 mg iron, 79 mg calcium

Muffin Tops
Pour batter into muffin top pans (available in kitchen specialty stores). Bake at 375°F about 15 minutes.

🍎 HONEY ALMOND BRAN-ANA MUFFINS

These luscious dairy-free muffins are not too sweet and are full of fiber and flavor. The whole-grain cereal, ground almonds, and flaxseed or wheat germ, make them a great choice for a healthy breakfast or snack. Did you know that a cup of almonds contains the same amount of calcium as a cup of milk?

2 large eggs
2 Tbsp canola oil
1/2 cup honey
1 tsp pure vanilla extract
1 cup All-Bran cereal
3 very ripe medium bananas
   (about 11/2 cups mashed)
2 Tbsp water
1 cup whole wheat flour
1/2 cup finely ground almonds
   (see Almond Meal, page 390)
3 Tbsp ground flaxseed or wheat germ
2 tsp baking powder
1/2 tsp baking soda

1. Preheat the oven to 375°F. Spray the compartments of a muffin pan with cooking spray.

2. In a food processor fitted with the steel blade (or in a large bowl and using an electric mixer), combine the eggs, oil, honey, and vanilla; process for 2 minutes or until light in color. Add the bran, bananas, and water; mix well. Add the flour, ground almonds, flaxseed, baking powder, and baking soda; process just until blended.

3. Scoop the batter into the prepared muffin pan, filling each compartment three-quarters full. Bake for 20 to 25 minutes or until the tops are golden brown and spring back when lightly touched.

Yield: 12 muffins. Freezes well for up to 3 months.

185 calories per muffin, 31.1 g carbohydrate, 4.7 g fiber, 5 g protein, 6.6 g fat (0.8 g saturated), 35 mg cholesterol, 160 mg sodium, 240 mg potassium, 2 mg iron, 89 mg calcium

Honey Almond Bran-ana Loaf
Pour batter into a sprayed 9- × 5-inch loaf pan and spread evenly. Bake at 350°F for 50 to 60 minutes. When done, a cake tester or toothpick, when inserted into the center, should come out clean.

"Nut"-rition Notes
• Nuts about Almonds! Just one ounce of almonds contains half the daily requirement for vitamin E. Almonds are also a good source of magnesium, dietary fiber, and plant compounds that can help control blood cholesterol. The brown skin on almonds contains flavonoids, but almonds without the skin are also a healthy choice.

🍎 MANGO MADNESS MUFFINS

You'll go mad for these marvelous muffins. They're light as a cloud and much lower in calories and fat than commercial muffins. Absolutely addictive!

3/4 cup granulated sugar
1/4 cup canola oil
1 large egg
1/2 tsp pure vanilla extract
2/3 cup whole wheat flour
2/3 cup all-purpose flour
1/2 tsp baking soda
1/2 tsp baking powder
1/8 tsp salt
1/2 tsp ground cinnamon
1/2 cup plain nonfat yogurt or light sour cream
1 cup chopped mango mixed
   with 1 Tbsp all-purpose flour

Oatmeal Topping:

2 Tbsp rolled oats
2 tsp brown sugar

1. Preheat the oven to 350°F. Line the compartments of a muffin pan with paper liners (or spray with cooking spray).

2. In a food processor fitted with the steel blade, combine the sugar, oil, egg, and vanilla; mix well. In a small bowl, combine the flours, baking soda, baking powder, salt, and cinnamon. Add the dry ingredients to the batter along with the yogurt. Process with quick on/off pulses, just until combined. Add the mango; process with 2 or 3 quick on/off pulses, just until combined.

3. Scoop the batter into the prepared muffin pan, filling each compartment about two-thirds full. Combine the oats and brown sugar in a small bowl. Lightly sprinkle the

muffin batter with the mixture. Bake for 25 to 30 minutes or until the tops are golden brown and spring back when lightly touched.

Yield: 12 muffins. Freezes well for up to 3 months.

165 calories per muffin, 27.5 g carbohydrate, 1.4 g fiber, 3 g protein, 5.4 g fat (0.5 g saturated), 18 mg cholesterol, 105 mg sodium, 65 mg potassium, 1 mg iron, 36 mg calcium

Mini Mango Muffins
Spoon batter into sprayed mini muffin pans and sprinkle with topping. Bake at 350°F for 15 to 18 minutes. Recipe makes 3 dozen miniatures. Three minis equal 1 regular muffin. Kids love these!

❤ PUMPKIN CRANBERRY MUFFINS

These light, moist muffins are adapted from Kathy Guttman's recipe from her delightful cookbook, *Whop Biscuits and Fried Apple Pie*. If you have leftover canned pumpkin after making Pumpkin Hummus (page 49), these delicious muffins are a wonderful way to use it up.

2/3 cup granulated sugar
1/3 cup canola oil
1 large egg
3/4 cup canned pumpkin
   or Pumpkin Puree (page 309)
3/4 cup whole wheat flour
1/2 cup all-purpose flour
1 tsp baking powder
1 tsp baking soda
1/4 tsp ground cloves
1/2 tsp ground cinnamon
1/8 tsp salt
1/2 cup dried cranberries (raisins
   or chocolate chips can be substituted)
Pumpkin seeds, for garnish (optional)

1. Preheat the the oven to 350°F. Line the compartments of a muffin pan with paper liners (or spray with cooking spray).

2. In a food processor fitted with the steel blade (or in a large bowl and using an electric mixer), process (or beat) the sugar and oil until light, about 1 minute. Add the egg and pumpkin and process 30 to 45 seconds longer or until well blended. Add the flours, baking powder, baking soda, cloves, cinnamon, and salt; process just until combined. Batter will be thick. Stir in the cranberries with a rubber spatula.

3. Scoop the batter into the prepared muffin pan, filling each compartment about two-thirds full. Top the batter with a few pumpkin seeds, if using.

4. Bake for 20 to 25 minutes or until the tops are golden brown and spring back when lightly touched.

Yield: 12 muffins. Freezes well for up to 3 months.

171 calories per muffin, 26.2 g carbohydrate, 1.8 g fiber, 2 g protein, 6.9 g fat (0.6 g saturated), 18 mg cholesterol, 167 mg sodium, 76 mg potassium, 1 mg iron, 40 mg calcium

❤ SWEET POTATO BRAN MUFFINS

Caryn Bloomberg of Columbus, Ohio, modified several recipes before she came up with these moist, flour-free muffins. Their texture is similar to a souffle—they taste almost like pumpkin pie! Caryn freezes them, then heats one a day in her toaster oven because she loves them warm. These muffins make a super sugar-free snack for carb-watchers.

1 medium sweet potato
  (enough for 1 cup mashed)
1/2 cup skim milk
2 egg whites
2 Tbsp canola oil
2 1/4 cups raisin bran cereal
1 Tbsp baking powder
1/2 tsp ground cinnamon
1/8 tsp ground nutmeg
1 Tbsp granular Splenda

1. Preheat the oven to 350°F. Spray 10 compartments of a 12-compartment muffin pan with cooking spray. Fill the 2 empty compartments with water.

2. Pierce the sweet potato in several places with a sharp knife. Microwave it on high for 5 to 7 minutes or until tender. Cool slightly, then cut in half and remove the pulp; you'll need 1 cup. Discard the skin.

3. Place the sweet potato pulp in a food processor fitted with the steel blade. Add the milk, egg whites, and oil; process for 6 to 8 seconds or until combined. Add the cereal, baking powder, cinnamon, nutmeg, and Splenda; process with quick on/off pulses, just until blended.

4. Scoop the batter into the prepared muffin pan, filling each compartment about two-thirds full. Bake for 20 to 25 minutes or until the tops are golden brown and spring back when lightly touched.

Yield: 10 muffins. Freezes well for up to 1 month.

103 calories per muffin, 17.6 g carbohydrate, 2.5 g fiber, g protein, 3.2 g fat (0.3 g saturated), 0 mg cholesterol, 254 mg sodium, 191 mg potassium, 1 mg iron, 114 mg calcium

Chef's Secret
• Size Counts! Caryn makes 12 small muffins, so each one contains 86 calories, 14.6 g carbohydrate, 2.1 g fiber, 2.7 g fat (0.3 g saturated). Baking time is slightly shorter.

cakes & cookies

CAKES AND COOKIES

FAT FACTS:

Butter or Margarine? Butter and margarine contain the same number of calories (about 100 calories per tablespoon). However, soft margarine, sold in plastic tubs, is lower in saturated fat and cholesterol than butter. Food manufacturers now produce many trans-fat-free brands.

Fat Chance! For baking, I use canola oil or soft tub margarine instead of butter, unless I'm making something very decadent. I use either Becel soft tub margarine (which contains dairy ingredients), Earth Balance buttery spread (which is dairy-free), or Fleischmann's pareve soft tub margarine (which is available unsalted and is also dairy-free).

Spreading the News: Reduced fat/low-calorie margarine and butter are fine to use as spreads but don't work properly in most baking recipes because they have a high water content.

How Low Can You Go? To reduce fat, replace half the fat in your recipe with fruit purée. For example, replace 1 cup of oil with 1/2 cup oil and 1/2 cup unsweetened applesauce, Banana Purée, or Prune Purée (see Fruit Purées on this page). Mashed sweet potatoes or squash can also be used. You might be able to reduce the fat further, but with less fat, baked goods may be denser, with a rubbery texture. Some experimentation will be necessary.

FRUIT PURÉES:

Prune Purée: Combine 2 cups pitted prunes (about 3 dozen) with 1 cup hot water in a bowl. Cover and let stand for 5 minutes or until plump. Process in a food processor fitted with the steel blade until puréed, about 1 minute. Scrape down the sides of the bowl several times during processing. Transfer to a container, cover, and refrigerate up to 3 months or freeze for up to 6 months. Makes about 2 cups.

In a Jam? Prune Purée can also be used as sugar-free jam. One tablespoon contains 20 calories, 0 g fat, and 5 g carbohydrate.

Dare to Compare! One cup of Prune Purée contains 304 calories and less than 1 gram of fat. One cup of butter contains 1628 calories and 184 g fat. One cup of canola oil contains 1927 calories and 218 g fat, but it is mainly monounsaturated.

Slash the Fat! Prune Purée is excellent as a replacement for up to half the fat in chocolate cakes, brownies, muffins, and quick breads. It helps keep them moist. Don't use Prune Purée if you want to make crispy cookies—the cookies will be too soft.

Banana Purée: Purée or mash ripe bananas and use them to replace up to half the fat in cakes, muffins, and quick breads, but not in cookie batters. Whenever you have ripe bananas, freeze them whole and still in the peel. When needed, place the frozen bananas under hot running water for 20 to 30 seconds (or microwave them on high for 20 seconds), and then remove the peel with a paring knife. Two medium bananas yield about 1 cup purée.

cakes &
cookies

DAIRY SUBSTITUTES:

Dairy-Free: Instead of milk in baking recipes, use soy or rice milk—they're both dairy-free. You can also use water or juice, but you may need to add a little extra oil—about 1 tsp for each cup of liquid.

GI Go! Milk, whether regular, low-fat, or skim, has a low glycemic index (27 to 34). Soymilk, preferably calcium-fortified and reduced fat, has a slightly higher glycemic index (36 to 44). Rice milk has a high glycemic index (79) and is not a good substitute for those following a low GI diet.

No Buttermilk? Mix together equal parts of nonfat plain yogurt and skim milk or water. Or measure 1 Tbsp lemon juice or vinegar into a measuring cup, then add enough skim or 1% milk to make 1 cup.

Dairy-Free Buttermilk: Measure 1 Tbsp lemon juice or vinegar into a measuring cup then add enough soy or rice milk to make 1 cup. If possible, choose low-fat soy or rice milk. You can also use this mixture as a dairy-free substitute for yogurt in baking.

EGG SUBSTITUTES:

Eggs-actly! I use eggs enriched with Omega-3 in my baking and cooking. If you're concerned about cholesterol, you can substitute 2 egg whites for 1 large egg (or 2 large eggs plus 2 egg whites for 3 large eggs). Don't replace more than half the eggs in a recipe with only whites or the texture may be affected.

No Yolk-ing! Feed leftover egg yolks to your dog to make his or her coat shiny. Or mix yolks with water and add them to your plants to help them thrive.

Egg Replacers: Use either low-cholesterol liquid egg substitute or pasteurized liquid egg whites as a substitute for whole eggs. They come in a carton and are available in most supermarkets. For each large egg, use 3 Tbsp plus 1 tsp egg substitute (or a scant 1/4 cup).

A Matter of Flax: For each large egg, combine 1 tsp ground flaxseed with 3 Tbsp hot water. Let stand until cool and thick, about 5 minutes. Baked goods will be somewhat heavier and may require a slightly longer baking time.

Vegan Alternative: For each egg, use 1/4 cup silken tofu. Blend tofu with the liquid called for in the recipe, using a food processor or blender. The mixture should be completely smooth and creamy before adding it to your recipe. Cakes, cookies, or quick breads baked with tofu will be very moist, with a somewhat heavier texture, and they won't brown as much.

FLOUR FACTS:

Flour Power! You can replace all-purpose flour with equal amounts of all-purpose and whole wheat flours in baking recipes. For lighter cakes, you can use whole wheat pastry flour instead of all-purpose flour. However, don't use whole wheat pastry flour in yeast breads as its protein content is too low and your bread won't hold its shape.

Carb Alert! Be aware that most of the carbs in baked goods come from flour, not sugar!

Gluten-Free Flours: You can buy gluten-free flour mixes, such as Bob's Red Mill or

Arrowhead Mills, in health food stores or many large supermarkets. Tammy Friedman of Riverdale, New York, adds 1 tsp xanthan gum for each cup of gluten-free flour in cake and cookie recipes. (The xanthan gum acts as a gluten substitute.) She also makes her own gluten-free mix using 2 parts brown rice flour, 1 part sweet sorghum flour, and 1 part tapioca starch. Specialty cookbooks and the Internet offer additional suggestions for making gluten-free flour mixes.

What about Spelt? Spelt is technically a form of wheat and works well as a substitute for flour in most baking and cooking recipes. Some—but not all—people who are gluten-intolerant are able to tolerate spelt instead of regular flour.

Nuts and Oats: You can replace 25% to 50% of the flour with Almond Meal (page 390) or Oat Flour (page 355), but some experimentation may be needed. They help lower the GI of baked goods.

Soy Secrets: Soy flour works well in baked goods containing nuts, fruits, or chocolate, which camouflage its "bean-y" flavor. Soy flour lacks gluten so you can only substitute it for 25% of the flour called for in recipes. (Protein whey powder can also be used in the same ratio.) Soy flour is best when combined with other flours such as rice flour or whole wheat flour. Baked goods will brown quickly and may appear dark without being burnt. Use light-colored heavy pans and reduce the oven temperature by 25°F. Soy flour makes a crispy coating for breading and is higher in protein and fat than other flours. It should be kept refrigerated or frozen.

HOW SWEET IT IS:

Short on Sugar? Instead of 1 cup sugar, use ³/4 cup honey or maple syrup and reduce the total amount of liquid called for in the recipe by 1/4 cup. If using honey, add 1/4 tsp baking soda per cup of honey. If using maple syrup, add 1/8 tsp baking soda per cup of maple syrup. Reduce the oven temperature by 25°F to prevent over browning.

White or Brown? Brown sugar can be substituted for white sugar, but baked goods will be slightly darker in color. If using dark brown instead of light brown sugar, watch carefully to prevent baked goods from getting too brown. It may be necessary to reduce the baking time slightly, or to cover the baked goods loosely with foil to prevent overbrowning.

Got Lumps? If your brown sugar is hard and lumpy, process it in a food processor fitted with the steel blade until it's finely ground. Or place half an apple in the brown sugar container, close tightly, and refrigerate for a day or two. Discard the apple. To keep brown sugar soft, store it in a tightly closed container in the refrigerator.

Microwave Magic! Place a slice of bread or half an apple, cut-side up, on top of the hardened brown sugar in a microwaveable dish. Cover and microwave on high for 30 to 60 seconds, or until softened.

No Brown Sugar? You can use 1 cup granulated sugar plus 2 Tbsp molasses.

How Low Can You Go? You can reduce the amount of sugar called for in recipes by up to 25%. However the moisture, texture, and color of baked goods may be affected.

cakes & cookies

SUGAR SUBSTITUTES:

So Many Choices: There are many alternative sweeteners available and each person has their favorite brand. Sweeteners can be helpful for dieters or people with diabetes who want to reduce their calorie and/or carbohydrate intake.

Here's the Scoop! Artificial sweeteners don't add texture or bulk to baked goods. They work best in dishes such as fruit crisps that don't depend on sugar for color, texture, or moistness. (Cakes and cookies that are made with sugar will be higher in volume, more moist, and become golden brown.) Many artificial sweeteners break down when heated for long periods and lose their sweetness.

Sweet Choice: I prefer to use granular Splenda when I want to replace part or all of the sugar in my recipes. Granular Splenda measures exactly like sugar, and its taste is not affected by heat.

Split the Splenda! When a recipe calls for 1 cup sugar, you can use 1/2 cup granulated sugar and 1/2 cup granular Splenda. The volume may be slightly lower and the color may be paler, but cakes or cookies baked with a mix of sugar and Splenda will still taste terrific. If you substitute Splenda completely for sugar, baked goods will be drier, lower in volume, and paler in color. If you use other brands of artificial sweeteners, rather than Splenda, your recipes will probably require adjusting, so it's better to use recipes that have been developed by the manufacturer for their specific brand of artificial sweetener.

Half, Half, Half! Two fairly new products on the market are Splenda Sugar Blend for Baking and Splenda Brown Sugar Blend, which tastes delicious on your breakfast oatmeal. These products contain half the sugar, half the calories and half the carbs of regular sugar. To replace 1 cup white or brown sugar in recipes, use 1/2 cup of the desired Splenda Sugar Blend. Although these products are convenient to use, they are also more expensive than using a combination of half sugar (or brown sugar) and half granular Splenda in recipes.

What's the Difference? Granular Splenda, sold loose in the box, contains sucralose and maltodextrin, which is a bulking agent. Individual packets of Splenda contain dextrose in addition to sucralose and maltodextrin. Refer to Splenda Conversions (page 24).

A Spoonful of Sugar: One individual packet (1 g) of Splenda has the same sweetening power as 2 tsp of granular Splenda or granulated sugar. A teaspoon of granular Splenda has 2 calories per teaspoon (sugar has 16). Not all brands of sugar substitute are created equal. Some packets of sugar substitute are equivalent to 1 teaspoon of sugar, so check the label.

Timely Tip: Baking time may be shorter with Splenda than with sugar. For cakes, check 7 to 10 minutes before the completion of the recipe's expected baking time. For cookies, check 3 to 5 minutes before the completion of the recipe's expected baking time.

Puddin' on the Ritz: Sugar-free, fat-free pudding makes a delicious icing or topping for cakes and cupcakes.

cakes & cookies

DARK CHOCOLATE SECRETS:

Deep, Dark Secrets! Dark chocolate provides the highest antioxidant content of any food. The darker the chocolate, the less sugar it contains. Chocolate also makes you feel good, so what more could you ask for?

Milk or White Chocolate: Milk chocolate contains only about 1/3 the amount of antioxidants of dark chocolate, whereas white chocolate doesn't contain any antioxidants.

Super News! Dark chocolate is considered a super-food because of its extremely high antioxidant content and its heart-protecting benefits. The darker the chocolate, the higher its antioxidant content and the lower its sugar content. A one-ounce serving of dark chocolate (70% and higher) contains 2 to 3 grams of fiber, depending on the brand.

What's in Store: Choose the best quality dark chocolate you can. The terms "bittersweet" and "semi-sweet" are interchangeable, so you can use either kind. Different brands taste different, so choose the one you like the best. More expensive brands usually contain more cocoa butter, which is the main source of fat. Cocoa butter is high in stearic acid, which raises LDL (bad) cholesterol less than other fats do, and also raises HDL (good) cholesterol.

GI Go! The average glycemic index (GI) of dark chocolate is around 45. That's because the high fat content slows down the rate that the sugar is digested, so most chocolates don't have a big impact on blood sugar levels. Although chocolate sweetened with sugar substitute is lower in carbs and calories, it often has a laxative effect, so I would rather enjoy a good-quality brand of dark chocolate made with sugar, and watch my portions.

How Much Is Enough? Chocolate makes you feel good, but if you indulge too much, you will bulge—then you won't feel so good! We think an ounce a day is a good thing!

Chip Chip Hooray! In recipes that call for chocolate chips, use pure semi-sweet or dark chocolate chips, not chocolate-flavored chips.

Chocolate in Bloom: If chocolate is stored above 70°F, it will "bloom" (get white streaks). The streaks will disappear when the chocolate is melted.

Go for Cocoa: Unsweetened cocoa powder is lower in fat and calories than dark chocolate. Refer to Cooking and Baking Substitutions (page 40) for more information on how to substitute.

More Dark Secrets! Refer to Chef's Secrets: Be a Chocolate Maven (page 391), and Calling all Chocoholics (page 410).

BAKE SOMEONE HAPPY:

Pan-tastic! If you use a glass baking dish instead of a metal pan, reduce the oven temperature by 25°F. If a recipe calls for a glass baking dish, there's no need to adjust the oven temperature.

The Paper Chase: Line pans with parchment paper: it's environmentally friendly, doesn't need to be sprayed, can be reused, and is safe up to 400°F.

cakes & cookies

Silver Lining: I use foil when baking at temperatures higher than 400°F. Line baking trays and cookie sheets with foil, then spray with cooking spray.

Position Is Everything: Bake cookies, cakes and muffins on the middle rack of your oven. If baking two pans at once and they both don't fit on the same rack, place the racks so that they divide the oven space evenly into thirds. For even browning, switch (from top to bottom) and rotate the pans (from back to front) for the last few minutes of baking.

The Power of Convection: When baking on the convection cycle, reduce the temperature by 25°F. Baking time will be about 25% shorter. A recipe that takes 30 minutes conventionally will take 20 to 25 minutes on the convection cycle. A recipe that takes 1 hour conventionally will take about 45 minutes. Check for doneness and note the baking time on your recipe for future reference.

THE COOKIE MONSTER:

Flat and Crispy or Soft and Chewy? Everyone has their own personal preference as to how they like their chocolate chip cookies. I prefer flat and crispy cookies. The following tips will help you achieve the type of results you want.

"Chews" Correctly: Using more brown sugar produces softer, chewier cookies. That's because brown sugar has a higher moisture content than granular sugar, with about 1/3 more moisture. Using more white sugar produces cookies that are flatter and crispier. If you replace part of the sugar with sugar substitute, you will probably need to flatten cookies before baking to help them spread.

Flour Power! Measure flour properly, with a dip-and-sweep method. Use nested, dry measuring cups, not glass measuring cups (e.g. Pyrex), which are meant for liquids. Don't shake the dry measuring cup or bang it to level off the flour. If you do, the flour will get packed down, resulting in dry, tough cookies.

Here's the Scoop! Use a small ice-cream scoop to shape the dough — it will produce cookies that bake evenly since they are uniform in size. When placing the cookie dough on the baking sheet, leave 1 to 2 inches between each cookie since the dough will spread during baking.

The Cold Facts: If you chill your cookie dough before baking, cookies will spread more slowly during baking. That's because the oven's heat sets the cookie while it's still thick, producing a denser, chewier cookie. Warm dough spreads more quickly in the oven, producing a thinner, crispier cookie. If your cookie sheets are hot when you add the next batch of cookie batter, your cookies will spread, so for chewy cookies, use cool baking sheets.

Pan-tastic! Bake cookies on light-colored cookie sheets lined with parchment paper. Dark cookie sheets absorb more heat, causing the cookies to brown more quickly.

Bottoms Up! Cookies bake more evenly on baking sheets without sides because the heat flow over the cookies is more even. If you only have baking trays with sides and not baking sheets, turn the pan over and bake the cookies on the bottom side.

cakes & cookies

Freeze with Ease: Cookie dough can be frozen for 3 to 4 months. Once the dough is made, just shape it into cookies, then freeze until solid. Transfer the frozen cookies to freezer containers; cover and freeze. When ready to use, there's no need to defrost the cookie dough. However, baking time will be 2 or 3 minutes longer. You can take out as many cookies as you need—this helps with portion control!

APPLE-LICIOUS CAKE

This is a higher-fiber, lower-carb version of the fabulous low-fat apple cake that appears in my cookbook *Healthy Helpings* originally published as *MealLeaniYumm!* Ground almonds replace part of the flour, making it a smarter choice for those on a low GI diet. Although the fat content is slightly higher, it contains healthy monounsaturated fats from the almonds and canola oil. An apple a day will keep the doctor a-weigh!

Filling:

5 to 6 large apples, peeled, cored and
   thinly sliced
3 to 4 Tbsp brown sugar
   or granular Splenda
2 tsp ground cinnamon

Batter:

1/2 cup whole blanched almonds
   or 1/2 cup Almond Meal (page 390)
1 large egg plus 2 egg whites
   (or 2 large eggs)
3/4 cup granulated sugar
1 tsp pure vanilla extract
1/4 cup canola oil
1/2 cup unsweetened applesauce
11/4 cups whole wheat flour
2 tsp baking powder
1/2 tsp ground cinnamon

1. Preheat the oven to 350°F. Spray a 7- × 11-inch glass baking dish with cooking spray.

2. In a large bowl, combine the apples with the brown sugar and cinnamon. Mix well and set aside.

3. In a food processor fitted with the steel blade, process the whole almonds until

finely ground, about 25 to 30 seconds. Transfer the ground almonds to a bowl and set aside.

4. Add the egg, egg whites, sugar, vanilla extract, oil, and applesauce to the food processor; process for 2 minutes or until smooth and creamy. Don't insert the pusher into the feed tube while processing. Add the reserved ground almonds along with the flour, baking powder, and cinnamon; process just until combined.

5. Spread half the batter into the prepared pan. Spread the apple filling evenly over the batter. Top with the remaining batter and spread evenly. Some of the apples will peek through, but that's okay! Bake for 45 to 55 minutes or until the top is golden brown.

Yield: 12 servings. If frozen, the cake will become very moist. If you reheat it uncovered in a preheated 350°F oven for 10 minutes, it will taste just-baked!

238 calories per serving, 39.0 g carbohydrate, 4.7 g fiber, 4 g protein, 8.6 g fat (0.8 g saturated), 18 mg cholesterol, 101 mg sodium, 220 mg potassium, 1 mg iron, 79 mg calcium

Nutrition Notes
• Nut Alert! If you have nut allergies, replace the almonds with either 1/2 cup wheat germ or all-purpose flour.

• Spicy News: Recent studies have shown that as little as 1/4 tsp ground cinnamon daily may improve blood glucose control. Spice up your life with cinnamon with this sinless cake!

• GI Go! The increased soluble fiber content of this cake comes from the addition of apples and applesauce. Increasing the soluble fiber helps to reduce the GI of baked goods. Replacing part of the flour with ground almonds helps to lower the carbohydrate content.

⬤ APPLES 'N HONEY CAKE

This high, moist cake is ideal for the Jewish High Holidays because it combines three traditional ingredients—apples, carrot, and honey. A food processor helps speed up preparation. If you don't have a large food processor, see Chef's Secret on page 381. This cake is much lower in carbs than a traditional honey cake and has the added benefit of soluble fiber from the apples and carrot.

3 large eggs
  (or 2 large eggs plus 2 egg whites)
1/2 cup canola oil
1 cup honey
1/2 cup lightly packed brown sugar
2 tsp pure vanilla extract or brandy
1 1/2 cups whole wheat flour
1 3/4 cups all-purpose flour
2 tsp baking powder
1 tsp baking soda
2 tsp ground cinnamon
1/8 tsp salt
3/4 cup cold tea (green tea is a great choice)
1/4 cup orange juice (preferably fresh)
2 medium apples, peeled, cored, and grated
  (about 1 cup grated)
1 medium carrot, grated
  (about 1/2 cup grated)

1. Preheat the oven to 350°F. Spray a 12-cup fluted tube pan with cooking spray.

2. In a food processor fitted with the steel blade, process the eggs, oil, honey, brown sugar, and vanilla extract for 2 to 3 minutes

or until smooth and creamy. Don't insert the pusher into the feed tube while processing.

3. Add the flours, baking powder, baking soda, cinnamon, and salt to the processor bowl. Then add the tea and orange juice and process with several on/off pulses, just until combined. Add the grated apples and carrot and process with several quick on/off pulses, until combined.

4. Pour the batter into the prepared pan and spread evenly. Bake for 65 to 70 minutes or until a cake tester or toothpick inserted into the center of the cake comes out clean. Let cool for 15 minutes before inverting the pan and unmolding the cake onto a serving plate.

Yield: 20 servings. Freezes well for up to 3 months.

206 calories per serving, 34.8 g carbohydrate, 1.8 g fiber, 3 g protein, 6.7 g fat (0.7 g saturated), 32 mg cholesterol, 142 mg sodium, 108 mg potassium, 1 mg iron, 45 mg calcium

Chef's Secret

• Too much batter? If there's too much batter to fit in your processor, process the eggs, oil, honey, brown sugar, and vanilla extract for 2 to 3 minutes. Transfer mixture to a large mixing bowl. Add the dry ingredients, tea and orange juice to the bowl; mix just until blended. Stir in the grated apples and carrot and bake as directed.

⏺ CARROT PINEAPPLE CAKE

Bake this "grate" dairy-free cake in an oblong pan for everyday fare. For entertaining, use a fluted Bundt pan and glaze with Chocolate Glaze (page 389).

2 large eggs (or 1 large egg plus 2 whites)
1/4 cup canola oil
1 cup lightly packed brown sugar
1/2 cup granulated sugar
2 tsp pure vanilla extract
6 medium carrots, grated
    (about 3 cups grated)
1 can (8 oz/227 ml) crushed pineapple,
    drained (about 3/4 cup)
1 1/4 cups all-purpose flour
1 1/4 cups whole wheat flour
1/4 cup ground flaxseed or wheat germ
1 1/2 tsp baking powder
1 1/2 tsp baking soda
1 Tbsp ground cinnamon
1/2 tsp ground ginger
1/2 cup chopped walnuts,
    semi-sweet chocolate chips, raisins,
    or dried cranberries

1. Preheat the oven to 350°F. Spray a 12-cup fluted tube pan or 9- × 13-inch baking pan with cooking spray.

2. Combine the eggs, oil, sugars, and vanilla extract in a food processor fitted with the steel blade. Process until smooth and creamy, about 2 to 3 minutes. Don't insert the pusher into the feed tube while processing. Add the grated carrots and pineapple and mix until combined, about 10 seconds. Add the flours, flaxseed, baking powder, baking soda, cinnamon, and ginger. Using quick on/off pulses, process just until combined. Add the nuts, and process with several more quick on/off pulses.

3. Pour the batter into the prepared pan and spread evenly. Bake for 55 to 60 minutes or until golden brown and a cake tester or toothpick inserted into the center of the cake comes out clean.

4. If using a Bundt pan, cool for 15 minutes before carefully inverting the pan and unmolding the cake onto a serving plate. If using a 9- × 13-inch pan, serve the cake directly from the pan.

Yield: 18 servings. Freezes well for up to 3 months.

207 calories per serving, 34.7 g carbohydrate, 2.8 g fiber, 4 g protein, 6.6 g fat (0.6 g saturated), 24 mg cholesterol, 172 mg sodium, 181 mg potassium, 2 mg iron, 58 mg calcium

Carrot Zucchini Cake

Use a combination of grated carrots and zucchini to equal 3 cups.

Carrot Cupcakes

Prepare batter and bake in sprayed muffin pans at 375°F for 20 to 25 minutes. Makes 16 to 18 cupcakes. They're delicious topped with a swirl of Cream Cheese Frosting (page 389).

DOUBLE CHOCOLATE ZUCCHINI LOAF

My amazing assistant Elaine Kaplan, who is a chocoholic, adores this moist, decadent-tasting loaf. You'll never know it contains zucchini. For special occasions, top it with Chocolate Glaze (page 389).

1 small zucchini (do not peel)
3/4 cup whole wheat flour
1/2 cup all-purpose flour
1 cup granulated sugar
2 Tbsp unsweetened cocoa powder
1 tsp ground cinnamon
1 tsp baking soda
1/2 tsp baking powder
1 large egg
1/4 cup orange juice (preferably fresh)
1/4 cup canola oil
1 tsp pure vanilla extract
1/3 to 1/2 cup semi-sweet chocolate chips

1. Preheat the oven to 350°F. Spray a 9- × 5-inch loaf pan with cooking spray. Grate zucchini; you should have about 1 cup lightly packed. Set aside.

2. In a food processor fitted with the steel blade, process flours, sugar, cocoa, cinnamon, baking soda, and baking powder until blended, about 10 seconds. Add the egg, orange juice, oil, and vanilla extract. Process 15 to 20 seconds or until blended. Add the reserved zucchini; process 10 seconds longer or until combined. Stir in chocolate chips with a rubber spatula. Pour batter into prepared pan and spread evenly.

3. Bake for 45 to 50 minutes. Top will spring back when lightly touched.

Yield: 12 servings. Freezes well for up to 3 months.

186 calories per serving, 30.7 g carbohydrate, 1.9 g fiber, 3 g protein, 6.8 g fat (1.4 g saturated), 18 mg cholesterol, 133 mg sodium, 110 mg potassium, 1 mg iron, 24 mg calcium

CHOCO-LATTE CAKE

Perk It Up! This decadent chocolate cake is made with a double hit of chocolate plus equal parts coffee and milk. It's a variation of my mom's delicious chocolate cake, updated for today's healthier kitchen. For additional decadence, frost it with Quick Chocolate Frosting (page 389).

2 oz (60 g) dark chocolate
   (bittersweet or semi-sweet)
1/2 cup soft tub margarine
1 cup granulated sugar
2 large eggs
1 tsp pure vanilla extract
1/2 cup skim or soymilk
1/2 cup brewed coffee or espresso
   (or 1/2 tsp instant coffee or espresso
   dissolved in 1/2 cup boiling water)
1 1/2 cups all-purpose flour (you can use
   half whole wheat pastry flour)
2 Tbsp unsweetened cocoa powder
1 tsp ground cinnamon
2 tsp baking powder
1/4 tsp baking soda

1. Preheat the oven to 350°F. Spray a
7- × 11-inch glass baking dish with cooking
spray.

2. Melt chocolate (about 2 minutes on medium, uncovered, in the microwave). Cool
slightly.

3. In a food processor fitted with the steel
blade, process margarine, sugar, eggs, and vanilla extract for 2 to 3 minutes or until smooth
and creamy. Don't insert the pusher into the
feed tube while processing. Add the reserved
melted chocolate, milk, and coffee; process
10 to 12 seconds longer. Add the flour, cocoa,
cinnamon, baking powder, and baking soda.
Process with several quick on/off pulses, just
until combined. Don't overprocess.

4. Pour batter into prepared dish and spread
evenly. Bake for 40 to 45 minutes or until
a cake tester or toothpick inserted into the
center of the cake comes out clean.

Yield: 12 servings. Freezes well for up to 3
months.

232 calories per serving (without frosting), 33.1 g
carbohydrate, 1.1 g fiber, 4 g protein, 10.1 g fat (2.3 g
saturated), 35 mg cholesterol, 227 mg sodium, 87 mg
potassium, 1 mg iron, 71 mg calcium

Chocolate Cupcakes

Bake in sprayed muffin pans at 375°F for 20
to 25 minutes. Makes 12 cupcakes.

Decadent Variation

• With frosting, one serving contains 291
calories, 43.6 g carbohydrate, and 12.1 g fat
(2.6 g saturated).

Lighter Variation

• Use 1/4 cup soft tub margarine and 1/4 cup
unsweetened applesauce or Prune Purée (page
373). Instead of 2 eggs, use 1 egg plus 2 egg
whites. One serving contains 197 calories, 33.7 g
carbohydrate, and 5.9 g fat (1.6 g saturated).

● COFFEE STREUSEL CAKE

This sinfully good-tasting cake is made with
ingredients that make it glycemic-index
friendly, including rolled oats, yogurt, applesauce, and cinnamon. Chocolate lovers will
love the variation on page 384. I believe
that food that's good for you should taste
good—and this cake tastes terrific!

Streusel Mixture:

1/4 cup flour (whole wheat or all-purpose)
1/4 cup lightly packed brown sugar
1/2 cup rolled oats
1/4 cup chopped pecans, walnuts, or almonds
2 Tbsp toasted wheat germ (optional)
1 Tbsp unsweetened cocoa powder
2 tsp ground cinnamon
2 Tbsp canola oil

Batter:

1 cup rolled oats
1 cup nonfat plain yogurt
   (or 1 Tbsp lemon juice plus soymilk
   or skim milk to equal 1 cup)
1/2 cup unsweetened applesauce
3 large eggs (or 2 large eggs
   plus 2 egg whites)
1 1/4 cups granulated sugar
1/3 cup canola oil or soft tub margarine
2 tsp pure vanilla extract
1 cup whole wheat flour
1 cup all-purpose flour
1 1/2 tsp baking powder
1 1/2 tsp baking soda

1. Preheat the oven to 350°F. Spray a 12-cup fluted tube pan with cooking spray.

2. In a medium bowl, combine ingredients for streusel mixture and mix until crumbly. Set aside.

3. In another bowl, mix together oats, yogurt, and applesauce. Let stand for 3 or 4 minutes.

4. In a food processor fitted with the steel blade, process eggs, sugar, oil, and vanilla extract until smooth and creamy, about 2 to 3 minutes. Don't insert the pusher into the feed tube while processing. Add the reserved oats mixture, and process until blended. Add the flours, baking powder, and baking soda. Process with several quick on/off pulses, just until combined.

5. Pour half the batter into the prepared pan. Sprinkle with half the streusel mixture. Repeat with the remaining batter and streusel mixture. Bake for 50 to 55 minutes or until a cake tester or toothpick inserted into the center of the cake comes out clean. Let cool for 15 minutes before carefully inverting the pan to unmold the cake onto a serving plate. If desired, carefully turn the cake over so that the filling is on top.

Yield: 20 servings. Freezes well for up to 3 months.

205 calories per serving, 31.2 g carbohydrate, 2.2 g fiber, 4 g protein, 7.7 g fat (0.7 g saturated), 32 mg cholesterol, 150 mg sodium, 70 mg potassium, 1 mg iron, 53 mg calcium

Chocolate Chip Coffee Cake

At the end of Step 4, fold 1/2 cup of semi-sweet chocolate chips or grated dark chocolate into the batter. One serving contains 225 calories, 33.8 g carbohydrate, 2.4 fiber, and 8.9 g fat (1.5 g saturated).

🍎 HIDDEN TREASURE LEMON DELIGHTS

I developed this recipe for my neighbor Lesley Walsh, when she needed a light and elegant dessert for her guests. Everyone loved it. Lesley used canned lemon pie filling and real whipped cream, but this lighter version works very well. These baby cakes are almost like mini trifles.

Lemon Filling/Topping:

1 pkg (7 1/2 oz/212 g) lemon pie filling
   (the kind you cook)
1 cup frozen light whipped topping, thawed
   or Almost Whipped Cream (page 410)
1 cup fresh or frozen blueberries

cakes & cookies

Batter:

1 cup all-purpose flour
2/3 cup whole wheat flour
1 1/2 tsp baking powder
1/2 tsp baking soda
1 Tbsp grated lemon rind
2 large eggs
3/4 cup granulated sugar
3 Tbsp canola oil
1/2 cup unsweetened applesauce
1/4 cup lemon juice (preferably fresh)
1/2 cup nonfat plain yogurt

1. Prepare the pie filling according to package directions; cool completely. (The pie filling can be made up to a day in advance and refrigerated.) Reserve 1 cup lemon filling—this will be the "hidden treasure" inside the cupcakes. Fold the remaining lemon filling into the whipped topping; chill in the refrigerator until serving time. (This lemon cream mixture will be used to garnish the baked cupcakes.)

2. Preheat the oven to 350°F. Spray the compartments of a muffin pan with cooking spray.

3. In a large bowl, mix together the flours, baking powder, baking soda, and lemon rind.

4. In a food processor fitted with the steel blade, process the eggs, sugar, oil, and applesauce until smooth and creamy, about 2 to 3 minutes. Don't insert the pusher into the feed tube while processing. Add the flour mixture, lemon juice, and yogurt and mix together with quick on/off pulses, just until combined.

5. Spoon half of batter into prepared muffin pan compartments. Top each one with a tablespoon of reserved lemon filling. (Don't let filling touch edges of pan.) Add the remaining batter, covering lemon filling completely. Bake for 25 minutes. Cool 10 to 15 minutes, then remove carefully from pan.

6. At serving time, garnish each cupcake with a dollop of chilled lemon cream and a few blueberries.

Yield: 12 servings. Refrigerate leftovers (if you have any!) or freeze them for up to 2 months.

247 calories per serving, 44.1 g carbohydrate, 1.7 g fiber, 5 g protein, 6.5 g fat (1.5 g saturated), 59 mg cholesterol, 155 mg sodium, 96 mg potassium, 1 mg iron, 61 mg calcium

◖ MANGO CAKE

Mangoes are so juicy some people think you should eat them in the bathtub! Frozen mangoes are convenient when fresh mangoes aren't easily available. Did you know that you can chop frozen mango chunks in the food processor even while they are frozen? Now that's cool!

1 large mango, peeled and pitted,
    or 1 cup chopped frozen mango
1/4 cup canola oil
3/4 cup granulated sugar
2 large eggs (or 1 large egg
    plus 2 egg whites)
1 tsp pure vanilla extract
1 cup whole wheat flour
1 cup all-purpose flour
1 tsp baking powder
1 tsp baking soda
1/2 cup mango juice or nectar
    (or orange juice, preferably fresh)
1 Tbsp lemon juice (preferably fresh)
1/2 cup chopped pecans, if desired

1. Preheat the oven to 350°F. Spray a 7- × 11-inch glass baking dish with cooking spray.

2. In a food processor fitted with the steel blade, process the mango with several quick on/off pulses, until coarsely chopped. Remove from the bowl and set aside. You should have about 1 cup packed chopped mango.

3. Process the oil, sugar, eggs, and vanilla until smooth and creamy, about 2 minutes. Don't insert the pusher into the feed tube while processing. Add the reserved mango and process for 8 to 10 seconds, just until combined. Add the flours, baking powder, baking soda, mango juice, and lemon juice. Process with quick on/off pulses, just until blended. Add the pecans and process with 2 or 3 quick on/off pulses to combine.

4. Spread the batter evenly in the prepared pan. Bake for 40 to 45 minutes or until golden brown and the cake tests done.

Yield: 15 servings. Freezes well for up to 3 months.

154 calories per serving, 25.9 g carbohydrate, 1.5 g fiber, 3 g protein, 4.7 g fat (0.5 g saturated), 28 mg cholesterol, 129 mg sodium, 74 mg potassium, 1 mg iron, 28 mg calcium

Chocolate Chip Mango Cake
Add ³/4 cup semi-sweet chocolate chips to batter at the end of Step 3. One serving contains 194 calories, 31.2 g carbohydrate, 1.9 g fiber, and 7.2 g fat (2.0 g saturated).

Mango Layer Cake
Bake cake in two layer pans. Cool completely. Spread lightly with a double recipe of Cream Cheese Frosting (page 389) or light whipped dessert topping between the layers and on top of the cake. Garnish with chopped mango and shredded unsweetened coconut.

Chef's Secrets
• Shopping Secrets: When selecting mangoes, use the sniff-and-squeeze (but not squish!) test. They should smell aromatic and sweet, and the flesh should yield when gently pressed. Mangoes can be green, red, orange, or pinkish gold, and can be round, oval, or kidney-shaped.

• Ripe for the Eating: To ripen, put mangoes in a paper bag and leave them on your counter for a day or two until ripe. Adding an apple or banana to the bag will speed up the ripening process. Ripe mangoes will keep in the refrigerator for up to 5 or 6 days.

• Nice Dice! To dice mango, use a sharp knife and cut down one side, feeling for the pit with your knife. Repeat on the other side. Discard the pit. You will have 2 large halves. Score the flesh of each half by cutting parallel lines from top to bottom, first lengthways and then crossways, ¹/2-inch apart, without cutting through the peel. Turn the mango halves inside out so that the peel is on the inside and the cut mango is almost released. Carefully cut the flesh away from the skin. One mango yields about 1 cup diced.

• Frozen Assets: Mangoes freeze very well, so buy extras when they are in season, cut in slices or chunks, and freeze for later use. Add mango to cereals, smoothies, salsas, salads, yogurt, ice cream, and even stir-fries!

Nutrition Notes

• Mangoes are rich in vitamins A, C, and E, beta carotene, potassium, and fiber. One mango contains 135 calories, 35.2 g carbohydrate, 3.7 g fiber, and 0.6 g fat.

• Go, Man-go! Mango is packed with antioxidants and nutrients and has an average glycemic index of 51.

🍑 PLUM CRAZY CAKE

You'll go plum-crazy over this delectable, reduced-carbohydrate cake. It's a delightful dessert for people with diabetes or anyone who is watching their carbs. It's hard to believe it's made with only 1 cup of flour and very little sugar. Even if you make it with all sugar, the carbohydrate content is still quite low. Serve it for breakfast or enjoy it with guests. Little Jack Horner would say "Stick in your thumb and pull out a plum—yum!"

Fruit Mixture:

12 firm, ripe plums, pitted and sliced
   (do not peel)
2 Tbsp granular Splenda or granulated sugar
1 tsp ground cinnamon

Batter:

1/2 cup canola oil
1/2 cup unsweetened applesauce
1/4 cup granulated sugar
   plus 1/4 cup granular Splenda
   (or use 1/2 cup granulated sugar)
1 tsp pure vanilla extract
2 large eggs
   (or 1 large egg plus 2 egg whites)
1 cup whole wheat flour
1 tsp baking powder
1/4 tsp salt

1. Preheat the oven to 350°F. Spray a 9- × 13-inch glass baking pan with cooking spray.

2. Spread the plums in a single layer in the prepared baking pan. In a small bowl, mix together the Splenda and cinnamon; sprinkle over the plums.

3. In a food processor fitted with the steel blade, combine the oil, applesauce, sugar, Splenda, vanilla extract, and eggs. Process for 1 minute or until smooth and creamy. Don't insert the pusher into the feed tube while processing. Add the flour, baking powder, and salt; process with 3 or 4 quick on/off pulses, just until blended. Pour the batter evenly over the plums.

4. Bake for 45 to 55 minutes or until golden.

Yield: 15 servings. Don't freeze: the cake will get soggy if it is frozen and then thawed.

147 calories per serving, 16.9 g carbohydrate, 1.8 g fiber, 2 g protein, 8.4 g fat (0.8 g saturated), 28 mg cholesterol, 81 mg sodium, 131 mg potassium, 1 mg iron, 28 mg calcium

Variations

• Instead of plums, substitute with 3 lb (1.4 kg) nectarines, peaches, apricots, pears, or apples.

Nutrition Note

• Sweet Choice: If made completely with sugar instead of Splenda, one serving contains 164 calories and 21.3 g carbohydrate.

◔ ZUCCHINI CAKE WITH ALMONDS AND RAISINS

This large, moist cake contains whole wheat flour, vegetables, fruit, and nuts, with half the sugar of a traditional zucchini cake. Zucchini is a terrific source of lutein, which helps prevent macular degeneration. You'll see how quickly this cake disappears.

1 cup all-purpose flour
1 cup plus 2 Tbsp whole wheat flour
2 tsp baking powder
1 tsp baking soda
1/8 tsp salt
1 Tbsp ground cinnamon
1 unpeeled medium zucchini,
   ends trimmed (about 2 cups grated)
2 large eggs plus 2 egg whites
   (or 3 large eggs)
1 cup lightly packed brown sugar
1/2 cup canola oil
1/2 cup unsweetened applesauce
2 tsp pure vanilla extract
2 Tbsp lemon or orange juice
   (preferably fresh)
1/2 cup slivered almonds
1/2 cup raisins

1. Preheat the oven to 350°F. Spray a 12-cup fluted tube pan with cooking spray.

2. In a food processor fitted with the steel blade, process the flours, baking powder, baking soda, salt, and cinnamon for 10 seconds or until blended. Transfer to a bowl.

3. Grate the zucchini; you should end up with about 2 cups, loosely packed.

4. In the food processor, process the eggs, brown sugar, oil, applesauce, and vanilla extract for 2 minutes or until smooth and creamy. Don't insert the pusher into the feed tube while processing. Add the grated zucchini and lemon juice; process 10 seconds longer. Add the reserved dry ingredients; process with several quick on/off pulses, just until blended. Add the almonds and raisins; process with 2 or 3 quick on/off pulses to combine. Pour the batter into the prepared tube pan and spread evenly.

5. Bake for 50 to 60 minutes or until a cake tester or toothpick inserted into the center comes out clean. Cool the cake in the pan for 15 minutes before inverting onto a cake plate and removing it from the pan.

Yield: 18 servings. Freezes well for up to 3 months.

200 calories per serving, 28.4 g carbohydrate, 2.1 g fiber, 4 g protein, 8.6 g fat (0.8 g saturated), 24 mg cholesterol, 162 mg sodium, 192 mg potassium, 1 mg iron, 64 mg calcium

Variation
• Substitute walnuts for almonds and dried cranberries or semi-sweet chocolate chips for raisins.

Chef's Secrets
• Company's Coming! Sift 2 Tbsp icing sugar on top of the cooled cake. Alternatively, prepare Cream Cheese Frosting (page 389), adding a little extra lemon juice until it reaches the consistency of a glaze. Drizzle the glaze over the cooled cake—your guests will go "glazy" over it!

cakes & cookies

♥ CHOCOLATE GLAZE

This makes enough glaze for a large Bundt cake and is also excellent drizzled over brownies or cupcakes.

1/2 cup semi-sweet chocolate chips
   (or 3 oz/85 g dark chocolate, chopped)
3 Tbsp water or brewed coffee
1 tsp canola oil
1 tsp honey
1/2 tsp pure vanilla extract

1. Combine the chocolate, water, oil, and honey in a 2-cup glass measuring cup. Microwave, uncovered, on medium for 1 minute. Stir well. Microwave for 30 to 45 seconds longer, then stir again until smooth. Stir in the vanilla extract.

2. Drizzle the glaze on top of your favorite cake, allowing some of the glaze to drip down the sides.

Yield: About 3/4 cup (12 servings). The glaze may crack if frozen.

39 calories per serving, 4.9 g carbohydrate, 0.4 g fiber, 0 g protein, 2.5 g fat (1.3 g saturated), 0 mg cholesterol, 1 mg sodium, 26 mg potassium, 0 mg iron, 2 mg calcium

♥ QUICK CHOCOLATE FROSTING

This frosting is delicious on your favorite chocolate cake or brownies—save it for special occasions.

1 cup icing sugar
2 Tbsp soft tub margarine
2 Tbsp unsweetened cocoa powder
2 Tbsp brewed coffee, milk, or soymilk
1/2 tsp pure vanilla extract

1. In a food processor fitted with the steel blade, process all ingredients for 10 to 12 seconds. Scrape down the sides of the bowl as needed. Spread on cooled cake.

Yield: 12 servings (for a 7- × 11-inch cake). Freezes well for up to 3 months.

58 calories per serving (1/12th of the recipe), 10.5 g carbohydrate, 0.3 g fiber, 0 g protein, 2.0 g fat (0.3 g saturated), 0 mg cholesterol, 26 mg sodium, 16 mg potassium, 0 mg iron, 2 mg calcium

♥ CREAM CHEESE FROSTING

This creamy frosting is delicious on Mango Cake (page 385) or swirled onto Carrot Cupcakes (page 382). To turn it into a delicious glaze, add a little extra lemon juice or milk and drizzle it over your favorite Bundt cake. The Dairy-Free Variation is on page 390.

1 cup light cream cheese or
   Homemade Cottage Cheese
   (page 177)
1/2 cup icing sugar
1 tsp lemon juice (preferably fresh)
   or mango juice

1. Combine all ingredients in a food processor fitted with the steel blade. Process until smooth, about 10 to 12 seconds.

Yield: 1 1/4 cups frosting. For a 7- × 11-inch cake or two 9-inch layers. Freezes well for up to 3 months. Recipe doubles easily.

39 calories per Tbsp, 3.8 g carbohydrate, 0 g fiber, 1 g protein, 2.1 g fat (1.3 g saturated), 7 mg cholesterol, 36 mg sodium, 20 mg potassium, 0 mg iron, 13 mg calcium

cakes & cookies

Dairy-Free Variation

• Instead of cream cheese, substitute imitation cream cheese (e.g., Tofutti). The nutrition count will be very similar.

🍎 ALMOND MEAL

"Nutting" could be easier! This is a fantastic alternative to flour for low-carb baking. You can use other nuts, but for best results, at least half the mixture should be almonds.

1 cup whole blanched almonds

1. Place the almonds in a food processor fitted with the steel blade. Process with several quick on/off pulses to start, then let the motor run until finely ground, about 20 to 25 seconds. Don't overprocess or you will get almond butter! (You can also pulse small amounts of nuts in an electric coffee grinder.)

Yield: 1 cup. Store in a re-sealable plastic bag in the refrigerator for 3 months. Freezes well for up to 1 year.

40 calories per Tbsp, 1.5 g carbohydrate, 0.8 g fiber, 2 g protein, 3.5 g fat (0.2 g saturated), 0 mg cholesterol, 2 mg sodium, 60 mg potassium, 0 mg iron, 15 mg calcium

Chef's Secrets

• The Daily Grind: You can buy good-quality almond meal, such as Bob's Red Mill, in most supermarkets if you don't want to grind it yourself.

• Nut Knowledge: Almond meal can replace flour in low-carb baking recipes but some experimentation will be needed. A good starting point is to replace half the flour with almond meal. If a recipe calls for 2 cups flour, use 1 cup flour and 1 cup almond meal. The carbs will be lower but the fat and protein content will be higher.

• The Right Switch! Almond meal can be used instead of flour or cookie crumbs to make a delicious nut crust for pies, cheesecakes, and other desserts. It's perfect for Passover.

• Calci-Yum! Did you know that 1 cup of almonds contains the same amount of calcium as 1 cup of milk?

🍎 CHOCOLATE BLUEBERRY BLOBS

These are "berry" easy to make. What a decadent way to eat your fruit!

2 cups fresh blueberries
8 oz good-quality dark chocolate,
　broken up into chunks

1. Line a baking tray or sheet with parchment paper. Rinse the blueberries and pat completely dry.

2. Meanwhile, microwave the chocolate in a microwaveable bowl on medium until melted, about 2 minutes, stirring every minute.

3. Remove the chocolate from the microwave. Let cool to lukewarm before gently mixing in the blueberries with a rubber spatula. Continue gently mixing until the berries are well coated with chocolate. Drop teaspoonfuls of the mixture onto the lined tray, about 2 inches apart. Refrigerate until firm, about 1 hour.

Yield: 30 pieces. Keeps about a day in the refrigerator, if they last that long! Don't freeze.

43 calories each, 5.2 g carbohydrate, 0.8 g fiber, 1 g protein, 3.3 g fat (1.6 g saturated), 0 mg cholesterol, 0 mg sodium, 7 mg potassium, 0 mg iron, 1 mg calcium

Chef's Secrets

• Berry Important! Dry the blueberries thoroughly before adding them to the chocolate. If any moisture gets into the chocolate, it will seize (get thick and lumpy).

• Dark Secret! Instead of bittersweet chocolate, substitute with 1 1/3 cups semi-sweet chocolate chips and 2 tsp canola or vegetable oil.

Nutrition Notes

• For more information about chocolate, see page 377 and pages 391–92. For more information about blueberries, see page 431.

🍎 CHOCOLATE ROCKS

These treats really rock! That was the opinion of my young helper, Shoshana Beer. Although Shoshana says she prefers milk chocolate, she definitely had no trouble devouring these.

6 oz (180 to 200 g) good-quality
   dark chocolate, chopped into chunks
   (or 1 cup semi-sweet chocolate chips)
1 tsp canola oil
1 1/3 cups Special K cereal
   or any crunchy breakfast cereal
1/2 cup raisins or dried cranberries

1. Combine the chocolate and oil in a medium glass bowl. Microwave, uncovered, on medium for 2 to 3 minutes or until the chocolate has just melted, stirring every minute.

2. Remove the bowl from the microwave and let the chocolate cool slightly before stirring in the cereal and raisins.

3. Line a large baking sheet with parchment paper. Drop the mixture by rounded teaspoonfuls onto the baking sheet. Refrigerate for 30 to 45 minutes or until firm. Once firm, transfer them to an airtight container, separating each layer with parchment or waxed paper. Store in the refrigerator.

Yield: 24 pieces. Keeps about 2 weeks in the refrigerator, if well hidden! Freezes well for up to 3 months.

52 calories per piece, 8.1 g carbohydrate, 0.7 g fiber, 1 g protein, 2.4 g fat (1.2 g saturated), 0 mg cholesterol, 15 mg sodium, 28 mg potassium, 1 mg iron, 2 mg calcium

Chef's Secrets: Be a Chocolate Maven!

• Got Milk? Dark chocolate (either bittersweet or semi-sweet) is not always dairy-free, so check labels carefully if this is a concern.

• Melting Moments: Use a bowl that is completely wiped dry, and don't cover it when melting chocolate or the chocolate can "seize" (become solid and grainy). The mixing spoon should also be dry.

• Chocolate Rescue: If chocolate seizes, add canola oil, a teaspoon at a time, and stir until smooth. Another solution is to add an equal volume of hot liquid, such as milk or coffee, plus a few drops of pure vanilla extract or liqueur—instant chocolate sauce!

• Meltdown! I used to melt chocolate in the microwave oven on high power, but since newer microwave ovens are more powerful, I now use medium power (50%). One or two ounces takes 2 to 3 minutes. Eight to sixteen ounces takes 3 to 4 minutes. Stir every minute to help chocolate melt evenly, and prevent scorching. Melting time may vary with different brands of chocolate, and from one brand of microwave oven to another.

• Store It Right! To protect chocolate from absorbing odors, wrap it in plastic wrap, then in foil, and store in a cool, dry, dark place, but not in the refrigerator. If properly stored, chocolate will keep up to 3 years.

• White's Alright! Chocolate will develop white streaks known as "bloom" if stored in a warm place but will still taste delicious. Once you melt it, the white streaks will disappear.

🍎 HOMEMADE CEREAL BARS

These make a great snack for adults and kids alike. They're packed with dried fruit, cereal, and nuts or seeds, as well as chocolate chips for a special taste treat. Most schools are now peanut-free zones, so if you are packing these in a child's lunch box, omit the nuts and substitute with sunflower or pumpkin seeds.

3 Tbsp soft tub margarine
40 large marshmallows
4 1/2 cups toasted oat cereal
   (such as Cheerios or bran flakes)
3/4 cup dried cranberries or raisins
   (or a combination)
3/4 cup chopped dried apricots
1/2 cup toasted sliced almonds,
   peanuts, sunflower,
   or pumpkin seeds
1/2 to 3/4 cup semi-sweet chocolate chips

1. In a large saucepan, melt the margarine and marshmallows together over low heat. Stir until the marshmallows are melted; remove from heat and cool slightly. (Or microwave in a large glass microwaveable bowl on high for 2 to 3 minutes, stirring every minute, until melted.)

2. Add the cereal, dried fruit, and almonds to the cooled marshmallow mixture; mix well to combine. Quickly stir in the chocolate chips.

3. Spoon the mixture into a sprayed 9- × 13-inch glass baking dish. Dampen your hands and press the mixture evenly into the pan. Chill in the refrigerator for 1/2 hour or until set. Cut into bars with a sharp knife. If you wait too long, they will be difficult to slice. Store in a covered container at room temperature.

Yield: 24 bars. These cereal bars freeze well for up to 3 months, but be sure to slice them first before freezing.

122 calories per serving, 22.2 g carbohydrate, 1.6 g fiber, 2 g protein, 3.9 g fat (1.0 g saturated), 0 mg cholesterol, 70 mg sodium, 116 mg potassium, 2 mg iron, 32 mg calcium

Chef's Secrets
• A Cut above the Rest: Apricots are a good source of beta carotene and add lovely color to this recipe. The easiest way to cut up dried apricots is with kitchen scissors.

• Nuts to You! Did you know that a cup of almonds contains the same amount of calcium as a cup of milk? Almonds and sunflower seeds are also excellent sources of Vitamin E.

cakes & cookies

• The Seedy Truth: Pumpkin seeds, with their sweet, nutty flavor, are available shelled and toasted, making them a quick, convenient, and healthy snack. They are a very good source of zinc and magnesium. You can add pumpkin seeds to baked goods, stir-fries, salads, and grains. To maintain their freshness, store pumpkin seeds in an airtight container in the refrigerator or freezer. They'll keep for several months.

CINNAMON TORTILLA TRIANGLES

This recipe can be doubled or tripled easily. If you have frozen tortillas on hand, you can make a batch of these crisp treats in minutes.

2 egg whites, lightly beaten
4 large (10-inch) whole wheat
    or flour tortillas
4 Tbsp sesame seeds
1 tsp ground cinnamon mixed with 4 Tbsp
    granulated sugar or granular Splenda

1. Preheat the oven to 400°F. Line a large baking sheet with parchment paper.

2. Using a pastry brush or paper towel, brush a light coating of egg white on one side of each tortilla. Sprinkle the brushed side with sesame seeds and the cinnamon-sugar mixture. Pile the tortillas in a stack, brushed-side up, and cut into triangles with a pizza wheel or sharp knife. (First cut the stack in half, then into quarters, then into eighths, like cutting a pizza into wedges.) Each tortilla will make 8 pie-shaped wedges.

3. Arrange the triangles in a single layer on the prepared baking sheet. Bake for 8 to 10 minutes or until crisp and golden. Watch carefully to prevent burning.

Yield: 32 triangles. Freezes well for up to 3 months.

23 calories per triangle, 4.3 g carbohydrate, 0.1 g fiber, 1 g protein, 0.6 g fat (0 g saturated), 0 mg cholesterol, 27 mg sodium, 14 mg potassium, 0 mg iron, 6 mg calcium

Cinnamon Wonton Triangles

Use 24 wonton wrappers; defrost if frozen. Brush one side of each wrapper with egg white; sprinkle with sesame seeds and the cinnamon-sugar mixture. Cut each wrapper in half to make 2 triangles. Place in a single layer on a baking sheet. Bake at 350°F for 5 to 7 minutes or until crisp and golden. Makes 48 triangles.

Chef's Secrets

• Crisp-less? If these triangles lose their crispness, place them on a baking sheet in a single layer and reheat at 350°F for a few minutes. They'll taste just-baked!

• Pack It Right: If freezing, pack and store carefully in rigid freezer containers as they are somewhat fragile.

Nutrition Note

• Sweet Choice: With Splenda, one tortilla triangle contains 18 calories and 2.9 g carbohydrate. The calorie and carbohydrate count is similar for the wonton triangles.

ANYTIME BREAKFAST COOKIES

Thanks to my friend Anne Perrelli for sharing her recipe for scrumptious snacking cookies. They're great for kids of all ages and make a healthy breakfast or snack. For that just-baked taste, reheat them briefly in the toaster oven before serving.

2 cups coarsely crushed bran flakes
2 cups rolled oats (preferably large flake)
2 Tbsp ground flaxseed or wheat germ
1 Tbsp ground cinnamon
1 cup unsweetened applesauce
1/2 cup nonfat plain yogurt
   (or substitute with your favorite flavor)
1 tsp pure vanilla extract
1/3 cup honey or maple syrup
1 large egg
1/2 cup skim milk powder
1 tsp baking powder
1 tsp baking soda
1/4 cup dried cranberries or raisins
1/3 cup coarsely chopped dried apricots
1/2 cup chopped walnuts, almonds,
   or pecans
1/4 cup sunflower seeds — choc. chips?

1. Preheat the oven to 350°F. Line two large baking sheets with parchment paper.

2. In a medium-sized bowl, combine the bran flakes, oats, flaxseed, and cinnamon; set aside.

3. In a large mixing bowl, combine the applesauce, yogurt, vanilla, honey, egg, and skim milk powder; mix well. Add the baking powder and baking soda; mix until combined. Gradually add the reserved bran flake mixture to the applesauce mixture. Add the dried fruit, nuts, and sunflower seeds; mix well. Drop by rounded teaspoonfuls onto the prepared baking sheets.

4. Bake for 15 minutes or until golden.

Yield: About 5 1/2 dozen cookies. Freezes well for up to 4 months; reheats well.

38 calories per cookie, 6.0 g carbohydrate, 0.8 g fiber, 1 g protein, 1.2 g fat (0.1 g saturated), 3 mg cholesterol, 41 mg sodium, 51 mg potassium, 1 mg iron, 20 mg calcium

Chef's Secret
• Got Milk? Add skim milk powder to smoothies and soups for a calcium boost.

🍫 BROWNIE COOKIES

Instead of baking brownies in a baking pan, drop them, by teaspoonfuls, onto a cookie sheet. These crispy cookies are flatter but larger in diameter than square-cut brownies, so you get more bites for the same number of calories. You'll definitely get brownie points for making these!

1/4 cup soft tub margarine
1/4 cup unsweetened applesauce
1/2 cup granulated sugar
1/2 cup lightly packed brown sugar
2 large eggs (or 1 large egg
   plus 2 egg whites)
1 tsp pure vanilla extract
3/4 cup whole wheat or all-purpose flour
1/2 cup unsweetened cocoa powder
1/2 tsp baking powder
1/8 tsp salt
25 walnut or pecan halves

1. Preheat the oven to 350°F. Line a baking sheet with parchment paper.

2. In a food processor fitted with the steel blade, combine the margarine, applesauce, sugars, eggs, and vanilla; process for 1 minute or until well-blended. Add the flour, cocoa, baking powder, and salt; process with several quick on/off pulses, just until blended. Don't overprocess.

3. Drop the batter from a tablespoon onto the prepared baking sheet, leaving 3 inches between each mound. Place a walnut on top of each mound.

4. Bake for 13 to 15 minutes or until the tops are set when touched with your fingertips; don't overbake. Cool for 5 minutes before removing from the pan.

Yield: 25 cookies. Freezes well for up to 4 months.

78 calories per cookie/brownie, 11.0 g carbohydrate, 1.2 g fiber, 2 g protein, 3.7 g fat (0. 6g saturated), 8 mg cholesterol, 55 mg sodium, 70 mg potassium, 1 mg iron, 15 mg calcium

Brownies

Melt the margarine, then prepare the batter as directed. Spread evenly in a sprayed, 8-inch square glass baking dish. Place the nuts 5 across and 5 down. Bake at 350°F for 25 minutes. When done, the top will be set when touched with your fingertips and a cake tester or toothpick inserted into the center of the cake will come out slightly moist. Don't overbake. Once cooled, cut into 25 small squares. If desired, drizzle with Chocolate Glaze (page 389)

Chef's Secrets

• No Nuts for You! Without nuts, one cookie/brownie contains 65 calories, and 2.3 g fat (0.5 g saturated).

• Kidding Around: Instead of nuts, top each cookie/brownie with an M&M. Mmmm!

• Super-Size Me! If you want bigger brownies, cut them into 16 squares. One brownie with nuts contains 114 calories, 17.1 g carbohydrate, 1.8 g fiber, and 5.0 g fat (0.9 saturated).

🍎 CHOCOLATE CHIP COOKIES

Oat-so-good! This recipe comes from my favorite (and only) daughter, Jodi Sprackman, who is an excellent cook and baker. My granddaughters call them "Jodi's Oaties!" Lauren and Camille love to bake and are showing great potential as future chefs.

1/2 cup soft tub margarine
1/2 cup lightly packed brown sugar
1/4 cup granulated sugar
1 large egg
1 tsp pure vanilla extract
3/4 cup whole wheat flour
1/2 tsp baking soda
1/4 tsp salt
1 1/2 cups quick-cooking oats
  (preferably large flake)
3/4 to 1 cup semi-sweet chocolate chips

1. Preheat the oven to 350°F. Line 2 large baking sheets with parchment paper.

2. In a food processor fitted with the steel blade, combine the margarine, sugars, egg, and vanilla; process for 2 minutes or until well-blended. Add the flour, baking soda, salt, and oats; process with quick on/off pulses, just until combined. Stir in the chocolate chips with a rubber spatula.

3. Drop from a teaspoon onto the prepared baking sheets, leaving 2 inches between each cookie. Bake for 12 to 15 minutes or until golden. Cool for 5 minutes, then remove from pan.

Yield: About 44 cookies. Recipe can be doubled easily. Freezes well for up to 4 months.

cakes & cookies

62 calories per cookie, 7.9 g carbohydrate, 0.7 g fiber, 1 g protein, 3.3 g fat (0.9 g saturated), 5 mg cholesterol, 58 mg sodium, 37 mg potassium, 0 mg iron, 6 mg calcium

Variations
• Use only 1/2 cup chocolate chips and add 1/2 cup chopped pecans or walnuts.

• Instead of nuts, substitute with dried cherries, cranberries, or raisins.

● BEST OATMEAL COOKIES

These scrumptious cookies are a new twist on an old favorite. They're "oat" of this world! For dairy-free cookies, choose a brand of chocolate chips that contain no dairy products.

1/2 cup canola oil
2 egg whites (or 1 large egg)
1/3 cup lightly packed brown sugar
1/3 cup granulated sugar
2 Tbsp water
1 tsp pure vanilla extract
3/4 cup whole wheat flour
1 1/2 cups rolled oats (preferably large flake)
1/4 cup wheat germ
1/2 tsp baking soda
1 tsp ground cinnamon
1/8 tsp salt
1/3 cup semi-sweet chocolate chips
1/3 cup raisins or dried cranberries
1/3 cup sunflower seeds or chopped
  almonds, walnuts, or pecans (optional)

1. Place the oven rack in the middle of the oven and preheat to 350°F. Line two large baking sheets with parchment paper.

2. In a food processor fitted with the steel blade (or in a large bowl and using an electric mixer), beat the oil, egg whites, sugars, water, and vanilla until well-blended, about 1 minute. Add the flour, rolled oats, wheat germ, baking soda, cinnamon, and salt; mix well. If using a food processor, transfer the batter to a large bowl. Stir in the chocolate chips, raisins, and seeds or nuts.

3. Drop the batter from a teaspoon onto the prepared baking sheets. Bake for 10 to 12 minutes or until golden.

Yield: About 3 1/2 dozen cookies. Store in a covered container. Freezes well for up to 4 months.

66 calories per cookie, 8.3 g carbohydrate, 0.8 g fiber, 1 g protein, 3.4 g fat (0.5 g saturated), 0 mg cholesterol, 26 mg sodium, 46 mg potassium, 0 mg iron, 5 mg calcium

Nutrition Notes
• Wheat germ or wheat bran—what's the difference? They're separate parts of the same grain: the bran is the outer coating and the wheat germ is the inner part. Wheat germ supplies nutrients such as protein, B vitamins, and vitamin E, whereas wheat bran has more fiber. So include both in your diet for good health.

● CRANBERRY OATMEAL FLAX COOKIES

These yummy cookies come from Shayla Goldstein of Toronto, and they've become one of my favorites. I've reduced the sugar and added pumpkin seeds and cinnamon. What a delicious way to incorporate flax-seed into your diet! They are fairly high in calories, so enjoy in moderation.

1/2 cup less 1 Tbsp canola oil
1/3 cup packed brown sugar
1/3 cup granulated sugar
1 large egg (or 2 egg whites)
1 tsp pure vanilla extract
1/2 tsp ground cinnamon
1/4 cup all-purpose flour
1/4 cup whole wheat flour
1 cup rolled oats (preferably large flake)
1/2 cup ground flaxseed
1/2 tsp baking soda
1/2 cup dried cranberries
1/3 cup pumpkin seeds

1. Preheat the oven to 350°F. Line a large baking sheet with parchment paper.

2. In a food processor fitted with the steel blade, combine the oil, sugars, egg, vanilla, and cinnamon. Process for 1 minute or until well-blended. Add the flours, rolled oats, flaxseed, and baking soda; process with quick on/off pulses, just until combined. Stir in the cranberries and pumpkin seeds with a rubber spatula.

3. Drop the batter by rounded teaspoonfuls onto the prepared baking sheet, leaving 2 inches between each cookie. Flatten each mound with the tines of a fork. Bake for 10 to 12 minutes or until golden.

Yield: About 36 cookies. Freezes well for up to 4 months.

79 calories per cookie, 8.5 g carbohydrate, 0.8 g fiber, 1 g protein, 4.5 g fat (0.4 g saturated), 6 mg cholesterol, 20 mg sodium, 15 mg potassium, 0 mg iron, 3 mg calcium

Variations
• Substitute raisins for dried cranberries. Substitute chopped walnuts, pistachios, or pecans for pumpkin seeds. Add 1/2 to 3/4 cup semi-sweet chocolate chips.

Chef's Secrets
• Be "Flax"-ible! Flaxseed increases in volume when ground, so you'll need 6 Tbsp of whole flaxseed to get 1/2 cup ground. Grind flaxseed in a clean coffee grinder or mini processor. If you grind too many, don't worry. Just place the extra ground flaxseed in a re-sealable plastic bag and refrigerate or freeze. Ground flaxseed will keep for several months in the refrigerator or freezer.

● PEANUT BUTTER COOKIES

Three ingredients, three minutes to mix up the batter, and less than three minutes before they're gone! You can make these gluten-free cookies with sugar or Splenda, but either way they might turn you into a glutton, so practice portion control and save these as an occasional treat.

1 cup creamy
   or crunchy natural peanut butter
3/4 cup granulated sugar or granular Splenda
1 large egg

1. Preheat the oven to 325°F. Line a large baking sheet with parchment paper.

2. In a mixing bowl, combine the peanut butter, sugar, and egg; mix well. Drop by rounded teaspoonfuls onto the prepared baking sheet, leaving 2 inches between each cookie. (If you use Splenda, place a piece of parchment or wax paper on top of the unbaked cookies and press gently to flatten them before baking; see Chef's Secrets, page 398.) Uncover before baking.

3. Bake for 10 minutes or until cookies are golden. Remove from the oven and let cool on the baking sheet for 10 to 15 minutes. The cookies will firm up as they cool.

cakes &
cookies

Yield: 26 cookies (if made with sugar) or 21 cookies (if made with Splenda). Freezes well for up to 4 months.

87 calories per cookie (with sugar), 7.9 g carbohydrate, 0.6 g fiber, 2 g protein, 5.1 g fat (0.7 g saturated), 8 mg cholesterol, 40 mg sodium, 3 mg potassium, 0 mg iron, 1 mg calcium

83 calories per cookie (with Splenda), 3.5 g carbohydrate, 0.8 g fiber, 3 g protein, 6.3 g fat (0.8 g saturated), 10 mg cholesterol, 49 mg sodium, 3 mg potassium, 0 mg iron, 1 mg calcium

Chef's Secrets
• What's the Spread? Cookies made with sugar will spread during baking, whereas cookies made with Splenda will stay in a mound and won't spread unless you flatten them before baking.

• Batter Up! You get more batter (and cookies) when using sugar, but less batter (and cookies) with Splenda. That's the way the cookie crumbles!

🍎 SUGAR-FREE MERINGUE COOKIES

My foodie-friend Wendy Baker, of New York, sent this recipe to me and wrote: "Eureka! At last, a light meringue cookie that works without sugar and that still holds up in baking! These are more fragile than meringue cookies made with sugar, so handle them with care." This recipe is a modified version of one she got from a diabetes support newsgroup.

3 egg whites (at room temperature)
1/8 tsp cream of tartar
1 tsp pure vanilla or almond extract
1/2 cup granular Splenda
2 Tbsp grated orange rind
24 semi-sweet chocolate chips

1. Preheat the oven to 350°F. Line a large baking sheet with parchment paper.

2. In a large bowl and using an electric mixer, beat the egg whites on medium-high speed until foamy. Add the cream of tartar and vanilla and beat until soft peaks form. Reduce the speed to low and gradually beat in the Splenda. Increase the speed to high and beat until stiff peaks form. Using a rubber spatula, carefully fold in the rind.

3. Drop in mounds from a teaspoon onto the prepared baking sheet. Top each mound with a chocolate chip. Bake for 10 minutes. Turn off the oven and keep the door closed for 30 minutes to let the meringues dry. (No peeking allowed!) When cool, store in a loosely covered container so the meringues will stay crisp.

Yield: 24 cookies. Don't freeze: the Splenda makes the meringues too fragile.

7 calories per cookie, 1.0 g carbohydrate, 0.1 g fiber, trace protein, 0.1 g fat (0.1 g saturated), 0 mg cholesterol, 7 mg sodium, 12 mg potassium, 0 mg iron, 1 mg calcium

Chef's Secret
• Freeze with Ease: If you substitute 6 Tbsp sugar for the Splenda, you will be able to freeze these because meringues made with sugar aren't as fragile.

Nutrition Note
• Sweet Choice: If made with sugar, 1 cookie contains 18 calories and 3.6 g carbohydrate.

♠ DOUBLE ALMOND MANDEL BREAD

Once you taste these, you'll go "almond-lutely" nuts! Mandel bread is the Jewish version of biscotti. I reduced the carbs by more than one-third by substituting Splenda for part of the sugar and replacing all-purpose flour with a mixture of whole wheat flour, oat bran, and finely ground almonds. This is a great choice for people with diabetes.

1/2 cup finely ground almonds
    or Almond Meal (page 390)
3 large eggs (or 2 large eggs plus 2 whites)
1/2 cup granulated sugar
1/2 cup granular Splenda
    or granulated sugar
1/2 cup canola oil
1 cup whole wheat flour
1/2 cup oat bran
2 cups Special K cereal
2 tsp baking powder
1 tsp ground cinnamon
1/2 cup sliced almonds

1. Preheat the oven to 350°F. Line a large baking sheet with parchment paper. If making Almond Meal, prepare as directed.

2. In a large bowl, beat the eggs with sugar, Splenda, and oil until well mixed. Add the flour, oat bran, and ground almonds; mix well. Add the Special K, baking powder, and cinnamon. Mix well. Stir in the sliced almonds. If the mixture is somewhat sticky, refrigerate for 15 minutes for easier handling.

3. Divide the dough evenly into 3 long, narrow rolls (about 18- × 2-inches) directly on the prepared baking sheet. Leave at least 3 inches between each roll as they will spread during baking. Flour your hands for easier handling. Using a rubber spatula, smooth the tops, and make the edges neat.

4. Bake on the middle rack of the oven for 20 to 25 minutes or until the rolls are pale golden. Remove the pan from the oven; let cool for 5 minutes.

5. Reduce the oven temperature to 250°F. Using a sharp knife, slice the cooled rolls on a slight angle into 1/2-inch slices. Place, cut-side down, on the baking sheet. Bake for 30 to 40 minutes or until the slices are dry and crisp.

Yield: About 54 slices. Store, loosely covered, in cookie tins for up to 1 month. If tightly covered, the cookies will get soft. Freezes well for up to 4 months.

55 calories per slice, 5.6 g carbohydrate, 0.7 g fiber, 1 g protein, 3.4 g fat (0.3 g saturated), 12 mg cholesterol, 33 mg sodium, 38 mg potassium, 1 mg iron, 12 mg calcium

Variations
• Add 2 Tbsp wheat germ or unsweetened cocoa powder to batter along with the dry ingredients.

• In Step 5, sprinkle the slices with 2 tsp ground cinnamon mixed with 1/4 cup sugar or Splenda. Bake as directed.

Nutrition Note
• Sweet Choice: If you omit Splenda and use 1 cup sugar, one slice contains 62 calories and 7.4 g carbohydrate.

cakes & cookies

🍎 SKINNY LEMON BISCOTTI

These thin, crisp biscotti have a lovely lemon flavor and are packed with almonds and dried fruit. You'll go nuts over them!

4 egg whites (or 2 large eggs)
1/2 cup granulated sugar
2 Tbsp canola oil
1 tsp pure vanilla extract
1 Tbsp grated lemon rind
1 Tbsp lemon juice (preferably fresh)
1 cup whole wheat flour
1/2 tsp baking powder
2/3 cup slivered almonds
2/3 cup chopped dried apricots
1/2 tsp ground cinnamon mixed
   with 1 Tbsp granulated sugar

1. Preheat the oven to 350°F. Spray a small (8- × 4-inch) loaf pan with cooking spray.

2. Beat the egg whites with sugar, oil, and vanilla until well mixed, about 2 minutes. Add the lemon rind, juice, flour, and baking powder. Stir in almonds and apricots and mix until combined. Pour into the prepared pan and spread evenly.

3. Bake for 30 to 35 minutes or until golden. Let cool for 10 to 15 minutes, then invert and remove the loaf from the pan. Wrap in foil and refrigerate overnight (or up to 2 days).

4. Unwrap the loaf and slice as thinly as possible, about 1/4-inch thick, with a sharp serrated knife. Arrange slices in a single layer on parchment-lined baking sheet(s). Sprinkle lightly with cinnamon-sugar mixture. Bake in a preheated 250°F oven for 30 to 40 minutes, until crisp and toasted.

Yield: About 32 slices. Store in a loosely covered container. Freezes well for up to 4 months.

58 calories per slice, 8.8 g carbohydrate, 1.0 g fiber, 2 g protein, 2.1 g fat (0.2 g saturated), 0 mg cholesterol, 15 mg sodium, 75 mg potassium, 0 mg iron, 14 mg calcium

Variations
• Instead of almonds, substitute with flaked Brazil nuts or coarsely chopped walnuts.

• Instead of dried apricots, substitute with dried cranberries or raisins.

🍎 TRAIL MIX BISCOTTI

Everyone will beat a trail to your door when you make these skinny, addictive biscotti. When I asked Sandra Gitlin of Toronto for her recipe, she said she had given her word that she wouldn't share it with anyone. I did some detective work and produced this yummy version. Happy and healthy trails!

3 large eggs (or 2 large eggs
   plus 2 egg whites)
3/4 cup granulated sugar
1 Tbsp grated orange rind
1 tsp grated lemon rind
Juice of 1 orange (about 3 Tbsp)
3/4 cup all-purpose flour
3/4 cup whole wheat flour
1/2 tsp baking powder
1/2 to 3/4 cup shelled pistachios
1/2 to 3/4 cup whole almonds
1/2 to 3/4 cup raisins
1/2 to 3/4 cup dried cranberries

1. Preheat the oven to 350°F. Spray a 9- × 5-inch loaf pan with cooking spray.

2. In a food processor fitted with the steel blade, process the eggs with sugar for 2 to 3 minutes or until well mixed. Add the grated rinds, orange juice, flours, and baking pow-

der; process just until combined. Transfer the batter to a large bowl. Stir in the nuts, raisins, and dried cranberries. Pour into the prepared pan and spread evenly.

3. Bake for 50 to 55 minutes or until golden. Remove from the oven and let stand for 10 minutes before removing from the pan. (The loaf can be prepared up to this stage, wrapped tightly in foil, and refrigerated for 1 to 2 days. This makes slicing easier.)

4. Slice the baked loaf as thinly as possible, about 1/4 inch thick, using a sharp, serrated knife. Arrange the slices in a single layer on foil-lined cookie sheets. Bake in a preheated 250°F oven for 30 minutes or until crisp and lightly toasted.

Yield: About 48 slices. Store in cookie tins, and hide them in a safe place or they won't last very long! Freezes well for up to 4 months.

56 calories per slice, 9.2 g carbohydrate, 0.7 g fiber, 2 g protein, 1.8 g fat (0.2 g saturated), 13 mg cholesterol, 10 mg sodium, 54 mg potassium, 0 mg iron, 11 mg calcium

Variations
• Mix It Up: Instead of raisins and cranberries, add pumpkin and/or sunflower seeds, and instead of pistachios, add cashews. You can also try these with 1/2 to 3/4 cup chocolate chips.

Chef's Secrets
• "Fat-Astic" News! There's no oil added to these biscotti. The only fat in this recipe comes from the nuts.

• Nuts to You! Always store your nuts and seeds in the refrigerator or freezer so they won't become rancid.

🍎 MOM'S KICHEL

Even if you can't pronounce the word "kichel," you'll love these light and crispy cookies—they're so addictive! My mom pats out the dough exactly the same way her mother did, bringing back marvelous memories from my childhood. These are great for people with diabetes—or anyone at all!

Batter:

3 large eggs
2 Tbsp granulated sugar or granular Splenda
1/3 cup canola oil
1/2 cup all-purpose flour
1/2 cup whole wheat flour

Topping:

1 Tbsp canola oil (to brush on top of dough)
1 to 2 Tbsp granulated sugar
    or granular Splenda
1/4 cup sesame seeds

1. Preheat the oven to 500°F. Move the oven rack to the middle position. Line a large baking sheet (or 2 smaller ones) with foil and spray with cooking spray.

2. In a food processor fitted with the steel blade, process the eggs and sugar until frothy, about 1 minute. Add the oil through the feed tube while the motor is running; process for 1 minute longer or until light in color. Add the flours by heaping tablespoons through the feed tube while the motor is still running; process for 30 to 45 seconds longer. (While it's processing, the dough will be very sticky, and the processor may shut off automatically. This is normal, so don't worry.) Use a rubber spatula to scrape out the dough from the bowl onto a well-floured surface.

3. Pat out into a long, thin rectangle, approximately 48 inches × 6 inches, flouring your hands for easier handling. (If you don't have enough counter space, divide the dough in half, and work in batches; pat out each piece of dough into a rectangle about 24 inches × 6 inches.)

4. Topping: Brush the top of the dough lightly with the oil. Sprinkle the sugar and the sesame seeds evenly over the dough. Cut into 24 pieces, about 2 inches × 3 inches. Place them on the prepared baking sheet, leaving 2 inches between each one as they will expand during baking.

5. Reduce the oven temperature to 400°F. Place the pan on the middle rack and shut the door quickly; bake for 7 to 8 minutes. Reduce the heat to 300°F and bake for 10 to 12 minutes longer. Don't open the oven door during baking! If your oven has a glass window in the door, peek through and see if the cookies have expanded and puffed up. Turn off the heat and leave the kichel in the oven for 15 to 20 minutes longer or until dry and crispy.

Yield: About 24 large kichel. Store loosely covered in a bowl so they will stay crisp. Freezes well for up to 4 months (but they never last very long).

74 calories per cookie, 5.6 g carbohydrate, 0.5 g fiber, 2 g protein, 5.1 g fat (0.5 g saturated), 26 mg cholesterol, 12 mg sodium, 21 mg potassium, 0 mg iron, 9 mg calcium

Chef's Secrets
• Hot Stuff! Newer ovens are better insulated, so they hold the heat longer. If you have a newer oven, you may have to reduce the heat and time to prevent the kichel from burning. If your oven door has a window, peek and check, but don't open the door!

• Warning Light: If the temperature light of your oven turns on during baking, drop the temperature slightly or until the light turns off—otherwise your kichel will burn!

• Quick Clean-up: To remove the sticky dough from the processor bowl and steel blade, place the processor bowl and blade back onto the base. Add a few drops of dish-washing detergent, then add enough hot water to almost reach the top of the blade. Process for 8 to 10 seconds—clean cuisine!

• Cute Tip: A cotton swab will remove the sticky dough from the hole on the underside of the steel blade.

Nutrition Note
• Sweet Choice: With Splenda, one kichel contains 69 calories and 4.3 g carbohydrate.

● CREAM CHEESE PASTRY DOUGH

If you hate making pastry because you have trouble rolling out the dough, you'll love this foolproof recipe. I've been making different versions of this for years because it's so versatile. I've also included a dairy-free version on page 403. Dough, baby, dough!

1 cup soft tub margarine (or butter
    substitute such as Earth Balance)
1 cup light cream cheese (or pressed
    dry cottage cheese), well-chilled
2 cups all-purpose flour

1. Freeze the margarine for several hours or overnight. When ready to use, remove from

the freezer and let stand at room temperature for 10 minutes.

2. Cut the margarine and cream cheese into 1-inch chunks; place in a food processor fitted with the steel blade. Add the flour and process with several quick on/off pulses, then let the motor run for about 18 to 20 seconds, just until the mixture gathers together and forms a ball around the blades. Don't overprocess or the dough will be tough. If the dough is too soft, add an extra tablespoon of flour.

3. Divide the dough into 4 balls. Flatten each ball into a disk, place in a re-sealable plastic bag, and chill for 30 minutes or for up to 2 days in the refrigerator.

4. Flour each piece of dough lightly. Roll the dough out thinly on a lightly floured surface or on a floured pastry cloth. Use in recipes calling for pastry dough.

Yield: Four 9-inch circles (enough for 48 cookies). Freezes well for up to 3 months. Recipe can be halved.

65 calories per serving, 4.3 g carbohydrate, 0.1 g fiber, 1 g protein, 4.7 g fat (1.1 g saturated), 3 mg cholesterol, 76 mg sodium, 17 mg potassium, 0 mg iron, 9 mg calcium

Dairy-Free Pastry Dough

Use imitation cream cheese, such as Tofutti, instead of cream cheese. Use dairy-free soft tub margarine. (The nutrients found in dairy-free pastry dough are almost identical to the dairy version above.)

Chef's Secrets

• Dough It Right! My secret to making flaky dough is to use frozen margarine. Earth Balance Buttery Spread works very well. It's non-hydrogenated but has a buttery flavor. Don't use reduced-fat margarine in this recipe; if you do, the results will be disappointing.

• Your Choice: This dough is excellent for Heavenly Hamentaschen (page 405), Raspberry Rogelach (page 404), Cookie Cut-Outs (below), or your favorite pie or quiche.

🍎 COOKIE CUT-OUTS

Let the kids help cut out different shapes to develop their motor skills. Have them count how many cookies they get from a batch. Smart cookies!

Cream Cheese Pastry Dough or Dairy-Free Pastry Dough (pages 402–03)
2 egg whites, lightly beaten
1/2 cup granulated sugar
  or cinnamon-sugar, for sprinkling

1. Prepare the dough as directed, and chill for 30 minutes (or refrigerate for up to 2 days). Preheat the oven to 375°F. Line 2 large baking sheets with parchment paper.

2. Flour each piece of dough lightly. Roll out each piece on a lightly floured surface to 1/4-inch thickness. Cut into various shapes with assorted cookie cutters. (Or use a fluted pastry wheel and cut into squares, triangles or whatever shape you like.) Brush with egg white and then sprinkle lightly with sugar.

3. Place on the prepared baking sheets. Bake for 8 to 10 minutes or until golden. (Baking time will depend on the size of your cookies, which can vary if the children are helping.)

Yield: About 4 dozen. Freezes well for up to 4 months.

73 calories per cookie, 6.4 g carbohydrate, 0.1 g fiber, 1 g protein, 4.7 g fat (1.1 g saturated), 2 mg cholesterol, 78 mg sodium, 19 mg potassium, 0 mg iron, 9 mg calcium

Chef's Secrets

• Roll It Right: For easier handling, roll out the chilled dough on parchment-lined baking sheets. Cut into desired shapes. Remove any scraps of dough with a floured spatula and set aside.

• Not So Tough: Save all the scraps until the end, then gather them together in a ball and re-roll to make more cookies. This helps prevent tough cookies.

• Top Notch: Sprinkle the chilled dough with sesame seeds, finely chopped nuts, or grated chocolate. Press the topping into the dough gently with a rolling pin so that the topping won't fall off. Brush the tops with egg white, and then sprinkle lightly with sugar. Cut into desired shapes, then bake. If desired, dip one end of the baked, cooled cookies in melted chocolate. Place cookies on a rack to dry.

• No-Roll Cookies: Shape the dough into 1-inch balls and place on parchment-lined baking sheets. Flatten with a fork, making a criss-cross pattern, and bake.

• Pan-tastic! Not enough cookie sheets? While the first batch of cookies is in the oven, place the next batch of cookie dough on a sheet of parchment paper. When the first batch of cookies is baked, slide the parchment paper (with the baked cookies still on top) off the pan. Cool the pan slightly, then replace with the next batch and bake. (This method also saves on clean-ups!)

• Double Without Trouble: If baking 2 sheets of cookies at once, place the oven racks so they divide the space inside the oven into thirds. For even browning, switch the baking sheets (top to bottom and front to back) for the last few minutes of baking.

❧ RASPBERRY ROGELACH

These sugar-free treats are perfect for any special occasion. They can be enjoyed by those with diabetes or anyone watching their carb intake. How sweet is that! They're fairly high in calories and fat, so watch those portions.

Cream Cheese Pastry Dough or Dairy-Free Pastry Dough (pages 402–03)
1 cup all-fruit raspberry preserves
1 cup slivered or chopped almonds (or chopped pecans or walnuts)
1 large egg (or 2 egg whites, lightly beaten)

1. Prepare dough as directed. Chill for 30 minutes (or for up to 2 days) in the refrigerator.

2. Preheat the oven to 375°F. Line baking sheet(s) with parchment paper.

3. Flour each piece of dough lightly. Roll out the chilled dough thinly on a lightly floured surface into a 9-inch circle. Spread with 1/4 cup preserves and sprinkle with 1/4 cup nuts. Cut with a sharp knife or pastry wheel into 12 wedges. Roll up from the outside edge towards the center. Place on prepared baking sheet(s). Repeat with remaining dough, jam, and nuts. Brush lightly with beaten egg.

cakes & cookies

4. Bake for 18 to 20 minutes or until lightly browned.

Yield: 4 dozen. Freezes well for up to 4 months.

82 calories per cookie, 6.5 g carbohydrate, 0.4 g fiber, 2 g protein, 5.9 g fat (1.2 g saturated), 7 mg cholesterol, 78 mg sodium, 35 mg potassium, 0 mg iron, 15 mg calcium

Apricot Cranberry Rogelach

Substitute apricot preserves for raspberry preserves. Instead of almonds, sprinkle dough with dried cranberries. For an attractive presentation, sprinkle the baked rogelach lightly with icing sugar once they have cooled—but they won't be sugar-free!

Variations

• Substitute strawberry jam or orange marmalade for the raspberry preserves. Instead of almonds, substitute chopped pecans, walnuts, or filberts (hazelnuts).

Chef's Secrets

• Frozen Assets! Place the unbaked rogelach on a cookie sheet and freeze. Transfer to freezer containers, separating the layers with parchment paper. Seal tightly and store in the freezer until needed. You can bake them from frozen—they'll take 2 or 3 minutes longer to bake.

HEAVENLY HAMENTASCHEN

Everyone loves these triangular-shaped treats for Purim. They're fit for a queen—or a king!

Cream Cheese Pastry Dough or Dairy-Free
    Pastry Dough (pages 402–03)
Hamentaschen Fillings (pages 406–07)
1 large egg, lightly beaten

1. Prepare the dough and filling as directed and chill for 30 minutes (or for up to 2 days) in the refrigerator. Preheat the oven to 400°F. Line 2 large baking sheets with parchment paper.

2. Flour each piece of dough lightly. Roll out each piece on a lightly floured surface to 1/4-inch thickness. Use a 3-inch-round cookie cutter and cut the dough into circles. Place a teaspoonful of filling in the center of each circle. Bring 3 sides of the dough upwards over the filling, until the 3 sides are barely touching, then pinch the edges of dough together to form a triangle. Repeat with remaining dough and filling.

3. Place the filled triangles onto the prepared baking sheets. Brush the tops and sides of each triangle with the beaten egg. Bake for 15 to 18 minutes or until golden.

Yield: About 3 1/2 to 4 dozen. Freezes well for up to 4 months.

89 calories per serving, 11.7 g carbohydrate, 0.7 g fiber, 1 g protein, 4.2 g fat (1.0 g saturated), 7 mg cholesterol, 69 mg sodium, 89 mg potassium, 0 mg iron, 12 mg calcium

cakes & cookies

Chocolate Hamentaschen

Roll out the dough as directed. Instead of fruit filling, place an unwrapped chocolate kiss or a teaspoon of Nutella in the center of each circle. (Or place a dab of natural peanut butter on the dough, then top with a few semi-sweet chocolate chips.) Shape as directed. Reduce the baking temperature to 375°F to prevent burning.

Variation

• All-Fruit Cranberry Sauce (page 102) also makes an excellent filling.

Chef's Secrets

• Yes, You Can! If you don't have a round cookie cutter, use an empty can that has been well rinsed. It works perfectly!

• Tough Stuff! If you re-roll the scraps too many times, the pastry will become tough. Give the dough scraps to the kids and let them have fun.

🍑 FRUIT FILLING FOR HAMENTASCHEN

This fiber-packed fruit mixture is absolutely scrumptious. It also makes a delicious spread for wholegrain toast as an alternative to jam.

1/2 of a medium, seedless orange (thin-skinned)
1/2 cup raisins
1 cup dried cranberries
1 cup dried apricots
1 cup pitted prunes
1 Tbsp honey

1. Wash the orange well. Cut away both the navel and the stem end, but don't peel. Cut into chunks.

2. In a food processor fitted with the steel blade, combine all the ingredients. Process with several quick on/off pulses, then let the motor run for 20 to 30 seconds or until the fruit is finely ground. Scrape down the sides of the bowl as necessary.

3. Transfer to a container, cover, and refrigerate until ready to use.

Yield: About 4 cups. Will keep up to 2 to 3 weeks in the refrigerator. Freezes well for up to 4 months.

36 calories per Tbsp, 9.0 g carbohydrate, 0.7 g fiber, 0 g protein, 0 g fat (0 g saturated), 0 mg cholesterol, 1 mg sodium, 82 mg potassium, 0 mg iron, 4 mg calcium

Dried Fruit Truffles

Shape filling into 1-inch balls and roll in finely chopped almonds. Store in the refrigerator or freezer. Perfect for leftover filling.

Variations

• Other dried fruits, such as dried cherries, blueberries, dates, or mangoes can be substituted. Chopped almonds or pecans also make tasty additions to the filling.

Chef's Secret

• Fill 'em Up! One cup of filling is enough to fill 12 hamentaschen, depending on their size.

🍑 JAM AND NUT FILLING FOR HAMENTASCHEN

Cheryl Goldberg shared this treasure from her late Aunt Bella Uger's recipe collection. Many of her aunt's recipes were hand-written on scraps of paper while others were organized in a tattered, black three-ring binder. Cheryl said: "My aunt would make these jam-packed treats just for me! She would fill a cake box full to the brim and I would eat them all!"

1/2 cup apricot jam
1/2 cup marmalade
1/2 cup raisins
Rind of half a lemon
Rind of half an orange
2 tsp lemon juice (preferably fresh)
1/2 cup chopped walnuts

1. Combine the jam, marmalade, raisins, rinds, juice, and walnuts into a medium bowl and mix well.

Yield: About 2 cups. Keeps in the refrigerator for 2 to 3 weeks. Freezes well for up to 4 months.

37 calories per Tbsp, 6.4 g carbohydrate, 0.3 g fiber, 0 g protein, 1.2 g fat (0.1 g saturated), 0 mg cholesterol, 0 mg sodium, 28 mg potassium, 0 mg iron, 4 mg calcium

Chef's Secrets
• In a Jam? Some brands of jam and marmalade are low in sugar or are all-fruit. They aren't as thick as regular jam. If this happens, thicken the filling by heating it for a minute or two, either in the microwave or in a saucepan on top of the stove.

cakes & cookies

desserts & beverages

DESSERTS AND BEVERAGES

DELECTABLE DESSERTS:

Feeling Desserted? Sweets add pleasure to your life. Unfortunately, most desserts go straight from your eyes to your thighs! Choose wisely so you can have your cake and eat it too! You'll find many delectable desserts in this chapter that will satisfy your sweet tooth and still provide nutritional benefits. Refer to Cakes and Cookies (pages 373–407) and Breads and Muffins (pages 341–70) for more ideas and recipes.

Portion Distortion: The problem with many sweet treats is that they taste so good, you just can't stop at one serving. The solution? Share dessert—you'll also share the calories, carbs, and fat. One plate—two forks! Or try to save some for another day if you can control yourself.

Born to be Sweet: We are born with an innate desire for sweetness, beginning with mother's milk. It's when we progress to mom's apple pie à la mode that we get into trouble!

Root for Fruit: Fruits contain an abundance of vitamins, minerals, phytochemicals, antioxidants, and fiber that help reduce the risks of disease.

Stay on Route: There are many routes to fruit enjoyment—roasting, grilling, poaching—or just eating it fresh or frozen!

Go Local: Whenever possible, buy locally grown fruits. They are picked at the height of ripeness and will likely have the best flavor, as well as optimal nutritional benefits. Produce that's shipped from long distances may lose some of its flavor or nutritional value.

Clean Cuisine: Peel fruit or wash it thoroughly in a solution of water mixed with 2 or 3 drops of liquid dish detergent to remove pesticides and other harmful chemicals.

Melon-choly? Always wash melons such as cantaloupe, honeydew, and watermelon before cutting.

Lemon Aid: To prevent fresh fruit from discoloring, sprinkle with lemon juice.

Stick It To 'Em! Serve cubes of fruit on skewers and arrange them on a serving platter for a pleasing presentation. If you plan on grilling the fruit, soak wooden skewers in water for at least 20 minutes before using them on the grill.

"Wooden-it" be Loverly! Denise Levin of Toronto soaks whole packages of wooden skewers, and then stores them in a re-sealable bag in the freezer. They're ready when you are.

Platter Power: Arrange chunks, wedges, or slices of fresh fruit, such as watermelon, pineapple, kiwi, strawberries, mangoes, plums, or nectarines, on a large serving platter. Garnish with sliced star fruit for an absolutely stellar dessert.

Dip Tip: For a delicious dip for fresh fruit, mix 1 cup nonfat plain yogurt with a drizzle of honey. Or melt dark chocolate in a small microwaveable bowl. Place the dip in the center of the platter, surrounded by a colorful array of fruit. Dip a-weigh!

desserts & beverages

Chocolate-Dipped Apricots: Dip the tips of dried apricots in melted chocolate, then coat with chopped pistachios, almonds, or walnuts. Place on parchment paper until set.

It's a Date! Stuff the hollow in pitted dates with whole, unblanched almonds. Dust lightly with icing sugar.

Stem Sells: For an elegant presentation, serve mousses, puddings, parfaits, and sherbets in stemmed wine glasses. Alternate layers of fruit with mousse, etc. for additional color and fiber.

Puddin' on the Ritz! For a quick fix, combine sugar-free pudding mix with nonfat milk as per package directions. Top with fresh fruit or dark chocolate shavings.

Whipped Cream Substitutes: Instead of whipped cream, I've used frozen light whipped topping in many of my desserts because it's convenient, but it contains many chemicals. You can substitute firm silken tofu or Almost Whipped Cream (see my next tip). Soft Yogurt Cheese (page 178) also makes a super substitute.

Almost Whipped Cream: In a food processor fitted with the steel blade, process 1 cup of light ricotta cheese or low-fat cottage cheese for 2 to 3 minutes or until silky smooth. Add 2 Tbsp icing sugar and 1/4 tsp pure vanilla extract (or 1 tsp orange, chocolate, or almond liqueur). Chill before serving.

Cheesed Off? Firm Yogurt Cheese (page 178), Homemade Cottage Cheese (page 177), or pressed cottage cheese make excellent alternatives to cream cheese in cheesecakes and creamy desserts. Light ricotta cheese is another option.

Mock-Sicles: For an easy treat, freeze individual containers of sugar-free nonfat yogurt. Insert a wooden stick before freezing and wrap well. Enjoy!

Calling all Chocoholics! Although chocolate is high in fat, it doesn't raise blood cholesterol because of the type of saturated fat (stearic acid) that it contains. Dark chocolate has one of the highest antioxidant contents of any food. The darker the chocolate, the higher the antioxidant content. Dark chocolate can provide as much as 3 grams of fiber in a 1-oz serving. The dark side is that chocolate is high in calories, so watch your portions! Read Dark Chocolate Secrets (page 377).

Chocolate Meltdown: Microwave 1 to 2 ounces of chocolate (or 1 cup chocolate chips) uncovered on medium for 2 to 3 minutes, stirring every minute. Your bowl must be dry and the chocolate shouldn't be covered or it will "seize" (become lumpy and grainy).

GI Go! To reduce the glycemic index (GI) of a dessert, add foods that have a low GI value, such as berries or other fruit, rolled oats, wheat germ, yogurt, or lemon juice.

The Light Switch: Instead of pie, make the switch to fruit crisp. A crisp, with its juicy fruit filling and crunchy topping of rolled oats and nuts, is lower in fat and calories. No rolling of dough is required—and you'll have fewer rolls around your middle.

Dough Man Dough! Phyllo dough is wonderful in desserts. You can still enjoy crispy dough, but with less calories, carbs, and fat. See recipes for Phyllo Nests (page 62) and Apple Pear Strudel (page 422).

🍑 MINI CHEESECAKES

These muffin-sized cheesecakes are a ter-rific "weigh" to exercise portion control—if you can stop at one! Try the variations and expand your repertoire without expanding your hips!

⅓ cup finely chopped almonds or pecans
2 cups (1 lb/500 g) light cream cheese
  (half cottage cheese can be used)
⅔ cup granulated sugar
  or granular Splenda
1 egg plus 2 egg whites (or 2 eggs)
1 Tbsp lemon juice (preferably fresh)
12 large whole strawberries, hulled

1. Preheat the oven to 350°F. Line each compartment of a muffin pan with paper liners and sprinkle some chopped nuts in the bottom of each one.

2. In a food processor fitted with the steel blade, process the cheese with sugar until blended, about 15 seconds. Add the egg, egg whites, and lemon juice; process for 20 to 30 seconds or until smooth and creamy. Spoon the batter into the prepared muffin pan.

3. Bake for 10 to 12 minutes or until set. When cooled, top each cheesecake with a whole strawberry and refrigerate for 3 to 4 hours, or overnight. Serve chilled.

Yield: 12 mini cheesecakes. Keeps for up to 2 to 3 days in the refrigerator. You can freeze these, but add the strawberries at serving time.

161 calories per cheesecake, 15.8 g carbohydrate, 0.7 g fiber, 6 g protein, 8.5 g fat (4.4 g saturated), 39 mg cholesterol, 127 mg sodium, 126 mg potassium, 1 mg iron, 55 mg calcium

Praline Mini Cheesecakes
Replace sugar with brown sugar. Instead of strawberries, top each cheesecake with a pecan half. Each cheesecake contains 152 calories, 11.1 g carbohydrate, and 9.4 g fat (4.5 g saturated).

Marbled Mini Cheesecakes
Place ⅓ cup semi-sweet chocolate chips in a 2-cup glass measure. Microwave on medium for 1 minute or until melted. Stir ¾ cup of cheesecake batter into melted chocolate. Spoon the remaining batter into paper-lined muffin pan compartments. Drizzle chocolate mixture over white mix-ture. Cut through the batter with a knife to marble it. Bake as directed. Garnish with Chocolate-Dipped Strawberries (page 428). Each cheesecake (with Splenda) contains 167 calories, 11.8 g carbohydrate, and 1.3 g fiber.

Nutrition Note
• Sweet Choice: If you use Splenda instead of sugar, each mini cheesecake contains 123 calories and 6.1 g carbo-hydrate.

🍑 MANGO CHEESECAKE

This easy, no-bake cheesecake comes from Elena Eder of Miami, who is a dessert maven. It's mango-licious! I've modified her recipe slightly and used fat-free cream cheese to reduce the fat.

desserts & beverages

1 ripe mango, peeled
3 cups (1½ lb/750 g) fat-free
  or light cream cheese
½ cup granulated sugar
  or granular Splenda
2 cups frozen light whipped topping,
  partially thawed
9-inch Graham Wafer Pie Crust
  (page 412)
Additional light whipped topping,
  or Almost Whipped Cream (page 410)
  for garnish

1. Cut a slice off each side of the mango, lengthwise, as close to the seed as possible. Cut 8 thin slices from the two halves and reserve to use as a garnish. Cut the remaining mango into chunks.

2. In a food processor fitted with the steel blade, combine the mango chunks, cream cheese, and sugar. Process until well-blended, scraping down the sides of the bowl as needed. Add the whipped topping and process a few seconds longer or until combined.

3. Pour the mixture into the prepared pie crust. Cover with plastic wrap and refrigerate for at least 2 hours, or preferably overnight. When ready to serve, garnish the cheesecake with a little whipped topping around the edges. Top with the reserved mango slices.

Yield: 10 servings. Keeps for up to 2 to 3 days in the refrigerator. Don't freeze.

216 calories per serving, 30.1 g carbohydrate, 0.7 g fiber, 11 g protein, 6.1 g fat (2.8 g saturated), 6 mg cholesterol, 463 mg sodium, 172 mg potassium, 1 mg iron, 143 mg calcium

Chef's Secrets
• Quick Switch! Instead of a graham wafer crust, use baked wonton tart shells (see Quick Tarts on page 422).

• Count Down! To reduce the carbs and calories, use granular Splenda instead of sugar and omit the crust. Pour mixture into 8 parfait glasses. (This makes a more generous serving.) One serving contains 146 calories, 15.3 g carbohydrate, 0.5 g fiber, and 3.7 g fat (2.9 saturated).

🍎 GRAHAM WAFER PIE CRUST

This crust is much lower in calories and fat than a regular pie crust.

1 cup graham wafer crumbs
2 Tbsp melted soft tub margarine or
  canola oil
2 Tbsp granulated sugar or granular Splenda
½ tsp ground cinnamon

1. Preheat the oven to 375°F. Combine the crumbs, margarine, sugar, and cinnamon in a medium bowl and mix well. Press the mixture into the bottom of a sprayed 9-inch glass pie plate.

2. Bake for 7 to 8 minutes (or microwave uncovered on high for 2 minutes) until set. Let cool before filling the crust.

Yield: One 9-inch pie crust (8 to 10 servings). The pie crust can be made a day or two in advance and stored in the refrigerator. Don't freeze: if frozen, crust won't be as crisp.

82 calories per serving (1/8th of recipe), 11.3 g carbohydrate, 0.4 g fiber, 1 g protein, 3.9 g fat (0.6 g saturated), 0 mg cholesterol, 102 mg sodium, 16 mg potassium, 0 mg iron, 5 mg calcium

Nutrition Note
• Sweet Choice: If you use Splenda instead of sugar, one serving contains 72 calories and 8.6 g carbohydrate.

🍎 PUMPKIN CHEESECAKE

This scrumptious pumpkin cheesecake can be made lighter by using half cream cheese and half cottage cheese. Or you can make it dairy-free by using imitation cream cheese. It's perfect for Thanksgiving—your guests will be so thankful!

Crust:

1 cup graham wafer or gingersnap
   cookie crumbs
2 Tbsp canola oil
1 Tbsp brown sugar or granular Splenda

Filling:

3 cups (1 1/2 lb/750 g) light cream cheese
   or imitation cream cheese such as Tofutti
1 cup granulated sugar
   or granular Splenda
1 cup canned pumpkin
   or Pumpkin Purée (page 309)
3 eggs (or 3/4 cup liquid eggs)
1 tsp pure vanilla extract
1 tsp pumpkin pie spice

1. Preheat the oven to 350°F. Spray a 9-inch springform pan with cooking spray. Place a pie plate, half-filled with water, on the lowest rack of the oven. (This helps prevent the cheesecake from cracking.)

2. Crust: Combine the crumbs with the oil and brown sugar in a bowl; mix well. Pat into the bottom of the prepared pan.

3. Filling: In a food processor fitted with the steel blade, process the cream cheese, sugar, and pumpkin until blended, about 20 seconds. Add the eggs, vanilla, and pumpkin pie spice; process until smooth and creamy, 20 to 30 seconds longer. Pour over crust.

4. Place the cheesecake on the middle rack. Bake for 40 to 45 minutes. When done, the edges will be set, but the center will jiggle slightly.

5. Turn off the heat and let the cheesecake cool in the oven with the door partly open for 1 hour. The cheesecake will firm up during this time. Remove the cheesecake from the oven and let cool. Cover and refrigerate overnight, or for up to 2 days. When ready to serve, remove the sides of the pan from the chilled cheesecake and transfer to a serving plate.

Yield: 12 servings. Keeps for up to 2 to 3 days in the refrigerator. Don't freeze: if frozen, the crust will become soggy.

275 calories per serving, 28.6 g carbohydrate, 0.8 g fiber, 8 g protein, 14.3 g fat (7.1 g saturated), 85 mg cholesterol, 229 mg sodium, 167 mg potassium, 2 mg iron, 79 mg calcium

Nutrition Note
• Sweet Choice: If you use Splenda instead of sugar, one serving contains 216 calories and 13.4 g carbohydrate.

Chef's Secrets
• No pumpkin pie spice? Combine 1/2 tsp ground cinnamon, 1/4 tsp ground nutmeg, and 1/4 tsp ground allspice.

desserts &
beverages

• Top It Up! If your cheesecake develops cracks in the top during baking, don't worry. Combine 1 cup light sour cream, 2 Tbsp granulated sugar or Splenda, and 1 tsp pure vanilla extract; mix well. Pour carefully on top of the cheesecake and bake 6 to 8 minutes longer. Topping will firm up when chilled.

Dairy-Free Variation
• Make the cheesecake with imitation cream cheese. Brush the top of the baked cheesecake with 1/4 cup melted apricot preserves and sprinkle with 1/2 cup toasted sliced almonds. It will taste just like regular cheesecake.

♨ FASTER THAN PUMPKIN PIE

This tastes like pumpkin pie without the crust. When you don't have time to bake, this is a snap to make. Kids love to help—and eat it too!

2 pkgs instant vanilla pudding mix
   (4 serving size)
1 can (12 oz/385 ml) 2% evaporated milk
1 can (15 oz/425 ml) canned pumpkin
   or Pumpkin Purée (page 309)
1 tsp pumpkin pie spice
Frozen light whipped topping
   or Almost Whipped Cream (page 410)
   and pecan halves, for garnish

1. Combine the pudding mix and evaporated milk in a large mixing bowl; blend with a whisk until smooth. Transfer to the refrigerator and chill for 5 to 10 minutes or until thickened.

2. When chilled, add the canned pumpkin and pumpkin pie spice and mix well.

3. Divide the pumpkin-pudding mixture into eight parfait dishes. Refrigerate for at least 10 minutes before serving. Serve chilled; garnish each serving with a dollop of whipped topping and a pecan half.

Yield: 8 servings. Keeps for up to 2 to 3 days in the refrigerator. Freezes well for up to 2 months. See Frozen Pumpkin Pops (below).

157 calories per serving (without garnish), 33.1 g carbohydrate, 1.7 g fiber, 4 g protein, 1.3 g fat (0.7 g saturated), 4 mg cholesterol, 414 mg sodium, 277 mg potassium, 1 mg iron, 154 mg calcium

Pumpkin Parfaits
Blend 2 cups of light whipped topping or Almost Whipped Cream (page 410) into pumpkin mixture at the end of Step 1. Spoon into parfait or wine glasses; garnish with whipped topping and chopped pecans.

Frozen Pumpkin Pops
In Step 3, pour mixture into individual popsicle molds and freeze until needed. Serve frozen.

Lighter Variation
• Substitute sugar-free, fat-free instant vanilla pudding and fat-free evaporated milk. One serving contains 89 calories, 16.1 g carbohydrate, and 1.1 g fat (0.7 saturated).

Chef's Secrets
• Feeling Crusty? Fill baked wonton tart shells with pumpkin mixture. (See Quick Tarts, page 422.)

• No instant pudding? No problem—just substitute the kind you cook. (We discovered that by accident.) Combine the pudding mix with evaporated milk in an 8 cup microwaveable bowl; blend well. Microwave, uncovered, on high for 3 minutes; stir well. Microwave for 3 to 4 minutes longer or until boiling and thickened. Cover the surface of the hot pudding with parchment paper to prevent a skin from forming on top. When cool, blend in canned pumpkin and pumpkin pie spice.

• Can-Can! We accidently made this recipe using canned pumpkin pie filling instead of canned pure pumpkin. It turned out yummy, although it was sweeter.

• No pumpkin pie spice? See page 413.

Nutrition Notes

• Nuts to You! Pecans contain more antioxidants than any other nut. They are nutrient-dense, offering vitamin E, calcium, magnesium, potassium, zinc, protein, and fiber. A handful (15 halves) makes a satisfying snack, with 147 calories, 2.9 g carbs, 2 g fiber, and 2 g protein. One pecan half contains 1 g fat, but it's heart-healthy fat.

🍎 HEAVENLY PUMPKIN TRIFLE

This guilt-free trifle is as easy as pie and makes a delectable dessert for a crowd. Your guests will shout "What a 'BOO-tiful' treat!"

Faster Than Pumpkin Pie (page 414)
4 cups frozen light whipped topping, thawed or Almost Whipped Cream (page 410)
9-inch angel food cake (store-bought or homemade), cut in 1-inch chunks
1/2 cup pecan halves, for garnish

1. Prepare the Faster Than Pumpkin Pie mixture as directed. Blend in 1 cup of the whipped topping.

2. Place half the cake chunks in a 3-quart glass serving bowl. Add half the pumpkin mixture and spread evenly. Spread half the whipped topping over the pumpkin mixture. Repeat with the remaining cake chunks, pumpkin mixture, and whipped topping. Garnish with pecans. Chill for several hours or overnight before serving.

Yield: 18 to 20 servings. Keeps for up to 2 to 3 days in the refrigerator. Don't freeze.

174 calories per serving, 29.9 g carbohydrate, 1.3 g fiber, 3 g protein, 4.4 g fat (2.2 g saturated), 1 mg cholesterol, 326 mg sodium, 155 mg potassium, <1 mg iron, 99 mg calcium

Lighter Variation

• If you use the lighter variation of Faster Than Pumpkin Pie to make this trifle, one serving contains 145 calories, 22.4 g carbohydrate, and 4.3 g fat (2.2. g saturated).

🍎 TIRAMISU

Tiramisu, with its light and creamy layers alternating with ladyfingers, is often referred to as Italian trifle. However, tiramisu isn't so light when it comes to fat and calories! This is a lighter version of a recipe shared by Elena Eder of Miami. Tiramisu means "pick me up" and when you taste this decadent dessert, you'll be tempted to pick up another helping! This is a wonderful dessert to enjoy for special occasions.

1 cup (8 oz/250 g) light cream cheese,
   cut into chunks
3/4 cup granulated sugar
2 Tbsp skim milk
2 Tbsp coffee-flavored liqueur or brandy
1 1/2 tsp pure vanilla extract
4 cups frozen light whipped topping, thawed
   or Almost Whipped Cream (page 410)
1 1/2 cups strong coffee
   mixed with 1 tsp granulated sugar
   and 1 Tbsp coffee liqueur or brandy
2 pkgs ladyfingers (about 36 to 40)
1 Tbsp unsweetened cocoa powder

1. In a food processor fitted with the steel blade, combine the cream cheese, sugar, and milk; process until smooth, about 15 seconds. Blend in the liqueur and vanilla, scraping down the sides of the bowl as necessary.

2. Add the whipped topping to the cream cheese mixture and process with several quick on/off pulses, just until combined.

3. Pour the coffee mixture into a shallow bowl. Quickly dip each ladyfinger into the coffee mixture. Work quickly so that the ladyfingers don't get soggy and fall apart. Arrange a layer of ladyfingers in a 9- × 13-inch glass baking dish. Spread with half the cheese mixture. Repeat with another layer of ladyfingers, then with the remaining cheese mixture.

4. Using a fine mesh strainer, lightly sprinkle the cocoa powder on top of the dessert and refrigerate or freeze overnight. Serve chilled or frozen.

Yield: 15 servings. Keeps for up to 2 days in the refrigerator. Freezes well for up to 2 months.

229 calories per serving, 33.3 g carbohydrate, 0.4 g fiber, 5 g protein, 7.8 g fat (4.9 g saturated), 105 mg cholesterol, 100 mg sodium, 94 mg potassium, 1 mg iron, 47 mg calcium

Passover Variation
• Use stale Passover sponge cake instead of ladyfingers. Cut the cake into strips in the shape of ladyfingers. Use Passover whipped topping instead of frozen light whipped topping, and substitute Passover wine for brandy.

Tiramisu Mousse
Omit the ladyfingers. Pour the cheese mixture into 10 parfait glasses and garnish each one with a strawberry. One serving contains 197 calories and 25.6 g carbohydrate.

🍐 LUSCIOUS LEMON BERRY MOUSSE

Picture perfect! This creamy, lemony dessert is like trifle without the cake. The best time to make this dessert is in the summertime, when fresh berries are plentiful and inexpensive. Your guests will think it's so decadent.

1 pkg (7 1/2 oz/212 g) lemon pie filling
   (the kind you cook)
1 1/2 cups softened fat-free
   or light cream cheese
3 cups frozen light whipped topping, thawed
   or Almost Whipped Cream (page 410)
3 cups fresh blueberries
2 cups raspberries or strawberries,
   hulled and halved

1. Prepare the pie filling according to the package directions. (To microwave the filling, cook on high in an 8-cup glass batter bowl for 3 to 4 minutes, stirring once or twice, until bubbly and thick.) Cool for 5 to 10 minutes.

2. Add the cream cheese, by heaping tablespoonfuls, to the hot lemon mixture, whisking well after each addition. Continue whisking until smooth and blended. Cover and refrigerate for 1 hour.

3. When the mixture is fully chilled, whisk in the whipped topping. Pour 1/3 of the lemon mixture into a large glass serving bowl and layer with half the blueberries. Add another 1/3 of the lemon mixture and layer with most of the raspberries. Top with the remaining lemon mixture and arrange the remaining blueberries around the edge of the bowl and the raspberries in the center. Cover and store in the refrigerator overnight. Serve chilled.

Yield: 12 servings. Keeps for up to 2 to 3 days in the refrigerator. Don't freeze.

161 calories per serving, 28.1 g carbohydrate, 2.3 g fiber, 6 g protein, 3.7 g fat (2.6 g saturated), 26 mg cholesterol, 182 mg sodium, 97 mg potassium, 0 mg iron, 63 mg calcium

Chef's Secrets
• Say Cheese! The Lemon Berry Mousse can also be made with Firm Yogurt Cheese (page 178) instead of cream cheese. However, it takes 4 hours to drain the yogurt, so allow sufficient time. The nutrient content is almost the same as with fat-free cream cheese.

• How Light? This recipe can also be made with light cream cheese, but the saturated fat content is significantly higher. One serving contains 204 calories and 8.3 g fat (5.8 g saturated).

🍓 BERRY FOOL

A fool is a creamy dessert traditionally made with whipped cream and fruit. This light, calcium-packed version tastes decadent, but you can enjoy it without the guilt (no fooling)! Drained yogurt replaces the whipped cream. Feel free to use any soft-textured, ripe berries or fruit such as peaches, nectarines, or bananas.

3 cups nonfat plain natural yogurt
   (without gelatin or stabilizers)
3 cups whole strawberries (hulled),
   raspberries, or blackberries
3 to 4 Tbsp granulated sugar, maple syrup,
   or granular Splenda

1. Line a fine mesh strainer with a paper coffee filter, a paper towel, or cheesecloth. Place the lined strainer over a glass bowl or large measuring cup. Spoon the yogurt into the lined strainer, cover, and refrigerate. Let drain for 2 hours. When done, you'll have 2 cups of thick yogurt in the strainer and 1 cup of liquid whey in the bowl. Discard the liquid whey or store it in the refrigerator, covered, and use in recipes as a substitute for buttermilk.

2. Set aside 1 cup of the berries. (If using strawberries, thinly slice 1 cup and set aside.) In a food processor fitted with the steel blade, process the remaining berries until puréed, about 15 to 20 seconds. Add the drained yogurt and the sugar; process with several quick on/off pulses, just until combined.

desserts & beverages

3. Pour half the mixture into four parfait glasses, and then top with a layer of the reserved berries. Repeat with the remaining mixture and another layer of berries. Chill for at least 1 to 2 hours before serving.

Yield: 4 servings. Keeps for up to 2 days in the refrigerator. Don't freeze.

151 calories per serving, 33.2 g carbohydrate, 2.5 g fiber, 8 g protein, 0.4 g fat (0 g saturated), 4 mg cholesterol, 102 mg sodium, 191 mg potassium, 1 mg iron, 245 mg calcium

Mango Fool
Instead of strawberries, substitute with 3 peeled and pitted mangoes. Slice 1 mango and set aside; purée the remaining two. Prepare as directed above.

Chef's Secrets
• Whey to Go! Save the drained liquid (whey) and use it instead of buttermilk when baking muffins and cakes. It will keep up to 2 weeks in the refrigerator.

• Measure Up: To measure how much yogurt you've got after draining, measure the drained whey. Three cups of yogurt yield 1 cup of whey and 2 cups of drained yogurt. If the drained yogurt is too firm, don't worry. Just stir some of the whey back in.

desserts & beverages

Nutrition Note
• Sweet Choice: With Splenda, one serving contains 119 calories and 24.9 g carbohydrate.

● BERRY MANGO SHERBET

Keep frozen fruit on hand in your freezer so you can make this guilt-free dessert in moments. It's "berry" refreshing—great for friends and family!

3 cups frozen strawberries, blueberries, and/or raspberries
1 cup frozen mango chunks
1/4 to 1/3 cup granulated sugar or granular Splenda
1 cup plain yogurt (nonfat or low-fat)

1. In a food processor fitted with the steel blade, process the frozen berries, mango, and sugar with several quick on/off pulses. Continue running the motor until the mixture has the texture of snow. Add the yogurt and process until very smooth, scraping down the sides of the bowl as needed.

2. Serve immediately in parfait glasses or transfer to a bowl, cover, and freeze. About 30 minutes before serving, remove from the freezer and place in the refrigerator to soften. Scoop into parfait or wine glasses and serve.

Yield: About 4 cups (6 servings of 2/3 cup each).

90 calories per serving, 21.8 g carbohydrate, 2.5 g fiber, 2 g protein, 0.1 g fat (0 g saturated), 1 mg cholesterol, 23 mg sodium, 43 mg potassium, 0 mg iron, 63 mg calcium

Chef's Secrets
• Mix It Up! You can create different flavors by using a total of 4 cups frozen mixed fruit.

• Berry Easy! To make a small batch, use 1 cup frozen fruit, 1 Tbsp granulated sugar or Splenda, and 1/4 cup yogurt.

Nutrition Note

• Sweet Choice: If you use Splenda instead of sugar, one serving contains 74 calories and 16.8 g carbohydrate.

🍓 STRAWBERRY KIWI PARFAITS

Love that layered look! These colorful, fiber-filled parfaits are perfect for company.

1 cup fat-free or low-fat cottage cheese
1 cup nonfat or low-fat plain yogurt
3 Tbsp granulated sugar or granular Splenda
1/2 tsp pure vanilla extract
4 cups strawberries, hulled and sliced
4 kiwifruit, peeled and diced
6 whole strawberries, for garnish

1. In a food processor fitted with the steel blade, combine the cottage cheese, yogurt, sugar, vanilla, and 2 cups of strawberries. Process until very smooth, scraping down the sides of the bowl as needed.

2. Layer the remaining sliced strawberries in the bottom of four parfait glasses. Follow with a layer of half the cheese mixture, a layer of kiwifruit, then the remaining cheese mixture. Top each parfait with a whole strawberry. Cover and refrigerate for 1 to 2 hours, or until well chilled.

Yield: 6 servings. Recipe doubles or triples easily. Keeps in the refrigerator for a day or two. Don't freeze.

144 calories per serving, 29.4 g carbohydrate, 4.1 g fiber, 7 g protein, 0.6 g fat (0 g saturated), 4 mg cholesterol, 175 mg sodium, 356 mg potassium, 1 mg iron, 115 mg calcium

Nutrition Notes

• Sweet Choice: If you use granular Splenda instead of sugar, one serving contains 123 calories and 23.9 g carbohydrate.

• Kiwifruit (GI 53) is high in vision-saving lutein, vitamin C, and fiber. It is a good source of vitamin E and potassium.

• Strawberries (GI 40) are high in vitamin C, potassium, fiber, folate, and antioxidants. Too many can have a diuretic and laxative effect.

🍓 FROZEN PEANUT BUTTER MOUSSE

This sugar-free dessert tastes like ice cream. However, even though there's no added sugar, it's still quite high in calories and saturated fat because of the peanut butter, so save it for special occasions.

1 cup 1% cottage cheese
    or light cream cheese
1 cup natural peanut butter
3/4 cup granular Splenda
2 cups frozen light whipped topping, thawed
    or Almost Whipped Cream (page 410)
1 tsp pure vanilla extract

1. In a food processor fitted with the steel blade, process the cottage cheese until smooth and creamy, about 2 minutes, scraping down the sides of the bowl as needed.

2. Add the peanut butter, Splenda, whipped topping, and vanilla; process until well blended, about 25 to 30 seconds. Divide the mixture into individual serving dishes; cover and freeze.

desserts & beverages

Yield: 8 servings. Freezes well for up to 1 month.

271 calories per serving, 16.1 g carbohydrate, 2.0 g fiber, 11 g protein, 18.3 g fat (4.2 g saturated), 1 mg cholesterol, 235 mg sodium, 25 mg potassium, 0 mg iron, 17 mg calcium

Dairy-Free Variation

• Replace the cream cheese with Tofutti imitation cream cheese and instead of light whipped topping, use non-dairy topping that has been whipped in an electric mixer until stiff.

Nutrition Note

• Sweet Choice: If you use sugar instead of Splenda, one serving contains 334 calories and 32.6 g carbohydrate.

◖ CHOCOLATE TOFU MOUSSE

Cocoa and tofu makes for a delicious pairing, and they have more in common than you'd think. Both come from beans (cocoa beans and soybeans), both are relatively healthy, and both are scrumptious in desserts. So, if you can keep a secret, no one will ever guess this luscious dessert has anything to do with tofu, unless of course you tell them!

1 pkg (16 oz/500 g) extra-firm
    or firm silken tofu, well-drained
3/4 cup granular Splenda
    or granulated sugar
2/3 cup unsweetened cocoa powder
1 tsp pure vanilla or almond extract
Frozen light whipped topping
    or Almost Whipped Cream (page 410) and
    grated semi-sweet chocolate, for garnish

1. In a food processor fitted with the steel blade, process the tofu for 1 to 2 minutes or until very smooth. Scrape down the sides of the bowl as needed. Add Splenda, cocoa and vanilla and process until blended, about 20 seconds longer.

2. Transfer the mixture into four parfait or wine glasses; garnish with whipped topping and grated chocolate. Chill for 1 to 2 hours, or until serving time.

Yield: 4 servings. Keeps for up to 2 to 3 days in the refrigerator. Don't freeze.

96 calories per serving, 13.6 g carbohydrate, 4.3 g fiber, 11 g protein, 2.7 g fat (1.2 g saturated), 0 mg cholesterol, 114 mg sodium, 426 mg potassium, 3 mg iron, 65 mg calcium

Chef's Secrets

• Doubly Delicious: Some brands of silken tofu come in a 12-oz/340-g package. Use 2 packages and make 1 1/2 times the recipe (6 servings). You'll be glad you did!

• Smooth as Silk: Silken tofu is dairy-free, cholesterol-free, and silky smooth. It provides a wonderful creamy texture that's creamier than cream itself! You can use it instead of whipped cream or whipped dessert topping in desserts.

Nutrition Note

• Sweet Choice: If you use sugar instead of Splenda, one serving contains 168 calories and 36.1 g carbohydrate.

● HOMEMADE CHOCOLATE PUDDING

Chocolate pudding always brings back memories of my childhood. This calcium-packed dessert is true comfort food. I love it hot from the pot, but it's also delicious cold. So nutritious, so delicious!

2 cups skim or 1% milk
1/3 cup unsweetened cocoa powder
6 Tbsp granulated sugar
2 Tbsp cornstarch
1/8 tsp salt
2 large eggs (or 1 egg plus 2 egg whites)
1 tsp pure vanilla extract

1. Microwave the milk in a 2-cup glass measure for 4 minutes on high or until piping hot. Combine the cocoa, sugar, cornstarch, and salt in a heavy-bottomed, 2-quart saucepan. Gradually whisk the hot milk into the saucepan and mix well. Place over medium heat and cook for 2 to 3 minutes or until thick, whisking to prevent sticking.

2. Combine the eggs and vanilla in the same measuring cup used to heat the milk (this saves on clean-up). Whisk in 1 cup of the hot chocolate mixture; continue whisking until well blended. Pour the mixture back into the saucepan and cook on low, whisking constantly, for 1 to 2 minutes longer or until thickened.

3. When thickened, transfer to four dessert dishes. Serve immediately or chill in the refrigerator until ready to serve: it's delicious hot, warm, or cold.

Yield: 4 servings. Keeps for up to 2 days in the refrigerator. Don't freeze.

187 calories per serving, 32.6 g carbohydrate, 2.4 g fiber, 9 g protein, 3.7 g fat (1.5 g saturated), 108 mg cholesterol, 173 mg sodium, 348 mg potassium, 2 mg iron, 174 mg calcium

Chef's Secrets
• Fill 'em Up! This makes a delicious filling for Quick Tarts (page 422) or Phyllo Nests (page 62).

● CHOCOLATE PUDDING FOR ONE

Nutritious and satisfying, this calcium-packed, sugar-free dessert is perfect when you have a craving for chocolate.

2 tsp cornstarch
1 Tbsp unsweetened cocoa powder
4 tsp granular Splenda (or 2 packets)
1/2 cup skim milk
Dash of pure vanilla extract

1. Combine the cornstarch, cocoa, Splenda, and milk in a 2-cup glass measure. Blend well.

2. Microwave, uncovered, on high for 1 minute; stir well. Microwave on high for another 30 seconds or until the mixture is thick and bubbly.

3. Stir in the vanilla. Serve immediately or chill in the refrigerator until ready to serve: it's delicious hot, warm, or cold.

Yield: 1 serving. Keeps for up to 1 to 2 days in the refrigerator. Freezes well for up to a month (see Frozen Pudding on a Stick, below).

85 calories per serving, 15.8 g carbohydrate, 1.8 g fiber, 5 g protein, 1.0 g fat (0.6 g saturated), 2 mg cholesterol, 65 mg sodium, 285 mg potassium, 1 mg iron, 158 mg calcium

desserts & beverages

Frozen Pudding on a Stick
Pour the cooked pudding into a small paper cup. Cover the paper cup with foil and insert a wooden stick in the center of the cup by making a slit in the foil. Freeze for at least 2 hours. Remove the foil and peel away the paper cup at serving time. Freezes for up to a month.

Nutrition Note
• Sweet Choice: If you prefer to use 4 tsp of sugar instead of granular Splenda, one serving contains 142 calories and 30.5 g carbohydrate.

🍎 QUICK TARTS

You can make the tart shells for this recipe in advance, but it's best to fill them just before serving so they won't become soggy.

12 wonton wrappers (defrost if frozen)
2 Tbsp low-sugar apricot preserves
3 cups sliced strawberries (other berries
 or cut-up fruit can be substituted)
1 cup nonfat yogurt
 (choose your favorite flavor)

1. Preheat the oven to 375°F. Spray the compartments of a standard muffin pan with cooking spray.

2. Press each wonton wrapper into the compartments of the muffin pan, allowing the corners of the dough to stand up over the edges of the pan.

3. Bake for 5 to 6 minutes, or until golden. Cool slightly. Carefully remove the shells from the pans and cool on a wire rack. (These shells can be prepared in advance and kept for up to 1 week in the refrigerator in an airtight container.)

4. In a small saucepan, heat the apricot preserves on low for 2 to 3 minutes (or microwave for 30 to 45 seconds), until melted. Brush the insides of the tart shells with the melted preserves. Fill the shells with strawberries and top each one with a spoonful of yogurt shortly before serving.

Yield: 12 servings. Recipe doubles or triples easily. Filled tart shells are best served within a few hours of assembly.

49 calories per serving, 10.4 g carbohydrate, 1.0 g fiber, 2 g protein, 0.2 g fat (0 g saturated), 1 mg cholesterol, 57 mg sodium, 70 mg potassium, 0 mg iron, 35 mg calcium

Chef's Secrets
• Fill 'em Up! Delicious filled with your favorite flavor of pudding and topped with your favorite fruit. Toasted sliced almonds or chopped pistachios make a great garnish.

• Easy Elegance: Fill tart shells with any of the following: Mango Cheesecake (page 411), Faster Than Pumpkin Pie (page 414), Chocolate Tofu Mousse (page 420), or Homemade Chocolate Pudding (page 421).

🍎 APPLE PEAR STRUDEL

The aroma of apples, pears, and cinnamon will warm both your heart and your home. This delicious combination contains two of my favorite fruits, but you can substitute your own favorites. Easy, yet elegant!

4 large baking apples, peeled, cored,
 and sliced
2 firm ripe pears, peeled, cored, and sliced
1 Tbsp lemon juice (preferably fresh)
1/4 cup brown sugar or granular Splenda
2 tsp ground cinnamon
2 Tbsp whole wheat or all-purpose flour
8 sheets phyllo dough
2 to 3 Tbsp canola oil
 or melted tub margarine
1 cup Special K cereal, finely crushed
1 Tbsp granulated sugar or granular Splenda
 mixed with 1/4 tsp ground cinnamon,
 for sprinkling

1. Preheat the oven to 375°F. Line a large baking sheet with parchment paper.

2. In a large bowl, combine the apples, pears, lemon juice, brown sugar, cinnamon, and flour; toss to combine.

3. Place one sheet of phyllo dough on a dry work surface, with the longer side facing you. (Keep the remaining phyllo covered with plastic wrap to prevent it from drying out.) Brush the top side lightly with oil, and then sprinkle lightly with the crushed cereal. Place another sheet of phyllo on top of the first one; brush with oil and sprinkle with crushed cereal. Repeat until you have 3 layers, then top with a fourth layer of phyllo. Don't brush the top layer with oil or add the crumbs. Spoon half of the filling in a line along the bottom edge of the phyllo layers, leaving a 1½-inch border at the bottom and on the sides. Fold both of the shorter sides inwards and, starting with the bottom, carefully roll up the phyllo. Place the roll, seam-side down, on the prepared baking sheet.

4. Repeat Step 3 with the remaining phyllo dough and filling to make a second strudel. Brush the tops of the strudels lightly with oil and sprinkle with the cinnamon-sugar mixture. Use a sharp knife to cut partially through the top of the dough, but not through the filling, marking 6 slices per strudel.

5. Bake for 30 minutes or until the pastry is golden. Fruit should be tender when strudel is pierced with a knife. At serving time, use a serrated knife to slice completely through.

Yield: 12 servings. Will keep in the refrigerator for up to 2 days; reheats well. It can be frozen for up 2 months: it will be delicious, but the dough won't be as crisp.

142 calories per serving, 27.9 g carbohydrate, 3.2 g fiber, 2 g protein, 3.3. g fat (0.4 g saturated), 0 mg cholesterol, 82 mg sodium, 142 mg potassium, 2 mg iron, 17 mg calcium

Chef's Secrets
• Heat and Eat: To reheat the strudel, bake it uncovered at 350°F for 10 to 12 minutes. Don't microwave the strudel or the dough will be soggy. It's delicious topped with low-fat ice cream or frozen yogurt.

• Mix It Up! Instead of pears, experiment with other fruits such as plums, pears, peaches, nectarines, blueberries, and pitted cherries.

• Go Nuts! Instead of crushed cereal, substitute ½ cup Almond Meal (page 390) and sprinkle lightly between the phyllo layers.

• Phyllo Facts: See Chef's Secrets—Phyllo Facts (page 61).

Nutrition Note
• Sweet Choice: With Splenda, one serving contains 129 calories and 24.5 g carbohydrate.

BLUEBERRY CRUMBLE

Your guests won't mumble—they'll scream for more of this crispy crumble! It's terrific topped with frozen yogurt or ice cream.

desserts & beverages

Filling:

4 cups fresh or frozen blueberries
  (no need to thaw)
1/3 cup granulated sugar
  or granular Splenda
1/3 cup water
2 Tbsp cornstarch
2 Tbsp orange juice (preferably fresh),
  or cranberry or pomegranate juice

Topping:

1/2 cup whole wheat or all-purpose flour
1/2 cup rolled oats (preferably large flake)
1/3 cup lightly packed brown sugar
  or granular Splenda
3 Tbsp canola oil
1/2 tsp ground cinnamon

1. Preheat the oven to 350°F. Spray a 10-inch ceramic or glass pie plate with cooking spray.

2. Filling: Combine the blueberries, sugar, and water in a medium saucepan. Bring to a boil. Reduce heat and simmer for 5 minutes, stirring occasionally. In a small bowl, dissolve the cornstarch in the juice; stir into the blueberry mixture. Cook for 1 to 2 minutes longer or until the filling is thick and glossy. Pour into the sprayed pie plate.

3. Topping: Combine the flour, oats, sugar, oil, and cinnamon in a large bowl and mix together until crumbly. Sprinkle evenly over the hot blueberry mixture.

4. Bake for 30 minutes or until golden. Serve warm or at room temperature.

Yield: 10 servings. Keeps for up to 2 to 3 days in the refrigerator; reheats well. Freezes well for up to 3 months.

154 calories per serving, 28.5 g carbohydrate, 2.6 g fiber, 2 g protein, 4.8 g fat (0.4 g saturated), 0 mg cholesterol, 1 mg sodium, 90 mg potassium, 1 mg iron, 9 mg calcium

Variations
• Instead of blueberries, substitute with 4 cups of frozen mixed berries. Sliced peaches, nectarines, pears, or apples can replace part of the berries.

• Go Nuts! Add 1/2 cup slivered almonds to the topping mixture.

Nutrition Note
• Sweet Choice: If you're using Splenda instead of sugar, one serving contains 120 calories and 18.9 g carbohydrate, making this an excellent diabetic choice.

❧ FABULOUS FRUIT CRISP

This delectable dairy-free dessert is very versatile. It can be baked in the oven or in the microwave, and it can be made sugar-free or nut-free without compromising its fabulous flavor. That's my kind of recipe! I keep several bags of frozen berries in my freezer so I can always prepare this dessert in minutes . . . and it disappears just as quickly.

Filling:

7 to 8 cups frozen mixed berries
  (try blueberries, strawberries, raspberries,
  and/or blackberries)
1/3 cup whole wheat flour
1/4 cup granulated sugar
  or granular Splenda
1 tsp ground cinnamon

Topping:

1 cup rolled oats (preferably large flake)
1/3 cup lightly packed brown sugar
   or granular Splenda
1/4 cup whole wheat flour
1/4 cup sliced almonds or filberts (optional)
1/4 cup canola oil
   or melted soft tub margarine
1 tsp ground cinnamon

1. Preheat the oven to 375°F. Combine the ingredients for the filling in a large bowl and mix well. (The berries can be added while still frozen.) Pour into a sprayed 10-inch ceramic quiche dish or 7- × 11-inch glass baking dish, and spread evenly.

2. Using the same large bowl (no washing required), combine the ingredients for the topping and mix until crumbly. Sprinkle the topping over the filling in the baking dish.

3. Bake for 40 to 45 minutes or until the topping is golden brown. To test for doneness, insert a knife into the center of the crisp. It should be hot to the touch when you remove it. Serve warm or cold.

Yield: 10 servings. Leftovers (if any) will keep for up to 3 or 4 days in the refrigerator; reheats well. Freezes well for up to 4 months.

194 calories per serving, 32.1 g carbohydrate, 4.8 g fiber, 3 g protein, 6.4 g fat (0.4 g saturated), 0 mg cholesterol, 2 mg sodium, 47 mg potassium, 2 mg iron, 32 mg calcium

Any Kinda Crisp
Use a total of 7 to 8 cups fruit (sliced apples, pears, peaches, plums, nectarines, strawberries, and/or rhubarb); or combine 4 cups frozen mixed berries with 3 cups frozen cubed mango. Your choice!

Chef's Secrets
• Microwave Magic: Place a large sheet of parchment paper under the quiche dish to catch any spills while it's baking. Microwave, uncovered, on high for 12 to 14 minutes or until the filling is bubbly and the topping is golden.

• Double Up! Double the recipe, using a 9- × 13-inch glass baking dish that has been sprayed with cooking spray. Bake the assembled crisp in a 375°F oven for 45 to 55 minutes. Great for a crowd.

• Frozen Assets: Make up batches of the topping and store it in re-sealable plastic bags in the freezer. There's no need to thaw it before using—it's ready when you are.

Nutrition Note
• Sweet Choice: If you use Splenda instead of sugar, one serving contains 162 calories and 23.8 g carbohydrate.

🍑 MIXED FRUIT COMPOTE

This delicious compote is perfect for people with diabetes. It's also a terrific topping for pancakes or a scrumptious sauce over frozen yogurt or ice cream. If you're short of one fruit, just use more of another one.

2 cups blueberries or blackberries
2 cups strawberries, hulled and halved
3 plums, pitted and sliced
3 nectarines or peaches, pitted and sliced
3 large apples (try Cortland, Spartan,
   or Gala), peeled, cored, and cut in chunks
1 1/2 cups water
1/2 cup granular Splenda (or to taste)
1 tsp ground cinnamon

1. Combine the berries, plums, nectarines, and apples in a large pot. You should have 8 to 9 cups of fruit. Add the water and bring to a boil. Reduce heat and simmer, partially covered, for about 20 to 25 minutes or until tender, stirring occasionally.

2. Remove from the heat and stir in the Splenda and cinnamon. When cool, transfer to glass jars or freezer containers. Cover and refrigerate. Serve chilled.

Yield: About 8 cups (16 servings of 1/2 cup each). Keeps for up to 10 days in the refrigerator; reheats well. Freezes well for up to 4 months.

58 calories per serving, 14.7 g carbohydrate, 2.5 g fiber, 1 g protein, 0.3 g fat (0 g saturated), 0 mg cholesterol, 1 mg sodium, 160 mg potassium, 0 mg iron, 11 mg calcium

Variations
• Raspberries, cranberries, and/or peeled peaches or pears can be substituted for any of the fruits. Frozen mixed berries are also delicious in this compote.

Nutrition Note
• Sweet Choice: If made with sugar instead of Splenda, one serving contains 79 calories and 20.2 g carbohydrate.

✎ ROASTED FRUIT MEDLEY

Roast and boast! Roasting brings out the best in fruit, intensifying the flavor by caramelizing their natural sugars. This fruit medley is absolutely amazing over ice cream or frozen yogurt. What a fabulous "weigh" to increase your fruit intake!

2 lb (1 kg) plums, nectarines,
  and/or peaches (about 5 cups sliced)
1 Tbsp lemon juice (preferably fresh)
3 Tbsp maple syrup, honey,
  or granular Splenda
3 to 4 Tbsp water or pomegranate juice

1. Preheat the oven to 375°F. Arrange the fruit in a large, sprayed baking dish. Drizzle with lemon juice and maple syrup. Add the water to the baking dish.

2. Roast uncovered, basting occasionally, about 20 to 25 minutes. When done, the fruit should be tender and the pan juices thick and syrupy. If the pan juices evaporate too quickly, add a little extra water to the baking dish. Serve warm or chilled.

Yield: 6 servings. Recipe doubles or triples easily. Keeps for up to 3 to 4 days in the refrigerator; reheats well. Freezes well for up to 3 months.

92 calories per serving, 23.2 g carbohydrate, 2.0 g fiber, 1 g protein, 0.4 g fat (0 g saturated), 0 mg cholesterol, 1 mg sodium, 247 mg potassium, 0 mg iron, 15 mg calcium

Chef's Secrets
• Your Choice: Roasting works well for many kinds of fruit, including apples, apricots, mangoes, peaches, pears, pineapples, plums, and strawberries.

• Time to Cook: Softer fruits such as strawberries or apricots take 20 to 25 minutes. Harder fruits such as apples or pears will take 35 to 40 minutes.

Nutrition Note
• Sweet Choice: If you use Splenda instead of maple syrup or honey, one serving contains 69 calories and 17.2 g carbohydrate.

🍎 GRILLED PINEAPPLE

Many supermarkets sell pineapple already peeled and cored—now that's "a-peel-ing!" Other fruits can be grilled successfully—try peaches, nectarines, or mangoes.

1 ripe pineapple, peeled and cored
Cooking spray or canola oil

1. Core and slice the pineapple into circles about 3/4-inch thick. You should have about 8 slices. Spray the slices lightly with cooking spray on both sides or brush lightly with oil.

2. Place the slices on a hot grill and cook on medium-high heat for 3 to 4 minutes per side, until just heated through and grill marks appear. Serve immediately.

Yield: 4 servings of 2 slices per person.

58 calories per serving (2 slices), 14.9 g carbohydrate, 1.7 g fiber, 0 g protein, 0.3 g fat (0 g saturated), 0 mg cholesterol, 1 mg sodium, 136 mg potassium, 0 mg iron, 15 mg calcium

Pineapple Strawberry Kabobs

Soak wooden skewers in water for 20 minutes to prevent them from burning on the grill. Chop a pineapple into 2-inch chunks and push onto the pre-soaked skewers, alternating with whole, hulled strawberries; you should have about 3 pineapple chunks and 3 strawberries on each skewer. Drizzle lightly with honey or maple syrup. Grill over medium heat for 5 to 6 minutes, turning occasionally, until the edges of the pineapple are golden brown. Serve warm.

Grilled Strawberries

Place firm, ripe hulled strawberries in a bowl; drizzle lightly with balsamic vinegar, and maple syrup or honey. Let stand 10 minutes, then thread onto the pre-soaked wooden skewers. (To keep the strawberries from spinning around when you turn them over, it's best to double-skewer them.) Grill over medium heat for 4 to 5 minutes, turning occasionally, until they are almost tender and grill marks appear. Scrumptious over ice cream.

Chef's Secrets

• Leftovers? Refrigerate and use leftover grilled fruit in smoothies (pages 433–37), fruit salad, or Pineapple Salsa (page 105).

• Ripe for the Picking: Pineapple must be picked ripe because the starch won't convert to sugar once it has been picked. If pineapple isn't quite ripe enough when you buy it, store it at room temperature for a few days to reduce its acidity.

• Weighing In: An average pineapple weighs 2 to 4 lb (1 to 2 kg). When buying, choose one that's slightly soft to the touch, with no soft or dark areas. The center leaves on top should pull out easily and the pineapple should smell sweet. Store it in the refrigerator for 3 to 4 days.

Nutrition Notes

• Pineapple is a good source of fiber, contains vitamins A and C, and is low in calories. Because it's a tropical fruit, it has a medium GI value (around 59), but its glycemic load is low because pineapple is low in carbohydrate, so enjoy it often.

desserts & beverages

FROZEN GRAPES

These make a refreshing, super snack straight from the freezer. Grape idea!

Green or red seedless grapes

1. Wash the grapes thoroughly and pat dry. Remove from stems and place in a single layer on a tray. Store, uncovered, in the freezer for 1 to 2 hours, or until frozen. Transfer to re-sealable freezer bags and store in the freezer for up to a month.

Yield: 16 grapes make 1 serving.

58 calories per serving, 15.0 g carbohydrate, 0.7 g fiber, <1 g protein, 0.1 g fat (0 g saturated), 0 mg cholesterol, 2 mg sodium, 159 mg potassium, 0 mg iron, 8 mg calcium

Nutrition Notes
• People with kidney problems who are on a fluid-restricted diet can enjoy these without worry. Frozen grapes don't count as fluid and will help quench your thirst. Thanks to dietitian Ilana Kobric of Toronto for this terrific tip.

CHOCOLATE-DIPPED STRAWBERRIES

This makes a "berry" delicious low-calorie treat.

24 large strawberries, hulled
4 oz/125 g dark, (semi-sweet or bittersweet) chocolate (preferably 70% or higher)

1. Rinse the strawberries and pat dry with paper towels.

2. Melt the chocolate in the microwave for 2 minutes on medium (50%), stirring at half time. Make sure no water gets into the chocolate or it will turn hard and lumpy. Remove and cool slightly.

3. Dip the tip of each strawberry in melted chocolate. Place on a parchment paper-lined baking sheet and refrigerate until set. These can be made several hours in advance.

Yield: 2 dozen. Don't freeze. These should be eaten the same day they are made.

28 calories per strawberry, 4.2 g carbohydrate, 0.7 g fiber, 0 g protein, 1.5 g fat (0.8 g saturated), 0 mg cholesterol, 2 mg sodium, 28 mg potassium, 0 mg iron, 3 mg calcium

Variation
• Coat chocolate-dipped strawberries in chopped walnuts, almonds, or pecans. Chopped pistachios make an attractive presentation. Go nuts!

Chef's Secrets
• Chilling News: If chocolate is refrigerated, it may sweat when it returns to room temperature. Don't worry—this doesn't affect its taste!

• White's Alright! The white streaks that develop on chocolate is the cocoa butter coming to the surface. This doesn't compromise its taste or quality. The "bloom" disappears when it melts—providing a perfect reason to coat strawberries with melted chocolate that has lost its shine!

• For more on chocolate, see Chef's Secrets—Be a Chocolate Maven (page 391).

Nutrition Notes
• Deep, Dark Secrets! Dark chocolate is very high in antioxidants. The darker the

chocolate, the less sugar it contains, and the higher its antioxidant content. Chocolate also makes you feel good—but if you indulge too much, you'll bulge—then you won't feel so good! We think up to an ounce a day is a good thing.

• Super News: Dark chocolate is considered a super-food because of its extremely high antioxidant content and its heart-protecting benefits. A 1 oz serving of dark chocolate (70% and higher) contains 2 to 3 g fiber, depending on the brand.

🍎 MAPLE BALSAMIC STRAWBERRIES

This is a beautiful blend of flavors. So berry good!

4 cups strawberries
2 Tbsp balsamic vinegar
2 Tbsp maple syrup

1. Rinse the strawberries thoroughly, then hull and slice.

2. Combine the sliced strawberries with balsamic vinegar and maple syrup in a medium bowl and mix gently.

3. Cover and refrigerate for at least 1 hour before serving. (The longer they marinate, the better they taste.) Serve chilled in stemmed wine glasses.

Yield: 4 servings.

84 calories per serving, 20.6 g carbohydrate, 3.3 g fiber, 1 g protein, 0.5 g fat (0 g saturated), 0 mg cholesterol, 4 mg sodium, 280 mg potassium, 1 mg iron, 36 mg calcium

Chef's Secrets
• A Different Twist! Add a grinding or two of black pepper to add a kick!

• For Passover, use honey or sugar instead of maple syrup.

🍎 POACHED PEARS

Juicy fruit! Pears take on a lovely rosy hue from the cooking juices in this easy, elegant dessert.

1 cup cranberry juice (low-calorie or regular)
1 cinnamon stick
   or 1/4 tsp ground cinnamon
1 Tbsp honey
1 tsp lemon juice (preferably fresh)
4 firm ripe pears such as Bosc or Anjou

1. Combine the cranberry juice, cinnamon, honey, and lemon juice in a large skillet over high heat; bring to a boil. Reduce heat to low and simmer for 2 minutes.

2. Peel the pears and cut in half lengthwise. Remove the cores with a melon baller. Place, cut-side down, in the skillet, with the narrow ends pointing inwards.

3. Cover and continue simmering for 8 to 10 minutes, basting occasionally. When done, the pears should hold their shape but be tender and easily pierced with a knife. Serve warm or chilled, with the sauce spooned over the pears.

Yield: 4 servings. Keeps for up to 3 to 4 days in the refrigerator. Don't freeze.

109 calories per serving, 28.9 g carbohydrate, 4.5 g fiber, 1 g protein, 0.2 g fat (0 g saturated), 0 mg cholesterol, 5 mg sodium, 197 mg potassium, 1 mg iron, 21 mg calcium

desserts & beverages

Chef's Secrets

• Wing It! Place 2 poached pear halves on each dessert dish, with their stem ends touching. Slice each half lengthwise, from the wide end to just past the middle, so that each sliced piece is still attached at the narrow end. Fan out the sliced ends; you will have an appealing butterfly design.

• "Nut"-ritious: At serving time, sprinkle the poached pears with toasted slivered almonds.

• Juice It Up! Instead of cranberry juice, use pomegranate juice and increase the amount of honey to 2 Tbsp. Other juice options to consider are apple-raspberry, cranberry-orange, cran-raspberry, or cran-blueberry juice. Juggle your juices!

• Leftovers? Slice any leftover pears and combine with your favorite flavor of nonfat yogurt for breakfast. Or serve pears with vanilla frozen yogurt for dessert—a drizzle of chocolate couldn't hurt!

APPLE BLUE-PEARY SAUCE

This fiber-packed dessert can be enjoyed hot or cold, chunky or smooth. It also makes a terrific topping over frozen yogurt, ice cream, or pancakes.

4 large apples, peeled, cored, and
  cut in chunks
2 cups blueberries (frozen or fresh)
2 pears, peeled, cored, and cut in chunks
1/3 cup water
3 Tbsp brown sugar or granular Splenda
1 tsp ground cinnamon
1 tsp lemon juice (preferably fresh)

1. Combine all the ingredients in a large microwaveable bowl. Cover and microwave on high for 6 to 8 minutes or until the fruit is tender, stirring once or twice during cooking.

2. Mash with a potato masher for a smoother consistency, or don't mash and leave it chunky. Serve hot or cold.

Yield: 6 to 8 servings. Keeps for up to a week to 10 days in the refrigerator. Freezes well for up to 3 months.

150 calories per serving, 39.1 g carbohydrate, 6.7 g fiber, 1 g protein, 0.6 g fat (0.1 g saturated), 0 mg cholesterol, 4 mg sodium, 264 mg potassium, 1 mg iron, 26 mg calcium

Nutrition Note

• Sweet Choice: If you use granular Splenda instead of brown sugar, one serving contains 136 calories, 35.5 g carbohydrate, and 6.7 g fiber.

WARM MIXED BERRY SAUCE

This is so quick and simple to prepare. It's fabulous over frozen yogurt, ice cream, or Roasted Fruit Medley (page 426). Berries are supposed to help your memory, so, for a memorable brunch dish, spoon it over Cheese Pancakes (page 173).

4 cups mixed berries (try blueberries,
  strawberries, and blackberries)
2 to 3 Tbsp granulated sugar, honey,
  maple syrup, or granular Splenda
1 to 2 tsp kirsch or cherry brandy (optional)

1. In a large nonstick skillet, combine the berries with sugar. Cook over high heat, stirring occasionally, for about 2 to 3 minutes or until the berries start to release their juices but still hold their shape.

2. Taste the fruit to test for sweetness, adding more sugar if necessary. Stir in the kirsch or cherry brandy, if using. Serve warm (although it's also delicious when chilled).

Yield: 6 servings Keeps for up to 3 to 4 days in the refrigerator. Freezes well for up to 3 months.

60 calories per serving, 14.8 g carbohydrate, 3.2 g fiber, 1 g protein, 0.4 g fat (0 g saturated), 0 mg cholesterol, 1 mg sodium, 134 mg potassium, 1 mg iron, 17 mg calcium

Chef's Secrets
• Frozen Assets: When berries aren't in season, substitute with frozen mixed berries. Cooking time for frozen berries will be 3 to 5 minutes. When fresh berries are expensive, frozen are usually more economical.

• Freeze with Ease: Don't rinse fresh berries if you are freezing them. Spread them in a single layer on a tray and freeze, then transfer them to re-sealable plastic bags. Freeze for up to 3 months. There's no need to defrost them before using—they thaw very quickly. Rinse before using.

• Berry Versatile: Try berries in fruit crisps, smoothies, muffins, quick breads, pancakes, and fruit salad. Use them as a topping for your breakfast cereal or as a satisfying snack. Berry good!

Nutrition Notes
• Berry Boost: Boost your berry intake and enjoy them several times a week. Berries are rich in vitamin C, fiber, and are packed with antioxidants, but they're low in calories. The less you cook them, the more nutrients they retain.

• So Blue-tiful! Blueberries contain the most health-protecting antioxidants of all fruits because of their high level of anthocyanins, the pigment that makes blueberries blue. A cup of blueberries contains about $1/3$ of your daily requirement for vitamin C.

• Get Cultivated! Fresh blueberries are cultivated and are larger and sweeter than wild ones.

• Go Wild! Wild blueberries may be tiny, but they're mighty good for you. Wild blueberries are packed with more phytonutrients than cultivated ones.

• True Blue: Blueberries are a great source of fiber, with almost 3 grams in a half-cup serving. Like cranberries, blueberries may protect against bladder infections because they contain compounds that prevent bacteria from adhering to the walls of the bladder.

• Sweet Choice: If you use granular Splenda instead of sugar, one serving contains 46 calories and 11.2 g carbohydrate. If using honey or maple syrup, the nutrient analysis will be similar to using granulated sugar.

desserts & beverages

BEST BEVERAGES:

• Thirst Is First: Think you're hungry? It's possible you're just thirsty. Before you indulge in a snack, drink a glass of water or have a cup of hot tea. Go for green or black tea, which are packed with antioxidants. Herbal teas, hot water with a wedge of lemon, sugar-free iced tea, or Lemonade (page 432) are also satisfying beverages.

• Eau my Goodness! Water is your best choice for quenching thirst and it's calorie-free. Aim for 8 or 9 glasses of fluid a day, including water and other beverages. Intake should be distributed throughout the day. Add a wedge of lemon, lime, or orange for a flavor boost.

• Drink Up! Club soda, seltzer, and mineral water will add a little sparkle to your day. Soups and other beverages count as part of your daily fluid intake. When you increase your intake of fiber, be sure to drink more liquids.

• Fruit Spritzer: Dilute fruit juice with club soda or mineral water—half the carbs and calories.

• Sugar Blues: Replace sugary drinks with water or calorie-free beverages. Did you know that a 12-ounce can of regular (not diet) coke or ginger ale contains 150 calories and the equivalent of 12 teaspoons of sugar? One can a day is equivalent to 12 pounds (up or down!) a year.

• Coffee Break: Coffee is an excellent source of antioxidants. To boost your calcium intake, enjoy Skinny Café au Lait (page 16).

• Smooth Sailing: Smoothies (pages 433–37) make a satisfying and healthy treat and are nutrition-packed. Experiment with some of the variations within each recipe for a more "fruit-full" experience. They make an excellent, nutritious breakfast or snack. Here's to your health!

🍊 LEMONADE

Enjoy this refreshing beverage for a low-calorie treat.

1 Tbsp lemon juice (preferably fresh)
1 cup cold water
2 tsp granular Splenda (or 1 packet)
3 or 4 ice cubes
Lemon slice, for garnish

1. Combine the lemon juice, water, Splenda, and ice cubes in a tall glass and mix well.

2. Garnish with the lemon slice and serve immediately.

Yield: 1 serving. Recipe easily doubles or triples.

8 calories per serving, 2.3 g carbohydrate, 0.1 g fiber, 0 g protein, 0 g fat (0 g saturated), 0 mg cholesterol, 0 mg sodium, 19 mg potassium, 0 mg iron, 1 mg calcium

Chef's Secrets
• Free Lemonade! When you eat in a restaurant, ask your server to give you a lemon wedge for your water. Squeeze the juice into the glass, add a packet of sweetener or sugar, and you've got a free lemonade! (My friend Rita Busman showed me this trick.)

desserts & beverages

• Time for Lime: Substitute lime for lemon.

• Sparkling Lemonade: Use 1/2 cup cold water and 1/2 cup soda water for a sparkling version.

Nutrition Note
• Sweet Choice: With sugar, one serving of lemonade contains 24 calories and 7.3 g carbohydrate.

🍎 CHOCOLATE BANANA SMOOTHIE

You'll go bananas over this nutritious, scrumptious smoothie. It's guaranteed to please kids of all ages. If you don't have a frozen banana, use a fresh one and add a few more ice cubes.

1 frozen banana, peeled and
   cut in 1-inch chunks
1 1/2 cups skim milk or soymilk
1 Tbsp unsweetened cocoa powder
1/2 tsp pure vanilla extract
3 or 4 ice cubes

1. Combine all the ingredients in a blender or food processor; blend or process until smooth and creamy.

2. Serve immediately or cover and refrigerate for a day or two. If you do make this ahead, shake it well before serving.

Yield: 2 servings.

126 calories per serving, 24.0 g carbohydrate, 2.4 g fiber, 7 g protein, 0.9 g fat (0.5 g saturated), 3 mg cholesterol, 97 mg sodium, 558 mg potassium, 1 mg iron, 235 mg calcium

Chef's Secrets
• Frozen Assets: Keep ripe bananas in a plastic freezer bag and store them in the freezer—there's no need to peel them first. When needed, remove from the freezer and place under warm running water for 10 to 15 seconds. This will make them very easy to peel with a sharp knife. How a-peeling!

• Shake Your Smoothies! You can make smoothies in advance and store them for a couple of days in the refrigerator, in a tightly covered container. However, they do have a tendency to separate, so shake well (or stir) before serving. How's that for getting some extra exercise!

• Protein Power: Add a tablespoon of whey protein powder for an additional protein boost.

• Flax Facts! Add a tablespoon of ground flaxseed for additional fiber. Wheat germ also works well.

🍎 MANGO BERRY SMOOTHIE

Dairy-free and flavorful: go man-go! If you keep frozen fruit in the freezer, you can make this 3-ingredient smoothie in a matter of seconds.

1 cup chopped frozen mango
   (or 1 mango, peeled, pitted, and
   cut in 1-inch chunks)
1 cup mixed frozen berries (try blueberries,
   strawberries, and/or blackberries)
1 cup mango, cranberry, or apple juice

1. Combine all the ingredients in a blender or food processor; blend or process until thick and creamy. If too thick, thin with a little juice or water.

2. Serve immediately or cover and refrigerate for a day or two. If you do make this ahead, shake it well before serving.

Yield: 3 servings of approximately 1 cup each.

127 calories per serving, 31.1 g carbohydrate, 3.2 g fiber, 1 g protein, 0.2 g fat (0 g saturated), 0 mg cholesterol, 25 mg sodium, 108 mg potassium, 1 mg iron, 30 mg calcium

Variations
• Instead of mango, you can substitute with 1 frozen banana. I always have frozen ripe bananas on hand, so when mangoes are out of season and expensive, bananas are an economical alternative.

• Instead of berries, substitute with peeled peaches, nectarines, kiwi, pineapple, or papaya, cut in chunks.

• Try pineapple, orange, pomegranate, cranberry, or guava juice as the liquid. Leftover whey from making Cottage Cheese (page 177) or Yogurt Cheese (page 178) can be added to smoothies as part of the liquid.

• Soymilk is excellent in smoothies. Just add a drizzle of honey to round out the flavor.

• Protein Power: To boost the protein, add 1 to 2 Tbsp of whey protein powder.

☂ MANGO LASSI

A lassi is a refreshing chilled drink popular in India that tastes like a healthy milkshake. It can be made with other fruits, but mango is mmm-marvelous!

1 cup mango, peeled and
   cut in 1-inch chunks
1 cup nonfat plain or vanilla yogurt
1/2 cup ice cubes
Mint leaves, for garnish

1. Combine all the ingredients in a blender or food processor; blend or process until thick and frothy. If too thick, thin with a little skim milk or water.

2. Garnish with mint and serve immediately, or cover and refrigerate for a day or two. If you do make this ahead, shake it well before serving, then garnish with mint.

Yield: 2 servings.

117 calories per serving, 27.1 g carbohydrate, 1.9 g fiber, 6 g protein, 0.3 g fat (0.1 g saturated), 2 mg cholesterol, 71 mg sodium, 162 mg potassium, 0 mg iron, 162 mg calcium

Variation
• For a decadent version, use low-calorie vanilla ice cream instead of yogurt.

☂ POMEGRANATE POWER SMOOTHIE

This power-packed drink is perfect to serve at a brunch. Pomegranates are popular because of their health benefits, despite the mess factor. When my son-in-law Paul Sprackman was very young, he always ate pomegranates outside, wearing a raincoat, so he wouldn't stain his clothes! Read my mess-less way to remove seeds (see Chef's Secrets on page 435).

1 pomegranate
1 cup blueberries, strawberries,
   or raspberries
1 mango, peeled and cut in 1-inch chunks

1 frozen banana, peeled and
  cut in 1-inch chunks
1 cup nonfat plain or vanilla yogurt
1 cup skim milk, or orange
  or pomegranate juice
1/2 cup cold water
2 tsp honey, granulated sugar,
  or granular Splenda

1. Remove the seeds from the pomegranate
(see Chef's Secrets).

2. Combine the pomegranate seeds with all
the remaining ingredients in a blender or
food processor. Blend or process for 1 or 2
minutes or until smooth and creamy. (You
may have to do this in 2 batches.)

3. Serve immediately or cover and refrigerate for a day or two. If you do make this
ahead, shake it well before serving.

Yield: About 6 cups. Recipe can be halved.

109 calories per cup, 25.0 g carbohydrate, 2.0 g fiber,
4 g protein, 0.5 g fat (0.1 g saturated), 2 mg cholesterol,
46 mg sodium, 274 mg potassium, 0 mg iron, 108 mg
calcium

Variations
• Instead of mango, substitute with peeled
peaches, nectarines, papaya, pineapple, or
pears.

• Dairy-Free: Omit the yogurt and milk and
substitute with 2 cups soymilk. You could
also make this with apple, cranberry, grape,
guava, pineapple, or pomegranate blueberry
juice.

• For a protein boost, add 2 Tbsp of soy
protein powder.

Chef's Secrets
• No-Mess Method to Removing Seeds: Cut
off the pomegranate's crown, then cut into
quarters. Place in a bowl of water. Using
your fingers, scoop out the juice sacs (arils)
from the spongy white membrane. The
seeds will sink and the rind and membrane
will float. With a slotted spoon, gather the
seeds and discard everything else. Only the
seeds are edible.

• The Seedy Truth! Pomegranate seeds look
like ruby-red jewels and have a sweet-tart
flavor. One pomegranate contains about 3/4
cup seeds. Some people spit out the seeds
after enjoying their juice, but most of the
fiber is in the seeds, so crunch away!

• Food for Thought! Eat the seeds as a
snack or sprinkle them over salads, cereals, grains, vegetables, fish, or poultry. Use
pomegranate seeds in parfaits and other
fruit desserts or add them to muffin, waffle,
or pancake batter. For a decorative touch,
sprinkle a few seeds into the water when
making ice cubes.

• Pomegranate Juice: Blend or process
pomegranate seeds in a blender or food
processor until minced. Strain pulp through
a cheesecloth or a fine sieve. One medium
pomegranate yields about 1/2 cup juice.

• Store It Right! Store pomegranates at
room temperature in a dark, cool place, or
up to 2 months in the refrigerator. Once
removed from the fruit, the seeds will keep
about 3 days in the refrigerator. You can
freeze the seeds in an airtight container
for up to 6 months. Use the frozen seeds to
make juice.

**desserts &
beverages**

Nutrition Note
• One pomegranate has about 105 calories. Pomegranates are a good source of fiber, potassium, vitamin C, and niacin. They are also an excellent source of antioxidants and ellagic acid, which are both potent anti-carcinogens.

🍎 STRAWBERRY ORANGE SMOOTHIE

Quick, refreshing, and healthy as a snack or a breakfast treat! I always have some frozen ripe bananas on hand, and this is a delicious way to use them up.

1 frozen banana, cut in 1-inch chunks
1 cup frozen unsweetened strawberries
   (do not thaw)
1/2 cup frozen unsweetened orange
   concentrate (do not thaw)
1/2 cup cold water
1/2 cup nonfat plain yogurt
1 cup skim milk
2 tsp honey, granulated sugar,
   or granular Splenda
1 tsp pure vanilla extract

1. Combine all the ingredients in a blender or food processor; blend or process until smooth and creamy.

2. Serve immediately or cover and refrigerate for a day or two. If you do make this ahead, shake it well before serving.

Yield: 4 servings of approximately 1 cup each.

150 calories per serving, 33.7 g carbohydrate, 1.9 g fiber, 5 g protein, 0.3 g fat (0.1 g saturated), 2 mg cholesterol, 51 mg sodium, 532 mg potassium, 1 mg iron, 135 mg calcium

Variation
• Instead of strawberries, substitute with frozen raspberries, blueberries, or mixed frozen berries.

🍎 TOFU BERRY SMOOTHIE

You won't believe this smoothie is dairy-free! It makes an excellent breakfast-in-a-glass or is perfect as a nutritious snack.

1 pkg (10 oz/300 g) low-fat silken tofu
2 cups frozen blueberries
1 frozen banana, peeled and
   cut in 1-inch chunks
3/4 cup unsweetened apple juice
2 tsp honey, maple syrup,
   or granular Splenda

1. Combine all the ingredients in a blender or food processor; blend or process until smooth and creamy.

2. Serve immediately or cover and refrigerate for a day or two. If you do make this ahead, shake it well before serving.

Yield: 4 servings of approximately 1 cup.

125 calories per serving, 25.3 g carbohydrate, 2.9 g fiber, 5 g protein, 1.2 g fat (0.2 g saturated), 0 mg cholesterol, 64 mg sodium, 249 mg potassium, 1 mg iron, 37 mg calcium

Mock-sicles
Pour the tofu mixture into popsicle molds (or use paper cups and insert a wooden or plastic stick in each one). Freeze until needed. Cool idea!

Variations

• No frozen blueberries? Add a few ice cubes along with fresh blueberries or strawberries and process until thick and creamy.

• No tofu? Substitute with 1¼ cups nonfat vanilla or plain yogurt.

• Use 2 cups frozen mixed berries such as a combination of raspberries, blackberries, and strawberries.

• For a tropical twist, use a combination of pineapple chunks, mango, and kiwi.

• "Melon-choly?" Combine chunks of cantaloupe, honey dew, watermelon, or your favorite melon with strawberries or raspberries.

• Use 1 cup blueberries or strawberries and add 1 or 2 peaches or nectarines, peeled, and pitted.

• Instead of apple juice, substitute with any of the following: cranberry, grape, guava, mango, orange, pineapple, or pomegranate juice.

Nutrition Notes

• Berry Healthy! Read Nutrition Notes (see page 431).

• For a nutritional boost, add 1 to 2 Tbsp ground flaxseed or wheat germ. For a protein boost, add a tablespoon or two of vanilla whey protein powder.

• Sweet Choice! With Splenda, one serving contains 115 calories, 22.6 g carbs, and 2.9 g fiber.

desserts &
beverages

passover pleasures

PASSOVER PLEASURES

PASSOVER RECIPE LIST

To make this book Passover-friendly, here is a list of recipes found in this chapter, as well as recipes from other chapters that can be used for Passover. Modifications are listed where appropriate.

Some of the recipes have variations that are not suitable for Passover as they contain ingredients that are not Kosher for Passover.

Availability of Passover products varies from year to year. Consult your local Kashruth authority.

Splenda isn't available for Passover use, so use granulated sugar, brown sugar, or Passover sugar substitute (e.g., Gefen Sweet N'Low). One packet of sugar substitute is equal to 2 tsp sugar or granular Splenda. Passover sweeteners are not heat stable—hopefully this will change.

Imitation Passover Dijon mustard is available, but it is inferior in taste to Dijon mustard.

RECIPE	PAGE	MODIFICATION
APPETIZERS AND STARTERS		
Aioli	46	
Tzatziki	52	Dairy version
Roasted Eggplant Spread	53	
Mushroom Mock Chopped Liver	56	
Smoked Salmon Pinwheels	57	
Best Bruschetta	63	Replace crostini with matzo crackers
Mediterranean Stuffed Mushrooms	66	Omit sun-dried tomatoes
Mini Veggie Latkes with Smoked Salmon	67	
Tomato Tidbits	70	
Charoset	453	
Eggplant Mock Chopped Liver	453	
Vegetable Fricassee (or Loaves)	454	

passover pleasures

RECIPE	PAGE	MODIFICATION

SOUPS

SAUCES AND MARINADES

passover pleasures

RECIPE PAGE MODIFICATION

FISH

Fast Fish Salad	121	
Three-Color Gefilte Fish Loaf	123	
Halibut with Tiny Roasted Tomatoes	124	
Pesto Salmon or Halibut	125	
Aioli Salmon/Halibut	126–27	
Lemon Dill Salmon	131	
Thyme for Lime Salmon	136	
Snapper Balsamico with Grape Tomatoes and Mushrooms	138	Replace maple syrup with honey
Fish Fillets in Parchment	139	
Stuffed Sole Duxelles	139	Replace bread with $1/2$ cup matzo meal
Tilapia Mediterrania	140	Omit capers
Seder Salmon	457	
Glazed Stuffed Salmon	457	

MEAT

Cranberry Brisket with Caramelized Onions	186	Use canned Passover jellied cranberry sauce
Cranberry Veal Brisket	187	
Saucy Brisket	187	
Holiday Brisket	458	
Roast Veal with Lemon Gremolata	459	

GROUND MEAT/POULTRY

Better Burgers	189	Replace rolled oats with matzo meal
Mighty Good Meatballs/Meat Loaf	190	Replace rolled oats with matzo meal
Barbecue Meat Loaf	191	Replace rolled oats with matzo meal
Mushroom Turkey Loaf	193	See Passover variation
Sweet Potato Shepherd's Pie	194	
Unstuffed Cabbage	195	Omit rice. Replace rolled oats with matzo meal
Passover Meat Lasagna	462	

passover pleasures

RECIPE	PAGE	MODIFICATION

POULTRY

RECIPE	PAGE	MODIFICATION
Cheater Chicken	198	Replace chutney with duck sauce
Chicken Marvelosa	200	Omit sun-dried tomatoes
Pomegranate Chicken	205	Use cranberry juice if pomegranate is unavailable
Rosemary Maple Chicken	206	Replace maple syrup with honey
Oven-Fried Chicken	208	See Passover variation
Almond Mandarin Chicken Breasts	209	Omit soy sauce. Replace cornstarch with potato starch
Stuffed Chicken Breasts	214	
Quick Chicken Cacciatore	219	Omit red pepper flakes
Citrus Roast Turkey	221	
Rolled Stuffed Turkey Breast	224	
Stuffed Turkey London Broil	224	
Chicken Duxelles	302	
Exodus Chicken	460	
Honey 'n Herb Turkey Breast	461	
Turkey (or Chicken) Scaloppini with Mushrooms	462	

MAKE IT MEATLESS

RECIPE	PAGE	MODIFICATION
Pasta Primavera	161	Replace pasta with Passover noodles
Spaghetti Squash with Roasted Vegetables	163	Omit sesame seeds from Roasted Vegetables
Eggplant Stacks	164	
Eggplant Mock Pizzas	165	
Portobello Mushroom Pizzas	166	
Shakshuka	167	Omit cumin and cayenne
Yogurt Cheese	178	
Sweet Potato and Mushroom Lasagna	464	
Meatless Moussaka	465	
Crustless Spinach Quiche (or Tuna Quiche)	466	
Passover Blueberry Cheese Pancakes (or Apple)	472–73	
Passover Cheese Muffins	473	

passover
pleasures

RECIPE PAGE MODIFICATION

GRAINS AND SIDE DISHES

Orzo with Spinach and Asparagus	330	See Passover Variation with Quinoa
Pretend Potato Kugel	335	Replace flour with potato starch
Broccoli Spinach Kugel	335	Replace flour with potato starch
Winter Vegetable Latkes	337	Use matzo meal instead of flour. Replace grapeseed or canola oil with vegetable oil
Spinach and Mushroom Stuffing	339	
Farfel and Broccoli Kugel	467	
Faux-Tato Kugel	468	
Passover Vegetable Muffins	469	
Vegetable Kishka	469	
Matzo and Vegetable Stuffing	469	
Cauliflower Latkes (or Broccoli)	470–71	
Quinoa Pilaf	471	
Farfel Pilaf	472	

VEGETABLES

Oven Roasted Asparagus	287	
Roasted Broccoli	289	Omit sesame seeds
Steamed Broccoli with Olive Oil and Garlic	290	
Garlic-Roasted Carrots (and Potatoes)	292	
Garlic-Roasted Parsnips	293	
Honey-Glazed Carrots	293	Use apricot jam
Carrot and Sweet Potato Tzimmes	294	Omit Splenda
Creamy Garlic Mashed Faux-tatoes (or Potatoes)	295	Replace Tofutti with light cream cheese
Popcorn Cauliflower	297	
Passover Faux Fried Rice	299	
Mushroom Duxelles	302	
Roasted Portobello Mushrooms	303	
Roasted New Potatoes	305	
Potato Fans	305	
Roasted Sweet Potatoes	305	
Smashed Potato "Latkes"	306	Omit Montreal-Style steak spice

passover
pleasures

passover
pleasures

**passover
pleasures**

passover pleasures

PASSOVER MEMORIES

With apologies to Barbra Streisand, here is
our version of "Memories" to sing at your
Seder!

Memories
Of the chicken soup we ate
Tasty golden-colored memories,
Of the "weigh" we were!

Oy, those memories
Of Mom's special matzo balls
Light and fluffy in our soup bowl
Oy, the "weigh" we were!

Can it be that it was all so simple then?
When schmaltz and calories didn't count!
Oy, if we could only eat like that again,
Tell me, would we? Could we?

Memories
May be beautiful and yet,
We're so lucky to remember
Seder meals we can't forget.

It's our traditions
We will remember
Whenever we remember…
The "weigh" we were…
The "weigh" we were!

Tradition, Tradition: Passover is the eight
day spring festival that commemorates the
exodus of the Jews from Egyptian slavery
more than 3,000 years ago. All over the
world, Jewish families gather around the
table for the Seders on the first two nights
of Passover. Israelis only observe the first
night of Passover. We eat the traditional
foods which include matzo, bitter herbs, and
Charoset (page 453), drink four cups of wine,
and read the Passover story. Then the festive
meal is served—let the calories begin!

The Meaning of Matzo: In their haste to
leave Egypt, the Jews did not have time to let
their dough rise. The resulting unleavened
bread became the first matzos. Matzo is
made from special wheat flour, but it must be
prepared and baked in less than 18 minutes,
under strict supervision. This prevents the
flour and water mixture from absorbing wild
yeast cells from the air and from fermenting
(the sourdough principle of bread baking).
Shmurah matzo, which is handmade and
round, is served by many families. Although
whole wheat matzo is a healthier choice, it is
traditional to eat plain matzo at the Seders.

Chometz: During Passover, chometz
(fermented or leavened products) are not
allowed. Chometz includes any foods made
from wheat, oats, barley, rye or spelt—
except matzo.

Kitniyot: Ashkenazi (Eastern European)
Jews don't eat kitniyot, which includes
legumes (e.g., lentils, beans, chickpeas, peanuts), rice, corn, buckwheat/kasha, mustard,
peas, string beans, soy, cumin, coriander,
sesame seeds, poppy seeds, and sunflower
seeds. Sephardi Jews follow a different tradition, which permits kitniyot.

**passover
pleasures**

Gebrochts: Some Jews follow the tradition of no gebrochts—foods that mix matzo or matzo products (e.g., matzo meal, cake meal, farfel) with liquid. In this way, they will not eat food that could possibly ferment. Potato starch is allowed.

The Grain That's Not a Grain: Although quinoa resembles a grain, it is technically a grass. It is very high in protein and is an excellent option for those who won't eat gebrochts. Quinoa is available in health food stores and bulk stores. Check that it comes from a closed container that has been newly opened for Passover. It requires Passover certification.

The Passover Challenge: Most traditional Passover recipes are high in calories, carbs, and fat but low in fiber. However, traditions are hard to break and favorite foods are hard to "pass up" during Passover. Refer to the Passover Recipe List (page 439) for a comprehensive listing of healthy recipes found in this chapter, plus recipes in other chapters that are suitable for Passover or can be modified easily.

Passover Substitutions: Check the charts for Cooking and Baking Substitutions (pages 450–52).

Availability: Passover products change from year to year and from community to community. Consult your local Kashrut authority or visit www.ou.org, www.cor.org, or other reliable internet sites for a current list of approved Kosher for Passover products.

Plan Ahead: Each year, go through your favorite recipes, photocopy those that are "keepers," and note any necessary adjustments. Keep your menus and grocery lists as a helpful guide and store them in clear plastic page protectors. In this way, you will be organized and know what ingredients you will need to buy for Passover. Don't be afraid to try new recipes, but it's a good idea to try them ahead of the Seders to ensure your family will like them.

Shop Smart: Fill your grocery cart with fresh fruits and vegetables, lean meats, poultry, and fish, plus low-fat dairy products. Beware of packaged products—they are often loaded with fat, carbs, and sodium. Don't shop when you are hungry—you'll buy too much junk food.

Boost the Fiber: Choose whole wheat matzo when possible. Whole wheat matzo contains 3 to 4 grams of fiber per sheet, whereas plain matzo contains only 1 gram of fiber. Eat lots of fresh fruits and vegetables. Soups, salads, and vegetable dishes are healthier options than traditional starchy Passover dishes.

Portion Distortion: You don't need to eat everything on the table! Choose lower GI foods and lower fat dishes when possible. Chicken, turkey, and fish are leaner protein choices than meat. Eat slowly—it takes 20 minutes for your brain to know that your stomach is full.

Dessert Dilemma: Focus on fruit. Most fruits are low in calories, and they also have a low GI value. Berries are best. When choosing a high GI value dessert, top it with fruit to bring the glycemic index down to a moderate zone. It's okay to indulge but keep those portions small. In this book, I've focused on smaller desserts and finger foods.

Sweet Choices: Sugar is okay in small amounts—use it wisely. Splenda isn't available for Passover. Use a heat-stable sugar substitute. Cinnamon and lemon or orange juice help mask the taste of artificial sweeteners.

Quick Chicken Salad: Too much boiled chicken? Chop 1 small onion, 2 stalks celery, and 1/2 of a red pepper in your food processor, using several quick on/off pulses. Add 2 cups leftover cooked chicken (but remove the skin and bones). Process with quick on/off pulses, until combined. Season with salt and pepper. Serve on salad greens, use it as a sandwich filling on Passover Rolls (page 473), or spread it on matzo.

Wine Not: The sugar content of dry wine is lower than sweet wine. Wine or alcohol does not generally raise blood sugar levels—it can actually lower them instead. Wine stops the liver from making the sugar it needs, which can result in lower blood sugar. An afternoon snack helps counteract this effect. Dilute the wine with club soda or water, especially the first cup, as you are drinking it on an empty stomach.

Leftover Wine? Refrigerate leftover wine or freeze it in ice cube trays, then store the cubes in re-sealable freezer bags. Wine adds flavor to meat, poultry, and sauces.

BREAKFAST IDEAS

Breakfast Bonanza: Here are some breakfast ideas that will make you wish Passover would last longer than 8 days!

Chocolate Banana Smoothie (page 433)

Mango Lassi (page 434)

Strawberry Orange Smoothie (page 436)

Quinoa (page 472) with cinnamon, berries, and nonfat or low-fat yogurt

Passover Granola (page 486)

Passover Blueberry Cheese Pancakes (page 472)

Passover Cheese Muffins (page 473)

Passover Fruit Crisp (page 476)

Poached Pears (page 429) with nonfat or low-fat cottage cheese

Mixed Fruit Compote (page 425) with nonfat or low-fat yogurt or cottage cheese

Passover Rolls (page 473) with light cream cheese and smoked salmon

Passover Rolls (page 473) with chopped egg, tuna, or salmon

Crustless Spinach Quiche (page 466)

Whole wheat matzo spread with Prune Purée (page 373), Nut Butter (page 487), or leftover Charoset (page 453)

Let Them Eat Cake: One slice of Never-Fail Passover Sponge Cake (page 474) has about the same number of calories and carbs as one sheet of plain matzo. So enjoy a slice of sponge cake with fresh berries and nonfat yogurt for breakfast as an occasional treat. Stale sponge cake makes fantastic French toast—top it with fresh fruit, applesauce, or fruit compote. Great for kids!

PASSOVER COOKING SUBSTITUTIONS

FOR:	USE:
1 cup breadcrumbs (for breading)	1 cup matzo meal OR 1/2 cup matzo meal and 1/2 cup ground nuts OR 1 cup finely ground mandlen (Passover soup nuts)
1 cup matzo meal	1 cup Whole Wheat Matzo Meal (page 487) OR 3 matzos, finely ground OR 2 cups matzo farfel, finely ground
2 cups matzo farfel	2 cups whole wheat matzo farfel OR 3 matzos (whole wheat or plain), coarsely crumbled
1/4 cup oatmeal (in ground meat mixtures)	1/4 cup Whole Wheat Matzo Meal (page 487) OR 1/4 cup matzo meal
1/4 cup matzo meal (in ground meat mixtures)	1/4 cup whole wheat matzo meal OR 1/4 cup grated potato or sweet potato
1 Tbsp cornstarch or 2 Tbsp all-purpose flour	1 Tbsp potato starch
1 Tbsp all-purpose flour (to thicken sauces)	1/2 Tbsp potato starch
lasagna noodles	whole wheat or regular matzos, moistened under cold water (cut them to fit baking dish)
1 cup rice (3 cups cooked)	1 cup quinoa (3 cups cooked, page 323)
1 tsp Italian seasoning	1/3 tsp each dried basil, oregano, and thyme
1 clove garlic	1/4 tsp garlic powder or 1 tsp bottled minced garlic
1 cup chicken or vegetable broth	1/2 to 1 tsp instant pareve chicken soup mix dissolved in 1 cup hot or boiling water
1/2 cup mango or apricot chutney	1/2 cup Passover duck sauce
light margarine	Process 1 cup soft tub margarine in a food processor until smooth. Add 1/2 cup cold water through feed tube while machine is running. Process 2 to 3 minutes, until light. (Don't use for baking.)

passover
pleasures

Norene's Healthy Kitchen

PASSOVER COOKING SUBSTITUTIONS *(Continued)*

FOR:	USE:
2 tsp granulated sugar or granular Splenda	1 packet (1 g) Passover sugar substitute (e.g., Gefen Sweet N'Low)
sour cream (in cooking/baking)	Process 1 to 2 cups small-curd low-fat (1%) cottage cheese in a food processor for 2 to 3 minutes, until smooth. Blend in 1 to 2 Tbsp granulated sugar
alcoholic beverages (in cooking/baking)	apple, orange, grape juice, chicken broth, vegetable broth, or wine in the same amount, depending on the recipe

PASSOVER BAKING SUBSTITUTIONS

FOR:	USE:
1 large egg (in baking/cooking)	2 egg whites OR 1/4 cup Passover liquid egg substitute
2 large eggs	1 large egg plus 2 egg whites
1 cup all-purpose flour	5/8 cup potato starch or cake meal (or a combination sifted together) OR 3/4 cup ground almonds plus 1/4 cup potato starch (Some experimentation may be needed)
1 cup cake meal	1 cup finely ground almonds (Almond Meal, page 390)
1 cup cookie crumbs	1 cup crushed Passover mandel bread, egg kichel or macaroons
chopped nuts (for nut allergies)	Coarsely crushed Cheerio-style Passover cereal or soup nuts (mandlen)
1 cup brown sugar	1 cup Passover brown sugar or granulated sugar

passover
pleasures

FOR:	USE:
1 cup icing (confectioners) sugar	1 cup minus 1 Tbsp granulated sugar, plus 1 Tbsp potato starch (Process in the food processor on the steel blade for 2 to 3 minutes, until pulverized)
vanilla sugar	Bury a split vanilla bean pod in granulated sugar. (Use 1 bean per pound of sugar.) Store in container for a week, then remove vanilla bean. You can reuse it for up to 6 months
1 tsp pure vanilla extract	1 Tbsp Passover liqueur, brandy, or wine (Pure vanilla extract isn't available, and artificial vanilla extract is inferior in flavor)
1 tsp baking powder	1 tsp Passover baking powder
$1/8$ tsp cream of tartar	1 tsp lemon juice
1 cup buttermilk (in baking)	1 Tbsp lemon juice or vinegar plus skim or 1% milk to equal 1 cup OR equal parts of nonfat plain yogurt or light sour cream, mixed with skim milk or water
1 cup whipped cream	1 cup lightly sweetened Soft Yogurt Cheese (page 178)
1 oz (30 g) unsweetened baking chocolate	3 Tbsp unsweetened cocoa powder plus $1/2$ Tbsp vegetable oil OR $1^{1}/_2$ oz dark, semi-sweet or bittersweet chocolate (reduce sugar in recipe by 2 Tbsp)
6 oz (170 g) dark, semi-sweet, or bittersweet chocolate (these terms are interchangeable)	1 cup semi-sweet or pure chocolate chips
2 cups semi-sweet chocolate chips	12 oz (350 g) dark, semi-sweet, or bittersweet chocolate, broken up (Passover dark chocolate usually comes in 100 g packages)

**passover
pleasures**

🍎 CHAROSET

This sweet, nutty mixture is served at Passover Seders all over the world. It's symbolic of the mortar used in making bricks for the Pharaoh, when the Jews were slaves in Egypt. This version, which has a low glycemic index (GI), also makes a tasty spread for matzos.

1/2 cup almonds (or any nuts you like)
3 medium apples (McIntosh
   or Cortland), peeled and cored
1 to 2 tsp lemon juice (preferably fresh)
2 Tbsp Passover red wine
2 Tbsp honey
1/2 tsp ground cinnamon

1. In a food processor fitted with the steel blade, process the almonds with 5 or 6 quick on/off pulses, until coarsely chopped. Transfer the almonds to a bowl.

2. Process the apples until minced, about 10 seconds; sprinkle with lemon juice. Add the nuts back to the food processor, along with the wine, honey, and cinnamon; process with quick on/off pulses, just until combined. (Be careful not to overprocess.) Refrigerate until serving time.

Yield: 2 1/2 cups. Recipe easily doubles and triples. Keeps for up to 3 to 4 days in the refrigerator. Don't freeze.

21 calories per Tbsp, 2.8 g carbohydrate, 0.4 g fiber, 0 g protein, 1.0 g fat (0.1 g saturated), 0 mg cholesterol, 0 mg sodium, 26 mg potassium, 0 mg iron, 6 mg calcium

Chef's Secrets
• Nut Allergies? Instead of nuts, use Cheerio-style Passover cereal or leave them out.

🍎 EGGPLANT MOCK CHOPPED LIVER

This easy, tasty vegetarian spread is unusual because it's made without legumes. Enjoy it on Passover—or any time! Serve this as a spread or on salad greens as an appetizer.

1 large eggplant (about 1 1/2 lb/750 g)
2 large onions, cut in chunks
2 cups mushrooms
2 Tbsp extra virgin olive oil
4 hard-boiled large eggs, halved
1/2 cup walnuts or pecans
Salt and freshly ground black pepper

1. Prick the eggplant with a fork. Microwave on high for 7 to 8 minutes, until soft. Let cool. (Or cut in half lengthwise and place cut side down on a broiling rack. Broil the eggplant about 4 inches from heat for 15 minutes. Don't turn it over.)

2. In a food processor fitted with the steel blade, coarsely chop the onions and mushrooms, using 4 or 5 quick on/off pulses.

3. Heat the oil in a skillet on medium high heat. Transfer the onions and mushrooms to the skillet and sauté until nicely browned, about 7 to 8 minutes.

4. Scoop out the eggplant pulp with a spoon and place in the processor bowl. Discard the skin. Add the onions, mushrooms, eggs, nuts, salt, and pepper. Process with quick on/off pulses, just until combined. Chill several hours or overnight for the best flavor.

Yield: 8 servings of 1/2 cup each. Keeps for up to 3 or 4 days in the refrigerator. Don't freeze.

165 calories per serving, 12.8 g carbohydrate, 3.3 g fiber, 6 g protein, 11.2 g fat (1.8 g saturated), 106 mg cholesterol, 33 mg sodium, 262 mg potassium, 1 mg iron, 34 mg calcium

passover pleasures

Nutrition Note
• To reduce the cholesterol and fat, make 6 hard-boiled eggs and discard 4 of the yolks. (You'll use 2 eggs and 4 egg whites for this recipe.) One serving contains 154 calories, 9.9 g fat (1.4 g saturated), and 53 mg cholesterol. Eggs-actly half the cholesterol!

● VEGETABLE FRICASSEE

This vegetarian version of sweet and sour meatballs comes from my friend Cheryl Goldberg. It's always devoured by vegetarians and meat-eaters alike! The recipe was originally developed by Cynthia Gassner and Esther Schwartz for the Kashruth Council of Canada. I've added basil and oregano and reduced the sugar.

Sauce:

2 1/2 cups tomato-mushroom sauce
1 cup vegetable broth
2 Tbsp lemon juice (preferably fresh)
1 tsp dried basil
1 tsp dried oregano
1 Tbsp granulated sugar (or to taste)

Veggie Balls:

2 Tbsp olive oil
1 clove garlic (about 1 tsp minced)
1 onion, chopped
2 stalks celery, chopped
1 carrot, grated
2 parsnips, grated (about 3 cups)
2 1/2 cups chopped mushrooms (8 oz/227 g)
2 large eggs, lightly beaten
Salt and freshly ground black pepper
1 tsp dried basil
2 to 3 Tbsp chopped fresh parsley
1 1/2 cups matzo meal
   or Whole Wheat Matzo Meal (page 487)

1. In a large saucepan, combine all the ingredients for the sauce and heat slowly.

2. Heat the oil in a large skillet on medium high heat. Sauté the garlic, onion, and celery for 5 minutes or until golden. Add the carrot and parsnips; sauté for 5 minutes longer. Add the mushrooms and sauté for 3 to 4 minutes longer. Remove from the heat and let cool for 5 to 10 minutes. Add the eggs, salt, pepper, basil, parsley, and matzo meal; mix well.

3. Form into 1-inch balls, wetting your hands for easier handling. Add to the tomato sauce, partially cover, and simmer for 20 to 25 minutes, shaking the pot gently every few minutes to prevent sticking.

Yield: About 4 dozen (12 servings as an appetizer or 6 servings as a main dish). Keeps for up to 3 to 4 days in the refrigerator; reheats well. Freezes well for up to 3 months.

113 calories as an appetizer, 22.6 g carbohydrate, 4.0 g fiber, 4 g protein, 1.7 g fat (0.4 g saturated), 35 mg cholesterol, 356 mg sodium, 438 mg potassium, 2 mg iron, 39 mg calcium

Vegetable Loaves
Instead of shaping the mixture into balls in Step 3, shape into 2 loaves and place in a large sprayed casserole dish, leaving 3 inches between the loaves. Pour the heated sauce over the loaves. Bake in a preheated 350°F oven for 50 to 60 minutes. Serve as a vegetarian main dish.

● MATZO BALLS

Be sure to use a large pot so the matzo balls can expand while cooking. To make "floaters" (light, fluffy matzo balls), use club soda or ginger ale. If your family prefers "sinkers," add 2 to 3 Tbsp additional matzo meal.

3/4 cup matzo meal
   or Whole Wheat Matzo Meal (page 487)
3/4 tsp salt
1/4 tsp freshly ground black pepper
2 large eggs plus 2 egg whites
   (or 3 large eggs)
3 Tbsp club soda, ginger ale, or water
2 tsp olive or vegetable oil
2 Tbsp minced fresh dillweed or parsley
16 cups (4 quarts/liters) salted water

1. In a large mixing bowl or a food processor, combine the matzo meal, salt, and pepper; mix or process well. Add the eggs, egg whites, club soda, oil, and dill; mix or process until blended. Cover and refrigerate for 30 to 60 minutes; the mixture will thicken.

2. In a large pot, bring the salted water to a boil. Wet your hands for easier shaping. Form the mixture into 1-inch balls. Carefully add the matzo balls to the pot of boiling water; cover tightly and cook for 40 to 45 minutes. No peeking allowed!

3. With a slotted spoon, carefully remove the matzo balls from the water and transfer to hot chicken soup or vegetable broth.

Yield: 18 matzo balls. Keeps for up to 3 or 4 days in the refrigerator; reheats well. Freezes well for up to 3 months.

36 calories per matzo ball, 4.6 g carbohydrate, trace fiber, 2 g protein, 1.1 g fat (0.2 g saturated), 24 mg cholesterol, 111 mg sodium, 22 mg potassium, 0 mg iron, 4 mg calcium

Chef's Secrets
• Hidden Treasure: When shaping the matzo balls, poke a hole in the center of each one with your finger. Stuff with any of the following: shredded carrots, finely minced parsley, cooked chopped spinach, sautéed chopped mushrooms, and/or onions. Close the opening and re-roll the matzo balls so that the filling is hidden.

• Frozen Assets: Matzo balls can be cooked in advance, then frozen in chicken soup. Or you can freeze them in a single layer on a cookie sheet or in muffin tins until firm. Transfer them to plastic freezer bags and freeze until needed. There's no need to thaw first—just reheat them directly in the simmering soup! They will take about 10 minutes to defrost and heat through.

● MINIATURE "NOTSA" BALLS (CHICKEN KNEIDLACH)

These low-carb chicken kneidlach (matzo balls) are a luscious alternative to regular matzo balls. For people who aren't able to use matzo meal, these can be made with ground almonds, making them gluten-free.

1 medium onion, cut into chunks
1 stalk celery, cut into chunks
2 Tbsp fresh dillweed
1 lb (500 g) lean ground chicken or turkey
1 large egg
1 Tbsp vegetable or olive oil
3 Tbsp matzo meal (or ground almonds)
1/2 tsp salt
Freshly ground black pepper
2 Tbsp club soda or cold water
10 cups salted water

1. In a food processor using the steel blade, process the onion, celery, and dill until minced, about 10 seconds. Add the ground chicken, egg, oil, matzo meal or almonds, salt, pepper, and club soda; process just until mixed. Transfer to a bowl, cover, and chill for 20 to 30 minutes.

2. In a large pot, bring the salted water to a boil. Wet your hands and shape the mixture into walnut-sized balls. Drop into boiling water, cover tightly, and simmer for 20 to 25 minutes or until cooked through. Using a slotted spoon, carefully remove the balls from the water and transfer to bowls of hot chicken soup or vegetable broth.

Yield: 2 dozen miniatures. Keeps for up to 2 days in the refrigerator; reheats well. Freezes well for up to 3 months.

39 calories each, 1.4 g carbohydrate, 0.1 g fiber, 3 g protein, 2.3 g fat (0.6 g saturated), 21 mg cholesterol, 65 mg sodium, 17 mg potassium, 0 mg iron, 3 mg calcium

Chef's Secrets
• Freeze with Ease: See Frozen Assets (page 455).

• Grind It Right: Ground chicken usually contains dark meat, increasing the fat content. Ask your butcher to grind skinless, trimmed chicken breasts. You can also grind them yourself in a food processor. Cut 1 lb (500 g) chilled boneless, skinless chicken breasts into 1-inch chunks; process 15 to 20 seconds, until minced.

Nutrition Note
• With ground almonds, each ball contains 40 calories, 0.7 grams carbohydrate, and 2.6 g fat.

◉ "NOTSA" BALLS FROM A MIX

This tasty, low-carb recipe (which makes a larger quantity than the previous recipe) uses a packet of matzo ball mix. Serve these in chicken soup or as a side dish. "Notsa" balls taste terrific when reheated in the defatted pan juices from brisket or roast chicken.

1 lb (500 g) lean ground raw chicken
2 large eggs (or 1 large egg
   plus 2 egg whites)
1 Tbsp oil
3 Tbsp water or club soda
1 Tbsp minced fresh dillweed
1 packet matzo ball mix
10 cups salted water

1. In a large bowl, combine the ground chicken with the eggs, oil, water, dillweed, and matzo ball mix; combine well. Cover and chill for 20 to 30 minutes.

2. In a large pot, bring the salted water to a boil. Wet your hands and shape the mixture into 1-inch balls. Drop into the boiling water, cover tightly, and simmer for 40 to 45 minutes or until cooked through. Don't peek! Using a slotted spoon, carefully remove the balls from the water and transfer to bowls of hot chicken soup or vegetable broth.

Yield: 3 dozen miniatures. Keeps for up to 2 days in the refrigerator. Freezes well for up to 3 months.

30 calories each, 1.4 g carbohydrate, 0.1 g fiber, 2.0 g protein, 1.7 g fat (0.4 g saturated), 20 mg cholesterol, 97 mg sodium, 4 mg potassium, 0 mg iron, 6 mg calcium

🍎 SEDER SALMON

This dish will bring rave reviews from your guests and makes a wonderful alternative to brisket or chicken. It's also ideal served cold for Shabbat lunch, along with a selection of salads. If you make Decadent Marbled Cheesecake (page 475) for dessert, everyone can have their cake and eat it too!

Glaze:

1/4 cup apricot jam or preserves
   (low-sugar or all-fruit)
2 Tbsp lemon juice (preferably fresh)
2 Tbsp extra virgin olive oil
2 Tbsp honey or brown sugar
2 cloves garlic (about 2 tsp minced)
1/4 cup chopped fresh dillweed or parsley

1 fillet of salmon (about 3 lb/1.4 kg)
Salt and freshly ground black pepper
Paprika
Lemon slices, dillweed, and grape tomatoes,
   for garnish

1. In a small bowl, combine the preserves, lemon juice, oil, honey, garlic, and dillweed; mix well. (The glaze can be prepared in advance and refrigerated for 1 to 2 days.)

2. Preheat the oven to 425°F. Line a large baking sheet (without sides) with foil; spray with cooking spray.

3. Rinse the salmon well and pat dry. Place, skin-side down, on the prepared baking sheet. Sprinkle with salt and pepper to taste. Spread the glaze over the salmon; sprinkle with paprika. Marinate for 30 minutes or up to 2 hours in the refrigerator.

4. Bake, uncovered, for 15 to 18 minutes or until glazed and golden, basting occasionally with the pan juices. Remove from the oven and cool slightly before carefully transferring the salmon to a large serving platter. Garnish with the lemon slices, dillweed, and grape tomatoes. Serve hot or cold.

Yield: 10 servings. Recipe easily doubles and triples. Refrigerate leftovers for 2 to 3 days, or freeze them for up to 2 months.

270 calories per serving, 6.4 g carbohydrate, 0 g fiber, 31 g protein, 12.7 g fat (1.9 g saturated), 86 mg cholesterol, 68 mg sodium, 771 mg potassium, 1 mg iron, 20 mg calcium

Glazed Stuffed Salmon

Place the salmon fillet, skin-side down, on the prepared baking sheet. Cut horizontally through the salmon, leaving it hinged on one side so that it opens flat, like a book. Sprinkle inside and out with salt and pepper. Stuff with Matzo and Vegetable Stuffing (page 469) or Spinach and Mushroom Stuffing (page 339) and then "close the book" to cover the stuffing. Spread the glaze over the top of the salmon. Bake, uncovered, at 425°F for about 25 minutes, until glazed and golden. Stuffing must be cooked until it reaches 165°F on an instant-read thermometer. Serve hot.

Chef's Secrets
• No Bitter Herbs: Experiment with different herbs such as rosemary, basil, or thyme.

• Pan-tastic! To transfer the salmon to a serving platter, use a cookie sheet without sides as a giant spatula. Otherwise, use 2 large wide metal spatulas.

• It's a Slice: Slice the salmon into individual portions. Baking time will be 12 to 15 minutes at 425°F. If the salmon is stuffed, baking time for individual slices will be 18 to 20 minutes.

passover pleasures

⚫ HOLIDAY BRISKET

This dish is wonderful for holiday celebrations, when most people like to serve meat as a special treat. Kosher cuts of beef are often higher in fat than non-Kosher cuts, so eat moderate portions and pray that the carbs, fat, and calories don't add up too high. Of course, with all the extra exercise you'll get cooking and preparing for the holidays, it's okay to indulge a little.

4 onions, chopped
1 lean beef brisket, well trimmed (4 lb/2 kg)
Salt, freshly ground black pepper,
    and paprika
4 cloves garlic (about 4 tsp minced)
1/2 cup orange juice (preferably fresh)
1/2 cup sugar-free ginger ale or cola
1/2 cup barbecue or tomato sauce
5 to 6 large potatoes, peeled and
    cut into chunks
5 carrots, peeled and sliced
1/2 lb (250 g) sliced mushrooms

1. Spray a large roasting pan with cooking spray. Place the onions in the bottom of the pan and place the brisket on top of the onions. Season both sides of the brisket with salt, pepper, paprika, and garlic.

2. Combine the orange juice, ginger ale, and barbecue sauce in a large measuring cup and mix well. Pour the liquid over and around the meat; cover with foil. (The brisket may be prepared in advance up to this point and refrigerated overnight, or for up to 2 days.)

3. Preheat the oven to 325°F. Cook the brisket, covered, calculating 45 minutes per lb. The total cooking time will be about 3 hours. During the last hour of cooking, add the potatoes, carrots, and mushrooms. Cover the pan loosely with foil and baste occasionally. If desired, uncover the pan the last 20 to 30 minutes of cooking so the potatoes will brown. The meat and vegetables should be tender when pierced with a fork.

4. Cool completely and refrigerate overnight. A half hour before serving, discard the congealed fat from the gravy. Slice the brisket thinly across the grain, trimming away the fat. Reheat the sliced brisket in the gravy at 350°F for 25 to 30 minutes in a covered casserole.

Yield: 10 servings. Keeps for up to 3 to 4 days in the refrigerator; reheats well. Freezes well for up to 4 months; omit the potatoes if freezing.

428 calories per serving, 44.8 g carbohydrate, 5.5 g fiber, 43 g protein, 8.5 g fat (3.1 g saturated), 77 mg cholesterol, 203 mg sodium, 1393 mg potassium, 5 mg iron, 71 mg calcium

Low Glycemic Variation
• Omit the ginger ale, barbecue sauce, and potatoes. Add 2 cups canned tomatoes (don't drain). One serving contains 293 calories, 14.7 g carbohydrate, 2.6 g fiber, and 677 mg potassium.

Chef's Secret
• For more information about brisket read Chef's Secrets on page 187.

ROAST VEAL WITH LEMON GREMOLATA

This elegant main dish is excellent for a Passover Seder or any special occasion. The Gremolata adds a lotta flavor without overwhelming the dish—veal-ly!

3 medium onions, sliced
3 stalks celery, sliced
2 cups baby carrots
1 boneless veal roast (about 5 lb/2.3 kg)
2 tsp Kosher salt
1 tsp freshly ground black pepper
2 tsp dried thyme or rosemary
2 tsp dried basil
4 cloves garlic (about 4 tsp minced)
1 can (28 oz/796 ml) tomatoes (don't drain)
1/2 cup white wine

Lemon Gremolata

3 Tbsp grated lemon rind
1/2 cup tightly packed fresh parsley
3 cloves garlic

1. Spray a large roasting pan with cooking spray. Place the onions, celery, and carrots in the bottom of the pan.

2. Rub the roast with salt, pepper, thyme, basil, and garlic. Place in the roasting pan on top of the vegetables. Add the tomatoes and wine, crushing the tomatoes with the back of a spoon. If you have time, let marinate for 1 hour before cooking (or up to 2 days in the refrigerator).

3. Preheat the oven to 300°F. Bake, covered, for 3 1/2 hours. Uncover and roast for 45 to 60 minutes longer, basting occasionally, until fork tender.

4. Remove from the oven. Let the roast stand for 20 minutes before slicing, or slice when cold and reheat in the pan gravy.

5. In a food processor fitted with the steel blade, process the lemon, parsley, and garlic until finely minced, about 10 seconds.

6. When ready to serve, place the meat on a large serving platter, spoon sauce on top, and sprinkle with gremolata.

Yield: 10 to 12 servings. Keeps for up to 3 to 4 days in the refrigerator; reheats well. Freezes well for up to 4 months. Don't freeze the Gremolata.

356 calories per serving, 11.0 g carbohydrate, 2.6 g fiber, 42 g protein, 14.2 g fat (5.6 g saturated), 188 mg cholesterol, 450 mg sodium, 786 mg potassium, 6 mg iron, 103 mg calcium

Variation
• Add 20 to 24 unpeeled baby potatoes to the roast after uncovering it in Step 3. Roast 45 minutes longer, basting occasionally. If the potatoes are large, cut them in half. Don't freeze the potatoes.

Chef's Secrets
• The Low-Down: The low cooking temperature is important. Allow 50 to 60 minutes per pound of veal and cook until fork tender.

• Saucy Secrets: For a richer, thicker sauce, purée the pan juices with the cooked carrots, onions, and celery in a food processor, using the steel blade.

passover pleasures

☙ EXODUS CHICKEN

This tender, succulent chicken is made with 40 cloves of garlic to commemorate the Israelites wandering in the desert for 40 years after their exodus from Egypt. When you serve this, there won't be an exodus from your Seder table! The garlic becomes mild and mellow from the long, slow cooking, and is also wonderful spread on matzo.

40 cloves garlic (3 whole heads)
2 medium onions, chopped
4 stalks celery, chopped
2 chickens (3¹/2 lb/1.4 kg each),
  cut into pieces
2 tsp Kosher salt (or to taste)
1 tsp freshly ground black pepper
2 tsp paprika
2 Tbsp chopped fresh thyme or 2 tsp dried
¹/4 cup chopped fresh parsley
  or 1 Tbsp dried
2 Tbsp olive oil
³/4 to 1 cup dry white wine
  or chicken broth
Additional fresh thyme, for garnish

1. Preheat the oven to 375°F. Spray a large roasting pan with cooking spray.

2. Drop the garlic cloves into a pot of boiling water for 1 minute; drain well. (Or place the whole garlic bulbs in a microwaveable bowl and sprinkle with water. Cover and microwave on high for 1 minute.) Squeeze the garlic cloves out of their skins—they'll pop right out. Set aside.

3. Place the onions and celery in the bottom of the prepared roasting pan. Rinse the chicken pieces well and trim any excess fat. Place the chicken pieces in a single layer in the prepared roasting pan. Season with salt, pep-

per, paprika, thyme, and parsley, then drizzle with oil. Tuck the reserved garlic cloves around and between the chicken pieces. Pour wine on top and cover tightly with foil. (If desired, the chicken can be prepared up to this point and refrigerated overnight.)

4. Bake, tightly covered, for 1¹/2 hours. Remove the foil and bake for 30 to 40 minutes longer, until nicely browned, basting occasionally.

5. Transfer the chicken and garlic to a large serving platter and drizzle with the pan juices. Garnish with thyme, and serve.

Yield: 10 to 12 servings. Keeps for up to 2 to 3 days in the refrigerator; reheats well. Freezes well for up to 4 months.

302 calories per serving (without skin), 7.8 g carbohydrate, 1.1 g fiber, 36 g protein, 11.9 g fat (2.9 g saturated), 108 mg cholesterol, 377 mg sodium, 440 mg potassium, 5 mg iron, 57 mg calcium

Variations
• Use 10 to 12 single chicken breasts, with bone and skin. Bake covered for 1 hour, then uncover and bake 20 minutes longer.

• Garlic Alert: Some people won't use garlic during Passover. Instead, add 1 additional chopped onion, 2 chopped red peppers, and 2 cups sliced mushrooms.

Chef's Secrets
• The Numbers Game: Did you know that an average head of garlic contains 15 to 16 cloves?

• Skinny Secrets: If desired, remove the skin from the chicken before cooking. However, if you want to serve the chicken the next day, cook it with the skin on, then refrigerate

passover
pleasures

overnight. Discard the congealed fat before reheating. Remove the skin before eating.

❧ HONEY 'N HERB TURKEY BREAST

Honey and Herb (and all the other couples at your table) will gobble this up! Mango juice adds a mmm-marvelous flavor, but orange juice will also add its own special twist. Great for Passover or any special occasion!

Marinade:

2 Tbsp extra virgin olive oil
2 Tbsp lemon juice (preferably fresh)
2 cloves garlic (about 2 tsp minced)
2 to 3 Tbsp honey
1/2 tsp dried basil
1/2 tsp dried thyme

3 onions, thinly sliced
1 red pepper, seeded and sliced
1 boneless rolled turkey breast
   (about 4 lb/1.8 kg)
Salt, freshly ground black pepper
   and paprika
1 cup mango or orange juice

1. In a small bowl, combine the olive oil, lemon juice, garlic, honey, basil, and thyme; mix well.

2. Spray a roasting pan with cooking spray. Place the onions and red pepper in the bottom of the pan. Rinse the turkey breast and pat dry. Place the turkey on top of the vegetables; season with salt, pepper, and paprika. Drizzle with marinade, coating the turkey on all sides. Drizzle the mango juice over and around the turkey. Cover and refrigerate for 1 hour or up to 2 days, basting occasionally. Remove from the refrigerator about 1/2 hour before cooking.

3. Preheat the oven to 350°F. Roast the turkey, covered, calculating 25 to 30 minutes per pound as the cooking time. The total cooking time will be about 2 hours. Uncover the turkey the last 30 minutes of cooking; baste occasionally. When done, the juices will run clear when pierced with a fork, and a meat thermometer, when inserted into the thickest part of the bird, should register an internal temperature of 165 to 170°F.

4. Remove the pan from the oven, cover, and let stand for 20 minutes before thinly slicing. Serve with the pan juices.

Yield: 10 servings. Keeps for up to 2 to 3 days in the refrigerator; reheats well. Freezes well for up to 4 months.

263 calories per serving, 11.3 g carbohydrate, 0.7 g fiber, 44 g protein, 3.9 g fat (0.7 g saturated), 119 mg cholesterol, 83 mg sodium, 498 mg potassium, 3 mg iron, 33 mg calcium

Chef's Secrets

• Be Prepared: Prepare and cook the turkey breast as directed. Slice thinly and place in a casserole; top with pan juices. Refrigerate for 1 to 2 days. Reheat covered for 20 minutes at 350°F.

• No Bones About It: If a rolled turkey breast isn't available, use an unrolled turkey breast, allowing 20 to 25 minutes per pound. If you can't find one large turkey breast, use 2 smaller ones. Use an instant read thermometer to prevent overcooking.

• Expecting a Crowd? See recipe for Citrus Roast Turkey (page 221).

• Let's Talk Turkey: For more tips on cooking turkey, see pages 183–84.

🍎 TURKEY SCALOPPINI WITH MUSHROOMS

My friend Cheryl Goldberg of Toronto made this simple, fabulous dish for a dinner party, and we're all still thanking her for inviting us. So tender, so juicy—everyone had second helpings and some guests even went back for thirds! I've adapted her recipe for Passover, using potato starch instead of flour and adding garlic, which I love.

2 lb (1 kg) turkey scaloppini, thinly sliced
    (8 to 12 slices)
Salt, freshly ground black pepper, basil,
    and paprika
1 large egg plus 2 Tbsp water, lightly beaten
1/3 cup potato starch
4 Tbsp olive oil
3 medium onions, sliced
1 lb (500 g) mushrooms, sliced
3 to 4 cloves garlic (about 3 to 4 tsp minced)
1/2 cup chicken broth or water
1/2 cup Passover Marsala cooking wine
    (or your favorite red wine)

1. Preheat the oven to 350°F. Spray a large, oblong casserole dish with cooking spray.

2. Rinse the turkey scallopini and pat dry. Sprinkle both sides with salt, pepper, basil, and paprika. Dip both sides in egg, then in potato starch.

3. Heat 2 Tbsp of the oil in a nonstick skillet over medium high heat. Sauté the turkey in batches for 2 minutes on each side, until no longer pink. Transfer to the prepared casserole.

4. In the same skillet, heat the remaining 2 Tbsp oil over medium high heat. Add the onions, mushrooms, and garlic and sauté for 6 to 8 minutes, until golden brown. Add the broth and wine; simmer 2 minutes longer, stirring to prevent sticking.

5. Pour the mushroom mixture over the turkey and cover with foil. (Can be prepared in advance and refrigerated several hours or overnight.) Bake for 30 minutes or until very tender.

Yield: 8 servings. Recipe easily doubles and triples. Keeps for up to 2 days in the refrigerator; reheats well. Freezes well for up to 4 months.

254 calories per serving, 12.7 g carbohydrate, 1.5 g fiber, 30 g protein, 8.2 g fat (1.2 g saturated), 71 mg cholesterol, 116 mg sodium, 251 mg potassium, 3 mg iron, 19 mg calcium

Chicken Scaloppini

Substitute boneless, skinless chicken fillets for turkey scaloppini. In Step 3, sauté the chicken breasts for 3 to 4 minutes on each side, until no longer pink. Continue as directed above.

🍎 PASSOVER MEAT LASAGNA

Don't "pass over" this recipe because of the long list of ingredients; it's so scrumptious you'll soon be passing it on to your friends and family. You won't believe there are no noodles in this luscious lasagna, which comes from Esther Schwartz, of Toronto. I've modified it slightly to reduce the fat and salt. It's perfect for a crowd.

passover pleasures

Meat Sauce:

2 Tbsp olive or vegetable oil
2 large onions, chopped
1 clove garlic (about 1 tsp minced)
1/2 cup chopped green pepper
2 lb (1 kg) extra-lean ground beef
2 cans (11 oz/312 g each) tomato-
    mushroom sauce
Salt and freshly ground black pepper
2 Tbsp granulated sugar
1 medium carrot, peeled and grated

Matzo Layers:

6 large eggs (or 4 large eggs and
    4 egg whites)
3/4 cup white wine
8 matzos

Mushroom Sauce:

2 Tbsp olive or vegetable oil
1 Spanish onion, finely chopped
1 lb (500 g) mushrooms, sliced
2 Tbsp potato starch
2 cups water or clear chicken soup
1/4 tsp salt
1/8 tsp freshly ground black pepper

1. Meat Sauce: Heat the oil in a large non-stick pot on medium high heat. Add the onions and garlic and sauté for 5 to 7 minutes or until golden. Add the green pepper and sauté for 3 or 4 minutes longer. Add the meat and brown slowly for 10 minutes, stirring often, until the beef loses its red color. Stir in the tomato-mushroom sauce, salt, pepper, sugar, and carrot. Simmer, uncovered, stirring occasionally, for 2 hours. (If desired, the sauce can be prepared up to this point and refrigerated overnight.)

2. Preheat the oven to 375°F. Spray a 10- × 15- × 2-inch glass baking dish or a disposable foil pan with cooking spray.

3. Matzo Layers: In a medium bowl, beat the eggs together with the wine until frothy. Dip each matzo briefly in the egg-wine mixture. Place two matzos side-by-side in the bottom of the prepared baking dish. Top with 1/3 of the meat sauce. Repeat the dipping and layering of the matzos and meat sauce, ending with a layer of matzos. Pour any remaining egg-wine mixture over the lasagna. Cover the pan with foil.

4. Bake for 30 minutes. While this bakes, make the mushroom sauce.

5. Mushroom Sauce: Heat the oil in a large skillet on medium high heat. Sauté the onion until tender, about 5 to 7 minutes. Add the mushrooms and sauté 5 to 7 minutes longer, until tender. If the vegetables begin to stick, add a little water. Dissolve the potato starch in water and add it slowly to the skillet. Add salt and pepper. Cook until bubbling and thickened, stirring constantly.

6. After the lasagna has baked for 30 minutes, remove the foil and pour the mushroom sauce overtop. Bake, uncovered, for 15 to 20 minutes longer.

Yield: 10 servings. Keeps for up to 2 to 3 days in the refrigerator; reheats well. Freezes well for up to 3 months.

439 calories per serving, 36.6 g carbohydrate, 2.6 g fiber, 27 g protein, 19.2 g fat (5.4 g saturated), 186 mg cholesterol, 590 mg sodium, 586 mg potassium, 6 mg iron, 43 mg calcium

passover pleasures

◖ SWEET POTATO AND MUSHROOM LASAGNA

"Pass over" the pasta with this noodle-free lasagna! It's delicious any time of the year. Although there are several steps to this recipe, it's easy to make and can be prepared in advance. A food processor helps speed up preparation time.

Sauce:

2 medium onions
3 cups mushrooms
1 red pepper
1 to 2 Tbsp olive oil
3 cloves garlic (about 1 Tbsp minced)
1/2 cup lightly packed fresh parsley
2 Tbsp fresh basil or 1 tsp dried
3 cups Italian-style tomato sauce
　or pasta sauce
Salt and freshly ground black pepper

3 large sweet potatoes

Filling:

3 cups light ricotta cheese
　(or 1% pressed cottage cheese)
1 cup grated Parmesan cheese
1 large egg
1/2 tsp salt (or to taste)
Freshly ground black pepper
1 tsp dried basil
1/2 tsp dried oregano
2 cups grated low-fat mozzarella cheese

1. Cut the onions, mushrooms, and red pepper in chunks. Process in batches in a food processor, using quick on/off pulses, until coarsely chopped. Spray a large pot with cooking spray. Add the oil and heat on medium high heat. Add the vegetables and sauté for 5 to 7 minutes or until golden.

2. Process the garlic, parsley, and basil until minced, about 10 seconds. Add to the pot along with the tomato sauce, salt, and pepper to taste. Bring the sauce to a simmer and cook, uncovered, stirring occasionally, for 10 minutes. (The sauce can be made a day in advance and refrigerated.)

3. Pierce the sweet potatoes with a sharp knife. Microwave on high for 6 to 8 minutes or until partially cooked. Cool slightly before peeling; cut into thin slices with a sharp knife. You should have about 6 cups. Transfer to a bowl and sprinkle with additional salt and pepper.

4. Insert the steel blade in the processor bowl. Add ricotta cheese, 1/2 cup Parmesan, egg, and seasonings. Process with quick on/off pulses, until combined, scraping down the sides of the bowl as needed.

5. Place one-third of the sauce in the bottom of a sprayed 9- × 13-inch baking dish. Arrange one-third of the sweet potatoes over the sauce. Spread with half the ricotta cheese mixture. Sprinkle with 1/4 cup Parmesan cheese and 2/3 cup mozzarella cheese. Repeat the layering once more. Top with remaining sweet potatoes, sauce, and mozzarella. Cover the lasagna with foil that has been sprayed on the underside with cooking spray. (If desired, the lasagna can be prepared in advance up to this point and refrigerated overnight.)

6. Preheat the oven to 350°F. Place the baking dish on a foil-lined baking sheet to catch any spills. Bake, covered, for 45 minutes. Uncover and bake for 15 to 20 minutes longer or until golden brown. The sweet potatoes should be tender when you insert a knife. Remove from the oven and

let the lasagna sit for 10 minutes for easier slicing.

Yield: 12 servings. Keeps for up to 2 to 3 days in the refrigerator; reheats well. Freezing isn't recommended.

257 calories per serving, 22.6 g carbohydrate, 3.6 g fiber, 17 g protein, 11.6 g fat (6.4 g saturated), 55 mg cholesterol, 740 mg sodium, 468 mg potassium, 2 mg iron, 426 mg calcium

🍎 MEATLESS MOUSSAKA

Thanks to my friend Micki Grossman of Farmington Hills, Michigan, for sharing this fabulous moussaka, which has a lot less grease than the traditional version. The recipe seems complicated but it's really not. Making this takes much less time than a flight to Athens!

1 medium eggplant (1 1/2 lb/750 g), peeled
1 medium zucchini, unpeeled
Salt
2 Tbsp olive oil
1 medium onion, chopped
1 clove garlic (about 1 tsp minced)
1 Tbsp potato starch
2 plum tomatoes, thinly sliced
1 1/2 to 2 cups grated low-fat
  mozzarella cheese
2 tsp instant pareve soup mix
1/3 cup warm water
2 Tbsp tomato paste

Topping:

1 large egg, lightly beaten
1 Tbsp additional potato starch
3/4 cup nonfat plain yogurt
  or light sour cream

1. Preheat the oven to 375°F. Line a large baking sheet with parchment paper.

2. Slice the eggplant and the zucchini into 1/4-inch-thick rounds. Place in a single layer on paper towels and sprinkle lightly with salt. Let stand for 30 minutes to release excess moisture. Rinse and pat dry. Reserve the zucchini.

3. Place the eggplant slices on the prepared baking sheet and brush lightly with oil on both sides, using 1 Tbsp oil. Bake at 375°F for 5 to 6 minutes per side, until softened.

4. Heat the remaining tablespoon of oil in a large nonstick skillet on medium high heat. Sauté the onion and the garlic until softened, about 3 to 4 minutes.

5. Spray a 7- × 11-inch baking dish with cooking spray. Place half the eggplant slices in bottom of the baking dish. Sprinkle lightly with the potato starch. Top with the tomatoes, then the reserved zucchini, then the onion mixture. Sprinkle with half the cheese. Top with the remaining eggplant slices and sprinkle with the remaining cheese. Dissolve the soup mix in the warm water and stir in the tomato paste; drizzle over the cheese.

6. Bake, uncovered, for 35 minutes. Mix together the ingredients for the topping. Drop by teaspoonfuls on top of the moussaka and bake 10 to 15 minutes longer or until golden brown.

Yield: 6 servings. Keeps for up to 3 to 4 days in the refrigerator and reheats well. Freezing isn't recommended.

190 calories per serving, 16.0 g carbohydrate, 4.2 g fiber, 11 g protein, 10.2 g fat (3.8 g saturated), 54 mg cholesterol, 440 mg sodium, 434 mg potassium, 1 mg iron, 283 mg calcium

CRUSTLESS SPINACH QUICHE

It's so easy eating green! This delicious, low-carb dish is packed with vitamins, minerals, and flavor, and makes a wonderful brunch or lunch dish. It's perfect for Passover or any time of year.

6 green onions, trimmed
   or 1 medium onion, cut into chunks
1 red pepper, cut into chunks
1 Tbsp olive oil
1/2 cup fresh dillweed
1 pkg (10 oz/300 g) frozen chopped
   spinach, thawed and squeezed dry
3 large eggs (or 2 large eggs
   plus 2 egg whites)
2/3 cup milk (skim or 1%)
1 cup grated low-fat Swiss or cheddar cheese
3/4 tsp salt (or to taste)
Freshly ground black pepper
3 Tbsp grated Parmesan cheese

1. Preheat the oven to 375°F. Spray a 10-inch ceramic quiche dish or a deep 9-inch pie plate with cooking spray.

2. In a food processor using the steel blade, process the green onions and the red pepper with quick on/off pulses, until coarsely chopped. Heat the oil in a nonstick skillet on medium high heat. Add the vegetables and sauté for 5 minutes or until golden. Remove from heat and cool slightly.

3. Process the dillweed and spinach on the steel blade until minced, about 10 seconds. Add the sautéed vegetables, eggs, milk, cheese, salt, and pepper to taste. Process with quick on/off pulses, just until combined.

4. Spread the mixture in the prepared pan and sprinkle with Parmesan cheese. Bake for 35 to 40 minutes or until puffed and golden.

Yield: 6 servings. Keeps for up to 2 to 3 days in the refrigerator; reheats well. Freezes well for up to 2 months.

135 calories per serving, 7.4 g carbohydrate, 2.1 g fiber, 12 g protein, 6.6 g fat (2.2 g saturated), 115 mg cholesterol, 460 mg sodium, 265 mg potassium, 2 mg iron, 311 mg calcium

Crustless Tuna Quiche
Omit spinach. In Step 3, add 1 can (6 oz/170 g) flaked tuna, well-drained, to the vegetable mixture. One serving contains 161 calories, 5.8 g carbohydrate, 1.0 g fiber, 18 g protein, and 7.3 g fat (2.4 g saturated).

BEST-EVER SCALLOPED SWEET POTATOES

This is a healthier version of the scalloped potato recipe in my food processor cookbook. It's nutrition-packed and gluten-free. You'll be known as the "scalloping gourmet" after you serve this dish!

2 medium onions, sliced
6 medium sweet potatoes, peeled and sliced
Salt and freshly ground black pepper
2 Tbsp extra virgin olive oil
2 Tbsp potato starch
2 tsp instant pareve soup mix
2 cups boiling water
Paprika

1. Preheat the oven to 375°F. Spray a 9- × 13-inch glass baking dish with cooking spray.

2. Layer the onions and the sweet potatoes in the prepared baking dish, ending with sweet potatoes, sprinkling each layer with salt and pepper to taste.

Norene's Healthy Kitchen

3. In a 4-cup glass measure, mix together the oil, potato starch, and soup mix. Gradually whisk in the boiling water and mix until smooth. Microwave on high for 1 to 1½ minutes or until bubbly and thick, stirring once or twice. Pour over the sweet potatoes and sprinkle with paprika.

4. Bake, uncovered, for 1 to 1¼ hours or until tender and golden brown.

Yield: 8 servings. Keeps for up to 2 to 3 days in the refrigerator; reheats well. Freezing isn't recommended.

138 calories per serving, 25.0 g carbohydrate, 3.2 g fiber, 2 g protein, 3.7 g fat (0.6 g saturated), 0 mg cholesterol, 173 mg sodium, 301 mg potassium, 1 mg iron, 37 mg calcium

Variations
• Use a mixture of sweet potatoes, carrots, parsnips, and/or regular potatoes. Instead of soup mix and boiling water, use 2 cups of chicken soup. If desired, add 1 to 2 Tbsp chopped fresh dillweed, basil, or thyme—or your favorite herbs.

• Non-Passover Variation: Substitute ¼ cup whole wheat or all-purpose flour for the potato starch. Substitute hot skim milk or soymilk for the boiling water.

🍎 FARFEL AND BROCCOLI KUGEL

A similar version of this recipe first appeared in my cookbook *MicroWays*, which is now out of print. This kugel serves a large crowd, making it perfect for Passover entertaining.

4 cups matzo farfel (or 6 whole wheat matzos, coarsely crumbled)
3 cups vegetable or chicken broth
3 cups chopped broccoli
2 medium onions, chopped
1 red pepper, seeded and chopped
2 cups sliced mushrooms
2 cloves garlic (about 2 tsp minced)
2 Tbsp olive oil
½ cup chopped fresh parsley
1½ tsp salt (or to taste)
½ tsp freshly ground black pepper
5 large eggs (or 3 large eggs plus 4 egg whites)
Paprika, for garnish

1. Preheat the oven to 375°F. Spray a 9- × 13-inch baking dish with cooking spray.

2. In a large bowl, combine the matzo farfel with the broth. Let stand for 10 minutes or until the liquid is absorbed.

3. Meanwhile, in a 4-cup glass measuring cup or bowl, microwave the broccoli, covered, on high for 4 minutes, until tender-crisp. (Parchment paper or a small plate makes a perfect cover.) Let stand covered for 1 minute. Uncover carefully and let cool.

4. Combine the onions, red pepper, mushrooms, garlic, and oil in a large microwaveable bowl. Microwave uncovered on high for 5 minutes or until tender-crisp, stirring at half time. Cool slightly.

5. Add the cooked vegetables, parsley, salt, pepper, and eggs to the farfel; mix well. Spread the mixture evenly in the prepared baking dish and sprinkle with paprika.

6. Bake, uncovered, for 45 to 55 minutes. When done, the kugel will be golden and crusty.

Yield: 12 servings. Keeps for up to 3 to 4 days in the refrigerator; reheats well. Freezes well for up to 2 months.

129 calories per serving, 17.4 g carbohydrate, 3.2 g fiber, 6 g protein, 4.8 g fat (1.0 g saturated), 88 mg cholesterol, 445 mg sodium, 217 mg potassium, 2 mg iron, 37 mg calcium

Variations
• Instead of broccoli, substitute cauliflower florets. Instead of onions, use 4 chopped shallots. Use a mixture of wild mushrooms (e.g., cremini, shiitake, portobello).

Mini Farfel Kugels
Fill sprayed muffin pans three-quarters full. Bake at 375°F about 25 minutes, until golden. Great for portion control!

● FAUX-TATO KUGEL

This kugel should be called "the great pretender!" It's a wonderful way to cut back on calories and carbohydrates.

1 large cauliflower, cut into florets
    (about 8 cups)
2 Tbsp olive oil
1 medium onion, cut into chunks
2 large eggs
1 tsp salt (or to taste)
1/4 tsp freshly ground black pepper
1/4 cup matzo meal (whole wheat
    or regular)

1. Pour 1 inch of water into a large saucepan. Place the cauliflower florets in a steamer basket and transfer the basket to the saucepan, making sure the florets don't touch the water. Cover the pan and bring to a boil. Reduce heat to low and steam until tender, about 12 to 15 minutes. Drain well and pat dry with paper towels. Let cool.

2. Preheat the oven to 375°F. Pour the oil into a 7- × 11-inch glass baking dish. Place the dish in the oven and heat until the oil is piping hot, about 5 minutes.

3. In a food processor fitted with the steel blade, process onion for about 10 seconds or until minced. Scrape down the sides of the bowl before adding the cauliflower, eggs, salt, pepper, and matzo meal; process until mixed, about 10 to 15 seconds. Carefully add half the hot oil to the cauliflower mixture and mix well.

4. Pour the mixture into the prepared baking dish and spread evenly. Sprinkle a little additional oil on top. Bake, uncovered, for 45 to 55 minutes or until nicely browned.

Yield: 8 servings. Keeps for up to 2 to 3 days in the refrigerator; reheats well. Freezes well for up to 2 months (see Chef's Secrets).

93 calories per serving, 8.9 g carbohydrate, 2.8 g fiber, 4 g protein, 5.1 g fat (0.9 g saturated), 53 mg cholesterol, 323 mg sodium, 181 mg potassium, 1 mg iron, 26 mg calcium

Chef's Secrets
• Frozen Assets: If you want to make this in advance and freeze it, bake it in a disposable foil pan. When cool, wrap tightly and freeze. When needed, reheat the frozen kugel, uncovered, in a preheated 375°F oven for 20 to 25 minutes or until piping hot. Don't defrost it first or it will be too soft. If the kugel begins to brown too much while baking, cover it loosely with foil.

🍎 PASSOVER VEGETABLE MUFFINS

Vegetarian heaven from Cheryl Goldberg's kitchen! These colorful veggie muffins make an excellent side dish or are perfect as a healthy snack. I added garlic, extra red pepper, and fresh dillweed to the original recipe and used my food processor to speed up the preparation.

2 Tbsp olive oil
1 medium onion, chopped
1 clove garlic (about 1 tsp minced)
1/2 red or green pepper, seeded and chopped
1 stalk celery, chopped
1 1/2 cups grated carrots
1 cup grated zucchini, well-drained
    (about 1 small zucchini)
3 large eggs, lightly beaten
3/4 tsp salt
1/4 tsp freshly ground black pepper
3/4 cup matzo meal
1 Tbsp chopped fresh dill or 1 tsp dried

1. Preheat the oven to 375°F. Spray 10 compartments of a muffin pan with cooking spray and fill 2 compartments with water.

2. Heat the oil in a large nonstick skillet on medium high heat. Sauté the onion and garlic in hot oil for 5 minutes or until golden. Add the bell pepper, celery, carrots, and zucchini. Reduce heat to medium and sauté for 5 to 7 minutes longer, until tender, stirring occasionally. Let cool.

3. Stir in the eggs, salt, pepper, and matzo meal; mix well. Scoop the batter into the compartments of the muffin pan. Bake for 35 to 40 minutes or until golden brown. Cool slightly, then carefully remove from the pan.

Yield: 10 muffins. Recipe easily doubles and triples. Keeps for up to 3 to 4 days in the refrigerator; reheats well. Freezes well for up to 2 months.

100 calories per muffin, 11.6 g carbohydrate, 0.8 g fiber, 3 g protein, 4.4 g fat (0.8 g saturated), 63 mg cholesterol, 269 mg sodium, 128 mg potassium, 1 mg iron, 19 mg calcium

Vegetable Kishka

Prepare the vegetable mixture as directed. Spoon half of the mixture onto a sheet of foil that has been well-sprayed with cooking spray. Wet your hands for easier handling. Form the mixture into a long roll about 2 inches in diameter and wrap well. Repeat with the remaining mixture. Place both rolls on a baking sheet. Bake at 375°F about 45 minutes. Unwrap and cut into 1/2-inch slices.

Variations

• Instead of carrots, use parsnips. Instead of zucchini, use chopped broccoli. Instead of dill, use basil, parsley, or your favorite herbs.

🍎 MATZO AND VEGETABLE STUFFING

This makes a scrumptious stuffing for a turkey breast, fillet of salmon, veal roast, or boneless chicken breasts—but try not to overstuff yourself!

2 Tbsp olive oil
1 medium onion, chopped
1 clove garlic (about 1 tsp minced)
1/2 red pepper, seeded and chopped
1 medium zucchini, chopped
2 cups chopped mushrooms
3 matzos (whole wheat or regular)
1/2 to 3/4 cup vegetable or chicken broth
    (as needed)
1 tsp salt
1/2 tsp freshly ground black pepper
1 Tbsp minced fresh basil (or 1 tsp dried)

1. In a large nonstick skillet, heat the oil on medium high. Sauté the onion and garlic for 3 minutes. Add the red pepper, zucchini, and mushrooms; sauté 3 minutes longer. If the vegetables begin to stick, add 2 or 3 Tbsp water to the skillet.

2. Moisten the matzos briefly under luke-warm running water, and then crumble them into the skillet. Add the broth and seasonings; mix well (the mixture should be moist but not soggy). Cool before using.

Yield: 8 servings. Recipe easily doubles and triples. Keeps for up to 2 days in the refrigerator. Freezing isn't recommended.

72 calories per serving, 12.5 g carbohydrate, 2.2 g fiber, 2 g protein, 2.0 g fat (0.3 g saturated), 0 mg cholesterol, 323 mg sodium, 183 mg potassium, 1 mg iron, 15 mg calcium

Variations
• Experiment with other vegetables such as chopped celery, broccoli, or spinach. Chopped dried apricots or grated apple make delicious additions. Use your imagination!

Chef's Secrets
• Crumb-y News: Finally, here's a way to use up all those broken matzos! Each matzo yields about 2/3 cup. If you prefer, use 2 cups matzo farfel instead of 3 matzos.

• Safe Stuff: Don't stuff meat, poultry, or fish until just before cooking.

• Leftovers? For safe storage, remove the stuffing from cooked meat or poultry and store it separately in the refrigerator.

• Get Stuffed: Use this stuffing for Stuffed Chicken Breasts (page 214), Rolled Stuffed Turkey Breast (page 224), or Seder Salmon (page 457). Or have your butcher cut a pocket in a veal roast or brisket. Stuff it, then prepare as directed in the recipe for Roast Veal with Lemon Gremolata (page 459).

• On the Side: Make a double batch of stuffing. Instead of stuffing a whole turkey, put the stuffing into a sprayed 2-quart casserole dish. Cover and bake at 325°F for 50 to 60 minutes, until piping hot. Serve with Citrus Roast Turkey (page 221).

• The Right Stuff: For more helpful tips, see page 184.

CAULIFLOWER LATKES

These luscious, low-carb latkes are a delicious alternative to traditional potato latkes. They're excellent for Passover, Chanukah, or any time of year.

1/2 medium cauliflower, cut into florets
   (about 4 cups)
1 medium onion, chopped
1 clove garlic (about 1 tsp minced)
1 large egg
1/4 cup matzo meal (preferably
   whole wheat)
2 Tbsp minced fresh dillweed
3/4 tsp salt (or to taste)
1/4 tsp freshly ground black pepper
2 Tbsp vegetable oil, for frying

1. Steam the cauliflower for 10 minutes or until tender. (Or microwave covered on high for 6 to 7 minutes.) You should have about 3 cups once it's cooked.

2. In a food processor fitted with the steel blade, process the cauliflower until mashed, about 10 to 12 seconds. Add the remaining

ingredients except the oil; process with quick on/off pulses to combine. If the mixture seems too loose, add a little extra matzo meal.

3. Heat the oil in a large nonstick skillet over medium heat. Drop the mixture by rounded spoonfuls into the hot oil to form pancakes. Flatten each one slightly with the back of the spoon. Brown 4 to 5 minutes on each side or until golden brown and cooked through. Spray the skillet with cooking spray between batches and add more oil as needed. Drain the cooked latkes well on paper towels to absorb extra oil.

Yield: 14 latkes. Recipe easily doubles and triples. Reheats well (see Chef's Secrets). Freezing isn't recommended.

42 calories per latke, 3.9 g carbohydrate, 0.8 g fiber, 1 g protein, 2.5 g fat (0.3 g saturated), 15 mg cholesterol, 134 mg sodium, 5 mg potassium, 0 mg iron, 9 mg calcium

Broccoli Latkes
Substitute 4 cups of broccoli florets for cauliflower.

Non-Passover Variation
• Substitute breadcrumbs (preferably multigrain) for matzo meal.

Chef's Secrets
• Don't Flip Out! If the latkes aren't thoroughly cooked, they'll fall apart when you try to flip them over.

• Hot Stuff: To reheat, arrange the latkes in a single layer on a foil-lined baking sheet. Bake uncovered in a preheated 375°F oven for 8 to 10 minutes, until hot and crispy.

◖ QUINOA PILAF

This dish is excellent for Passover, when it's nearly impossible to find grains that are allowed as a side dish. Lemon juice and parsley pair perfectly with the quinoa and vegetables. Quinoa also makes a terrific Passover breakfast cereal (see Breakfast Bonanza on page 472).

1 cup quinoa
2 cups water
1 Tbsp olive oil
1 medium red onion, chopped
1 cup seeded and chopped red pepper
2 cups sliced mushrooms
2 cloves garlic (about 2 tsp minced)
1 tsp salt
1/2 tsp freshly ground black pepper
2 Tbsp fresh chopped basil or 1 tsp dried
Juice of 1/2 lemon (about 2 Tbsp)
1/4 cup chopped fresh parsley, for garnish

1. Place the quinoa in a fine-meshed strainer; rinse and drain thoroughly. Transfer to a medium saucepan, add the water and bring to a boil. Reduce heat to low and simmer, covered, for 15 minutes. Remove from the heat and let stand, covered, for 5 to 10 minutes. Fluff with a fork.

2. Heat the oil in a large nonstick skillet on medium heat. Add the onion, red pepper, mushrooms, and garlic and sauté for 6 to 8 minutes or until golden.

3. Add the cooked quinoa, salt, pepper, basil, and lemon juice. Cook over low heat, stirring often, for about 5 minutes or until heated through. Transfer to a serving dish and sprinkle with parsley.

Yield: 6 to 8 servings. Recipe easily doubles and triples. Keeps for up to 2 to 3 days in the refrigerator and reheats well. Don't freeze.

150 calories per serving, 25.0 g carbohydrate, 2.9 g fiber, 5 g protein, 4.1 g fat (0.5 g saturated), 0 mg cholesterol, 398 mg sodium, 377 mg potassium, 3 mg iron, 35 mg calcium

Farfel Pilaf

Substitute 3$\frac{1}{2}$ cups matzo farfel for the quinoa and omit the water. Omit Step 1. Sauté the vegetables as directed in Step 2. In Step 3, add the matzo farfel to the sautéed vegetables and stir until lightly browned. Gradually stir in 2 cups chicken or vegetable broth. Add the seasonings and lemon juice and cook over low heat, stirring often, until all the liquid has been absorbed, about 5 to 10 minutes. Sprinkle with parsley.

Chef's Secrets

• Breakfast Bonanza: Cook 2 cups of quinoa in 4 cups water as directed in Step 1. Use half the quinoa for the recipe above. Use the other half as a breakfast cereal. Add a drizzle of honey, some raisins or dried cranberries, and a sprinkling of cinnamon. Fresh strawberries or blueberries are another delicious option as a topping. Serve with skim milk or yogurt.

◔ PASSOVER BLUEBERRY CHEESE PANCAKES

These gluten-free pancakes are delicious for breakfast, brunch, or as a snack. Blueberries should be cooked as little as possible to retain their maximum nutritional benefits, so adding them to pancakes is a berry good idea!

1 cup low-fat dry (pressed) cottage cheese
3 large eggs (or 2 large eggs
   plus 2 egg whites)
2 Tbsp granulated sugar
2 Tbsp vegetable oil
$\frac{1}{4}$ cup nonfat plain yogurt or skim milk
$\frac{1}{2}$ cup potato starch
$\frac{1}{8}$ tsp salt
$\frac{1}{2}$ tsp ground cinnamon
1 cup blueberries (no need to defrost
   if frozen)

1. In a food processor, combine all the ingredients except the blueberries. Process the mixture until well blended, about 30 seconds. Carefully stir in the blueberries with a rubber spatula. Let the batter stand for 5 to 10 minutes. If mixture gets too thick, thin with a little milk.

2. Spray a large nonstick skillet with cooking spray. Heat on medium heat for 2 minutes or until a drop of water skips on its surface. Spoon the batter onto the hot pan, forming pancakes about 3 inches in diameter. Continue cooking on medium heat until the bottom of the pancakes are lightly browned, about 2 to 3 minutes. Small bubbles will appear on the surface of the pancakes. Carefully flip the pancakes and brown the other side. Transfer to a plate and keep warm.

3. Repeat with the remaining batter, spraying the pan between batches.

Yield: 16 pancakes. Keeps for up to 2 to 3 days in the refrigerator; reheats well. Freezes well for up to 2 months.

89 calories per pancake, 10.2 g carbohydrate, 0.3 g fiber, 4 g protein, 3.8 g fat (0.8 g saturated), 54 mg cholesterol, 121 mg sodium, 43 mg potassium, 0 mg iron, 26 mg calcium

Passover Apple Cheese Pancakes

No blueberries? Don't be blue—just substitute 1 cup coarsely chopped apple.

Chef's Secrets

• Tip-Top: These pancakes are delicious topped with yogurt, berries, and/or all-fruit apricot jam. For a special treat, top with Warm Mixed Berry Sauce (page 430).

• Hot Stuff: Place the cooked pancakes in a 250°F oven to keep warm. Or reheat the pancakes in the microwave, allowing 15 seconds per pancake on high.

🍎 PASSOVER CHEESE MUFFINS

These easy muffins are low in carbs and high in protein, so don't pass them up, pass them around the table! They make a quick and delicious breakfast for kids and adults alike. Keep some in the freezer for an easy, handy snack.

2 cups low-fat dry (pressed) cottage cheese
1/4 cup vegetable oil
3 large eggs
1/3 cup granulated sugar
1/2 cup cake meal
1 tsp Passover baking powder
1/2 tsp ground cinnamon

1. Preheat the oven to 350°F. Spray the compartments of a muffin pan generously with cooking spray.

2. In a food processor fitted with the steel blade, or in a large bowl, combine the cheese, oil, eggs, and sugar; process or beat until well-blended. Add the cake meal, baking powder, and cinnamon. Process (or mix) just until combined. The batter will be thick.

Scoop the batter into the prepared muffin pan, filling the compartments two-thirds full.

3. Bake for 35 to 40 minutes or until nicely browned. Let cool for 10 minutes before removing carefully from the pan.

Yield: 12 muffins. Keeps for up to 2 to 3 days in the refrigerator. Freezes well for up to 2 months.

137 calories per muffin, 11.6 g carbohydrate, 0.1 g fiber, 9 g protein, 6.2 g fat (1.0 g saturated), 56 mg cholesterol, 63 mg sodium, 39 mg potassium, 1 mg iron, 42 mg calcium

🍎 PASSOVER ROLLS

These rolls have a crisp exterior and aren't doughy inside. I've used half the amount of matzo meal and sugar called for in my original Passover recipe. Believe it or not, my Asian home-stay students loved these rolls and never complained that they couldn't eat bread during Passover!

1/2 cup olive or vegetable oil
1 cup water
1 tsp salt
1 tsp granulated sugar
1 cup matzo meal (regular or whole wheat)
4 large eggs

1. Preheat the oven to 400°F. Line a large baking sheet with foil and spray with cooking spray.

2. In a large saucepan, combine the oil, water, salt, and sugar. Bring to a boil over high heat. Remove the pan from the heat and add the matzo meal. Stir vigorously with a wooden spoon until the mixture pulls away from the sides of the pan. Let cool for 5 minutes.

3. Add the eggs, one at a time, beating well after each addition. (Or transfer the mixture to a food processor fitted with the steel blade; drop the eggs through the feed tube one at a time while the motor is running. Process for about 20 to 30 seconds, until smooth.)

4. Drop the mixture from a large spoon onto the prepared baking sheet. Wet your hands and shape into rolls. Leave about 2 inches between the rolls as they will expand during baking.

5. Bake for 15 minutes. Reduce heat to 350°F and bake for 30 minutes longer or until nicely browned. (No peeking allowed!)

6. Remove the baking sheet from the oven and make a small slit on the side of each roll to let the steam escape.

Yield: 10 rolls. Keeps for up to 2 days in a loosely covered container. Freezes well for up to 2 months.

172 calories per roll, 11.3 g carbohydrate, 0.4 g fiber, 4 g protein, 12.9 g fat (2.1 g saturated), 85 mg cholesterol, 262 mg sodium, 27 mg potassium, 1 mg iron, 11 mg calcium

Nutrition Notes

• These rolls contain half the carbohydrates of my original recipe but are still high in calories and fat, so control those portions. It's a good thing Passover lasts for only 8 days because these are very addictive! My original Passover rolls each contain 219 calories and 22.4 grams of carbohydrate. You'll save 47 calories and 11 grams of carbohydrate if you choose this lighter version.

🍎 NEVER-FAIL PASSOVER SPONGE CAKE

If you hate the hassle of separating eggs, this is the cake for you. Thanks to Micki Grossman of Farmington Hills, Michigan, for sharing her recipe. It takes a while to beat the eggs, so use an electric stand mixer so you can do other things during the process. Or, you can beat the eggs by hand and get a very good workout, which entitles you to eat more cake!

9 large eggs (at room temperature)
1 1/4 cups granulated sugar
3/4 cup cake meal
1/4 cup potato starch
1/8 tsp salt
Grated rind of 1 lemon (about 2 tsp)
Grated rind of 1 orange (about 2 Tbsp)
Juice of 1 orange (about 1/2 cup)

1. Preheat the oven to 325°F. Use an ungreased 10-inch tube pan with a removable bottom.

2. Beat the eggs in the large bowl of an electric mixer on high speed for 15 minutes or until the batter is very light in color. Gradually add the sugar and beat for 5 minutes longer.

3. Combine the cake meal, potato starch, salt, and lemon and orange rind in a small bowl. Reduce the mixer speed to the lowest setting. Gradually add the cake meal mixture alternately with the orange juice to the batter. Mix just until combined.

4. Pour the batter into the ungreased pan. Bake the cake on the center rack of the oven for 1 hour and 5 minutes. When done, the top of the cake should be golden and will spring back when lightly touched. A cake tester should come out clean.

5. Remove the pan from the oven and immediately invert. Cool completely, about 1 1/2 hours. If your tube pan doesn't have little feet, invert the cake onto a cooling rack to allow for air circulation.

6. To remove the cake from the pan, slide a thin-bladed knife between the pan and the sides of the cake. Push up the bottom of the pan and remove the sides of the pan. Carefully loosen the cake from the center tube and the bottom of the pan with the knife. Invert the cake onto a large, round serving platter.

Yield: 16 servings. Keeps for up to 3 to 4 days if well wrapped. If freezing, pack the cake carefully in a rigid container as it's very delicate. Freezes well for up to 2 months.

115 calories per serving, 19.6 g carbohydrate, 0.1 g fiber, 4 g protein, 2.9 g fat (0.9 g saturated), 119 mg cholesterol, 58 mg sodium, 65 mg potassium, 1 mg iron, 17 mg calcium

Passover Lemon Roll

Line a 10- × 15-inch jelly roll pan with parchment paper. Spread the cake batter in the pan. Bake at 375°F for 15 minutes. Invert the cake immediately onto a towel sprinkled with icing sugar. Carefully peel off the parchment paper. Roll up the hot cake in the towel and let cool. When fully cooled, unroll, remove the towel, and fill the cake with Passover Lemon Filling (page 478). Roll up the cake and place on an oblong platter. One serving contains 199 calories, 35.4 g carbohydrate, 0.2 g fiber, and 4.4 g fat (1.3 saturated).

Grated Chocolate Sponge Cake

Fold 1/2 cup grated bittersweet or dark chocolate into the batter at the end of Step 3. One serving contains 133 calories, 21.3 g carbohydrate, 0.4 g fiber, and 4.4 g fat (1.6 saturated).

Nutrition Note

• Let Them Eat Cake! One slice of sponge cake has a similar nutrient analysis to 1 sheet of plain matzo. One matzo contains 112 calories, 23.7 g carbohydrates, 0.9 g fiber, 3 g protein, 0.4 g fat (0.1 g saturated), and 0 mg cholesterol.

☙ DECADENT MARBLED CHEESECAKE

This is such a gorgeous dessert to serve following a dairy meal. Everyone will smile and say "Cheesecake, please!" I've kept the portions small to keep the calories, carbohydrates, and fat down.

1 lb (500 g) light cream cheese,
   cut in chunks
1/2 lb (250 g) nonfat pressed (smooth)
   cottage cheese, cut in chunks
1 cup granulated sugar
2 large eggs plus 2 egg whites
   (or 3 large eggs)
1 Tbsp Passover brandy or liqueur
3 oz (75 g) dark/bittersweet chocolate,
   melted (or 1/2 cup chocolate chips)

1. Preheat the oven to 350°F. Fill a baking pan half-full with water and place it on the bottom rack of the oven. (The steam helps prevent the cheesecake from cracking.) Spray a 10-inch ceramic quiche dish with cooking spray.

2. In a food processor fitted with the steel blade, process the cream cheese, cottage cheese, and sugar until smooth, about 30 seconds. Add the eggs and brandy; process until well mixed, about 25 to 30 seconds longer. (Be careful not to overprocess.) Remove 1 cup of the batter and mix with the melted chocolate until blended.

3. Pour the white batter into the prepared baking dish. Pour the chocolate batter over the white batter in a wide circle, about 1/2-inch in from the sides of the pan; there should be a bulls-eye of white batter in the center. Cut through the batter carefully with a knife to create a marbled effect. Don't blend the batter too much or the marbled effect will disappear.

4. Bake on the middle rack of the oven for 30 to 35 minutes. When done, the center will jiggle slightly when you shake the baking dish, but the cheesecake won't be sticky when touched lightly with your fingertips.

5. Remove the cheesecake from the oven and let cool. When completely cool, cover with plastic wrap and refrigerate.

Yield: 12 servings. Keeps for up to 3 to 4 days in the refrigerator. Leftovers, if any, can be frozen.

220 calories per serving, 23.3 g carbohydrate, 0.6 g fiber, 9 g protein, 9.8 g fat (5.7 g saturated), 58 mg cholesterol, 135 mg sodium, 90 mg potassium, 1 mg iron, 53 mg calcium

Chef's Secrets
• Crumb-y News: If you want a thin crust, sprinkle a handful of coarsely crushed Passover mandel bread or ground almonds in the bottom of the sprayed baking dish, then carefully pour in the batter.

• Pan-tastic! To bake the cheesecake in a springform pan, you need a crust or the batter will leak out. Prepare Almond Crust (page 479) as directed and press into a sprayed 9-inch springform pan. Top with the batter and bake as directed.

• Cool News: To help prevent the baked cheesecake from cracking, invert a large bowl on top of the cheesecake as soon as you remove it from the oven.

PASSOVER FRUIT CRISP

This crowd-pleaser makes an easy, light dessert for your Passover Seder. Leftovers, if any, are excellent for breakfast. Delicious warm or cold.

Filling:

3 cups strawberries, hulled and sliced
5 to 6 large apples, peeled and sliced
1 mango or 2 pears, peeled and sliced
1 Tbsp lemon juice (preferably fresh)
1/4 cup potato starch
1/2 cup granulated sugar
1 tsp ground cinnamon
1/2 tsp ground ginger

Topping:

2 cups matzo meal
1/3 cup granulated sugar
2 tsp ground cinnamon
1/4 cup chopped walnuts or almonds
1/3 cup vegetable oil
   or melted tub margarine

1. Preheat the oven to 375°F. Spray a 9- × 13-inch glass baking dish with cooking spray.

2. Combine the filling ingredients in a large mixing bowl and mix well. Spread evenly in the prepared pan.

3. Combine the topping ingredients in the same bowl (no need to wash it). Mix until crumbly. Spread the topping evenly over the filling. Bake for 50 to 55 minutes, until golden and bubbly.

Yield: 15 servings. Keeps for up to 2 days in the refrigerator. Freezes well for up to 3 months.

235 calories per serving, 43.1 g carbohydrate, 3.0 g fiber, 2 g protein, 6.8 g fat (0.5 g saturated), 0 mg cholesterol, 2 mg sodium, 188 mg potassium, 1 mg iron, 19 mg calcium

Variations
• Instead of mango or pears, add 4 pitted sliced plums, or use 4 cups strawberries and 6 apples. Instead of matzo meal, use 2 cups of crushed Passover cookie crumbs. Omit nuts if there are allergy concerns.

Chef's Secrets
• Frozen Assets: The topping mixture can be prepared in advance and frozen in a re-sealable plastic bag. When needed, sprinkle the topping over the filling (there's no need to thaw) and bake.

• Store It Right: Although this dessert actually keeps for up to 4 to 5 days, it will start to get soggy—and then you can't call it a crisp! It tastes best when eaten within a day or two of baking.

• Be Prepared: Bake in a disposable foil pan. When cool, wrap well and freeze.

● HEAVENLY LEMON PAVLOVA

A traditional pavlova is a meringue shell topped with whipped cream and fruit. In this version, a luscious lemon filling replaces the whipped cream. This eye catching dessert is sure to impress your Seder guests.

One 10-inch Meringue Shell
(page 478)
Passover Lemon Filling (page 478)
3 cups strawberries, halved
2 kiwis, peeled and sliced

1. Prepare the meringue shell and the filling as directed. (The meringue shell can be made up to a week in advance and the filling can be made a day in advance.)

2. Up to 4 hours before serving, fill the meringue shell with the lemon filling. Arrange the strawberry halves around the outside edge, placing them cut-side down. Arrange an inner circle of kiwi slices. Serve within a few hours.

Yield: 10 servings. Keeps for up to 1 to 2 days in the refrigerator. Don't freeze.

211 calories per serving, 46.5 g carbohydrate, 1.6 g fiber, 2 g protein, 2.7 g fat (0.6 g saturated), 61 mg cholesterol, 64 mg sodium, 160 mg potassium, 0 mg iron, 23 mg calcium

Mini Pavlovas
Make 10 individual meringue shells. Fill with lemon filling. Top each one with a strawberry or a slice of kiwi, cut in half, making 2 "wings." Heavenly de-light!

passover pleasures

PASSOVER LEMON FILLING

This light and luscious lemon filling is absolutely addictive. It's delicious in Heavenly Lemon Pavlova (page 477) or Lemon Trifle (page 478). It also makes a fabulous filling for Passover sponge cake or ready-made chocolate shells.

1 cup granulated sugar
1/3 cup potato starch
1/8 tsp salt
2 cups cold water
3 egg yolks
6 Tbsp lemon juice (preferably fresh)
1 Tbsp grated lemon rind
1 Tbsp soft tub margarine

1. In a heavy-bottomed saucepan, whisk together the sugar, potato starch, and salt. Gradually whisk in the water. Add the egg yolks, lemon juice, and rind; mix well. Cook and stir over medium heat until bubbly. Boil and stir for 1 minute more before removing from the heat.

2. Stir in the margarine and let cool. Transfer to a medium bowl, cover with plastic wrap, and chill for 1 to 2 hours before using.

Yield: 3 cups. Keeps for up to a day in the refrigerator (then it starts to separate and weep). Don't freeze.

102 calories per 1/4 cup serving, 21.1 g carbohydrate, 0.1 g fiber, 1 g protein, 2.1 g fat (0.5 g saturated), 51 mg cholesterol, 39 mg sodium, 16 mg potassium, 0 mg iron, 7 mg calcium

Passover Lemon Mousse
Combine the cooled filling with 1 1/2 cups nonfat vanilla yogurt and blend well. Serve chilled in parfait glasses and garnish with strawberries or blueberries. So refreshing!

Heavenly Lemon Trifle
In a large glass bowl, alternate layers of Passover sponge cake cubes (homemade or store-bought) with Passover Lemon Filling or Lemon Mousse and fruit (e.g., sliced strawberries, mangoes, kiwis, blueberries). If desired, sprinkle the cake with Passover wine or brandy when assembling the trifle. This serves a large crowd.

MERINGUE SHELL(S)

This is the ultimate fat-free pie shell! Make one large shell or ten smaller shells for easy portion control. The outside of the meringue shell will be crisp and the inside will be soft and chewy.

3 large egg whites (at room temperature)
1 tsp lemon juice (preferably fresh)
3/4 cup granulated sugar

1. Preheat the oven to 250°F. Line a large baking sheet with parchment paper.

2. In the large bowl of a stand mixer, beat the egg whites on high speed until frothy. Drizzle in the lemon juice and beat until soft peaks form. Gradually beat in the sugar, 1 Tbsp at a time. Continue to beat until the egg whites are stiff and glossy. The mixture should look like marshmallow.

3. Spread the meringue on the prepared baking sheet and form one 10-inch circle (or 10 smaller circles). Using the back of a large spoon, build up the sides to form a shell.

4. Bake on the middle rack of the oven for about 1 hour or until crisp. Don't let the meringue brown. Turn off the heat and keep the oven door closed; let meringue(s) dry in the oven for 1 hour.

Yield: 10 servings. Keeps in an air-tight container, in a cool, dry place, for up to a week. Freezes well for up to a month. Pack carefully in a rigid container to prevent breakage.

63 calories per serving, 15.1 g carbohydrate, 0 g fiber, 1 g protein, 0 g fat (0 g saturated), 0 mg cholesterol, 17 mg sodium, 17 mg potassium, 0 mg iron, 1 mg calcium

Chef's Secrets

• Them's the Breaks: If your meringue shell crumbles and breaks, don't fall apart! Break the meringue into chunks, and layer with Passover Lemon Mousse (page 478) and cut-up fruit in parfait glasses.

• Egg White Wisdom: Make sure no yolks get into the whites or they won't whip properly. Separate each egg white into a small bowl before adding to the rest of the whites. That way, if a drop of yolk gets into the white from one egg, it can be removed easily with a piece of egg shell. Eggs separate best when they are cold and whip best when they are at room temperature.

• Bowl Them Over: Use a stainless steel or glass mixing bowl to beat egg whites; they won't whip properly in a plastic bowl. The beaters must be clean and grease-free. Even a trace of grease will keep the whites from whipping properly. When egg whites are properly beaten, you should be able to turn the bowl upside down without the whites falling out.

• How to Test if an Egg is Fresh: Place the egg in a bowl of cold water. A fresh egg will lie flat on the bottom of the bowl. An egg that's a week old will tilt up, its larger end rising because the air pocket inside expands as it ages. When an egg is about 2 weeks old, the air pocket has expanded all around the inside of the shell, and the larger end will point straight up when you put the egg in a bowl of water. If the egg floats, forget about it—it's probably rotten!

ALMOND CRUST

This low-carbohydrate crust is perfect for those who are watching their carb intake. Even though it's fairly high in fat, almond crust contains mainly heart-healthy unsaturated fat. It's a scrumptious base for your favorite cheesecake or pie any time of year.

1½ cups finely ground almonds
2 Tbsp granulated sugar
1 tsp ground cinnamon
1 Tbsp vegetable oil
1 egg white

1. Preheat the oven to 350°F. Spray a 9-inch glass pie plate with cooking spray.

2. In a mixing bowl, combine the almonds, sugar, and cinnamon. Add the oil and egg white and mix well. Pat the mixture evenly into the bottom and part-way up the sides of the prepared pan.

3. Bake for 10 to 12 minutes or until lightly browned. Fill as desired.

Yield: 8 to 10 servings. Keeps for up to 2 to 3 days in the refrigerator. Don't freeze: the crust may become soggy if frozen.

133 calories per serving, 6.3 g carbohydrate, 1.9 g fiber, 4 g protein, 11.2 g fat (0.8 g saturated), 0 mg cholesterol, 12 mg sodium, 7 mg potassium, 1 mg iron, 39 mg calcium

Almond Crumb Crust
Replace half the nuts with crushed Passover mandel bread and increase the oil to 2 Tbsp.

Chocolate Almond Crust
Add 2 Tbsp unsweetened cocoa powder to the nut mixture.

Chocolate Pie
Prepare Homemade Chocolate Pudding (page 424), but substitute potato starch for cornstarch. Pour the cooled mixture into the baked crust and refrigerate. At serving time, garnish with Chocolate-Dipped Strawberries (page 428).

Lemon Pie
Prepare Passover Lemon Filling (page 478). Pour the cooled mixture into the baked crust and refrigerate.

Chef's Secrets
• Pan-tastic! You can also bake this crust in a 9- or 10-inch springform pan and use it for your favorite cheesecake. If you line the pan with parchment paper first, it will be easier to remove the finished crust from the pan.

• Nuts to You: Replace half the ground almonds with other nuts (e.g., ground walnuts, pecans, or hazelnuts).

FRUIT SHERBET

So cool! This is a great "weigh" to meet your fruit quota for the day. To double or triple this recipe, process in batches.

1 can (15 oz/425 g) apricots,
    pineapple chunks,
    or peaches in light syrup
2 Tbsp orange liqueur

1. Cut the fruit into small chunks. Spoon the fruit and its juices into ice cube trays. Cover with plastic wrap, and freeze for 2 to 3 hours or until needed.

2. Just before serving time, place all the "ice cubes" with the liqueur in a food processor fitted with the steel blade; process for 30 seconds or until it reaches the texture of sherbet. Scrape down the sides of the bowl 2 or 3 times while processing. Serve immediately.

Yield: 3 servings. Recipe easily doubles and triples.

103 calories per serving, 21.9 g carbohydrate, 2.3 g fiber, 1 g protein, 0.2 g fat (0 g saturated), 0 mg cholesterol, 3 mg sodium, 200 mg potassium, 0 mg iron, 14 mg calcium

Chef's Secrets
• Yes You Can! Instead of placing the fruit and juice in ice cube trays, remove the top of the can and cover with plastic wrap, securing it well with an elastic band. Freeze for 10 to 12 hours. When needed, place the can under warm running water for 2 to 3 minutes and then invert the contents into the processor bowl. Use a metal spoon to break the fruit into chunks. Process as directed in Step 2.

🍎 CHOCOLATE ALMOND APRICOT CLUSTERS

These are so good, you'll need to pray that they'll last throughout Passover! Chocolate lifts your spirits when you're feeling tired and overwhelmed with Passover preparations, and these no-bake treats are the perfect "pick-me-upper." These are also a wonderful and easy gift to bring to a Seder. Everyone will cluster around you when you bring these to the table!

10 oz (300 g) good-quality dark chocolate (bittersweet or semi-sweet)
1 Tbsp vegetable oil
2 cups toasted sliced or slivered almonds
1 1/2 cups (8 oz/250 g) cut-up dried apricots (scissors work best)

1. Break up the chocolate into chunks and place in a large dry microwaveable bowl. Microwave, uncovered, on medium for 2 minutes, then stir. Continue microwaving on medium for 1 to 2 minutes longer, just until melted; stir well. Cool slightly before stirring in oil, almonds, and apricots.

2. Drop by teaspoonfuls onto parchment paper-lined baking sheets. Refrigerate for 30 to 45 minutes or until firm. Transfer to an airtight container, separating the layers with parchment or waxed paper.

Yield: 48 pieces. Keeps for up to 2 to 3 weeks in the refrigerator, if you hide them well! Freezes well for up to 4 months.

66 calories per piece, 6.7 g carbohydrate, 1.2 g fiber, 1 g protein, 4.9 g fat (1.5 g saturated), 0 mg cholesterol, 1 mg sodium, 84 mg potassium, 0 mg iron, 12 mg calcium

🍎 CHOCOLATE FARFEL NUT CLUSTERS

These easy, no-bake treats come from my cousin Nancy Gordon of Toronto. They're a Passover version of a family favorite that my late Aunt Adele made using coconut and dried chow mein noodles. Even kids can make these!

2 cups chocolate chips
1/2 to 2/3 cup chopped walnuts or raisins (other nuts can be substituted)
1 cup matzo farfel

1. Place the chocolate chips in a large microwaveable bowl. (Be sure that the bowl is completely dry.) Microwave on medium for 2 to 3 minutes or until melted, stirring every minute. Cool slightly.

2. Add the nuts and farfel; mix to combine. Drop by teaspoonfuls onto a cookie sheet lined with parchment or waxed paper. Refrigerate for 30 minutes or until firm. Transfer to an airtight container, separating the layers with parchment or waxed paper. Store in a cool place or in the refrigerator.

Yield: About 30 pieces. Keeps for up to 2 months if you hide them well! Freezes well for up to 4 months.

76 calories per piece, 9.4 g carbohydrate, 0.8 g fiber, 1 g protein, 4.7 g fat (2.1 g saturated), 0 mg cholesterol, 1 mg sodium, 54 mg potassium, 1 mg iron, 6 mg calcium

Chef's Secrets
• Dark Secret: Instead of chocolate chips, use 350 grams of good-quality dark chocolate, broken up. Dark chocolate is available for Passover in 100 gram packages and is usually dairy-free (pareve). Dark chocolate, bittersweet chocolate, and semi-sweet chocolate are all interchangeable.

• Crumb-y News: No matzo farfel? Break up matzos (whole wheat or regular) into small pieces.

• No Nuts? Use unsweetened coconut or dried cranberries.

🍎 ROCKY ROAD BARK

Your guests will be barking for more! If you are watching your calories, try to choose the smaller chunks, or see Chef's Secrets for tips on portion control.

1 lb (500 g) good-quality dark chocolate
   (bittersweet or semi-sweet)
1¼ cups toasted slivered almonds
   or chopped pecans
1½ cups miniature
   or cut-up marshmallows
3 oz (85 g) milk chocolate (dark
   or white chocolate can be substituted)

1. Break the dark chocolate into chunks and place in a large dry microwavable bowl. Microwave uncovered on medium for 2 minutes, then stir. Microwave on medium 1 to 2 minutes longer, just until melted; stir well. Let cool for 5 minutes. Stir in 1 cup each of the nuts and marshmallows.

2. Spread the chocolate mixture in a thin layer on a parchment-lined baking sheet. Sprinkle with the remaining nuts and marshmallows, pressing them into the chocolate mixture.

3. Melt the milk chocolate on medium for 2 minutes; stir well. If necessary, microwave for 30 seconds longer or until melted. Dip a fork into the melted milk chocolate and drizzle it over the bark in a zig-zag design.

4. Refrigerate for 30 to 45 minutes, until hard. Break into small chunks and transfer to an airtight container, separating the layers with parchment or waxed paper. Store in a cool place or in the refrigerator.

Yield: About 1¾ lb, approximately 50 pieces. Keeps for up to 2 to 3 weeks in the refrigerator. Freezes well for up to 4 months.

75 calories per piece, 7.3 g carbohydrate, 1.0 g fiber, 1 g protein, 5.8 g fat (2.4 g saturated), 0 mg cholesterol, 3 mg sodium, 20 mg potassium, 0 mg iron, 9 mg calcium

Chef's Secrets
• Instant Portion Control: In Step 2, instead of spreading mixture onto baking sheet, drop by teaspoonfuls into equal-size mounds. (Hopefully, that should help prevent your hips from spreading!)

• Allergic to Nuts? Substitute Passover ready-to-eat cereal, raisins, or dried cranberries.

🍎 ALMOND COCONUT CRUNCHIES

There's no need to beat the egg whites for these crunchy chocolate cookies—and you can't beat that! Although coconut is high in saturated fat, it's okay to enjoy it in moderation. Coconut provides texture and taste, but use unsweetened coconut rather than the sweetened version to avoid extra sugar.

2 large egg whites
½ cup granulated sugar
1 tsp vanilla extract or Passover brandy
2 Tbsp unsweetened cocoa powder
½ tsp ground cinnamon
2 cups sliced almonds
1 cup shredded unsweetened coconut

1. Preheat the oven to 350°F. Line a large baking sheet with parchment paper.

2. In a large mixing bowl, combine the egg whites, sugar, and vanilla; mix well with a wooden spoon. Add the cocoa, cinnamon, almonds, and coconut; stir to combine.

3. Drop the mixture from a tablespoon onto the prepared baking sheet, making small mounds.

4. Bake on the middle rack of the oven for 15 minutes or until firm. Cool for 15 minutes before removing from the pan.

Yield: About 30 cookies. Store in a loosely covered container. Freezes well for up to 4 months.

68 calories per cookie, 5.4 g carbohydrate, 1.3 g fiber, 2 g protein, 4.9 g fat (1.7 g saturated), 0 mg cholesterol, 5 mg sodium, 69 mg potassium, 0 mg iron, 17 mg calcium

🍎 PASSOVER DATE AND NUT COOKIES

Bev Corber of Vancouver, B.C., shared this favorite recipe that she got from her friend's mother-in-law, Muriel Goldman. I find that dates are very sweet, so I prefer making these cookies with dried apricots. Either way, you'll go nuts over these.

2 egg whites (at room temperature)
1/2 cup Passover icing sugar, store-bought
   or homemade (page 452)
1/2 cup ground walnuts or pecans
1/2 cup ground almonds
1/2 cup chopped pitted dates
   or dried apricots

1. Preheat the oven to 300°F. Line a large baking sheet with parchment paper.

2. In the large bowl of a stand mixer, beat the egg whites on high speed until stiff and glossy. Reduce the speed and gradually beat in the icing sugar, 1 Tbsp at a time. Carefully fold in the nuts and dates.

3. Drop the mixture from a tablespoon onto the prepared baking sheet, making small mounds.

4. Bake on the middle rack of the oven for 30 minutes or until firm.

Yield: About 24 cookies. Recipe easily doubles and triples. Store in a loosely covered container. Freezes well for up to 3 months.

44 calories per cookie, 5.8 g carbohydrate, 0.6 g fiber, 1 g protein, 2.1 g fat (0.2 g saturated), 0 mg cholesterol, 5 mg sodium, 48 mg potassium, 0 mg iron, 8 mg calcium

🍎 DOUBLE CHOCOLATE DELIGHTS

Double your pleasure with this double hit of chocolate—it's doubly delicious! These cookies are perfect for Passover or any time of year.

1 large egg plus 2 egg whites
   (or 2 large eggs)
3/4 cup granulated sugar
1 tsp pure vanilla extract
2 Tbsp unsweetened cocoa powder
3 cups slivered and/or chopped almonds
   (I like a combination of chopped
   and slivered)
1 cup chocolate chips

1. Preheat the oven to 350°F. Line a large baking sheet with parchment paper.

2. In a large mixing bowl, combine the egg, egg whites, sugar, and vanilla; mix well. Add the cocoa, almonds, and chocolate chips and stir to combine.

3. Drop the mixture from a tablespoon onto the prepared baking sheet, making small mounds. These don't spread during baking.

4. Bake on the middle rack of the oven for 15 minutes or until firm. Cool for 15 minutes before removing from the pan.

Yield: About 4 dozen cookies. Store in a loosely covered container. Freezes well for up to 3 months.

71 calories per cookie, 6.8 g carbohydrate, 1.1 g fiber, 2 g protein, 4.6 g fat (0.9 g saturated), 4 mg cholesterol, 4 mg sodium, 69 mg potassium, 0 mg iron, 19 mg calcium

PASSOVER NOTHINGS

These Nothings are really something—they look and taste like the kind you make with regular flour! The secret to these cookies is to start them off in a hot oven so they will expand, then when they've finished baking, leave them in the oven so the insides will dry out, and the cookies won't collapse.

3 large eggs
2 Tbsp granulated sugar
1/8 tsp salt
1/2 cup vegetable oil
1/2 cup cake meal
1 Tbsp potato starch
2 Tbsp additional granulated sugar, for sprinkling

1. Preheat the oven to 450°F. Line a large baking sheet with foil and spray with cooking spray.

2. In a food processor fitted with the steel blade, process the eggs with the sugar and salt for 1 minute or until light. While the motor is running, pour the oil through the feed tube in a steady stream; process for 1 minute longer. Add the cake meal and potato starch; process for 2 to 3 minutes longer—the batter will become thicker as you beat it.

3. Drop the batter by scant teaspoonfuls onto the prepared baking sheet, using a second spoon to push it off. Leave about 2 inches between cookies for expansion. Sprinkle the tops of the cookies lightly with additional sugar.

4. Reduce the heat to 400°F. Place the cookies on the middle rack of the oven and bake for 7 to 8 minutes. Reduce the heat to 300°F and bake for 10 to 12 minutes longer. Turn off the oven and leave the cookies in the oven for 20 to 30 minutes longer to dry.

Yield: About 28 cookies. Store in a loosely covered container. Freezes well for up to 2 months.

59 calories per cookie, 4.0 g carbohydrate, 0 g fiber, 1 g protein, 4.5 g fat (0.5 g saturated), 23 mg cholesterol, 18 mg sodium, 11 mg potassium, 0 mg iron, 3 mg calcium

Chef's Secrets

• Hot Stuff: Newer ovens are better insulated, so they hold the heat longer. You may have to reduce the heat and baking time to prevent these cookies from burning. If your oven door has a window, peek and check, but don't open the door!

• Warning Light: If the temperature light of your oven turns on during baking, drop the temperature slightly, until the light turns off. Otherwise, your cookies will be too dark.

Norene's Healthy Kitchen

• Cute Tip: A cotton swab will remove sticky dough from the hole on the underside of the steel blade.

🍎 PASSOVER ALMOND KOMISH

Komish is the Winnipeg term for mandel bread, which is also known as Jewish biscotti. This treasured recipe comes from my cousin Nancy Gordon. Her late mom, my Aunt Adele Rykiss, made these crispy treats for Passover. I was able to reduce the fat without compromising the flavor. This komish is delish, but enjoy it in moderation.

3 large eggs
  (or 2 large eggs plus 2 egg whites)
3/4 cup granulated sugar
1/2 cup vegetable oil
3/4 cup cake meal
1/4 cup matzo meal
2 Tbsp potato starch
1 tsp ground cinnamon
1/4 tsp salt
3/4 cup slivered or chopped almonds

1. Combine the eggs, sugar, and oil in a large mixing bowl and mix until well blended, about 1 minute. Add the remaining ingredients; mix well. Cover and refrigerate for 1 hour so the mixture will thicken.

2. Preheat the oven to 350°F. Line a large baking sheet with parchment paper.

3. Form the batter into 2 long, narrow rolls on the prepared baking sheet. Leave at least 4 inches between the rolls as they will spread during baking. If the rolls begin to lose their shape, use a rubber spatula to reshape them.

4. Bake for 25 minutes or until golden. Remove from the oven and let cool for 5 minutes. Reduce the oven temperature to 200°F.

5. Using a sharp knife, slice the rolls diagonally into 1/2-inch pieces. Place the slices, cut-side down, on the baking sheet. Bake at 200°F for 1 hour or until dry and crisp.

Yield: About 32 slices. Recipe easily doubles and triples. Store in an airtight container. Freezes well for up to 4 months.

88 calories per slice, 9.2 g carbohydrate, 0.3 g fiber, 2 g protein, 5.2 g fat (0.5 g saturated), 20 mg cholesterol, 25 mg sodium, 31 mg potassium, 0 mg iron, 14 mg calcium

Variations
• Add 3/4 cup grated bittersweet chocolate in Step 1. Instead of almonds, substitute chopped filberts, walnuts, or pecans.

• For a gourmet touch, dip the tip of each cookie in melted bittersweet chocolate.

🍎 PASSOVER JAM KOMISH

Thanks to my friend Micki Grossman of Farmington Hills, Michigan, for this scrumptious recipe. This cake-like cookie is a cross between biscotti and roly poly. It's like a slice of heaven. Micki reduced the sugar and I reduced the fat, but these are still somewhat high in calories, so enjoy in moderation. Micki sprinkles cinnamon-sugar on top, but I think they are sweet enough without it.

3 large eggs
3/4 cup granulated sugar
3/4 cup vegetable oil
1 1/2 cups cake meal
1/4 tsp salt
3/4 cup apricot or strawberry jam
  (preferably low-sugar)
2 Tbsp granulated sugar
  plus 1/2 tsp ground cinnamon (optional)

1. Preheat the oven to 350°F. Line a large baking sheet with parchment paper.

2. In a food processor fitted with the steel blade, or in a large mixing bowl, process or beat the eggs, sugar, and oil for about 2 minutes or until light and fluffy. Add the cake meal and salt; mix just until combined. Cover and refrigerate for 20 to 30 minutes; the batter will thicken and firm up for easier handling.

3. Once chilled, divide the mixture into 3 long, narrow rolls on the prepared baking sheet, leaving 3 inches between each roll as they will spread during baking. Make a narrow ridge down the center of each roll. (The handle of a wooden spoon works well.)

4. Bake for 10 minutes. Remove the pan from the oven, and fill each ridge with 1/4 cup jam. If desired, sprinkle the top of each roll with cinnamon-sugar. Bake for 15 to 18 minutes longer or until golden. Remove from the oven; let cool for 10 to 15 minutes.

5. Using a sharp knife, slice the rolls into 1/2-inch pieces. Arrange the slices in a single layer on the baking sheet. Return the slices to the oven for 5 minutes so they will be crispier.

Yield: About 3 dozen slices. Store in a loosely covered container. Freezes well for up to 4 months if you are fast enough!

92 calories per slice, 10.7 g carbohydrate, 0 g fiber, 1 g protein, 5.0 g fat (0.5 g saturated), 18 mg cholesterol, 22 mg sodium, 14 mg potassium, 0 mg iron, 2 mg calcium

⬤ PASSOVER GRANOLA

With the addition of milk or yogurt and a topping of fresh berries, this makes a tasty breakfast cereal for kids of all ages and is healthier than commercial granola. If you eat it plain, it also makes a super snack.

3 Tbsp vegetable oil
1/2 cup honey
3 cups matzo farfel
1/2 cup chopped almonds
1/2 cup chopped walnuts or pecans
1/2 cup coconut (preferably unsweetened)
1 tsp ground cinnamon
1/2 cup raisins or dried cranberries
1/2 cup chocolate chips

1. Preheat the oven to 350°F. Line a large baking sheet with parchment paper.

2. In a large bowl, combine the oil and honey. Add the matzo farfel, almonds, walnuts, coconut, and cinnamon; mix well. Spread the mixture out on the prepared baking sheet.

3. Bake, uncovered, for 30 minutes or until toasted, stirring every 10 minutes. Watch carefully for the last few minutes to prevent burning.

4. Remove from the oven and transfer the hot mixture to a large bowl. Cool completely, stirring with a fork occasionally to break up any clumps. Stir in the raisins and chocolate chips.

Yield: About 6 cups (12 servings of 1/2 cup). Store in an airtight container, in a cool, dry place, for up to 2 to 3 weeks. Freezes well for up to 3 months.

247 calories per serving, 31.8 g carbohydrate, 3.5 g fiber, 4 g protein, 13.7 g fat (3.8 g saturated), 0 mg cholesterol, 4 mg sodium, 191 mg potassium, 1 mg iron, 30 mg calcium

Variation
• For non-Passover use, substitute rolled oats for matzo farfel.

Chef's Secrets
• Crumb-y News: Whole wheat matzo farfel is now available. If you can't find it, coarsely crumble 4 1/2 to 5 sheets of whole wheat matzo to make 3 cups farfel. Don't crumble it too much or you will have matzo meal!

NUT BUTTER

This makes a tasty spread instead of peanut butter on matzo. Peanuts are legumes so Ashkenazic Jews aren't allowed to eat them during Passover. Make sure the nuts are totally fresh for best results. We've figured out a way to include a chocolate version, of course!

2 cups unsalted almonds or cashews
 (or a combination)
1 to 2 Tbsp vegetable oil (as needed)
Pinch of salt

1. In a food processor fitted with the steel blade, process the nuts for 30 seconds or until coarsely ground.

2. Add 1 Tbsp oil and salt; process for 2 minutes longer or until smooth and creamy, stopping the motor several times during processing to scrape down the sides of the bowl. If the mixture seems dry, add additional oil and process until smooth. Transfer to an airtight container, cover, and refrigerate.

Yield: 1 generous cup. Recipe easily doubles and triples. Keeps for up to 2 months in the refrigerator. Don't freeze.

89 calories per Tbsp, 2.8 g carbohydrate, 1.5 g fiber, 3 g protein, 7.9 g fat (0.6 g saturated), 0 mg cholesterol, 18 mg sodium, 98 mg potassium, 1 mg iron, 231 mg calcium

Chocolate Nut Butter
Use 1 1/2 cups nuts and 1/2 cup chocolate chips. Omit the oil. Process for 2 to 3 minutes or until smooth and creamy.

WHOLE WHEAT MATZO MEAL

Use whole wheat matzo meal in your favorite recipes to boost the fiber. Make this a part of your regular Passover routine.

3 sheets whole wheat matzo

1. Break matzo into chunks. Process on the steel blade of the food processor until fine, about 1 minute.

Yield: About 1 cup. Recipe easily doubles and triples. Store in a tightly sealed jar in your pantry for up to 3 months. Freezes well for up to 4 months.

102 calories per 1/4 cup, 22.9 g carbohydrate, 3.4 g fiber, 4.0 g protein, 0.4 g fat (0.1 g saturated), 0 mg cholesterol, 1 mg sodium, 92 mg potassium, 1 mg iron, 7 mg calcium

Nutrition Note
• Whole wheat matzo is made from whole wheat flour and contains 3 to 4 grams of fiber per sheet, depending on the brand, whereas plain matzo contains only 1 gram of fiber.

BIBLIOGRAPHY

Agatston, Arthur, MD
The South Beach Diet: The Delicious, Doctor-Designed, Foolproof Plan for Fast & Healthy Weight Loss
Rodale, 2003

Bishop, Jack
Vegetables Every Day
HarperCollins Publishers, 2001

Brand-Miller, Jennie, PhD
Wolever, Thomas M. S., MD, PhD
Foster-Powell, Kay, M. Nutrition & Diet
Colagiuri, Stephen, MD
The New Glucose Revolution: The Authoritative Guide to the Glycemic Index, Revised and Expanded
Marlowe & Company, 2003

Brand-Miller, Dr. Jennie
Foster-Powell, Kaye
McMillan-Price, Joanna
The Low GI Diet Revolution: The Definitive Science-Based Weight Loss Plan
Marlowe & Company, 2003

Corriher, Shirley O.
Cookwise: The Hows and Whys of Successful Cooking
William Morrow and Company, 1997

Gallop, Rick
The G.I. Diet (Revised Edition): The Green-Light Way to Permanent Weight Loss
Random House Canada 2005

Herbst, Sharon Tyler
The New Food Lover's Companion, Third Edition
Barron's Educational Series, Inc., 2001

Jacobi, Dana
12 Best Foods Cookbook: Over 200 Delicious Recipes Featuring the 12 Healthiest Foods
Rodale, 2005

Newman, Bettina, RD
Joachim. David
Lose Weight the Smart Low-Carb Weigh: 200 High-Flavor Recipes & a 7-Step Plan to Stay Slim Forever
Rodale, 2002

Ornish, Dean, MD
Eat More, Weigh Less, Revised & Updated
Quill/HarperCollins Publishers, 2001

Ostmann, Barbara Gibbs
Baker, Jane L.
The Recipe Writer's Handbook, Revised and Expanded
Wiley, 2001

Pearson, Liz, RD
Smith, Mairlyn, H.Ec
The Ultimate Healthy Eating Plan: That Still Leaves Room for Chocolate
Whitecap Books, 2002

Podleski, Janet and Greta
Eat, Shrink & Be Merry: Great-Tasting Food That Won't Go from your Lips to your Hips!
Granet Publishing Inc., 2005

Polin, Bonnie Sanders, PhD
Giedt, Frances Towner
Nutrition Services Staff, Joslin Diabetes Center
The Joslin Diabetes Healthy Carbohydrate Cookbook
Fireside/Simon & Schuster, 2001

Roizen, Michael F., MD
Oz, Mehmet C., MD
YOU on a Diet: The Owner's Manual for Waist Management
Free Press/Simon & Schuster, 2006

Rolls, Barbara, PhD
The Volumetrics Eating Plan: Techniques & Recipes for Feeling Full on Fewer Calories
HarperCollins Publishers, 2005

Weil, Andrew, MD
Daley, Rosie
The Healthy Kitchen: Recipes for a Better Body, Life, & Spirit
Alfred A. Knopf, 2002

Willett, Walter, MD
Katzen, Mollie
Eat, Drink, & Weigh Less: A Flexible and Delicious Way to Shrink Your Waist Without Going Hungry
Hyperion, 2006

Willett, Walter, MD with The Harvard School of Public Health
Eat, Drink, & Be Healthy: The Harvard Medical School Guide to Healthy Eating
Free Press/Simon & Schuster, Inc., 2001

INDEX

Color entries indicate glycemic index (GI) information.
*Asterisks indicate sugar-free or low sugar recipes/choices.
Italicized entries indicate nutritional/general information.

index

index

index

index

index

index

index

index

index

index

index

index

index